# Designing Positive Psychology

## Series in Positive Psychology

Christopher Peterson, Series Editor

*Oxford Handbook of Positive Psychology, 2nd Edition*
Shane J. Lopez and C. R. Snyder

*International Differences in Well-Being*
Ed Diener, John F. Helliwell, and Daniel Kahneman

*Well-Being for Public Policy*
Ed Diener, Richard E. Lucas, Ulrich Schimmack, and John Helliwell

*Oxford Handbook of Methods in Positive Psychology*
Anthony D. Ong

*A Primer in Positive Psychology*
Christopher Peterson

*A Life Worth Living: Contributions to Positive Psychology*
Mihaly Csikszentmihalyi

# Designing Positive Psychology

## Taking Stock and Moving Forward

*Edited by*

Kennon M. Sheldon, PhD
Professor of Psychological Sciences
University of Missouri
Columbia, MO

Todd B. Kashdan, PhD
Associate Professor of Psychology
George Mason University
Fairfax, VA

Michael F. Steger, PhD
Assistant Professor of Applied Social Psychology and
Counseling Psychology
Colorado State University
Fort Collins, CO

OXFORD
UNIVERSITY PRESS
2011

Oxford University Press, Inc., publishes works that further
Oxford University's objective of excellence
in research, scholarship, and education.

Oxford   New York
Auckland   Cape Town   Dar es Salaam   Hong Kong   Karachi
Kuala Lumpur   Madrid   Melbourne   Mexico City   Nairobi
New Delhi   Shanghai   Taipei   Toronto

With offices in
Argentina   Austria   Brazil   Chile   Czech Republic   France   Greece
Guatemala   Hungary   Italy   Japan   Poland   Portugal   Singapore
South Korea   Switzerland   Thailand   Turkey   Ukraine   Vietnam

Published by Oxford University Press, Inc.
198 Madison Avenue, New York, New York 10016

www.oup.com

Oxford is a registered trademark of Oxford University Press, Inc.

Library of Congress Cataloging-in-Publication Data
Designing Positive Psychology: Taking Stock and Moving
Forward/edited by Kennon M. Sheldon, Todd B. Kashdan, Michael F. Steger.
     p.; cm.
 Includes bibliographical references and index.
 ISBN 978-0-19-537358-5 (hardcover)
    1. Positive psychology.    I. Sheldon, Kennon M. (Kennon Marshall)
II. Kashdan, Todd.    III. Steger, Michael F.
[DNLM: 1. Psychology—methods.    2. Attitude.    3. Emotion.
4. Personality.    5. Psychophysiology—methods.]
BF204.6.D475 2011
150.19'88—dc22       2010016830

Printed in the United States of America
on acid-free paper

*Sheldon: To Melanie, the great love and facilitator of my life.*

*Kashdan: To the three women who add color, depth, and stability to my life: Sarah, Raven, and Chloe.*

*Steger: To LeAnn, Rowan, and Ava…who continually design my optimal future.*

# Preface

Positive psychology exploded into public consciousness 10 years ago and has continued to capture attention around the world ever since. The movement promised to study positive human nature, using only the most rigorous scientific tools and theories.

How well has this promise been fulfilled? The book you hold in your hands evaluates the first decade of this fledgling field of study, from the perspective of nearly every leading researcher in the field. Chapter authors, each an expert in an area of deep importance to positive psychology, were asked to "take stock" of their field, bearing in mind the original goals of the movement that were laid out in a "Positive Psychology Manifesto" authored in 1999 (reprinted as an appendix to this book). Authors were enjoined not simply to review their field and pet theories, but instead to stretch themselves—to provide honest, critical evaluations of the flaws, problems, and untapped potential of this field of inquiry. We also asked them to provide a critical analysis of the role of problems, stressors, and difficulties for bringing about optimal outcomes—issues that have perhaps received short shrift in past positive psychology books.

After taking stock of the past, authors were then asked to "brainstorm the blue sky"—to design the optimal future of the field. Given what we now know, what is it that we most need to know next? What gaps, biases, or methodological limitations have become apparent and need to be patched and, more important, what whole new vistas have opened up that need exploring?

These 31 chapters include an introduction to and a historical account of the positive psychology movement by one of its co-founders, Csikszentmihalyi with Nakamura, as well as an additional introductory chapter by Kashdan and Steger. The book is then organized in a bottom-to-top approach, to highlight the unique challenges and opportunities that exist at multiple levels of analysis, and also to provide an easy way for readers to see how research and inquiry can advance through integration and cross-germination throughout these levels.

First, Suzanne Segerstrom, Julienne Bower, and Jaak Panksepp and their colleagues use their respective chapters to consider the biological processes that may underlie positive functioning, such as psychophysiology, self-regulation, and primary process affects. Next, James Gross, Shige Oishi, and Barbara Fredrickson (and colleagues) consider positive emotionality and emotion regulation; of course, emotions lie between the biological and the cognitive. Next, Mark Leary, Kirk Brown, Michael Robinson, and Roy Baumeister (and colleagues) examine the social-cognitive underpinnings of optimal functioning, examining self-processes, experiential processes, task-focused processes, and the role of conscious experience.

The focus then shifts to the level of personality, as Robert McCrae, Richard Robins, Brian Little, and Robert Emmons (and colleagues) weigh in on the nature of positive personality functioning. The next section then transcends the individual, as Shelly Gable, Frank Fincham, and Anthony Grant (and colleagues) summarize and criticize what is known about positive relationship and coaching processes.

Following this, the focus shifts to applied relationship science, in the guise of clinical psychological theory; here, Thomas Joiner, Crystal Park, and Ruth Baer (and colleagues) supply wisdom concerning the importance of "negative" factors, as well as the importance of the search for meaning, mindfulness, and growth within the clinical context.

The book's attention then moves even higher up the hierarchy, to organizational psychology; here, Fred Luthans and Alex Linley (and colleagues) evaluate what is known. Finally, the societal level is reached; here, Ruut Veenhoven, Richard Florida, and Robert Biswas-Diener (and colleagues) discuss positive psychology's influence on public policy and social change.

The book concludes with summary chapters by Sheldon, who discusses the importance of multi-level perspectives in detail; by Rozin and colleagues, who discuss the importance of including non-Western cultural wisdom within positive psychology; by Laura King, who considers the stumbling blocks of positive psychology and suggestions for a more constructive, durable future; and by Simonton, who uses historiometric analyses of past scientific movements to forecast the possible future(s) of positive psychology.

# Contents

Contributors      xi

## I: Introductory Perspectives

1. Positive Psychology: Where Did It Come From, Where Is It Going?
   *Mihaly Csikszentmihalyi & Jeanne Nakamura*      3
2. Challenges, Pitfalls, and Aspirations for Positive Psychology
   *Todd B. Kashdan & Michael F. Steger*      9

## II: Biological Perspectives

3. Positive Psychophysiology: The Body and Self-Regulation
   *Suzanne C. Segerstrom, Timothy W. Smith, & Tory A. Eisenlohr-Moul*      25
4. Positive Psychological States and Biological Processes
   *Carissa A. Low, Julienne E. Bower, Judith T. Moskowitz, & Elissa S. Epel*      41
5. The Primary Process Affects in Human Development, Happiness, and Thriving
   *Jaak Panksepp*      51

## III: Emotional Perspectives

6. Beyond Pleasure and Pain? Emotion Regulation and Positive Psychology
   *Maya Tamir & James J. Gross*      89

7. The Positive Psychology of Positive Emotions: An Avuncular View
   *Shigehiro Oishi & Jaime L. Kurtz*      101
8. The Future of Emotions Research within Positive Psychology
   *Sara B. Algoe, Barbara L. Fredrickson, & Sy-Miin Chow*      115

## IV: Social-Cognitive Perspectives

9. The Role of Hypo-egoic Self-Processes in Optimal Functioning and Subjective Well-Being
   *Mark R. Leary & Jennifer Guadagno*      135
10. Experiential Processing and the Integration of Bright and Dark Sides of the Human Psyche
    *Kirk Warren Brown & Melissa Holt*      147
11. A Task-Focused Mind Is a Happy and Productive Mind: A Processing Perspective
    *Michael D. Robinson & Maya Tamir*      160
12. Finding Positive Value in Human Consciousness: Conscious Thought Serves Participation in Society and Culture
    *E. J. Masicampo & Roy F. Baumeister*      175

## V: Personality Perspectives

13. Personality Traits and the Potential of Positive Psychology
    *Robert R. McCrae*      193

14. Character and Personality: Connections
between Positive Psychology and
Personality Psychology
*Erik E. Noftle, Sarah A. Schnitker, &
Richard W. Robins*    207
15. Personality Science and the Northern Tilt:
As Positive as Possible Under the
Circumstances
*Brian R. Little*    228
16. Why Gratitude Enhances Well-Being:
What We Know, What We Need
to Know
*Robert A. Emmons &
Anjali Mishra*    248

**VI:  Relationship Perspectives**

17. The Positive Side of Close
Relationships
*Shelly L. Gable &
Courtney L. Gosnell*    265
18. Positive Relationship Science: A New
Frontier for Positive Psychology?
*Nathaniel M. Lambert,
Frank D. Fincham,
A. Marlea Gwinn, &
Christine A. Ajayi*    280
19. Coaching and Positive Psychology
*Anthony M. Grant &
Michael J. Cavanagh*    293

**VII:  Clinical Perspectives**

20. The Dog Woman, Addie Bundren,
and the Ninth Circle of Hell: Positive
Psychology Should Be More
Open to the Negative
*Jennifer L. Hames &
Thomas E. Joiner Jr.*    313
21. Meaning and Growth within Positive
Psychology: Toward a More Complete
Understanding
*Crystal L. Park*    324
22. Mindfulness and Positive Psychological
Functioning
*Ruth A. Baer & Emily L. B. Lykins*    335

**VIII:  Organizational Perspectives**

23. Positive Psychological Capital in the
Workplace: Where We Are and
Where We Need to Go
*Carolyn M. Youssef &
Fred Luthans*    351

24. Organizational Applications of Positive
Psychology: Taking Stock and a
Research/Practice Roadmap for
the Future
*P. Alex Linley, Nicky Garcea,
Susan Harrington,
Emma Trenier, & Gurpal Minhas*    365

**IX:  Societal Perspectives**

25. Place and Well-Being
*Richard Florida &
Peter J. Rentfrow*    385
26. Greater Happiness for a Greater
Number: Is That Possible? If So, How?
*Ruut Veenhoven*    396
27. Positive Psychology as a Force for
Social Change
*Robert Biswas-Diener, P. Alex Linley,
Reena Govindji, & Linda Woolston*    410

**X:  Summary Perspectives**

28. What's Positive about Positive
Psychology? Reducing Value-Bias and
Enhancing Integration within the Field
*Kennon M. Sheldon*    421
29. To Celebrate Positive Psychology and
Extend Its Horizons
*Gordon Bermant, Charu Talwar, &
Paul Rozin*    430
30. Are We There Yet? What Happened
on the Way to the Demise of
Positive Psychology
*Laura A. King*    439
31. Positive Psychology in Historical and
Philosophical Perspective: Predicting Its
Future from the Past
*Dean Keith Simonton*    447

Appendix    455

Index    457

# Contributors

**Christine A. Ajayi,** Department of Family and Child Sciences, Florida State University

**Sara B. Algoe,** Department of Psychology, The University of North Carolina at Chapel Hill

**Ruth A. Baer,** Department of Psychology, University of Kentucky

**Roy F. Baumeister,** Department of Psychology, Florida State University

**Gordon Bermant,** Department of Psychology, University of Pennsylvania

**Robert Biswas-Diener,** Centre of Applied Positive Psychology, Coventry, UK

**Julienne E. Bower,** Department of Psychology, University of California, Los Angeles

**Kirk Warren Brown,** Department of Psychology, Virginia Commonwealth University

**Michael J. Cavanagh,** Coaching Psychology Unit, Department of Psychology, University of Sydney

**Sy-Miin Chow,** Department of Psychology, The University of North Carolina at Chapel Hill

**Mihaly Csikszentmihalyi,** School of Behavioral and Organizational Sciences, Claremont Graduate University

**Tory A. Eisenlohr-Moul,** Department of Psychology, University of Kentucky

**Robert A. Emmons,** Department of Psychology, University of California, Davis

**Elissa S. Epel,** Department of Psychiatry, University of California, San Francisco

**Frank D. Fincham,** Family Institute, Florida State University

**Richard Florida,** Rotman School of Management, University of Toronto

**Barbara L. Fredrickson,** Department of Psychology, The University of North Carolina at Chapel Hill

**Shelly L. Gable,** Department of Psychology, University of California, Santa Barabara

**Nicky Garcea,** Centre of Applied Positive Psychology, Coventry, UK

**Courtney Gosnell,** Department of Psychology, University of California, Santa Barbara

**Reena Govindji,** Centre of Applied Positive Psychology, Coventry, UK

**Anthony M. Grant,** Coaching Psychology Unit, School of Psychology, University of Sydney

**James J. Gross,** Department of Psychology, Stanford University

**Jennifer Guadagno,** Department of Psychology, Duke University

**A. Marlea Gwinn,** Department of Psychology,, Florida State University

**Jennifer L. Hames,** Department of Psychology,Florida State University

**Susan Harrington,** School of Psychology, University of Leicester

**Melissa Holt,** Department of Psychology, Virginia Commonwealth University

**Thomas E. Joiner, Jr.,** Department of Psychology, Florida State University

**Todd B. Kashdan,** Department of Psychology, George Mason University

**Laura A. King,** Department of Psychological Sciences, University of Missouri

**Jaime L. Kurtz,** Department of Psychology, James Madison University

**Nathaniel M. Lambert,** Department of Psychology, Florida State University

**Mark R. Leary,** Department of Psychology and Neuroscience, Duke University

**P. Alex Linley,** Centre of Applied Positive Psychology, Coventry, UK

**Brian R. Little,** Fitzwilliam College, Cambridge University; Department of Psychology, Carleton University

**Carissa A. Low,** Department of Psychology, University of California, Los Angeles

**Fred Luthans,** College of Business Administration, University of Nebraska – Lincoln

**Emily L. B. Lykins,** Department of Psychology, University of Kentucky

**E.J. Masicampo,** Department of Psychology, Tufts University

**Robert R. McCrae,** Baltimore, Maryland

**Gurpal Minhas,** Centre of Applied Positive Psychology, Coventry, UK

**Anjali Mishra,** Department of Psychology, University of California, Davis

**Judith T. Moskowitz,** Osher Center for Integrative Medicine, University of California, San Francisco

**Jeanne Nakamura,** School of Behavioral and Organizational Sciences, Claremont Graduate University

**Erik E. Noftle,** Department of Psychology, Willamette University

**Shigehiro Oishi,** Department of Psychology, University of Virginia

**Jaak Panksepp,** Department of Veterinary Comparative Anatomy, Physiology, and Pharmacology, Washington State University

**Crystal L. Park,** Department of Psychology, University of Connecticut

**Peter J. Rentfrow,** Department of Social and Developmental Psychology, University of Cambridge

**Richard W. Robins,** Department of Psychology, University of California, Davis

**Michael D. Robinson,** Department of Psychology, North Dakota State University

**Paul Rozin,** Department of Psychology, University of Pennsylvania

**Sarah A. Schnitker,** Department of Psychology, University of California, Davis

**Suzanne C. Segerstrom,** Department of Psychology, University of Kentucky

**Kennon M. Sheldon,** Department of Psychology, University of Missouri

**Dean Keith Simonton,** Department of Psychology, University of California, Davis

**Timothy W. Smith,** Department of Psychology, University of Utah

**Michael F. Steger,** Department of Psychology, Colorado State University

**Charu Talwar,** Department of Psychology, University of Pennsylvania

**Maya Tamir,** Department of Psychology, The Hebrew University of Jerusalem

**Emma Trenier,** Centre of Applied Positive Psychology, Coventry, UK

**Ruut Veenhoven,** Department of Social Sciences, Erasmus University

**Linda Woolston,** Centre of Applied Positive Psychology, Coventry, UK

**Carolyn M. Youssef,** College of Business Bellevue University

# Designing Positive Psychology

# I

---

# Introductory Perspectives

# 1

# Positive Psychology: Where Did It Come from, Where Is It Going?

*Mihaly Csikszentmihalyi and Jeanne Nakamura*

## The Prehistory

It is very strange to be caught up trying to describe, let alone explain, a historical change of which one has been a part. One comes away with renewed respect for the Herculean task historians are trying to accomplish, and with a better understanding of how psychological processes are involved in reporting the past for a future audience.

Ten years ago my wife and I (the first author) took a week off in the middle of winter and rented a tropical hut at a resort on the Big Island of Hawaii. After a few days, completely unexpectedly, I ran into a hearty fellow walking along the beach who introduced himself as Marty Seligman. Of course we knew about each other's work, and we had passed each other at conferences before, but we had never really had a chance to talk.

It turned out that Marty and his family were spending a week at the same resort we were. For the rest of our stay, at breakfast, lunch, and dinner, we exchanged ideas as to what we thought the future of psychology ought to be. This question was especially timely for Marty because the

following year he was going to take over the presidency of the American Psychological Association, and he was thinking about the kind of legacy he would like to leave behind.

We both had had somewhat unusual careers as psychologists. Marty made his fame at Cornell with his studies of learned helplessness in dogs, which turned out to be among the last nails hammered into the coffin of pure behaviorism. After discovering that dogs could develop what amounted to a pessimistic worldview if they were shocked often enough, he realized that the opposite could also be true: namely, if an organism was consistently rewarded, it would develop an optimistic disposition. This conclusion fit better with his value system (Marty occasionally wishes he had become a rabbi when he grew up), and so he was ready to pursue the implications of what he had come to call *learned optimism*.

As for myself, I had always been interested in how to improve the quality of life. Perhaps because after a fairly idyllic childhood I witnessed some of the misery of World War II, I came to an early belief that life can be either rather pleasant, or horrible—and that the difference usually hinges on human choice. I had become interested in psychology after reading Carl Jung, who looked at the tragic predicament of humankind with an unflinching yet hopeful gaze.

After more than three decades as a psychologist, however, I had become dissatisfied with much of what I was teaching my graduate students. Most of the research, and the conceptual framework that generated it, seemed artificial—constrained by the very experimental methodology that was supposed to vouch for the validity of the findings. And the basic assumptions about human beings seemed to be that we were randomly assembled organisms that had to enact passively the behaviors that were programmed into our genes.

So it turned out that Marty and I had much to talk about. Our basic concerns zeroed in on one question: What could we do to bring back into the discourse of psychology some of the concepts we found were so important to understand for a life worth living, yet were so rarely addressed by psychology, such as courage, generosity, creativity, joy, and gratitude?

The rest, as they say, is history—perhaps only the history of psychology, but in some small way perhaps also part of the history of our culture as well.

This is the easy part. But the more difficult questions to answer are: Why did we embark on this path? What exactly were we hoping to accomplish? What did we do to make it happen? How does what has happened resemble our intentions? What is likely to happen next?

I can certainly try to answer some of these questions, but by no means all. Of course the answers are going to be shaped by my own personal experiences, and so in no sense are they going to be objective, impartial, or true in some absolute sense.

Before starting on this task of remembering and recording, I would like to share a perception of cultural change that I think is valid and that colors everything I have to say about this matter from now on. It concerns a distinction that some philosophers make between *the world as history* and *the world as nature*. The claim is that when a successful change is introduced into society, those involved in it see that change as their own doing—their actions made history. But after a generation or two, the change has become so much a part of everyday life that people see it as part of nature—like the weather, or the shape of the ground on which they live.

A good example is the creation of the American Constitution. The Founding Fathers who put their signatures to it believed that the document represented their true beliefs, their aspirations, and their reasoned knowledge about human nature and about society. They were aware that they were making history, but I don't think there is evidence that they thought the Constitution was supposed to be taken as a law of nature—like the tides or like gravity. That fundamentalist attitude developed later.

There are very few institutions, if any, that do not go through such a reversal in perspective—being seen by the founders as the result of human agency, to be changed as conditions and knowledge change, and then gradually becoming more and more of a rigid and closed system. It happened to Christianity and to the Boy Scouts; to Frank Lloyd Wright's architectural style and to Socialism as a form of government; to General Motors and to IBM. I hope against hope that it will not happen to positive psychology.

The problem with the transition from the world as history to the world as nature is that the original energy that created the change becomes reified into a dogma, a church, a form of government, or an artistic style. And more often than not, in the process of reification, the spirit that animated the change drops into the background, while the superficial forms come to the foreground. No matter how liberating Christianity was originally, it took only a few generations before it became in its turn an institution embroiled in greed and oppression.

How does this apply to positive psychology? Well, for instance, one of the motives that prompted Marty Seligman to change psychology from deficit-orientation to strength-orientation was that he believed psychologists could contribute much more than what they were doing at the time. "There is so much work for psychologists to do," he kept saying, "and so few jobs for psychologists." I thought this was a perceptive observation, one that added an important reason to push for change.

So, 10 years later, Seligman's wish (and mine) has been in part realized. Hundreds of new life coaches are spreading the good news of positive psychology far and wide, and presumably making a living at it. The problem is that when a person charges for a specific service, he or she cannot be as critical of it, lest the clients begin to suspect that the goods provided are not as advertised. So life coaches need theories of happiness, and interventions that produce them, that are beyond change and improvement. Whether they can resist this pressure or not remains to be seen.

If they do not, it will create a tension that will, in a small way, recapitulate the tension that resulted in psychology at large when the needs of clinicians began to take precedence over those of scholars and researchers.

So this is where the development of positive psychology replicates the development of institutions in general. The Christian Church, for example, began to feel this kind of pressure as soon as it became successful—a few hundred years after its tentative beginnings. When the emperor Constantine converted in 313 AD and became patron of the church, suddenly quite a lot of real estate became available to the formerly embattled religion. Large fields were given to bishops, smaller plots to the lower clergy. But who qualified to receive them? Could anyone stand up and say, "I am a good Christian and willing to be a good shepherd to my flock; please give me a parish plus a horse, two cows, and four pigs"? No, that could get awkward—a lot of phonies would benefit from the emperor's largesse. So the church elders decided that they had to develop rules and procedures for consecrating priests and bishops.

Does that sound familiar? These days, of course, instead of Holy Roman Emperors we have NIMH, insurance companies, and HMOs, but the question is very much the same: Who is qualified to provide therapy, or coaching, and what does such a person need to be like? If we are not careful, that question is likely to lead to a premature rigidity about what should be the priority of positive psychology—to understand what makes life better and society more uplifting. But I am digressing… let us return to consider the flow of events.

### Next Moves

Having agreed with Marty that something should be done to redress the imbalance between negative and positive perspectives in psychology, the question became, what should we do? The very first decisions we made in retrospect seem to have been sound.

First of all, we never thought of this new development as being in any way antagonistic to existing psychology. It was to be an enrichment of the status quo, not a rejection of it. Neither one of us even thought of abandoning the scientific method or ignoring the history of past findings. Although at the time we did not discuss it, this decision set the course of positive psychology

apart from that of its predecessor, humanistic psychology, which from its inception harbored a deep suspicion of the scientific method as applied to human affairs.

Second, we decided that the best course would be to concentrate on involving young scholars rather than established ones. This was based, at least in part, on Thomas Kuhn's dictum that senior scholars will rarely adopt a paradigm shift in their own lifetime. Although we did not think of what we were doing as shifting paradigms, it made sense to expect that there would be more excitement about these ideas among young scholars who had not already devoted their careers to an alternative perspective.

So Marty and I wrote letters to 50 of the most influential psychologists in the country, asking them if they would nominate a former student of theirs who was still under 40 years of age, who was in sympathy with what we were trying to do, and who had a good chance to be the head of a psychology department by the time he or she was in the fifth decade of his or her life. Every one responded to the request, and we invited the 50 nominees to send us a CV and some writings if they were interested in joining us for a relaxing week of conversations on an undeveloped beach on the "Riviera Maya" of Mexico. Forty-five of the nominees sent in materials, and we selected 18 of them.

This is what resulted in Akumal I, a delightful and stimulating meeting conducted mostly in swimsuits and flip-flops in a trio of adjacent villas, one of which originally belonged to the Grateful Dead. Besides the 18 who were invited, we also had with us Dr. and Mrs. Don Clifton and Dr. and Mrs. Ray Fowler. Don Clifton was the CEO of Gallup and had developed an approach to management based on developing one's strengths rather than fixing one's weaknesses. Ray Fowler was the supremely qualified CEO of the American Psychological Association.

This meeting (and Akumal II a year later) established a strong foundation for what later became positive psychology. The style of meetings was itself an attempt to break the mold of the typical psychology meetings: alternating informal but intense conversations with walks on the beach and snorkeling; good local dishes in the evening followed by volunteers reading their favorite poetry; and discussing it in a circle around the living room… I can speak only for myself, but after the Akumal experience I realized that believing in the importance of positive psychology leads to the conclusion that there is nothing about our ways of doing business that needs to be boring, constricting, and alienating— not the way we talk to each other, the way we teach, or the way we express ideas.

The success of Akumal I convinced Marty and me that we had been right: there was a need for bringing back virtues, strengths, and values into mainstream psychology. This began a period of heavy lifting, done mostly by Marty, which resulted in putting the perspective on a more secure footing.

## From 1999 to 2009: The First Decade

What Marty accomplished in these years was nothing short of incredible. Helped at first by the "bully pulpit" of his APA presidency, he was able to convince foundations (starting with the Templeton Foundation) of the importance of our ideas. The funds helped to defray the costs of the two Akumal meetings; a series of summer workshops at which other young scholars were exposed to positive psychology by Akumal veterans; and the positive psychology prizes that went to young investigators (which, with a top prize of $100,000, were the most lavish of their kind in psychology). In other words, these funds helped to create a *field*, or the human infrastructure that is needed to carry a set of ideas forward.

But a field by itself cannot carry an idea forward without being able to draw on a *domain*, which is the set of rules, procedures, and knowledge that distinguishes one set of ideas from another. In many ways, the domain had already been maturing, even if not self-consciously, in parallel with the development of psychology at large. The writings of Maslow, Antonovsky, and Rogers, to name just a few, had kept alive a dimension of psychological thought that was eclipsed for so long under the hegemony first of behaviorism and psychoanalytic thought, and later of cognitive psychology.

More recent psychologists like Ed Diener, David Myers, Marty Seligman, and Rick Snyder— again to mention only a few—were also writing about what now we would consider to be "positive psychology." However, because these various scholars did not consciously identify themselves with a particular perspective, their work remained isolated and peculiar exceptions to the main domain, without an identity of their own.

But it did not take long for a younger generation of researchers to change this state of affairs

after Akumal presented an alternative. The first decade has been extraordinarily rich in contributions to what will eventually become the domain of positive psychology. The names of the young Akumal participants have become stars of this new field: Shane Lopez, Ursula Staudinger, Lisa Aspinwall, and Corey Keyes have edited collections, handbooks, and encyclopedias; Sonja Lyubomirsky, Jon Haidt, Ken Sheldon, and Barbara Fredrickson have written important books that have become centerpieces of the positive psychology reading list.

Having just taught the first year of the first doctoral program in positive psychology, which we have started at Claremont Graduate University, it seems clear that a domain is in the process of evolving. The database that Marty Seligman and Chris Peterson have collected on human strengths and virtues provides an enormously rich empirical foundation with important implications for clinical psychology, coaching, and interventions for improving the quality of life. Topics like savoring, mindfulness, flow, forgiveness, and humor—among others— are becoming legitimate concepts in the discipline, generating new research and applications.

## The Future

If it is difficult to describe the past, it is of course impossible to describe what is yet to be. As a graduate student, I (the second author) watched the first stirrings of positive psychology with avid interest. I recall seeing listeners moved to tears during Martin Seligman's presidential call to arms at the 1998 American Psychological Association meeting in San Francisco. I remember seeing them rise to applaud at its conclusion. A decade later, against such a backdrop, it is tempting to think not in terms of whether there will be a future, but of what the best future might be.

As a prologue to peering into the future, it is worth dwelling on one exceptional feature of the launching of positive psychology that also provides a useful tool for thinking about what that future is likely to be. Seligman and Csikszentmihalyi made a deliberate decision at the outset of their undertaking to apply the systems model of creativity (Csikszentmihalyi, 1988) to the seeding of positive psychology. The model suggested that the birth of a self-conscious subdiscipline would require doing two things: first, delineating the domain—a body of knowledge, collection of accepted tools, and set of animating questions and commitments—and second, mobilizing a field that would attract individuals to work in the domain and encourage and reward promising contributions to the body of knowledge. As the first half of the present chapter detailed, those efforts gained traction rapidly on both fronts, and the result has been a broadly defined subdiscipline, significant new knowledge, and an engaged, increasingly global community.

Looking ahead, one can envision various negative futures, of course, ranging from waning of interest to excessive enthusiasm that leads to premature implementations and exaggerated expectations. Ideas can lose credibility for a variety of reasons: because they fail to stand up to public scrutiny, because they promise much and deliver little, or because their proponents are self-serving and use the ideas to their personal advantage. All of these developments, and more, could derail the growth of positive psychology. Therefore, it is not too early to consider what needs to be done for this perspective to survive and prosper.

Keeping in mind the systems model, what might it take to create a positive future for positive psychology—to keep it vibrant and relevant while moving forward? What are the priorities— to nurture the domain, the field, or both? And toward what ends?

Different futures have been proposed with respect to the domain. According to some, positive psychology should seek to move toward a body of knowledge that is unified by a single, overarching theory of human flourishing. The goal: a fully fleshed out and scientifically grounded psychology of well-being.

According to others, the study of positive phenomena, and a positive perspective on psychological functioning, should ultimately be integrated with the rest of the knowledge in established subdisciplines such as social psychology, the psychology of the emotions, clinical psychology, and organizational psychology. Within this view, neither a single universal theory, nor even the persistence of a separate positive psychology, is the goal. Instead, the ultimate aim is the balanced understanding of each sphere of functioning. What these two views have in common is an effort to define now how the domain should look in the future.

A third possible look ahead eschews this telic perspective. Instead, the best future for the domain—whatever it might be—will arise from rallying around a shared purpose and a shared set of questions or problems and letting the domain evolve organically.

These different futures of the *domain* imply different agendas for the *field* of positive psychology. Unless the domain of positive psychology ultimately is completely absorbed into existing subdisciplines, it seems likely that the majority of positive psychologists will continue to hold "dual citizenship," belonging to the positive psychology community and to the community of (for example) cognitive psychologists, personality psychologists, or developmental psychologists. In other words, there will continue to be a vigorous, cooperative community of positive psychologists, actively engaged in exchange about the many aspects of human flourishing and its conditions. In addition, if the present predicts the future, this field will continue to be an increasingly global community.

Positive psychology is shaped not only by its own internal dynamics but also by interaction with external systems. What does this imply for its possible futures? One reason for the rapid growth of positive psychology has been the tremendous interest in "positive interventions." In any sustainable future, positive psychologists will have to maintain a healthy interaction between advances in basic knowledge and the development and deployment of applications of this knowledge. The eagerness for application can protect the basic science of positive psychology from the kind of insularity that leads to self-referentiality and even irrelevance. At the same time, premature application can pose a threat to good basic science, which takes time, and needs to remain willing to discard promising ideas that don't hold up under scrutiny.

In the United States, positive psychology's most salient reference point in applied psychology has been clinical; as a result, the field has been fastest to respond to the demand for interventions targeted at the direct increase of individual well-being, for example, through coaching and personal exercises. In the positive psychology community as a whole, it seems clear that the future of applied work will encompass both these interventions at the individual level and ones aimed at the institutional and aggregate levels. Efforts to develop national indicators of well-being and a positive psychology of environmental stewardship are examples. That is, the best future for positive psychology may be as heralding a positive social science, contributing directly to the enhancement of individual well-being and to the creation of flourishing institutions, and improving societal conditions in ways that impact individual well-being indirectly but on a wider scale.

These conditions include, but are not limited to, the family, the school, the workplace, cultural institutions, and the community. The argument can be made that by improving such conditions of existence we can achieve the goals of positive psychology as well as, if not better than, by focusing on individual traits such as optimism, hope, or gratitude. At the very least, it is clear that the two directions of research and intervention—the first focusing on the person, the second on the conditions of life—are mutually supportive of each other.

Thus far, positive psychology has only begun to enter the second of these realms of research and practice. Most headway has been made in the application of positive psychology principles to the workplace. Positive organizational psychology has become another vital subfield in the U.S., with an emphasis on the improvement of working life. Education is also beginning to receive significant attention.

But the potential applications of positive psychology are almost limitless, ranging from the design of computer games to that of urban communities, from political decisions to the protection of the environment. Of course, the very vastness of the scope of applications should be sobering to those who pursue this second direction because it invites shallowness and grandiosity. We must be aware of the huge responsibility attending the great promise and proceed with creative humility (two of the VIA virtues).

Some of the insights of positive psychology seem ready-made to help build a positive future. First, we have learned that positive emotions open up new ways of thinking and acting (Fredrickson, 2009). Positive psychology began in Akumal in a spirit of joy and curiosity. This spirit has been replicated on much larger stages—for instance, at the Fourth European Conference on Positive Psychology held in Opatija, Croatia, in 2008, where more than 500 participants from all over the world were joined by a common focus and excitement about each other's work; or the symposium held in 2009 at our campus in Claremont, attended by 650 enthusiastic participants and 150 more who followed the event by webcast. In the interest of the growth of the

domain, one hopes this spirit will continue to prevail.

Second is the blindingly simple fact that—to invoke Chris Peterson's (2006) words—*other people matter*. Positive psychology has been a notably collegial community, particularly for one originated by a group of senior scientists from very different backgrounds, all eminent in their own rights. Perhaps this is in part because of their deliberate emphasis on nurturing rising generations of scholars from the outset, through training institutes and fellowships. In the interest of the health of the field, may it continue to be so.

Third is the importance of hope, and a sense of meaning and purpose achieved through working for the welfare of others (e.g., Emmons, 2003). Looking ahead, we suggest that the most desirable future of positive psychology will encompass a vibrant, rigorous basic science joined to the applied purpose of contributing in multiple ways to positive human development, and the increase of global well-being.

*References*

Csikszentmihalyi, M. (1988). Society, culture, and person: A systems view of creativity. In R. J. Sternberg (Ed.), *The nature of creativity* (pp. 325–339). Cambridge: Cambridge University Press.

Emmons, R. A. (2003). Personal goals, life meaning, and virtue: Wellsprings of a positive life. In C. L. M. Keyes & J. Haidt (Eds.), *Flourishing: Positive psychology and the life well-lived* (pp. 105–128). Washington, DC: American Psychological Association.

Fredrickson, B. (2009). *Positivity*. New York: Crown.

Haidt, J. (2006). *The Happiness hypothesis*. New York: Basic Books.

Lyubomirsky, S. (2007). *The How of happiness*. New York: Penguin Press.

Lopez, S. (2009). *The encyclopedia of positive psychology*. New York: Wiley-Blackwell.

Peterson, C. (2006). *A primer in positive psychology*. New York: Oxford University Press.

Staudinger, U. & Aspinwall, L. (2002). *A psychology of human strengths*. Washington, DC: APA Publications.

# 2

# Challenges, Pitfalls, and Aspirations for Positive Psychology

*Todd B. Kashdan and Michael F. Steger*

This book roughly coincides with the completion of the first decade of the popular "positive psychology" movement (conceived in Seligman, 1998, and kicked off with Seligman & Csikszentmihalyi, 2000). In this relatively brief time frame, several demonstrable accomplishments have been marked, ranging from the development of efficacious interventions to influencing several countries to use well-being rather than economic indicators to assess societal progress. It has been an exciting decade, and in the chapters that follow this preface, the reader will find an impressive array of scientific discoveries. In addition, an enormously compelling picture of the future of positive psychology is laid out in these wide-ranging contributions, offering glimpses of the biological, social, psychological, organizational, and evolutionary landscape of "optimal human being" (cf. Sheldon, 2004). However, the goal of this book is not boosterism but rather to take the opportunity to take stock of 10 years of positive psychology. Along with impressive advancements, we find that a sober appraisal suggests that the movement is facing challenges as the second decade of its existence approaches.

An initial challenge is the lack of clarity on which research topics constitute "positive psychology." One common feeling is that positive psychology is the scientific effort to improve people's lives. Research on a variety of desirable human qualities has proliferated under the banner of positive psychology, and few would argue that learning how to instill meaning, curiosity, hope, and motivation fails to work toward this goal. But aren't those who study cognitive errors, biases, or mental health disorders also trying to improve people's quality of life? Can't the study of human frailty also fit under this constitution of positive psychology? If nearly all research can be construed as positive psychology, though, then the label is meaningless. But if studying only trendy-sounding topics counts as positive psychology research, the movement may fail to generate sound, comprehensive science and will quickly drift toward the fringe. Given the shift in government funding priorities away from the positive back to the treatment of mental disorders, this may already be occurring.

For many positive psychology researchers, there is often a one-sided focus on desirable-sounding constructs and topics, with new, exotic terms like *self-compassion* or *state cheerfulness* proliferating. Surely "negative" human experiences and characteristics, such as regret or perfectionism, are not just bad things to be avoided and minimized—they may also be essential challenges, springboards to higher peaks. Just as the possible benefits of the bad often seem neglected, the limits of the good are rarely considered. Too much curiosity could lead to obsessions and nosiness; too little guilt could lead to antisocial behavior and a failure to learn from mistakes; and too much purpose in life could lead to monomaniacal obsession. To date, positive psychology researchers have had little to say about the yin and yang of positive and negative, the dialectical tension between stress and growth. Marcus Aurelius said, "in all things, moderation," and Aristotle extolled the golden mean. Does this apply to an optimal balance or sequence of positive and negative? We suspect one reason for neglect of the negative is the designation of happiness as the ultimate criterion of life.

## From the Happiness Obsession to a Matrix of Well-Being Dimensions

We realize that it smacks of blasphemy to challenge the notion that happiness for ourselves and other people is a desirable outcome. More importantly, the data are convincing that there are reliable, robust salutary effects for happiness (Lyubomirsky, King, & Diener, 2005). Happy people are more sociable, attracting other people and developing a greater number of lasting, significant, meaningful relationships. Beyond the social world, happy people are healthy (from pain tolerance to quicker immunological responses), creative, productive, successful, and live longer than their less happy peers. So what's the problem?

To begin, we need to specify a clear, coherent definition of happiness. Unless you subscribe to "bracket creep," where people conflate the sources or contributors to happiness (such as love, religiosity, feelings of autonomy and belonging, and personal growth) with the experience itself (Biswas-Diener, Kashdan, & King, 2009; Kashdan, Biswas-Diener, & King, 2008), happiness can be reliably defined and measured. Most scientists and laypeople agree that happiness is primarily a cognitive evaluation that one's life is satisfying and includes the presence of frequent positive and infrequent negative emotions (Diener, Suh, Lucas, & Smith, 1999).

Essentially, it is a simple barometer that life is moving in a desired direction. The problem with happiness arises when people ascribe it to be the primary objective of their life (which reflects the vast majority of people; Oishi, Diener, & Lucas, 2007).

In the pursuit of an optimal concoction of thoughts and feelings to become happy, human begins face an uphill struggle. To become happier, to think more positively, and to feel better, a person naturally tries to control, purge, or avoid negative thoughts and feelings. This is often counterproductive because deliberate attempts to suppress or avoid certain thoughts and feelings only increase their persistence (Wegner, 1994). Attempts to dispute and challenge pain, anxiety, sadness, anger, or loneliness and replace them with more positively valenced private experiences (e.g., Longmore & Worrell, 2007; Seligman, 1998) increase the psychological importance of unwanted experiences. In addition, by elaborating on the negative thoughts, their accessibility increases through new connections made with other thoughts and meaning systems. Anxiety provides a great example. Greater attentional resources are devoted to indicators of anxiety (e.g., short breaths, sweaty palms) that only intensify anxious feelings and reduce awareness of whatever else is going on in the present moment. Essentially, the struggle to feel less negativity and greater positivity steals time and effort away from other strivings to do what is most interesting and valued (Hayes, Luoma, Bond, Masuda, & Lillis, 2006; Kashdan, Breen, & Julian, 2010).

Besides the counterproductive nature of trying to control thoughts and feelings in the brain, there are other problems with happiness as the fundamental aim of life. Our ability to predict what we will feel in the future is flawed at best. We regularly underestimate our ability to tolerate pain and adversity (Gilbert, Pinel, Wilson, Blumberg, & Wheatley, 1998) and neglect peripheral factors that profoundly influence our quality of life. For instance, when deciding to purchase a house, we decide that the number of bedrooms and size of the backyard are of paramount importance but fail to consider how annoying the neighbors might be or the extent by which the distance from our friends will detract from our quality of life (Wilson, Wheatley, Meyers, Gilbert, & Axsom, 2000). In addition, we often lack explicit control over what we feel. Consider well-meaning friends that suggest you "just relax" prior to giving a speech to an audience. If it was this easy to change the content or frequency of our thoughts and feelings, would we need them? Surely part of the purpose of thoughts and feelings is to alert us to important features or changes in our environments; maybe thoughts and feelings shouldn't be infinitely labile. Our brains are plastic but not that plastic. Forces outside of our immediate conscious awareness influence what we think, feel, and do; whether it is hormonal activity, temperature, or reflexive reactions to subtle environmental cues (e.g., meeting someone with the same name as a friend from childhood that was abusive can put us in a foul mood) (Bargh & Williams, 2006). Taken together, we often lack explicit knowledge about what satisfies us and what triggers positive and negative emotions. Despite this ignorance, anticipated happiness is often used as an imprecise compass to direct us among competing options for how to allocate finite time, attention, energy, and money.

Mirroring the general public, positive psychology researchers far too often rely on the pursuit of happiness as the ultimate criterion. An alternative perspective has been gaining steam, however, marked by an influx of attention to mindfulness, acceptance, and values, but this work often occurs in isolation from people interested in positive psychology (Brown, Ryan, & Creswell, 2007; Leary, Adams, & Tate, 2006; Wilson & Murrell, 2004). Because of this separation, complex issues such as how happiness goals might be diametrically opposed to mindfulness are often ignored. Again, it is useful to consider how the vast body of research that has focused on psychopathology exemplifies the challenges facing positive psychology. In several variants of cognitive therapy—not to mention optimism training—clients are informed that certain thoughts are dysfunctional. The first step is to increase self-monitoring and awareness of thoughts. The second step is to pinpoint thoughts that are dysfunctional with appropriate labels. The third step is to refute or challenge the validity of these thoughts. The final step is to replace these negative dysfunctional thoughts with more positive, constructive thoughts and thereby lessen the amount of negative emotion experienced. Essentially, some negative emotions and thoughts are problematic and need to be purged and hopefully replaced with more positive emotions and thoughts. In contrast, in mindfulness- and acceptance-based interventions, clients are taught that thoughts are thoughts, neither good nor bad, and they can be observed and explored without getting snagged into a resource-depleting struggle for control. In cognitive therapies the goal is to modify the content of one's thoughts and feelings. The goal of acceptance- and mindfulness-based approaches is to change relationships with thoughts and feelings—taking steps toward meaningful strivings while observing and being receptive to whatever internal experiences accompany the journey. While both perspectives share features such as insight about how automatic, habitual mental reactions can increase stressful reactions, a person cannot be nonjudgmental, open, and curious toward thoughts while simultaneously holding the belief that well-being stems from refuting negative thoughts and then replacing them with more positive thoughts. Despite a few incompatible philosophical differences, there is an important general insight to be gleaned from this example: individual differences matter, and it remains to be seen which strategy is most effective for particular people in particular circumstances. Scientific inquiry will be enhanced when both the similarities and differences among constructs and theories are appreciated at both conceptual and practical levels of how different people have varying responses.

Despite an intuitive appeal, the happiness obsession has a downside. Besides a few everyday problems that might result when regular people attempt to follow positive psychology's prescriptions (more about that in a bit), there is a theoretical problem inherent to the happiness obsession. A narrow approach to well-being that is circumscribed to happiness might be less advantageous than a broader approach that includes happiness as only one of several dimensions within a matrix. Other dimensions in this broad, matrix approach include meaning and purpose in life, mindfulness, achievement, life balance and flexibility, and psychological needs for belonging, competence, and autonomy, among others. There are several immediate benefits of this broadened approach to well-being. The synergy among different dimensions of this matrix offers a wide range of interesting hypotheses, such as how the immediate experience of positive emotions can alter people's judgments of meaning in their lives (King, Hicks, Krull, & Del Gaiso, 2006). In addition, there is merit in studying configurations of different dimensions instead of studying happiness or any other positive experience or strength in a vacuum (as if other personal qualities do not exist). Unfortunately, these latter strategies still dominate positive psychology research, and happiness is given prominence over other dimensions of well-being. Instead of loading everything that is good as a constituent element of happiness, we believe that distinct constructs are best organized as separate dimensions of well-being. This preserves opportunities to research similarities, differences, and synergistic relationships in understanding the multiple pathways to positive outcomes. Several contributors in this volume offer thought-provoking questions about these perspectives, offering interesting alternatives (that are often complementary).

### Reconsidering the Nature and Assessment of Strengths and Personality

The bar of what constitutes satisfactory research questions and methodologies changes as a field evolves. Simply naming new constructs and creating questionnaires to measure them is unlikely to be fruitful in the long term, although it has been a logical beginning given the many previously ignored positive phenomena. An examination of past research offers an entry point to designing the best future research agenda for positive psychology.

Besides happiness, strengths of character have quickly surfaced as one of the most popular subjects in positive psychology. Strengths have been defined as pre-existing qualities that reflect an authentic version of the self and, when used, are intrinsically desirable and energizing, thereby increasing the probability of healthy outcomes (Linley, 2008; Peterson & Seligman, 2004). In one of the foremost achievements in positive psychology, Peterson and Seligman created a catalog of strengths of character that are purported to be invariant across history and culture. Their efforts led to a final tally of 24 strengths and the creation of an extensive battery of assessment tools including a 240-item self-report questionnaire—Values in Action Inventory of Strengths (VIA-IS; Peterson & Seligman, 2004). The popularity of this scale in basic research and coaching work (to help people and organizations reach their potential) has been unprecedented. In a mere six years, more than a million people completed the VIA-IS.

With the advent of Web-based survey technology, to date, scientists have uncovered strengths with the largest positive correlations with well-being (Park, Peterson, & Seligman, 2004; Peterson et al., 2007), effective recovery

from illness (Peterson, Park, & Seligman, 2006), and perceived psychological growth following adversity (Peterson, Park, Pole, D'Andrea, & Seligman, 2008). Taken together, strengths of character appear to contribute to fulfilling outcomes at personal, relational, and organizational levels. To build on these promising findings, we consider the default methodological approach to strengths and many of the constructs in positive psychology.

Global surveys provide useful information about how people differ from each other. In the VIA-IS, people are asked the degree to which general statements characterize them. Each person gets a score for a particular strength, and this can be compared to other people (inter-individual), or relative scores on other strengths (intra-individual). The latter approach allows each person to receive a personalized profile of strengths that are the least and most endorsed. From this matrix, an array of interventions can be provided to increase the probability that endorsed strengths are used more regularly and in new ways, and in what ways lesser strengths of personal value can be enhanced. An implicit assumption in this assessment device and any subsequent use of the information is that more is better. We wonder whether the evidence supports this lynchpin of applied positive psychology. For instance, it could be argued that psychological balance offers benefits above and beyond the amount of particular strengths. Also, we wonder when it is advantageous to study strengths at a more molecular level of analysis. Strengths assessed at the global level seem to offer greater utility when the interest is in comparisons among people across lengthy periods of time (e.g., comparing young adults after college on their ability to achieve successful balance among work, family, and leisure). For shorter-term outcomes such as effectiveness in a given situation, assessing within-person behavior patterns might be more appropriate. Only by collecting information on what people actually think and do in the moment can we capture dynamic concepts such as the degree to which people are flexible and versatile in their deployment of strengths to match the demand and potential rewards within a given situation.

Going forward, researchers can assess strengths as situationally based judgments, behaviors, and reactions as a complement to a trait approach. That is, both the endorsement and use of strengths in a given moment can vary depending on what is happening in a given moment. Possessing strengths is not synonymous with using strengths. This is because people might fail to recognize situations to use their strengths or for a number of reasons (including self-efficacy and poor insight) or fail to bring their strengths to the forefront. While a person might feel energized and intrinsically motivated to use their strengths, this does not mean they are adept. Moreover, we believe there is a potentially meaningful difference between the volitional wielding of strengths compared with a more passive approach where other people or the situation "pulls" strengths into action (e.g., consider impulsive versus deliberate courage to stand up for a colleague being bullied by management). Because these are empirical questions, if we fail to operationalize the nuances of the various ways that strengths might operate, these and other questions cannot be formally tested.

Assessing states and behaviors in the context of people's natural environment is a more difficult, resource-intensive strategy than asking people to complete a one-time questionnaire. However, the relation is often slight, or insignificant, between retrospective reports of personality and online assessments of personality behaviors on multiple occasions across multiple days. In the emotion literature, a consistent finding is that the frequency of positive emotions in daily life outweighs the intensity of positive emotions in the prediction of well-being (e.g., Diener, Sandvik, & Pavot, 1990). With global surveys such as the VIA-IS, researchers are unable to parse out frequency, intensity, and context sensitivity to understand how strengths of character operate in daily life.

A parsimonious way to describe our point is that context matters when studying and trying to modify people's personality—regardless of whether the target is momentary states, basic behavioral tendencies, strivings, or life narratives. If positive psychology is going to progress at the scientific and applied level, context can no longer be underappreciated, ignored, and untreated. An additional benefit of addressing people in context is that we can begin to truly address change as it naturally unfolds from one time point or situation to the next (Stone, Shiffman, Atienza & Nebeling, 2007). When something beneficial happens in one situation and not another, we can uncover the psychological, social, and biological mechanisms that account for this variability. If context is not directly modeled, then we are making an assumption that

people are invariant across situations. We know this is untrue. This is not a controversial statement.

How we address personality matters, and we can contrast business as usual—between-person trait approaches such as the Big Five factors of personality and the VIA-IS strength model—with within-person approaches. Between-person approaches are static, designed to classify people with qualities that are relatively stable across time and situations. By extension, research driven by this approach is designed to predict what a person does in a given situation compared to another person in that situation; arguably, there are more sensitive approaches to map out how a single person changes according to different situational parameters. We suspect that most scientists are interested in what people do in a given situation and, for clinicians and coaches, helping people modify what they do with the aim of extracting more pleasure and meaning from life. This begs the question of why between-person approaches to positive emotions and strengths dominate. A contextualized approach to strengths requires more fine-tuned assessment strategies.

Within-person approaches have different assumptions. Critical to a within-person approach is that differences among people include but go beyond differences in average response tendencies (such as endorsed kindness, mindfulness, or courage). People differ in mean response tendencies, yet they also differ in variability in responses across situations (Cervone, 2005). These patterns are often idiosyncratic. For instance, I might experience more intense and lasting gratitude when given gifts by friends as opposed to strangers; you might have the opposite pattern. Sometimes these response patterns to situations are relatively uniform. For instance, people's behavior responses tend to show greater fluctuations when with other people versus when alone (Diener & Larsen, 1984). Existing findings suggest that the situation should often be part of the process of assessing personality (Cervone & Shoda, 1999; Mischel & Shoda, 1998). The ingredients of a situation activate what we think and do, and what we think and do might differ from person to person. That is, our goals, competencies, values, expectations, emotions, and self-regulatory strategies interact with the ingredients of a situation, and these interactions can vary from one person to the next. Links between these mental units and situations, together, form our signature personality pattern.

To be clear, both approaches to personality are correct. Generally, different people routinely act in different ways on a given dimension of behavior (between-person trait approach). When trying to describe how a person is on average over long periods of time, traits suffice. When trying to explain and predict behavior in daily life, within-person approaches are necessary. This is because there is a near-zero correlation between how people act during one hour of the day and how they act in a different hour of the day (Fleeson, 2001). Moreover, the degree of variability in how the typical person behaves across situations is substantially greater than how they differ from other people. As an example of the large variability in the behavioral manifestation of personality across situations, consider a comparison to emotions. Emotions are commonly believed to vary extensively such that scientists often conceive them to be fleeting psychological states rather than stable personality traits. Interestingly, the amount of within-person variability in how people exhibit openness and curiosity, conscientiousness, agreeableness, and neuroticism (the Big Five personality traits represented as behaviors) is just as large as the within-person variability in positive emotions and distress (Fleeson, 2001). To understand what makes people act differently from one moment to the next, we can examine the ingredients of situations and whether there are stable combinations for a particular person.

While several researchers have adopted a within-person approach to well-being, few have applied this approach to strengths of character that are central to positive psychology theory, research, and interventions (for exceptions, see Campbell, Simpson, Stewart, & Manning, 2003; Cervone, 1997; Heppner et al., 2008). Suppose a person is morally courageous in sticking up for herself when her husband argues with her but docile when this happens at work or around people viewed as authority figures. If these patterns are relatively stable, for all intents and purposes, the situational contingencies are part of her personality. To ignore or discount these contingencies is to miss opportunities to explain variance in well-being and uncover the most effective targets of intervention.

### Preventing a Tool-Based Discipline

Our research questions, discoveries, and interventions are limited by the tools at our disposal. Despite this, it is important that we should not be complacent and become a tool-based science. Rather than letting existing tools dictate our scientific approach, research questions should dictate the tools and methods to be used. If the tools are inadequate to address unresolved issues, then new tools require creation. If we believe that strengths and well-being are dynamic, flexible, broad concepts, then our tools need to be sensitive to these dimensions (and global surveys are, by design, insensitive to time and context). If we believe that self-regulation often occurs outside of conscious awareness, then we are going to require non-obtrusive, implicit measures and not rely solely on face-valid, explicit measures. If we are interested in how generosity and kindness impact work productivity, our measurement strategy might change depending on whether we want to know if people endorsing these strengths are different from people who do not, whether people who are kind and compassionate on a particular day are more productive on the same day, or whether being kind and compassionate outside of work has a spillover effect on work performance. Depending on the specific research question, the ideal measurement strategy could be global questionnaires such as the VIA-IS, global questionnaires with item content modified to be explicitly linked to work settings, experience sampling of daily behaviors over multiple days, or behavioral observations by coworkers and supervisors. Instead of selecting assessment techniques because they are new, popular, easy to implement, and cost-effective, researchers and practitioners should continually return to the territory that they hope to explore and relentlessly seek better ways of gathering information.

### Questioning a Variable-Centric Universe

As researchers make inroads into why certain people are able to create lives that are most worth living, an endless array of variables enter the mix. There are temporary states such as positive emotions, flow, mindfulness, and the act of savoring a meaningful event. There are perceptions of whether basic psychological needs are satisfied such that a person feels autonomous, competent, and a sense of belonging (Deci & Ryan, 2000). There are personal strengths such as courage, curiosity, gratitude, forgiveness, hope, and optimism. There are social conditions that enable positive states, psychological needs, and strengths such as capitalization and autonomy support. And if we seriously consider the multiple levels that characterize a person, from their personality traits to their goals and life narratives, and the biological and social factors that influence each level (McAdams, 1996; Sheldon, 2004), the list of models to account for happiness, meaning in life, and other elements of well-being is nothing short of paralyzing.

We suggest that certain psychological variables are more important than others for staying on course toward a fulfilling life despite obstacles, failures, and the absence of positive feedback. This point is not controversial. However, far too much work in the field of positive psychology, no different than other areas of psychology, is what we call "variable-centric." That is, far too much scientific attention is devoted to working with singular variables in isolation from the rest. Consider a simple outcome such as physical health. A PsycInfo literature search restricted to peer-reviewed articles published over the past decade corroborated this claim where more than 2,500 articles were found with physical health as the outcome, and more than 500 variables (e.g., alcohol consumption, depression, HIV, etc.) from approximately 10 different general classes of causes (e.g., health behaviors, mental health, physical health, etc.) were identified as predictors of the outcome. In most cases, a single variable was studied as the focal cause of changes in physical health. Evident from these results is the common restriction to one or a few variables of interest rather than more comprehensive examinations of people. Existing VIA-IS research is noteworthy for relying on a matrix of trait dimensions, avoiding the trend of scientists focusing on a single strength—whether it be forgiveness, optimism, curiosity, religiosity, or another—to conduct a programmatic line of research to understand health and success.

We ourselves have developed numerous measures of psychological variables and understand the desire to delve deeper into what can be learned about a single variable. The traditional way to do this is to chart a somewhat familiar path of relations with other existing variables. This path is a worthy starting point; it is, after all, the heart of construct validation for measurement. Yet, we find it valuable to constantly remind ourselves that our primary interest is in understanding the lives of people (not an unending queue of abstract statistical relations among variables).

Variable-centric research may miss the underlying causal structure simply due to the fact that a small subset of known variables is being addressed. Besides the mere number of variables that are studied together, there is an issue concerning the level of analysis used to get to know another person, whether a research participant or client. Once again, positive psychology is dominated by research on positive experiences (particularly affects) and strengths. While useful, there are other levels of analysis where a person's mental concerns, strivings, and integrated life narratives offer a portal into the nature of a person in context and across longer periods of time. Broader conceptions of personality reflecting strivings, purpose in life, and life narratives offer additional insight (beyond positive experiences and strengths) into how and why certain people are healthy and successful in the long term (Emmons, 1999; Little, Salmela-Aro, & Phillips, 2007; McAdams, 2008; McKnight & Kashdan, 2009). We look forward to the continuing integration of multiple variables at different levels of analysis to address people in research and practice.

Psychological contributions to well-being are often studied without an appreciation of heterogeneity. Complementary to variable-centric research is what is termed a "person-centered" approach that focuses on different subsets of people and how they differ as a function of prespecified characteristics (e.g., Boniwell, Osin, Linley, & Ivanchenko, 2010; Keyes, Shmotkin, & Ryff, 2002; Singer, Ryff, Carr, & Magee, 1998). This approach is quite useful when there is the potential for meaningful heterogeneity that is lost when the focus is limited to response means. For instance, in an effort to understand well-being, it is probably insufficient to simply regard people who report being religious as a homogeneous group to be compared with a supposedly homogeneous group of people who are not religious. We suspect that the reason that religiosity has a small correlation with indices of happiness and meaning in life is that groups with distinct motivations, behavioral commitment, and well-being outcomes are being merged together. With a person-centric approach, we can empirically determine whether there are cases of religious people that are qualitatively different from each other on meaningful strings of variables such as the degree to which they are intrinsically or extrinsically motivated, the degree to which there is behavioral commitment on a daily basis toward prayer and sacrifice, and the degree to which choices regarding leisure, socializing, and work are dictated by religious beliefs. With a person-centered approach, scientists can test whether there are distinct, meaningful subsets of people whose characteristics correspond to significant differences in well-being or moral behavior or any other relevant outcome (see Westen & Shedler, 2007 for an example of empirically derived personality configurations with implications for moving positive psychology forward). As long as inquiry is not restricted to a small subset of the population of interest, as long as relevant variables are chosen in the quest to map out potentially neglected heterogeneity, and as long as replications are relatively consistent, person-centered approaches preserve human beings as the unit of analysis improving inferences that can be made about the dynamic complexity of people. On their own, neither approach offers the scope of synthesis of a broad theory. To do this, a perspective is needed that includes the majority of relevant indicators at both the predictor and outcome levels and thus combines variable-centric and person-centric approaches. To do anything less is to increase the propensity to find spurious effects, sending researchers and practitioners down empty roads to understand and improve people's lives.

Our hope is that a future agenda for positive psychology is broad enough to include various approaches, with various methods, guided (but not governed) by strong theoretical frameworks. Instead of grabbing a single body part of the proverbial elephant, science will progress faster when we realize that no positive construct exists in a vacuum. Before we make claims on the value of a specific construct, we need to carefully consider whether any benefits are better accounted for by other well-established or parsimonious constructs. For instance, does emotional creativity offer any additional understanding to how people navigate their social world than emotional valence, awareness, and clarity? Is religiosity in adults linked to well-being because of something particular to religious beliefs and practice or is it better accounted for by mundane mechanisms such as social support and the presence of a clearly defined purpose in life? We also require links between the intrapersonal and interpersonal world. The research on how people respond to partners that share good news, termed capitalization, has been one of the most valuable discoveries in positive psychology in that it has been shown to be predictive of relationship love and commitment even after accounting for how supportive partners are during difficult times (social support). With the establishment of this construct, we can now turn to the qualities of the people that enter situations where partners share positive events to understand how personality, self-regulation, and context operate in this equation. Similarly, seemingly intrapersonal strengths such as wisdom, creativity, and perseverance are rarely considered in the context of social interactions and relationships. The merger of the intrapersonal and interpersonal is a fruitful direction because outside of the laboratory and paper-and-pencil questionnaires, people cannot be divorced from the ebb and flow of social situations (even if it just imagining or fantasizing about other people).

## Additional Challenges

### Integrating Biological Perspectives

A couple of other issues loom as challenges for positive psychology. The first is to remember what we're studying. We're studying people, and people are organisms. There's a captivating field of research that looks at what happens to people when they are reminded of their beastly natures. Here we're not referring to Freud's id-based drives, but rather to what researchers call our "creatureliness" (e.g., Goldenberg et al., 2001). When people are asked to reflect on the biological processes they share with other animals, they get uncomfortable, with terror management theory explaining that reminders of our biology underscore the truth that biological things die, and upon dying fail to appear as special as they once did. We often resist the notion that our cherished existence will cease and that upon death our bodies will become as inert as packaged meat in the grocery store. Is it possible for a field of science to have a similar reaction to the fact that we are studying biological organisms, no matter how complex they appear to be? The great appeal of psychology is the fact that by studying human behavior, there are very good reasons for trying to understand what happens at the subcellular level as well as what happens at the social collective or even cultural level. Our interests span the scope of human creation and endeavor, yet our positive psychology research often spans only the breadth of cognitive processing required to choose a number between one and seven to register our attitudes on a self-report survey. This is not intended as a critique of using self-report measures. Rather, efforts should be made to integrate lower-level biological perspectives into our research and, in turn, seek ways to make our research relevant to the biological perspective. There exists a temptation in positive psychology to perhaps overly ennoble the human being and neglect the biological organism.

Many researchers integrate some degree of biological underpinnings to their work. The best of this work has charted metabolic markers of psychological states in the brain, hormonal indicators of stress and affiliation, physiological arousal, or immune cell reflections of disease progression. But for most people interested in positive psychology, a rather familiar and routine incorporation of the biological perspective seems to peter out a couple pages into an article after mentioning hemispheric asymmetry (left prefrontal cortex slants being associated with exploratory behavior), the orbitofrontal cortex, oxytocin, or dopamine. The contributions in the biological section of this book will radically open the eyes of people who are content to cite *de rigeur* the trendiest imaging or brain lesion study (see Low, Bower, Moskowitz, & Epel; Segerstrom & Smith; and Panksepp, this volume). Of course, biological measures are subject to the same problems as other variable-centric or tool-bound methods. They do not necessarily reflect the phenomenon of interest, they do not always inform the question at hand, and they may force research questions to conform to their use rather than the theory being pursued. However, the 20th century provided an inescapable conclusion: human psychology is a biological process at its fundamental level of reduction. Although we are in agreement that the characteristics and experiences of greatest interest to positive psychologists might not be reducible to a biological level, and that positive psychology might gain the most traction by focusing on personality and higher levels of organization (see Sheldon, this volume), this experience cannot be divorced from the organ or cellular level any more than our physical health can be divorced from how organs and cells are functioning. It makes a lot of sense to work both up and down the levels of organization within a human being, from character strengths down to autonomic arousal, hormonal levels, and the integrity of RNA transcription; from positive affect up to happiness contagion, collective self-esteem, and legacy-building generativity.

Not everyone has access to a Seven Tesla fMRI magnet, or a blood assay machine, or a grant to obtain those services (neither of us currently do). That should not prevent any psychological researcher—positive or otherwise—from enriching his or her conceptualization of well-being, strengths, belongingness, or any other phenomenon through a responsive grounding in biological science. This does not have to mean that character strengths always need to be explained in terms of neurotransmitter action or brain amorphisms. One of the best examples of how biological science can be done without needing to be an expert in comparative psychology or having a place to store blood samples is likely to be familiar to most readers. In Baumeister and Leary's (1995) classic article about the need to belong, a massive amount of contemporary psychological science concerning the influence of social relationships on individual functioning was firmly rooted in an evolutionary perspective. By developing hypotheses based on best estimates of our species' ancestral environments, a robust vision of why the social world is important emerged, providing leverage for the venerable observations of Cooley (1902) and Mead (1934). A similar task remains for many of the topics central to positive psychology (emotions are an obvious example). Why did strengths evolve? What advantage might curiosity confer for survival? Might meaning and purpose in life have served an organizing function in the small bands of ancestral hominids that gave eventual rise to us? Can human greatness and flourishing truly be understood without also understanding the biological needs and origins of our species?

Another advantage of directing more of our attention to the biological machinery running our show is that attempting to get up to speed with this exploding area of research is very humbling and is an excellent exercise in demonstrating that there is so much we do not know! Socrates' famously deflected accolades that pegged him as the wisest man in Athens by saying that his only wisdom came from his appreciation of the fact that he knew nothing. A subtle seduction of gaining a platform as successful and prominent as positive psychology is that a flavor of cognitive dissonance could set it. Given how hard each of us likely works at building our expertise, we become deeply tempted by our investment to think we are right. To the contrary, good science demands that we not only entertain the possibility that our pet theories are wrong, but actively consider alternative explanations, being open to the story borne out by the data apart from our expectations and aspirations.

At present, in the rush of excitement to share new knowledge about the positive nature of humanity and how to achieve it, the importance of replications and bending over backward to test alternative explanations have often been skipped over. It is doubly important to put pressure on our notions if we are contemplating interventions designed to change people.

## Taking Positive Psychology to Market (Too Soon)

It is hard to think of a precedent for the rapid assimilation of positive psychology into the mainstream imagination. Clearly, that is the mark of a powerful, or at least powerfully compelling, idea. Most clinicians these days take it for granted that cognitive-behavioral therapies are efficacious approaches for a variety of psychological problems. However, if one traces the core ideas back as far as Albert Ellis' rational emotive behavioral therapy (e.g., Ellis, 1969), it is rather shocking to see this approach battling Perls' gestalt therapy for legitimacy in the legendary "Gloria" psychotherapy training tapes (with many years to go before reaching the current exalted status). Positive psychology was inaugurated to stimulate an empirical study of human excellence, and the appeal of that directive brought a hungry market. As a collective, positive psychology has been only too happy (pun intended) to meet that demand. For example, the seminal popular book on positive psychology, Seligman's (2002) *Authentic Happiness*, was published only two years after the call was made in the *American Psychologist* to start studying what makes life most worth living. Within the next five years, more than a dozen conceptually similar books had been written by other scientists for the same general audience.

The desire to give away our science is a big part of the identity of positive psychologists, and it is easy to forget sometimes just how revelatory some of the knowledge that we take for granted is for many people outside our profession. Even the most basic inference drawn from 40 years of studying well-being—good relationships are good for us—is in fact a novel insight to some. We are both clinicians by training, and this experience helps keep us from taking our knowledge for granted. Translating basic science into what the largest portion of the market wants—namely, solutions to vexing problems—

is not always straightforward, and that challenge has often been met with wisdom, prudence, temperance, and a clear statement about the empirical support for any suggested interventions. However, not all efforts in the name of positive psychology have been sound. There is an enormous flood of "aftermarket" positive psychology products out there, and more seem to be generated every month. Consumers can get their hands on "positive" books, services, unlicensed life coaches, motivational CD programs, and even bracelets and rocks! Surely if anything undermines the mission of forging a better science of human greatness, it is the hollow promise created by hawkers of the psychological equivalent of the Sham-Wow. The first 10 entries returned from an Internet search on "positive psychology products" consisted of a seminal textbook by C. R. Snyder and Shane Lopez, a transpersonal psychology conference in Palm Springs, an applied positive psychology center, a Web page for a coach who follows the "Law of the Garbage Truck," a positive psychology "store" where you can buy space to advertise your latest self-help book, and more sites peddling books and coaching services. Who knows, maybe all of these are quality offerings. The more salient point is that, to the public, the face of positive psychology is someone with very white teeth selling the secrets to everything we ever wanted.

There is probably little that true positive psychologists can do to defend the science from the more vulgar marketers, but the field should aggressively promote a clear vision of what science is, and what science is when it is applied to positive psychology. The first data on rigorously tested positive psychology interventions have only recently begun to show up in journals, yet people have been offering to "apply" positive psychology for several years already. What kind of message does this convey about the scientific endeavor of positive psychology? Is it any wonder that positive psychology is often dismissed as "happiology" or the equivalent of accepting a Dixie cup of Kool-Aid from Jim Jones?

Offering suggestions, giving the science away, attempting to apply the very best psychological science to the problems people face are all noble aims and extremely defensible. But, in the long run, it is even more important to clearly convey in what ways positive psychology is a science and in what ways much of what is done in the name of positive psychology is unscientific. This is not a job that can be completed in a year or two. This aim will require patience and persistence over the next decade, when we hope that positive psychology develops an increasingly strong scientific foundation and serves as an ambitious, hopeful, clear-minded chart of the human condition. We hope that the insights and visions crafted by the authors of the chapters that follow chart a clear course toward these aims.

## General Aims

We are interested in how positive psychology fits in the larger picture of science and how to make this happen to an even greater degree; what inroads still need to be made (besides perfunctory statements on how positive institutions are neglected or how we need to study harder outcomes); what areas are being neglected and misunderstood; and what sort of directions need to be modified with the goal of advancing the quality of the science and how it is applied. In this context, we would like to emphasize that criticisms and critiques should be constructive, a means to an end rather than an end in themselves.

In this book we hope to deepen positive psychology and enhance its longevity. We invited leading developmental, biological, social, personality, and clinical psychologists from around the world to weigh in on what we know and help design a template of where positive psychology needs to go in the future in order to best realize its huge potential. It is our hope that this book will provide a radical integrative advance for the positive psychology movement, enhancing its conceptual complexity, its explanatory potential, and its underlying connectivity to the broader research base of psychology. The list of contributors might surprise a few readers. The work of several contributors has been neglected at the cost of missing potential preconditions for the most optimally positive results to occur. Our aim was to create a critical analysis of where we are and a guidebook of where to go.

*References*

Bargh, J. A., & Williams, E. L. (2006). The automaticity of social life. *Current Directions in Psychological Science, 15*, 1–4.

Baumeister, R. F., & Leary, M. R. (1995). The need to belong: Desire for interpersonal attachments as a fundamental human motivation. *Psychological Bulletin, 117*, 497–529.

Biswas-Diener, R., Kashdan, T. B., & King, L. A. (2009). Two traditions of happiness research, not two distinct types of happiness. *Journal of Positive Psychology, 4*, 208–211.

Boniwell, I., Osin, E., Linley, P. A., & Ivanchenko, G. (2010). A question of balance: Examining relationships between time perspective and measures of well-being in the British and Russian student samples. *Journal of Positive Psychology, 5*, 24–40.

Brown, K. W., Ryan, R. M., & Creswell, J. D. (2007). Mindfulness: Theoretical foundations and evidence for its salutary effects. *Psychological Inquiry, 18*, 211–237.

Campbell, L., Simpson, J. A., Stewart, M., & Manning, J. G. (2003). Putting personality in social context: Extraversion, emergent leadership, and the availability of rewards. *Personality and Social Psychology Bulletin, 29*, 1547–1559.

Cervone, D. (1997). Social-cognitive mechanisms and personality coherence: Self-knowledge, situational beliefs, and cross-situational coherence in perceived self-efficacy. *Psychological Science, 8*, 43–50.

Cervone, D. (2005). Personality architecture: Within-person structures and processes. *Annual Review of Psychology, 56*, 423–452.

Cervone, D., & Shoda, Y. (Eds.). (1999). *The coherence of personality: Social-cognitive bases of consistency, variability, and organization*. New York: Guilford Press.

Cooley, C. H. (1902). *Human nature and the social order*. New York: Scribners.

Deci, E., & Ryan, R. (2000). The "what" and "why" of goal pursuits: Human needs and the self-determination of behavior. *Psychological Inquiry, 11*, 227–268.

Diener, E. & Larsen, R. J. (1984). Temporal stability and cross-situational consistency of affective, cognitive, and behavioral responses. *Journal of Personality and Social Psychology, 47*, 871–883.

Diener, E., Sandvik, E., & Pavot, W. G. (1990). Happiness is the frequency, not intensity, of positive versus negative affect. In F. Strack, M. Argyle, & N. Schwarz (Eds.), *The social psychology of subjective well-being* (119–139). Elmsford, NY: Pergamon Press.

Diener, E., Suh, E. M., Lucas, R. E., & Smith, H. L. (1999). Subjective well-being: Three decades of progress. *Psychological Bulletin, 125*, 276–302.

Ellis, A. (1969). Rational emotive therapy. *Journal of Contemporary Psychotherapy, 1*, 82–90.

Emmons, R. (1999). *The psychology of ultimate concerns: Motivation and spirituality in personality*. New York: Guilford Press.

Fleeson, W. (2001). Toward a structure- and process-integrated view of personality: Traits as density distributions of states. *Journal of Personality and Social Psychology, 80,* 1011–1027.

Gilbert, D. T., Pinel, E. C., Wilson, T. D., Blumberg, S. J., & Wheatley, T. (1998). Immune neglect: A source of durability bias in affective forecasting. *Journal of Personality and Social Psychology, 75,* 617–638.

Goldenberg, J. L., Pyszczynski, T., Greenberg, J., Solomon, S., Kluck, B., & Cornwell, R. (2001). I am NOT an animal: Mortality salience, disgust, and the denial of human creatureliness. *Journal of Experimental Psychology: General, 130,* 427–435.

Hayes, S. C., Luoma, J. B., Bond, F. W., Masuda, A., & Lillis, J. (2006). Acceptance and Commitment Therapy: Model, processes, and outcomes. *Behaviour Research and Therapy, 44,* 1–25.

Heppner, W. L., Kernis, M. H., Nezlek, J. B., Foster, J., Lakey, C. E., & Goldman, B. M. (2008). Within-person relationships between daily self-esteem, need satisfaction, and authenticity. *Psychological Science, 19,* 1140–1145.

Kashdan, T. B., Biswas-Diener, R., & King, L. A. (2008). Reconsidering happiness: The costs of distinguishing between hedonics and eudaimonia. *Journal of Positive Psychology, 3,* 219–233.

Kashdan, T. B., Breen, W. E., & Julian, T. (2010). Everyday strivings in combat veterans with posttraumatic stress disorder: Problems arise when avoidance and emotion regulation dominate. *Behavior Therapy, 41,* 350–363.

Keyes, C. L. M., Shmotkin, D., & Ryff, C. D. (2002). Optimizing well-being: The empirical encounter of two traditions. *Journal of Personality and Social Psychology, 82,* 1007–1022.

King, L. A., Hicks, J. A., Krull, J., & Baker, A. G. (2006). Positive affect and the experience of meaning in life. *Journal of Personality and Social Psychology, 90,* 179–196.

Leary, M. R., Adams, C. E., & Tate, E. B. (2006). Hypo-egoic self-regulation: Exercising self-control by diminishing the influence of the self. *Journal of Personality, 74,* 1803–1831.

Linley, A. (2008). *Average to A+: Realising strengths in yourself and others*. London: CAPP Press.

Little, B., Salemla-Aro, K., & Phillips, S. (2007). *Personal project pursuit: Goals, action and human flourishing*. Mahwah, NJ: Erlbaum.

Longmore, R., & Worrell, M. (2007). Do we need to challenge thoughts in cognitive behavior therapy? *Clinical Psychology Review, 27,* 173–187.

Lyubomirsky, S., King, L., & Diener, E. (2005). The benefits of frequent positive affect: Does happiness lead to success? *Psychological Bulletin, 131,* 803–855.

McAdams, D. P. (1996). Personality, modernity, and the storied self: A contemporary framework for studying persons. *Psychological Inquiry, 7,* 295–321.

McAdams, D. P. (2008). Personal narratives and the life story. In O. John, R. Robins, and L. Pervin (Eds.), *Handbook of personality: Theory and research* (3rd Ed., pp. 241–261). New York: Guilford Press.

Mead, G. H. (1934). *Mind, self, and society,* Chicago: University of Chicago.

Mischel, W., & Shoda, Y. (1998). Reconciling processing dynamics and personality dispositions. *Annual Review of Psychology, 49,* 229–258.

McKnight, P. E., & Kashdan, T. B. (2009). Purpose in life as a system that creates and sustains health and well-being: An integrative, testable theory. *Review of General Psychology, 13,* 242–251.

Oishi, S., Diener, E., & Lucas, R. (2007). The optimum level of well-being: Can people be too happy? *Perspectives on Psychological Science, 2,* 346–360.

Park, N., Peterson, C., & Seligman, M. E. P. (2004). Strengths of character and wellbeing. *Journal of Social and Clinical Psychology, 23,* 603–619.

Peterson, C., Park, N., Pole, N., D'Andrea, W., & Seligman, M. E. P. (2008). Strengths of character and posttraumatic growth. *Journal of Traumatic Stress, 21,* 214–217.

Peterson, C., Park, N., & Seligman, M. E. P. (2006). Greater strengths of character and recovery from illness. *Journal of Positive Psychology, 1,* 17–26.

Peterson, C., Ruch, W., Beermann, U., Park, N., & Seligman, M. E. P. (2007). Strengths of character, orientations to happiness, and life satisfaction. *Journal of Positive Psychology, 2,* 149–156.

Peterson, C., & Seligman, M. E. P. (2004). *Character strengths and virtues: A handbook of classification*. New York: Oxford University Press.

Seligman, M. E. P. (1998). *Learned optimism*. New York: Pocket Books (Simon and Schuster).

Seligman, M. E. P. (2002). *Authentic happiness*. New York: Free Press.

Seligman, M. E. P., & Csikszentmihalyi, M. (Eds.). (2000). Positive psychology [Special issue]. *American Psychologist, 55.*

Sheldon, K. M. (2004). *Optimal human being: An integrated multi-level perspective*. Mahwah, NJ: Lawrence Erlbaum Associates.

Singer, B., Ryff, C. D., Carr, D., & Magee, W. J. (1998). Life histories and mental health: A person-centered strategy. In A. Raftery (Ed.),

*Sociological Methodology* (pp. 1–51). Washington, DC: American Sociological Association.

Stone, A. A., Shiffman, S., Atienza, A. A., & Nebeling, L. (2007). *The science of real-time data capture*. New York: Oxford University Press.

Wegner, D. M. (1994). Ironic processes of mental control. *Psychological Review, 101*, 34–52.

Westen, D., & Shedler, J. (2007). Personality diagnosis with the Shedler-Westen Assessment Procedure (SWAP): Integrating clinical and statistical measurement and prediction. *Journal of Abnormal Psychology, 116*, 810–822.

Wilson, K. G. & Murrell, A. R. (2004). Values work in acceptance and commitment therapy: Setting a course for behavioral treatment. In Hayes, S. C., Follette, V. M., & Linehan, M. (Eds.), *Mindfulness and acceptance: Expanding the cognitive-behavioral tradition* (pp. 120–151). New York: Guilford.

Wilson, T. D., Wheatley, T. P., Meyers, J. M., Gilbert, D. T., & Axsom, D. (2000). Focalism: A source of durability bias in affective forecasting. *Journal of Personality and Social Psychology, 78*, 821–836.

# II

**Biological Perspectives**

# 3

# Positive Psychophysiology: The Body and Self-Regulation

*Suzanne C. Segerstrom, Timothy W. Smith, and*
*Tory A. Eisenlohr-Moul*

## Introduction

Self-regulation refers to control over one's emotions, thoughts, and behaviors. Failure of self-regulation is cited as contributing to many important individual and societal problems, including problems with eating, spending, interpersonal violence, sexual promiscuity, and alcohol and drug use (Baumeister & Vohs, 2004). It is less commonly recognized that self-regulation is also important for optimal functioning. At an individual level, enhancing positive emotion as well as dampening negative emotion appears to require regulatory strength (Demaree, Robinson, Everhart, & Schmeichel, 2004). Savoring positive experiences, for example, both amplifies associated positive affect and requires control over one's attention and stream of thought to do so (Bryant, 2003; Segerstrom, Roach, Evans, Schipper, & Darville, 2010). At an interpersonal level, the abilities to avoid offense, help, cooperate, and manage self-presentation both contribute to more positive social interactions and require self-regulatory strength (e.g., Finkel et al., 2006; Muraven, 2008; Vohs, Baumeister, & Ciarocco, 2005).

Self-regulation can also contribute to resilience in the face of negative experience. Resilience can arise from several sources: limited exposure to negative experiences, diminished emotional and physiologic reactivity to negative experiences, accelerated recovery from negative experiences, and greater restoration of adaptive resources after such experiences (A. Smith & Baum, 2003; Uchino et al., 2007; Williams et al., in press). For example, effective self-regulation of stress and emotion is evident in people's choices of situations to enter and avoid, as well as in their active management of their expressive behavior during social interactions that might otherwise become strained (Gross, 2001; Williams et al., in press). Some self-regulatory strategies (e.g., attentional redeployment, cognitive reappraisal) can attenuate negative emotional responses and physiological reactivity during demanding or threatening situations, as well as facilitate a more rapid and complete return of those responses to normal, pre-stressor levels following such situations. Self-regulation also influences subsequent restorative processes that rebuild the individual's adaptive resources, such as high-quality sleep (Hall et al., 2008), exposure to natural environments (Parsons, 2007), and social interactions that induce positive moods and affirm a sense of connection and care (A. Smith & Baum, 2003). Hence, individual differences in resilience reflect effects of self-regulation on exposure, reactivity, recovery, and restoration, ultimately moderating otherwise unhealthy effects of negative experiences.

An abundance of empirical evidence points to factors that cause limitations in the ability to self-regulate. For example, the ability to self-regulate is impaired after an initial act of self-regulation, a phenomenon called self-regulatory fatigue or "ego depletion" (Muraven & Baumeister, 2000). This fatigue is not limited to particular domains—regulation of any domain (including, for example, emotion, behavior, speech, attention, or choice) can result in fatigue in any other domain. Therefore, the evidence points to a general pool of self-regulatory capacity. In the present chapter, we suggest that this capacity depends on, is reflected in, and affects physiology. That is, self-regulation is literally embodied. This assertion seems obvious with regard to the central nervous system (e.g., Compton et al., 2008; Inzlicht & Gutsell, 2007), but less so with regard to peripheral physiology. Nonetheless, there is evidence that peripheral regulation of physiological parameters such as blood glucose and heart rate is intertwined with central regulation of the self. Therefore, we focus here on these peripheral processes. We give a brief overview of physiological systems involved in self-regulation, review the empirical links between self-regulation and physiology in several domains, and then suggest directions for future research.

## Measurement and Meaning of Physiological Parameters Related to Self-Regulation

Because readers may not be familiar with how physiological parameters that we later relate to self-regulation are measured, manipulated, and interpreted, we provide a brief orientation to three parameters: one metabolic (blood glucose and glucose regulation), one neuroendocrine (cortisol), and one cardiovascular (heart rate variability). This is clearly not an exhaustive list of physiological parameters that *may* be relevant to self-regulation, but it is nearly exhaustive of the parameters that *have* been linked to self-regulation. Later, we expand on this narrowness as something to be remedied as this research moves forward.

## Glucose

All brain processes rely on the metabolism of glucose for fuel (Siesjö, 1978). Though the brain constitutes only 2% of the body's mass, it consumes roughly 21% of the blood's glucose (Elia, 1992). Furthermore, there is evidence that higher-order, goal-oriented functions such as self-regulation rank among the most energetically expensive of the brain's processes, making glucose availability and transport particularly relevant to these tasks (Fairclough & Houston, 2004).

Blood glucose levels are typically measured in milligrams per deciliter (mg/dL) using a glucose meter to analyze a small drop of blood. Blood glucose can be also manipulated by glucose injection or ingestion, most precisely through the use of a glucose clamp technique in which blood glucose levels are "clamped" at hypoglycemic, euglycemic, or hyperglycemic levels by the intravenous administration of glucose or insulin (Defronzo, Tobin, & Andres, 1979). The latter technique allows for the systematic study of physiological, cognitive, and emotional phenomena associated with different blood glucose levels. Because people with diabetes frequently experience low blood glucose and exhibit poor glucose tolerance, some studies of the relationship between blood glucose and self-regulation compare people with and without diabetes.

Blood glucose tolerance, a measure of the effectiveness of glucose transport into cells, is measured after an overnight fast by the administration of glucose followed by periodic assessment of blood glucose levels. A pattern of high blood glucose after glucose administration followed by a return to baseline levels indicates good glucose tolerance, whereas a pattern of abnormally high blood glucose levels after glucose administration followed by a dip below baseline indicates poor glucose tolerance. Glycosylated hemoglobin (hemoglobin A1c) is a long-term measure of the effectiveness of blood glucose control, assessing effectiveness over the last 2–3 months (Koenig et al., 1976). Because it is less sensitive to short-term changes, this measure is especially useful for identifying those with less effective use of glucose. It has been suggested that levels of A1c not exceed 6% for normal individuals (American Diabetes Association, 2008). A1c can be measured using a simple A1c monitor to analyze a small drop of blood.

## Cortisol

The primary function of cortisol is to mobilize glucose for use in the body by initiating its release from the liver and muscles (Lovallo & Thomas, 2000). Cortisol release follows a normal diurnal pattern, peaking in the morning and falling throughout the day with slight increases associated with meal times. The spontaneous release of additional cortisol by the hypothalamic-pituitary-adrenal (HPA) axis in response to environmental stimuli is most often attributed to a "stress response" elicited by physical or psychosocial stressors (Hennessey & Levine, 1979). However, cortisol levels and patterns of release may also be associated with energy regulation in general. First, cortisol release may change the energetic priorities in the body even in the absence of stress. Second, cortisol release during the exertion of self-regulatory effort may compensate for or anticipate energy that might be required for "fight or flight" or "pause and plan," that is, self-regulation (Segerstrom, Hardy, Evans, & Fantini, in press). Although the spontaneous release of additional cortisol makes a short-term increase in energy possible, it does so in part by slowing or inhibiting long-term processes such as tissue repair, digestion, and reproduction.

Cortisol levels can be manipulated pharmacologically by administering metyraprone, an inhibitor of glucocorticoid synthesis that decreases cortisol levels, and hydrocortisone, a synthetic glucocorticoid (e.g., Lupien et al., 2002). Cortisol may be measured in blood, urine, and saliva. Only 3%–5% of total blood cortisol is unbound and biologically active; in urine and saliva, only this active free cortisol is present. If measurement by blood sample is necessary, Lovallo and Thomas (2000) recommend an indwelling catheter, inserted 45–60 minutes before the first blood sample is taken. Urine, collected most often in 24-hour samples, may also be used to measure cortisol. Urinary cortisol, which shows good correlations with plasma levels of free cortisol (Moleman et al., 1992), is often used in research examining chronic stressors, as it allows for time-integrated sampling. Salivary cortisol, which also correlates highly with plasma levels of free cortisol (Aardal & Holm, 1995), can be assessed using various simple collection methods. Given the accuracy, ease, and noninvasiveness of salivary cortisol measurement, it is generally considered to be the most desirable way to measure cortisol, especially when one is interested in transitory changes in HPA activity (Kirschbaum & Hellhammer, 1989).

## Autonomic Nervous System

Although the process of self-regulation and its physiological outcomes have been assessed through a variety of aspects of autonomic nervous system responses, cardiac parasympathetic activity plays a central role in current theory and research. The heart is dually innervated by the sympathetic and parasympathetic branches of the autonomic nervous system, with opposing effects on heart rate. At rest, parasympathetic influences predominate, as combined pharmacological blockade or surgical denervation of sympathetic and parasympathetic inputs results in increased heart rate. Respiratory sinus arrhythmia (RSA) provides a noninvasive index of parasympathetic activation of the heart. Heart rate accelerates as an individual inhales because the parasympathetic inhibition of the heart is briefly dampened. Heart rate slows down again as parasympathetic inhibition returns when the individual exhales. This oscillation in heart rate across respiratory cycles is RSA, and its magnitude in turn can be used to measure the magnitude of parasympathetic activity. A variety of specific methods are used to measure RSA, though the most common and readily accessible methods quantify the degree of variability in heart rate that falls within the likely frequency range of respiration (i.e., 9–24 cycles per minute). This index, called high frequency heart rate variability (HRV), is the most commonly used index of parasympathetic activation. It can be obtained with relatively simple psychophysiological assessment methods for measuring heart rate and software for extracting the degree of HRV corresponding to the respiratory cycle (for a review, see Thayer, Hansen, & Johnsen, 2008). RSA is the primary contributor to total variability in heart rate, as specific measures of high frequency HRV (i.e., RSA) correlate highly with other, less specific measures such as the root mean square of the successive differences in the interbeat interval (Allen, Chambers, & Towers, 2007; Berntson, Lozano, & Chen, 2005). In the rest of this chapter, we will use the more general label of HRV to refer to results of the relevant empirical studies, which used various means of extracting the parasympathetically controlled variability in heart rate.

## Taking Stock

What do we know so far about the relationship of self-regulation to physiology? We begin by reviewing relevant theories that link heart rate variability and glucose, respectively, to self-regulatory ability. We then turn to the empirical evidence. Although this is a relatively new area of research, there are studies that address physiological correlates and predictors of self-regulation in several domains: executive cognitive function, repetitive thought (e.g., worry), emotion, and social relationships.

### Psychophysiological Theories of Self-Regulation: Polyvagal Theory and Neurovisceral Integration

Two prominent models of the psychophysiology of self-regulation emphasize the close connections of parasympathetic processes in general and HRV in particular to the brain bases of self-regulation. Polyvagal Theory (Porges, 2001, 2007) and the Neurovisceral Integration Model (Hagemann, Waldstein, & Thayer, 2003; Thayer & Lane, 2000) both note that a set of structures and circuits within the pre-frontal regions of the brain called the *ventral vagus complex* plays a key role in parasympathetic nervous system modulation of emotion and expressive behavior, as well as related physiological responses. Efferent parasympathetic nerves innervate the specific organs involved in expressive behavior (e.g., facial expressions and vocalization). These aspects of emotion and expressiveness, in turn, are central in social interaction. Ongoing parasympathetic inhibition of these responses can be altered quickly as individuals vary the level and tone of their engagement with the social environment. In these perspectives, relatively stable resting levels of HRV reflect the individual's capacity for regulation, whereas short-term changes reflect temporary application (i.e., HRV increase) or withdrawal (i.e., HRV decrease) of the parasympathetic "brake" on sympathetic activation and related expressive behavior (c.f., Segerstrom & Solberg Nes, 2007). For example, HRV increases as individuals attempt to regulate the experience or expression of negative emotion in response to aversive stimuli (Butler et al., 2006).

The Polyvagal and Neurovisceral Integration perspectives are based in large part on the fact that neural circuits supporting self-regulation of emotion and social behavior and parasympathetic influences on the heart are co-localized in the brain, comprising an integrated system (Porges, 2007; Thayer & Lane, 2009). Anesthesia of the pre-frontal cortex region involved in regulation of emotion and expressive behavior decreases HRV and increases heart rate as parasympathetic inhibition is withdrawn (Ahern et al., 2001). These brain regions also support aspects of attention and response inhibition that are central in executive cognitive functions, which are essential cognitive underpinnings of the modulation of emotional expression and social behavior (Ochsner & Gross, 2007; Posner & Rothbart, 2007; von Hippel, 2007). Further, HRV is correlated with performance on executive cognitive functioning tasks (Hansen, Johnsen & Thayer, 2003), and the degree of activation of related brain structures (e.g., anterior cingulate cortex) correlates with levels of HRV during performance of such tasks (Gianaros, Van Der Veen, & Jennings, 2004; Matthews et al., 2004). Hence, readily available, inexpensive, and noninvasive measures of parasympathetic influences on the heart can provide a physiologic window through which to observe self-regulatory processes.

### Psychophysiological Theories of Self-Regulation: The Energy Metaphor

As the empirical evidence below will attest, higher levels of blood glucose and better glucose regulation are associated with better self-regulation and more positive and less negative outcomes related to self-regulation. Based on these findings, Gailliot and colleagues have proposed that blood glucose is a literal measure of the capacity to self-regulate (Gailliot & Baumeister, 2007; Gailliot et al., 2007). However, there are physiological complexities that suggest a more nuanced interpretation. First, glucose regulation in the brain is different than in the periphery. Most glucose transporters in the periphery (i.e., GLUT4) are insulin-regulated and not highly saturable. In contrast, most glucose transporters in the brain (i.e., GLUT3) are not insulin-regulated, are highly saturable, and therefore are completely saturated at a wide range of blood glucose levels, although transporters at the blood-brain barrier (i.e., GLUT1) are less saturable (Frayne, 2003). Second, glucose ingestion elicits a host of complex regulatory responses. For example, increases in blood glucose correlate with an increase in sympathetic nervous system activity, and this relationship may be bidirectional, as both feeding and stress can initiate this change. Therefore, with regard to the energy theory of blood glucose,

> The strength of this notion lies in its common-sense plausibility, not in scientific evidence, and so the effects may well be epiphenomenal… a plethora of neurohormonal responses are activated for glycaemic homeostasis (Gibson & Green, 2002, p. 185).

Although blood glucose may be a good marker, it is entirely possible that the effects on self-regulatory ability are not due to blood glucose per se, but to the indirect effects of blood glucose on neurohormonal responses, to its ability to index qualities of glucose metabolism and regulation, or to both. The empirical findings reviewed below should be considered in this light.

## Empirical Findings: Regulation of Executive Cognitive Functions

Control over basic cognitive processes such as attention is attributed to the central executive; hence, executive cognitive functioning has been proposed as both an example of and a capability essential to self-regulation. Supporting this proposal, self-regulatory fatigue selectively and adversely affects fluid and executive cognitive functions (Schmeichel et al., 2003, 2007). Conversely, people with stronger executive cognitive functions (e.g., error control, working memory) are more effective self-regulators and experience higher levels of well-being (Hofmann, Gschwendner, Friese, Wiers, & Schmitt, 2008; Robinson, 2007).

Evidence suggests that higher availability of blood glucose, a more responsive cortisol system, and higher heart rate variability may all contribute to more effective executive control. Gailliot and Baumeister (2007) provide a review of the literature linking blood glucose to attentional control. For example, blood glucose dropped during performance of the Stroop color-word task, a test of selective attention; Stroop performance correlated inversely with blood glucose; and performance could be restored with a glucose drink (Fairclough & Houston, 2004; Gailliot et al., 2007). Other studies have linked low blood glucose and poor glucose tolerance to impaired performance on difficult, complex, or effortful tasks (Benton and Owens, 1993; Benton, Owens, and Parker, 1994; Fairclough and Houston, 2004;

Owens and Benton, 1994; Schultes et al., 2005) and to many forms of self-regulatory failure (see Gailliot and Baumeister, 2007, for review).

A number of medical conditions are associated with deficits on neuropsychological measures of executive functions (Schillerstrom, Horton, & Royall, 2005). Non-insulin-dependent diabetes and insulin resistance are particularly interesting insofar as these conditions reflect poor glucose regulation. A number of large, population-based studies in several countries have found that individuals with diabetes perform more poorly on tests of executive functions and inductive reasoning (Abbatecola et al., 2004; Kuo et al., 2005; Kumari & Marmot, 2005; Qiu et al., 2006; Vanhanen et al., 1999). However, it is not clear whether these deficits are specific to executive cognitive functions (versus general cognitive functioning) or diabetes (versus hypertension). However, one study found that insulin resistance associated with poorer performance on the Trail Making Test, a test of cognitive flexibility, after controlling for Mini-Mental State Examination scores and a host of demographic and medical covariates including age, BMI, physical activity, and hypertension (Abbatecola et al., 1999).

A study examining the relationship of cortisol to executive functioning in preschoolers found a positive relationship between HPA activation and performance (Blair, Granger, and Razza, 2005). Another study found that higher levels of pretask cortisol were associated with poorer executive functioning in women but better executive functioning in men (as measured by the Wisconsin Card Sorting Test; McCormick, Lewis, Somley, & Kaham, 2007). As noted above, cortisol release could either facilitate glucose release or reflect a compensatory response to hypoglycemia.

Finally, high HRV has been associated with better performance at executive cognitive tasks. In a small sample of children in Head Start, higher HRV at rest and increases in HRV during testing were positively, albeit nonsignificantly, associated with peg-tapping and Stroop performance ($r = .15$–.28; Blair, 2003). Luft, Takase, and Darby (2009) found that HRV was higher during "executive" working memory tasks than in simple attention and reaction time tasks in adults. Another small study of male Norwegian Navy sailors found positive relationships between resting HRV and working memory and continuous performance test reaction time and accuracy (Hansen, Johnsen, & Thayer, 2003).

When a subgroup of sailors was restricted from physical activity (due to deployment on a submarine), their HRV and executive cognitive performance both declined relative to the subgroup that continued physical training (Hansen, Johnsen, Sollers, Stenvik, & Thayer, 2004). However, one recent population-based study (Whitehall II) did not find any relationship between HRV and cognitive performance, including executive functions (Britton et al., 2008).

In general, then, it seems that blood glucose and glucose regulation are important correlates of executive cognitive functions, including attentional control and cognitive flexibility. Furthermore, HRV seems to index the capacity to effect these functions, and the slower heart rate associated with vagal inhibition may reduce glucose consumption in the periphery and thereby affect glucoregulatory processes. Therefore, these parameters may be important for cognitive abilities that in turn help people control their thoughts, emotions, and relationships, to which we turn next. These relationships, however, are more evident in small-scale studies than in population-based studies. The smaller studies tend to be of younger people with few or none of the comorbid conditions that may complicate the relationship between physiology and cognitive self-regulatory capacity.

## Empirical Findings: Regulation of Repetitive Thought

Poor self-regulation manifests in thoughts as repetitive, uncontrolled, negative thought such as worry, rumination, and intrusive thoughts. Although fewer studies have addressed the physiological substrates of these naturalistic cognitions than cognitive function as measured with neuropsychological testing (as reviewed above), there is some evidence that peripheral physiology contributes to control over naturally occurring cognition.

In one study, adults with Type 1 (insulin-dependent) diabetes had blood glucose maintained at euglycemic or hypoglycemic levels by means of the glucose clamp technique. Under hypoglycemic conditions, participants were significantly more likely to report "task-irrelevant" cognitions such as "I thought about personal worries." Other cognitive variables such as concentration and confidence were unaffected, suggesting that control over worries is particularly correlated with blood glucose (McAulay, Deary, Sommerfield, Matthews, & Frier, 2006).

HRV has also been linked to poor control over one's thoughts. Alcoholics with lower resting HRV also were more bothered by unwanted and intrusive thoughts (Ingaldsson, Laberg, & Thayer, 2003). Resting HRV (HF power) correlated with cognitive accessibility of intelligence words after experimentally manipulated failure at a purported intelligence test (but not after success); higher accessibility of words related to failure suggests less inhibitory control over failure-related thoughts (Geisler & Kubiak, 2009). In an ambulatory study, worry episodes were characterized by low HRV (Pieper, Brosschot, van der Leeden, & Thayer, 2007). One question is whether worry creates subjective stress, which might lower HRV, or whether episodes of HRV are permissive for worry. One piece of support for the latter interpretation is that although both stress and worry increased HR, only worry was associated with low HRV.

## Empirical Findings: Regulation of Emotion

Emotion regulation refers to the process by which individuals "influence which emotions they have, when they have them, and how they experience and express these emotions" (Gross, 1998). Because emotion regulation relies on the same fatigable resources as other forms of self-regulation, it exhibits the same intraindividual variability in strength—variability that may be explained in part physiologically. Specifically, heart rate variability, blood glucose level, the effective use of glucose, and cortisol levels and patterns of release have been associated with one's ability to regulate emotion.

A growing body of literature indicates that one is more likely to both experience and express negative emotions when blood glucose becomes low due to natural processes or experimental manipulation. In one study, blood glucose was manipulated and maintained at hypoglycemic or euglycemic levels using a hyperinsulinemic glucose clamp technique (Gold, MacLeod, Frier, & Deary, 1995). During acute hypoglycemia, subjects reported lower hedonic tone (less happiness), an increase in tense arousal, and a decrease in energy relative to their euglycemic state. In another study, individuals with diabetes who were prone to hypoglycemic attacks reported higher anxiety and lower levels of happiness than individuals with diabetes alone (Wredling, Theorell, Roll, Lins, & Adamson, 1992). In a series of studies, higher blood glucose levels—either naturally occurring or due to the effects of a glucose drink—were associated with feeling less tense and giving fewer negative responses during a frustrating situation (Benton & Owens, 1993). Not surprisingly, the ineffective use of glucose has also been linked to poor emotion regulation. Poor glucose tolerance has been associated with many forms of psychopathology involving emotion dysregulation, especially depression (Winokur, Maislin, Phillips, & Amsterdam, 1988). Taken together, work in this area suggests that adequate glucoregulation is required for active regulation of experienced and expressed emotion.

While research addressing the relationship of cortisol and cortisol patterns to specific emotion regulation processes is virtually nonexistent, there is evidence that deviation from normal levels and patterns of secretion is associated with many disorders involving emotion dysregulation. For example, in one large cohort study, individuals with current or remitted major depressive disorder had a higher cortisol wakening response (increase in cortisol during the first 20–30 minutes of wakefulness) than those without current or remitted depression, suggesting that those with normal patterns of cortisol release may be less likely to experience major depression (Vreeburg et al., 2009). In another study, individuals with Borderline Personality Disorder—a disorder characterized by chronic and intense emotion dysregulation—had higher cortisol wakening response and higher total daily cortisol levels than healthy controls (Lieb et al., 2004). Although higher levels of real or perceived stress are likely to account for at least part of the relationship between psychopathology and abnormal cortisol values, it is also possible that chronic attempts to regulate negative affect influence cortisol release.

HRV has also predicted the ability to regulate emotions in naturalistic and laboratory settings. Higher resting vagal tone has been associated with self-reported ability to regulate emotion, lower frustration levels, and lower emotional arousal in response to daily stressors over a two-week period (Fabes & Eisenberg, 1997). Another study found that HRV mediated the relationship between perception of security in current relationships and effective recovery from a laboratory anger-recall task used to induce anger (Diamond & Hicks, 2005). Further, higher HRV has been linked to more emotional control and less hostility in romantic conflicts among those highly sensitive to rejection (Gyurak & Ayduk, 2008), as well as more approach motivation and

less defensiveness among normal subjects (Movius & Allen, 2005).

Higher heart rate variability has also been associated with startle responses to acoustic startle stimuli (Ruiz-Padial, Sollers, Vila, & Thayer, 2003). The acoustic startle reflex is ordinarily potentiated by the presentation of pleasant stimuli and inhibited by the presentation of aversive stimuli. In those with low heart rate variability, however, pleasant stimuli potentiated, rather than inhibited, the startle reflex, suggesting that those with low heart rate variability do not adequately differentiate between emotional cues. Such lack of differentiation means that, for those with lower HRV, emotional cues could have less functional significance and emotion regulation could be impaired (Persad & Polivy, 1993; c.f., Barrett, Gross, Christensen, & Bevenuto, 2001). When subjects in another study were shown a film of a slaughterhouse intended to induce negative emotion, higher resting HRV predicted less negative facial response to the film as well as greater ability to exaggerate facial responses to the film (Demaree, Robinson, Everhart, & Schmeichel, 2004). In a replication and extension of this study, higher resting HRV was once again associated with less negative facial expression in the negative-mood condition (Demaree, Pu, Robinson, Schmeichel, & Everhart, 2006). Notably, self-report measures of emotional reaction to the slaughterhouse film and physiological measures of sympathetic activation during the film were similar across levels of HRV. Because self-reported negative mood and measures of sympathetic activation are associated with emotional experience, emotion per se cannot account for the finding that higher resting HRV was associated with regulation of facial expression (Gross & Levenson, 1993, 1997).

Given the relatively consistent finding that higher HRV corresponds to better emotion regulation, it is not surprising that heart rate variability is associated with many forms of psychopathology involving emotion dysregulation, including generalized anxiety disorder (GAD; Thayer, Friedman, & Borkovec, 1996), panic disorder (Friedman & Thayer, 1998), bulimia nervosa (Kennedy & Heslegrave, 1989), anorexia nervosa (Melanson, Donahoo, Krantz, Poirier, & Mehler, 2004), post-traumatic stress disorder (Blechert, Michael, Grossman, Lajtman, & Wilhelm, 2007), bipolar I disorder (Cohen et al., 2003), major depression (Agelink, Boz, Ullrich, & Andrich, 2002), and borderline personality disorder (Weinberg, Klonsky, & Hajcak, in press). Furthermore, increases in heart rate variability have been associated with successful treatment outcomes in patients with major depressive disorder (Balogh, Fitzpatrick, Hendricks, & Paige, 1993; Chambers & Allen, 2002).

## Empirical Findings: Regulation of Relationships

Warm and rewarding close relationships can be a source of resilience, but the maintenance of relationship quality often requires considerable self-regulatory effort (Snyder, Simpson, & Hughes, 2006). For example, protecting and enhancing the quality of close relationships such as marriage often requires efforts to manage the tone of potentially conflictual interactions (Halford, Lizzio, Wilson, & Occhipinti, 2007), so as to avoid the negative interaction cycles that typify troubled relationships (Fincham & Beach, 1999; Snyder, Heyman, & Haynes, 2005). Such efforts include the inhibition of angry or aggressive impulses, suppression of verbal or facial expressions of negative affect, self-calming, pursuit of more constructive problem-solving, and attempts to calm one's partner.

As discussed above, if self-regulatory effort fatigues this limited resource, the individual may be temporarily susceptible to lapses in self-control during interactions with close relationship partners (Baumeister, Bratslavsky, Muraven, & Tice, 1998; Muraven & Baumeister, 2000). Effortful self-regulation in social interactions outside of close relationships has been shown to lead to lapses in self-control during later, unrelated contexts. Further, prior self-regulation during non-social tasks can disrupt subsequent social functioning in several ways, including relaxing restraints on aggressive impulses, impairing self-presentation, and attenuating the tendency to be accommodating to interaction partners (DeWall, Baumeister, Stillman, & Gailliot, 2007; Finkel & Campbell, 2001; Stucke & Baumeister, 2006; Vohs, Baumeister, & Ciarocco, 2005). Given the likely greater importance relative to interactions with partners, these effects of self-regulation should be particularly apparent in interactions with strangers. However, relatively few studies have examined these behavioral processes in established relationships, and few have examined the physiological correlates of those processes.

Low resting levels of HRV are associated with insecurity in romantic relationships (Diamond & Hicks, 2005), greater social isolation (Horsten et al., 1999), and antagonistic social interaction

styles (Demaree & Everhart, 2004; Sloan et al., 1994). However, one study found that stress-related decreases in HRV, but not tonic levels, were associated with the quality of social relationships (Egizio et al., 2008). In contrast, in a study of young married couples, resting HRV was positively associated with marital quality (Smith et al., in press). Further, in animal models that manipulate social isolation, disruption of social bonds reduces HRV (Grippo, Lamb, Carter, & Porges, 2007). Obviously, the association of tonic HRV as an index of self-regulatory capacity and the quality of close relationships requires additional research.

One recent study of young married couples provides an illustration of how HRV predicts and reflects social regulation in close relationships. A negative interaction task evoked a significant decrease in resting HRV from before to after the task, compared with either a positive or neutral task (Smith et al., under review). Importantly, this effect was apparent only for wives. During a discussion of an ongoing marital problem (e.g., money, in-laws, children, household responsibilities) a few minutes after this first task, wives who had previously participated in the negative interaction displayed a significant increase in HRV while discussing the issue. In contrast, women who had participated in the prior neutral or positive task displayed a significant decrease in HRV typical of stressful experiences, as did husbands regardless of the type of prior interaction. Hence, there was evidence of a depleting effect of negative interactions on self-regulatory capacity as measured by resting HRV among women but not men, as well as evidence of increased regulatory effort by these women during a subsequent marital conflict discussion. The greater effects on tonic and reactive HRV among women as compared with men could reflect the fact that in close relationships women are often more attentive to relationship quality (Acitelli, 1992; Nolen-Hoeksema & Jackson, 2001) and more active in seeking change and managing disagreements (Denton & Burleson, 2007; Vogel et al., 2007). Greater expenditure of regulatory effort by women in close relationships could contribute to sex differences in the health benefits of marriage (Kiecolt-Glaser & Newton, 2001). That is, women might benefit less from close relationships than do men, in part because their regulatory reserves are more frequently depleted by their greater effort to manage the quality of the relationship. Interestingly, in the study described above

(Smith et al., in press), a positive interaction with their spouse produced a small but significant increase in women's resting HRV, suggesting perhaps that some of the health benefits of higher-quality close relationships could occur through the mechanism of restoring or augmenting the capacity for self-regulation.

## Summary

It could be argued that effective self-regulation is a prerequisite to living the "good life." Happiness and well-being, as well as the things that seem to bring them, especially good social relationships, are not the result of passivity but rely on active management to avoid and ameliorate the negative (e.g., sadness, conflict) and amplify the positive (e.g., happiness, cooperation). This active management is literally embodied.

The clearest theoretical model and most substantive empirical evidence is for a relationship between tonic HRV and better self-regulatory function across a wide range of domains, from performance on neuropsychological tests of executive functions to reports of marital quality. There is also preliminary evidence for a correlation between self-regulatory effort and phasic HRV (Butler et al., 2006; Segerstrom & Solberg Nes, 2007; Smith et al., in press). Overlap between the central structures that subserve self-regulation and cardiac regulation provides an anatomical rationale for this relationship, and the role of the vagus in modulating aspects of emotional and social behavior (e.g., emotional expression) provides a functional rationale. The fairly direct neurological pathway that the vagus provides between central structures and the heart, furthermore, means that HRV can be interpreted in a straightforward way as efferent parasympathetic outflow.

For the glucoregulatory parameters, including cortisol and blood glucose, both theory and evidence are suggestive but not as clear as for HRV. Low blood glucose appears to compromise performance on neuropsychological tests, particularly executive cognitive function, control over intrusive thoughts, and emotional stability. Although the studies reviewed here focused on adults, it has been argued that children are more vulnerable than adults to the cognitive effects of low blood glucose secondary to fasting because they have less capacity for glucose storage and later release (Gibson & Green, 2002). This developmental difference points to the complexity of glucoregulation. Cortisol and blood glucose are part of a larger glucoregulatory system that includes glucose transporters, an astrocytic glucose "buffer" in the brain, the sympathetic nervous system, and energy use by a host of organs whose energetic priority may be affected. As such, it may be surprising that a simple measure such as blood glucose has predictive power at all. It is possible that this measure, while not a literal indicator of self-regulatory "energy," does reflect a regulatory state that facilitates or inhibits self-regulatory function.

## Moving Forward

The study of psychophysiology has been largely dominated by a focus on negative experience, that is, stress. The literature reviewed above indicates that psychophysiology is also inextricably intertwined with the positive experiences associated with the ability to self-regulate: better cognitive function, less worry and rumination, more positive emotion, and smoother social interactions. Compared with stress psychophysiology, however, self-regulation psychophysiology is in its infancy. Moving forward, then, will require first and foremost the accumulation of work that expands and refines these early studies.

Appropriately for this stage of research, most of the extant research employs simple, noninvasive measures such as blood glucose or HRV, and studies that manipulate these measures are fewer than those that focus on naturalistic individual differences. One important question going forward is whether psychophysiological correlates of self-regulation are markers or determinants of self-regulatory capacity, and this question can be answered only with experimental studies. For example, models of the relationship between HRV and self-regulation posit that HRV merely reflects central processes that are driving self-regulatory activity. However, it is possible that, given the importance of glucose for these central processes, parasympathetic slowing of the heart is not an epiphenomenon but an important redistribution of the energetic demands of the body. The heart consists of 0.5% of the body's mass but accounts for 9% of its caloric expenditures (Elia, 1992). Pharmacological blockade of the parasympathetic nervous system could begin to answer the question of whether cardiac slowing during self-regulation is an epiphenomenon or an important contributor to self-regulatory capacity.

The heart and brain are not the only energetically demanding organs. Others include visceral organs, in particular the liver (2.2% of body mass; 19% of caloric expenditure) and kidneys (0.4% of body mass; 8% of caloric expenditure). It has been known for decades that during sympathetic nervous system activation associated with stress or exercise, blood flow to these organs decreases dramatically (e.g., by 50–75% in the case of the kidney) (Papillo & Shapiro, 1990) while blood flow and the fuel it carries is redistributed to large muscles. If there is a similar redistribution occurring during self-regulation, it is possible that there are peripheral changes in organs other than the heart.

For example, the immune system comprises a large, integrated system of organs (e.g., spleen), cells (e.g., natural killer cells), and molecules (e.g., cytokines) (see Clark, 2008, for an accessible overview.) Although the immune system is probably not a necessary substrate of self-regulation per se, it provides an example of how organ systems are affected by and in turn may affect self-regulation. Almost every function of the immune system, beginning with physical mobilization of cells and their relocation to the site of infection and ending with production of the proteins that will effect immunity, requires energy (Demas, 2004; Elia, 1992; Lochmiller & Deerenberg, 2000). For example, it has been recognized for almost a century that fever comes at a metabolic cost, estimated at 7–13% of total metabolism per degree Celsius. As a consequence of the energetic demands of immunity, energy availability significantly impacts immune function: Energy restriction in the diet and reductions in body fat lead to suppression of immune functions and increased risk of infection. Self-regulation and the immune system may compete. Sometimes the immune system "wins" this competition; the immune system can signal the brain about the presence of infection, and these signals adversely affect motivation to expend energy in other pursuits. In the absence of infection, however, self-regulation and motivation to pursue other goals "win," resulting in lower immune function (Segerstrom, 2007). However, what happens to other peripheral organs during self-regulation is not known.

Also appropriately for this stage of research, most studies have focused on a single physiological parameter, such as HRV, salivary cortisol, or blood glucose, to study the relationship between physiology and self-regulatory effort and capacity. Moving forward, research should recognize how closely intertwined these parameters are and their abilities to affect each other. For example, cortisol and glucose clearly counter-regulate, so acute increases in cortisol might either reflect hypoglycemia or proactively increase glucose. Parasympathetic nervous system activity has anti-inflammatory effects, slowing not only the heart but this energetically costly function of the immune system. How these systems interact when the brain is working hard will take us beyond snapshots of the physiology of self-regulation and start to show the bigger picture.

Perhaps most important to the forward progress of this area is the recognition that demanding tasks or circumstances differ in both self-regulatory demand (i.e., the degree to which they require control over thoughts, emotions, or behavior) and stressfulness (i.e., the degree to which they elicit negative experience). When self-regulation and stress coexist, apparently perplexing results can be obtained. For example, Fairclough and Houston (2004) characterized falling glucose levels and increasing HRV during a prolonged Stroop task as "contradictory" (p. 185) insofar as the parasympathetic component was interpreted as an inverse measure of stress and effort. However, it appears that the well-characterized cardiac stress effect of the Stroop (i.e., increased heart rate) was eventually overridden by the cardiac self-regulation effect. Another example comes from the literature on stuttering. In laboratory public speaking tasks, people who stutter have a "paradoxical" reduction of heart rate compared with people who do not stutter that can be as large as 20 beats/minute (Alm, 2004, p.123). This lower heart rate has been attributed variously to anticipatory anxiety or to psychodynamic mechanisms in which stuttering is a cathartic activity or a means of need fulfillment (Alm, 2004). Again, this perplexing result is more understandable if cardiac slowing is occurring as a consequence of the self-regulatory effort associated with the attempt to inhibit stuttering. That is, decreases in heart rate among people who stutter as they face a potentially evaluative audience might reflect the increased parasympathetic inhibition of the heart accompanying effortful self-regulation. This hypothesis could be tested directly by measuring HRV. These examples serve to illustrate the importance of understanding the psychological characteristics of laboratory tasks along multiple dimensions rather than the single dimension of "stressfulness." It may also be important to identify tasks that are relatively pure along these dimensions in order to isolate their sometimes contradictory effects on physiological systems (Segerstrom & Solberg Nes, 2007).

Effects of evaluative threat on stress and self-regulation also illustrate the importance of studying the social psychophysiology of self-regulation. Many of our most important self-regulatory challenges—and many of the most important sources of both the positive and the negative qualities of our lives—involve personal relationships. Hence, the social psychophysiology (Cacioppo & Petty, 1983; Smith & Gerin, 1998) of self- and other regulation during interactions in important relationships is an important topic for future research. The capacity for such regulation, the manner and skill with which it is exerted, and the degree of success of such efforts are likely to be important influences of this central aspect of health and well-being. Further, the physiological processes outlined here can provide useful windows on these processes, as well as plausible links to health outcomes. Integrative measurement of physiological processes as described previously (e.g., HRV, glucose, cortisol), related cognitive processes (e.g., individual differences in executive function), and behavioral manipulations and measurements of regulatory effort in social interactions could help address important questions on the role of regulatory capacity and effort in the personal relationships. For example, do self-regulatory capacity and its fatigue contribute to well-known findings in relationship research, such as the fact that cycles of negative reciprocity in couple interactions predict negative relationship outcomes (Snyder et al., 2005)? Further, as suggested by preliminary findings described previously (Smith et al., in press), can positive relationship interactions enhance self-regulatory capacity? Lastly, do efforts to increase regulatory capacity and improve the effectiveness of regulatory effort enhance positivity in close relationships and promote related emotional and physical health benefits? Hence, a *positive* social psychophysiology of self-regulation and relationships is a promising future direction.

Finally, we (Segerstrom & Smith, 2006; Smith, 2006) have previously called for more research that links short- or medium-term changes in physiology to health endpoints. As research in this area advances, the link to health should be established. There is already evidence that personality dimensions associated with good self-regulation, such as conscientiousness, predict mortality (see Roberts, Kuncel, Shiner, Caspi, &

Goldberg, 2007, for a meta-analytic review). Positive psychophysiology may provide the link between being good living and longevity.

*References*

Aardal, E., & Holm, A. C. (1995). Cortisol in saliva—reference ranges and relation to cortisol in serum. *European Journal of Clinical Chemistry and Clinical Biochemistry, 33,* 927–932.

Abbatecola, A. M., Paolisso, G., Lamponi, M., Bandinelli, S. Lauretani, F., Launer, L., & Ferrucci, L. (1999). Insulin resistance and executive dysfunction in older persons. *Journal of the American Geriatrics Society, 52,* 1713–1718.

Acitelli, L. K. (1992). Gender differences in relationship awareness and marital satisfaction among young married couples. *Personality and Social Psychology Bulletin, 18,* 102–110.

Agelink, M. W., Boz, C., Ullrich, H., & Andrich, J. (2002). Relationship between major depression and heart rate variability: Clinical consequences and implications for antidepressive treatment. *Psychiatry Research, 113,* 139–149.

Ahern, G.L., Sollers, J.J., Lane, R.D., Labiner, D.M., Herring, A.M., Weinand, M.E., Hutzler, R., & Thayer, J.F. (2001). Heart rate and heart rate variability changes in the intracarotid sodium amobarbital test. *Epilepsia, 42,* 912– 921.

Allen, J. J. B., Chambers, A. S., & Towers, D. N. (2007). The many metrics of cardiac chronotropy: A pragmatic primer and a brief comparison of metrics. *Biological Psychology, 74,* 243–262.

Alm, P. A. (2004). Stuttering, emotions, and heart rate during anticipatory anxiety: A critical review. *Journal of Fluency Disorders, 29,* 123–133.

American Diabetes Association (2008). Standards of medical care in diabetes: Clinical practice recommendations 2008. *Diabetes Care, 31,* S12–S54.

Balogh, S., Fitzpatrick, D. F., Hendricks, S. E., & Paige, S. R. (1993). Increases in heart rate variability with successful treatment in patients with major depressive disorder. *Psychopharmacology Bulletin, 29,* 201–206.

Barrett, L. F., Gross, J., Christensen, T. C., & Benvenuto, M. (2001). Knowing what you're feeling and knowing what to do about it: Mapping the relation between emotion differentiation and emotion regulation. *Cognition and Emotion, 15,* 713–724.

Baumeister, R. F., Bratslavsky, E., Muraven, M., & Tice, D. M. (1998). Ego depletion: Is the active self a limited resource? *Journal of Personality and Social Psychology, 74,* 1252–1265.

Baumeister, R. F., Heatherton, T. F., & Tice, D. M. (1994). *Losing control: How and why people fail at self-regulation*. San Diego, CA: Academic Press.

Baumeister, R. F., & Vohs, K. D. (Eds.) (2004). *Handbook of self-regulation: Research, theory, and applications*. New York: Guilford.

Benton, D., & Owens, D. A. (1993). Blood glucose and human memory. *Psychopharmacology, 113*, 83–88.

Benton, D., Owens, D. A., & Parker, P. Y. (1994). Blood glucose influences memory and attention in young adults. *Neuropsychologia, 32*, 595–607.

Berntson, G. G., Lozano, D. L., & Chen, Y. J. (2005). Filter properties of root mean square successive difference (rMSSD) for heart rate. *Psychophysiology, 42*, 246–252.

Blair, C. (2003). Behavioral inhibition and behavioral activation in young children: Relations with self-regulation and adaptation to preschool in children attending Head Start. *Developmental Psychobiology, 42*, 301–311.

Blair, C., Granger, D., & Razza, R. P. (2005). Cortisol reactivity is positively related to executive function in preschool children attending Head Start. *Child Development, 76*, 554–567.

Blechert, J., Michael, T., Grossman, P., Lajtman, M., & Wilhelm, F. H. (2007). Autonomic and respiratory characteristics of post-traumatic stress disorder and panic disorder. *Psychosomatic Medicine, 69*, 935–943.

Britton, A., Singh-Manoux, A., Hnatkova, K., Malik, M., Marmot, M. G., & Shipley, M. (2008). The association between heart rate variability and cognitive impairment in middle-aged men and women: The Whitehall II Cohort Study. *Neuroepidemiology, 31*, 115–121.

Bryant, F. B. (2003). Savoring Beliefs Inventory (SBI): A scale for measuring beliefs about savouring. *Journal of Mental Health, 12*, 175–196.

Butler, E. A., Wilhelm, F. H., & Gross, J. J. (2006). Respiratory sinus arrhythmia, emotion, and emotion regulation during social interaction. *Psychophysiology, 43*, 612–622.

Cacioppo, J. T., & Petty, R. E. (Eds.) (1983). *Social psychophysiology*. New York: Guilford Press.

Chambers, A. S., & Allen, J. J. B. (2002). Vagal tone as an indicator of treatment response in major depression. *Psychophysiology, 39*, 861–864.

Clark, W.R. (2008). *In defense of self: How the immune system really works*. New York: Oxford University Press.

Cohen, H., Kaplan, Z., Kotler, M., Mittelman, I., Osher, Y., & Bersudsky, Y. (2003). Impaired heart rate variability in euthymic bipolar patients. *Bipolar Disorders, 5*, 138–143.

Compton, R. J., Robinson, M. D., Ode, S., Quandt, L. C., Fineman, S. L., & Carp, J. (2008). Error-monitoring ability predicts daily stress regulation. *Psychological Science, 19*, 702–708.

De Fronzo, R., Tobin, J. D., Andres, R. (1979). Glucose clamp technique: A method for quantifying insulin secretion and resistance. *American Journal of Physiology, 273*, E214–E223.

Demas, G.E. (2004). The energetics of immunity: A neuroendocrine link between energy balance and immune function. *Hormones and Behavior, 45*, 173–180.

Demaree, H. A., & Everhart, D. E. (2004). Healthy high-hostiles: Reduced parasympathetic activity and decreased sympathovagal flexibility during negative emotional processing. *Personality and Individual Differences, 36*, 457–469.

Demaree, H. A., Pu, J., Robinson, J., Schmeichel, B. J., & Everhart, E. (2006). Predicting facial valence to negative stimuli from resting RSA: Not a function of active emotion regulation. *Cognition and Emotion, 20*, 161–176.

Denton, W. H., & Burleson, B. R. (2007). The Initiator Style Questionnaire: A scale to assess initiator tendency in couples. *Personal Relationships, 14*, 245–268.

DeWall, C. N., Baumeister, R. F., Stillman, T. F., & Gailliot, M. T. (2007). Violence restrained: Effects of self-regulation and its depletion on aggression. *Journal of Experimental Social Psychology, 43*, 62–76.

Diamond, L. M., & Hicks, A. M. (2005). Attachment style, current relationship security, and negative emotions: The mediating role of physiological regulation. *Journal of Social and Personal Relationships, 22*, 499–518.

Egizio, V. B., Jennings, J. R., Christie, I. C., Sheu, L. K., Matthews, K. A., & Gianaros, P. J. (2008). Cardiac vagal activity during psychosocial stress varies with social functioning in older women. *Psychophysiology, 45*, 1046–1054.

Elia, M. (1992). Organ and tissue contribution to metabolic rate. In J. M. Kenny & H. N. Tucker (Eds.), *Energy metabolism: Tissue determinants and cellular corollaries* (pp. 61–79). New York: Raven Press.

Fabes, R. A., & Eisenberg, N. (1997). Regulatory control and adults' stress-related responses to daily life events. *Journal of Personality and Social Psychology, 73*, 1107–1117.

Fairclough, S. H., & Houston, K. (2004). A metabolic measure of mental effort. *Biological Psychology, 66*, 177–190.

Fincham, F. D., & Beach, S. R. H. (1999). Conflict in marriage: Implications for working with couples. *Annual Review of Psychology, 50*, 47–77.

Finkel, E. J., & Campbell, W. K. (2001). Self-control and accommodation in close relationships: An interdependence analysis. *Journal of Personality and Social Psychology, 81*, 263–277.

Finkel, E. J., Campbell, W. K., Brunell, A. B., Dalton, A. N., Scarbeck, S. J., & Chartrand, T. L. (2006). High-maintenance interaction: Inefficient social coordination impairs self-regulation. *Journal of Personality and Social Psychology, 91*, 456–475.

Frayn, K. (2003). *Metabolic regulation: A human perspective*. Malden, MA: Blackwell Science.

Friedman, B. H., & Thayer, J. F. (1998). Autonomic balance revisited: Panic anxiety and heart rate variability. *Journal of Psychosomatic Research, 44*, 133–151.

Gailliot, M. T., & Baumeister, R. F. (2007). The physiology of willpower: Linking blood glucose to self-control. *Personality and Social Psychology Review, 11*, 303–327.

Gailliot, M. T., Baumeister, R. F., DeWall, C. N., Maner, J. K., Plant, E. A., Tice, D. M., Brewer, L. E., & Schmeichel, B. J. (2007). Self-control relies on glucose as a limited energy source: Willpower is more than a metaphor. *Journal of Personality and Social Psychology, 92*, 325–336.

Geisler, F. C. M., & Kubiak, T. (2009). Heart rate variability predicts self-control in goal pursuit. *European Journal of Personality, 23*, 623–633.

Gianaros, P. J., Van Der Veen, F. M., & Jennings, J. R. (2004). Regional cerebral blood flow correlates with heart period and high-frequency heart period variability during working-memory tasks: Implications for the cortical and subcortical regulation of cardiac autonomic activity. *Psychophysiology, 41*, 521–530.

Gibson, E. L., & Green, M. W. (2002). Nutritional influences on cognitive function: Mechanisms of susceptibility. *Nutrition Research Reviews, 15*, 169–206.

Gold, A. E., MacLeod, K. M., Frier, B. M., & Deary, I. J. (1995). Changes in mood during acute hypoglycemia in healthy participants. *Journal of Personality and Social Psychology, 68*, 498–503.

Grippo, A. J., Lamb, D. G., Carter, C. S., & Porges, S. W. (2007). Social isolation disrupts autonomic regulation of the heart and influences negative affective behaviors. *Biological Psychiatry, 62*, 1162–1170.

Gross, J. J. (1998). The emerging field of emotion regulation: An integrative review. *Review of General Psychology, 2*, 271–299.

Gross, J.J. (2001). Emotion regulation in adulthood: Timing is everything. *Current Directions in Psychological Science, 10*, 214–219.

Gross, J. J., & Levenson, R. W. (1993). Emotional suppression: Physiology, self-report, and expressive behavior. *Journal of Personality and Social Psychology, 64*, 970–986.

Gross, J. J., & Levenson, R. W. (1997). Hiding feelings: The acute effects of inhibiting negative and positive emotion. *Journal of Abnormal Psychology, 106*, 95–103.

Gyurak, A., & Ayduk, O. (2008). Resting respiratory sinus arrhythmia buffers against rejection sensitivity via emotion control. *Emotion, 8*, 458–467.

Hagemann, D., Waldstein, S. R., & Thayer, J. F. (2003). Central and autonomic nervous system integration in emotion. *Brain and Cognition, 52*, 79–87.

Halford, W. K., Lizzio, A., Wilson, K. L., & Occhipinti, S. (2007). Does working at your marriage help? Couple relationship self-regulation and satisfaction in the first 4 years of marriage. *Journal of Family Psychology, 21*, 185–194.

Hall, M., Okun, M.L., Atwood, C.W., Buysse, D.J., & Strollo, P.J. (2008). Measurement of sleep by polysomnography. In L.J. Lueken and L.C. Gallo (Eds.), *Handbook of physiological research methods in health psychology* (pp. 341–367). Thousand Oaks, CA: Sage Publications.

Hansen, A. L., Johnsen, B. H., & Thayer, J. F. (2003). Vagal influence on working memory and attention. *International Journal of Psychophysiology, 48*, 263–274.

Hansen, A. L., Johnsen, B. H., Sollers, J. J., Stenvik, K., & Thayer, J. F. (2004). Heart rate variability and its relation to prefrontal cognitive function: The effects of training and detraining. *European Journal of Applied Physiology, 93*, 263–272.

Hennessey, J., & Levine, S. (1979). Stress, arousal, and the pituitary-adrenal system: A psychoendocrine hypothesis. *Progress in Psychobiology and Physiological Psychology, 8*, 133–178.

Hofmann, W., Gschwendner, T., Friese, M., Wiers, R.W., & Schmitt, M. (2008). Working memory capacity and self-regulatory behavior: Toward an individual differences perspective on behavior determination by automatic versus controlled processes. *Journal of Personality and Social Psychology, 95*, 962–977.

Horsten, M., Ericson, M., Perski, A., Wamala, S. P., Schenck-Gustafsson, K., & Orth-Gomer, K. (1999). Psychosocial factors and heart rate variability in healthy women. *Psychosomatic Medicine, 61*, 49–57.

Ingjaldsson, J. T., Laberg, J. C., & Thayer, J. F. (2003). Reduced heart rate variability in chronic alcohol abuse: Relationship with negative mood, chronic thought suppression, and compulsive drinking. *Biological Psychiatry, 54*, 1427–1436.

Inzlicht, M., & Gutsell, J. N. (2007). Running on empty: Neural signals for self-control failure. *Psychological Science, 18*, 933–937.

Kennedy, S. H., & Heslegrave, R. J. (1989). Cardiac regulation in bulimia nervosa. *Journal of Psychiatric Research, 23*, 267–273.

Kiecolt-Glaser, J. K., & Newton, T. L. (2001). Marriage and health: His and hers. *Psychological Bulletin, 127*, 472–503.

Kirschbaum, C., & Hellhammer, D. H. (1989). Salivary cortisol in psychobiological research: An overview. *Neuropsychobiology, 22*, 150–169.

Koenig, R. J., Peterson, C. M., Jones, R. L., Saudek, C., Lehrman, M., & Cerami, A. (1976). Correlation of glucose regulation and hemoglobin A1c in diabetes mellitus. *The New England Journal of Medicine, 295*, 417–420.

Kumari, M., & Marmot, M. (2005). Diabetes and cognitive dysfunction in a middle-aged cohort: Findings from the Whitehall II study. *Neurology, 65*, 1597–1603.

Kuo, H. K., Jones, R. M., Milberg, W. P., Tennstedt, S., Talbot, L., Morris, J. N., & Lipsitz, L. A. (2005). Effect of blood pressure and diabetes mellitus on cognitive and physical functions in older adults: A longitudinal analysis of the Advanced Cognitive Training for Independent and Vital Elderly cohort. *Journal of the American Geriatrics Society, 53*, 1154–1161.

Lieb, K., Rexhausen, J. E., Kahl, K. G., Schweiger, U., Philipsen, A., Hellhammer, D. H., & Bohus, M. (2004). Increased diurnal salivary cortisol in women with borderline personality disorder. *Journal of Psychiatric Research, 38*, 559–565.

Lochmiller, R. L., & Deerenberg, C. (2000). Trade-offs in evolutionary immunology: Just what is the cost of immunity? *OIKOS, 88*, 87–98.

Lovallo, W. R., & Thomas, T. L. (2000). Stress hormones in psychophysiological research: Emotional, behavioral, and cognitive implications. In J. T. Cacioppo, L. G. Tassinary, & G. G. Berntson (Eds.), *Handbook of psychophysiology* (2nd ed., pp. 342–367). Cambridge, Massachusetts: Cambridge University Press.

Luft, C. D., Takase, E., & Darby, D. (2009). Heart rate variability and cognitive function: Effects of physical effort. *Biological Psychology, 82*, 196–201.

Lupien, S. J., Wilkinson, C. W., Briere, S., Menard, C., Ng Ying Kin, N. M., & Nair, N. P. (2002). The modulatory effects of corticosteroids on cognition: Studies in young human populations. *Psychoneuroendocrinology, 27*, 401–416.

Matthews, S. C., Paulus, M. P., Simmons, A. N., Nelesen, R. A., & Dimsdale, J. E. (2004). Functional subdivisions within anterior cingulate cortex and their relationship to autonomic nervous system function. *Neuroimage, 22*, 1151–1156.

McAulay, V., Deary, I. J., Sommerfield, A. J., Matthews, G., & Frier, B. M. (2006). Effects of acute hypoglycemia on motivation and cognitive interference in people with Type I diabetes. *Journal of Clinical Psychopharmacology, 26*, 143–151.

McCormick, C. M., Lewis, E., Somley, B., & Kahan, T. A. (2007). Individual differences in cortisol levels and performance on a test of executive function in men and women. *Physiology & Behavior, 91*, 87–94.

Melanson, E. L., Donahoo, W. T., Krantz, M. J., Poirier, P., and Mehler, P. S. (2004). Resting and ambulatory heart rate variability in chronic anorexia nervosa. *The American Journal of Cardiology, 94*, 1217–1220.

Moleman, P., Tulen, J. H. M., Blankstijn, P. J., Man in t' Veld, A. J., & Boomsma, F. (1992). Urinary excretion of catecholamines and their metabolites in relation to circulating catecholamines. *Archives of General Psychiatry, 49*, 568–572.

Movius, H. L, & Allen, J. B. (2005). Cardiac vagal tone, defensiveness, and motivational style. *Biological Psychology, 58*, 147–162.

Muraven, M. (2008). Prejudice as self-control failure. *Journal of Applied Social Psychology, 38*, 314–333.

Muraven, M., & Baumeister, R. F. (2000). Self-regulation and depletion of limited resources: Does self-control resemble a muscle? *Psychological Bulletin, 126*, 247–259.

Nolen-Hoeksema, S., & Jackson, B. (2001). Mediators of the gender difference in rumination. *Psychology of Women Quarterly, 25*, 37–47.

Ochsner, K. N., & Gross, J. J. (2007). The neural architecture of emotion regulation. In J. J. Gross (Ed.), *Handbook of Emotion Regulation* (pp. 351–372). New York: Guilford Press.

Owens, D. S. & Benton, D. (1994). The impact of raising blood glucose on reaction times. *Neuropsychobiology, 30*, 106–113.

Persad, S. M., & Polivy, J. (1993). Differences between depressed and nondepressed individuals in the recognition of and response to facial emotional cues. *Journal of Abnormal Psychology, 102*, 358–368.

Papillo, J., & Shapiro, D. (1990). The cardiovascular system. In J. T. Cacioppo & L. G. Tassinary (Eds.), *Principles of psychophysiology: Physical, social and inferential elements* (pp. 456–511). New York: Cambridge University Press.

Parsons, R. J. (2007). Environmental psychophysiology. In J. T. Cacioppo, L. G. Tassinary, & G. G. Berntson (Eds.), *Handbook of psychophysiology* (3rd Ed.) (pp. 752-786). New York: Cambridge University Press.

Pieper, S., Brosschot, J. F., van der Leened, R., & Thayer, J. F. (2007). Cardiac effects of momentary assessed worry episodes and stressful events. *Psychosomatic Medicine, 69,* 901–909.

Porges, S. (2007). The polyvagal perspective. *Biological Psychology, 74,* 116–143.

Porges, S. W. (2001). The polyvagal theory: Phylogenetic substrates of a social nervous system. *International Journal of Psychophysiology, 42,* 123–146.

Posner, M. I., & Rothbart, M. K. (2007). Research on attention networks as a model for the integration of psychological science. *Annual Review of Psychology, 58,* 1–23.

Qiu, W. Q., Price, L. L., Hibberd, P., Buell, J., Collins, L., Leins, D., Mwamburi, D. M., Rosenberg, I., Smaldone, L., Scott, T. M., Siegel, R. D., Summergrad, P., Sun, X., Wagner, C., Wang, L., Yee, J., Tucker, K. L., & Folstein, M. (2006). Executive dysfunction in homebound older people with diabetes mellitus. *Journal of the American Geriatrics Society, 54,* 496–501.

Roberts, B. W., Kuncel, N. R., Shiner, R., Caspi, A., & Goldberg, L. R. (2007). The power of personality: The comparative validity of personality traits, socioeconomic status, and cognitive ability for predicting important life outcomes. *Perspectives on Psychological Science, 2,* 313–345.

Robinson, M. D. (2007). Gassing, braking, and self-regulating: Error self-regulation, well-being, and goal-related processes. *Journal of Experimental Social Psychology, 43,* 1–16.

Ruiz-Padial, E., Sollers, J. J., Vila, J., & Thayer, J. F. (2003). The rhythm of the heart in the blink of an eye: Emotion-modulated startle magnitude covaries with heart rate variability. *Psychophysiology, 40,* 306–313.

Schillerstrom, J. E., Horton, M. S., & Royall, D. R. (2005). The impact of medical illness on executive function. *Psychosomatics, 46,* 508–516.

Schmeichel, B. J. (2007). Attention control, memory updating, and emotion regulation temporarily reduce the capacity for executive control. *Journal of Experimental Psychology: General, 136,* 241–255.

Schmeichel, B. J., Vohs, K. D., & Baumeister, R. F. (2003). Intellectual performance and ego depletion: Role of the self in logical reasoning and other information processing. *Journal of Personality and Social Psychology, 85,* 33–46.

Schultes, B., Peters, A. Kern, W., Gais, S., Oltmanns, K. M., Fehm, H. L., & Born, J. (2005). Processing of food stimuli is selectively enhanced during insulin-induced hypoglycemia in healthy men. *Psychoneuroendocrinology, 30,* 496–504.

Segerstrom, S. C. (2007). Stress, energy, and immunity: An ecological view. *Current Directions in Psychological Science, 16,* 326–330.

Segerstrom, S. C., Hardy, J. K., Evans, D. R., & Winters, N. F. (in press). "Pause and plan": Self-regulation and the heart. In G. Gendolla & R. Wright (Eds.), *Motivational perspectives on cardiovascular response.* Washington, DC: American Psychological Association.

Segerstrom, S. C., Roach, A. R., Evans, D. R., Schipper, L. J., & Darville, A. K. (2010). The structure, validity, and correlates of trait repetitive thought in older adults. *Psychology and Aging, 25,* 505–515.

Segerstrom, S. C., & Smith, T. W. (2006). Physiological pathways from personality to health: The cardiovascular and immune systems. In M. Vollrath (Ed.), *Handbook of Personality and Health* (pp. 175–194). New York: Wiley.

Segerstrom, S. C., & Solberg Nes, L. (2007). Heart rate variability reflects self-regulatory strength, effort, and fatigue. *Psychological Science, 18,* 275–281.

Siesjö, B. (1978). *Brain Energy Metabolism.* New York: Wiley.

Sloan, R. P., Shapiro, P. A., Bigger, J. T., Bagiella, E., Steinman, R. C., & Gorman, J. C. (1994). Cardiac autonomic control and hostility in healthy subjects. *American Journal of Cardiology, 74,* 298–300.

Smith, A. W., & Baum, A. (2003). The influence of psychological factors on restorative function in health and illness. In J. Suls & K. Wallston (Eds.), *Social psychological foundations of health and illness* (pp. 432–457). UK: Blackwell Publishers.

Smith, T. W. (2006). Personality as risk and resilience in physical health. *Current Directions in Psychological Science, 15,* 227–231.

Smith, T. W., Cribbet, M. R., Nealey-Moore, J. N., Uchino, B. N., Williams, P. G., MacKenzie, J., & Thayer, J. F. (in press). Matter of the variable heart: Respiratory sinus arrhythmia response to marital interaction and associations with marital quality. *Journal of Personality and Social Psychology.*

Smith, T. W., & Gerin, W. (1998). The social psychophysiology of cardiovascular response: An introduction to the special issue. *Annals of Behavioral Medicine, 20,* 243–246.

Snyder, D. K., Heyman, R. E., & Haynes, S. N. (2005) Evidence-based approaches to assessing couple distress. *Psychological Assessment, 17,* 288–307.

Snyder, D. K., Simpson, J., & Hughes, J. (Eds.) (2006). *Emotion regulation in couples and families: Pathways to dysfunction and health.* Washington, DC: American Psychological Association.

Stucke, T. S., & Baumeister, R. F. (2006). Ego depletion and aggressive behavior: Is the inhibition of aggression a limited resource? *European Journal of Social Psychology, 36,* 1–13.

Thayer, J. F., Friedman, B. H., & Borkovec, B. H. (1996). Autonomic characteristics of generalized anxiety disorder and worry. *Biological Psychiatry, 39,* 255–266.

Thayer, J. F., Hansen, A. L., & Johnsen, B. H. (2008). Noninvasive assessment of autonomic influences on the heart: Impedance cardiography and heart rate variability. In L. Leuken and L. C. Gallo (Eds.), *Handbook of physiological research methods in health psychology* (pp. 183–209). Thousand Oaks, CA: Sage.

Thayer, J. F., & Lane, R. D. (2000). A model of neurovisceral integration in emotion regulation and dysregulation. *Journal of Affective Disorders, 61,* 201–216.

Thayer, J. F., & Lane, R. D. (2009). Claude Bernard and the heart-brain connection: Further elaboration of a model of neurovisceral integration. *Neuroscience and Biobehavioral Reviews, 33,* 81–88.

Timonen, M., Laakso, M., Jokelainen, J., Rajala, U., Meyer-Rochow, V. B., & Keinanen-Kiukaanniemi, S. (2005). Insulin resistance and depression: Cross sectional study. *British Medical Journal, 330,* 17–18.

Uchino, B. N., Smith, T. W., Holt-Lunstead, J., Campo, R. A., & Reblin, M. (2007). Stress and illness. In J. T. Cacioppo, L. G. Tassinary, & G. G. Bertson (Eds)., *Handbook of psychophysiology* (pp. 608–632). New York, NY: Cambridge University Press.

Vanhanen, M., Kuusisto, J., Koivisto, K., Mykkanen, L., Helkala, E. L., Hanninene, T., Riekkinen, P.,

Soininen, H., & Laakso, M. (1999). Type 2 diabetes and cognitive function in a non-demented population. *Acta Neurologica Scandinavica, 100,* 97–101.

Vogel, D. L., Murphy, M. J., Werner-Wilson, R. J., Cutrona, C. E., & Seeman, J. (2007). Sex differences in the use of demand and withdraw behavior in marriage: Examining the social structure hypothesis. *Journal of Counseling Psychology, 54,* 165–177.

Vohs, K. D., Baumeister, R. F., & Ciarocco, N. J. (2005). Self-regulation, self-presentation: Regulatory resource depletion impairs impression management and effortful self-presentation depletes regulatory resources. *Journal of Personality and Social Psychology, 88,* 632–657.

von Hippel, W. (2007). Aging, executive functioning, and social control. *Current Directions in Psychological Science, 16,* 240–244.

Vreeburg, S. A., Hoogendijk, W. J. G., van Pelt, J., DeRijk, R. H., Verhagen, J. C. M., van Dyck, R., Smit, J. H., Zitman, F. G., & Penninx, B. W. (2009). Major depressive disorder and hypothalamic-pituitary-adrenal axis activity: Results from a large cohort study. *Archives of General Psychiatry, 66,* 617–626.

Weinberg, A., Klonsky, E. D., & Hajcak, G. (2009). Autonomic impairment in borderline personality disorder: A laboratory investigation. *Brain and Cognition, 71,* 279–286.

Williams, P. G., Smith, T. W., Gunn, H., & Uchino, B. N. (2010). Personality and stress: Individual differences in exposure, reactivity, recovery, and restoration. In R. Contrada & A. Baum (Eds.), *Handbook of stress science: Biology, psychology, and health.* New York, NY: Springer.

Winokur, A., Maislin, G., Phillips, J. L., & Amsterdam, J. D. (1988). Insulin resistance after oral glucose tolerance testing in patients with major depression. *American Journal of Psychiatry, 145,* 325–330.

Wredling, R. A., Theorell, P. G., Roll, H. M., Lins, P. E., & Adamson, UK (1992). Psychosocial state of patients with IDDM prone to recurrent episodes of severe hypoglycemia. *Diabetes Care, 15,* 518–521.

# 4

# Positive Psychological States and Biological Processes

*Carissa A. Low, Julienne E. Bower, Judith T. Moskowitz, and Elissa S. Epel*

## Taking Stock

Mounting scientific evidence indicates that positive psychological states are reflected in biological processes, objective physical health, and mortality. Several recent reviews have comprehensively summarized the growing literature on positive psychology and physical health (Lyubomirsky, King, & Diener, 2005; Pressman & Cohen, 2005), and our goal is not to reiterate these excellent overviews. Rather, this chapter will focus on the mechanisms through which positive psychological states influence physical health outcomes, focusing on biological processes. To that end, we first review the literature on the effect of positive psychological states on neuroendocrine and immune system function with a focus on hypothalamic-pituitary-adrenal (HPA) and inflammatory processes. Second, we describe our conceptual model of "enhanced allostasis" as a mechanism linking positive psychological states with physical health. Finally, we identify questions that remain unanswered and outline testable hypotheses guided by both existing literature and the enhanced allostasis model. For the purposes of this chapter, we use the term "positive psychological states" broadly to include positive affect, active coping processes, benefit finding, and other positive resources such as optimism, self-esteem, and resilience.

## Positive Psychological States and Neuroendocrine Function

Cortisol is released by the hypothalamic-pituitary-adrenal (HPA) axis in response to psychological stress. Although activation of the HPA system prepares the organism to respond to threat and is adaptive in the short term, exaggerated or prolonged activation of this stress response may lead to excessive secretion of cortisol, which can cause wear and tear on the body and increased risk for disease (McEwen, 1998). In healthy individuals, cortisol exhibits a distinct diurnal rhythm, peaking in the early morning and declining steadily throughout the day. Thus, dysregulation of the HPA axis may be reflected in high overall levels of cortisol, dysregulation of the diurnal rhythm (e.g., no decline in cortisol in the evening), or exaggerated or prolonged cortisol responses to stress.

Several studies have demonstrated an association between positive psychological states and HPA axis activity, as measured by total cortisol excretion and diurnal cortisol regulation. For example, reporting benefits or positive life changes as a result of living with HIV infection was associated with lower 24-hour urinary free cortisol output in a large sample of HIV+ men and women (Carrico et al., 2006). Both positive affect and approach-oriented coping style have been inversely associated with average salivary cortisol levels across the day (O'Donnell, Badrick, Kumari, & Steptoe, 2008; Steptoe et al., 2008). Within subjects, reports of positive affect were associated with lower salivary cortisol levels regardless of time of day (Smyth et al., 1998). There is also evidence that both optimism (Lai et al., 2005) and positive affect are associated with lower salivary cortisol secretion in the morning (Polk et al., 2005; Steptoe, Gibson, Hamer, & Wardle, 2007), resulting in a low, flat diurnal rhythm.

Positive psychological states have also been examined as moderators of the cortisol response to acute stress. Self-esteem has been demonstrated to buffer cortisol responses to experimental psychological stress in older adults (Seeman et al., 1995), as has affirmation of personal values in younger adults (Creswell et al., 2005). Emotional intelligence, an individual's perceived ability to recognize and regulate his or her emotions, has also been associated with reduced cortisol reactivity to laboratory stress (Mikolajczak et al., 2007). In a study of healthy young men, those who scored higher on a measure of psychological resilience exhibited lower cortisol levels in anticipation of a public speech task (Mikolajczak et al., 2008). A recent meta-analysis examining the effect of chronic psychological states on cortisol reactivity found that positive affect and other positive psychological factors (but not negative affect) were associated with reduced HPA reactivity (Chida & Hamer, 2008). Because uncontrollable, social-evaluative threats are most evocative of HPA responses (Dickerson & Kemeny, 2004), such positive psychological resources as favorable view of oneself or ability to regulate negative emotions may result in less perceived threat when encountering acute social stressors (e.g., a laboratory speech task). Positive psychological resources may also affect biological adaptation to repeated stressful situations. For example, in a study that exposed younger adults to repeated social stressors, those who reported higher self-esteem

showed more rapid neuroendocrine habituation (i.e., decreased response magnitude to repeated presentation of a stressor; Kirschbaum et al., 1995). Another study examining HPA habituation to repeated laboratory stressors found that healthy women who reported positive benefits as a result of their most stressful life event habituated more quickly than women who did not (Epel et al., 1998). Thus, positive psychological states may reduce basal HPA activity, buffer individuals from stress-induced HPA activation, and facilitate more rapid HPA habituation to repeated stressors, all of which result in decreased exposure of tissues to the potentially damaging effects of cortisol.

Other endocrine markers have received less attention in relation to positive psychological states, but several warrant mention. Of particular relevance are anabolic hormones. In contrast to catabolic hormones such as cortisol, which break down molecules to produce energy, anabolic hormones stimulate protein synthesis and tissue growth. The prototypical anabolic hormones include dehydroepiandrosterone (DHEA), which may protect tissues from the deleterious effects of cortisol, as well as hormones of the growth hormone axis (growth hormone (GH) and insulin-like growth factor (IGF)). Other hormones that can be considered anabolic and may also be important for health include oxytocin and neuropeptide Y (NPY). To date, positive psychological correlates of anabolic hormones have been examined in only a handful of studies. Positive affect and active coping have been correlated with higher levels of growth hormone (Epel, Adler, Ickovics, & McEwen, 1999; Epel, Adler, Ickovics, McEwen, & Clayton, 2001), and IGF-1 was positively correlated with social well-being among younger adults (Unden et al., 2002). Positive social emotions such as love and trust are associated with oxytocin (Gonzaga, Turner, Keltner, Campos, & Altemus, 2006; Kosfeld, Heinrichs, Zak, Fischbacher, & Fehr, 2005). Anabolic hormones have also been linked to positive psychological processes in the context of stress. In two recent studies of veterans, DHEA was associated with total coping scores as well as recovery from combat trauma (i.e., PTSD symptom improvement) whereas NPY was associated with approach-oriented coping and resilience to combat trauma (defined as combat exposure without PTSD; Yehuda, Brand, Golier, & Yang, 2006; Yehuda, Brand, & Yang, 2006). NPY has also been associated with resilience to psychological distress among military personnel undergoing survival training (Morgan et al., 2002). These preliminary findings implicate anabolic hormones in resilience to psychological stress.

## Positive Psychological States and Immune Function

In the field of psychoneuroimmunology, research has generally focused on the relationship between immunity and negative psychological states such as stress and depression. A small and growing field of literature highlights the importance of positive psychological states for immune function as well, generally supporting the hypothesis that positive psychological states are related to superior immune functioning (Marsland et al., 2007). For example, trait positive affect has been associated with a higher level of Hepatitis B antibody production after vaccination (Marsland et al., 2006) and higher levels of natural killer cell activity (Valdimarsdottir & Bovbjerg, 1997). The relationship between positive psychological states and immune function has also been examined in the context of immune disorders, particularly HIV/AIDS, with studies showing beneficial effects of benefit finding and other positive states on CD4 T cell levels and viral load (Bower et al., 1998; Ickovics et al., 2006; Ironson & Haward, 2008; Milam, 2006). In this section, we focus our discussion on the links between positive psychosocial factors and inflammatory processes, given growing evidence of their importance for physical health.

Inflammation is associated with a variety of negative health outcomes, including cardiovascular disease (Ross, 1999), diabetes (Hotamisligil, Shargill, & Spiegelman, 1993), and cancer (Coussens & Werb, 2002). Several recent studies have examined the cross-sectional association between positive psychological states and inflammatory activity. In general, most report an inverse correlation between positive moods or resources and markers of inflammation, including proinflammatory cytokines (e.g., IL-6, TNF-$\alpha$), and markers of cytokine activity (e.g., C-reactive protein (CRP), soluble IL-6 receptor). For example, positive affect was associated with lower plasma levels of IL-6 and CRP in women (Steptoe et al., 2008), and life purpose was associated with lower levels of soluble IL-6 receptor in older women (Friedman et al., 2007). A study examining the capacity of immune cells to produce cytokines when stimulated with

lipopolysaccharide found that positive affective style was inversely correlated with IL-6 production and with production of the anti-inflammatory cytokine IL-10 (Prather et al., 2007). Of note, the findings in this emerging area are not entirely consistent; for example, studies have shown effects in women but not men (Steptoe et al., 2008), for some positive states but not others (Friedman et al., 2007), and for some inflammatory markers but not others (Friedman et al., 2007; Prather et al., 2007).

Acute psychological stress is associated with increased circulating inflammatory markers and stimulated cytokine production (Steptoe, Hamer, & Chida, 2007), and there is also evidence that positive psychological processes may buffer this inflammatory reactivity to acute stress. Optimism buffered the effect of stress on IL-6 levels after controlling for age, body mass index, and depressive symptoms (Brydon et al., 2009). Self-esteem was also associated with smaller TNF-$\alpha$ and IL-1 receptor antagonist (IL-1RA) responses immediately post-stress and lower IL-1RA levels 45 minutes after stress (O'Donnell et al., 2008). Emotional approach coping (i.e., coping by processing or expressing emotions) was associated with less pronounced TNF-$\alpha$ responses to acute stress (but not related to IL-6 or cortisol reactivity; Master et al., 2009). In a study examining fibrinogen responses to experimental stress, individuals who reported higher levels of happiness showed lower responses (Steptoe, Wardle, & Marmot, 2005). Thus, positive moods and psychological resources have been associated with both lower levels of baseline systemic inflammation as well as attenuated inflammatory reactivity to acute stress.

## Summary and Limitations of Existing Literature

Taken together, this growing literature suggests that positive psychological states and resources are associated with reduced HPA and inflammatory activity. A handful of studies also support an association between positive psychological states and higher levels of anabolic hormones such as DHEA and GH. However, several important limitations of these studies must be addressed by future science.

First, the mechanisms that link positive psychological states and biological processes have not been articulated. How might positive affect, or purpose in life, influence circulating levels of inflammatory cytokines? Do these states have direct effects on physiological systems, or do they act primarily as stress buffers, mitigating the detrimental impact of stressful life experiences on neuroendocrine and immune function? Are effects primarily mediated by behavioral confounds, such as sleep, social engagement, and adherence to medical regimens? Surprisingly few studies have directly tested these questions, which are critical for advancing our understanding of the "biology" of positive psychology.

Second, most existing studies examine cross-sectional associations, but longitudinal studies will be necessary to disentangle causal and temporal relationships between positive psychological factors and biomarkers. Bidirectionality must also be considered, particularly with regard to inflammatory activity, as proinflammatory cytokines can elicit increases in depressed mood (Reichenberg et al., 2001) and reductions in positive affect (Janicki-Deverts et al., 2007; Spath-Schwalbe et al., 1998).

Third, although the HPA axis and inflammatory activity are implicated in a wide range of diseases, the relationships between positive psychological states and endocrine/immune activity are rarely examined in combination with clinically relevant outcomes. A recent meta-analysis of 70 prospective studies supported a significant effect of positive well-being on mortality outcomes among healthy populations and clinical populations, independent of negative affect and measured behavioral covariates (Chida & Steptoe, 2008). Positive affect has also been associated with protection from the development of stroke (Ostir, Markides, Peek, & Goodwin, 2001) and infectious diseases (Cohen et al., 2003). However, these outcomes have not been investigated in concert with potential biological mediators.

Relatedly, it will be important to identify for which clinical populations positive psychological states matter. The strongest evidence for the benefit of positive psychological states exists for HIV (Ironson & Hayward, 2008; Moskowitz, 2003). In contrast, there is less evidence of beneficial effect of positive well-being among cancer patients (Brown et al., 2000). In their review, Pressman and Cohen (2005) suggest that positive affect may be more beneficial for patients for whom behavioral factors (e.g., exercise, medication adherence) are more closely linked to the disease process.

Fourth, existing studies also provide limited insight into which specific positive psychological states are beneficial for physiological functioning. It has been suggested that eudaimonic (e.g., purpose and meaning in life) rather than hedonic (e.g., positive moods reflecting pleasure and contentment) states may be more closely tied to health (Friedman et al., 2007), although empirical support for this hypothesis is mixed. A variety of positive psychological states have been linked to health outcomes, including optimism, self-esteem, positive mood, and finding benefit in stressful life events. Because most investigators focus on only one or two of these constructs in their analyses, it remains unclear which positive states or traits are most relevant to physical health, or whether constellations of traits may be most predictive of health outcomes.

Finally, to determine whether positive psychological states have unique implications for biological health beyond negative psychological states, it is important to determine whether the variance accounted for by positive psychological states overlaps with that explained by negative moods. Not all studies control for the effect of negative psychological states. However, it is encouraging that several recent studies have found evidence of a unique contribution of positive affect independent of negative mood (Brydon et al., 2009; Marsland et al., 2006; Moskowitz, 2003; Moskowitz, Epel, & Acree, 2008; Prather et al., 2007).

## The Enhanced Allostasis Model

We recently described a conceptual model termed "enhanced allostasis," which we argue provides a useful framework for understanding the biological underpinnings of positive psychological states (Bower et al., 2009; Epel, McEwen, & Ickovics, 1998). Enhanced allostasis refers to highly adaptive physiological response to stressors and biological regulation of allostatic systems. The enhanced allostasis theory is an extension of the allostatic load model (McEwen, 1998). According to the allostatic load model, frequent or chronic stress causes repeated or prolonged fluctuations of physiological stress response systems, which may exact a cumulative toll on homeostatic systems such as the HPA axis. As a result, these overburdened stress response systems may exhibit less flexible or salutary responding over time (e.g., slower recovery, inadequate habituation), accelerating disease processes.

In contrast, enhanced allostasis describes adaptive responding to stress that may accompany positive psychological responses to challenge (Bower et al., 2009; Epel et al., 1998). With enhanced allostasis, physiological responses to stress are more efficient, circumscribed, and tightly regulated than normal, reducing wear and tear and protecting individuals from diseases of stress and age. Figure 4.1 depicts four response profiles reflective of enhanced allostasis. The first panel illustrates fewer "hits," or fewer physiological responses to frequent stressors. The second panel illustrates **rapid physiological habituation** to repeated stress exposure. In this case, an individual mounts a full physiologic response when first exposed to a stressor but quickly adapts when re-exposed to a stressor of the same type. The third panel focuses on response to an individual stressor and is characterized by a peak response with **rapid recovery** following termination of the stressor. In addition, as depicted in the fourth panel, enhanced allostasis may be reflected in health-enhancing

changes in **baseline restorative processes** (e.g., higher heart rate variability, higher levels of anabolic hormones) that result in lower tonic physiological arousal. All four profiles limit the body's exposure to excessive and/or prolonged levels of stress hormones.

Positive psychological processes figure prominently in the enhanced allostasis model, as more efficient responses to stress are thought to follow from more positive appraisals of potential stressors, use of approach-oriented coping strategies, employment of positive coping resources (e.g., self-esteem, optimism), and experience of positive mood. An example here would be an individual who shows a physiological reaction to the stress of an argument with a friend but whose effective coping efforts in the aftermath of the argument limit the duration of HPA activation. A key aspect of the enhanced allostasis model is

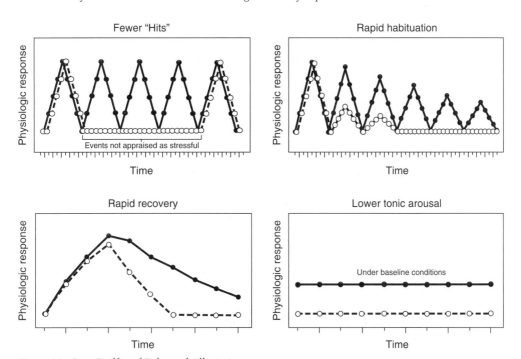

Figure 4.1. Four Profiles of Enhanced Allostasis.
These panels depict four physiological profiles illustrative of enhanced allostasis. Enhanced allostasis describes a pattern of adaptive, more efficient physiological responding to stress which we hypothesize may be a consequence of positive psychological processes. In the top left panel, the dashed line depicts a pattern of fewer physiological responses ("hits") to external stressors than normally occur (solid line). In the top right panel, the dashed line depicts a pattern of more rapid habituation of physiological responses to repeated stressors. The dashed line in the bottom left panel depicts a pattern of peak response with rapid recovery to baseline following termination of a stressor, and the dashed line in the bottom right panel depicts a pattern of lower tonic arousal in physiological stress systems due to baseline differences in restorative physiological processes.
Reprinted from Bower, J. E., Low, C. A., Moskowitz, J., Sepah, S., & Epel, E. (2009). Benefit finding and physical health: Positive psychological changes and enhanced allostasis. *Social and Personality Psychology Compass, 2*, 223–244. Used with permission from John Wiley and Sons.

the idea that positive psychological processes may be reflected in biological regulation that is healthier than normal. Just as positive psychology is not merely the absence of psychopathology or negative psychological states, the biology of positive psychology likely involves physiological processes that are not merely the absence of pathogenic processes and ill health (Charney et al., 2004). Enhanced allostasis and other indicators of better than normal physiological functioning may mediate the observed effects of positive psychological states and traits on disease relevant outcomes.

### Moving Forward

Existing data support the hypothesis that positive psychological states matter for health and physiological processes. The enhanced allostasis model provides a conceptual framework suggesting why this might be the case. In this exciting area of research, many important questions remain to be addressed. Guided by both existing literature and the enhanced allostasis model, we suggest specific, testable hypotheses that represent priority areas of inquiry for current and future researchers if we are to advance the field of positive health psychology.

### Positive Psychological Processes Affect Physiological Processes Such as HPA and Inflammatory Activity, Independent of the Effects of Negative Psychological Processes

The extant literature provides suggestive cross-sectional evidence that positive psychological processes are associated with reduced HPA and inflammatory activity. We hypothesize that these effects are causal and will be detectable in future longitudinal and experimental studies. Given preliminary findings that cross-sectional effects are independent of negative mood, we further predict that longitudinal effects will persist when negative psychological states such as depression are controlled. For example, we hypothesize that the relationship between positive affect and the rapid physiological recovery characteristic of enhanced allostasis will remain significant even after statistical models are adjusted for negative affect.

The mechanisms underlying these causal relationships will be an important area for future investigations. We hypothesize that some of the benefits of positive psychological states on physiology are mediated by improvements in health behaviors, specifically sleep, physical activity, and adherence to medical regimens. Guided by the enhanced allostasis model, we suspect that benefits are also partially mediated by the buffering role of positive psychological states in the context of stress. To test this pathway, it will be important for future studies to test interactions between positive states and stress to determine whether the effects of positive mood, optimism, or other positive factors on physiology are most significant under conditions of stress. Prospective research that examines whether positive factors protect individuals from the pathogenic effects of subsequent stressors will also be important.

### Positive Psychological Processes Affect Markers of Positive Physiological Functioning

In addition to their inverse association with markers of dysfunction and predictors of negative health (e.g., reduced HPA and inflammatory activity), we predict that positive psychological processes will also be positively correlated with indicators of positive physiological functioning, including heart rate variability and anabolic hormones. Although anabolic hormones such as DHEA and growth hormone have received limited empirical attention by health psychologists, we hypothesize that these restorative, homeostatic biomarkers are closely related to psychological and physiological resilience to stress. Thus, we predict that positive psychological processes will be causally linked to higher levels of these hormones at baseline and in response to stress.

### The Effects of Positive Psychological Processes on Physiology Are Clinically Significant

Previous research has demonstrated that positive psychological processes are related to (a) physiological processes including neuroendocrine and immune activity and (b) clinical outcomes such as disease incidence and mortality. Too few studies have examined both of these relationships to test whether changes in physiology are clinically significant and mediate effects on health outcomes. At this point, it remains unclear whether positive psychological processes induce changes in physiology that are of the type, magnitude, and duration to significantly affect long-term health outcomes. We hypothesize that the neuroendocrine and immune effects of positive psychological processes will predict health outcomes, including both protection from negative outcomes such as disease and death as well as positive outcomes such as successful aging and vitality. That said, we predict that these relationships will become clear only when researchers take a more dynamic, fine-grained look at these physiological processes. Increasing or decreasing levels of cortisol or specific cytokines are difficult to interpret in isolation, and a more nuanced view of the dynamic regulation inherent in these systems should become a goal of future research. In addition, it will be important to examine physiological processes that are known to be relevant for a particular health outcome (e.g., inflammation and cardiovascular disease or metabolic peptides/hormones and obesity) to draw conclusions about mechanistic pathways.

## Positive Psychological Processes Are More Beneficial for Some Individuals Under Some Conditions

As the literature on positive psychological states and biological processes continues to grow, the conditions under which such psychological variables are most beneficial for physical health will emerge. Based on the enhanced allostasis model, we hypothesize that positive psychological states will be most relevant to health for populations at risk for allostatic load and disease (e.g., older adults or individuals under chronic stress) and for clinical populations. With regard to clinical populations, there is some evidence that positive psychological states matter most in the context of conditions where behavioral factors are closely related to disease processes (Pressman & Cohen, 2005). For example, positive affect predicts mortality for adults with AIDS (Moskowitz, 2003) and diabetes (Moskowitz, Epel, & Acree, 2008) as well as incidence of coronary heart disease (Kubzansky & Thurston, 2007). All three of these disorders require considerable adherence to medical regimens and recommended changes in health behavior (e.g., exercise), which positive psychological processes such as self-esteem and positive mood may motivate and sustain. However, there is less evidence for a benefit of positive psychological states in the context of cancer, where behavioral factors might account for less variance in disease progression.

We also hypothesize that trait positive psychological factors will be more beneficial than

more short-lived positive mood states, providing cumulative benefits of health behaviors, stress-buffering, and physiological changes. The existing literature also more strongly supports the importance of trait vs. state factors (Pressman & Cohen, 2005).

## Different Positive Psychological Processes Affect Physical Health through Different Pathways

It will be important for future research to consider whether different kinds of positive psychological processes affect physical health outcomes through different pathways. For example, different psychological processes may regulate different components of the stress response, where positive appraisals are particularly important for regulating initial responses to stress as people weigh what is at stake for them when confronted with a potential stressor. If they appraise a situation as not relevant to their goals, they are less likely to respond physiologically. On the other hand, coping and positive emotion may play a stronger role in recovery, allowing an individual who positively reframes a stressful situation to return to a physiological baseline quickly once a stress response has been initiated. Other psychological processes such as self-efficacy may be especially important for motivating and sustaining positive health behaviors.

## Interventions Aimed at Enhancing Positive Psychological Processes Will Affect Physiology and Consequent Physical Health

The development of clinical interventions designed to enhance positive psychological states, traits, and processes is a key objective for future applied research in this field. To date, randomized controlled trials of positive psychological interventions are limited, but existing evidence is encouraging. For example, Stanton and colleagues (2002) assigned women with early-stage breast cancer to write about positive thoughts and feelings about their experience with breast cancer (benefit finding condition), their deepest thoughts and feelings about breast cancer (emotional disclosure condition), or facts of their breast cancer experience (control condition). Those in both the benefit finding and emotional disclosure conditions had significantly fewer medical appointments for cancer-related problems than those in the control condition at the three-month follow-up, although neuroendocrine or immune mediators were not measured in this study. Antoni and colleagues (2001) found a significant increase in benefit finding among women after a 10-week cognitive behavioral intervention (Antoni et al., 2001) that was correlated with decreases in serum cortisol (Cruess et al., 2000) and with increases in lymphocyte proliferation (McGregor et al., 2004) in small subgroup analyses (although note that this intervention was not aimed explicitly at positive psychological processes). An intervention that asked students to list weekly "things in your life that you are grateful or thankful for" found that randomization to this condition was associated with reductions in self-reported physical symptoms, relative to students who listed hassles or more neutral events, although, again, neuroendocrine or immune mediators of this effect were not assessed (Emmons & McCullough, 2003). Taken together, these preliminary studies suggest that interventions specifically designed to increase positive moods (e.g., gratitude) or coping resources (e.g., positive reappraisal coping) hold promise as cost-effective strategies for improving neuroendocrine and immune function as well as physical health (Moskowitz, in press).

In conclusion, there is increasing attention to positive psychological constructs and their importance for mental and physical well-being. We are heartened by this proliferation of scientific investigation into the biology of positive psychology and also cognizant of the limitations of existing research and the rigorous longitudinal and theoretically guided work that remains to be done. Existing data support our general hypothesis that positive psychological processes are beneficial for health and for neuroendocrine and immune function in particular. Based on these findings, we advance the enhanced allostasis model to guide future research and integrate findings in this area. Overall, we believe that identification of the physiological pathways through which positive psychological processes influence physiological processes and physical health are an important topic for future research.

*References*

Antoni, M. H., Lehman, J. M., Klibourn, K. M., Boyers, A. E., Culver, J. L., Alferi, S. M. et al. (2001). Cognitive-behavioral stress management intervention decreases the prevalence of depression and enhances benefit finding among women under treatment for early-stage breast cancer. *Health Psychology, 20,* 20–32.

Bower, J. E., Kemeny, M. E., Taylor, S. E., & Fahey, J. L. (1998). Cognitive processing, discovery of meaning, CD4 decline, and AIDS-related mortality among bereaved HIV-seropositive men. *Journal of Consulting and Clinical Psychology, 66,* 979–986.

Bower, J. E., Low, C. A., Moskowitz, J., Sepah, S., & Epel, E. (2009). Benefit finding and physical health: Positive psychological changes and enhanced allostasis. *Social and Personality Psychology Compass, 2,* 223–244.

Brown, J. E., Butow, P. N., Culjak, G., Coates, A. S., & Dunn, S. M. (2000). Psychosocial predictors of outcome: Time to relapse and survival in patients with early stage melanoma. *British Journal of Cancer, 83,* 1448–1453.

Brydon, L., Walker, C., Wawrzyniak, A. J., Chart, H., & Steptoe, A. (2009). Dispositional optimism and stress-induced changes in immunity and mood. *Brain, Behavior, and Immunity*.

Carrico, A. W., Ironson, G., Antoni, M. H., Lechner, S. C., Duran, R. E., Kumar, M., & Schneiderman, N., (2006). A path model of the effects of spirituality on depressive symptoms and 24-hour urinary free cortisol in HIV-positive persons. *Journal of Psychosomatic Research, 61,* 51–58.

Charney, D. S. (2004). Psychobiological mechanisms of resilience and vulnerability: implications for successful adapation to extreme stress. *Focus, 2,* 368–391.

Chida, Y., & Hamer, M. (2008). Chronic psychosocial factors and acute physiological responses to laboratory-induced stress in healthy populations: A quantitative review of 30 years of investigation. *Psychological Bulletin, 134,* 829–885.

Cohen, S., Doyle, W. J., Turner, R. B., Alper, C. M., & Skoner, D. P. (2003). Emotional style and susceptibility to the common cold. *Psychosomatic Medicine, 65,* 652–657.

Coussens, L. M. & Werb, Z. (2002). Inflammation and cancer. *Nature, 420,* 860–867.

Creswell, J. D., Welch, W. T., Taylor, S. E., Sherman, D. K., Gruenewald, T. L., & Mann, T. (2005). Affirmation of personal values buffers neuroendocrine and psychological stress responses. *Psychological Science, 16,* 846–851.

Cruess, D. G., Antoni, M. H., McGregor, B. A., Kilbourn, K. M., Boyers, A. E., Alferi, S. M. et al. (2000). Cognitive-behavioral stress management reduces serum cortisol by enhancing benefit finding among women being treated for early stage breast cancer. *Psychosomatic Medicine, 62,* 304–308.

Dickerson, S. S., & Kemeny, M. E. (2004). Acute stressors and cortisol responses: A theoretical integration and synthesis of laboratory research. *Psychological Bulletin, 130,* 355–391.

Epel, E., McEwen, B., & Ickovics, J. (1998). Embodying psychological thriving: Physical thriving in response to stress. *Journal of Social Issues, 54,* 301–322.

Epel, E., Adler, N., ickovics, J., & McEwen, B. (1999). Social status, anabolic activity, and fat distribution. *Annals of the New York Academy of Sciences, 896,* 424–426.

Epel, E., Adler, N., Ickovics, J., McEwen, B., & Clayton, P. (2001). Stress-induced reductions in nocturnal growth hormone: preliminary evidence and relations with fat distribution. Poster presentation at the annual meeting of the endocrine society. Denver, Colorado.

Emmons, R. A., & McCullough, M. E. (2003). Counting blessings versus burdens: An experimental investigation of gratitude and subjective well-being in daily life. *Journal of Personality and Social Psychology, 84,* 377–389.

Friedman, E. M., Hayney, M., Love, G. D., Singer, B. H., & Ryff, C. D. (2007). Plasma interleukin-6 and soluble IL-6 receptors are associated with psychological well-being in aging women. *Health Psychology, 26,* 305–313.

Gonzaga, G. C., Turner, R. A., Keltner, D., Campos, B., & Altemus, M. (2006). Romantic love and sexual desire in close relationships. *Emotion, 6,* 163–179.

Hotamisligil, G. S., Shargill, N. S., & Spiegelman, B. M. (1993). Adipose expression of tumor necrosis factor-alpha: direct role in obesity-linked insulin resistance. *Science, 259,* 87–91.

Ickovics, J. R., Milan, S., Boland, R., Schoenbaum, E., Schuman, P., & Vlahov, D. (2006). Psychological resources protect health: 5-year survival and immune function among HIV-infected women from four US cities. *AIDS, 20,* 1851–1860.

Ironson, G. H., & Hayward, H. (2008). Do positive psychosocial factors predict disease progression in HIV-1? A review of the evidence. *Psychosomatic Medicine, 70,* 546–554.

Janicki-Deverts, D., Cohen, S., Doyle, W. J., Turner, R. B., & Treanor, J. J. (2007). Infection-induced proinflammatory cytokines are associated with decreases in positive affect, but not increases in negative affect. *Brain, Behavior, & Immunity, 21,* 301–307.

Kirschbaum, C., Prussner, J. C., Stone, A. A., Federenko, I., Gaab, J., Lintz, D. et al. (1995). Persistent high cortisol responses to repeated psychological stress in a subpopulation of healthy men. *Psychosomatic Medicine, 57,* 468–474.

Koh, K. B., Choe, E., Song, J. E., & Lee, E. H. (2006). Effect of coping on endocrinoimmune functions in different stress situations. *Psychiatry Research, 143,* 223–234.

Kosfeld, M., Heinrichs, M., Zak, P. J., Fischbacher, U., & Fehr, E. (2005). Oxytocin increases trust in humans. *Nature, 435,* 673–676.

Kubzansky, L. D., & Thurston, R. C. (2007). Emotional vitality and incident coronary artery disease: Benefits of healthy psychological functioning. *Archives of General Psychiatry, 64,* 1393–1401.

Lai, J. C. L., Evans, P. D., Ng, S. H., et al. (2005). Optimism, positive affectivity, and salivary cortisol. *British Journal of Health Psychology, 10,* 467–484.

Lyubomirsky, S., King, L., & Diener, E. (2005). The benefits of frequent positive affect: Does happiness lead to success? *Psychological Bulletin, 131,* 803–855.

Marsland, A. L., Cohen, S., Rabin, B. S., & Manuck, S. B. (2006). Trait positive affect and antibody response to hepatitis b vaccination. *Brain, Behavior, & Immunity, 20,* 261–269.

Marsland, A. L., Pressman, S., & Cohen, S., 2007. Positive affect and immune function. In R. Ader (Ed.), *Psychoneuroimmunology* (4th ed., vol. 2, pp. 761–779). San Diego, CA: Elsevier.

Master, S. L., Amodio, D. M., Stanton, A. L., Yee, C. M., Hilmert, C. J., & Taylor, S. E. (2009). Neurobiological correlates of coping through emotional approach. *Brain, Behavior, & Immunity, 23,* 27–35.

McEwen, B. S. (1998). Protective and damaging effects of stress mediators. *New England Journal of Medicine, 338,* 171–179.

McGregor, B. A., Antoni, M. H., Boyers, A., Alferi, S. M., Blomberg, B. B., & Carver, C. S. (2004). Cognitive-behavioral stress management increases benefit finding and immune function among women with early-stage breast cancer. *Journal of Psychosomatic Research, 56,* 1–8.

Mikolajczak, M., Roy, E., Luminet, O., Fillée, C., & de Timary, P. (2007). The moderating impact of emotional intelligence on free cortisol responses to stress. *Psychoneuroendocrinology, 32,* 1000–1012.

Mikolajczak, M., Roy, E., Luminet, O., & de Timary, P. (2008). Resilience and hypothlamaic-pituitary adrenal axis reactivity under acute stress in young men. *Stress, 11,* 477–482.

Milam, J. (2006). Posttraumatic growth and HIV disease progression. *Journal of Consulting and Clinical Psychology, 74,* 817–827.

Morgan, C. A., III, Rasmusson, A. M., Wang, S., Hoyt, G., Hauger, R. L., & Hazlett, G. (2002). Neuropeptide-Y, cortisol, and subjective distress in humans exposed to acute stress: Replication and extension of previous report. *Biological Psychiatry, 52,* 136–142.

Moskowitz, J. T. (in press). Positive affect at the onset of chronic illness: Planting the seeds of resilience. In Reich, J. W., A. J. Zautra, & J. Hall, (Eds.) *Handbook of Adult Resilience.* New York: Guilford.

Moskowitz, J. T. (2003). Positive affect predicts lower risk of AIDS mortality. *Psychosomatic Medicine, 65,* 620–626.

Moskowitz, J. T., Epel, E. S., & Acree, M. (2008). Positive affect uniquely predicts lower risk of mortality in people with diabetes. *Health Psychology, 27,* S73–S82.

O'Donnell, K., Badrick, E., Kumari, M., & Steptoe, A. (2008). Psychological coping styles and cortisol over the day in healthy older adults. *Psychoneuroendocrinology, 33,* 601–611.

O'Donnell, K., Brydon, L., Wright, C. E., & Steptoe, A. (2008). Self-esteem levels and cardiovascular and inflammatory responses to acute stress. *Brain, Behavior, and Immunity, 22,* 1241–1247.

Ostir, G. V., Markides, K. S., Peek, M. K., & Goodwin, J. S. (2001). The association between emotional well-being and the incidence of stroke in older adults. *Psychosomatic Medicine, 63,* 210–215.

Polk, D. E., Cohen, S., Doyle, W. J., Skoner, W. P., & Kirschbaum, C. (2005). State and trait affect as predictors of salivary cortisol in healthy adults. *Psychoneuroendocrinology, 30,* 261–272.

Prather, A. A., Marsland, A. L., Muldoon, M. F., & Manuck, S. B. (2007). Positive affective style covaries with stimulated IL-6 and IL-10 production in a middle-aged community sample. *Brain, Behavior, & Immunity, 21,* 1033–1037.

Pressman, S. D., & Cohen, S. (2005). Does positive affect influence health? *Psychological Bulletin, 131,* 925–971.

Reichenberg, A., Yirmiya, R., Schuld, A., Kraus, T., Haack, M., Morag, A., & Pollmacher, T. (2001). Cytokine-associated emotional and cognitive disturbances in humans. *Archives of General Psychiatry, 58,* 445–452.

Ross, R. (1999). Atherosclerosis—an inflammatory disease. *New England Journal of Medicine, 340,* 115–126.

Seeman, T. E., Berkman, L. F., Gulanski, B. I., Robbins, R. J., Greenspan, S. L., Charpentier, P. A. et al. (1995). Self-esteem and neuroendocrine response to challenge: MacArthur studies of successful aging. *Journal of Psychosomatic Research, 39,* 69–84.

Smyth, J., Ockenfels, M. C., Porter, L., Kirschbaum, C., Hellhammer, D. H., & Stone, A. A. (1998). Stressors and mood measured on a momentary basis are associated with salivary cortisol secretion. *Psychoneuroendocrinology, 23,* 353–370.

Spath-Schwalbe, E., Hansen, K., Schmidt, F., Schrezenmeier, H., Marshall, L., Burger, K., Fehm, H. L., & Born, J. (1998). Acute effects of recombinant human interleukin-6 on endocrine and central nervous sleep functions in healthy men. *Journal of Clinical Endocrinology and Metabolism, 83,* 1573–1579.

Stanton, A. L., Danoff-Burg, S., Sworowski, L. A., Collins, C. A., Branstetter, A. D., Rodriguez-Hanley, A. et al. (2002). Randomized, controlled trial of written emotional expression and benefit finding in breast cancer patients. *Journal of Clinical Oncology, 20,* 4160–4168.

Steptoe, A. Gibson, E. L., Hamer, M., & Wardle, J. (2007). Neuroendocrine and cardiovascular correlates of positive mood assessed by ecological momentary assessment and questionnaire. *Psychoneuroendocrinology, 32,* 56–64.

Steptoe, A., Hamer, M., & Chida, Y. (2007). The effects of acute psychological stress on circulating inflammatory markers in humans: A review and meta-analysis. *Brain, Behavior, & Immunity, 21,* 901–912.

Steptoe, A., O'Donnell, K., Badrick, E., Kumari, M., & Marmot, M. (2008). Neuroendocrine and inflammatory factors associated with positive affect in healthy men and women: The Whitehall II study. *American Journal of Epidemiology, 167,* 96–102.

Unden, A. L., Elofsson, S., Knox, S., Lewitt, M. S., & Brismar, K. (2002). IGF-1 in a normal population: Relation to psychosocial factors. *Clinical Endocrinology, 57,* 793–803.

Valdimarsdottir, H. B., & Bovbjerg, D. H. (1997). Positive and negative mood: Association with natural killer cell activity. *Psychology & Health, 12,* 319–327.

Yehuda, R., Brand, S., & Yang, R. K. (2006). Plasma neuropeptide Y concentrations in combat exposed veterans: Relationship to trauma exposure, recovery from PTSD, and coping. *Biological Psychiatry, 59,* 660–663.

Yehuda, R., Brand, S. R., Golier, J. A., & Yang, R. K. (2006). Clinical correlates of DHEA associated with post-traumatic stress disorder. *Acta Psychiatrica Scandinavia, 114,* 187–193.

# 5

# The Primary Process Affects in Human Development, Happiness, and Thriving

*Jaak Panksepp*

## Introduction

As Jeremy Bentham, the father of utilitarianism, noted—"utility" reflects "that property in any object, whereby it tends to produce benefit, advantage, pleasure, good, or happiness . . . or . . . to prevent the happening of mischief, pain, evil, or unhappiness" (*Introduction to the Principles of Morals and Legislation,* 1789). Since presumably the material world outside living bodies contains no feelings, the most momentous question in all positive psychology research is: What are *those properties in "objects"?* A reasonable provisional answer is the capacity of various world events to evoke affective feelings within our brains. All affective (valenced) feelings, as they arise either intrinsically (unconditionally) or via learned associations, have much utility for survival. They arise from the psychobiological properties of our brains and minds and bodies (henceforth BrainMinds as well as occasionally BrainMindBody functions[1]).

Brains elaborate several distinct forms of primary-process affective experience. Some arise from the way we perceive the world with our externally directed senses (*sensory affects*).

Others arise from the way our brains *interoceptively* monitor what is happening inside our bodies (*homeostatic affects*). Yet others reflect intrinsic activities of our brain (*emotional affects*). They all presumably contribute to our lingering *moods.* Thus our affective feelings come in many forms, and the failure to distinguish them causes much confusion in emotion research and affective science. Here, I will focus mostly on those most mysterious feelings that originate within the brain itself—the emotional affects that are not tightly restricted to specific exteroceptive and interoceptive body state channels like the sensory and homeostatic varieties. This is not to say that emotional affects are not modulated by sensory and homeostatic inputs; they surely are, but that BrainMindBody "higher-order psychological insights" (most of which remain to be well studied) do not help that much in explaining the mystery of the various basic types of *emotional experiences* we have, but rather their tertiary-process complexities (*vide infra*).

Right now, one of the greatest scientific mysteries is: *What is happening in the brain when we are having these various types of affective feelings?*

Clearly, some arise as intrinsic unconditioned properties of our brains (primary-process affects). Others arise more from learned associations (secondary-process affects). Yet others arise from these "simpler" processes interacting with our capacity for language, thought, and reflections (*tertiary-process affects*). The biggest part of the mystery seems to reside in the *intrinsic MindBrain functions* that give our perceptual experiences their affective feeling tone. This is most poignant for emotional feelings, since there are initially (before learning) only a few external stimuli that can evoke emotional feelings—the so-called *unconditioned stimuli* of behavioristic learning paradigms.

There are many reasons we know so little about how our valenced feelings—the various positive and negative affects—are created within the brain. Some are taken in by the illusion that affects are just "sensations" or "perceptions" that arise largely from, as opposed to just being triggered and modulated by, external events. People are generally not accustomed to viewing their primary-process affective states as being ancestral "memories"—qualities of mind that they inherited from an ancestral past, ancient brain functions still shared with all other mammals in general principles if not the precise details. Scientists have at times also been searching for the mechanisms of affect in the wrong places, especially the expanded neocortical-cognitive terrain of human beings, not to mention higher brain interpretation of bodily states (i.e., the many James-Lange types of theories of emotion). Regrettably few investigators envision the scientific problem in hierarchical terms, ranging from various unconditioned *foundational* "primary-process" issues—best studied in animal models—to a great variety of higher-order thought-penetrated MindBrain processes best studied in humans.

## Conceptual Perspectives

The continuing failure of psychology to cultivate a cross-mammalian sub-neocortical locus of control for human emotional feelings can be placed directly at the doorstep of influential behaviorists, largely interested in *secondary* behavioral processes (i.e., learning) who have long claimed that the emotions "are excellent examples of the fictional causes to which we commonly attribute behavior" (p. 160, Skinner, 1953). This kind of thinking within the modern era also goes back to Cartesian dualism whereby animals were

envisioned as "machines" while humans possessed immortal souls from which the gift of mental life arises. Nonsense. To this day, such historical mistakes still lead prominent investigators studying fear-learning in animals, using traditional foot-shock classical-conditioning procedures in animal models, to assert that their animals feel nothing (e.g., LeDoux, 1996 (p. 302), but see his 2009 for a slight re-tuning). In any event, work on the unconditioned neural mechanisms of raw affective experiences in animal models, especially positive emotions, has not been encouraged within our current Zeitgeist. As George Vaillant (2008) noted: "The first article specifically on the neurobiology of the positive emotions (Burgdorf and Panksepp, 2006) has only been published in the last year." Meanwhile hundreds if not thousands of papers have been published on fear conditioning under the guise that they are clarifying the fundamental nature of emotional processes of the brain, while they have clarified only some of the secondary-processes of fear conditioning, and perhaps not the core of the mechanisms, which may be more linked to the intrinsic "world grasping" properties of the unconditioned emotional response pathways than how unconditioned stimuli promote the creation of conditioned stimuli. I will focus here on how an understanding of the primary-process (unconditioned response) nature of human emotional affects may be achieved through the use of animal models, which may set the stage for more realistic emotional learning theories that have broader implications for positive psychology.

Positive psychological science and practice may benefit from empirically based neuroscientific visions of how core, primary-process affective processes arise from mammalian brains.[2] Useful strands of positive psychobiological knowledge should arise especially from our emerging understanding of the primary-process positive and negative emotional qualia of mental life that arise from our ancestral mammalian nature, as recently illuminated by affective neuroscience research. The evidence now speaks loudly—raw affects are intimately intermeshed with the ancient (sub-neocortical) neural circuits that generate natural-instinctual (unconditioned) emotional behaviors (Panksepp, 1982, 1998a, 2005a).

As used here, *primary-process emotions* are the evolutionary "givens" of mental life; they encode various unconditional affective responses of the brain that were designed to code key survival values of life—they intrinsically *anticipate* universal survival issues. They are evolved tools for living—internal affective states that immediately provide guidance for behaviors; they have an intrinsic capacity to sustain life. They are guides for living from our ancestral past. From a slightly different vantage, they are strongly experienced intrinsic "memories" (unconditioned responses) that can rapidly shift organisms' bodily and mental attitudes to environmental events. In other words, raw emotional-affective experiences arise from the same sub-neocortical brain networks that generate coherent instinctual action displays. The data for that is compelling (Panksepp, 1998a, 2005a, 2010a), which, through a dual-aspect monism strategy (Panksepp, 2005b), now allows us to utilize emotional-instinctual actions as proxies for animal feelings. This chapter will advance the view that an understanding of such intrinsic affective "voices" of our minds can usefully link up with and structure our rapidly increasing higher-order understanding of positive psychology issues. Such a view can also beneficially restructure our discussions of many emotional-motivational issues of increasing interest within scientific psychology. Many debates in academic psychology are muddied by not keeping hierarchical MindBrain issues in sight—for instance, debates between dimensional-constructivist views and "basic emotion" views.

To reiterate this critical point: *Secondary emotional processes* reflect how those basic mechanisms for living interact with learning mechanisms such as operant and classical conditioning (LeDoux, 2000). *Tertiary processes*, as used here, reflect emotional interactions with thoughts and appraisals, the level of analysis at which most psychologists study mental life. For instance, the key concept of *happiness* in positive psychology clearly arises at the highest tertiary levels of affective processing. In contrast, the raw nature of pleasure and pain, and various raw emotional feelings, are foundational issues. Here I will also develop the view that a fundamental understanding of our negative primary-process emotions and feelings in the brain may be as important for understanding as the positive psychological insights concerning the nature of happiness in the brain.

Once we link what we are talking about affectively at a foundational level to brain circuits and specific neurochemical systems that constitute our core emotional processes, we may better envision their interactions within our vast general-purpose cognitive abilities that parse our "given" affective life into innumerable idiographic nuances

(i.e., the experiential construction of adult human emotions, with considerable cultural variety). As we begin to understand the cross-species foundational issues, we can potentially achieve a deep psychobiological understanding of the underlying dynamics of positive psychological processes, from the garden varieties of daily joys and satisfactions to ecstatic delights. We may also achieve better clarity about many hard-to-treat psychiatric disorders, especially treatment resistant anxieties and depressions, full of psychic turmoil and various discontents (Panksepp, 2004a, b). Thereby we should better understand how our basic feelings control our aspirations for satisfying lives—namely how the various ancestral roots of animal joys and various forms of distress are also the raw materials from which we construct our lives. In short, the primary-process issues are more nomothetic (universal) than the higher-order complexities of human mental life that are constructed from more idiographic, highly variable societal and cultural influences (Panksepp & Northoff, 2009; Vandekerckhove & Panksepp, 2009).

This does not mean that the details of emotionality across species are identical. They obviously are not. The diversity of emotional details across mammalian species may be as great as the variability of their bodies. The only claim is that *general principles* concerning types of emotions and their general organization in the brain have been conserved, as indicated by abundant brain research conducted during the second half of the 20th century. Such foundational issues never fully penetrated the psychological sciences, but there is increasing interest in such complex neuro-evolutionary psychological issues. My aim here is not to overload interested readers with the abundant details (Panksepp, 1998a, 2005a, 2010a), but to highlight the general principles that may satisfy our hunger for something stable at the very ground of our affective existence, positive and otherwise.

Since the beginning of modern psychology, a central dilemma has been how to develop ways to scientifically understand what we mean by affective-emotional experiences—those evolutionarily honed, energetic aspects of mind that can color our very being. At one time, psychology almost gave up on ever trying to scientifically specify how affects emerge from our brains, and discarded our animalian instincts and psychological "energies" from consideration, replacing them with a pantheon of more cognitive concepts. The cognitive-propositional (tertiary) side of affective life seemed more empirically tractable than the raw feeling side. At least our languages are better designed to talk about them. Thus, the very nature of affective experience has remained more mysterious, some say empirically intractable. Although that is wrong, that central scientific problem continues to be, well, problematic, to the present time. Our ignorance has become especially poignant now that psychology no longer dwells almost exclusively on the negative side of affective life but also on the positive aspects. Still, somehow *anger* and *fear* seemed easier to understand than loving *care* and *joy*, perhaps because the Walter Cannon gave us such a clear, albeit conflated, "fight-flight" concept as a behavioral bookmarker for future developments.

While we have been harvesting abundant evidence about the bodily psychophysiological, surface behavioral and cognitive features of human suffering and more recently happiness—very broad and multidimensional higher-order processes—the neural nature of the various core positive and negative affects, and the resulting implications for understanding human nature and human problems, has gradually become more tractable. Although experienced affects have been implicitly accepted as psychological primitives, we are now well situated to unpack their neuro-evolutionary nature and cultural implications. But the conversation has barely begun about how the brain truly generates affects and whether at the foundation there are only some primitive dimensions of valence and arousal or a more evolutionarily resolved affective life (for a forthcoming extensive debate on this issue, see Zachar & Ellis, 2010, in press).

## More Personal Perspectives

For more than 40 years, since terminating my clinical psychology training as a graduate student (in frustration over our lack of knowledge and work on understanding emotional feelings—for synopsis, see Panksepp 2010b), my scientific goal has been to promote evidence-based discourse and research on the affective infrastructure of the human BrainMind, through evolutionarily informed cross-species brain research. In the late 1960s I concluded that the only way we can understand the basic affective nature of our own minds was through *physiological psychology* research on the emotional brains and behaviors of our fellow animals, where key neural questions

could be addressed. However, such a conversation in psychology was modest in the '60s and became increasingly impoverished in the '70s, as behaviorists, who earlier had little interest in the brain, learned to follow the money with the onslaught of the cognitive revolution. Indeed, my field itself was renamed *behavioral neuroscience*. Work on the memory of sea snails was accepted and lauded (Kandel, 2000), but work on the passions of the animal mind were neglected, if not explicitly discouraged: Federal funding for research to understand emotional feelings in animals remains unavailable to this day. It was implicitly agreed, in line with behaviorist dogma, that research on experiences of animals was close to nonsense talk—beyond the ken of science. That continues to be a major intellectual-scientific tragedy, but hopefully the times are changing (Panksepp, 2010a). The evidence is sufficient! Animals do have emotional feelings (*vide infra*).

In any event, after receiving tenure, I decided to inquire how a study of the unconditioned (i.e., evolved) primary-process emotional response circuits of mammalian brains might illuminate the principles by which human brains create raw affective states (e.g., Panksepp, 1982, 1985, 1991, 1998a, 2005a). The most general principle that emerged was that wherever in the brain one could arouse coherent emotional-instinctual behavior patterns, using electrical or chemical stimulation of specific sub-neocortical regions, the same stimulation could serve as "rewards" and "punishments" in learning paradigms. This highlighted which circuits we need to focus on to understand the various primary-process emotional feelings. I relied on the intuition and data-based probability that rewards and punishments were effective in the brain only because of their capacity to engender internal affective states. That continues to be a radical, some believe untenable, position. The argument should become more compelling as one realizes that rewards and punishments—long defined as environmental events—logically have to be brain events. And if one provides mere electrical "noise" to the brain in the emotional networks, there is no existing behavioristic or psychological theory that would predict that they would consistently serve to "reinforce" learning. But such effects are abundant in animal brain research, and just at the locations where brain stimulation in humans evokes the strongest emotional feelings (Panksepp, 1985).

In my estimation, "reinforcement"—from a brain perspective—is a content-free "placeholder" for the way affect-generating circuits mediate learning. If brain stimulation evoked no affects, surely it would have little capacity to mediate learning. Indeed, this suggests that fear conditioning and appetitive conditioning may work only because unconditioned FEAR and SEEKING networks open up glutamatergic gateways from associated (conditional stimulus as well as, probably, cognitive) pathways to the emotional primes. And this gate-opening function may arise largely from the unconditioned emotional system networks of the brain, allowing learned synaptic changes to be created (a totally novel way to envision and study conditioning).

To help clarify nomenclature issues, major emotional systems arising from affective neuroscience evidence are now capitalized in my work to emphasize that the referents are to specific networks of the brain that concurrently help orchestrate i) coherent behavioral emotional responses (of the ethological variety that Darwin (1872) studied); ii) the autonomic-visceral, immunological and other bodily changes to support such distinct emotional states; and iii) the feeling tone of each emotion, which signals intrinsic survival values to the organism in ways that motivate the emergence of higher emotional-cognitive processes. This last attribute, the affective feel of emotions, can be phenomenologically described by humans, in multi-tiered semantic complexities (with no agreed-upon rules; Zachar & Ellis, 2010), but surely their neurobiological basis is only readily studied in animal models. Thus, if one wishes to clarify the primary-process level of affective life, one has few options but neurobehavioral research on other animals (with all the ethical compromises that this entails).

It bears repeating: Artificial arousal of such brain circuits—typically with localized electrical and chemical stimulation of the brain—can serve as diverse rewards and punishments in the acquisition and molding of new learned responses and modes of being. In other words, primary-process affects are the unconditioned responses necessary for emotional learning! The fact that diverse neural systems exist in sub-neocortical regions of the brain (Panksepp, 1982, 1998a, 2005a) has empirically clarified the primary-process neural infrastructure of the emotional-affective BrainMind, apparently shared by all mammals. Another reason for capitalizing these core emotional-affective primes is to reduce mereological fallacies (part-whole conflations) that are otherwise rampant in our use of psychological language, especially in the cognitive neurosciences

(Bennett & Hacker, 2003). Although an understanding of the primary affective processes does not automatically inform us how they percolate through higher cognitive processes, it is reasonable to theorize that they might be necessary foundations for those higher developments, especially if consciousness depends on core affective/emotional mechanisms (Holstege & Saper, 2005, Panksepp, 1998b, 2005b, 2007a, 2008a, 2009a).

Of course, as already noted, there are also primary-process affects other than "emotional" varieties, for instance the various sensory (e.g., pain, taste, etc.) and homeostatic affects (e.g., from air hunger to energy hunger, thirst, thermoregulation, etc.). The menagerie of evolved affects surely needs to be distinguished from each other in various ways. For instance, the sensory and homeostatic affects are aroused by various unconditioned stimuli that guide and energize learning. In contrast, the emotional affects are intimately linked to within-brain action tendencies, with only a few "trigger stimuli" (sign-stimuli in the parlance of ethology; unconditioned stimuli in behavioral theory) that arouse the underlying emotional action substrates, that remain to be worked out in fine detail. But a substantive beginning has been made.

All primary-process affects, whether emotional, sensory, or homeostatic, are ancestral memories—evolved ways of being and feeling—that help all mammals anticipate survival needs. Affective "ancestral *memories!?*" you might ask. Perhaps this concept is easiest to grasp with the homeostatic affect of HUNGER. These pangs don't tell us that we have terribly depleted body energy stores (we can survive for months without much more to eat). HUNGER is an anticipatory affect indicating that taking meals, as opportunities arise, is a wise investment for one's long-term energy budget. This emphasizes that the most fundamental adaptive function of all the evolutionarily "given" primary-process affects is the ability to *anticipate* survival needs. First I will briefly consider the role of the two categories of non-emotional affects—namely sensory and homeostatic—in positive-affect regulation. Then I will proceed to the main theme of this chapter—the role of emotional affects in child development and positive psychology discourse.

## The Sensory Affects

Although there is insufficient room here to go into details, the pleasures of sensation (primarily value of tastes) were first intensively studied by Pfaffman (1960) and Young (1959). Those studies were refined by the breakthrough evolutionary research and thinking of Michelle Cabanac (1992), which highlighted that the same sensory stimulus can change from pleasantness to unpleasantness depending on the status of our bodies (i.e., hunger makes sweetness taste better). A penetrating neuroscientific understanding of the sensory affects was inaugurated by the seminal neurophysiological work of Edmund Rolls (2005) and subsequently through the neuroethological analysis of gustatory-facial responses of Kent Berridge (2000, 2004), and his colleagues (Peciña et al., 2006; Steiner et al., 2001) as well as others (Sewards & Sewards, 2000; Kringelbach, 2010).

There are many other sensory affects, ranging from the complex thermoregulatory dynamics of the mammalian brain to orgasmic delights (Holstege et al., 2003). Certain basic *sensory* affects such as nauseating DISGUST (Ellis & Toronchuk, 2005; Toronchuk & Ellis, 2007), can also presumably be used as a substrate for the construction of tertiary-process emotions such as social-disgust, albeit to my knowledge there is no neuroscientific evidence for any primary-process *emotional* DISGUST circuitry in the human brain (Panksepp, 2007a). At this level of the brain, core emotions are defined by their neural and affective properties.

The primary-process affects engendered by the internal states of the body (i.e., homeostatic affects), ranging from air hunger to food and water "hungers," so to speak, are also organized by the most medial sub-neocortical regions of the mammalian brain (Denton, 2006; Panksepp, 1998a; Sewards, 2004). The level of detailed understanding already achieved of the participating neural substrates is truly remarkable, albeit the accompanying experiences of the animals are rarely addressed in affective terms. The failure of animal investigators to discuss feelings of hunger and satiety in affective terms is detrimental to identifying knowledge from animal models that may be most useful for helping us find excellent appetite control agents (e.g., see Panksepp, 2010c, for discussion of tests that could be run but rarely are).

From a general neuro-geographic perspective, the various types of affect overlap and interpenetrate with each other within the medial regions of the midbrain, hypothalamus, and intimately interconnected old basal ganglia and paleo-cortical regions. This extended neural matrix is postulated

to be the neural grounding for the nomothetic core SELF, from which core affective consciousness emerges (Panksepp, 1998a, b, 2007d, 2009a), which is closely related to higher self-related processing in the brain (Northoff, et al., 2006; Panksepp & Northoff, 2009).

## From the Homeostatic and Emotional Affects to the Core SELF

Our provisional understanding of how raw affective experience arises from ancient brain activities, yielding a unified but unreflective sense of belonging to oneself, is based upon a postulated medial sub-neocortical core SELF substrate that is deeply homologous across mammalian species (Northoff & Panksepp, 2008). This substrate provides coherence-creating networks for both affective experience (perhaps the first glimmer of mind in brain evolution) and instinctual emotional responses of body for all mammals. These primary-process substrates, as they interact with the many secondary and tertiary processes of the MindBrain, especially the medial neocortical regions that are most tightly linked to the primary-process affective substrates, generate the varieties of idiographic passionate and ruminative selves that are manifested within the higher regions of the brain (Panksepp & Northoff, 2009), issues on which we have dwelt elsewhere (Vandekerckhove & Panksepp, 2009).

Although all of these affects contribute substantially to the quality of lived lives, it would be foolish to seek the major sources of human happiness within the simple-minded dictates of sensory and homeostatic affects. Happiness surely requires wisdom—what Aristotle called *phronesis*—the ability to have nuanced feelings that are well measured (regulated) by our cognitive abilities. Wisdom through the ages has affirmed that it is not the maximizations of sensory pleasures or bodily satisfactions that elevate us toward human happiness, but the prosocial emotional qualities of our lives.

Still, happiness is hard to find in the midst of any kind of psychic pain, including ravaging hungers and sensory disgusts. However, positive psychology can thrive in the midst of good-enough sensory pleasures, the ability to subsist bodily without too much distress, but rarely without solid SEEKING urges, and the sharing, empathic grace of well-cultivated prosocial emotions of LUST, CARE, and PLAY, as well as the full appreciation of the profound sting of PANIC/GRIEF that tells us "loudly" how much we value each other, promoting mother-infant as well as adult social bonding (Panksepp, 1981, 2010e; Swain et al., 2007).

Those simple infantile beginnings of an affirmative mental life can be cultivated into the exquisite complexities of adult happiness as well as miseries within the epigenetic-developmental engravings of those ancestral values into the idiographic thoughtful higher regions of the mind—more easily observed in humans because of our capacity to speak. I expect that many contributors to this volume will focus our attention to those higher, tertiary-process affective-cognitive qualities of happy minds (as have many philosophers down through the ages). Regrettably, human research has little access to the *nature* of the primary-process affective substrates. What basic cross-species neuroscience can now provide is a lasting knowledge about these ancient brain processes that can either fertilize or derail individual passages toward mature happiness. The nature of our primary-process emotional traits can help refocus our attention toward the basic affective tools needed to pursue happiness (SEEKING, LUST, CARE, and PLAY), and to highlight the kinds of social structures and developmental supports we need in early life to optimally cultivate our higher affective potentials. An excess of negative primary-process emotional affects early in life (RAGE, FEAR, and PANIC/GRIEF) can demolish such potentials. If so, a positive psychology without an understanding of both the desirable and undesirable core *emotional* experiences may remain more speculative than is desirable.

This vision of primary-process emotional life also helps us understand why our affective feelings are so self-centered. At the primary and probably secondary-process levels they are most intimately intertwined with our core SELVES, laid out largely in primitive visceral and somatic action coordinates. Once these affects are re-represented in higher MindBrain regions, they tend to remain idiographically self-centered, and much of emotional education as well as psychotherapy may need to proceed by "deconditioning" and "recontextualization" of emotional self-centeredness. That allows one to accept one's negative feelings as one's own, and not of others' making. This allows positive psychological attitudes to have a broader reach toward close others as well as into an ever-wider outside community. This would surely be enhanced if therapists explicitly try to facilitate "reconsolidation" of new ways of viewing life in the context of more positive feelings,

and this may be better effected if one brings back troublesome autobiographical memories gently in the context of positive emotional arousals, which should be especially effective if primary-process affective-emotional networks of the brain actually lead to the "reinforcement-consolidation" processes that control affective-cognitive learning linkages in the brain.

## The Emotional Primes: Seven Evolutionary Tools for Affective Life

The most compelling evidence for the existence of seven ancestral basic emotional systems, shared by all mammals, is our ability to artificially activate distinct kinds of emotional patterns by applying the appropriate kinds of chemical or electrical stimulation to specific subneocortical regions of the brain in every species studied. Such "sweet" and "sour" affective spots (highlighting poorly understood networks) of animal brains also affect human higher-order mentation. Stimulation of these same brain regions arouses more intense emotional affects in humans, with full "ownership" of experience, than stimulations of any other regions of the human brain (Heath, 1996; Panksepp, 1985). They are experienced completely as one's own emotional feelings. Since epistemological and phenomenological evidence for these systems is detailed elsewhere (Austin, 1998; MacLean, 1990; Panksepp, 1998a, 2005a, 2010a), archival referencing in the following thumbnail descriptions will be used sparingly. I will simply highlight one or two recent reviews as each system is introduced.

The basic emotional systems can be used in ways that promote lifelong happiness or lifelong problems, and such possibilities will be my main focus here. Our understanding of human happiness should increase as we consider how these seven ancestral tools for living can promote lives well lived—with positive affects becoming part of a child's emerging character and the intrinsic negative affects becoming part of a cognitive understanding that can hopefully mute their long-term sting. So let's briefly focus on each of these systems from a positive psychology perspective. In line with my interest in the role of these systems in child well-being (Panksepp, 2001a, b), after each system is introduced, I will briefly highlight the potential role of each in positive childhood development.

In general, a goal of emotional-social intelligence should be to promote psychological flexibility and the capacity to use emotions in the furtherance of positive prosocial habits and fair, life-affirming goals. Following time-honored wisdom, we should encourage children gradually to become masters of their negative emotions rather than servants of them. For instance, understanding what information anger is providing in one's mental life and its deep potential for destructive self-defeating actions should be part of one's emotional education. Helping children to master the many affective tools, especially negative ones, often allows them to move more effectively toward valued goals.

According to the nomenclature convention already described, I employ uppercase for labeling each system but then, as didactically needed, shift to the lowercase vernacular, since the primary-process affects are no doubt major influences in the many vernacular concepts we humans readily use to discuss emotions, with interesting variability across cultures. These systems may be primordial endophenotypes that may need to be understood in order to understand psychiatric disorders (Panksepp, 2006a). Additional developmental issues will be considered in the ensuing "Moving Forward" section.

1) **The SEEKING/Desire System** (Alcaro et al., 2007; Panksepp & Moskal, 2008). This general-purpose appetitive-motivational system, driven by the mesolimbic dopamine system, is foundational for many other emotional systems to operate effectively (e.g., LUST, CARE, and PLAY). Ascending dopamine pathways innervate the medial frontal cortical regions in all mammals, but in human brain evolution they have proceeded to grow much further into the forebrain, innervating the sensory-perceptual regions of the brain, suggesting a more profound mental role for this system that promotes psychomotor energization in humans than in most other mammals (Panksepp, 1998a). SEEKING arousal may be a major source of the directed "mental energy" that has at times been called "libido"—it generally promotes an energized positive affective presence that resembles what might be commonly called, from low to high arousal respectively, interest, enthusiasm, exhilaration, and euphoria. It is an addictive quality within the BrainMind. It induces animals to be intensely engaged in exploring their world—searching inquisitively for the fruits of survival and entertainment. Along with the automatic anticipatory learning that results from periodic (i.e., fixed interval) as well as cue-related arousal of this system, the SEEKING urge spontaneously leads

animals to become excited when they are about to get what they desire (i.e., yielding expectancy-arousal to conditioned stimuli). Animals use this system to get their daily food and fun. Thus, rather than preferring to "freeload" when freely available food is well-provisioned, all species of mammals tested would rather eagerly work for their food if such interesting options are made available. This psychic energy, one that promotes dreams (Solms & Turnbull, 2002 can easily lead to delusional thinking, which can lead to impulsive sensation seeking (as exemplified most prolifically by Internet addictions in our children) and at its worst can lead to various addictions (from obsessive Internet "pecking" to drug delights to greedy hoarding as well as the suspicions of paranoid schizophrenia). This highlights how a very desirable (a potentially "good") affective system can become the bane of one's existence and thus brings into relief the concept of emotional balance (Aristotle's *phronesis*) in lives well lived. At its best, the SEEKING urge promotes our creativity and search for knowledge (Reuter et al., 2005) and the construction of highly engaging personality structures.

In short, the SEEKING system allows animals to exhibit an intensely engaged curiosity—to find and eagerly anticipate all kinds of resources they need for survival. Each day the system devotes needed efforts toward the pursuit of all the traditional rewards of the world—water, food, warmth, or coolness depending on the status of thermoregulatory systems, and it promotes the ultimate evolutionarily dictated mammalian social-emotional survival needs—sexual gratification, maternal care, and social bonding. When bodily needs are fulfilled, it promotes enthusiastic exploration of the world, helping to create new knowledge and promote new interests (Silvia & Kashdan, 2009). However, it is also essential for obtaining resources when negative affects are aroused such as FEAR, which can, as already noted, promote the seeking of safety.

Neuroanatomically, the SEEKING system corresponds to the major self-stimulation system that runs from the dopamine-rich midbrain Ventral Tegmental Area (VTA) up to the nucleus accumbens and medial frontal cortex via the Medial Forebrain Bundle (MFB). Animals will activate this dopamine-fired system readily, whether with drugs of abuse such as cocaine or direct electrical or chemical stimulation of the brain (after they have been surgically prepared with the necessary delivery devices, of course). Ever since its discovery by Jim Olds and

Peter Milner in 1954, long before the discovery of dopamine networks in the brain, this emotional system has been poorly conceptualized as a *Reward, Pleasure, or Reinforcement System* of the brain.

This has stifled creative and accurate neuroethological thinking. Instead, it appears to be a general-purpose neuronal system that coaxes animals and humans to move energetically from where they are presently situated to the places where they can find and consume resources needed for survival. However, it is so well connected with other regions of the brain that most brain activities, including thoughts, can surely come to tickle this system. This energy can be used in psychologically serious or playful ways. Indeed, our discovery of rat "laughter" (Panksepp, 2007b)—a 50 kHz chirping abundant during their social play as well as when we humans tickle them—has been mapped to the trajectory of the SEEKING system and is distinctly controlled by brain dopamine release (Burgdorf et al., 2007).

The SEEKING system promotes learning by readily engendering predictive reward relationships in the world. As noted, a critically important chemical in this system is dopamine, but SEEKING is also regulated by practically all other brain synaptic chemistries, including neuropeptides such as endogenous opioids, neurotensin, oxytocin, and orexin (a novel brain arousal system, all of whose neurons are clustered smack in the middle of the MFB). Many of these peptides participate in several other basic emotional and motivational processes, and diverse forms of affect may be engendered by their various brain sites of action. In any event, dopamine-energized SEEKING circuits can energize and coordinate the functions of many higher brain areas that mediate planning and foresight. As noted, this system has more extensive cortical innervation in hominid brains than more simple-minded mammals. The SEEKING urge promotes normal states of anticipatory eagerness and apparent purpose in both humans and animals. This is the closest we have to a generalized positive-affect system in the brain, but there are many other chemistries that promote distinct forms of positive affect, including prominently, among many less prolific players, endogenous opioids and serotonin.

In any event, when fully aroused, the SEEKING urge fills the mind with interest and motivates organisms to move their bodies seemingly effortlessly in search of the things they

need, crave, and desire—from gambling or shopping (Knutson, et al., 2001; Knutson & Wimmer, 2007) to being moved by the yearnings evoked by music (Blood & Zattore, 2001). In short, this system generates and sustains our curiosity from the mundane to our highest intellectual pursuits (Kashdan, 2009; Silvia, 2006). When this system becomes underactive for various reasons, such as drug withdrawal, chronic helplessness/stress, or neural deficits of old age, a form of depression results (a state promoted by brain dynorphin dominance in mesolimbic dopamine pathways), which is currently figuring heavily in our understanding of clinical depression (Nestler & Carlezon, 2006). When the SEEKING urge becomes spontaneously overactive, which can happen as a result of various drugs, as already noted, thoughts and behaviors can become excessive and stereotyped, yielding manic obsessions, guided often by psychotic delusions and confabulations.

*Implications for a life well lived:* Affectively, the SEEKING urge, albeit in the positive-affective domain, is a double-edged sword: Balanced activity can promote a positive world engagement, while excessive activity can generate an addictive "too-muchness"—a mania that is detrimental to a balanced, positive life. It may be hard to understand that this critically important "rewarding" MindBrain system also has a dark side, as already noted above. It can promote human misery because it draws "psychic energy" away from the more productive life activities into narcissistic self-engagements. Many drug addictions that operate through this system, including amphetamines and cocaine, not to mention gambling and sex addictions, can destroy lives. At milder, socially acceptable levels, just consider the addictive qualities of "Facebook" and other electronic social-networking tools, now available to so many of our adolescents, who often find ways to cyber-stalk and marginalize others. Clearly, happiness requires a balanced life, where one deploys this psychological energy in judicious ways that enhance creative, fair, life-affirming activities. Nothing inside our brains mandates that path, and this is where culture and education need to lend a hand to promote optimal positive character development.

Optimal child development is surely promoted by abundant positive life-affirming experiences, especially during childhood, providing perhaps a lasting "tonic" for affectively positive personality development. In sum, presumably the SEEKING urge can be strengthened (sensitized) and channeled to mold positive characterological habits, or negative ones, through early experiences. If one has been reared in the midst of hunger and poverty, this system, as already noted, may promote a lifetime of greed and hoarding. One can become addictively captivated by material things and lose the capacity for a deeply spiritual grounding. With guidance into scientific-humanistic curiosity and the arts, one can develop a storehouse of world perspectives that can establish life paths that reflect the better side of the human spirit. It cannot be overemphasized: Much of this depends on the environments in which children are reared.

However, this system also highlights how certain intrinsic psychobiological motive urges—perhaps all of the non-social emotional systems—do not have any intrinsic sense of morality or perspective taking on what must constitute a balanced, happy life. It is important to recognize the negative aspects of this system. If deployed judiciously, with all the societal supports needed to guide young people onto productive paths, we can easily envision how abundantly culture and education need to utilize and guide this system toward the creation of balanced, happy lives. Books have been written on how a better understanding of the positive psychic energy of this system can promote the emergence of deep meaning in life; the ability to have healthy, fun-filled, give-and-take relationships; and the generation of the cognitive wherewithal for greater tolerance, compassion, and tolerance of uncertainty (Kashdan, 2009; Silvia, 2006). Surely some of the paths to human happiness through creative, productive lives are through the diverse learning potentials of this system.

In sum, the SEEKING system "knows" nothing on its own. It is born naïve, engendering the simple urge to go out and explore the world, with exhilaration and gusto. It can promote mindful knowledge as well as mindless tragedies. As all emotional primes, SEEKING is born *anoetic* (without knowledge; "objectless" in a manner of speaking); the system needs to be shaped by early experiences for optimal thriving.

2) The RAGE/Anger System (Haller & Kruk, 2006, Siegel, 2005; Panksepp & Zellner, 2004). Working in tandem with, often in opposition to, SEEKING is an emotional system that helps organisms defend and procure resources when there is competition; it probably mediates what is typically called "anger" in the vernacular. RAGE is aroused by frustration arising from any attempts to curtail an animal's freedom of action or aspirations to fulfill one's desires. It has long

been known that one can enrage both animals and humans by stimulating very specific circuits of the brain—running from medial amygdala through the hypothalamus to the Periaqueductal gray (PAG). The RAGE system invigorates aggressive behaviors when animals are irritated or restrained and also helps animals defend themselves by arousing fear in their opponents. Chronic overactivity of this system should be envisioned to be a major source of irritable psychiatric disorders, but such conditions are not explicitly recognized in current diagnostic manuals (e.g., DSM-IV). This has discouraged the pharmaceutical industry from developing anti-anger medications. Hence, there is no medically condoned market for such agents, retarding medicinal discovery. But if we consider anger turned inward, common in depressive disorders, we may better understand some of the sources of suicide.

There are a number of well-documented cases where humans stimulated in these brain regions have exhibited sudden, intense RAGE attacks, with no external provocations (Panksepp, 1985). But it should also be recognized that this system can also work in tandem with appetitive SEEKING urges, especially in higher regions of the BrainMind (Harmon-Jones, 2007). Key regulatory chemistries in the RAGE system are the neuropeptide, Substance P, and glutamate, which promote arousal of anger, and endogenous opioids, which inhibit the system. However, these chemistries (especially glutamate and opioids) also participate in many other emotional-affective states, and their functions are so broad that peripherally administered drugs would have little pharmacological specificity, suggesting the existence of a generalized positive-affect system (just like dopamine); however, the specificity of such neurochemicals is determined by local actions within the specific emotional systems in which they operate. Future medications based on more specific neuropeptide regulators of each emotional prime may allow us to more precisely target each of the individual emotional systems (Panksepp & Harro, 2004). Thus, novel medicines to control angry behavior in humans and animals could presumably be developed through further detailed understanding of the underlying brain for instance, Substance P antagonists such as aprepitant deserve to be analyzed for their anti-anger properties in dysregulated humans and other domestic animals (the existing preclinical data is promising: Gregg & Siegel, 2001; Katsouni et al., 2009).

*Implications for a life well lived:* Raw anger does have a *mind of its own.* When neuroscientists get around to it, they will better understand how repeated arousal of this system can be epigenetically strengthened by repeated use (Adamec & Young, 2000). Thus kids exposed to violence in the media may emulate what they have seen at deeper affective MindBrain levels than their cognitions (Feshbach & Tangney, 2008). Relevant gene-expression patterns may be modified in this emotional system, as already dramatically found with the epigenetic consequences of early experiences with the CARE system. For example, long ago Ginsburg & Allee (1942) demonstrated that levels of stress early in life influence whether mice would show peaceful or hyper-aggressive temperaments as adults. When dads physically play with their children, those who too readily take a submissive role seem to promote future aggression in their kids, while dads who show their confident authority in the midst of playful fun do not (Flanders et al., 2009). Of course, more research is needed before we can be confident of a causal tie between such parenting and child outcomes.

Children should be given instruction in anger management, preferably at the earliest opportunities, especially in the midst of the physical play that they adore. As Aristotle said in advancing his concept of *phronesis*: "Anybody can become angry—that is easy; but to be angry with the right person, and to the right degree, and at the right time, and for the right purpose, and in the right way—that is not within everybody's power and is not easy." That requires an accurate cognitive appraisal of all relevant facts and perspectives, often a rare commodity, providing many opportunities for assistance through cognitive behavioral therapies. Surely, a better understanding of one's intrinsic potential for anger can be a positive force in self-regulation and the emergence of mindfulness and psychological flexibility (but such issues need to be evaluated by future research).

As with all other emotional systems, optimal affective education needs to highlight how even this negatively valenced system can be used in the service of human well-being, as in righteous indignation that can serve as a platform for creative social change: Consider the biblical dictum (Old Testament: Fourth of Psalms): "Irascimini, et nolite peccare" ("Be angry and sin not"). A difficult task, for sure. But this is a fine goal for early emotional education.

As the old saying goes, one can achieve his or her aims more easily with honey than vinegar.

Also, better understanding how repressed anger can promote chronic irritability, resentment, and suspicion should be a big part of emotional intelligence. Children should be encouraged to learn how to cognitively understand their anger and dissipate such destructive energies creatively. A child should understand that one of the main roles of anger in his or her life should be to learn to open the gates of "forgiveness," for that is the main path away from the sustained bitterness of anger and hate. Such cultural visions of optimal education may help promote the attainment of a more solid foundation for positive psychology in our children (e.g., Thoresen, Luskin & Harris, 1998).

3) **The FEAR/Anxiety System** (Panksepp, 1990, 2004a; Panksepp et al., 2010a). A coherently operating FEAR circuit was designed during brain evolution to help animals reduce pain and the possibility of destruction. When electrically stimulated at low current, this circuit initially promotes freezing (typically seen when animals are placed back into an environment in which they have been previously hurt or frightened), but with higher levels of stimulation animals flee in a coordinated fashion as if they are extremely scared. Humans stimulated in these same brain regions, coursing between the amygdala and PAG along a course that overlaps and interdigitates with the nearby FEAR system, are engulfed by an intense free-floating anxiety that appears to have no environmental cause. Key chemistries that regulate this system are Neuropeptide Y and Corticotrophin Releasing Factor (CRF); specific anti-anxiety agents such as the benzodiazepines inhibit this system.

Modest anxiety in rats can be monitored through their emission of 22 kHz ultrasonic vocalizations (USVs), but intense fear (i.e., impending foot-shock) terminates these alarm calls. Animals "sigh" (exhibit a double-inspiration) when given safety signals in the midst of the signaled punishments commonly used in fear-learning experiments (Soltysik & Jelen, 2005). We currently have no compelling animal models for "worry," but one might anticipate that more careful monitoring of more subtle emotional signs than those typically used in animals studies—e.g., more rapid shifting of eyes and body orientation during emotionally challenging tasks—might provide further insights that may be more relevant for human development (e.g., Berlyne, 1960) than the rather harsh fear-conditioning procedures so widely used in animal research.

*Implications for a life well lived:* Chronic arousal of this system in early development can promote chronic neuroticism, anxiety disorders, and depression (Heim, et al., 2008). Obviously, as with all other negative-affect systems, child mental well-being is optimized if the influences of early anxieties are minimized, albeit not totally absent from the banquet of development. This system, like all primary-process emotional systems, can be sensitized—experience dependent over-reactivity of specific types of emotional arousal, accompanied by epigenetic changes in gene-expression patterns (Szyf et al., 2008). We will focus more extensively on this principle when we come to the CARE system, where selected genetic aspects are worked out in considerable detail.

Assuming that the vicissitudes of early life have not already molded neurotic tendencies into young minds, as so often happens in war-torn regions of our world, titrated doses of anxiety may even promote emotional growth that is appropriate to local environmental and cultural context, but surely implementation of that in any systematic way would be no easy task. Probably the utility of fearfulness would need to be approached in as nuanced a manner as our potentials for RAGE. Fear is so intrinsically aversive that perhaps it will suffice for a child to simply better appreciate that everyone has this feeling in various situations. This is the feeling that tells us something is dangerous and that we should reconsider what we are about to do. If a young child feels anxious way too often, the child should gradually be coaxed to recognize that this is often due to the excessive richness of his or her imagination. It is conceivable that the power of the child's SEEKING system could be harnessed to help him or her find more pleasant psychic "pastures" in which to dwell, perhaps by harnessing mindfulness approaches or even the imaginative power of traditional children's stories. One can readily envision the development of new children's literature that is more optimally designed to help young ones become better versed in the nature of their negative emotions perhaps along the lines of Maurice Sendak's *Where the Wild Things Are.* Such possibilities need to be formally evaluated, along with new ideas on how children might be effectively "tutored" in the ways of courage. I suspect that PLAYful contexts will provide the ideal environments in which such enterprises could be best effected.

4) **The LUST/Sexual System** (Pfaff, 1999). Sexual urges are controlled by specific neurochemical circuits of the brain. The ruling chemistries are overlapping but also quite distinct for males and females. They are aroused by male and female sex hormones, which control the manifestations and maturations of social neuropeptide brain chemistries, especially two neuropeptides whose synthesis is regulated by sex hormones: Vasopressin transmission is promoted by testosterone in males. Oxytocin transmission is promoted by estrogen in females. These socio-sexual chemistries help create gender-specific sexual tendencies. Vasopressin promotes assertiveness and aggressiveness (sexual pushiness in male adolescents?), and perhaps jealous behaviors, in males. Oxytocin promotes sexual readiness postures and warm acceptance attitudes in females.

Distinct male and female sexual circuits are constructed early in life; they are activated by maturation of gonadal hormones at puberty. Because brain and bodily sex characteristics are independently organized, it is possible for animals that are externally male to have female-specific sexual urges and, likewise, for some to be female in external appearance but to manifest more male-like sexual urges. Acceptance of these differences has become a challenge for many modern societies.

*Implications for a life well lived:* There is a vast and growing body of literature on the roles of healthy intimate and/or sexual relationships in adolescence and adulthood for happiness and optimal functioning. Perhaps less has been said about younger children. Overall, kids surely never need to be shielded from loving adult relationships where nonsexual affection is abundantly displayed. Obviously they should never be sexually used or abused but encouraged to develop a healthy age-progressive regard for the life-affirming ways of human sexuality, and how such forces operate in most satisfying ways in the midst of solid social bonds. During early childhood it is probably best to educate by empathic example rather than cognitive instruction, with surely more explicit education in adolescence and young adulthood about the relevance of this basic human emotion for happiness and optimal functioning.

Perhaps an issue that deserves to be recognized more widely is that if husbands and wives have healthy, mutually supportive affectionate relationships, their children typically recognize this as their implicit positive ground of being (promoting secure-bonding), perhaps making the smothering attention problematic in increasingly common child-focused family practices (Code, 2009). Kids learn better by example than by any explicit instructions in how cooperative, loving relationships thrive. Clearly, the nature of human/mammalian social attachments looms heavily in the discussion of this as well as several other basic emotional processes (especially FEAR and PANIC promoting insecure attachments, while joint SEEKING and PLAY promote secure attachments). The role of parental sexuality and dominance in promoting or hindering childhood social attachments are clearly problematic and much underexplored facets of child development.

If adult (not to mention child) relationships are beset by major dominance issues, accompanied by excessive anger and fear, it is unlikely that either partner will find adequate emotional satisfaction from their relationships, and the positive affective development of the children is bound to be impaired. In this regard, future research may also need to consider the role of aggression systems in sexuality and bonding patterns across species, with the recognition that among our closest primate relatives, bonobos (once called pygmy chimpanzees) deploy liberal (promiscuous?) sexual greetings and interactions, leading to matriarchal solidarity as a staple of their overall social harmony (de Waal, 2009). In contrast, common chimpanzees exhibit more explicit male dominance, with more competitive social structures that often promote higher overall levels of aggression and conflict. No doubt, the modal human biological temperament is found somewhere in between.

5) **The CARE/Maternal Nurturance System** (Hrdy, 2009; Numan & Insel, 2003). Some of the chemistries of sexuality, for instance oxytocin, have been reused to mediate maternal CARE—nurturance and social bonding—suggesting that there is an intimate relationship between female sexual rewards and maternal devotions. Clearly, brain evolution has provided safeguards to ensure that parents (usually the mother) take care of offspring (but we have all seen the devotions of father penguins, warming and guarding "their" eggs through the harshest Antarctic winters).

The physiology of maternal urges has been worked out in considerable detail. The massive hormonal changes at the end of pregnancy (declining progesterone and increasing estrogen, prolactin, and oxytocin) set the stage for the activation of maternal urges a few days before the young are born. This symphony of hormonal and neurochemical changes, especially the heightened secretions of oxytocin and prolactin, facilitate maternal moods that assure strong social bonding with the offspring. Similar neurochemicals, especially oxytocin and endogenous opioids, promote infant bonding to the mother. These changes are foundational for one variant of tertiary-process love.

*Implications for a life well lived:* It can be easily argued that this system is foundational for key forms of human prosocial attitudes ranging from the establishment of a secure base for emotional maturation toward the emergence of broad-scale prosocial attitudes, ranging from the capacity and enthusiasm for sustained playful-friendly interactions to expertise with and refinement of all the pro-social capacities of our species (Nadel & Muir, 2005; Reddy, 2008) all the way to the depth of human empathy (for a full airing of evidence, see Decety & Ickes, (2009) and Watt (2007).

Overall, the major lesson from modern comparative neuroscience perspectives is as follows: Children that experience emotional distress and social loss early in life are less likely to live happy lives than those not beset by such vicissitudes (Heim et al., 2008). If parents learn to distribute their maternal care liberally, they will strengthen children's emotional fiber, multidimensionally, for a lifetime (see the stupendous work from Steve Suomi's lab at NIH for demonstrations of the lifetime benefits of early maternal as opposed to peer rearing). Likewise, Michael Meaney's group at McGill has demonstrated how dramatically maternal loving care benefits rat pups for a lifetime—better regulation of the pituitary-adrenal stress axis, and optimization of a diversity of positive, epigenetically promoted BrainMind changes too numerous to summarize here (see Champagne & Meaney, 2001; Szyf et al., 2008).

6) **The PANIC/GRIEF/Separation Distress System** (Freed & Mann, 2007; Swain et al., 2007; Watt & Panksepp, 2009). All young mammals are dependent on parental care, especially maternal care, for survival. Young mammals have a powerful emotional system to indicate they are in need of care, as reflected in their intense crying when lost or left alone in strange places. These separation calls alert caretakers, mothers typically, to seek out, retrieve, and attend to the needs of the offspring. This emotional system that motivates social togetherness engenders separation distress—a psychic pain—that motivates both mother and infant to seek each other (Panksepp, 2005 c, d, e; 2006b). This is a major system for the construction of social bonds (Nelson & Panksepp, 1998; Panksepp et al., 1985). The separation distress system has now been

mapped in several species, including human brain imaging (Panksepp, 2003a); it is powerfully inhibited by endogenous opioids, oxytocin, and prolactin—the major social-attachment, social-bonding chemistries of the mammalian brain. These basic separation-distress circuits are also aroused during human sadness, which is accompanied by low brain opioid activity. Sudden arousal of this system in humans may contribute to the psychiatric condition known as "panic attacks" (Panksepp, 2003a; Preter & Klein, 2008). It should be more widely recognized that the affects that characterize "panic attacks" probably emerge from quite different emotional networks than the FEAR system (see Panksepp et al.,1988 Panksepp, 1998a, p. 274–275).

*Implications for a life well lived:* Such issues—the role of sadness and grief in negative affect and depression—are almost too obvious to discuss, albeit it can be noted that Freud had great difficulty wrapping his fertile mind around such basic emotional processes of our social brains, believing humans had only two basic drives, aggression and lust. In any event, inadequate social bonds are a main source of insecure attachments, loneliness, and general feelings of negative affect in people's lives. Perhaps one that still needs attention in our modern society, where child-rearing was long guided by the "wisdom" of Dr. Spock, is the dubious advice that it is acceptable to have young children cry themselves to sleep and to sleep alone from the earliest days of life. The natural way for primate babies, indeed most mammalian babies, to sleep is by their mothers' sides. It has long been known that touch releases comfort-providing opioids (Keverne et al., 1989; Panksepp et al., 1980). The notion that the abundant everyday early isolation experiences have little effect on the emotional development of young children is not something that is empirically substantiated.

What is substantiated is that lifelong susceptibility to depression arises from too many early vicissitudes with emotional abuse, including over-arousal of the separation-distress system (for a full discussion of the neuroscience evidence, see Watt & Panksepp, 2009). Those whose lives are governed by the depressive psychic pain of PANIC/GRIEF are surely more likely to have suicidal thoughts. More subtle difficulties in living are manifested in higher rates of drug addictions, especially self-medication with opioids and short-term antidepressant drugs such as psychostimulants. There are now relatively safe ways to reduce arousability of this system, and

hence depressive affect, with remarkably low doses of opiate agonists-antagonists that are relatively non-addictive (Bodkin et al., 1995) and that can counter some of the depressive affects promoted by dynorphin (Bruchas et al., 2010). The ability of such agents to reduce suicidal ideation needs to be evaluated.

7) The PLAY/Joyful Rough-and-Tumble, Physical Social-Engagement System (Panksepp, 2007b; Pellis & Pellis, 1998; 2009). Young animals have strong urges for physical play. This takes the form of pouncing on each other, chasing, and wrestling. These actions can seem outwardly aggressive, but they are accompanied by positive affect—an intense social joy, reflected best in the happy sounds that our children (laughter) and young rats make, namely the high-frequency, ~50 kHz ultrasonic chirping sounds that resemble human laughter (Panksepp and Burgdorf, 2003). Indeed, there are similarities between the sub-neocortical brain circuits that mediate play-induced chirping in rats and neural controls of human laughter and joy (Panksepp, 2007b). In young rats these happy sounds are maximal when humans tickle them, leading to rapid social bonding. Young rats are strongly attracted to humans that tickle them (just like little kids), and if one stops, they vigorously solicit more tickling. In contrast, when negative feelings are aroused, animals begin to exhibit 22-kHz "complaint" type vocalizations and play temporarily ceases.

A key function of the social play system is to promote social exploration and gradually facilitate the natural emergence of confident social dominance. Play helps young animals to acquire subtle social interactions that are not genetically coded into the brain but must be learned—the ability to develop, appreciate, and hold on to friendships. Physical play is a major source of joy in early development, and the resulting friendships can diminish depression that can arise (or at least some data suggest) much more from childhood emotional abuse than either physical or sexual abuse (Powers et al., 2009).

The PLAY urge may be one of the major emotional forces that coaxes children to insistently explore intersubjective spaces (Tomasello, 2009), which help promote the cognitive and epigenetic construction of higher social brains, and some recent research advances will be summarized later. The fact that this is a distinct emotional system of the brain is revealed not only by the fact that young animals and humans tend to spontaneously exhibit various play activities, with many pro-social consequences for early development (for a most recent thorough summary, see Pellis & Pellis, 1998; 2009), but also by the fact that one can diminish play urges by brain lesions, such as in the parafascicular area of the thalamus (Siviy & Panksepp, 1987), that do not affect other basic emotions and motivations.

There is far too little research on human play, with our rough-and-tumble activities only recently being experimentally documented (Scott & Panksepp, 2003), but a good case can be made that absence of play in early human development can promote adult antisocial behaviors (Brown, 1998). Also, father-child play, which should be encouraged, is an ideal time for abundant positive affect and beneficial socialization, especially if well deployed.

*Implications for a life well lived:* Playfulness is the major source of human and animal joy. All other things being equal, those who do not cultivate ludic tendencies in early development, not to mention all other stages of living, cannot be as happy as those that do. The likelihood that this primal social-engagement process—surely fundamental for the emergence of social cooperation and friendships, not to mention empathy and the urge to imitate (learn from) others—is of critical importance for human happiness is obvious, but not all that well used by our society (i.e., recently our educational system regressed to strictly valuing basic educational skills (reading, writing, and arithmetic) without a comparable emphasis on the more playful arts and humanities (the substrates of joyful learning and living). We have developed the idea that some of our major childhood problems, such as Attention Deficit Hyperactivity Disorder (ADHD), are promoted by the impoverished play lives of our children (Panksepp, 1998b). The preclinical data indicate that we may be able to reduce ADHD-type life trajectories by promoting physical play throughout early development (Panksepp, 2007c, 2008b). Perhaps increased early playfulness can promote lifetime happiness. I will focus again on this system in the concluding section.

But how do we evaluate such basic emotional issues in the lives of mature humans? There are no agreed-upon ways. With this empirical lapse in our focus, we developed the Affective Neuroscience Personality Scales (Davis et al., 2003) in order to have a tool with which to help situate adult human lives within the spectrum of primary-process affects engendered by these ancestral systems for living. This scale evaluated all of the emotional primes described above

except for LUST/sexuality (we thought asking about people's erotic proclivities might make some uneasy, so we substituted another "s" concept important for human well-being—a SPIRITUALITY scale was added). Overall, it was quite easy to generate questions with distinct factor loadings for the three positive emotions (SEEKING, CARE, and PLAY) and the three negative ones (FEAR, RAGE, and PANIC/Separation Distress). Indeed, those clusters factored into two overall super-factors of overall positive and negative affect (Davis et al., 2003). This suggests how dimensional and basic emotion views of human nature can easily coexist (Panksepp, 2007e; Zachar & Ellis, 2011 In Press).

## The Evolved Sub-neocortical Foundations of Raw Emotional Feelings

Although we can be confident that the animalian emotional systems were built into our brains by evolution, the important point here is that their impact on lived lives is always guided by environmental contexts, learning, and culture. Each of these systems is refined and diversified by living in the world, and each has abundant implications for positive psychology and what it means to have a life well lived, in ways more subtle and diverse than can be discussed here.

Because of longstanding intellectual traditions that ascribed consciousness—the capacity to have and reflect upon one's experiences—strictly to the expanded neocortex of the human brain, few psychologically oriented investigators are currently considering the ancestral sources of our affective experiences that are concentrated in ancient brain regions shared homologously by all mammals. Thus, many still believe that human emotional feelings (affects) reflect higher brain "readout" of the unconscious arousals that sub-neocortical systems promote, but there is abundant available evidence to the contrary. The fact that affective feelings arise from these sub-neocortical neurodynamics is highlighted by the fact that animals are rarely neutral about such artificially induced emotional arousals. Animals are attracted to environmental locations where the various positive emotional expressions are aroused (SEEKING, LUST, CARE, and PLAY) and, given a chance, they self-activate (self-stimulate) such systems. In contrast, animals escape or avoid arousal of the negative emotional circuits (RAGE, FEAR, and PANIC). For instance, all brain sites that activate 50 kHz ultrasonic chirps, an apparent unconditional indicator of arousal of the SEEKING system in rodents, also support self-stimulation behavior (Burgdorf et al., 2007). Sites that arouse FEARful instinctual responses can be used to provoke escape and punish animals (Panksepp, 1990).

In lieu of contradictory evidence, the simplest explanation is that raw affective feelings are constituted substantially from sub-neocortical brain network activities—perhaps taking the form of "attractor landscapes" with dynamics that engender the visually evident instinctual emotional responses that have an intrinsic, raw feel to them (there is no hard evidence to indicate such ancient affective states need to be "read out" by the neocortex). In short, we now know that these brain networks are not "mere behavioral systems" in animals, but concurrently they also generate raw affective states. This conclusion is based on the fact that artificial arousal of such systems can serve as rewards and punishments in various simple learning paradigms.

These affective-emotional systems could be fundamental for engendering organismic coherence and underpinning all forms of human consciousness; for instance, brain-behavior studies have long indicated that extensive damage to brain regions in which these systems are concentrated, such as the Periaqueductal gray (PAG) of the midbrain, severely compromises the survival of animals. Such animals are in a "twilight state," no longer capable of looking after their own welfare (i.e., as highlighted first by the work of Bailey & Davis, 1942, 1943 with cats and primates that had suffered complete damage of the PAG). In contrast, radical decortication of animals at a very young age (surgical removal of the dorsal cerebral mantle, exposing many of the aforementioned brain structures) leaves all of the above emotional-instinctual urges intact, even though the capacity to learn new behavior patterns is severely impaired.

Emotional theories that fail to deal with the evidence for the existence of robust sub-neocortical emotional networks are profoundly incomplete from a cross-species neuropsychological perspective. Theories of positive emotions that do not consider the role of these nomothetic systems in the idiographic construction of human lives are ignoring a great deal of the MindBrain evidence. Because of the need to integrate all the relevant evidence, let me summarize the inadequacies of the prevailing views that believe the neocortex is where our emotional feelings are affectively experienced.

## "Read-out" theories of Emotional Feelings— The Fallacy That Affective Experiences Emerge from Neocortical "Awareness" Functions

A frank confrontation with the nature of the mind and our ancestral emotional nature has been delayed by the widespread belief that we could understand most of what we really wanted to know about the mind by focusing on sensory/ perceptual processes and learning. This led to an infatuation with peripheral theories of affect such as the James-Lange theory, which supposed that emotional feelings arise secondarily from the sensory inputs from the body to higher neocortical regions of the brain, a view that Antonio Damasio (2003) has to emphasize. Likewise, Joe LeDoux (1996) has situated the epicenter for affective experience within the higher working memory fields of human brains (dorsolateral frontal cortex). Edmund Rolls (2005) believes that conscious experiences, including affective feelings, arise only in creatures that have enough neocortex to talk and think about their lives. Although a good case can be made that our self-reflective awareness—the knowledge that we are having feelings (noetic consciousness)—arises from such higher brain regions, the supposition that emotional feelings themselves (anoetic consciousness) reflect higher neocortical functions is without any clear empirical support (for a wide-ranging discussion, see Vandekerckhove & Panksepp, 2009). The possibility that disgust and other sensory feelings arise from ancient cortices such as the insula is substantial.

The sub-neocortical locus of control for generation of diverse primary-process emotional feelings is rather enormous, but because of the types of biases just summarized, much neglected in cognitive neuroscience. As noted earlier, young animals bereft of their neocortical tissues remain highly affective animals. Indeed, they are incredibly lively and hyperemotional. They have all of the evolutionary tools for living except the higher brain regions that in humans engender ideas and insights about our lot in life. A more realistic program of research is to better understand how the higher brain functions that permit depth of perception, thought, reason, and morality arise developmentally in the neocortex as guided by our many evolutionarily provided sub-neocortical capacities for affective feelings— the diverse sensory, homeostatic, and emotional affects. With such a view, the manner in which basic affects are re-represented and elaborated further by higher brain mechanisms may provide a strategy for dealing with the enormous variety of socially constructed emotions—from negative ones, including guilt, jealousy, resentment, shame, etc., to positive ones such as love, hope, and pride, to moral ones such as empathy, feelings of fairness, and justice.

## The Epigenetic Neocortical Sources of Our Cognitive Sophistication

In fairness, it must be emphasized that the animal work is not well positioned to tell us how we should emotionally educate higher regions of the human brain (e.g., training in Aristotelian *phronesis*) to optimize human happiness and societal welfare. Such social-policy issues can be molded only by consideration of all level of analysis. However, animal models do allow superb causal analyses of the primary-process affects; they simply will never suffice to generate understanding of our higher mental-cognitive processes. I entertained the aforementioned implications for child development to promote the likelihood that such questions will be fleshed out through the needed human research. For instance, it is clear that abundant early negative experiences set up children and young animals for a lifetime of woe (e.g., Heim et al., 2008), which is not to say that humans and animals do not have remarkable resilience in the face of many adversities (Feder, et al., 2009; Masten, 2009).

The corollary that abundant primary-process positive feelings early in development can be harnessed to strengthen characterological traits needed for long-term happiness remains less studied. The fact that the earliest developing positive social emotional dynamics that give rise to social bonding, which arise from the intermixture of CARE and PANIC/GRIEF systems (Panksepp, 1998a), provide secure feelings and optimal frameworks for thriving is generally accepted, but not psycho-biologically well studied in humans. Likewise, the prominence of the SEEKING urge and childhood physical PLAY in early development suggests that these emotions may be better harnessed for helping higher brain regions to be programmed with positive, prosocial attitudes that can engender developmental landscapes filled with successful, happy living that may enrich cognitive mindsets and promote the construction of a better world.

One reason for investing in such developmental viewpoints is that the increasingly common belief that higher brain regions of the human BrainMind abound in evolutionary "modules" is probably as ill-informed as the supposition that our primary-process affects emerge from the neocortex. Although the neocortex becomes functionally specialized as a function of development in highly predictable ways, it is not modularized before prenatal experiences (e.g., hearing a mother's voice), with the most cortical programming surely emerging after birth. The evolution of the massive human neocortex may have been permitted by our genetic disposition for weak jaw muscles compared to the bigger and stronger jaw muscles of our primate cousins; that infirmity may allow human cranial plates the plasticity to accommodate sustained postnatal brain growth than could have been engendered with more stringent, muscle-bound cranial constraints. Such genetically promoted cranial changes, promoted perhaps by the discovery of cooking, allowed the implementation of other relatively simple genetic rules that supported sustained cortical neural proliferation of repetitive, self-similar cortical columns for longer periods of early development than would otherwise have been possible (for a discussion of these issues, see Gorman, 2008; Park et al., 2007).

In short, our massive general-purpose neocortical expansions seem to have emerged very rapidly in terms of evolutionary time. There may have been insufficient time for much additional intrinsic programming within these rapidly expanding tissues than was already present in ancestral primates. This would make much of our neocortex a generalized and highly plastic learning "machine," as many theoreticians have supposed (Doidge, 2007), rather than a repository of many specialized *evolved* functions. In other words, what may have evolved was simply much more general-purpose, working memory space adept at promoting complex learning, especially under the guidance of our genetically provided emotional abilities. An appropriate metaphor may be the rapid technology-driven expansions of random access memory (RAM) space that allowed our digital computers to become substantially more sophisticated, using quite similar types of operating systems, than the machines we had in the early 1980s with their limited RAM space (i.e., which resembled creatures with much smaller neocortices).

Thus, it is currently likely that much of what our neocortices achieve functionally has arisen from developmentally programming a much vaster RAM space rather than from any intrinsic (evolved) modular organization. In dramatic support of this view, consider the simple fact that even visual functions of the occipital cortex are developmentally, rather than evolutionarily, established: If posterior brain regions that typically become "visual cortex" are surgically removed *in utero* (in mice), the adjacent neocortical regions develop fine visual capacities (Sur & Rubenstein, 2005). Thus, it is not farfetched to believe that primary-process emotional systems, concentrated sub-neocortically, have a major role in helping to establish the executive and memorial functions of higher regions of the brain, especially frontal executive and temporal memory regions. After all, the ancient social-emotional networks innervate cingulate and medial frontal regions, as well as insular and orbitofrontal cortices more heavily than most other higher brain regions. Thus, what types of unique neuro-evolutionary functional engravings may exist in neocortical regions of the human brain currently remain unknown.

Although our expansive neocortex ultimately provides the brain power for the symbolic processing that permits humans to speak and think, those skills may arise as much from learning as any "language instinct" or any intrinsic cognitive-type dispositions for propositional logic—they may arise from the capacity of our emotional nature, as with the affective power of emotional vocalizations, especially of *motherese*, to promote our skill with, and love of, language (Panksepp, 2009a, b). As already noted, the assumption that the neocortex is needed for emotional feelings has remained a preeminent perspective within modern mind science, leading too many prominent investigators to continue to claim that *animals have emotional behaviors while humans have emotional feelings* (e.g., Damasio, 1994, 2003 and Dolan, 2002 2003; for critical analysis, see Panksepp, 2003b).

In fairness to Damasio, he has in other writings also acknowledged the affective nature of animal minds as he has puzzled over "neurosciences's reluctance to accept that complex non-human creatures have feelings—an attitude that goes beyond the necessary prudence over the fact that such creatures may or may not know they have such feelings" (Damasio, 1999, p. 39). Recently, LeDoux (2009, p. 265) has also acknowledged, while discussing my position on primal animalian affects, that animals may experience "coarse feeling states." But he proceeded to qualify "that a theory of human feelings needs to account for unique features of human consciousness made possible by, in fact defined by, the

unique feature of the brain the (*sic*) emerged with human evolution." Although I accept the vast complexity of human tertiary-process emotions, where propositional attitudes lead the way, unless we solve the primary-process issues, which most other neuroscientists interested in emotions have ignored, our understanding of higher human emotional processes will remain ungrounded.

To sum up this radical position: There is no data to suggest that at a primary-process level humans have depths of raw emotional feelings greater than other mammals, even though at a tertiary-process affective level we leave the other animals in the dust (e.g., the power of music; Panksepp & Trevarthen, 2008). Based on the sub-neocortical anatomies of emotional systems, the default assumption should be that all mammals share homologous primary-process affective substrates of mind, and if we do not understand these substrates, we will never understand the nature of emotional feelings as evolved processes.

To the extent that we can maximize primary-process positive affective feelings in our evolutionarily layered mind, we can promote the diverse dimensions of positive psychology in our adult lives (Keltner, 2009), in the lives of children (Sunderland, 2006), in our distraught, emotionally challenged clients (Fosha et al., 2009), and for the welfare of our fellow animals (Broom, 2001; Grandin, 2005, 2009; McMillan, 2005). For instance, I teach our veterinary students that they will have learned half of what they need to know if they are able to bring companion animals back into their affective "comfort zone" of living.

## Taking Stock

### Layers of Evolutionary Controls in the BrainMind and Implications for Positive Affect Research

Although the introductory remarks already "took stock" of the field, I will refocus on several key points in this section, including the simple fact that our ancestral minds contain the neural potentials for many types of affective experiences and that we may all be well served to consider mental processes as evolutionarily layered inter-digitations of older and newer parts of the BrainMind—from primary to tertiary processes, so to speak. This knowledge has the potential to minimize "culture wars" where some prefer to envision the cultural complexities of the human mind from top-down (where conceptualizations and cultural relativism lead the way), while others seek to more slowly proceed toward cultural complexities from a bottom-up view of our shared affective nature with other animals (Panksepp, 2007d, e). Perhaps this latter project is less in favor currently than the former. To advance integration, issues already raised will be elaborated here from slightly different perspectives, further emphasizing linguistic nomenclature problems in discussing such issues.

But it needs to be explicitly recognized how flawed our programs of research on the human emotional MindBrain may become if we do not integrate knowledge at all the relevant levels of analysis—from a discussion of cross-mammalian evolutionary "givens" to the acquired relativistic constructions of human culture-suffused minds. A big challenge is to empirically blend our best knowledge at all levels, with the primary processes necessarily explicated through animal brain research and the tertiary processes from human research. Here I will highlight how to envision clearly the lower emotional functions, largely homologous in all mammals, in the context of the many unique potentials of the human mind constructed within our higher cerebral spaces. An appreciation of our layered mind can promote the scientific maturation of academic psychology and foster conceptual-empirical progress in positive psychological science.

It has long been recognized by affective neuroscientists (MacLean, 1990; Panksepp, 1998a, 2005a, b) and increasing numbers of psychiatrists and clinicians dealing with emotional problems (Lane & Garfield, 2005), that the BrainMind, unlike the heart, viscera, and the rest of our bodies, is an evolutionarily layered organ. The failure to keep "levels of control" clear in psychological discussion is the cause of much controversy. Since the most important general function of the brain is to *anticipate* the future, we can focus on evolutionary layering as a way to better understand why all organisms have many basic (unlearned) affects that provide the motive forces for many kinds of learning. In themselves, raw affects promptly tell organisms that something they did is liable to promote or detract from survival, and such unconditioned responses apparently teach the memory-making mechanisms of the brain how to better anticipate the future.

Although it seems clear that organisms must be able to experience many affects to have veridical

unconditional signaling of diverse survival concerns, for healthy human maturation, those early simple-minded solutions have to be integrated with more sophisticated cognitive *potentials* permitted by more recently evolved BrainMind tissues. This allows organisms to *anticipate* ever more complex physical and social realms—allowing all to think and plan ahead partly by ruminating about the past and future—through learning and memory, yielding higher affective processes such as jealousy (Panksepp, 2010d). This layering of mind ultimately yielded the capacity for autonoetic consciousness, allowing us to travel forward and backward in time, as Endel Tulving phrased it (see Vandekerckhove & Panksepp, 2009, for a discussion of such higher mental processes).

Here is an image of our *primary-process* affective terrain in terms that may be more familiar to many psychologists, especially behaviorally oriented ones. We surely have no generally accepted words for pre-semantic mental concepts, and for that reason I have long favored the use of vernacular terms, with ambiguous and often excess meanings, as emotional labels, but capitalized to highlight that one is discussing neuro-evolutionary emotional primes (i.e., from SEEKING to PLAY, *vide supra*). This nomenclature aims to minimize part-whole confusions, so rampant in cognitive science (Bennett & Hacker, 2003), and also help highlight that we were discussing important evolutionary "parts" of complex human MindBrain "wholes" (Panksepp, 1998a, 2005a, b).

What traditional psychological concepts do the above labels relate to? Capitalized emotional primes are *unconditioned responses* (UCRs) that can initially be evoked by a limited number of *unconditioned stimuli* (UCSs), according to terminology developed in the era of behaviorism. The evidence strongly indicates that at least emotional UCR systems have raw experience as part of their inherited infrastructure.[3] For instance, emotional behavior patterns for the aforementioned seven emotional-instinctual processes can be evoked by localized electrical and chemical stimulation of specific neural networks concentrated in sub-neocortical regions of the brain (Panksepp, 1982, 1998a 2005a). We can surmise that these networks generate raw emotional feelings because they can be routinely used as "rewards" and "punishments" in various operant and instrumental learning tasks, especially ones like conditioned place preferences (Tzschentke, 2007). These "rewarding" and "punishing" effects do not require higher cerebral processing and have rarely been studied in humans. Also, behaviorists typically simply accepted the convenience of UCSs and UCRs in their learning paradigms, with little discussion about their underlying nature, especially in the brain.

The neglect of the many complex emotional UCRs of the MindBrain in academic psychology has led to many controversies. In earlier eras, this dilemma was exemplified poignantly by the marginalization of the emotional "instincts" by behavioral scientists, while implicitly accepting and explicitly using them in all their fine (albeit restrictive) behavioral paradigms. Because of such "concept battles," the fine work and thinking of early social psychologists such as McDougall (1871–1938), who in his *Introduction to Social Psychology* (1908) used every conceivable approach to understand the human mind. His development of instinct theory is a case in point. McDougall's way of thinking was eventually all but dismissed by the easy criticism that both human and animal behaviors are much more flexible than any primitive instinct theory would allow. This simply reflects that there are several levels of control in the brain, and it is important to emphasize that emotional instincts (both behavioral and affective) do not emerge from tertiary mental processes.

In McDougall's day, instinct theory was not especially popular, nor is it today. However, the primary-process affects of the BrainMind have to be instinctual—constructed out of a large number of positively and negatively experienced UCRs (arousals of intrinsic emotional networks) that are initially aroused by a very limited set of UCSs (which might have no affective impact were it not for their capacity to trigger various UCRs in the brain). In other words, raw emotions (UCRs) are born largely "objectless" (i.e., with only a few initial UCSs that can then be linked to an "infinitude" of CSs). This said, it should be noted again that there are other UCSs, such as taste, where affect is more intimately related to the sensory processing mechanisms, but even that supposition could be partly misleading since many resulting UCRs (chewing and swallowing) seem to amplify taste affect. In any event, all the needed neural networks for most UCSs and UCRs are concentrated in *sub-neocortical* brain regions—brain regions that we share homologously with other animals. This is compelling evidence for where raw affect is elaborated.

Although details are bound to differ among species, the general principles of operation are similar as far as we currently know. The appropriate analogy here is the genetic code, which we now know consists of ~23,000 self-similar genes in all mammalian species (not to emphasize even more lowly creatures), which are turned on at different times and different arrangements yielding both the many underlying similarities and surface diversities of vertebrate life. Learning and memory (secondary processes), along with thought and deliberation (tertiary processes) permit much more diversification. Still, an understanding of the basic affects—these foundational "tools for living"—are essential for understanding the developmental and epigenetic emergence of many higher-order forms of affect regulation and related psychological processes that arise from the massive expansions of our higher neocortical brains (to be addressed in the final section).

There is other evidence for the sub-neocortical locus of control for primary process affects. When we decorticate animals (i.e., surgically remove the whole neocortex) at a young age, they grow up to be quite stupid, but still they are to all appearances very coherent organisms, with a full spectrum of primary-process affective abilities whether animals (Kolb & Whishaw, 1990) or humans (as observed in human decorticates— anencephalic children reared in loving families: Shewmon et al., 1999). Decorticate rats even exhibit quite normal social play (Panksepp Normansell, et al., 1994). Indeed, because of diminished inhibitory control over behavior, they outperform neurologically intact animals on certain devilishly complex learning tasks, such as two-way avoidance where animals have to repeatedly shuttle between two chambers that shift repeatedly from safe (no shock, relief) areas to unsafe (I will get shocked) areas—a conundrum that has *never* existed in nature but is a common storyline in Hollywood horror flicks.

Neurologically intact rats get terrorized by this task and easily freeze up in seemingly hopeless conflicts (worries?). Accordingly, it commonly takes them many weeks of daily training to learn two-way avoidances, a learning that seems to require "paradoxical" rapid-eye-movement dreaming sleep. In contrast, quite simple-minded emotionally governed decorticate rats learn the task rapidly. They seem to learn one simple rule—life is bad; just keep running. This strategy is further promoted by the fact that removal of the neocortex has also made them super-active (i.e., disinhibited). In short, their super-aroused instincts allow them to perform in a situation that immobilizes normal animals.

Indeed, neonatally decorticate rats are so curious and engaged with the world that undergraduates in one of my laboratory courses selected three-quarters of the early decorticates (surgery at 3 days of age) to be the normal rats—namely, when forced to choose between the two animals provided to each student during a two-hour lab exercise at the end of a course on experimental methods (where they already conducted many animal experiments and learned much about natural behavior sequences). These decorticates are almost pure instinct in action. They have a terrible time learning complex mazes to get food that normal rats pick up in no time. But the important point is that they are fully coherent, emotionally rich organisms who have all of the basic evolutionary tools for living (practically all the UCRs and UCSs). But without a general-purpose neocortical "thinking cap," they never become smart in their decision making. They are like babies, and surely one reason we find babies to be so engaging (and at times exasperating) is their emotionally unfettered feelings-in-action (UCRs).

This existence of sub-neocortical emotional networks has been affirmed by hundreds of brain stimulation studies (Panksepp, 1982, 1998a, 2005a). Indeed, the primary-process emotional affects, including—contrary to common opinion—positive ones, are among the easiest to study neuroscientifically—because they are expressed so dramatically in easily observed motor actions. We can provoke characteristic emotional coherences with non-informational energy right out of any wall socket when applied to specific brain networks (stepped down, of course, to levels that cannot even be felt on our skin).

We can be confident that affective experiences are concurrently evoked since animals exhibit their likes or dislikes for such artificial arousals by various measures—i.e., operant reward and punishment paradigms as well as CPP and CPA procedures. In short, the most self-evident affective feelings with which all organisms come into the world are expressed within the neural networks that elaborate distinctively dynamic emotional actions. The predictions to human experience are clear-cut (Panksepp & Harro, 2004) but largely unstudied.

The ancestral message is this: In the beginning, MindBrain evolution created coherent organisms that were quite capable of showing a series of unconditioned emotional and motivational behaviors full of affect. These are the "primary psychobehavioral processes" of the mammalian BrainMind. All intact mammals are also able to learn many new responses with such evolutionarily provided UCRs and UCSs—from simple classical and operant conditioning and neural circuit sensitization and desensitization at the lowest levels of learning, to higher mental processes that are much harder to study neurologically. That is why a mental analysis, largely focused on what the neocortex can do, rules to this day in psychological science. But we must be very cautious in putting any "givens" within the neocortex. Most everything there is "learned," even sensory skills.

The expansion of the neocortex, which can be validly considered to be the neurobiological analog of random access memory (RAM) space in our computers, permitted the instantiation of more sophisticated software routines, eventually allowing forward-looking planning, thought, and even autonoetic consciousness—namely the vast and important varieties of tertiary MindBrain processes. However, at birth this higher BrainMind tissue is much closer to *tabula rasa*—seemingly endless, self-similar, repetitive cortical columns—resembling general-purpose learning chips—ready for learning, rather than the refinement of genetically modularized gardens of incipient cognitive skills. Here is usually where heated debate begins these days, but let us follow the evidence.

There is little evidence that those higher regions of the BrainMind have any evolutionarily dictated psychological modules (Panksepp & Panksepp, 2000), even though they readily become modularized by life experiences. Perhaps the "mirror neurons" learn especially rapidly. The mystery is why specific neocortical regions promote similar abilities across individuals, and I expect that is explained largely by their intrinsic (genetically determined) subcortical and intracortical connectivities.

Thus, for a forward-looking basic science of positive psychology, we might wish to invest more intensively on the primary-process affective nature of the BrainMind. In the 21st century, affects should no longer be relegated simply to the unanalyzed (perhaps unfathomable) "givens" of the mind. Rather, the neural-functional nature of these systems needs to be unraveled in detail. The needed tools are available. The detailed neuroscience approaches, necessarily using animal models, allow us to intensively study how such issues play out in the brain. There will be many empirical surprises, including types of plasticity in sub-neocortical primary-process systems—from a range of neuronal growth factors to experience-dependent conversion of "silent synapses" to active ones.

## The Strategy for Understanding the Nature of Primary Process Affects

In sum, for more than half a century, the animal work has affirmed that the sub-neocortical terrain of the brain contains a variety of complex and yet poorly understood networks that generate visually observable emotional-instinctual action schema. In other words, to the best of our knowledge, *primary-process* emotional feelings arise substantially from the same neural matrices that generate these coherent emotional behavior patterns (Panksepp, 1982, 1998a, 2005a). Every place in this rich and ancient neural terrain, wherever one evokes coherent emotional responses with localized electrical stimulation of the brain (ESB) or chemical stimulation of the brain (CSB), one also evokes feelings (affects), as indicated by the ability of such stimulation to serve as rewards or punishments in operant tasks as well as with other value-indicative choice measures such as Conditioned Place Preference (CPP) and Conditioned Place Aversion (CPA) tasks (CPP: Tzschentke, 2007). Namely, animals return to locations where positive feelings have been aroused, and they avoid those in which negative ones were evoked.

Modern (post-1950s) neuroscience, using ESBs and CSBs as rewards and punishments, now strongly implicates these *unconditioned, inbuilt* solutions to living—these ancestral tools (memories?) for survival—as the very ground for raw emotional feelings. The evidence strongly indicates that the various primary-process affective-emotional feelings arise somehow from the ancient central pattern generator neural matrices for emotional-instinctual behaviors. They are the coherent inbuilt UCRs to major challenges to living. There is no evidence that the rewarding and punishing properties of such arousals are due to affective interpretations made in the neocortex. In other words, core *emotional* affects are intimately linked to the arousal of ancient brain mechanisms that mediate emotional and organismic coherence.[4]

At this point, some readers may still be disturbed by concepts such as "primary-process affects" and the supposition that all mammalian brains harbor very similar ancestral memories within the affective infrastructures of their *MindBrains*. And they may continue to stumble on the last word of the previous sentence, for, despite the demise of Cartesian dualism, many have remained accustomed to envisioning "brain" and "mind" as sufficiently distinct conceptually so that the study of the former will not necessarily illuminate the latter. True enough! Indeed, that remains most true at the tertiary-process level—we have no comparable ability to link mind and brain with causal research in the "upstairs" cognitive regions of the human BrainMind as we have for the "downstairs" affective regions, shared by all mammals, that can be studied with animal models.

Among the new generation of revolutionaries with access to human brain imaging, one might begin to imagine that some solid bridges could finally be built between the two cultures—the animal behavioral-affective neurosciences and the human cognitive-affective neurosciences. Regrettably, fMRI technologies are beset by abundant interpretive problems (Vul et al., 2009) and generally much more robust for imaging cognitive than affective processes, simply because of dramatically higher neuronal firing rates in the relevant thalamo-cortical systems. Also, when one is simply harvesting neural correlates, as is almost invariably the case in human brain imaging, few feel comfortable with the total conflation of mind and brain functions. My main thesis is that the data now strongly indicate that at the primary-process level—the level shared homologously, through ancestral descent, by all mammals—the two concepts are integrally one and the same (yielding a dual-aspect monism ontology, similar to wave-particle dynamics in modern physics). Our inability to deal as effectively with higher MindBrain issues is also apparent. At tertiary (thought) process levels, the emergence of higher mind function from brain activities (operating especially in the real complexities of the world) are much harder to probe, partly because they are more idiographic than nomothetic.

## Hot Future Topics in Positive Psychology— From Empathy to Mirror Neurons

Modern "positive psychology" may be wise to embrace a cross-species understanding of the basic affects and their role in helping to developmentally program higher social MindBrain functions (e.g., Cacioppo, 2008; Goleman, 2007; Keltner, 2009). The neglect of foundational affective issues cannot give us a solid understanding of what we are talking about in positive psychology. Raw affects, quite simply, are ancestral tools for living that can be refined as they control and are reciprocally regulated by higher BrainMind processes. From a cross-species affective neuroscience vantage, the conflicts between i) basic emotion theorists and ii) those who espouse constructivist and dimensional visions of the human mind (e.g., Russell, 2003) are arising largely from different levels of analysis within hierarchically controlled BrainMind systems (Zachar & Ellis, 2010). The former are seeking to illuminate primary processes affects (Panksepp, 2007e) while the latter are typically studying tertiary processes.

Understandably, some of the findings and insights from a cross-species affective neuroscience do not fit easily into traditional approaches and understandings in psychology. But this is largely because the primary-process level of analysis has been woefully neglected in studies of emotions since the inception of academic psychology. Indeed, the "instincts" were marginalized early in the 20th century because they never seemed to exist "cleanly" in most animals in real-world situations. Behaviors were always subject to modification by learning. But that just indicated the power of the many UCSs and UCRs, which remained largely unanalyzed by everyone, while much effort was devoted to secondary processes by behaviorists and tertiary processes by cognitive and social psychologists. Those reflect important research endeavors, but for a coherent neuropsychological understanding of positive and negative affects, it is critically important to understand the primary-process infrastructure of the mammalian BrainMind. As we bring those evolutionary issues into the discussion, it could open up the possibility of abundant new scientific insights at higher levels, including a more solidly grounded evolutionary psychology. Indeed, this seems to be emerging gradually, for instance in the recognition of the role of oxytocinergic control of human and animal social-emotional processes (Panksepp, 2009b) as well as to some extent the role of endogenous opioids in the regulation of social affects (DePue & Collins, 1999; Panksepp, 1981; Zubieta et al., 2003).

However, unless one considers all relevant levels of analysis, mistakes can more easily be made. For instance, the animal data on oxytocinergic control of behavior has never synergized as well as it should have with simple-minded "love molecule" interpretations of oxytocinergic tone in the brain. For instance, i) oxytocin does not produce robust reward as monitored with conditioned place preference tasks, ii) oxytocin can reduce aggression without reducing dominance, and iii) it can promote more widespread exploratory activity in presumably insecure groups of young animals placed in new environments (Panksepp, 2009b). From a primary-process point of view, the concept that oxytocin promotes "confidence" may yield better theoretical coherence than a "love molecule" perspective. Such an affective reorientation may help us understand why oxytocin can promote "envy" and "gloating" in the human mind (Shamay-Tsoory et al., 2009).

To appreciate the role of primary-process subcortical affective systems such as oxytocin, and many other subcortical systems, in human tertiary-process psychological affairs would benefit from having more primary affective studies represented in the portfolio of relevant research approaches. As we come to appreciate the hierarchical, multidimensional nature of the human MindBrain, many investigators dedicated to pursuing tertiary process analyses may also be tempted to promote and pursue causal primary-process studies that can give us better empirical windows into the underlying evolutionary processes. In this respect, more studies of PLAY may be especially informative.

## PLAY and the Epigenetic Construction of the Social Brain

Our overall hypothesis is that the primary-process PLAY urges, when allowed free and abundant expression, help to construct and refine many of the higher regions of the social brain. In the midst of highly rewarding (joyous?) physical play, animals exercise an enormous number of social skills that probably allow them to positively coordinate with and predict the initially unpredictable actions and intentions of fellow creatures (Špinka et al., 2001). As a result, they get along with others better (pro-social effects), develop stronger friendships (Panksepp, 1988 Unpublished data), and generally become more assertive while being less aggressive (Pellis & Pellis, 1998; Power, 2000). Perhaps it is especially influential in programming our frontal cortical, executive networks that allow us to more effectively appreciate social nuances and develop better social strategies. In other words, PLAY might allow us to stop, look, listen, and feel the more subtle social pulse around us (Panksepp, 2001a).

Such developmental passages are beginning to be apparent in our animal models. Even though neocortex is not necessary for the normal emergence of PLAY urges (Panksepp, Normansell et al., 1994), playfulness generally activates the whole neocortical sheet (Panksepp, 1998a, p. 293, Figure 15.7) and has many positive consequences on the neocortex, which at birth *does* resemble *tabula rasa* much more than, as already noted, a bee's nest of evolutionarily dedicated *modules*. Playfulness has abundant effects on gene-expression patterns in the neocortex and other brain regions (Burgdorf et al., 2010). In recently completed microarray—that is, *gene-chip*—analyses of DNA transcription in neocortical regions of playing rats, the responses have been spectacular. Half an hour of rough-and-tumble play has induced about half of the twelve hundred genes we monitored to exhibit changed transcription levels in frontal or posterior neocortical regions by one hour after play, with many still exhibiting effects six hours after termination of play (Burgdorf et al., 2010). What a cornucopia of riches!

The best next step after such work is to evaluate whether some of these gene products actually do modulate positive affective processes. But which gene(s), from the all too many candidates, should be selected for initial functional follow-up studies? No laboratory could follow all the leads, or even a substantial subset, so we simply decided initially to pursue behavioral studies with the peptide product of the gene that exhibited the biggest, most sustained (i.e., changes evident at both 1 and 6 hours), and most widespread effects (i.e., brain changes evident in both frontal executive and posterior perceptual cortical areas). The winner in this lottery was the gene encoding Insulin-like Growth Factor-1 (IGF-1)—one of the oldest and most prominent brain "fertilizers"—and we proceeded to demonstrate that this peptide, along with its various transporters (molecules that promote IGF-1 functioning), were indeed elevated within rat brains following play. The existing literature in humans had already observed that this peptide was positively related to human cognitive and affective well-being as a function of age (Lasaite et al., 2004). Elevated positive affect and decreased depression are related to plasma IGF-1 levels, and intravenous IGF-1 supplementation can reduce anxiety and depression in humans (Stouthart et al., 2003; Thompson et al., 1998). Although little causal psychobiological work had been done with this growth factor in animal

models, we proceeded to evaluate the effects of intraventricularly administered IGF-1 as a modulator of affect when infused into the rat brain. Our results so far indicate that this growth factor promotes many positively motivated behaviors that may reflect some kind of good feelings in the BrainMind (Burgdorf et al., 2007, 2010). For instance, animals are less fearful in open-field exploration tests, and the peptide facilitates our prime index of positive affect in rats—50 kHz ultrasonic chirping—in response to tickling. There are bound to be many more such positive affect regulating factors within the brain to be found and studied, and currently we are especially interested to determine if the IGF-1 system may help mitigate devastating negative affects such as those that lead to depression.

Hopefully my point is clear. We marginalize our sub-neocortical affective mind at the peril of not really understanding what we are talking about. And we know so very little of how translation of our genetically promoted lower mind abilities helps to weave the rich tertiary-process tapestry of a well-trained, caring human mind (Ryff & Singer, 1998, with commentaries). Likewise, the way the vicissitudes and woes of existence leave their affective imprints on our higher minds is poorly understood, but when we start to invest in "complete" approaches, we may find totally new ways to conduct the therapy that is needed to make troubled minds more sanguine. All this does not mean that there are not any psycho-neuro-epistemological engravings in the higher reaches of the human brain, but if they exist, they are more likely to be found in the frontal executive regions of the brain than the sensory-perceptual ones. In sum, what our genetics do dictate are our primary-process emotional strengths and weaknesses, but these can be nourished in distinct ways by life experiences.

The scientific challenges ahead, both methodological and social, are great. Although the importance of inherited biological factors is now definitive, the epigenetic-developmental factors are looming ever larger as we learn more about not only cultural influences but also the nurturing ways of nature. Surely our genetic and neurobiological nature does not work against itself, but invests in every possible way to fit in ever better with the environment, social and physical, and our ever-increasing capacity to learn as our higher brain mushroomed in a very short time (perhaps because of the discovery of cooking, but that is another story).

As an ever-increasing number of studies are affirming, there is abundant evidence now for gene-environment (G x E) interactions in positive psychosocial development, related most prominently to an infant's early attachment relationships. Just to take one well-studied example: Identified polymorphisms of serotonin transporter (5-HTT) genes (i.e., short and long alleles) have measurable consequences on temperament, being related to how laid-back or emotionally temperamental humans and animals (Caspi & Moffitt, 2006) become, even though the results have been contested. These traits can influence aggressiveness as well as alcohol consumption, but they are magnified by the quality of early rearing—for example whether young rhesus monkeys are mother-reared or just with other infants in nursery settings. Secure maternal bonding protects individuals carrying risk-alleles that would otherwise promote various developmental problems, including early death (Suomi, 2006).

Various other such genetic interactions with social environments have now been characterized. Most famously, epigenetic gene-methylation patterns can promote "maternal buffering" effects in animals. The most important finding for us is that the greater tender loving care provided by mother rats (in the form of ano-genital licking of their pups) and maternal vs. peer rearing in monkeys has stupendous effects on gene-methylation patterns, especially in the hippocampal-pituitary-adrenal stress axis of animals. These protective effects often last a lifetime and can even be transmitted across generations through lasting methylation patterns in the germ line (Zhang & Meaney, 2010). Accordingly, we can now envision how many benefits of good upbringing operate through the positive affective mechanisms of primary-process social brain mechanisms.

## Moving Forward

I have sought to illuminate an important but rarely addressed psychological question: "What is the fundamental neurobiological nature of the *affects*, especially the positive ones?" For clarity, it is very important to respect different levels of analysis within the MindBrain axis. In the present usage, (1) primary-process emotions arise from evolutionarily provided sub-neocortical operating systems (which can surely be molded by life experiences to promote lifetime changes

in personality); (2) secondary-process emotions reflect basic emotional learning and memory processes as reflected, for example, in classical and operant conditioning (extremely well studied by the behavioristically oriented fear-conditioners, who have yet to acknowledge the psychological nature of the UCS pathways (e.g., FEAR System, perhaps because they do not want to allow "animal affects" to exist or be accepted) that allows them to do such exquisite (albeit insensitive) experimental work; and (3) tertiary processes are the higher emotional functions that include thought and deliberation often based on episodic/autobiographical memories and capacities for symbolic thought and communication (the endless phenomenological, bread-and-butter work of psychology). In general, at present much more research effort is devoted to the last level of analysis, and by far the least to the primary-process levels. This is because those "givens" of mental life are very hard to study systematically, and in any causal depth, in our own species (Zachar & Ellis, 2010, In press).

Basic emotional feelings are probably reflected within all levels of MindBrain organization, but the way we need to talk about these levels is bound to differ in yet-to-be-agreed-upon ways. A key goal of basic science, an aspiration that is rarely manifested in modern psychology, should be to get the foundational, primary processes described accurately, especially since tertiary processes—socially constructed, thought-penetrated emotions—arise from higher neocortical brain regions where culture-bound individualized learning creates endless idiographic complexities for psychological research (see Panksepp & Northoff, 2009). Fortunately, there is ever-increasing developmental research on how early childhood emotions can impact individuals developmentally as well as overall societal welfare.

Since primary-process emotional forces guide child development issues (Nadel & Muir, 2005; Panksepp, 2001a, b; Reddy, 2008), that is also the focus I will continue to take in this concluding section. Only a substantial start has been made in understanding how affective mind systems influence the trajectories of human lives. Ever since the demonstration of the tragic consequences of socially impoverished institutional life on child development, the overall theoretical vision provided by John Bowlby (1969) has guided child development research and has been a guiding light for neuroscientifically oriented psychologists who wish to understand the nature and long-term developmental consequence of excessive arousal of the diverse positive and negative affective processes in the brain (e.g., Watt & Panksepp, 2009). It probably does not need much emphasis that an overabundance of negative emotions, such as FEAR and RAGE, in the lives of children during early development tends to set them up for the emergence of negativistic self-images. In the most severe cases these can eventually promote borderline personality disorders and potentially lifelong chronic difficulties in handling social stressors, which can promote depression and other psychiatric disorders (Cirulli et al., 2009; Heim et al., 2008; Miller et al., 2009).

Indeed, as many investigators are studying the ramifications of emotional development in children's lives, often to maximize human welfare, few investigators are working to understand the unconditional nature of the primary-process emotional systems. I suspect that in order to fully understand simple forms of emotional learning (e.g., LeDoux, 2000), we must begin to focus on the permissive role of neurochemical influences of the Unconditioned Response networks of ancient emotional brains in promoting neuronal gateways to learning. There is currently little work from the bottom-up (emotion to cognition) perspectives. This may be due to the continuing hegemony of behavioristic biases in functional neuroscience using animal models, as well as more implicitly in much of human cognitive neuroscience.

Because of such biases, the SEEKING system is still mistakenly called the "brain reward system" by most active investigators, even though such a concept does not help to explain the unconditional behaviors and affects this system actually mediates (Panksepp & Moskal, 2008). Because of the shortage of investigators presently seeking to unravel the animalian-evolutionary sources of our human/mammalian nature, we have not developed conceptual systems capable of being deployed across species that can clarify various basic problems in positive psychology. We need to recognize that the SEEKING system is the foundation for all our goal-directed behaviors—it energizes gambling and shopping as well as the seeking of knowledge, artistic pursuits, and spiritual heights, so to speak. Fortunately, there are many psychologically oriented investigators who are studying the manifestations of such neural systems in human lives (Silvia & Kashdan, 2009). Still, the details of such a highly generalized

"motivational system" can be illuminated only through animal models.

This SEEKING system is critically important for most of our good and bad habits, for our aspiration and our desires, as well as for our addictions and repetition compulsions. Whether this system will be used in the service of enhancing a child's habit of focusing on commercial "mind-washing" TV and other mundane, noncreative activities, or for the development of more life-affirming artistic and interpersonal skills is surely a momentous developmental question. A child's long-term self-image is bound to be heavily intermeshed with how we emotionally raise our children. If the SEEKING system is not guided toward truly creative and positive life-affirming activities, it may easily regress toward pursuit of the lowest affective common denominators mediated by this system of self-gratification.

If our social bonds are deficient, and the PANIC/GRIEF system prevails (not to mention elevated levels of other distinct negative affects such as FEAR and RAGE), higher MindBrain regions are surely bound to be prepared for lives full of psychological pain on the one hand and perhaps increased tendencies for alexythymia, depression, and psychotic thinking on the other. Much of everyday human suffering arises because of the psychic sting of the PANIC/GRIEF system in the lives of people who do not have supportive bonds, whether short-term feelings arising from acute social exclusion (see Eisenberg chapter) or chronic negativistic feelings arising from deficient nurturance during early development (Bowlby, 1980). Even the presence of a pet animal has remarkable effects in alleviating chronic human loneliness, which from a primary-process point of view may arise substantially from excessive activity of the ancient mammalian separation-distress system. So far there has been very little work on how companion animals, under their direct care, influence children's social development and self-image development. Positive psychology studies are needed to evaluate how children's lives are improved, perhaps starting in the late preschool years, by the provision of small, young companion animals such as pre-acclimated, perhaps hand-play (e.g., tickle) acclimated domestic rats (Panksepp, 2007b). This may sound a bit shocking to many, but such animals are very safe, delightfully energetic, and highly entertaining—really rather superb pets, as many people already know (e.g., www.fancyrats.com). Such small child-friendly pets can also help promote a desperately needed reverence for life in our society.

As already noted, the study of adult empathy is currently on the rise (Decety & Ickes, 2009), but only a few are focusing on the development of affective CAREing attitudes in the emergence of compassionate convictions in the higher regions of the human mind (Watt, 2007). Mirror neurons are now widely recognized as key brain functions that participate in the emergence of prosocial cooperative brain networks (Iacoboni, 2008; Rizzolatti & Sinigaglia, 2008). However, animal models where the underlying causal issues can be studied will be essential for understanding how maternal love and CARE help to create the secure base that allows those higher brain functions to emerge developmentally. Our deep social nature arises from the primary-process mental "energies" we have inherited as ancestral tools for living—especially CARE and PANIC/GRIEF systems—all of which help mediate social bonding, opening up the developmental pathways to healthy expressions of adult LUST systems.

Still, the vast potential of a secure emotional base may need to be brought to fruition by primary-process emotional mechanisms that were evolutionarily designed to test and understand the complexities of the social terrain. The maturation of our best social qualities, permitting fulfilling adult lives, may be intimately linked to the learning and satisfaction that arise from the free exercises of PLAYful urges throughout early childhood. Such spontaneous social engagements surely promote positive development of balanced social expectations, refined social skills, and feelings of agency.

PLAY mechanisms of the brain, along with closely linked SEEKING urges, offer positive psychology some of the most important inbuilt emotional systems that can help clarify many relevant higher-order aspects of our social brain, from our love of camaraderie with abundant ribbing and humor to sports and the rough-and-tumble nature of power politics. An effective PLAY system may be one of the main sources of friendships and adult social bonding. As we diminish the influence of PLAY in our children's lives, a cultural dilemma we currently face, their future social aspirations and possibilities for lifelong happiness may be compromised (Panksepp, 2007c).

The primary-process PLAYfulness of young brains delightfully represents how our "simple" animalian emotions can help promote lifelong mental sophistication. Thus, in addition to promoting the maturation of the higher positive social emotions promoted by LUST and CARE, we are currently finding that PLAY urges are intimately related to how intensely various negative emotions can impact children's lives. The less play young animals have had, the more aggressive they will be; the more play they have had, the less likely they are to show depressive symptoms in adulthood as a result of stress (Panksepp lab: Unpublished observations).

Many psychologists may prefer to envision our playfulness as reflecting higher mind function, unique to humans, rather than the lower, more ancient functions we share with the other animals. The sooner we shift such anthropocentric perspectives and recognize the experience-expectant role of this universally important cross-mammalian BrainMind system, the sooner we may build cultural institutions that support our joyful *lower nature*, so important for mental health and age-appropriate education. As we aspire to promote our children's intellectual abilities through "No Child Left Behind" programs, we could also nurture their social intelligence through wiser PLAY policies. We should avoid stunting the beneficent nurturing and maturation of their human nature as we vigorously seek to develop children's *higher* mental abilities—too often by administering stale knowledge, too commonly in unpalatable ways that fail to promote higher social-brain development.

ADHD-type children are typically deficient in frontal lobe executive functions—in simple terms, as already noted, in their ability to stop, look, listen, and feel with consideration for others (Barkley, 1997). Indeed, when we damage the frontal lobes of rats, they exhibit extreme ADHD-type hyperkinetic, impulsive symptoms, which we can diminish by giving them abundant daily opportunities for play (Panksepp et al., 2003). We have strongly advocated for the development of "play sanctuaries" for our "glut" of PLAY-starved children in America (Panksepp, 2007c). After conducting the first systematic, well-controlled experimental study on the rough-and-tumble physical play of human children (Scott and Panksepp, 2003), we were chastened to have it rejected successively by three prominent developmental journals, with a single major criticism repeated like a mantra—"it was of no theoretical interest."

That the first formal description of play in our species was of so little interest to developmentalists was an eye-opener for us. After collecting pilot data within a community public school setting (Scott, 2001), we have sought support for a "play-sanctuary" study in human children for almost a decade, from both federal and private sources, without success. Meanwhile, the availability of "real" (self-initiated) physical play for children has been diminishing at an alarming rate in our school systems as well as part of children's free-time post-school activities. This potentially tragic shortsightedness in both our social and scientific fabric about the positive psychological influences of abundant early PLAY may have cross-generational epigenetic consequences for the mental health of our children for many years to come (e.g., Burgdorf et al., 2010). There are good reasons to believe that abundant happy social-physical play, in the context of joyous early education, will allow every child "to thrive by five." We expect that lots of free self-initiated social play will tend to produce more happy and productive citizens.

To help our children flourish affectively, we not only have to nurture them optimally psychologically, but we need to understand that in doing that we are also nurturing their genome. With abundant early positive affect that facilitates the development of a solid self-identity, we are providing a lifetime gift not only in terms of their implicit and explicit autobiographical memories, but also deep within the chromatin scaffolding of their DNA that can regulate beneficial (e.g., anti-stress) gene expressions for a lifetime, even across generations (Szyf et al., 2008; Zhang & Meaney, 2010).

The ability of environmentally promoted gene regulation has now revealed enormous epigenetic changes that result from different affective environments in which young animals (and presumably our children) are reared. The potential of such knowledge to lead to creative, life-affirming social "engineering" is vast. Once instituted, such forces could percolate through not only our social structures but also our epigenomes in ways that facilitate positive affective cultural developments. Perhaps, simply by paying better heed to the primary-process affective environments in which our children are reared, we could reap many societal benefits.

However, since different animals, even different strains of the same species, appear to exhibit different periods of epigenetic sensitivity to environmental factors, we must be concerned about scientifically determining the sensitive periods during which social benefits can optimize human development. In lieu of such difficult-to-obtain data, the default should be to provide abundant doses of positive experiences with all the positive emotions, with incremental age-appropriate challenges, as much as possible throughout early development.

In sum, through a better understanding the lifelong impacts of primary-process affective processes throughout the lifespan, we can begin to scientifically bridge and blend basic neuroscience research traditions that can reveal mammalian primary-process emotional systems with the human tertiary-process complexities that most psychologists focus upon. This will help us better translate the intrinsic capacities of our nomothetic core SELVES (Northoff & Panksepp, 2008; Panksepp, 1998b) with the vast idiographic potentials of our higher selves (Panksepp and Northoff, 2009).

In so doing, we will be able to better achieve optimal self-realization of a high level of social intelligence that Aristotle called *phronesis*—automatically appreciating how to do the correct things in the right ways at the most auspicious times, as one correctly appraises all the relevant contingencies. To do that well, we will have to have integrated scientific views of higher and lower BrainMind functions that do not yet exist in any mature forms either in our scientific research or our educational endeavors.

## Notes

1. I use this term (also MindBrain when stylistically desirable with no change in meaning), capitalized and without a space to highlight the necessity of viewing the brain as a unified organ with no dualities that have traditionally hindered our understanding.

2. Here, core affects are used as synonyms for the diverse primary-process forms of valenced feelings and can easily be distinguished from the unitary Core Affect concept recently developed by top-down dimensional emotional theorists such as James Russell (2003). The bottom-up neurobiological approach I advocate and summarize here differs markedly from such alternative approaches. These perspectives differ dramatically in the way they envision the foundational substrates of affective life (see Zachar and Ellis, 2010 for full coverage), and perhaps how higher mental processes gradually emerge from the lower evolutionary substrates. For me "basic," "core," and "raw" affects, used for semantic variety, are simply various synonyms for the primary-process affects. Secondary-processes in the brain reflect basic learning mechanisms, and tertiary-process affects reflect those arising from interactions with higher cognitive processes (e.g., thought, memory, deliberation).

3. This is not to deny that many unconditioned reflexes operate totally unconsciously and most are

more ancient than the evolution of the affective mind (e.g., spinal knee-jerk reflexes without any accompaniment that resembles "experience").

4. As noted, there are many other types of affects than emotional ones, for instance sensory as well as homeostatic ones, and it is not yet as clear that similar principles apply (but see Panksepp, 2007a). Those affects are, of course, relevant for understanding both positive and negative psychologies, and much of their affective intensity also arises from subcortical systems (Denton, 2006), but I will not focus on those issues here, simply because the emotional ones are really much more important for overall life quality and mental-health issues once bodily needs are taken care of.

## References

Adamec, R. E., & Young, B. (2000). Neuroplasticity in specific limbic system circuits may mediate specific kindling induced changes in animal affect-implications for understanding anxiety associated with epilepsy. *Neuroscience & Biobehavioral Reviews, 24,* 705–723.

Alcaro, A., Huber, R., & Panksepp, J. (2007). Behavioral functions of the mesolimbic dopaminergic system: An affective neuroethological perspective. *Brain Research Reviews, 56,* 283–321.

Austin, J. (1998). *Zen and the brain.* Cambridge, Mass: MIT Press.

Bailey, P., & Davis, E. W. (1942). Effects of lesions of the periaqueductal gray matter in the cat. *Journal of the Society for Experimental Biology and Medicine, 351,* 305–306.

Bailey, P., & Davis, E. W. (1943). Effects of lesions of the periaqueductal gray matter on the *Macaca mulatta. Journal of Neuropathology and Experimental Neurology, 3,* 69–72.

Barkley, R. A. (1997). *ADHD and the nature of self-control.* New York: Guilford Press.

Bennett, M. R., & Hacker, P. M. S. (2003). *Philosophical foundations of neuroscience.* Malden, MA: Blackwell.

Berlyne, D. E. (1960). *Conflict, arousal, and curiosity.* New York: McGraw Hill.

Berridge, K. C. (2000). Measuring hedonic impact in animals and infants: Microstructure of affective taste reactivity patterns. *Neuroscience and Biobehavioral Reviews, 24,* 173–198.

Berridge, K. (2004). Pleasure, unfelt affect, and irrational desire. In, A. S. R. Manstead, N. Frijda, & A. Fischer (Eds.) *Feelings and emotions: The Amsterdam Symposium* (pp. 243–262). Cambridge, UK: Cambridge University Press.

Blood, A., & Zatorre, R. J. (2001). Intensely pleasurable responses to music correlate with activity in brain regions implicated in reward and emotion. *Proceedings of the National Academy of Sciences, 98,* 11818–11823.

Bodkin, J. L., Zornberg, G. L., Lucas, S. E., & Cole, J. O. (1995). Buprenorphine treatment of refractory depression. *Journal of Clinical Psychopharmacology, 16,* 49–57.

Bowlby, J. (1969). *Attachment and loss, vol. 1: Attachment.* New York: Basic Books.

Bowlby, J. (1980). *Attachment and loss vol. III: Sadness and depression.* New York: Basic Books.

Broom, D. M. (Ed.) (2001). *Coping with challenge: Welfare in animals including humans.* Berlin: Dahlem University Press.

Brown, S. (1998). Play as an organizing principle: Clinical evidence and personal observations. In M Bekoff. & J. A. Beyer (Eds.) *Animal play: Evolutionary, comparative, and ecological perspectives* (pp. 242–251). Cambridge: Cambridge University Press.

Bruchas, M. R., Land, B. B., & Chavkin, C. (2010). The dynorphin/kappa opioid system as a modulator of stress-induced and pro-addictive behaviors. *Brain Research, 1314,* 44–55.

Burgdorf, J., & Panksepp, J (2006). The neurobiology of positive emotions. *Neuroscience and Biobehavioral Reviews, 30,* 173–187.

Burgdorf, J., Wood, P. L., Kroes, R. A., Moskal, J. R., & Panksepp, J. (2007). Neurobiology of 50-kHz ultrasonic vocalizations in rats: Electrode mapping, lesion, and pharmacology studies. *Behavioral Brain Research. 182,* 274–283.

Burgdorf, J., Kroes, R. A., Beinfeld, M. C., Panksepp, J., & Moskal, J. R., (2010). Uncovering the molecular basis of positive affect using rough-and-tumble play in rats: A role for insulin-like growth factor I. *Neuroscience, 163,* 769-777.

Cabanac, M. (1992). Pleasure: The common currency. *Journal of Theoretical Biology, 155,* 173–200.

Cacioppo, J. (2008). *Loneliness: Human nature and the need for social connection.* New York: Norton.

Caspi, A., & Moffitt, T. E. (2006). Gene-environment interactions in psychiatry: Joining forces with neuroscence. *Nature Reviews Neuroscience, 7,* 583–590.

Champagne, F., & Meaney, M. J. (2001). Like mother, like daughter: Evidence for non-genomic transmission of parental behavior and stress responsivity. *Progress in Brain Research, 133,* 287–302.

Cirulli, F., Francia, N., Berry, A., Aloe, L., Alleva, E., & Suomi SJ. (2009). Early life stress as a risk factor for mental health: Role of neurotrophins from rodents to non-human primates. *Neuroscience & Biobehavioral Reviews, 33,* 573–585.

Code, D. (2009), *To raise happy kids, put your marriage first*. New York: The Crossroad Pub. Co.

Damasio, A. R. (1994). *Descartes' error: Emotion, reason, and the human brain*. New York: Avon Books.

Damasio, A. R. (1999). Commentary (on J. Panksepp's Emotions as viewed by psychoanalysis and neuroscience: an exercise in consilience). *Neuropsychoanalysis, 1*, 38–39.

Damasio, A. (2003). *Looking for Spinoza: Joy, sorrow, and the feeling brain*. Orlando: Harcourt.

Darwin, C. (1872). *The expression of emotions in man and animals*. London: Murray.

Darwin, C. (1872/1998). *The expression of emotions in man and animals, 3rd edition*, New York: Oxford University Press.

Davis, K. L., Panksepp, J., & Normansell, L. (2003). The affective neuroscience personality scales: Normative data and implications. *Neuro-Psychoanalysis, 5*, 21–29.

Decety, J., & Ickes, W. (Eds.) (2009). *The social neuroscience of empathy*. Cambridge, MA: MIT Press.

Denton, D. (2006). *The primordial emotions: The dawning of consciousness*. New York: Oxford University Press.

Depue, R. A., & Collins, P. F. (1999). Neurobiology of the structure of personality: Dopamine, facilitation of incentive motivation, and extraversion. *Behavioral Brain Sciences, 22*, 491–517.

de Waal, F. (2009). *Primates and philosophers: How morality evolved*. Princeton, NJ: Princeton University Press.

Dolan, R. J. (2002). Emotion, cognition, and behavior. *Science, 298*, 1191–1194.

Dolan, R. J. (2003). Feeling emotional. *Nature, 421*, 893–894.

Doidge, N. (2007). *The brain that changes itself*. New York: Penguin.

Ellis, G. F. R., & Toronchuk, J. A. (2005). Neural development: Affective and immune system influences. In R. Ellis & N. Newton (Eds.), *Consciousness & emotions*, vol. 1 (pp. 81–119). Amsterdam: John Benjamins.

Feder, A., Nestler, E. J., & Charney, D. S. (2009). Psychobiology and molecular genetics of resilience. *Nature Reviews Neuroscience, 10*, 446–457.

Feshbach, S., & Tangney, J. (2008). Television viewing and aggression: Some alternative perspectives. *Perspectives on Psychological Science, 3*, 387–389.

Flanders, J. L., Simard, M., Paquette, D., Parent, S., Vitaro, F., Pihl, R. O., & Séguin, J. R. (2009). Rough-and-tumble play and the development of physical aggression and emotion regulation: A five-year follow-up study, *Journal of Family Violence, 25*, 357-367.

Fosha, D., Siegel, D., & Solomon, M. (Eds). (2009). *The embodied mind: Integration of the body, brain and mind in clinical practice*. New York: Norton.

Freed, P. J., & Mann, J. J. (2007). Sadness and loss: toward a neurobiopsychosocial model. *American Journal of Psychiatry, 164*, 28–34.

Ginsburg, B. E, & Allee, W. C. (1942). Some effects of conditioning on social dominance and subordination in inbred strains of mice." *Physiology and Zoology, 15*, 485–506.

Goleman, D. (2007). *Social intelligence: The new science of human relationships*. New York: Arrow.

Gorman, R. M. (2008). Cooking up bigger brains. *Scientific American, 298*, 104–105.

Grandin, T. (2005), *Animals in translation*. New York: Scribner.

Grandin, T. (2009), *Animals make us human*. New York: Houghton Mifflin.

Gregg, T. R., & Siegel, A. (2001) Brain structures and neurotransmitters regulating aggression in cats: implications for human aggression. *Progress in Neuro-Psychopharmacology & Biological Psychiatry, 25*, 91–140.

Haller, J., & Kruk, M. R. (2006). Normal and abnormal aggression: Human disorders and novel laboratory models. *Neuroscience and Biobehavioral Reviews, 30*, 292–303.

Harmon-Jones, E. (2007). Asymmetrical frontal cortical activity, affective valence, and motivational direction. In E. Harmon-Jones & P. Winkielman (Eds.), *Social Neuroscience* (pp. 137–156). New York: Guilford Press.

Heath, R. G. (1996), *Exploring the mind-body relationship*. Baton Rouge, LA: Moran Printing, Inc.

Heim, C., Newport, D. J., Mletzko, T., Miller, A. H., & Nemeroff, C. B. (2008). The link between childhood trauma and depression: insights from HPA axis studies in humans. *Psyconeuroendocrinology, 33*, 693–710.

Holstege G., Georgiadis J. R., Paans A. M., Meiners L. C., van der Graaf, F. H., & Reinders A. A. (2003). Brain activation during human male ejaculation. *Journal of Neuroscience, 23*, 9185–9193.

Holstege G. R., & Saper, C. B. (Eds.) (2005). Special issue entitled "The Anatomy of the Soul" *Journal of Comparative Neurology, 493*, 1–176.

Hrdy, S. (2009). *Mothers and others: The evolutionary origins of mutual understanding*. Cambridge, MA: Harvard Univ. Press.

Iacoboni, M. (2008). *Mirroring people: The new science of how we connect with others*. New York: Farrar, Strauss, and Giroux.

Kandel, E. R. (2000). The molecular biology of memory storage: A dialog between genes and synapses. Nobel Lecture, Dec. 8, 2000. http://nobelprize.org/nobel_prizes/medicine/laureates/2000/kandel-lecture.html

Kashdan, T. B. (2009). *Curious? Discover the missing ingredient to a fulfilling life.* New York: William Morrow.

Katsouni, E., Sakkas, P., Zarros, A., Skandali, N., & Liapi, C. (2009). The involvement of Substance P in the induction of aggressive behavior. *Peptides, 30,* 1586–1591.

Keltner, D. (2009). *Born to be good: The science of a meaningful life.* New York: Norton.

Keverne E.B., Martensz N.D., Tuite B. (1989) Beta-endorphin concentrations in cerebrospinal fluid of monkeys are influenced by grooming relationships. *Psychoneuroendocrinology, 14,* 155–161.

Knutson, B., Adams, C. M., Fong, G. W., & Hommer, D. (2001). Anticipation of increasing monetary reward selectively recruits nucleus accumbens, *Journal of Neuroscience, 21,* 1–5.

Knutson, B., & Wimmer, G. E. (2007). Reward: Neural circuitry and social valuation. In E. Harmon-Jones, & P. Winkielman (Eds.), *Social Neuroscience* (pp. 157–175). New York: Guilford Press.

Kolb & Whishaw, (1990). *The cerebral cortex of the rat.* Cambridge, MA: MIT Press.

Kringelbach, M. L. (2010). The hedonic brain: A functional neuroanatomy of human pleasure. In M. L. Kringelbach & K. C. Berridge (Eds.), *Pleasures of the brain.* (pp. 62-73). Oxford: Oxford University Press.

Lane, R. D., & Garfield, D. A. S. (2005). Becoming aware of feelings: Integration of cognitive-developmental, neuroscientific and psychoanalytic perspectives (with commentaries). *Neuropsychoanalysis, 7,* 5–70.

Lasaite, L., Bunevicius, R., Lasiene, D., Lasas, L. (2004). Psychological functioning after growth hormone therapy in adult growth hormone deficient patients: endocrine and body composition correlates. *Medicina (Kaunas) 40,* 740–744.

LeDoux, J. (1996). *The emotional brain.* New York: Simon & Schuster.

LeDoux, J. (2000). Emotion circuits in the brain. *Annual Review of Neuroscience, 23,* 155–184.

LeDoux, (2009). Emotions, scientific perspectives. In. T. Bayne, A. Cleeremans, & P. Wilken (Eds.), *The Oxford companion to consciousness* (pp. 262–266). Oxford: Oxford University Press.

MacLean, P. D. (1990), *The Triune Brain in Evolution.* New York: Plenum.

Masten, A. S. (2009). Ordinary Magic: Lessons from research on resilience in human development. *Education Canada, 49,* 28–32.

McMillan, F. (ed.) (2005). *Mental health and well-being in animals.* Oxford, UK: F. Blackwell Publishing.

Miller, A. H., Maletic, V., & Raison, C. L. (2009). Inflammation and its discontents: The role of cytokines in the pathophysiology of major depression. *Biological Psychiatry, 65,* 732–741.

Nadel, J., & R. Muir (Eds.). (2005). *Emotional development.* Oxford, UK: Oxford University Press.

Nelson, E. E., & Panksepp, J. (1998) Brain substrates of infant-mother attachment: Contributions of opioids, oxytocin, and norepinephrine. *Neuroscience & Biobehavioral Reviews, 22,* 437–452.

Nestler, E. J., & Carlezon, W. A. Jr. (2006). The mesolimbic dopamine reward circuit in depression. *Biological Psychiatry, 59,* 1151–1159.

Northoff, G., Henzel, A., de Greck, M., Bermpohl, F., Dobrowolny, H., & Panksepp, J. (2006). Self-referential processing in our brain—A meta-analysis of imaging studies of the self. *Neuroimage, 31,* 440–457.

Northoff, G., & Panksepp, J. (2008). The trans-species concept of self and the subcortical-cortical midline system. *Trends in Cognitive Sciences, 12,* 259–264.

Numan, M., & Insel, TR. (2003). *The neurobiology of parental behavior.* New York: Springer-Verlag.

Positive reinforcement produced by electrical stimulation of septal area and other regions of rat brain. *Journal of Comparative and Physiological Psychology, 47,* 419–427). London: Academic Press.

Panksepp, J. (1981). Brain opioids: A neurochemical substrate for narcotic and social dependence. In S. Cooper (Ed.). *Progress in theory in psychopharmacology.* (pp. 149–175). London: Academic Press.

Panksepp, J. (1982). Toward a general psychobiological theory of emotions. *The Behavioral and Brain Sciences, 5,* 407–467.

Panksepp, J. (1985). Mood changes. In P. Vinken, G. Bruyn, & H. Klawans (Eds.), *Handbook of clinical neurology,* vol. 45 (pp. 271–285). Amsterdam: Elsevier.

Panksepp, J. (1990). The psychoneurology of fear: Evolutionary perspectives and the role of animal models in understanding human anxiety. In G. D. Burrows, M. Roth, & R. Noyes Jr. (Eds.), *Handbook of anxiety, vol. 3, The neurobiology of anxiety* (pp. 3–58). Amsterdam: Elsevier/North-Holland Biomedical Press.

Panksepp, J. (1991). Affective Neuroscience: A conceptual framework for the neurobiological study of emotions. In K. Strongman (Ed.), *International Reviews of Emotion Research* (pp. 59–99). Chichester, England: Wiley.

Panksepp, J. (1998a). *Affective Neuroscience: The foundations of human and animal emotions.* New York: Oxford University Press.

Panksepp, J. (1998b). The periconscious substrates of consciousness: Affective states and the evolutionary origins of the SELF. *Journal of Consciousness Studies, 5,* 566–582.

Panksepp J. (2001a). The long-term psychobiological consequences of infant emotions: prescriptions for the 21st century. *Infant Mental Health Journal, 22,* 132–173.

Panksepp J. (2001b). The long-term psychobiological consequences of infant emotions: prescriptions for the 21st century (reprinting). *NeuroPsychoanalysis, 3,* 140–178.

Panksepp, J. (2003b). Trennungsschmerz als mogliche ursache fur panikattacken—neuropsychologische Uberlegungen und Befunde. *Personlichkeitsstorungen: Theorie und Therapie, 7,* 245–251.

Panksepp, J. (2003a). Feeling the pain of social loss. *Science, 302,* 237–239.

Panksepp, J. (Ed.) (2004a). *Textbook of biological psychiatry.* New York: Wiley.

Panksepp, J. (2004b). The emerging neuroscience of fear and anxiety disorders. In Panksepp J. (Ed.), *Textbook of biological psychiatry* (pp. 489–520). New York: Wiley.

Panksepp, J. (2005a). Affective consciousness: Core emotional feelings in animals and humans. *Consciousness & Cognition, 14,* 19–69.

Panksepp, J. (2005b). On the embodied neural nature of core emotional affects. *Journal of Consciousness Studies, 12,* 161–187.

Panksepp, J. (2005c). Feelings of social loss: The evolution of pain and the ache of a broken heart. In R. Ellis & N. Newton (Eds), *Consciousness & emotions,* vol. 1 (pp. 23–55). Amsterdam: John Benjamins.

Panksepp, J. (2005d). Why does separation distress hurt? A comment on MacDonald and Leary. *Psychological Bulletin, 131,* 224–230.

Panksepp, J. (2005e). Social support and pain: How does the brain feel the ache of a broke heart. *Journal of Cancer Pain & Symptom Palliation, 1,* 59–65.

Panksepp, J. (2006a). Emotional endophenotypes in evolutionary psychiatry. *Progress in Neuro-Psychopharmacology & Biological Psychiatry, 30,* 774–784.

Panksepp, J. (2006b). On the neuro-evolutionary nature of social pain, support, and empathy. In M. Aydede (Ed.), *Pain: New essays on its nature & the methodology of its study* (pp. 367–387). Cambridge, MA: The MIT Press.

Panksepp, J. (2007a). Criteria for basic emotions: Is DISGUST a primary "emotion"? *Cognition and Emotion, 21,* 1819–1828.

Panksepp J. (2007b). Neuroevolutionary sources of laughter and social joy: Modeling primal human laughter in laboratory rats. *Behavioral Brain Research, 182(2),* 231–244.

Panksepp, J., (2007c). Can PLAY diminish ADHD and facilitate the construction of the social brain. *Journal of the Canadian Academy of Child and Adolescent Psychiatry, 10,* 57–66.

Panksepp J. (2007d). Affective Consciousness. In M. Velmans and S. Schneider (Eds.), *The Blackwell companion to consciousness* (pp. 114–129). Malden, MA: Blackwell Publishing, Ltd.

Panksepp, J. (2007e). Neurologizing the psychology of affects: How appraisal-based constructivism and basic emotion theory can coexist. *Perspectives on Psychological Science, 2,* 281–296.

Panksepp, J. (2008a). The affective brain and core consciousness: How does neural activity generate emotional feelings? In M. Lewis, J. M. Haviland, & L. F. Barrett (Eds.), *Handbook of emotions* (pp. 47–67). New York: Guilford.

Panksepp, J. (2008b). Play, ADHD, and the construction of the social brain: Should the first class each day be recess? *American Journal of Play, 1,* 55–79.

Panksepp, J. (2009a). Core consciousness. In. T. Bayne, A. Cleeremans, & P. Wilken (Eds.), *The Oxford companion to consciousness* (pp. 198–200). Oxford, UK: Oxford University Press.

Panksepp, J. (2009b). Primary process affects and brain oxytocin. *Biological Psychiatry, 65,* 725–727.

Panksepp, J. (2010a). Perspectives on passages toward and affective neurobiology of mind? Foreword to the *Encyclopedia of Behavioral Neuroscience.* New York: Elsevier.

Panksepp, J. (2010b). The science of the brain as a gateway to understanding play. *American Journal for Play, 3,* 245–277.

Panksepp, J. (2010c). Energy is delight: The affective pleasures and pains of brain system for eating and energy regulation In, L. Dube, A. Bechara, A. Drewnowski, P. LeBel, P. James, & R. Y. Yada (Eds.), *Obesity prevention handbook* (p. 5-14). Amsterdam: Elsevier.

Panksepp, J. (2010d). The evolutionary sources of jealousy: Cross-species approaches to fundamental issues. In. S. L. Hart & M. Lagerstee (Eds.), *Handbook of jealousy: Theories, principles, and multidisciplinary approaches* (pp. 101–120). New York: Wiley-Blackwell.

Panksepp, J. (2011). The neurobiology of social loss in animals: Some keys to the puzzle of psychic pain in humans. In. L. A. Jensen-Campbell & G. MacDonald (Eds.), *Social pain: Neuropsychological and health implications of loss and exclusion* (pp 11-52). Washington, DC: American Psychological Association.

Panksepp, J., Bean, N. J., Bishop, P., Vilberg, T. and Sahley, T. L. (1980). Opioid blockade and social comfort in chicks. *Pharmacology Biochemistry & Behavior, 13*, 673–683.

Panksepp, J., & Burgdorf, J. (2003). "Laughing" rats and the evolutionary antecedents of human joy? *Physiology & Behavior, 79*, 533–547.

Panksepp, J., Burgdorf, J., Gordon, N., & Turner, C. (2003). Modeling ADHD-type arousal with unilateral frontal cortex damage in rats and beneficial effects of play therapy. *Brain and Cognition. 52*, 97–105.

Panksepp, J., & Harro, J. (2004). The future of neuropeptides in biological psychiatry and emotional psychopharmacology: Goals and strategies. In Panksepp J (Ed.) *Textbook of Biological Psychiatry* (pp. 627–660). New York: Wiley.

Panksepp, J., & Moskal, J. (2008). Dopamine and SEEKING: Sub-neocortical "reward" systems and appetitive urges. In A. Elliot (Ed.), *Handbook of approach and avoidance motivation* (pp. 67–87). New York: Taylor & Francis Group, LLC.

Panksepp, J. Nelson, E., & Siviy, S. (1994). Brain opioids and mother-infant social motivation. *Acta Paediatrica, 397*, 40–46.

Panksepp, J., Normansell, L. A., Herman, B., Bishop, P., & Crepeau, L. (1988). Neural and neurochemical control of the separation distress call. In J. D. Newman (Ed.). *The Physiological Control of Mammalian Vocalizations* (pp. 263–300). New York: Plenum.

Panksepp, J., Normansell, L. A., Cox, J. F., & Siviy, S. (1994). Effects of neonatal decortication on the social play of juvenile rats. *Physiology & Behavior, 56*, 429–443.

Panksepp, J., & Northoff, G. (2009). The Trans-species core self: The emergence of active cultural and neuro-ecological agents through self related processing within sub-neocortical-cortical midline networks. *Consciousness & Cognition, 18*, 193–215.

Panksepp, J., & Panksepp, J. B. (2000). The seven sins of evolutionary psychology. *Evolution & Cognition, 6*, 108–131.

Panksepp, J., Siviy, S. M., & Normansell, L. A. (1985). Brain opioids and social emotions. In M. Reite & T. Fields (Eds.), *The psychobiology of attachment and separation* (pp. 3–49). New York: Academic Press.

Panksepp, J., & Trevarthen, C. (2008). Motive impulse and emotion in acts of musicality and in sympathetic emotional response to music. In S. Maloch & C. Trevarthen (Eds.), *Communicative musicality* (pp. 105–146). Oxford, UK: Oxford University Press.

Panksepp, J., Fuchs, T., & Iacobucci, P. (2010). The basic neuroscience of emotional experiences: The case of FEAR and implications for clinical anxiety in animals and humans. *Applied Animal Ethology* (in press).

Panksepp, J., Sacks, D. S., Crepeau, L., & Abbott, B. B. (1991) The psycho- and neuro-biology of fear systems in the brain. In M. R. Denny (Ed.), *Aversive Events and Behavior* (pp. 7–59). New York: Lawrence Erlbaum Assocs. Inc. Publisher.

Panksepp, J., & Zellner, M. (2004). Toward a neurobiologically based unified theory of aggression. *Revue Internationale de Psychologie Sociale/ International Review of Social Psychology, 17*, 37–61.

Park, M. S., Nguyen, A. D., Aryan, H. E., Levy, M. L., & Semendeferi, K. (2007). Evolution of the human brain: Changing brain size and the fossil record. *Neurosurgery, 60*, 555–562.

Peciña, S., Smith, K., & Berridge, K. C. (2006). Hedonic hot spots in the brain. *The Neuroscientist, 12*, 500–511.

Pellis, S. M., & Pellis, V. C. (1998). Play fighting of rats in comparative perspective: A schema for neurobehavioral analysis. *Neuroscience and Biobehavioral Reviews, 23*, 87–101.

Pellis, S. M., & Pellis, V. C. (2009). *The playful brain: Venturing to the limits of neuroscience*. Oxford, UK: Oneworld Press.

Pfaff, D. W. (1999). *Drive: Neurobiological and molecular mechanisms of sexual behavior*. Cambridge, MA: MIT Press.

Pfaffman, C. (1960). The pleasure of sensation. *Psychological Review, 67*, 253–268.

Power, T. G. (2000). *Play and exploration in children and animals*. Hillsdale, NJ: Lawrence Erlbaum Associates.

Powers, A., Ressler, K. J., & Bradley, R. G. (2009). The protective role of friendship on the effects of childhood abuse and depression. *Depression and Anxiety, 26*, 46–53.

Preter, M., & Klein, D. F. (2008). Panic, suffocation false alarms, separation anxiety and endogenous opioids. *Progress in Neuropsychopharmacology and Biological Psychiatry, 32*, 603–612.

Reddy, V. (2008). *How infants know minds*. Cambridge, MA: Harvard University Press.

Reuter, M., Panksepp, J., Schnabel, N., Kellerhoff, N., Kempel, P., & Hennig, J. (2005). Personality and biological markers of creativity. *European Journal of Personality, 19,* 83–95.

Rizzolati, I., & Sinigaglia, (2008). *Mirrors in the brain: How our minds share actions, emotions, and experience.* Oxford, UK: Oxford University Press.

Rolls, E. T. (2005). *Emotions explained.* Oxford, UK: Oxford University Press.

Russell, J. A. (2003). Core Affect and the psychological construction of emotions. *Psychological Review, 110,* 145–173.

Ryff, C. D., & Singer, B. (1998). The contours of positive human health. *Psychological Inquiry, 9,* 1–28.

Scott, E. (2001). Toward a play program to benefit children's attention in the classroom. Unpublished Ph. D. Dissertation, Bowling Green State University, Bowling Green, Ohio.

Scott, E., & Panksepp, J. (2003). Rough-and-tumble play in human children. *Aggressive Behaviour, 29,* 539–551.

Sewards, T. V. (2004). Dual separate pathways for sensory and hedonic aspects of taste. *Brain Research Bulletin, 62,* 271–283.

Sewards, T. V., & Sewards, M. A. (2000). The awareness of thirst: Proposed neural correlates. *Consciousness and Cognition, 9,* 463–487.

Shamay-Tsoory, S. G., Fischer, M., Dvash, J., Harari, H., Perach-Bloom, N., & Levkovitz, Y. (2009). Intranasal administration of oxytocin increases envy and schadenfreude (gloating). *Biological Psychiatry, 66,* 864–870.

Shewmon, D. A., Holmse, D. A., & Byrne, P. A. (1999). Consciousness in congenitally decorticate children: developmental vegetative state as self-fulfilling prophecy. *Developmental Medicine and Child Neurology, 41,* 364–374.

Siviy, S. M., & Panksepp, J. (1987). Juvenile play in the rat: Thalamic and brain stem involvement. *Physiology & Behavior, 20,* 39–55.

Siegel, A. (2005). *The neurobiology of aggression and rage.* Boca Raton, FL: CRC Press.

Silvia, P. J. (2006). *Exploring the psychology of interest.* New York: Oxford Univ. Press.

Silvia, P. J., & Kashdan, T. B. (2009). Interesting things and curious people: Exploration and engagement as transient states and enduring strengths. *Social Psychology and Personality Compass, 3,* 785–797.

Skinner, B. F. (1953). *Science and human behavior.* New York: Macmillan.

Solms, M., & Turnbull, O. (2002). *The brain and the inner world.* New York: Other Press.

Soltysik, S., & Jelen, P. (2005). In rats, sighs correlate with relief. *Physiology & Behavior, 85,* 598–602.

Špinka, M., Newberry, R. C., & Bekoff, M. (2001). Mammalian play: Training for the unexpected. *The Quarterly Review of Biology, 76,* 141–168.

Steiner, J. E., Glaser, D., Hawilo, M. E., & Berridge, K. C. (2001). Comparative expression of hedonic impact: Affective reactions to taste by human infants and other primates. *Neuroscience and Biobehavioral Reviews, 25,* 53–74.

Stouthart, P. J., Deijen, J. B., Roffel, M., & Delemarre-van de Waal, H. A. (2003). Quality of life of growth hormone (GH) deficient young adults during discontinuation and restart of GH therapy. *Psychoneuroendocrinology, 28,* 612–626.

Sunderland, M. (2006). *The science of parenting.* London: Doring Kindersley Limited.

Suomi, S. J. (2006). Risk, resilience, and gene x environment interactions in rhesus monkeys. *Annals of the New York Academy of Sciences, 1094,* 52–62.

Sur, M., & Rubenstein, J. L. (2005). Patterning and plasticity of the cerebral cortex. *Science, 310,* 805–810.

Swain, J. E., Lorberbaum, J. P., Korse, S., & Strathearn, L. (2007). Brain basis of early parent-infant interactions: psychology, physiology, and in vivo function neuroimaging studies. *Journal of Child and Adolescent Psychiatry, 48,* 262–287.

Szyf, M., McGowan, P., & Meaney, M. J. (2008). The social environment and the epigenome. *Environmental and Molecular Mutagenesis, 49,* 46–60.

Toronchuk, J. A., & Ellis, G. F. R (2007). Disgust: Sensory affect or primary emotional system? *Cognition and Emotion, 21,* 1799–1818.

Thompson, J. L., Butterfield, G. E., Gylfadottir, U.K., Yesavage J., Marcus, R., Hintz, R. L., Pearman, A., & Hoffman, A. R. (1998). Effects of human growth hormone, insulin-like growth factor I, and diet and exercise on body composition of obese postmenopausal women. *Journal of Clinical Endocrinology & Metabolism, 83,* 1477–1484.

Thoresen, C. E., Luskin, F. M., & Harris, A. H. (1998). Science and forgiveness interventions: Reflections and recommendations. In E. L. Worthington, Jr. (Ed.), *Dimensions of forgiveness: Psychological research and theological perspectives* (pp. 163–190). Radnor, PA: Templeton Foundation Press.

Tomasello, M. (2009). Why we cooperate. Cambridge, MA: MIT Press.

Tzschentke, T. M. (2007). Measuring reward with the conditioned place preference (CPP) paradigm: Update of the last decade. *Addiction Biology, 12,* 227–462.

Vaillant, G. E. (2008). Positive emotions, spirituality and the practice of psychiatry. *Mental Health, Spirituality, Mind*, 6, 43–62.

Vandekerckhove, M., & Panksepp, J., (2009). The flow of anoetic to noetic and autonoetic consciousness: A vision of unknowing (anoetic) and knowing (noetic) consciousness in the remembrance of things past and imagined futures. *Consciousness & Cognition, 18*, 1018–1028.

Vul, E., Harris, C., Winkelman, P., & Pashler, H. (2009). Puzzlingly high correlations in fMRI studies of emotion, personality, and social cognition. *Perspectives on Psychological Science, 3*, 274–290.

Watt, D. F. (2007). Toward a neuroscience of empathy (with commentaries). *Neuro-Psychoanalysis, 9*, 119–172.

Watt, D. F., & Panksepp, J. (2009). Depression: An evolutionarily conserved mechanism to terminate separation distress? A review of aminergic, peptidergic, and neural network perspectives. *Neuropsychoanalysis, 11*, 11, 5–104.

Young, P. T. (1959). The role of affective processes in learning and motivation. *Psychological Review, 66*, 104–125.

Zachar, P., & Ellis, R. (Eds.) (2010, in press). *Emotional theories of Jaak Panksepp and Jim Russell*. Amsterdam: John Benjamins.

Zhang, T. Y., & Meaney, M. J. (2010). Epigenetics and the environmental regulation of the genome and its function. *Annual Review of Psychology, 61*, 439–466.

Zubieta, J. K., Ketter, T. A., Bueller, J. A., Xu, Y., Kilbourn, M. R., Young, E. A., & Koeppe, R. A. (2003). Regulation of human affective responses by anterior cingulate and limbic mu-opioid neurotransmission. *Archives of General Psychiatry, 60*, 1145–1153.

**III**

---

# Emotional Perspectives

# 6

# Beyond Pleasure and Pain? Emotion Regulation and Positive Psychology

*Maya Tamir and James J. Gross*

Emotion regulation and positive psychology are inextricably linked. Both fields seek to promote optimal human functioning, and because emotions play a pivotal role in optimal functioning, both fields seek to promote optimal emotional responding. Emotion regulation does this by studying the processes by which people influence which emotions they have, when they have them, and how they experience and express these emotions (Gross, 1998). Positive psychology does this by examining positive emotions, traits, and institutions (Seligman & Csikszentmihalyi, 2000). Research in both fields, therefore, is predicated on assumptions about the nature of optimal human functioning.

In this chapter, we argue that the fields of emotion regulation and positive psychology have been dominated by a hedonic view of optimal functioning. We first discuss the contributions of the hedonic view to both fields, and then consider its critical limitations. We then point to a broader conception of optimal functioning, which is based on a motivated view of human nature. We describe a new approach to emotion regulation that is based on this broader conception of optimal functioning and review related

empirical evidence. We conclude with the hope that the instrumental approach to emotion regulation might stimulate a similar shift in positive psychology, toward a broader view of optimal functioning that acknowledges—but moves beyond—pleasure and pain.

## The Hedonic View of Optimal Human Functioning

Since the dawn of human history, optimal functioning has been equated with the experience of pleasure and the absence of pain (e.g., Kahneman, 1999). Emotions are predominantly states of pleasure or pain involving both body and mind (e.g., Izard, 1977). Therefore, according to a hedonic view, the experience of pleasant emotions and the absence of unpleasant emotions are core components of optimal human functioning.

### The Short-Term Hedonic Approach to Emotion Regulation

The hedonic conception of optimal functioning has had a tremendous impact in the field of emotion regulation. The hedonic properties of emotions are their unique and most prominent defining feature (e.g., Averill, 1994; Barrett, Mesquita, Ochsner, & Gross, 2007). Such hedonic properties are relatively fixed across people and contexts (e.g., disgust usually feels bad), and they can be reliably measured and identified. Coupled with the powerful motivation to maximize pleasure and minimize pain (Freud, 1926/1959), the view of emotions as primarily hedonic states has led researchers to adopt a short-term hedonic approach to emotion regulation.

According to the short-term hedonic approach, when emotions are regulated, they are regulated primarily for short-term hedonic reasons. This has resulted in an explicit focus on emotion regulation as the process by which people decrease unpleasant emotions and increase pleasant emotions (e.g., Larsen & Prizmic, 2008). Guided by this approach, research in emotion regulation in the past few decades has made substantial contributions to our understanding of mental health and well-being, identifying adaptive ways in which people can influence their own emotional experiences (for reviews, see Denollet, Nyklicek, & Vingerhoets, 2008; Gross, 2007).

## The Hedonic Approach to Positive Psychology

The field of positive psychology has given rise to diverse definitions and operationalizations of well-being. Considerable attention has been given to two traditions—namely, the hedonic and the eudaimonic (Ryan & Deci, 2000). Both of these traditions have sprung from early philosophical conceptions of well-being in an attempt to translate them into empirical research. Although each tradition represents a simplified view of well-being, they are nonetheless highly important conceptual approaches that, to a large extent, have guided research in the field. In this chapter, we will describe both approaches and evaluate them critically. We begin in this section by briefly describing the hedonic view of well-being and some of the research it has given rise to.

The idea that optimal functioning involves the presence of pleasant emotions and absence of unpleasant emotions has dominated the field of positive psychology. In a seminal article that signaled the formation of positive psychology, the study of positive emotions was identified as one of the three target domains within the field (Seligman, 2003; Seligman & Csikszentmihalyi, 2000). The emphasis on pleasant emotions was soon linked to the hedonic philosophical tradition.

In fact, some of the leading figures in positive psychology went as far as labeling the study of well-being as "hedonic psychology" (Kahenman, Diener, & Schwarz, 1999). The role of pleasant feelings in hedonic conceptions of well-being has since been constantly reinforced by positive psychologists who use the terms "well-being," which typically refers to psychological welfare, and "happiness," which typically refers to a pleasant emotional state, interchangeably.

The emphasis on subjective hedonic experiences has given rise to the study of subjective well-being (Diener, 1984; Diener & Lucas, 2000). Subjective well-being assumes that well-being involves three distinct subjective experiences: satisfaction with life, the presence of pleasant feelings, and the absence of unpleasant feelings. Because of its emphasis on hedonic outcomes and its relative inattention to underlying processes, subjective well-being research has typically been viewed as reflecting the hedonic tradition, which argues that pleasure is a defining feature of the "good life" (Kahneman et al., 1999). Research on subjective well-being has made immense contributions to positive psychology, promoting our understanding of both the causes and consequences of happiness in individuals, cultures, and nations (for recent reviews, see Diener & Biswas-Diener, 2008; Eid & Larsen, 2008).

## Taking Stock

Despite its important contributions to the study of emotion regulation and to positive psychology, there is reason to believe that a purely hedonic view of human nature is too narrow to account for all aspects of optimal human functioning. In this section, we review the limitations of the hedonic approach for the study of emotion regulation as well as positive psychology.

### The Limitations of the Short-Term Hedonic Approach to Emotion Regulation

Although the short-term hedonic approach to emotion regulation has greatly contributed to our understanding of the role of emotion regulation in well-being, it suffers from several serious limitations. First, it views emotions as exclusively hedonic states. For example, excitement is pleasant whereas fear is unpleasant; therefore, people should be motivated to increase excitement and decrease fear at all times. Emotions, however, are more than states of pleasure or pain.

They influence physiology, cognition, and behavior and predispose people to act in goal-directed ways (e.g., Frijda, 1986). For example, excitement may predispose people to approach possible rewards (e.g., a potential mate), whereas fear may predispose people to avoid possible threats (e.g., a potential predator) (e.g., Gray, 1981).

By viewing emotions as exclusively hedonic states, the short-term hedonic approach to emotion regulation ignores the possibility that people may seek to regulate their emotions for reasons other than maximizing pleasure or minimizing pain. For instance, a person may try to increase her level of excitement not necessarily because it feels good, but because it might help her obtain a reward. The short-term hedonic approach is unable to account for such instrumental motives in emotion regulation.

Second, the short-term hedonic approach fails to account for all possible forms of emotion regulation. As mentioned above, emotions can be pleasant or unpleasant. Independent of their hedonic quality, emotions can also be useful by helping us respond to environmental challenges (Frijda, 1986; Levenson, 1994; Tooby & Cosmides, 1990). Emotions, however, can be harmful as well. The utility of emotions depends on an individual's goals as well as the characteristics of the context at hand. For instance, fear may be useful when it leads a person walking home at night to select a safe route over a dark alley. Fear may be harmful the next day, however, when it leads the person to freeze when giving an important presentation at work.

Both pleasant and unpleasant emotions, therefore, can be either useful or harmful, and there may be important benefits to accepting both types of emotional experiences in certain contexts (Hayes, Strosahl, & Wilson, 1999). To the extent that people seek to maximize both pleasure and utility, emotion regulation may be said to include four types of activities, ones that (1) increase pleasant emotions, (2) increase unpleasant emotions, (3) decrease pleasant emotions, or (4) decrease unpleasant emotions (Gross, 1998, 1999). Unfortunately, by focusing exclusively on hedonic considerations, the short-term hedonic approach to emotion regulation has led to a nearly exclusive focus on increasing pleasant and decreasing unpleasant emotions, neglecting to examine cases in which people seek to increase unpleasant or decrease pleasant emotions. This means that only two of these four possible types of emotion regulation have received substantive research attention (Parrott, 1993).

The short-term hedonic approach to emotion regulation, therefore, provides a relatively narrow and limited view of emotion regulation. In order to address its limitations, what is needed is an alternative approach that can explain different motives for experiencing emotions and account for all types of emotion regulation.

## The Limitations of the Hedonic Approach to Positive Psychology

Despite its broad impact in the field of positive psychology, the hedonic view has been extensively criticized almost since its inception (McMahon, 2006). In particular, many have argued that the hedonic approach fails to account for aspects of human functioning, such as self-fulfillment, virtue, and moral justice, that go beyond momentary subjective experiences (Ryan & Deci, 2000; Ryff, 1989; Waterman, 1993).

Building on a eudaimonic philosophical tradition, a different view of optimal functioning has distinguished well-being from subjective happiness (Ryan & Deci, 2000). In this view, optimal functioning depends on self-fulfillment, which involves a sense of autonomy, personal growth, self-acceptance, purpose in life, mastery, competence, and connection to others (Ryan & Deci, 2000; Ryff & Keyes, 1995; Ryff & Singer, 1998). According to the eudaimonic view, such processes are often associated with pleasant feelings, when successfully engaged in. Nonetheless, successful achievement of meaningful goals is viewed as conceptually independent of pleasure per se (Ryan & Huta, 2009).

Both the hedonic and the eudaimonic views of optimal functioning have merit. They complement each other and reflect non-overlapping aspects of optimal functioning (Compton, Smith, Cornish, & Qualls, 1996; King & Napa, 1998; Ryan & Deci, 2000). By emphasizing measurable hedonic outcomes, the hedonic view often neglects the conceptual processes that shape well-being. At the same time, by focusing on abstract philosophical constructs, the eudaimonic view underestimates the role of hedonic outcomes as indexing diverse aspects of well-being (Kashdan, Biswas-Diener, & King, 2008).

Neither the hedonic nor the eudaimonic views can independently account for the broad range of variables involved in well-being. This has even led some to question whether the distinction between these approaches is useful for advancing our understanding of well-being (Kashdan et al., 2008). As in the field of emotion regulation, what is needed in the field of positive psychology is a broad approach that can account for both hedonic and eudaimonic aspects of human functioning and tie them together.

## A Motivated View of Optimal Functioning

The hedonic and the eudaimonic views of optimal functioning highlight different aspects of human nature. But how do these aspects work together to account for the full range of optimal human functioning? A motivated view of human nature could potentially account for both approaches to well-being and highlight the potential links between them.

According to a motivated approach, optimal functioning is driven by the active pursuit of personal goals (e.g., Cantor & Sanderson, 1999). Such pursuit highlights two complementary elements: the process of goal pursuit and the outcomes of goal pursuit. From this perspective, eudaimonic approaches focus on the process of goal pursuit—namely, what people try to achieve as they pursue their goals. From this perspective, optimal functioning involves the pursuit of personally meaningful goals (Emmons, 2003) that satisfy intrinsic needs (Kasser & Ryan, 1996) and conform to people's values (Waterman, 1993; Ryan & Deci, 2000). The hedonic approach, on the other hand, focuses on how well people achieve their goals. From this perspective, optimal functioning involves success in goal pursuit, with pleasure reflecting success or progress toward goals and pain reflecting failure (Carver & Scheier, 1998).

According to a motivated view of optimal functioning, what has been viewed as two distinct approaches to well-being actually reflect different and complementary sides of the same coin. Research in the eudaimonic tradition typically focuses on the type of goals people pursue and how they pursue such goals, whereas research in the hedonic tradition typically focuses on subjective indices of progress in goal pursuit. It is not surprising, therefore, that eudaimonic and hedonic indices of well-being are often closely linked (e.g., King, Hicks, Krull, & Del Gaiso, 2006; Sheldon & Niemiec, 2006). A motivated approach to optimal functioning could explain when and why such overlap is likely and when it is not.

Such a motivated approach to optimal functioning has already informed the study of emotion regulation, by giving rise to a novel, instrumental approach (Tamir, 2009a). In the section below, we review the assumptions of the instrumental approach, highlight some of its main predictions, and review evidence in their support.

## An Instrumental Approach to Emotion Regulation

According to a motivated approach, optimal emotional experiences should be examined with respect to what people are trying to achieve when pursuing goals as well as how well they do so. When focusing on doing well, emotions can serve as desired end-states, or goals. Optimal experiences, in this respect, involve the presence of pleasant emotions and relatively low levels of unpleasant emotions. Such experiences can reflect progress or success in the pursuit of both hedonic goals (i.e., I want to feel good) and instrumental goals (e.g., I want to finish the assignment on time).

When focusing on what people try to achieve, however, emotions can serve either as ends or as means in goal pursuit. When the goal is to feel good, emotions serve as the desired end-state. When the goal is to finish the assignment on time, emotions may serve as means (e.g., by motivating the person to work harder). People may be motivated to experience an emotion, therefore, not in order to feel a certain way, but in order to attain a certain goal. Optimal experiences, in this respect, involve the presence of useful emotions (i.e., emotions that promote goal attainment) and the absence of harmful emotions, regardless of whether they are pleasant or unpleasant to experience.

According to the instrumental approach to emotion regulation, people regulate their emotions to optimize goal pursuit. People may be motivated to experience emotions for hedonic benefits (e.g., decreasing my level of worry would make me feel better) or for instrumental benefits (e.g., maintaining my level of worry would motivate me to work harder on my work assignment).

The idea that people regulate emotions for reasons other than immediate hedonic benefits is not novel (Parrott, 1993). For instance, it has long been acknowledged that people regulate the expression of their emotions to conform to social or cultural norms (Hochschild, 1979). They control their emotional expressions for strategic reasons in the workplace (e.g., Sutton, 1991), to convey strategic information in social interactions (e.g., Andrade & Ho, 2008; Barry, 1999), and to influence close relationships (Bell & Clarkins, 2000).

However, people can regulate the expression of emotion with little impact on the experience of emotion (Ekman, 1993). In contrast, a unique assumption of the instrumental approach to emotion regulation is that people regulate their emotional *experience* for instrumental reasons. The instrumental approach, therefore, contradicts the assumption that emotions are regulated primarily to satisfy short-term hedonic goals (e.g., Larsen, 2000; Thayer, 2000). It builds, instead, on the idea that emotions are regulated to satisfy any short- or long-term goal (Bonanno, 2001; Clore & Robinson, 2000; Erber & Erber, 2000; Mayer & Salovey, 1995; Parrott, 1993).

Because it is based on a motivated approach to optimal functioning, the instrumental approach grounds emotion regulation in the broader realm of self-regulation. In doing so, emotion regulation is subjected to the same set of principles that guide self-regulation, more broadly construed. Building on such broader principles, the instrumental approach to emotion regulation gives rise to three general hypotheses. First, to the extent that unpleasant emotions can be useful in particular contexts, people may be motivated to feel unpleasant emotions to promote their goal pursuit. Second, because the utility of emotions depends on the goals people pursue, people may be motivated to feel different emotions in different contexts. Third, because people differ in the goals they pursue, different people may be motivated to experience different emotions. Below, we review recent empirical research that addresses each of these predictions.

## People Are Sometimes Motivated to Feel Bad

Short-term goals are not always consistent with long-term goals. In the realm of self-regulation, for example, the goal to maximize pleasure by eating a slice of chocolate cake may be inconsistent with the goal of losing weight. Because people are often willing to forego immediate pleasure to maximize long-term benefits (Mischel, Shoda, & Rodriguez, 1989), a person who wants to lose weight may eat a salad instead of cake, despite the hedonic cost. Similarly, in the realm of emotion regulation, the goal to maximize immediate pleasure is not always consistent with long-term goals. For example, the goal to maximize pleasure by feeling happy is

inconsistent with the goal to reprimand a child for wrongdoing. In such cases, the instrumental approach predicts that people would be motivated to experience even unpleasant emotions if they promote long-term benefits. For example, a parent who wants to teach a child right from wrong by reprimanding her for wrongdoing may be motivated to increase his level of anger, despite the hedonic cost of doing so.

There is now empirical evidence to support this prediction. Specifically, we found that as people were preparing for a confrontational task, they tried to increase their experience of anger by engaging in anger-inducing activities (Tamir, Mitchell, & Gross, 2008). Such attempts to increase anger were found even when controlling for concurrent anger experiences, indicating that the effect was not driven by the feelings people were already experiencing (i.e., emotion-congruent effects). Furthermore, such attempts were found despite the fact that people found the anger-inducing activities to be significantly less pleasant than other potential activities. Finally, supporting the instrumental underpinnings of such regulatory behavior, increasing the level of anger people experienced led them to be more successful in the confrontational task. Thus, people were motivated to increase their level of anger when doing so was instrumental. Such findings are in stark contrast to the basic assumption of the short-term hedonic approach that people should *always* be motivated to feel good.

## People May Be Motivated to Feel Different Emotions in Different Contexts

As mentioned earlier, the instrumental nature of emotions is context-dependent. Therefore, according to the instrumental approach to emotion regulation, the emotions people want to feel should vary by context, as a function of the goals they pursue. A parent may be motivated to increase his anger when he wants to reprimand a child for wrongdoing, but decrease his anger when he wants to console a child hurt by another's wrongdoing.

There is now substantial evidence to demonstrate that what people want to feel varies by context. Initial evidence for this prediction was provided by Erber, Wegner, and Therriault (1996), who found that people try to neutralize their feelings when they expect to interact with a stranger, but not when they expect to work alone. Such findings led these authors to propose a contextual model of affect regulation and advocate the abandonment of simple hedonic assumptions (Erber & Erber, 2000). The instrumental approach to emotion regulation extends this contextual model by identifying the features of the situation that determine what people want to feel. According to the instrumental approach, what people want to feel in a particular context and how they subsequently regulate their emotions depend on the goals they pursue in that context.

In support of this argument, we have been able to predict what people want to feel by manipulating the goals they pursue. For instance, anger should facilitate successful confrontation (Frijda, 1986; Parrott, 2001). Consistent with this theoretical assumption, we found that people were more likely to try to increase their level of anger when pursuing a confrontational goal, compared to a non-confrontational goal (Tamir et al., 2008). Similarly, from a theoretical perspective, emotions such as fear and worry should facilitate successful avoidance of threats, whereas emotions such as excitement and happiness should facilitate successful approach of rewards (e.g., Carver, 2001). Consistent with these assumptions, we found that people were motivated to increase their level of fear when preparing to pursue avoidance goals, but they were motivated to increase their level of excitement when preparing to pursue approach goals (Tamir & Ford, 2009).

In a recent study, we demonstrated that what people want to feel is determined by goal accessibility, even when all other features of the situation remain constant (Tamir & Ford, 2010). Participants were told that they will complete a social interaction where they will play a landlord and another participant will play a tenant who hasn't paid rent. Before the interaction, some participants were told that their goal was to get the tenant to pay the debt quickly (i.e., a confrontational goal), while others were told their goal was to maintain a long-term relationship with the tenant (i.e., a collaboration goal).

Consistent with the idea that anger promotes confrontation, whereas happiness promotes collaboration (e.g., Barry, Fulmer, & Van Kleef, 2004), participants who were given the confrontational goal were more likely to try to increase their level of anger, whereas participants who were given a collaboration goal were more likely to try to increase their level of happiness before the interaction. Such findings demonstrate that what people want to feel depends on the goals they pursue in the given context. Such evidence is also at odds with the assumption of

the short-term hedonic approach that what people want to feel is fixed (i.e., high pleasure and low pain) across contexts.

## Different People May Be Motivated to Feel Different Emotions

Because people vary in the goals they pursue, the instrumental approach to emotion regulation predicts that people should vary in what they want to feel. The instrumental approach to emotion regulation expects people to differ in what they want to feel, as a function of the goals they pursue. In support of this prediction, we found consistent differences in what people want to feel as a function of two basic motivational dispositions: neuroticism and extraversion.

In a counterintuitive set of studies, we've shown that individuals who are highly motivated to avoid threats (i.e., high neurotics) were more likely to try to increase their level of worry before engaging in potentially threatening tasks (Tamir, 2005). Doing so, in turn, facilitated their performance. Individuals who prioritize the avoidance of threats, therefore, may be more likely to recruit emotions that help them do so successfully (e.g., worry). Similarly, we found that individuals who are highly motivated to approach rewards (i.e., high extraverts) were more likely to try to increase their level of happiness before potentially rewarding tasks (Tamir, 2009b). Taken together, such findings suggest that emotional preferences depend on the goals people are inclined to pursue.

Other laboratories have also found similar evidence in other domains of individual differences. For instance, people differ in their motivation to repair unpleasant affect as a function of self-esteem (Heimpel, Wood, Marshall, & Brown, 2002; Wood, Heimpel, & Michela, 2003). Specifically, people with low self-esteem are less motivated than their high self-esteem counterparts to decrease unpleasant feelings. Consistent with the instrumental approach to emotion regulation, such differences appear to be driven by self-verification goals (Wood, Stager, & Whittington, 2008).

People also differ in what they want to feel as a function of culture. Tsai, Knutsen, and Fung (2006) have shown that Americans value high-arousal pleasant emotions (e.g., excitement) more than Chinese, whereas Chinese value low-arousal pleasant emotions (e.g., calmness) more than Americans. When given the opportunity to regulate their feelings, Americans are more likely than Chinese to try to increase their excitement, as compared to calmness. Consistent with the predictions of the instrumental approach to emotion regulation, such cultural variation may be driven by differences in the propensity to pursue influence and adjustment goals (Tsai, Miao, Seppala, Fung, & Yeung, 2007).

Individual differences in what people want to feel depend not only on the goals people pursue. As highlighted in expectancy-value models of self-regulation, what people want depends on the outcomes they expect (e.g., Fishbein & Ajzen, 1975). In the case of emotion regulation, this implies that people might vary in what they want to feel, depending on their beliefs about the likely outcomes of their emotions. Consistent with this proposition, we found that the extent to which people wanted to feel an emotion depended on whether they believed it would be useful to them. For example, people who believed fear would be useful for a task were more likely to increase their level of fear before completing the task, whereas those who believed excitement would be useful were more likely to increase their level of excitement (Tamir & Ford, 2009). Interestingly, such beliefs about the instrumental nature of emotions may or may not be accessible to conscious awareness (Tamir, Chiu, & Gross, 2007).

Similar to the instrumental approach to emotion regulation, the short-term hedonic approach also predicts that people should vary in what they want to feel, but for different reasons. Whereas the instrumental approach attributes individual differences to differences in the goals people pursue or to differences in their beliefs about the utility of emotions, the short-term hedonic approach attributes such differences to variation in hedonic preferences.

According to the short-term hedonic approach, people vary in the level and type of emotional experiences they find most pleasurable (Larsen, 2000). For instance, individuals high in extraversion may find excitement more pleasant than calmness, whereas the opposite may be true for individuals low in extraversion (Rusting & Larsen, 1995). Such differences, in turn, would lead extraverts to prefer excitement and introverts to prefer calmness. Individual differences in hedonic preferences may explain some of the variance in what people want to feel. However, as indicated by the findings above, individual differences in what people want to feel also depend on the goals they pursue and their beliefs about the utility of emotions.

Taken together, the findings reviewed in this section provide direct empirical support for the three main predictions of the instrumental approach to emotion regulation—namely, that people can be motivated to feel bad, that people are motivated to feel different emotions in different contexts, and that different people may be motivated to feel different emotions. Whereas the instrumental approach can also account for cases of emotion regulation that are driven by short-term hedonic considerations (i.e., the increase of pleasant and decrease of unpleasant emotions), the short-term hedonic approach fails to account for cases of emotion regulation that are driven by instrumental considerations (e.g., the increase of unpleasant and decrease of pleasant emotions). Thus, the instrumental account of emotion regulation subsumes the short-term hedonic account and serves as a broader and more comprehensive approach to emotion regulation.

## Moving Forward

To date, both the hedonic and the eudaimonic views of optimal human functioning have made substantial contributions to the fields of emotion regulation and positive psychology. However, each approach has weaknesses that limit its potential to serve as a single framework for either emotion regulation or positive psychology. What is needed at this point is an overarching approach that subsumes the hedonic conception but moves us beyond a strictly pleasure-and-pain calculus.

In the domain of emotion regulation, the instrumental approach suggests how a single framework can account for both hedonic and eudaimonic aspects of optimal functioning. It also demonstrates how using such a framework can give rise to novel and testable predictions that shed light on new phenomena. We believe that by offering a broad and flexible view of optimal emotional functioning, the instrumental approach has the potential of making important contributions to the study of emotion and emotion regulation. Furthermore, the instrumental approach sets a new and exciting path for positive psychology. These possible contributions are detailed below.

### Moving the Study of Emotion Forward

By highlighting the expected implications of emotions for goal pursuit, the instrumental approach to emotion regulation revives the interest in the function of emotions. To describe healthy emotion regulation, it becomes crucial to identify not only which emotions are pleasant or unpleasant to experience, but also which emotions are adaptive for the pursuit of particular goals in a given context. For instance, if anger promotes confrontational behavior, it may be more adaptive to increase anger than to decrease it before a fight. The instrumental approach to emotion regulation highlights the importance of identifying which emotions are functional and at what level of intensity.

Perhaps even more importantly, the instrumental approach to emotion regulation highlights the idea that both pleasant and unpleasant emotions can be useful at times. Since the early days of our discipline, psychologists have studied the maladaptive nature of unpleasant emotions. With the rise of positive psychology, psychologists have begun to study the adaptive nature of pleasant emotions (Fredrickson, 1998, 2001; Lyubomirksy, King, & Diener, 2005). What remains to be studied in depth, however, is the adaptive nature of unpleasant emotions (e.g., de Hooge, Breugelmans, & Zeelenberg, 2008), as well as the maladaptive nature of pleasant emotions. The instrumental approach to emotion regulation propels emotion researchers to tackle this unchartered frontier and examine emotions not only as end-states but also as potentially useful means in goal pursuit.

## Moving the Study of Emotion Regulation Forward

The instrumental approach has the potential to advance the science of emotion regulation. First, the instrumental approach brings novel and important questions to the forefront. For example, because the short-term hedonic approach assumes that people want to feel good at any given moment, very few studies have examined what people actually want to feel. As reviewed above, however, people prefer different emotions in different contexts. Such preferences, in turn, set the course for the entire process of emotion regulation. Exploring the nature of such emotional preferences, what causes them, how they develop, and how they can be modified is an important avenue for future research.

Second, by placing emotion regulation in the broader realm of self-regulation, the instrumental approach renders theories of self-regulation applicable to the study of emotion regulation.

For instance, self-regulation research has shown that goals can guide behavior even when they operate outside of conscious awareness (Bargh, Gollwitzer, Lee-Chai, Barndollar, & Trotschel, 2001). By applying this principle to the emotion domain, the instrumental approach raises the possibility that emotion regulation can be propelled by goals operating outside of conscious awareness. Although it remains to be tested, support for this idea would have important pragmatic implications.

Third, whereas the short-term hedonic approach views emotion regulation as driven exclusively by hedonic goals, the instrumental approach accommodates the possibility of both hedonic and instrumental motives in emotion regulation. This implies that a person may be motivated to feel a particular emotion for either hedonic or instrumental reasons (or both). An interesting question, in this respect, is whether emotion regulation differs as a function of the motives that underlie it. For instance, is an attempt to increase happiness in order to feel good different from an attempt to increase happiness in order to obtain a reward? Future research could help clarify such matters.

Finally, the short-term hedonic approach fosters a relatively deterministic view of emotion regulation, where emotional preferences are nearly impossible to change. In contrast, the instrumental approach fosters a much more flexible and dynamic view of emotion regulation, where emotional preferences are malleable and context-dependent. What people try to feel, according to this perspective, depends not only on innate predispositions, but also on knowledge about emotions, values, and prior learning. This approach, we believe, is not only more promising scientifically, it is also more hopeful.

## Moving the Study of Positive Psychology Forward

Many positive psychologists and most emotion researchers use the terms "positive" and "pleasant" almost synonymously. But is positive psychology the psychology of pleasure? The answer is a resounding no. Both hedonic and eudaimonic approaches to well-being view optimal human functioning as going beyond pleasure per se (e.g., Kesebir & Diener, 2008). If unpleasant emotions can promote professional accomplishments, the maintenance of a supportive social network, self-fulfillment, and virtue—are these emotions truly "negative"?

Although many view unpleasant emotions as inherently negative and pleasant emotions as inherently positive, this view is slowly beginning to shift. For instance, there is now evidence showing that investment in personal goals, a crucial prerequisite of self-fulfillment, is associated with an increased level of worry (Pomerantz, Saxon, & Oishi, 2000). Self-fulfillment, therefore, may benefit from some degree of unpleasant emotions (Ryff & Singer, 1998). Similarly, recent evidence suggests that the people who report the highest level of happiness are actually not the ones who achieve the highest level of professional success, as indicated by levels of income and education (Oishi, Diener, & Lucas, 2007). Apparently, some degree of unpleasant emotions may be necessary to succeed. Even in the domain of interpersonal relationships, the expression of unpleasant emotions may carry certain benefits (Graham, Huang, Clark, & Helgeson, 2008).

Past research has shown that the experience of unpleasant emotions is strongly and negatively associated with well-being (e.g., Diener & Lucas, 2000). Yet, recent evidence demonstrates that the strength of this association varies by culture. Compared to collectivistic cultures, in individualistic cultures the experience of pleasant emotions is more strongly related to life satisfaction than the absence of unpleasant emotions (Kuppens, Realo, & Diener, 2008).

These findings resonate with an instrumental approach to emotion regulation, according to which all emotions can potentially contribute to well-being when they are experienced in the appropriate context, at the right level of intensity, and for an appropriate duration. "Positive," therefore, should not be defined as "pleasant" but as that which promotes optimal functioning. "Positive emotions," in turn, could be either pleasant or unpleasant, depending on their implications for well-being.

A motivated view of optimal functioning highlights the dual role of emotions in both the process and the outcome of well-being. In doing so, it can help bridge the hedonic and eudaimonic traditions. For instance, it can explain why indices of eudaimonic well-being are linked to pleasant emotions over time (e.g., Sheldon & Niemiec, 2006), why feeling pleasant emotions at all times may be less adaptive for well-being (e.g., Oishi et al., 2007), and why the experience of pleasant emotions can lead to perceptions of successful goal pursuit (e.g., King et al., 2006). It also points to the importance of studying the role of context in well-being (see also Ryan & Huta, 2009).

By providing a framework that integrates both the hedonic and the eudaimonic views of optimal functioning, the instrumental approach to emotion regulation offers a much more dynamic and sensitive view of optimal emotions. This view dramatically changes the role of emotion regulation in well-being. By following the path of the instrumental approach, positive psychology could be similarly transformed.

## Concluding Comment

The study of emotion regulation inevitably informs and is informed by positive psychology. In this chapter, we examined the parallel trajectories of emotion regulation and positive psychology in light of different conceptions of optimal functioning. We suggested that the hedonic view of optimal functioning, which has dominated research in emotion regulation as well as positive psychology, suffers from important limitations. We then briefly described a broader, motivated view of optimal functioning and reviewed the instrumental approach to emotion regulation as an approach that builds on this broader view and applies it to the study of emotion regulation.

By offering a theoretical framework that accounts for all types of emotion regulation, the instrumental approach significantly broadens our understanding of emotion, emotion regulation, and positive psychology. Furthermore, it demonstrates the benefits of a broader approach to optimal functioning and paves the way for bridging research on pleasure, emotion, and motivation. We are hopeful that positive psychologists will follow the lead of the instrumental approach to emotion regulation and formulate a similar approach to positive psychology that encompasses both hedonic and eudaimonic approaches. Such an approach, in turn, should highlight the positive nature of all emotional experiences and the role of emotion regulation in promoting emotional and psychological functioning, beyond pleasure and pain.

*References*

Andrade, E. B., & Ho, T. H. (2008). Gaming emotions. *Working paper*. University of California, Berkeley.

Averill, J. R. (1994). I feel, therefore I am—I think. In P. Ekman & R. J. Davidson (Eds.), *The nature of emotion: Fundamental questions* (pp. 379–385). New York, NY: Oxford University Press.

Bargh, J. A., Gollwitzer, P. M., Lee-Chai, A., Barndollar, K., & Trotschel, R. (2001). The automated will: Nonconscious activation and pursuit of behavioral goals. *Journal of Personality and Social Psychology, 81,* 1014–1027.

Barrett, L. F., Mesquita, B., Ochsner, K. N., & Gross, J. J. (2007). The experience of emotion. *Annual Review of Psychology, 58,* 373–403.

Barry, B. (1999). The tactical use of emotion in negotiation. In R. J. Bies, R. J. Lewicki, & B. H. Sheppard (Eds.), *Research in negotiation in organizations* (vol. 7, pp. 93–121). Elsevier Science.

Barry, B., Fulmer, I. S., & Van Kleef, G. A. (2004). I laughed, I cried, I settled: The role of emotion in negotiation. In M. J. Gelfand & J. M. Brett (Eds.), *The handbook of negotiation and culture* (pp. 71–94). Palo Alto, CA: Stanford University Press.

Bell, K. L., & Calkins, S. D. (2000). Relationships as inputs and outputs of emotion regulation. *Psychological Inquiry, 11,* 160–162.

Bonanno, G. A. (2001). Emotion self-regulation. In T. J. Mayne & G. A. Bonanno (Eds.), *Emotions: Current issues and future directions* (pp. 251–285). New York, NY: Guilford Press.

Cantor, N., & Sanderson, C. A. (1999). Life task participation and well-being: The importance of taking part in daily life. In D. Kahneman, E. Diener & N. Schwarz (Eds.), *Well-being: The foundations of hedonic psychology* (pp. 230–243). New York, NY: Russell Sage Foundation.

Carver, C. S. (2001). Affect and the functional bases of behavior: On the dimensional structure of affective experience. *Personality and Social Psychology Review, 5,* 345–356.

Carver, C. S., & Scheier, M. F. (1998). *On the self-regulation of behavior.* New York, NY: Cambridge University Press.

Clore, G. L., & Robinson, M. D. (2000). What is emotion regulation? In search of a phenomenon. *Psychological Inquiry, 11(3),* 163–166.

Compton, W. C., Smith, M. L., Cornish, K. A., & Qualls, D. L. (1996). Factor structure of mental health measures. *Journal of Personality and Social Psychology, 71,* 406–413.

de Hooge, I. E., Breugelmans, S. M., Zeelenberg, M. (2008). Not so ugly after all: When shame acts as a commitment device. *Journal of Personality and Social Psychology, 95,* 933–943.

Denollet, J., Nyklicek, I., & Vingerhoets, A. J. J. M. (2008). Introduction: Emotions, emotion regulation, and health. In A. J. J. M. Vingerhoets,

I. Nyklicek, & J. Denollet (Eds.), *Emotion regulation: Conceptual and clinical issues* (pp. 3–11). New York, NY: Springer.

Diener, E., (1984). Subjective well-being. *Psychological Bulletin, 95,* 542–575.

Diener, E., & Lucas, R. E. (2000). Subjective emotional well-being. In M. Lewis & J. M. Haviland-Jones (Eds.), *Handbook of emotions* (2nd ed., pp. 325–337). The Guilford Press.

Diener, E., & Biswas-Diener, R. (2008). *The science of optimal happiness.* Boston, MA: Blackwell Publishing.

Eid, M., & Larsen, R. J. (2008). *The science of subjective well-being.* New York, NY: Guilford Press.

Ekman, P. (1993). Facial expression and emotion. *American Psychologist, 48,* 384–392.

Emmons, R. A. (2003). Personal goals, life meaning, and virtue: Wellsprings of a positive life. In C. L. M. Keyes, & J. Haidt (Eds.), *Flourishing: Positive psychology and the life well-lived* (pp. 105–128). Washington, DC: The American Psychological Association.

Erber, R., & Erber, M. W. (2000). The self-regulation of moods: Second thoughts on the importance of happiness in everyday life. *Psychological Inquiry, 11(3),* 142–148.

Erber, R., Wegner, D. M., & Therriault, N. (1996). On being cool and collected: Mood regulation in anticipation of social interaction. *Journal of Personality and Social Psychology, 70,* 757–766.

Fishbein, M., & Ajzen, I. (1975). *Belief, attitude, intention, and behavior: An introduction to theory and research.* Reading, MA: Addison-Wesley.

Fredrickson, B. L. (1998). What good are positive emotions? *Review of General Psychology, 2,* 300–319.

Fredrickson, B. L. (2001). The role of positive emotions in positive psychology: The broaden-and-build theory of positive emotions. *American Psychologist, 56,* 218–226.

Freud, S. (1959). *Inhibitions, symptoms, anxiety* (J. Strachey, Ed., & A. Strachey, Trans.). New York: Norton. (Original work published 1926)

Frijda, N. H. (1986). *The emotions.* New York: Cambridge University Press.

Graham, S. M., Huang, J. Y., Clark, M. S., & Helgeson, V. S. (2008). The positives of negative emotions: Willingness to express negative emotions promotes relationships. *Personality and Social Psychology Bulletin, 34,* 394–406.

Gray, J. A. (1981). A critique of Eysenck's theory of personality. In H. J. Eysenck (Ed.), *A model of personality* (pp. 246–276). Berlin, Germany: Springer.

Gross, J. J. (1998). The emerging field of emotion regulation: An integrative review. *Review of General Psychology, 2,* 271–299.

Gross, J. J. (1999). Emotion regulation: Past, present, future. *Cognition and Emotion, 13,* 551–573.

Gross, J. J. (2007). *Handbook of emotion regulation.* New York, NY: Guilford Press.

Hayes, S. C., Strosahl, K. D., & Wilson, K. G. (1999) *Acceptance and commitment therapy: An experiential approach to behavior change.* New York: The Guilford Press.

Heimpel, S. A., Wood, J. V., Marshall, M. A., & Brown, J. D. (2002). Do people with low self-esteem really want to feel better? Self-esteem differences in motivation to repair negative moods. *Journal of Personality and Social Psychology, 82,* 128–147.

Hochschild, A. R. (1979). Emotion work, feeling rules, and social structure. *American Journal of Sociology, 85,* 551–575.

Izard, C. E. (1977). *Human emotion.* New York, NY: Plenum.

Kahneman, D. (1999). Objective happiness. In D. Kahneman, E. Diener, & N. Schwarz (Eds.), *Well-being: The foundations of hedonic psychology* (pp. 3–25). New York, NY: Russell Sage Foundation.

Kahneman, D., Diener, E., & Schwarz, N. (1999). *Well-being: The foundations of hedonic psychology.* New York, NY: Russell Sage Foundation.

Kashdan, T. B., Biswas-Diener, R., & King, L. A. (2008). Reconsidering happiness: The costs of distinguishing between hedonics and eudaimonia. *Journal of Positive Psychology, 3,* 219–233.

Kasser, T., & Ryan, R. M. (1996). A dark side of the American dream: Correlates of financial success as a central life aspiration. *Journal of Personality and Social Psychology, 65,* 410–422.

Kesebir, P., & Diener, Ed. (2008). In pursuit of happiness: Empirical answers to philosophical questions. *Perspectives on Psychological Science, 3,* 117–125.

King, L. A., Hicks, J. A., Krull, J. L., & Del Gaiso, A. K. (2006). Positive affect and the experience of meaning in life. *Journal of Personality and Social Psychology, 90,* 179–196.

King, L. A., & Napa, C. K. (1998). What makes life good? *Journal of Personality and Social Psychology, 75,* 156–165.

Kuppens, P., Realo, A., & Diener, E. (2008). The role of positive and negative emotions in life satisfaction judgment across nations. *Journal of Personality and Social Psychology, 95,* 66–75.

Larsen, R. J. (2000). Toward a science of mood regulation. *Psychological Inquiry, 11(3),* 129–141.

Larsen, R. J., & Prizmic, Z. (2008). Regulation of emotional well-being: Overcoming the hedonic treadmill. In M. Eid & R. J. Larsen (Eds.), *The science of subjective well-being* (pp. 258–289). New York, NY: Guilford Press.

Levenson, R. W. (1994). Human emotion: A functional view. In P. Ekman & R. J. Davidson (Eds.), *The nature of emotion: Fundamental questions* (pp. 123–126). New York, NY: Oxford University Press.

Lyubomirsky, S., King, L., & Diener, E. (2005). The benefits of frequent positive affect: Does happiness lead to success? *Psychological Bulletin, 131,* 803–855.

Mayer, J. D., & Salovey, P. (1995). Emotional intelligence and the construction and regulation of feelings. *Applied and Preventive Psychology, 4,* 197–208.

McMahon, D. M. (2006). *Happiness: A history.* New York, NY: Atlantic Monthly Press.

Mischel, W., Shoda, Y., & Rodriguez, M. L. (1989). Delay of gratification in children. *Science, 244,* 933–938.

Oishi, S., Diener, E., & Lucas, R. E. (2007). The optimum level of well-being: Can people be too happy? *Perspectives on Psychological Science, 2,* 346–360.

Parrott, W. G. (1993). Beyond hedonism: Motives for inhibiting good moods and for maintaining bad moods. In D. M. Wegner & J. W. Pennebaker (Eds.), *Handbook of mental control* (pp. 278–305). New Jersey: Prentice Hall.

Parrott, W. G. (2001). Implications of dysfunctional emotions for understanding how emotions function. *Review of General Psychology, 5,* 180–186.

Pomerantz, E., Saxon, J. L., & Oishi, S. (2000). The psychological trade-offs of goal investment. *Journal of Personality and Social Psychology, 79,* 617–630.

Rusting, C. L., & Larsen, R. J. (1995). Moods as sources of stimulation: Relationships between personality and desired mood states. *Personality and Individual Differences, 18,* 321–329.

Ryan, R. M., & Deci, E. L. (2000). On happiness and human potentials: A review of research on hedonic and eudaimonic well-being. *Annual Review of Psychology, 52,* 141–166.

Ryan, R. M., & Huta, V. (2009). Wellness as healthy functioning or wellness as happiness: The importance of eudaimonic thinking (A response to the Kashdan et al. and Waterman discussion). *The Journal of Positive Psychology, 4,* 202–204.

Ryff, C. D. (1989). Happiness is everything, or is it? Explorations on the meaning of psychological well-being. *Journal of Personality and Social Psychology, 57,* 1069–1081.

Ryff, C. D., & Keyes, C. L. M. (1995). The structure of psychological well-being revisited. *Journal of Personality and Social Psychology, 69,* 719–727.

Ryff, C. D., & Singer, B. (1998). The contours of positive human health. *Psychological Inquiry, 9,* 1–28.

Seligman, M. E. P. (2003). Foreword: The past and future of positive psychology. In C. L. M. Keyes & J. Haidt (Eds.), *Flourishing: Positive psychology and the life well-lived* (pp. xi-xx). Washington, DC: American Psychological Association.

Seligman, M. E. P., & Csikszentmihalyi, M. (2000). Positive psychology: An introduction. *American Psychologist, 55,* 5–14.

Sheldon, K. M., & Niemiec, C. (2006). It's not just the amount that counts: Balanced need-satisfaction also affects well-being. *Journal of Personality and Social Psychology, 91,* 331–341.

Sutton, R. I. (1991). Maintaining norms about expressed emotions: The case of bill collectors. *Administrative Science Quarterly, 36,* 245–268.

Tamir, M. (2009a). What do people want to feel and why? Pleasure and utility in emotion regulation. *Current Directions in Psychological Science, 18,* 101–105.

Tamir, M. (2009b). Differential preferences for happiness; Extraversion and trait-consistent emotion regulation. *Journal of Personality, 77,* 447–470.

Tamir, M. (2005). Don't worry, be happy? Neuroticism, trait-consistent affect regulation, and performance. *Journal of Personality and Social Psychology, 89,* 449–461.

Tamir, M., Chiu, C. Y., & Gross, J. J. (2007). Business or pleasure? Utilitarian versus hedonic consideration in emotion regulation. *Emotion, 7,* 546–554.

Tamir, M., & Ford, B. (2009). Choosing to be afraid: Preferences for fear as a function of goal pursuit. *Emotion., 9,* 488–497.

Tamir, M., & Ford, B. (2009). *Instrumental Emotion Regulation in Negotiations: Goals and the Expected Usefulness of Emotions.* Manuscript under review.

Tamir, M., Mitchell, C., & Gross, J. J. (2008). Hedonic and instrumental motives in anger regulation. *Psychological Science, 19,* 324–328.

Thayer, R. E. (2000). Mood regulation and general arousal systems. *Psychological Inquiry, 11,* 202–204.

Tooby, J., & Cosmides, L. (1990). The past explains the present: Emotional adaptations and the structure of ancestral environments. *Ethology and Sociobiology, 11,* 375–424.

Tsai, J. L., Knutson, B., & Fung, H. H. (2006). Cultural variation in affect valuation. *Journal of Personality and Social Psychology, 90,* 288–307.

Tsai, J. L., Miao, F. F., Seppala, E., Fung, H. H., & Yeung, D. Y. (2007). Influence and adjustment goals: Sources of cultural differences in ideal affect. *Journal of Personality and Social Psychology, 92,* 1102–1117.

Waterman, A. S. (1993). Two conceptions of happiness: Contrasts of personal expressiveness (eudaimonia) and hedonic enjoyment. *Journal of Personality and Social Psychology, 64,* 678–691.

Wood, J. V., Heimpel, S. A., & Michela, J. L. (2003). Savoring versus dampening: Self-esteem differences in regulating positive affect. *Journal of Personality and Social Psychology, 85,* 566–580.

Wood, J. V., Stager, P., & Whittington, E. J. (2008). *It's my party and I'll cry if I want to: Self-esteem differences in positive and negative affect regulation.* Talk given at the annual meeting of the Society for Personality and Social Psychology, Tampa, FL.

# 7

# The Positive Psychology of Positive Emotions: An Avuncular View

*Shigehiro Oishi and Jaime L. Kurtz*

## Introduction

Since its inception in the late 1990s, the positive psychology movement has inspired a wealth of new research on positive emotions (e.g., Emmons, 1999; Fredrickson, 1998, 2001; Seligman & Csikszentmihalyi, 2000). In particular, recent years have seen an explosion in the examination of positive moral emotions, including awe (e.g., Keltner, & Haidt, 2003), admiration (e.g., Haidt, & Seder, 2009), gratitude (e.g., McCullough, Tsang, & Emmons, 2004), and other related constructs such as hope (e.g., Snyder, 2002) and savoring (e.g., Bryant & Veroff, 2007). Also, whereas an earlier generation of positive emotion researchers had never engaged in intervention studies (perhaps to remain in the basic research areas), many positive psychologists have boldly delved into intervention studies to improve people's well-being (e.g., Emmons & McCullough, 2003; Lyubomirsky, Sousa, & Dickerhoof, 2006; Seligman, Steen, Park, & Peterson, 2005). Now academic psychologists can investigate moral emotions and/or conduct an intervention study without risking their academic reputation. This is a remarkable accomplishment

of the positive psychology movement, and the leaders of positive psychology (e.g., Martin Seligman, Christopher Peterson, Robert Emmons) should be congratulated for courageously breaking the taboo in academic psychology, paving a wider and smoother road for a younger generation of positive psychologists, and connecting psychological science with the concerns of ordinary citizens as well as those of policy makers. The mounting body of research puts positive psychology in the favorable position of being able to provide practical advice to an eager audience. However, it is important to take a step back and assess exactly how far the field has come and what it needs to focus on next.

In this chapter, we offer a critique of positive emotion research with the goal of suggesting specific ways positive psychology could move forward. Although research on positive emotion has made tremendous inroads in the past decade, we believe that several areas need further addressing. First, positive psychology often appears "thin" at this point, partially because it is not founded in a historical perspective (see Keltner & Haidt, 2003 for an exception). Because the leaders of positive psychology tend to frame positive psychology as a new endeavor, researchers do not pay enough tribute to an earlier generation of positive emotion researchers. We believe that positive psychologists must recognize the rich tradition of positive emotion research conducted since the early 1900s. A historical perspective will provide insight into what to study, how to study it, and how to avoid the demise of the entire scientific endeavor on emotion that took place in the 1940s and 1950s. Second, we believe that positive psychologists must make an explicit connection with other contemporary research on the topics relevant to positive psychology (e.g., empathy, willpower, cooperation) to broaden its intellectual base. Third, although most people in the U.S. want to be happier and most positive psychologists want to make people happier as well, we propose that it is critical to test the tacit assumption of positive psychology that the happier, the better. Fourth, we think it important for positive psychologists to acknowledge that negative emotions play a non-trivial role in a well-lived life, and to begin to fully examine how negative emotions fit into positive psychology. Fifth, although recent intervention studies were successful, it is important to examine the longer-term effects of these interventions in the future. Finally, we propose that more cross-cultural research is necessary to understand the universality of our findings.

## Taking Stock

### An Intellectual Ancestor of Positive Emotion Research

Psychologists have investigated positive emotions since the very beginning of psychological science. William James (1890/1950) famously proposed his theory of emotion in *The Principles of Psychology*, in which he distinguished "coarser emotions" such as love, joy, and pride from "subtler emotions" or moral, intellectual, and aesthetic feelings such as moral satisfaction, gratitude, and curiosity. For instance, James (1892/1963) discussed moral feelings by stating "the voice breaks and the eyes moisten when the moral truth is felt" (p. 340). It is obvious that these moral, intellectual, and aesthetic feelings capture one dominant force in positive psychology of today, namely Jonathan Haidt and colleagues' work on awe, admiration, and elevation (e.g., Haidt & Seder, 2009; Keltner & Haidt, 2003); Robert Emmons and colleagues' work on gratitude

(e.g., Emmons, & McCullough, 2004); and Todd Kashdan and colleagues' work on curiosity (e.g., Kashdan, Rose, & Fincham, 2004).

Another pioneering psychologist, William McDougall (1908/1921), made an important distinction between pleasure and various positive emotions (e.g., joy, happiness, admiration, gratitude) and envisioned the scientific study of human instincts, emotions, and the development of moral emotions to be the foundation of psychological science. He conceived curiosity and parental instincts (or tender emotions and sympathy) to be two of the most important instincts. In the chapter entitled "Nature of the Sentiments," McDougall further detailed various positive moral emotions. For instance, he described admiration as follows: "The primary condition of their excitement is the presence of a person bigger and more powerful than oneself; and, when we admire such an object as a picture of a machine, or other work of art, the emotion still has this social character and personal reference; the creator of minds as the object of our emotion, and often we say, 'what a wonderful man he is!' (p. 134). McDougall defined awe as "of many shades, ranging from that in which admiration is but slightly tinged with fear to that in which fear is but slightly tinged with admiration" (p. 135), reverence as "the religious emotion par excellence," and gratitude as "a binary compound of tender emotion and negative self-feeling" (p. 136).

In addition, McDougall (1908/1921) deemed these positive emotions to be central to the foundation of a civilized society. For instance, he stated that "aesthetic appreciation of the beauty of fine character and conduct may play a large part in the genesis of the ideal of conduct and of the sentiment of love for this ideal" (p. 233). In other words, similar to the current generation of positive psychologists, McDougall viewed positive emotions such as admiration, awe, and gratitude as important research topics and the critical building blocks of a well-functioning society. Moreover, he presented an idea that was a precursor to the current form of eudaimonic theory of well-being (e.g., Ryan & Deci, 2001; Seligman, 2002; Sheldon, 2004), stating that "happiness arises from the harmonious operation of all the sentiments of a well-organised and unified personality, one in which the principal sentiments support one another in a succession of actions all of which tend toward the same or closely allied and harmonious ends," and that "to add to the sum of happiness is not merely to add to the sum of pleasures, but is rather to contribute to the development of higher forms of personality, personalities capable, not merely of pleasure, as the animals are, but of happiness" (p. 160). In sum, although McDougall's book is often conceived as a theory of instincts today, it featured various prosocial positive emotions and foreshadowed the emergence of positive psychology eight decades later.

Whereas the central interests of James (1890/1950) and McDougall (1908/1921) were broader than positive emotions per se, there were several psychologists whose main interests centered squarely on positive emotions. For instance, the psychologist George Van Ness Dearborn published the book entitled *The Emotion of Joy* in 1899, summarizing the literature on the psychophysiology and psychobiology of positive emotions. In the book entitled *The Influence of Joy*, Dearborn (1916) went on to catalogue the effect of joy on digestion, blood circulation, and nervous system. This book also provided a primitive version of Isen's (1987) work on positive moods and creativity and Fredrickson's (2001) celebrated broaden-and-build theory of positive emotion by explicitly linking happiness and creativity. Furthermore, in the chapter entitled "The economics of happiness," Dearborn anticipated the positive consequences of happiness that Lyubomirsky, King, and Diener (2005) empirically documented nearly a century later by stating that "a happy girl in a paper-box factory will probably make at least five percent more boxes in a day than the same girl unhappy can pile up. Moreover, the work done under the stimulus of joy is not only faster but better in every way, for it means an attentive interest in the adjustments, making them more exact" (p. 197). Dearborn would be considered a positive psychologist today, as he was very much interested in improving ordinary people's levels of happiness. He stated, "We may cordially agree with sundry theorists that gladness as an effective agent in our behavior is eminently easy of cultivation. Were it not so, this book were of no use beyond its narrow and problematic scientific interest" (p. 218).

Moreover, a cursory look at the empirical literature makes it clear that there was a period of active research on positive emotions in the early 1900s (e.g., Gardiner, 1916). Most notably, the memory for happy events has been actively investigated at that time (see Oishi, 2000, for a review on this literature). For instance, Henderson (1911) showed that over the entire lifespan,

adults remembered more happy events than unhappy events (55.1% vs. 33.1%, 11.8% indifferent events). When asked immediately after a vacation period, schoolchildren recalled more happy experiences than unhappy experiences (Wohlgemuth, 1923). The first major review paper was published in *Psychological Review* in 1930, in which Meltzer examined all of the 25 empirical papers on memory for pleasant and unpleasant experiences. In 1938, Gilbert published the second review paper in *Psychological Review*, summarizing 20 empirical papers on the same topic since Meltzer's review. Combined with other empirical papers on sympathy (e.g., Meltzer, 1939), empathy (e.g., Gordon, 1917), gratitude (e.g., Baumgarten-Tramer, 1938), and curiosity (Kendrew, 1930), then, it can be said that the first generation of psychological scientists did study topics directly relevant to positive psychology of today.

The number of empirical papers on positive emotions became noticeably smaller, however, in the 1950s and 1960s, for several reasons. First, McDougall's (1908) theory of instincts was heavily influenced by Darwin, and Social Darwinism came under severe attack by social scientists and behavioral psychologists who believed in environmentalism in the 1920s and 1930s. Accordingly, McDougall's theory of instinct and emotion also fell out of favor and lost its influence (see Hilgard, 1987 for a historical review). Second, the concept of emotion came under attack by empirical psychologists in the 1930s and 1940s. For instance, Meyer (1933), after describing William James as a "poet and philosopher combined," criticized the lack of definition of emotion by stating that "Now, if anybody can find a textbook on psychology in which the term 'emotion' is introduced thus honestly, and not by the novelistic back door, he can make himself distinguished as the greatest discoverer in mankind" (p. 297). He went on to conclude his *Psychological Review* article by saying that "I predict: The 'will' has virtually passed out of our scientific psychology today; the 'emotion' is bound to do the same. In 1950, American psychologists will smile at both these terms as curiosities of the past" (p. 300, see also Duffy, 1934, 1941 for a similar view; Worcester, 1933 for the oppositional view).

Although American psychologists of today might smile at Meyer (1933) and Duffy (1934, 1941) as curiosities of the past, in 1950 most American psychologists indeed thought of both "will" and "emotion" as similarly antiquated.

In the heydays of behaviorism, all the fuzzy terms were questioned and deemed unworthy of scientific psychological investigations. This is why happiness, admiration, gratitude, curiosity, and other important positive emotions were neglected for an extended period of time in American psychology (see Arnold, 1960's chapter entitled "Some positive human emotions," however, in which she discussed love, admiration, happiness, love of beauty, empathy, sympathy, and laughter). The re-emergence of positive emotion also started with "coarser emotions" that were easily manipulated or observed first (e.g., Arnold, 1960; Ekman, 1964; Isen & Levine, 1972), before the fuzzier, more complex emotions were rediscovered much later. In our humble opinion, it is important to have a historical perspective on positive emotion research because (a) it explicates the critical importance of a sound definition and the steady establishment of the nomological network (Cronbach & Meehl, 1955), preferably with behavioral indicators; (b) it helps ground the current empirical endeavors in broader theories with a clear intellectual heritage (e.g., evolutionary perspective taken by William McDougall); and (c) it allows us to appreciate and be grateful for the favorable academic atmosphere of today for positive psychologists, which should not be taken for granted.

## Intellectual Cousins of Positive Psychology

In addition to positive emotion research in the first half of the 20th century, positive psychologists should pay tribute to positive psychologies advanced by researchers who do not necessarily identify themselves as positive psychologists. When emotion research was largely dormant from the 1950s to 1970s, various important discoveries were made on the topics relevant to positive psychology. For example, Walter Mischel and his colleagues examined willpower and self-regulation using the delay of gratification paradigm, finding empirical support for William James' (1890) assertion that willpower plays an indispensable role in an individual's successful functioning (e.g., Mischel & Gilligan, 1964; Mischel, Ebbesen, & Raskoff Zeiss, 1972; Mischel, Shoda, & Rodriquez, 1989; Shoda, Mischel, & Peake, 1990; see also Fabes et al., 1999; Tangney, Baumeister, & Boone, 2004). Muzafer Sherif, Elliot Aronson, and their colleagues discovered specific ways to improve intergroup relationships (Aronson & Bridgeman, 1979; Sherif, Harvey, White, Hood, & Sherif, 1954/1961).

Daniel Batson and his colleagues investigated altruism and empathy (e.g., Coke, Batson, & McDavis, 1978; see Batson, 1991 for a review) and empirically demonstrated a bright side of human nature. Elaine Hatfield, Robert Sternberg, Arthur Aron, and others successfully showed that love can be measured and scientifically investigated (e.g., Aron & Westbay, 1996; Hatfield, & Sprecher, 1986). Since the 1970s, secure attachment has been also shown to predict better interpersonal competence and relationship quality later in life (e.g., Waters, Wippman, & Sroufe, 1979; Simpson, 1990). Furthermore, over the last two decades psychological scientists have accumulated evidence that indicates that trust, cooperation, volunteerism, and other prosocial behaviors play an important role in the foundation of a well-functioning society (e.g., Dawes & Messick, 2000; Omoto & Snyder, 1995; Penner, Dovidio, Piliavin, & Schroeder, 2005; Van Vugt, Snyder, Tyler, & Biel, 2000).

Despite the obvious link between these research programs and positive psychology, research on willpower, empathy, love, attachment, trust, cooperation, volunteerism, and positive intergroup relations has not been generally part of the positive psychology movement. It is true that the *Handbook of Positive Psychology* (Snyder & Lopez, 2002) includes chapters on empathy and love. However, it appears to us that the positive psychology movement and existing research on positive emotions and related constructs summarized above have been poorly integrated, which has contributed to the relative isolation of the positive psychology movement from the rest of psychological science. It is desirable to consciously integrate new positive emotion research with older research programs on the aforementioned topics. We believe that such an integration will "thicken" the positive psychology movement and provide a broader and more stable base for the movement.

## More Is Not Always Better

As described above, the intervention studies conducted by positive psychologists (e.g., Lyubomirsky et al., 2006; Seligman et al., 2005) made an invaluable contribution to the science and the practice of positive psychology. These studies can help improve millions of ordinary people's levels of daily functioning and feelings of happiness. Underneath these intervention studies and the philosophy of the positive psychology movement in general are two tacit assumptions that happiness is good and that the happier one is, the better off he or she is. Lyubomirsky et al. (2005) conducted a comprehensive meta-analysis and found resounding support for the first assumption that happiness is good. Specifically, happiness is associated with various positive outcomes including higher income, better health, better job performance, and more stable relationships.

But just *how* happy should a person be? The second assumption of positive psychology—that the happier, the better—requires an empirical inquiry. Namely, it is important to test whether an increase in the level of happiness is monotonically associated with an increased number of positive outcomes. We (Oishi, Diener, & Lucas, 2007; Oishi & Koo, 2008) have recently examined this very question and found that this assumption was not tenable in terms of income and education. For instance, Diener, Nickerson, Lucas, and Sandvik (2002) analyzed a large set of longitudinal data on Americans who entered one of 25 elite colleges in 1976. In this study, participants reported their cheerfulness when they were incoming college freshmen on a 5-point scale (1 = lowest 10%; 2 = below average, 3 = average, 4 = above average, 5 = highest 10%) in 1976. In 1995, these participants reported their annual income. The most cheerful in 1976 ($65,023) were making substantially more money in 1995 than did the least cheerful ($49,770). More important, the researchers found a curvilinear relation between cheerfulness in 1976 and annual income in 1995 such that participants who rated themselves as "above average" on cheerfulness in 1976 earned $65,573 in 1995, slightly more than those who rated themselves as the "highest 10%" in cheerfulness. Thus, if we use income as a criterion, the optimal level of "cheerfulness" was not the highest possible level, but rather the "above average" level. In other words, the happier is not the better.

We (Oishi, Diener, & Lucas, 2007) analyzed the Australian Youth in Transition study, which is a longitudinal study of nationally representative cohorts of young people in Australia. The respondents in this study indicated their life satisfaction ("satisfaction with life as a whole") when they were 18 years old, in 1979. They also reported their gross income in 1994, when they were 33 years old (N = 1,166). Consistent with the findings of Diener et al. (2002), those who fell in the second-highest category of life satisfaction earned more money than those in the highest category. In addition, the curvilinear relationship

between life satisfaction at one point and income at later points was replicated in two large longitudinal studies: the German Socio-Economic Panel Study and the British Household Panel Study. Similarly, we (Oishi, Diener, & Lucas, 2007) examined the longitudinal association between life satisfaction and educational attainment in the Australian Youth in Transition study (the number of years of schooling they completed beyond high school in 1987, when they were 26 years old). Similar to the income findings, the moderately satisfied groups completed more education than did the most satisfied group. Thus, the optimal level of happiness in terms of future income and educational attainment was a moderate level of happiness, not the highest level of happiness: the happier is not the better.

Interestingly, however, when we examined the longitudinal relation between life satisfaction at age 18 in 1979 and the length of their intimate relationships in 1994 in the Australian dataset, the most satisfied group in 1979 were, on average, involved in a longer intimate relationship in 1994 than the second and third satisfied groups. In short, the highest level of satisfaction may in fact be optimal in terms of relationship stability, although the happier is not the better in terms of educational achievement and income later in life.

But why is the optimal level of happiness different between achievement domains (e.g., income, education) and relationship domains? We believe that self-critical motivation serves well in the achievement domains partly because this mindset makes it clear what needs to be done to improve skills and performance. In contrast, self-complacency prevents one from clearly seeing one's weaknesses and working on these weaknesses. The epitome of self-criticism and improvement motivation, Tiger Woods spent long hours practicing to improve his already-amazing shot after winning his first Masters. Similarly, Ichiro Suzuki is known to spend hours and hours improving his swing, even though he is already one of the best hitters in Major League Baseball.

This type of perfectionism and self-improvement often brings high performance, fame, status, and wealth. The same kind of motivation applied to an intimate relationship, however, does not work as well. This mindset could lead to a realization that the current partner is less than ideal, and that a better partner is somewhere out there. Indeed, idealization of the partner is associated with higher relationship satisfaction and stable relationship (e.g., Murray, Holmes, & Griffin, 2003). In other words, positive illusion serves well in romantic relationships, in which one might not want to pay too much attention to his or her partner's weaknesses. In the 1959 film *Some Like It Hot*, the millionaire Osgood Fielding III (played by Joe E. Brown) fell in love with Daphne (played by Jack Lemmon). In the memorable ending, Daphne confessed that she was actually a man. In response, Osgood famously said, "Well, nobody's perfect!" In sum, we hypothesize that the highest possible level of happiness is associated with idealization of the partner and positive illusion about the relationship itself, which in turn results in relationship stability. In an area in which nobody can be perfect, improvement motives can be toxic.

In a recent study, we also found the down side of chronic happiness (Oishi, Diener, Choi, Kim-Prieto, & Choi, 2007). In this study, participants in the U.S., Korea, and Japan completed a daily report of events and well-being for 21 days. We estimated the impact of positive versus negative events on participants' daily well-being and found that chronically happy individuals need more positive events to offset the detrimental effect of a negative event on daily life satisfaction. For instance, chronically happy American college students required roughly two compliments to overcome one critique, whereas moderately happy Japanese were able to recover one critique with one compliment. This study points to the greater sensitivity to negative events among chronically "very happy" individuals as compared to moderately happy individuals. Being "very happy" is like standing on a very steep slope near the summit. Moving further up is difficult and requires more positive events. Slipping backward is very easy with a few negative events.

In sum, although most Americans want to be happier and most positive psychologists want to make people happier, it is important to question whether making people happier indeed translates into better functioning. If one is already moderately happy, becoming even happier seems to come with few benefits and *might* even come with a price. Like having too many choices in life (Schwartz, 2005), having more happiness might not be always better. Extending the recent effort to re-examine the basic assumptions of positive psychology (Oishi, Diener, & Lucas, 2007; Oishi et al., 2007), it is important to test whether the happier is the better for more diverse life domains such as health in the future.

## The Positive Role of Negative Emotions

Although few psychologists would advise one to be continually "maxed out" on happiness, the casual student of positive psychology may conclude that experiencing the greatest amount of happiness for the longest time possible, while avoiding any form of negative emotion, is a reasonable and important goal. Therefore, it is important that positive psychology dispel this idea by acknowledging the benefits of certain negative emotions and more directly researching how they contribute to a well-lived life.

Sadness, for instance, serves an important function simply through contrast. In the same way that a sunny day is more fully appreciated when preceded by a week of rain, happiness is experienced more fully when it is contrasted with sadness. Experiencing sadness every now and then may help to undo hedonic adaptation (Brickman & Campbell, 1971; Diener, Lucas & Napa Scollon, 2006), the process through which events lose their emotional impact over time. But how much sadness is desirable? Because "bad is stronger than good" (Baumeister, Bratslavsky, Finkenauer & Vohs, 2001), having a one-to-one balance of happiness and sadness in life is not desirable. According to Fredrickson and Lasoda (2005), psychological well-being generally requires that this number be 2.9 to 1 or above. People who reported 2.9 or more instances of positive affect for every one instance of negative affect were more likely to fit the criteria for resiliency and flourishing. Notice, however, that negative affect *is* present in this ratio and that Fredrickson and Lasoda estimate that the positive-to-negative ratio of 11.6 to 1 or higher would result in negative consequences (i.e., too much positivity in the system to be functional). Clearly, negative emotions do serve some critical function when experienced to this degree, a fact that positive psychology needs to consider in greater depth.

The affect-as-information hypothesis claims that negative affect is a signal that something in our environment is awry and needs addressing. Whereas a happy mood fosters global, heuristic processing, people in sad moods have been shown to be more detail-focused and critical in their thinking, which is important for certain kinds of problem solving (Schwarz & Clore, 1983). State-trait congruity is also an important consideration. Those high in trait levels of negative affect (e.g., neurotics) are actually motivated to maintain higher levels of momentary negative affect because it is consistent with how they view themselves (Tamir, 2005). For all people, but especially those high in neuroticism and similar traits, negative emotions serve a critical informative function.

Also, from an evolutionary standpoint, negative emotions are quite functional (Damasio, 1994; Darwin, 1872). Anger mobilizes us to defend ourselves. Disgust signals that a certain food is potentially harmful (Rozin, Haidt, & McCauley, 1993). From a functionalist perspective, then, negative emotions are critical for ensuring our survival. They also serve important self-regulatory and social functions. Guilt, for instance, is an unpleasant affective state that creates a sense of accountability in relationships and can serve as negative reinforcement. For example, giving people false feedback indicating that they were racially prejudiced induced a sense of guilt that motivated them to read articles on how to reduce prejudice on both a personal and societal level (Amodio, Devine, & Harmon-Jones, 2007). According to Baumeister, Stillwell, and Heatherton (1994), guilt may also provide lower-status people with some power or leverage in social situations, and it helps redistribute negative affect from the victim of a transgression back to the source. In a sense, guilt serves as a psychological payback that may motivate people to regulate themselves in social situations. Other self-conscious states, such as social anxiety, shame, and embarrassment, are related to our real or imagined view of how others see us and therefore serve similar self-regulatory functions (Leary, 2007).

Negative life events also serve important functions. Of course, the vast majority of us would certainly choose to avoid disease, divorce, and death of loved ones, but it is traumas such as these that contribute to wisdom and meaning in life (Janoff-Bulman & Berger, 2000). Research shows that these desirable outcomes are often the result of trying experiences that are rife with negative emotion. For instance, McAdams (2001) has found that highly generative adults report life stories that contain redemptive sequences, in which they translate something negative into something positive and meaningful: "We started with nothing—I mean nothing. It was really, really terrible. It was all rigged against us. But we kept going, and we overcame." "If it hadn't been for my divorce, I would have never gone back to school. I put my life back together. I learned new skills. I left my old life behind, thank God. I am happy today because it all turned out for the best" (McAdams, 2006, pp. 40–41). Stories like

these abound in American culture, suggesting that, although so many of us report wanting to be happier, we also see great value in overcoming life's struggles. The "good life" comes not out of simply maximizing happiness but also from finding meaning through life's trials and tribulations.

One of life's most esteemed virtues is wisdom, which, again, comes not from a life of hedonic pursuits but through engagement with the full range of emotional experience. According to Kunzmann and Baltes (2003), those high in wisdom are less likely to endorse items related to pleasurable pursuits such as being well-to-do and having fun. Moreover, wisdom is correlated with lower levels of positive affect. Psychological adjustment requires much more than just maximizing happiness. From a lifespan developmental perspective, wisdom, meaning, and psychological health are the result of active engagement with all that life has to offer, the good and the bad (Ryff, 1989).

In sum, negative emotions contribute to a full and meaningful life. There does seem to be an implicit awareness of the importance of experiencing these emotions. After all, people seek out negative emotions when they willingly go to scary movies, read tragic love stories, or jump out of airplanes. However, the positive effects of negative emotions have received little attention from positive psychologists. As positive psychology moves forward, it is essential to begin to incorporate the full spectrum of affective experience into understanding what makes a life meaningful and fulfilling.

## Examining Long-Term Effects of Positive Interventions

One challenge inherent in research on wisdom, meaning, and other markers of a well-lived life is the fact that these studies are often correlational and retrospective. For example, people's life stories are reconstructed in an interview format and prone to memory biases (McAdams, 2001), making it difficult to really determine and give advice on how to develop a meaningful life. Given these limitations, a tremendous contribution of positive psychology has been the proliferation of longitudinal positive intervention studies, in which participants incorporate various cognitive strategies and behavioral changes into their daily lives, with the goal of increasing happiness and promoting optimal functioning. Fordyce (1977) pioneered this technique by randomly assigning a sample of non-depressed college students to one of the following: (1) an insight program, in which students read the author's book *Human Happiness: The Findings of Psychological Research*, which presented research findings on factors related to happiness, and try to apply the book's advice to their own lives; (2) the fundamentals program, in which participants were asked to apply nine specific pieces of advice on happiness (e.g., "become more present-oriented," "become more active," etc.) to their own lives; (3) the activities program, in which participants generated their own list of what makes them happy and tried to do them every day of the study; or (4) a control group. Although measurement of happiness was rudimentary at the time of this study, Fordyce found that the fundamentals and activities programs increased participants' happiness over the course of the study.

Although the twenty-odd years following Fordyce's work saw a sharp rise in the number of self-help books suggesting techniques on how to live a happier life, it was the advent of positive psychology that inspired researchers to study these techniques empirically. Armed with validated measures of happiness and related constructs, recent researchers have begun to establish evidence that it is indeed possible to make sustainable changes to one's level of happiness (Lyubomirsky, Sheldon, & Schkade, 2005).

Expressive writing is one technique that has been tested for its therapeutic nature. Specifically, writing about negative life experiences carries a variety of benefits, such as improved physical and mental health (Pennebaker, & Seagal, 1999; Lyubomirsky, Sousa, & Dickerhoof, 2006), presumably because participants are gaining closure and finding order and meaning in their difficulties. The results of writing about *positive* life experiences, however, are more mixed. In a variation on Pennebaker's paradigm, Burton and King (2004) found that writing about a very positive life experience for 20 minutes on three consecutive days created immediate increases in positive mood relative to controls. Also, this activity produced higher instances of physical health (as measured by fewer trips to the campus health center), even after three months. However, Lyubomirsky, Sousa, and Dickerhoof (2006) found that writing about positive life experiences was actually not as beneficial as thinking and reflecting on them. While more research on this is needed, Wilson and Gilbert (2008) offer a compelling reason for this discrepancy: Constructing a logical, ordered narrative about a positive experience might "explain it away."

Perhaps it is beneficial to keep positive experiences slightly mysterious or inexplicable so a person continues to dwell on them (Kurtz, Wilson, & Gilbert, 2007).

In another set of studies, Emmons and McCullough (2003) empirically tested the old adage "count your blessings" by randomly assigning participants to either list things they were grateful for, list daily hassles, or generate downward social comparisons. They found that expressing gratitude led to increased mood on both a daily and weekly basis. This strategy was effective for both undergraduates and adults suffering from neuromuscular disease. Sheldon and Lyubomirsky (2006) also randomly assigned a sample of college students to count their blessings and contrasted this with another activity: visualizing one's "best possible self." Doing both of these activities brought an immediate increase in positive affect when compared to a neutral condition ("reflect on the details of your day"). Moreover, these increases were maintained for the duration of the study (four weeks) but only when the activities were done regularly. Recent research by Lyubomirsky, Dickerhoof, Boehm, and Sheldon (2008) examined the effectiveness of two similar cognitive strategies: expressing optimism and practicing gratitude. College students were randomly assigned to practice one of these strategies or a neutral control once a week for eight weeks. These exercises significantly increased participants' happiness over the course of the study, but they were most beneficial for those who were motivated to become happier.

In what is possibly the most ambitious intervention study to date, Seligman and colleagues (2005) used a Web-based randomized controlled trial design to examine the effectiveness of six different activities over a six-month period. These activities were: paying someone a "gratitude visit," listing three good things that happened that day, imagining a time when the participant was at his or her best, identifying signature strengths (Peterson & Seligman, 2004), trying to use signature strengths in a new way, and a placebo control in which participants wrote about their early memories. Of these six activities, using signature strengths and listing three good things that happened that day increased happiness and reduced symptoms of depression over the course of the study, and the gratitude visit had similar benefits that lasted about a month. Not surprisingly, participants' willingness to continue with the activity played a large role in the degree to which it was effective.

Taken together, then, these studies make a fairly convincing argument for the idea that it is possible to make sustainable changes in happiness. However, some questions still remain. For instance, these studies ranged in time from several days to six months. It is unclear as to whether these activities and cognitive strategies would bring happiness over the long term. In fact, it is highly possible that these activities might be subject to hedonic adaptation (Brickman & Campbell, 1971; Wilson & Gilbert, 2008). For example, counting one's blessings might lose emotional power if the person runs out of blessings to count over time. Along these lines, once the blessings become difficult to generate, the activity could actually backfire (Schwarz, 1998). Therefore, it is important to examine whether these interventions are effective over a long period of time. As Lyubomirsky (2008) suggests, these happiness-increasing activities might have to be varied to continue to be beneficial, but further research should establish exactly *how* they should be varied.

While research on positive interventions certainly gives reason for optimism, one of the next steps for positive psychology is to move beyond speculation and convincingly determine the feasibility of these interventions in the long term. Also, future research should examine their utility at various stages in the lifespan. Do they work for children? For older people? Impressive as Seligman and colleagues' (2005) intervention is, it used a self-selected sample of people with Internet access who chose to visit a Web site with the goal of improving their happiness. They were largely middle-aged and well educated. The other interventions above examined mainly college students. These interventions might work better for certain people than others. More long-term studies should examine for whom they are most effective, and why. Although Sheldon and Lyubomirsky (2006) have found that happiness-increasing activities are most effective when the person feels a certain degree of "fit," or self-concordant motivation (e.g., extreme introverts might feel too uncomfortable to reap the benefits of paying someone a gratitude visit), if this research is to be truly prescriptive, more focus on this notion is needed. Positive interventions have also been proposed for the treatment of depression and anxiety (Seligman, Rashid, & Parks, 2006). Initial assessments of this positive psychotherapy, which involves activities similar to those described above, suggest that it is very effective in reducing the symptoms of anxiety and depression. However, the effects of it also need to be examined over longer periods of time.

Furthermore, future research should more closely examine the mechanisms through which positive interventions are effective. If doing random acts of kindness makes people happier, exactly why is that? Does it allow people to see themselves and kind and thoughtful? Does it build social capital and a sense of trust? Does it allow people to see just how fortunate they are, especially if they choose to help someone in need? Because these studies are often done on participants' own time rather than in the lab, assessing these processes may be difficult. However, it is important to understand exactly why they have such benefits. As positive longitudinal interventions are beginning to be applied in a clinical setting (Seligman et al., 2006), it is especially critical to more fully understand the nature of the processes underlying their apparent success.

## Testing Universality of Positive Psychology

As is the case with the rest of psychological research, most positive psychology research of today has been conducted in North America and Europe. There is a good reason to suspect that some theories and findings of positive psychology do not replicate universally, considering the cultural variation found in the related topics such as self-esteem (Heine, Lehman, Kitayama, & Markus, 1999), happiness (Oishi & Diener, 2001), and pride (Kitayama, Markus, & Kurokawa, 2000). First, what is "positive" varies to some extent across cultures. In the U.S. today, "pride" is considered positive by most. Children are taught to "take pride" in their accomplishments, for instance. Among East Asians, however, "pride" is not considered positive by most (Eid & Diener, 2001; Oishi, 2007). It is of course well known that Jane Austen used the term "pride" and "proud" in a negative light in her *Pride and Prejudice* (1813/1997), suggesting that "pride" was not considered positive even in the West until much later, and that the positivity of "pride" changed over time.

Similarly, the concept of "happiness" varies across cultures and historical periods. As seen in Saul Steinberg's famous *New Yorker* cover on January 17, 1959, happiness has been highly associated with prosperity in the U.S.—happiness is something you can attain via success in life. Implicitly, happiness is conceived as something that one can actively pursue in the U.S. today.

In contrast, the Chinese characters for happiness are as follows: 幸福. The first character indicates feeling happy, but the second character indicates luck and fortune. This is partly why East Asians are less likely to conceive of happiness as something that they can actively pursue; rather, they conceive of happiness as something they will feel if they are lucky and fortunate. To be sure, the Latin origin of happiness is "hap," which indicates luck, and historically "happiness" was defined in part as "good fortune and luck." Interestingly, however, the 1961 Webster's unabridged dictionary started to denote this definition as "archaic." That is, "happiness" used to be defined as "good fortune and luck" in the U.S., but not anymore. It is also interesting to note that, according to the influential moral philosopher Martha Nussbaum (1986), Aristotle conceived *eudaimonia* (happiness or flourishing in life) as vulnerable to external conditions and the power of luck and fortune, very much in line with current East Asian use of 幸福. Indeed, Aristotle used *eudaimonia* interchangeably with the Greek word *markarion*, which means "fortune," throughout his *Ethics* (Thomson, 1953). This also suggests that the current use of eudaimonia in positive psychology (which tends to be highly agentic) might not fully reflect Aristotle's concept of eudaimonia.

It should be noted that several positive psychologists have already begun to investigate universality of their theories. For instance, Park, Peterson, and Seligman (2006) collected data from 54 nations and showed that the rank-order of 24 character strengths is remarkably similar across nations. Similarly, Shimai, Otake, Park, Peterson, and Seligman (2006) showed that the patterns of correlations between character strengths and other related constructs were similar in the U.S. and Japan. Also, Otake, Shimai, Tanaka-Matsumi, Otsui, and Fredrickson (2006) demonstrated that the kindness intervention worked well in Japan. These research findings provide initial support for universality of character strengths and the effectiveness of the kindness intervention. However, researchers have also found some cultural variation in meaning of life. For instance, search for meaning was negatively associated with presence of meaning and life satisfaction in the U.S., whereas it was positively associated with presence of meaning and life satisfaction in Japan (Steger, Kawabata, Shimai, & Otake, 2008). In other words, search for meaning is more "positive" in Japan than in the U.S. It is important for positive psychologists to continue investigating universality of their theories and findings to find true universality of and cultural variation in positive psychological science (see Norenzayan & Heine, 2005 for a specific research approach).

## Moving Forward

As mentioned at the beginning of this chapter, it should be reiterated that the positive psychology movement has made considerable accomplishments in both research and practice. Some of the findings from positive psychology (e.g., Emmons & McCullough, 2003; Lyubomirsky, Sousa, & Dickerhoof, 2006; Seligman et al., 2005; Tugade & Fredrickson, 2004) are truly inspiring. We believe that positive psychology can move even further by attending to all six critiques presented above: namely, (1) cultivating the link with the early generation of positive emotion research, (2) cultivating the connection with other positive psychology research (e.g., empathy, willpower, love, trust, cooperation), (3) recognizing that more is not always better, (4) recognizing the positive in negative emotions, (5) investigating the long-term effect of interventions and identifying boundary conditions (e.g., "what works for whom?"), and (6) testing universality of the theories. In general, then, we suggest broadening our focus by incorporating complementary lines of research, considering our intellectual and historical roots, and acknowledging the cultural context of our findings while continuing to produce rigorous scientific research.

Positive psychology has made rapid and impressive progress in the past decade and is

TABLE 7.1 Six Recommendations for the Future Positive Psychology of Positive Emotion

1. Cultivate the link with the early generation of positive emotion research
2. Cultivate the connection with other positive psychology research (e.g., empathy, willpower, love, trust, cooperation)
3. Recognize that the happier is not always better
4. Recognize the positive in negative emotions
5. Investigate the long-term effect of interventions and identify boundary conditions (e.g., "what works for whom?")
6. Test universality of the theories (e.g., what is "positive"?)

now in the fortunate position to confidently suggest ways to put this research into practice to create better lives, more productive workplaces, and thriving societies. As we move forward, let us not forget that "with great power comes great responsibility." Stepping back to objectively assess our progress and re-examine our goals is but one of the responsibilities of a science that is both rigorous and highly prescriptive.

## References

Amodio, D. M., Devine, P. G., & Harmon-Jones, E. (2007). A dynamic model of guilt: Implications for motivation and self-regulation in the context of prejudice. *Psychological Science, 18*, 524–530.

Arnold, M. B. (*1960*). *Emotion* and personality. New York: Columbia University Press.

Aron, A., & Westbay, L. (1996). Dimensions of the prototype of love. *Journal of Personality and Social Psychology, 70*, 535–551.

Aronson, E., & Bridgeman, D. (1979). Jigsaw groups and the desegregated classroom: In pursuit of common goals. *Personality and Social Psychology Bulletin, 5*, 438–446.

Austen, J. (1813/1997). *Pride and prejudice*. Rutland, VT: Everyman.

Batson, C. D. (1991). *The altruism question: Toward a social-psychological answer*. Hillsdale, NJ: Erlbaum.

Baumgarten-Tramer, F. (1938). "Gratefulness" in children and young people. *Journal of Genetic Psychology, 53*, 53–66.

Baumeister, R. F., Stillwell, A. M., & Heatherton, T. F. (1994). Guilt: An interpersonal approach. *Psychological Bulletin, 115*, 243–267.

Baumeister, R. F., Bratslavsky, E., Finkenauer, C., & Vohs, K. D. (2001). Bad is stronger than good. *Review of General Psychology, 5*, 323–370.

Brickman, P., & Campbell, D. T. (1971). Hedonic relativism and planning the good society. In M. H. Appley (Ed.), Adaptation-level theory (pp. 287–305). New York: Academic Press.

Bryant, F. B., & Veroff, J. (2007). *Savoring: A new model of positive experience*. Lawrence Erlbaum Associates. Mahwah, NJ.

Burton, C. M., & King, L. A. (2004). The health benefits of writing about intensely positive experiences. *Journal of Research in Personality, 38*, 150–163.

Coke, J. S., Batson, C. D., & McDavis, K. (1978). Empathic mediation of helping: A twostage model. *Journal of Personality and Social Psychology, 36*, 752–766.

Cronbach, L. J., & Meehl, P. E. (1955). Construct validity in psychological tests. *Psychological Bulletin, 52*, 281–302.

Damasio, A. R. (1994). *Descartes' error: Emotion, reason, and the human brain*. New York: Putnam.

Darwin, C. (1872). *The expression of emotions in man and animals*. Chicago, IL: University of Chicago Press.

Dawes, R. M., & Messick, D. M. (2000). Social dilemmas. *International Journal of Psychology, 35*, 111–116.

Dearborn, G. V. N. (1899). *The emotion of joy*. New York: Macmillans.

Dearborn, G. V. N. (1916). *The influence of joy*. Boston, MA: Little, Brown, and Company.

Diener, E., Lucas, R. E., & Napa Scollon, C. (2006). Beyond the hedonic treadmill: Revising the adaptation theory of well-being. *American Psychologist, 61*, 305–314.

Diener, E., Nickerson, C., Lucas, R. E., & Sandvik, E. (2002). Dispositional affect and job outcome. *Social Indicators Research, 59*, 229–259.

Duffy, E. (1934). Is emotion a mere term of convenience? *Psychological Review, 41*, 103–104.

Duffy, E. (1941). The conceptual categories of psychology: A suggestion for revision. *Psychological Review, 48*, 177–203.

Eid, M., & Diener, E. (2001). Norms for experiencing emotions in different cultures: Inter- and intranational differences. *Journal of Personality and Social Psychology, 81*, 869–885.

Ekman, P. (1964). Body position, facial expression, and verbal behavior during interviews. *Journal of Abnormal and Social Psychology, 68*, 295–301.

Emmons, R.A. (1999). *The psychology of ultimate concerns: Motivation and spirituality in personality*. New York: The Guilford Press.

Emmons, R. A., & McCullough, M. E. (2003). Counting blessings versus burdens: An experimental investigation of gratitude and subjective well-being in daily life. *Journal of Personality and Social Psychology, 84*, 377–389.

Emmons, R. A., & McCullough, M. E. (Eds.). (2004) The psychology of gratitude. New York: Oxford University Press.

Fabes, R. A., Eisenberg, N., Jones, S., Smith, M., Guthrie, I., Poulin, R., Shepard, S., & Friedman, J. (1999). Regulation, emotionality, and preschoolers' socially competent peer interactions. *Child Development, 70*, 432–442.

Fordyce, M. (1977). Development of a program to increase personal happiness. *Journal of Counseling Psychology, 24*, 511–521.

Fredrickson, B. L. (1998). The role of positive emotions in positive psychology. *American Psychologist, 56,* 218–226.

Fredrickson, B. L. (2001). The role of positive emotions in positive psychology: The broaden-and-build theory of positive emotions. *American Psychologist, 56,* 218–226.

Fredrickson, B. L., & Losada, M. F. (2005). Positive affect and the complex dynamics of human flourishing. *American Psychologist, 60,* 678–686.

Gardiner, H. N. (1916). Affective phenomena-descriptive and theoretical. *Psychological Bulletin, 13,* 197–202.

Gilbert, G. M. (1938). The new status of experimental studies on the relationship of feeling to memory. *Psychological Review, 35,* 26–35.

Gordon, K. (1917). A device for demonstrating empathy. *Journal of Experimental Psychology, 17,* 892–893.

Haidt, J., & Seder, P. (2009) Admiration and awe. Entry for the *Oxford Companion to Affective Science* p. 4–5. New York: Oxford University Press.

Hatfield, E., & Sprecher, S. (1986). Measuring passionate love in intimate relations. *Journal of Adolescence, 9,* 383–410.

Heine, S., Lehman, D. R., Markus, H. R., & Kitayama, S. (1999). Is there a universal need for positive self-regard? *Psychological Review, 106,* 766–794.

Henderson, E. N. (1911). Do we forget the disagreeable? *Journal of Philosophy, Psychology, and Scientific Methods, 8,* 432–438.

Hilgard, E. R. (1987). *Psychology in America: A historical survey.* Orlando, FL: Harcourt Brace Jovanovich.

Isen, A. M. (1987). Positive affect, cognitive processes and social behavior. In L. Berkowitz (Ed.), Advances in experimental social psychology (pp. 203–253). New York: Academic Press.

Isen, A. M., & Levin, P. F. (1972). Effect of feeling good on helping: Cookies and kindness. *Journal of Personality and Social Psychology, 21,* 384–388.

James, W. (1890/1950). *The principles of psychology.* New York: Dover.

James, W. (1892/1963). *Psychology.* Greenwich, CT: Fawcett.

Janoff-Bulman, R., & Berger, A. R. (2000). The other side of trauma: Toward a psychology of appreciation. In J. H. Harvey & E. D. Miller (Eds.), Loss and trauma: General and close relationship perspectives (pp. 29–44). Philadelphia: Brunner-Routledge.

Kashdan, T. B., Rose, P., & Fincham, F. D. (2004). Curiosity and exploration: Facilitating positive subjective experiences and personal growth opportunities. *Journal of Personality Assessment, 82,* 291–305.

Keltner, D., & Haidt, J. (2003). Approaching awe, a moral, spiritual, and aesthetic emotion. *Cognition and Emotion, 17,* 297–314.

Kendrew, E. N. (1930). A further attempt to measure the strength of instincts. *British Journal of Psychology, 21,* 160–173.

Kitayama, S., Markus, H. R., & Kurokawa, M. (2000). Culture, emotion, and well-being: Good feelings in Japan and the United States. *Cognition & Emotion, 14,* 93–124.

Kunzmann, U., & Baltes, P (2003). Wisdom-related knowledge: Affective, motivational, and interpersonal correlates. *Personality and Social Psychology Bulletin, 29,* 1104–1119.

Kurtz, J. L., Wilson, T. D., & Gilbert, D. T. (2007). Quantity versus uncertainty: When winning one prize is better than winning two. *Journal of Experimental Social Psychology, 43,* 979–985.

Leary, M. (2007). Motivational and emotional aspects of the self. *Annual Review of Psychology, 58,* 317–344.

Lyubomirsky, S., King, L., & Diener, E. (2005). The Benefits of frequent positive affect: Does happiness lead to success? *Psychological Bulletin, 131,* 803–855.

Lyubomirsky, S., Sheldon, K. M., & Schkade, D. (2005). Pursuing happiness: The architecture of sustainable change. *Review of General Psychology, 9,* 111–131.

Lyubomirsky, S., Sousa, L., & Dickerhoof, R. (2006). The costs and benefits of writing, talking, and thinking about life's triumphs and defeats. *Journal of Personality and Social Psychology, 90,* 692–708.

Lyubomirsky, S. (2008). *The how of happiness. A scientific approach to getting the life you want.* New York: Penguin Press.

Lyubomirsky, S., Dickerhoof, R., Boehm, J. K., & Sheldon, K. M. (2008). *How and why do positive activities work to boost well-being? An experimental longitudinal investigation of regularly practicing optimism and gratitude.* Manuscript under review.

McAdams, D. (2001). The psychology of life stories. *Review of General Psychology, 5,* 100–121.

McAdams, D. (2006). *The redemptive self: Stories Americans live by.* New York: Oxford University Press.

McCullough, M. E., Tsang, J. T., & Emmons, R. A. (2004). Gratitude in intermediate affective terrain. *Journal of Personality and Social Psychology, 86,* 295–309.

McDougall, W. (1908/1921). *An introduction to social psychology*. Boston, MA: Luce.

Meltzer, H. (1930). The present status of experimental studies on the relationship of feeling to memory. *Psychological Review, 37*, 124–139.

Meltzer, H. (1939). Attitudes of American children toward peaceful and warlike nations in 1934 and 1938. *Journal of Psychology: Interdisciplinary and Applied, 7*, 369–384.

Meyer, M. F. (1933). That whale among the fishes— The theory of emotions. *Psychological Review, 40*, 292–300.

Mischel, W., & Gilligan, C. (1964). Delay of gratification, motivation for the prohibited gratification, and responses to temptation. *Journal of Abnormal and Social Psychology, 69*, 411–417.

Mischel, W., Ebbesen, E. B., & Raskoff Zeiss, A. (1972). Cognitive and attentional mechanisms in delay of gratification. *Journal of Personality and Social Psychology, 21*, 204–218.

Mischel, W., Shoda, Y., & Rodriguez, M. (1989). Delay of gratification in children. *Science, 244*, 933–938.

Murray, S. L., Holmes, J. G., & Griffin, D. W. (2003). Reflections on the self-fulfilling effects of positive illusions. *Psychological Inquiry, 14*, 289–295.

Norenzayan, A., & Heine, S. J. (2005). Psychological universals: What are they and how can we know? *Psychological Bulletin, 131*, 763–784.

Nussbaum, M. C. (1986). *The fragility of goodness: Luck and ethics in Greek tragedy and philosophy*. New York: Cambridge University.

Oishi, S. (2000). *Culture and memory for emotional experiences: On-line vs. retrospective judgments of subjective well-being*. A Dissertation Submitted to the University of Illinois at Urbana-Champaign.

Oishi, S. (2007). The application of structural equation modeling and item response theory to cross-cultural positive psychology research. In A. Ong, & M. van Dulmen (Eds.), Oxford Handbook of Methods in Positive Psychology (pp. 126–138). New York: Oxford University Press.

Oishi, S., & Diener, E. (2001). Goals, culture, and subjective well-being. *Personality and Social Psychology Bulletin, 27*, 1674–1682.

Oishi, S., Diener, E., Choi, D. W., Kim-Prieto, C., & Choi, I. (2007). The Dynamics of daily events and well-being across cultures: When less is more. *Journal of Personality and Social Psychology, 93*, 685–698.

Oishi, S., Diener, E., & Lucas, R. E. (2007). The optimal level of well-being: Can we be too happy? *Perspectives on Psychological Science, 2*, 346–360.

Oishi, S., & Koo, M. (2008). Two new questions about happiness: "Is happiness good?" and "Is happier better?" In M. Eid & R. J. Larsen. (Eds.), Handbook of subjective well-being (p. 290–306). New York: Oxford University Press.

Omoto, A. M., & Snyder, M. (1995). Sustained helping without obligation: Motivation, longevity of service, and perceived attitude change among AIDS volunteers. *Journal of Personality and Social Psychology, 68*, 671–686.

Otake, K., Shimai, S., Tanaka-Matsumi, J., Otsui, K., & Fredrickson, B. L. (2006). Happy people become happier through kindness: A counting kindnesses intervention. *Journal of Happiness Studies, 7*, 361–375.

Park, N., Peterson, C., & Seligman, M. E. P. (2006). Character strengths in fifty-four nations and the fifty US states. *Journal of Positive Psychology, 1*, 118–129.

Pennebaker, J. W., & Seagal, J. D. (1999). Forming a story: The health benefits of narrative. *Journal of Clinical Psychology, 55*, 1243–1254.

Penner, L. A., Dovidio, J. F., Piliavin, J. A., & Schroeder, D. A. (2005). Prosocial behavior: Multilevel perspectives. *Annual Review of Psychology, 56*, 365–392.

Peterson, C., & Seligman, M. E. P. (2004). *Character strengths and virtues: A handbook and classification*. New York: Oxford University Press.

Rozin, P., Haidt, J., & McCauley, C. (1993). Disgust. In M. Lewis & J. Haviland (Eds.), Handbook of emotions (pp. 575–594). New York: Guilford Press.

Ryan, R. M., & Deci, E. L. (2001). On happiness and human potentials: A review of research on hedonic and eudaimonic well-being. *Annual Review of Psychology, 52*, 141–166.

Ryff, C. D. (1989). Happiness is everything, or is it: Explorations on the meaning of psychological well-being. *Journal of Personality and Social Psychology, 57*, 1069–1081.

Schwartz, B. (2005). *The paradox of choice: Why more is less*. New York: Harper Collins.

Schwarz, N. (1998). Accessible content and accessibility experiences: The interplay of declarative and experiential information in judgment. *Personality and Social Psychology Review, 2*, 87–99.

Schwarz, N., & Clore, G. L. (1983). Mood, misattribution, and judgments of well-being: Informative and directive functions of affective states. *Journal of Personality and Social Psychology, 45*, 513–523.

Seligman, M. E. P. (2002). *Authentic happiness*. New York: Free Press.

Seligman, M. E. P., & Csikszentmihalyi, M. (2000). Positive psychology: An introduction. *American Psychologist, 55*, 5–14.

Seligman, M. E. P., Rashid, T., & Parks, A. C. (2006). Positive psychotherapy. *American Psychologist*, 61, 774–788.

Seligman, M. E. P., Steen, T. A., Park, N., & Peterson, C. (2005). Positive psychology progress: Empirical validation of interventions. *American Psychologist*, 60, 410–421.

Sheldon, K. M. (2004). *Optimal human being: An integrated multi-level perspective*. Mahwah, NJ: Lawrence Erlbaum Associates.

Sheldon, K. M., & Lyubomirsky, S. (2006). How to increase and sustain positive emotion: The effects of expressing gratitude and visualizing best possible selves. *The Journal of Positive Psychology*, 1, 73–82.

Sherif, M., Harvey, O. J., White, J., Hood, W. R., & Sherif, C. W. (1954/1961). *Intergroup conflict and cooperation: The Robbers cave experiment*. Norman, OK: University of Oklahoma.

Shimai, S., Otake, K., Park, N., Peterson, C., & Seligman, M. E. P. (2006). Convergence of character strengths in American and Japanese young adults. *Journal of Happiness Studies*, 7, 311–322.

Shoda, Y., Mischel, W., & Peake, P. K. (1990). Predicting adolescent cognitive and self-regulatory competencies from preschool delay of gratification: Identifying diagnostic conditions. *Developmental Psychology*, 26, 978–986.

Simpson, J. A. (1990). Influence of attachment styles on romantic relationships. *Journal of Personality and Social Psychology*, 59, 971–980.

Snyder, C. R. (2002). Hope theory: Rainbows of the mind. *Psychological Inquiry*, 13, 249–275.

Snyder, C. R., & Lopez, S. J (2002). *The handbook of positive psychology*. New York: Oxford University Press.

Steger, M. F., Kawabata, Y., Shimai, S., & Otake, K. (2008). The meaningful life in Japan and the United States: Levels and correlates of meaning in life. *Journal of Research in Personality*, 42, 660–678.

Sternberg, R. J. (1986). A triangular theory of love. *Psychological Review*, 93, 119–135.

Tamir, M. (2005). Don't worry, be happy? Neuroticism, trait-consistent affect regulation, and performance. *Journal of Personality and Social Psychology*, 89, 449–461.

Tangney, J. P., Baumeister, R. F., & Boone, A. L. (2004). High self-control predicts good adjustment, less pathology, better grades, and interpersonal success. *Journal of Personality*, 72, 271–324.

Thomson, J. A. K. (1953). *The ethics of Aristotle: The Nicomachean ethics*. London: Penguin Books.

Tugade, M. M., & Fredrickson, B. L. (2004). Resilient individuals use positive emotions to bounce back from negative emotional experiences. *Journal of Personality and Social Psychology*, 86, 320–333.

Van Vugt, M., Snyder, M., Tyler, T., & Biel, A. (2000). *Cooperation in modern society: Promoting the welfare of communities, states and organizations*. London, UK: Routledge.

Waters, E., Wippman, J., & Sroufe, L. A. (1979). Attachment, positive affect, and competence in the peer group: Two studies in construct validation. *Child Development*, 50, 821–829.

Wilson, T. D., & Gilbert, D. T. (2008). Explaining away: A model of affective adaptation. *Perspectives on Psychological Science*, 5, 370–386.

Wohlgemuth, A. (1923). The influence of feeling on memory. *British Journal of Psychology*, 8, 405–416.

Worcester, D. A. (1933). In defense of the whale—emotion is at least a term of convenience. *Psychological Review*, 40, 478–480.

# 8

# The Future of Emotions Research within Positive Psychology

*Sara B. Algoe, Barbara L. Fredrickson[1], and Sy-Miin Chow*

## Taking Stock

The task of taking stock of what's known about positive emotions is made far easier thanks to a landmark 2005 review paper published in the *Psychological Bulletin* by Sonja Lyubomirsky, Laura King, and Ed Diener. Their painstaking meta-analysis of some 300 studies plainly lays out the evidence that bears on the question of whether positive emotions are merely the pleasant consequences of good fortune, or whether they might also be consequential for creating future good fortunes. Culling all relevant empirical studies on positive emotions, positive affect, and happiness, and dividing them based both on the life domains they address (e.g., work life, social relationships, health) as well as on their empirical strength (into cross-sectional, longitudinal, and experimental studies), these authors concluded that although positive emotions certainly reflect success in life, they also produce success in life. This single paper offers superb one-stop shopping to gain appreciation for what's known already within positive psychology about positive emotions.

A clear implication of this work is that—whether for individuals or institutions—positive emotions are a worthy target of intervention. To the extent that positive emotions contribute to and cause human success, efforts to cultivate positive emotions promise to pay off handsomely within people's work, their relationships, and their personal growth more generally. Indeed, a chief aim of positive psychology has been to develop interventions that reliably raise positivity. The most promising approaches toward meeting this aim include ritualized gratitude exercises (Emmons & McCullough, 2003; Lyubomirsky, Sheldon, & Schkade, 2005; Seligman, Steen, Park, & Peterson, 2005), recrafting one's daily life to better draw on personal strengths (Seligman et al., 2005; Roberts, Dutton, Spreitzer, Heaphy, & Quinn, 2005), reflecting on or increasing kind actions (Lybomirsky, Sheldon et al., 2005; Otake, Shimai, Tanaka-Matsumi, Otsui, & Fredrickson, 2006), and mind training through meditation practice (Cohn & Fredrickson, in press; Davidson et al., 2003; Fredrickson, Cohn, Coffey, Pek, & Finkel, 2008; Kabat-Zinn, 1982; Teasdale et al., 2000).

Positive psychology interventions are often framed as ways of increasing happiness. Indeed, positive psychology founder Martin Seligman is fond of charging applied positive psychologists with the mission of increasing the "total tonnage of human happiness." It's worth noting, however, that scientists still debate how to adequately define the term "happiness." Should it be defined hedonically, as experienced pleasure (Kahneman, 1999) and/or satisfaction with life (Diener, Suh, Lucas, & Smith, 1999)? Or is it something more? Something that concerns meaning and purpose, as proponents of the eudaimonic view (Keyes, Shmotkin & Ryff, 2002; Ryan & Deci, 2001; Ryff & Singer, 1998) have long held? Much as Kashdan, Biswas-Diener, and King (2008), we view this persistent debate between hedonic and eudaimonic perspectives on happiness as distraction from fully understanding how key concepts within "the good life" interrelate. It's yet another instance in which "both-and" thinking can profitably supplant "either-or" thinking—happiness is *both* hedonic *and* eudaimonic.

Even so, how empirically minded positive psychologists resolve their view of the happiness debate is vital because it shapes the appropriate outcome measures for positive psychology interventions. Indeed, we believe we should concede as futile the search for a definitive understanding of the concept of happiness because, in pragmatic terms, how you define it depends on the function you want it to serve. By analogy, although you can certainly cup your two hands together to make an impromptu "vessel" to hold a bunch of grapes or water from a clear mountain stream, this makeshift "vessel" would be unsuitable for holding wine at the dinner table. Suitable definitions depend on the purpose at hand.

## Beyond Happiness

### Ban Scientific Use of the Term "Happiness"

Long-standing philosophical and scientific debates aside, another reason we should be suspicious of the term "happiness" within positive psychology is that even in the unlikely event that scientists were to agree on its meaning, such understanding could hardly compete with all multiple meanings of the word "happy" within common usage. At times "happy" is used to describe a momentary emotional state (as in "seeing you smile makes me happy"), yet that same feeling is often better described by a more specific term, like joy, relief, gratitude, or love, depending on the exact circumstances. People also use the word "happy" to describe someone's personality overall, as in the 2008 Mike Leigh film *Happy-Go-Lucky*, reflecting how the protagonist typically reacted to life's ups and downs. Still other times, happiness refers to an ultimate life goal, as in "I just want to be happy." Finally, happiness is also used to convey simple acceptance, as in "I'd be happy to go to the post office for you." Using a single word, like "happiness," in these various ways is not merely confusing; it violates the scientific necessity for precision in language use.

The strength of positive psychology rests on pulling apart the complex, dynamic processes by which momentary positive emotions arise and trigger psychological processes that ultimately place people on positive trajectories of growth. Two classic findings within positive psychology are that more frequent positive emotions day to day predict (1) being more satisfied with life overall (Diener et al, 1999) and (2) living longer (e.g., Danner, Snowdon & Friesen, 2001; Moskowitz, 2003). While the first finding may hardly stop the presses, the links to longevity certainly have. The key question, though, is *how*? How do fleeting momentary states like joy, gratitude, amusement, and the like contribute to overall life satisfaction and longevity?

The broaden-and-build theory can address this vital question about mechanisms (Fredrickson, 1998, Fredrickson & Cohn, 2008). In a recent paper entitled "Happiness Unpacked," we take the murky and overused concept of "happiness" and unpack it into its constituent parts, including momentary positive emotions, positive functioning, and life satisfaction (Cohn, Fredrickson, Brown, Mikels, & Conway, 2009). We then examine statistically how these more precisely defined constructs interrelate, looking for the underlying structure that characterizes the more complex happiness system. As predicted by the broaden-and-build theory, we found that daily positive emotions predict increases in positive functioning, as indexed by growth in the psychological resource of ego-resilience, which in turn forecasts increases in overall life satisfaction (Cohn et al., 2009). We observe similar patterns in our experimental tests of the effectiveness of the positive psychology intervention of learning meditation skills, namely loving-kindness meditation (Fredrickson et al., 2008). Daily positive emotions, increased by random assignment to the loving-kindness meditation group, produced increases in durable personal resources, which in turn produced increases in overall life satisfaction (see also Cohn & Fredrickson, in press). These data suggest that to make life itself more satisfying, it's better to focus on the present moment—on what activities or thought patterns might spark a positive emotion right now—rather than the long-range goal of pursuing "happiness" or global satisfaction with life more broadly. Positive emotions, unquestionably enjoyable in and of themselves, also unlock paths of growth that lead people to become better versions of themselves. By illuminating both the immediate effects of positive emotions and their long-range functions, the broaden-and-build theory (Fredrickson, 1998) bridges the chasm between hedonic and eudaimonic approaches to happiness. It exemplifies the "both-and" approach that Kashdan and colleagues (2008) call for.

## Specific Emotions Have Specific Effects

Recently, scientists have begun to put specific positive emotional moments under the microscope, and this work is revealing the rich texture that creates the fabric of our positive emotional life. Far from being one universal positive emotion (e.g., happiness or enjoyment), research into distinct positive emotions is demonstrating the unique ways that various moments of emotional positivity may lead to flourishing. In just the last decade, research on moments of **admiration** (Algoe & Haidt, 2009), **amusement** (many of the studies referenced in this section employ amusement as a comparison condition)[2], **awe** (Shiota, Keltner, & Mossman, 2007), **compassion** (Oveis, Horberg, & Keltner, 2010), moral **elevation** (Algoe & Haidt, 2009; Freeman, Aquino, & McFerran, 2008; Silvers & Haidt, 2008), **gratitude** (Algoe & Haidt, 2009; Algoe, Gable, & Maisel, 2010; Algoe, Haidt, & Gable, 2008; Bartlett & DeSteno, 2005; Tsang, 2006), **interest** (Silvia, 2005), **joy** (Agrawal, Menon, & Aaker, 2007; Algoe & Haidt, 2009; Shiota et al., 2007; Takahashi et al., 2008), **love** (Gonzaga, Turner, Keltner, Campos, & 2006), and **pride** (Aaker & Williams, 1998; Eyal & Fishbach, 2006; Oveis et al., 2010; Shiota et al., 2007; Tracy & Robins, 2004; 2008; Takahashi et al., 2008) has demonstrated the unique effects of these emotions, *compared to other positive emotional states*,[3] on such diverse aspects of emotional experience as appraisals, physiological activity, brain activation, nonverbal expression, cognitions, motivations, and behaviors.

Because an emotional reaction adds to a situation to both draw attention and coordinate a response to the situation (e.g., Tooby & Cosmides, 1990), the momentary changes produced by these distinct emotions shape subsequent decisions and interactions in distinct ways. It follows that the effects of specific emotions may cascade to have downstream consequences. Indeed, as one example, our recent prospective studies show that the emotion of gratitude is uniquely associated with consequential interpersonal outcomes, including a benefactor's time spent hanging out with the grateful individual and increased satisfaction about the relationship with the grateful individual, even after taking into account variance shared with other specific positive emotions (Algoe et al., 2008; Algoe et al., 2010).

Whereas emotions scholars long ago made empirical distinctions among the negative emotions, historically, to the extent that empirical research included examination of positive emotions, it tended to treat them as all the same (for key early exceptions, see Argyle & Crossland, 1987; de Rivera, Possell, Verette, & Weiner, 1989; and Ellsworth & Smith, 1988); that is, perhaps due to the fact that emotions research in its infancy focused on *expressions*, only "happiness" was often included in a study, alongside anger, fear, sadness, or disgust. We are not suggesting that the manipulations were inappropriate for their intended purposes. However, the rapidly emerging body of work on distinctions among positive emotions (which parallels prior work on negative emotions) suggests that advances to understanding the role of emotions in positive psychological processes and outcomes will depend on scientists taking seriously the *diversity* of potent emotional moments in everyday life, whether positive or negative.

## Negative Emotions Are Relevant to Positive Psychology Too

Alongside other affective scientists (Gottman, 1994; Schwartz, 1997; Larsen & Prizmic, 2008), we suggest that optimal human functioning is characterized by experiencing positive and negative emotions in a relative balance (Fredrickson & Losada, 2005). Notably, no affective scientist suggests that positive and negative emotions be balanced in a 1-to-1 fashion. Well-documented asymmetries between positive and negative states make such parity illogical. One such asymmetry is the *negativity bias* (Cacioppo, Gardner, & Berntson, 1999; Rozin & Royzman, 2001), or, as Baumeister and colleagues famously put it, "bad is stronger than good" (Baumeister, Bratslavsky, Finkenauer, & Vohs, 2001). Because of the greater potency of negative emotions, positive emotions need strength in numbers to etch a difference in people's lives. Another, often-overlooked asymmetry is the *positivity offset*, the fact the modal human experience is mildly positive (Cacioppo et al., 1999; Diener & Diener, 1996). In tandem, these two asymmetries set the stage for the optimal ratio of positive to negative emotions to be higher than 1 to 1. Based on mathematical modeling and tested against observed data from multiple laboratories, Fredrickson and Losada (2005) proposed that a ratio of about 3 to 1 is the tipping point beyond which humans begin to function at optimal levels.

Positivity ratios above 3 to 1 are wide enough to encompass the entire range of human emotions. Put differently, no emotion needs to be forever banished for humans to flourish. Just as affective scientists agree that positive and negative emotions should not be given equal airtime in a 1-to-1 ratio, they also agree that negative emotions are vital to optimal human functioning. What this means for the future of positive psychology is that negative emotions become the new frontier. Whether and how negative emotions contribute to optimal functioning depends not only on how frequently they are experienced relative to positive emotions, but also on whether they are necessary or gratuitous in a given context. We need better assessment tools for distinguishing necessary negativity from gratuitous negativity. One guiding principle is that necessary negativity is appropriate to the current circumstances in both content and scope, whereas gratuitous negativity is disproportionate, often overblown or inappropriately seeping into and dominating future circumstances (Fredrickson, 2009), perhaps reflecting what Gottman (1994) called an absorbing state. A new frontier for scientists working in positive psychology will be to discover when and how people's strategies for acknowledging and expressing their negative emotions contribute positively to well-being and when they detract from it (e.g., Graham, Huang, Clark, & Helgeson, 2008).

## Moving Forward

### Emotions Reside Within and Between People

What exactly *is* an emotion? Many affective scientists bypass tackling this primary question as

they proceed to address their own questions. There's nothing wrong with that approach so long as researchers provide at least some indication of their working definition of emotions so that others can interpret and situate their advances properly. This is a pragmatic approach because full agreement simply does not exist on the nature and structure of emotions, and we imagine areas of disagreement will continue for at least another decade (we see this as science at its best). One perhaps surprising point of debate concerns where emotions reside. That is, to whom does a given emotion belong? Most Westerners subscribe to the idea that emotions belong to individuals—that one person's interpretation of their current circumstances produces in them a cascade of responses, including (but not limited to) a particular subjective feeling state, changes in their heart rates and other physiological systems, characteristic facial and bodily movements, and urges to think and act in characteristic ways. With all these coordinated changes unfolding within them, it seems obvious to many that the emotion belongs to the person "having" it. It is a series of events unfolding within them, that they choose to express to others or not.

However obvious this conception of emotions may seem, it's worth underscoring that other possible locations of emotion exist. Affective scientists who study cultural differences have pointed out that in more communal or collectivist cultures, the notion that an emotion resides within a single person seems off-target. Within these cultures, emotions are taken to reside between and among people, not within individuals. Research shows that within collectivist contexts, emotions not only span the self-other boundary but are also taken as a shared and objective social reality rather than products of the private and subjective inner world of individuals (Mesquita, 2001).

This may be another place where a "both-and" perspective becomes more valuable than an "either-or" view. Perhaps each cultural norm reflects part of the whole, with traditional Western science magnifying the within-person effects of emotions and cultural psychologists amplifying the across-persons effects. The challenge for future positive psychologists will be to pursue this both-and perspective empirically, tracking both the within- and across-persons effects rigorously, even simultaneously. Research has already documented, for instance, that amusement-inspired laughter can shift a person's mindset (e.g., Johnson & Fredrickson, 2005) and release a cascade of neurochemicals (e.g., Kimata, 2007) within the person laughing. Yet research also shows that certain people who hear that other person laugh are more likely to feel positive emotions themselves (Bachorowski & Owren, 2001) and, because mirror neurons make laughter contagious (Gervais & Wilson, 2005), are more likely to themselves laugh (Smoski & Bachorowski, 2003). Shared laughter may in turn have its own cascade of relational effects, including an increased sense of safety and bondedness (Algoe, Kurtz, & Fredrickson, 2010; Gervais & Wilson, 2005), as well as ripple effects on other observers. It is perhaps more important to acknowledge and track this complex cascade of intra- and interpersonal events than to debate who "owns" the emotion per se.

## Emotion Specificity, Emotion Families

What you have read thus far is that there is much to be learned about emotions, and how they influence our lives, by thinking beyond the overarching categorization of "positive" or "negative." One reasonable place to start is to consider Ekman's concept of emotion "families" (1992). These are clusters of emotions that show similar characteristics and can be contrasted with other clusters of emotions. For example, Haidt (2003) has characterized the moral emotions into four primary families involving "other-praising" (admiration, gratitude, moral elevation), "other-condemning" (anger, contempt, disgust), "other-suffering" (compassion), and "self-conscious" (embarrassment, guilt, shame). Drawing on this classification, a recent expedition into the "other-praising" family of emotions showed distinctions between the "other-praising" and the "happiness" family (which was characterized by joy or amusement in these studies; Algoe & Haidt, 2009). For example, true to their name, compared to people in the control conditions, participants in the "other-praising" emotion conditions wanted to do just that: to praise the person who caused their positive emotion. This has important implications for how emotions from the "other-praising" family coordinate a person's interaction with the world. Indeed, relative to emotions from the "happiness" family, participants who experienced emotions from the "other-praising" family became focused on connecting with other people and seemed to see a path to self-improvement, whether it was in the domain of morality, relationships, or personal accomplishment (Algoe & Haidt, 2009).

Decades ago, Alice Isen demonstrated that people who are in positive moods are more likely to behave prosocially when given the opportunity compared to those in neutral control conditions (e.g., Isen & Levin, 1972). And now the latest research is honing that message to describe the *optimal* conditions under which prosociality may occur from positive emotions: experimental evidence from inductions of the other-praising positive emotions of gratitude or elevation shows that people who have recently experienced these emotions, compared to amusement or a different positive emotional state, are more likely to enact behaviors that will help even a stranger (Bartlett & DeSteno, 2005; Freeman et al., 2008; Tsang, 2006). Certain clusters of emotions may thus be better characterized as having "other-focused" effects.

Yet, the studies on other-praising emotions illustrate a second key point for positive psychologists to consider as well: even within an emotion family, important and useful distinctions can be made among positive emotions (Algoe & Haidt, 2009). A body of evidence is amassing to support the proposal that, because specific emotions arise from specific patterns of appraising a situation, one can predict consequences from emotions by paying attention to the appraisals (i.e., the "appraisal tendency theory" of Lerner & Keltner, 2000; 2001; see also Lerner & Tiedens, 2006). Indeed, our work on other-praising emotions has focused on identifying the key appraisals underlying the unique positive emotions of elevation, admiration, and gratitude, and using this information to predict the distinct consequences of these positive emotions, even when compared to each other (Algoe & Haidt, 2009; Algoe et al., 2008).

The bottom line is that more work is needed to discover the appraisals central to specific positive emotions; some of this work is already underway (e.g., Oveis et al., in press; Shiota et al., 2007; Silvia, 2005). Understanding the situational appraisals that contribute to specific emotions will go a long way toward understanding how those emotions uniquely coordinate a person's physiological, cognitive, and behavioral response to a situation. For example, even other-praising emotions have distinct interpersonal effects at times, in ways that can be predicted from understanding their underlying appraisals. One study showed that people who felt gratitude and were given a choice about a future interaction partner chose to interact with someone different than interaction partners chosen by people who felt admiration (Algoe & Haidt, 2009, Study 3), and prospective correlational evidence from a daily experience-sampling study with people in romantic relationships shows that the emotion of gratitude, but not admiration, from interactions with a romantic partner on a given day predicts *increases* in the participant's *and the partner's* positive feelings about the relationship from the prior day (Algoe et al., 2010). Our theory suggests that this is because, although admiration and gratitude both come from situations in which the other person is seen as praiseworthy, each has a different focus: admiration is about seeing skill or talent, while gratitude is about seeing relationship opportunities.

The themes regarding the negative emotions are similar to those in the paragraphs above: understanding the causes of specific negative emotions helps researchers better understand when a negative emotion should be context-appropriate and functional, rather than gratuitous and problematic. For example, feeling worried when a teenage child does not arrive home at the designated time may facilitate behaviors that will calm the fear, such as calling the child on the phone (who says, "I'm sitting in our driveway talking to my friend, who got in a fight with her parents today.") and taking steps to prevent the aversive situation in the future ("I appreciate that you were helping your friend, but please give me a call to let me know next time, because I worry about you."). Of course, excessive worry can lead to intrusive parenting, whereas lack of context-appropriate worry may give the opposite impression to the child. A parent who experiences sadness (or neglect) in this situation would have a different response altogether. New research on the expression of negative emotions is an example of important research that shows when and why negative emotions can be beneficial: In this research, willingness to express negative emotions was associated with *better* relationship outcomes (e.g., eliciting help, greater intimacy) across a variety of relationship types (Graham et al., 2008). When expressed in the appropriate context (e.g., concern over an upcoming exam) and to the appropriate people (e.g., friend compared to colleague), expressing one's negative emotions may facilitate the problem-solving that is often required from negative emotional experiences.

### Emotions within Relationships

One critical component of the experience of emotion is that the vast majority of emotional moments are caused by the real or imagined presence of other people. We are *social* creatures. This makes the social context a key consideration for understanding the causes and consequences of any given emotion. One way of thinking about social context is simply whether the emotion is appropriate to the situation. As one example, in contrast to common conceptions of pride as a vice, Williams and DeSteno (2008) recently demonstrated that pride, when experienced in the appropriate social context of a group problem-solving task, led to the adaptive outcomes of more dominance behavior during the task as well as higher ratings of liking for the proud individual by the other group members.

Yet social context might also shape expected outcomes if an interaction partner is a new or old acquaintance. Research on antiphonal laughter in dyads makes this point well; antiphonal laughs come when one person laughs in close temporal proximity to another person's laugh. Theorizing that laughter, as a behavioral manifestation of positive emotion, can become a conditioned response to the acoustic properties of the laugh of a relationship partner, Smoski and Bachorowski (2003) evaluated laughs in different types of relationship pairings. First, friendship pairs laughed more often than stranger pairs. Second, as predicted, their experiment showed that people who were better acquainted were more likely to laugh in close temporal proximity to the interaction partner's laugh. Because hearing a laugh *vocalized* produces positive emotions (Bachorowski & Owren, 2001), these findings have implications for understanding the role of laughter in positive relationship processes. As just one example, our own recent research suggests that moments of *shared laughter*—times when interaction partners are simultaneously laughing about the same thing—may lay the groundwork for feelings of trust and intimacy to advance a relationship (Algoe, Kurtz, & Fredrickson, 2010). Most research on amusement or humor has measured its effects (through videotaped induction) on an individual, but this emerging body of work suggests that amusement and laughter are relevant and perhaps most potent within interpersonal contexts.

Moreover, because emotions are characteristically experienced in the midst of this social milieu, they necessarily have short-term and possibly long-term consequences for interaction partners, whether it's an acquaintance, coworker, roommate, friend, romantic partner, or other family member. For example, researchers have long known that the experience of stressful events (and their associated negative valence) can permeate into social life, even spilling over from one domain to another context, such as work stress to family interaction (e.g., Repetti, 1989). Perhaps positive emotions permeate life as well, with different consequences. Indeed, recent work by Waugh and Fredrickson (2006) suggests this might be the case. In this study, they tested whether positive emotions, by expanding people's awareness (the broaden effect), would facilitate more rapid development of positive relationships with new roommates. Specifically, in a group of first-year college students, they measured positive (and negative) emotions at the end of each day for 28 days during the first month of school. At the beginning and end of this time period, they measured aspects of the relationship with the new roommate, to find that people experiencing more positive emotions demonstrated the largest increases in seeing overlap between themselves and their new roommates, as well as a more complex understanding of the roommate. This work drew on theory about positive emotions to make context-specific predictions (i.e., new roommate relationship) about their benefit to social life.

Beyond effects of the general categories of positive or negative emotions, certain specific emotions have been proposed to have specific social functions; that is, the motives and goals of the person experiencing the emotion are proposed to center on a specific function, such as remaining committed to a romantic partner (i.e., romantic love; Gonzaga, Keltner, Londahl, & Smith, 2001; Gonzaga et al., 2006) or appeasing social interaction partners when one has made a social gaffe (i.e., embarrassment; Keltner & Buswell, 1996). Recent research on the emotion of gratitude suggests that it is a detection-and-response system that functions to helps us *find, remind, and bind* ourselves to attentive other individuals (Algoe et al., 2008): it helps to build positive relationships. Using a variety of methods, this line of work examines the full interpersonal process starting with the provision of a benefit to a recipient, to the recipient's appraisal of the situation, emotional responses to receiving the benefit, change in cognitions about the benefactor, motivations toward the benefactor, expression of emotions to the benefactor, and future relationship consequences for the recipient *and* benefactor (Algoe & Haidt, 2009; Algoe et al., 2008; 2010; Algoe et al., under review). The novel contributions here involve recognition that, in addition to

evaluating the properties of the benefit itself (i.e., was it a *benefit?*), a recipient of a benefit inherently makes appraisals about the meaning of the benefactor's actions: what does the benefactor think about the nature of our relationship? The emotion of gratitude uniquely results when the benefactor is appraised as being responsive to the particular needs and preferences of the recipient (i.e., "thoughtful" in common language, related to the concept of "perceived responsiveness" in relationship science, Reis, Clark, & Holmes, 2004), (Algoe et al., 2008; 2010). In the moment of gratitude, thoughts and feelings about the new or old acquaintance who provided the benefit are refined, which has implications for relationship promotion in new friendships or romantic relationships.

The future of research that proposes specific social functions for specific emotions, as we see it, lies down two primary avenues: (1) study specific types of emotional moments within the relational contexts in which they are proposed to function, including, when possible, studying acquainted pairs of people together (i.e., roommates, coworkers, family members, romantic partners); (2) study the effects of one person's emotion on the interaction partner, which is to ask the obvious question, "Did the emotion have the social consequence I hypothesized?" These are not easy (or cheap) methodological endeavors that we propose, nor do we suggest that self-report questionnaires from the person feeling the emotion are irrelevant to our understanding of emotions and their social processes. However, we do think data from at least one of the avenues suggested above will provide the most *convincing* evidence to advance our understanding of how emotions work in the social world. To the extent that emotions are thought to influence social interactions and have downstream effect on relationships, emotions scholars interested in these questions must attend to the theoretical and methodological advances in studying such interpersonal processes from the literature on close relationships (e.g., Mashek & Aron, 2004; Vangelisti & Perlman, 2006)

### Emotions within Groups

Functional theories of emotions suggest that they originally evolved in the service of group living (e.g., Keltner & Haidt, 1999). A closer look at theories on the social functions of specific emotions makes this clear. For example, the social signal that comes from embarrassment

(Keltner & Buswell, 1996) helps to alleviate discomfort within a group that comes when a member has behaved inappropriately; it helps to restore equilibrium within the group. Empirical evidence for the social function of gratitude suggests that, in addition to helping us find, remind, and bind ourselves to attentive or caring other individuals in our lives, it may serve the good of the group as well. Specifically, one study examined a tradition of gift-giving in sororities: for a one-week period, new members of the sorority get pampered—showered with gifts—by an older member of the sorority, as a way to welcome the new members. In this study, the new members recorded the amount of gratitude that they felt for each benefit received during the week. In line with its proposed social function, the averaged gratitude from the week positively predicted the extent to which the new member said she *felt like an integral part of the sorority* when asked in a follow-up at the end of the week (Algoe et al., 2008). Beyond tying people into a group, research on other-praising emotions suggests that social expression of the emotion may also help the group's functioning. Specifically, the "praising" motivation associated with the other-praising emotions (Algoe & Haidt, 2009) helps to draw attention to culturally valued attributes (e.g., kindness). In addition, expressions of thanks may spread good deeds throughout a community (with potential snowball effects), in part through the emotional response they evoke in incidental witnesses (Silvers & Haidt, 2008; Freeman et al., 2008).

Although a thoroughly modern concept relative to hunter-gatherer tribes, the concept of individual emotions working for the good of the group can apply to other organizations beyond sororities. If taken seriously, little changes to increase the experience of certain positive emotions within the confines of a corporation or other organization may spread through to have downstream impact on the entire group. For example, Kanov and colleagues discuss the individual through group-level processes that are theorized to be associated with the enactment of compassion in organizational life (Kanov, Maitlis, Worline, Dutton, Frost, Lilius, 2004; see also, Dutton, Worline, Frost, & Lilius, 2006; Lilius, Worline, Maitlis, Kanov, Dutton, & Frost, 2008).

## Emotions within Cultural Contexts

Group and cultural contexts also contour the ways emotions are experienced (Mesquita, 2001).

Cultures shape people's values and, in doing so, they also shape whether or not given events trigger "good feelings." For instance, because Asian cultures value relational interdependence and social engagement to greater degrees, the associations between perceived emotional support/friendship and positive emotions are stronger in Asian than in Western cultures (Kitayama, Mesquita, & Karasawa, 2006; Uchida, Kitayama, Mesquita, Reyes, & Morling, 2008). Culture also shapes whether and to what degree specific emotions are valued, with implications for behavior (e.g., Tsai, 2007; Tsai, Knutson, & Fung, 2006; Tsai, Miao, & Seppala, 2007). Tsai and colleagues, for instance, have presented convincing evidence that the discrepancy between how people *want* to feel (i.e., ideal affect) and how people *actually* feel accounts for variation in depressive symptoms (Tsai et al., 2006). Importantly, this line of research shows that ideal affect varies by culture when it comes to valuing *high arousal positive* (HAP, valued more in Western cultures) compared to *low arousal positive* (LAP, valued more in Asian cultures) affective states. This has implications for behavior, because desired emotional states drive everyday and seemingly mundane decisions such as what to wear, buy, do, or even say at any given moment in time. Beyond differences in values, cultural and individual histories shape differences in global well-being, and by consequence also determine the likelihood of whether new experiences boost good feelings. Recent research documents that within Asian cultures, which are low in global well-being, the link between daily events and daily well-being is stronger than in Western cultures, which are higher in global well-being (Oishi, Diener, Choi, Kim-Prieto, & Choi, 2007).

Variations within a given culture must also be taken seriously. Within Western samples, for instance, women and those who endorse interdependent self-construals reap more positive emotional benefits from feeling understood by close others (Lun, Kesebir, & Oishi, 2008). The embedded lesson for positive psychologists is to appreciate the vital role of cultural values and personalized interpretations and appraisals in fostering positive emotions and well-being more generally. The search for viable and effective positive emotion interventions must recognize that no activity, event, or circumstance will invariably and universally trigger positive emotional responses in all. Rather, personally forged and culturally embedded appraisals of those activities, events, and circumstances are the levers that activate emotions.

## Individual Differences

There are innumerable ways in which individual differences might influence the appraisals and consequences of emotions, and there is not nearly enough space in this chapter to cover those ways. For example, we regret that we do not have space to discuss exciting new work in the parasympathetic nervous system (i.e., respiratory sinus arrhythmia, known also as RSA; Oveis et al., 2010; Kok & Fredrickson, in press). Instead, we take this opportunity to draw attention to two individual differences that we believe hold great promise for advancing understanding of the role of emotions in positive psychological processes. From our perspective, key contributions to emotions research from within the realm of positive psychology will not come from showing *that* people are different in the experience and expression of certain emotions, but from showing *why* and with what consequence those differences emerge. For example, individual differences may play a role in the effectiveness of positive emotion interventions (e.g., Froh, Kashdan, Ozimkowski, & Miller, 2009; also discussed in Kashdan, Mishra, Breen, & Froh, 2009).

*Active attention to cultivating positive emotions: Clues from aging research.* It has been long understood that "bad is stronger than good" (Baumeister et al., 2001); in the realm of emotions, this translates to the conclusion that negative emotions are more powerful and carry more weight than positive emotions. Given what we know about the good that comes from genuine positive emotions, this information feels like a heavy burden: in light of this pervasive negativity bias, how can we capitalize on positive emotions and tone down the effects of negative situations for enhanced well-being? Recent research by Carstensen and colleagues suggests that we may find clues from older adults. In a series of studies, these researchers have discovered what they term a "positivity effect" in older, relative to younger, adults (for review, see Carstensen & Mikels, 2005). Whereas younger adults (typically college-aged through 40) attend to and recall negative emotional stimuli more readily than positive emotional stimuli, this pattern is reversed in older adults (e.g., aged 65–90; Charles, Mather, & Carstensen, 2004). Why?

The theory of socioemotional selectivity suggests that an individual's goals are related to their current temporal context. When one feels that time is running out, attention is directed to the most emotionally meaningful aspects of life; however, when time is vast, one prepares for the future, including acquiring information and meeting new people. Given the strong link between old age and foreshortened futures, predictions from socioemotional selectivity theory are manifest through the individual difference of age. However, these effects can be reversed with experimental manipulation; for example, young people led to believe they have a short future (Fredrickson & Carstensen, 1990) show patterns of responding in line with positivity effects. One important lesson here is that older adults appear to use strategic self-regulation driven by their age-related goals. They actively attend to positive emotion-inducing stimuli and actively disengage from negative emotion-inducing stimuli (e.g., Charles & Carstensen, 2008). This line of work smashes long-held assumptions about the inevitable draw of negative emotions, while simultaneously creating a host of questions for future research about emotion regulation strategies, including whether and how they are learned, their automaticity, and their impact on health and well-being.

*Increased emotional reactivity to specific situations: Clues from gene-environment interactions.* Breakthrough research in genetics demonstrates the critical ways in which individual differences in gene expression may play a role in emotional responses to a given situation. When chronically experienced in reaction to similar and recurring situations, these emotional responses can have myriad cumulative consequences for long-term mental and physical health. One example of how this might play out for negative emotional reactivity comes from recent research on a polymorphism of the serotonin transporter gene, 5-HTTLPR. The gene that encodes the serotonin protein (5-HTT) has received much attention lately, in part because, through the regulation of serotonin, it is hypothesized to be associated with anxiety (Lesch et al.). Individual differences in 5-HTTLPR reveal the role it plays in emotional responses to stressful situations. Gunthert and colleagues (2007) hypothesized that the gene should have differential influence across varying situations of everyday life. Indeed, their research demonstrates that, on days when people were stressed, people with the allele that is less efficient at transcribing 5-HTT had greater anxiety, relative to people with the allele that is more efficient at transcribing 5-HTT. Research such as this, which considers the specific situations in which the gene is thought to be most relevant (here, stressful days), unveils key implications for the everyday experience of emotion and chronic emotional response styles.

For future research in emotions within the realm of positive psychology, the above approach provides a good working model for one way to think about and test the circumstances under which our genes may work to the *advantage* of our emotional life. The first empirical reports of gene-environment interaction related to positive emotions are just emerging. For example, Waugh and colleagues (2009) found that individual differences in a gene associated with social acceptance predicted variability in positive emotions before, during, and after a social stress task. Specifically, people with the variant associated with high social acceptance had higher reports of positive emotions during the stressor task compared to those with other variants. Drawing on the broaden-and-build theory of positive emotions, to the extent that a person can keep some dose of positive emotions in the face of crisis, this may help the person weather the storm (Fredrickson, Tugade, Waugh & Larkin, 2003). Research on gene-environment interactions in the experience and expression of emotion is a wide-open field of inquiry. As merely one speculative example, if emotion researchers can pair their understanding of psychological mechanisms associated with a given gene (e.g., social acceptance) with their understanding of the appraisals that underlie specific positive emotions, they might be able to predict the specific situations in which certain individuals will get the biggest boost in positive emotions. If so, perhaps positive emotion interventions could then be tailored to individuals, based on their genetic profiles, for maximum effectiveness.

## Biological Measures

Positive emotions—like all emotions—span both mind and body, and so they are true psychophysiological concepts that implicate psychological and biological systems in tandem. In the past decade or so, as the links between positive emotions and improved physical health have become more firmly established (Richman, Kubzansky, Maselko, Kawachi, Choo & Bauer, 2005; Moskowitz, 2003; Pressman & Cohen, 2005), rising questions concern plausible biological mechanisms: What are the physiological pathways through which positive emotions might contribute to physical health?

Given the history of psychology, it's not surprising that scientific understanding of the biological underpinnings of positive emotions lags behind that of negative emotions. In part, this reflects that biological measures refined to index negative emotions and stress (e.g., cardiovascular reactivity, cortisol, wound healing) are often less suitable for capturing the salubrious effects of positive emotions. That said, these same measures can at times reveal the presumably indirect effects of positive emotions, as they buffer against or undo the adverse effects of stress or negative emotional arousal (Fredrickson & Levenson, 1998; Fredrickson, Mancuso, Branigan & Tugade, 2000; Moskowitz & Epel, 2006; Robles, Brooks & Pressman, 2009).

Discovering the direct biological signatures of various positive emotions requires examining a wider array of biological systems and fine-tuning new emotion-related biological measures. For example, whereas cortisol has long been taken as a hormonal index of negative emotions and stress, new research suggests that increases in the hormone progesterone reflect positive emotions felt in connection with others (Brown, Fredrickson, Wirth, Poulin, Meier, Heaphy, & Schultheiss, 2009), as may oxytocin (Holt-Lunstad, Birmingham & Light, 2008), each as assayed from saliva samples. More generally, the balance of anabolic (e.g., oxytocin, DHEA, growth hormone) to catabolic hormones (e.g., cortisol) may reflect the body's ability to restore homeostasis and repair the damaging effects of stress (Bower, Epel & Moskowitz, 2009).

Another promising biological marker, here of cumulative emotional experiences over time, is leukocyte telomere length. Telomeres are the protective caps at the tips of chromosomes, and their length has been used to index biological age and predict disease risk and longevity (Epel, 2009). Whereas chronic stress predicts shortened telomere length, positive lifestyle interventions may actually lengthen telomeres, raising the possibility that telomere length may become a fruitful biomarker for positive emotion interventions intended to alter lifestyle (Epel, 2009).

The ways that positive emotions alter blood flow within specific brain areas is also vital to understand and can inspire and test theories within positive psychology. Recent fMRI studies, for instance, lend support to Fredrickson's broaden-and-build theory of positive emotions. Stroke patients with visual neglect, for instance, show expanded visual awareness when listening to pleasant music, relative to unpleasant or no music, an effect apparently mediated by functional coupling of emotional and attentional brain regions (Soto, Funes, Guzman-Garcia, Warbrick, Rotshtein, & Humphreys, 2009). Likewise, brain-based measures of breadth of visual encoding indicate that induced emotions bias early visual inputs, with positive emotions increasing and negative emotions decreasing field of view (Schmitz, De Rosa, & Anderson, 2009). With the new Templeton Positive Neuroscience Awards on the horizon, we should expect to see rapid growth in these areas.

## Dynamic Modeling of Emotions

In the study of affect and emotions, recent developments in dynamic systems modeling (Ford & Lerner, 1992) have led to renewed conceptualizations of emotions as dynamic processes. This stands in stark contrast to models that have dominated emotions research in the past two decades, one well-known example of which is the circumplex model (Watson & Tellegen, 1985; Russell, 1980; Feldman Barrett & Russell, 1998). Although the circumplex model has been well validated using self-reports and, more recently, neuroimaging data (Posner et al., 2008), much of the empirical support for the model has been garnered from factor analytic studies that focus on inter-individual difference (e.g., whether individuals who are prone to anger also have a higher tendency for sadness), as opposed to how different emotions covary *over time*.

Several key aspects of individual differences reside, however, in the dynamics of emotions. Previous research has shown that human beings tend to focus on duration when making judgments about sadness, but they are more likely to base their ratings of anger on magnitude, or so-called peak intensity (Gilboa & Revelle, 1994). Davidson (1998) has also argued that individual differences in emotion regulation may stem from differences in the threshold, peak, or amplitude associated with certain emotions, as well as an individual's rise time to peak and recovery time. Thus, an individual's overall emotional experience is related not only to the magnitude of a particular kind of emotion, but also to its duration and other temporal characteristics. Such time-specific features can help provide key insights into the development of psychopathology (Larsen, 2000) and individual differences in affective styles (Davidson, 1998).

Positive emotions, as mentioned previously, can also buffer against or "undo" the impact of negative emotions in our everyday lives (Fredrickson et al., 2000). Such effects can often be better understood by considering emotions as dynamic entities. In a daily diary study involving a group of older adults with Parkinson's disease, Chow, Nesselroade, Shifren, and McArdle (2004) fitted a dynamic factor model (i.e., a factor analysis model with time-based relationships among the factors) to the individuals' self-report affect ratings and found that high positive affect (PA) from yesterday tended to lower today's negative affect (NA). However, yesterday's NA *did not* affect today's PA. Furthermore, positive and negative affects, as measured using the Positive and Negative Affect Schedule (Watson, Lee, & Tellegen, 1988; Watson & Tellegen, 1985), became independent as they were originally conceived by Watson and Tellegen only after the lagged relationships within and between PA and NA were taken into account. Together, these findings indicate that our understanding of emotional processes may be compromised if supposedly dynamic processes are represented and analyzed as though they do not show any changes over time.

The study of emotions is thus at an exciting juncture. Whereas individuals' emotional experiences are described as analogous to snapshots, states, or, at times, stable traits, the very concept of emotion regulation presupposes that some sort of *process* is at work. To this end, Larsen (2000) postulated that emotion regulation can be conceived as a process through which the discrepancies between an individual's desired emotion state and his/her current emotion state are minimized. Larsen used the analogy of a "thermostat" to describe such dynamic processes. The concept of emotions as thermostats was formulated into a testable mathematical model by Chow, Ram, Boker, Fujita, and Clore (2005) and fitted to empirical data within a structural equation modeling framework. The thermostat analogy raises the intriguing question of whether the regulation of "good feelings" operates through a fundamentally different mechanism than that associated with the regulation of negative feelings. In the context of Larsen's (2000) model of an affective thermostat, several researchers have suggested that the same homeostatic principles can arguably be applied to the case of pleasant emotions, thus leading to the case of a "happy thermostat" (Erber & Erber, 2000; see also other commentaries in the same issue, e.g., Freitas & Salovey, 2000; Isen, 2000; Watson, 2000).

## Nonlinear Dynamic Models

The idea of a "happy thermostat" capitalizes heavily on the need to maintain a certain degree of emotional complexity and variability despite being in a generally good state. Central to this perspective is the view of change, as opposed to stability, as one of the goals of emotion regulation. The emphasis on change is consonant with that posited in a model of human flourishing adapted by Losada and colleagues (Fredrickson & Losada, 2005; Losada & Heaphy, 2004) from the famous Lorenz system. The Lorenz equation was originally proposed as a way to represent the weather system (Lorenz, 1963). Losada and colleagues argued that individuals who continue to excel and flourish are characterized by a "chaotic" behavioral profile. That is, rather than settling into a "languished" state, such individuals manifest psychological and behavioral resilience by constantly striving to change. Such resilience is directly attributable to a unique feature, referred to as *sensitive dependence on initial conditions* or the "butterfly effect," manifested by a special subclass of nonlinear dynamic systems known as chaotic systems, of which the Lorenz system is a famous special case. This refers to the feature that small differences in individuals' starting points (e.g., starting a particular day with a sense of hope and optimism vs. starting the day with bitterness and hostility) can cascade into remarkably discrepant trajectories later.

According to Fredrickson and Losada (2005), as an individual's ratio of positive to negative emotions reaches the critical tipping point of about 3 to 1, the individual's affective dynamics begin to show chaotic patterns that appear to repeat themselves (i.e., self-similar) over time; yet, their exact values can be very different with just slight differences in initial conditions. Methodologically, methods for fitting this type of nonlinear dynamic model directly to empirical data do now exist (Chow, Ferrer, & Nesselroade, 2007), although much remains to be done to make these tools more accessible to a broader audience.

In sum, much can be gained from expanding research questions in the field of positive psychology to better address issues concerning change over time, including linear as well as nonlinear changes. To benefit from the ideas and innovations of dynamic modeling techniques (Haken, 1977/83; Thelen, 1989), greater integration of theory-driven ideas with existing modeling tools is imperative. Timely solutions to this issue include theories and renewed ways of conceptualizing emotions as nonlinear processes (Vallacher & Nowak, 1994), as well as newer estimation techniques that allow researchers to assess dynamic models within a confirmatory, model-fitting framework (Boker, Neale, & Rausch, 2008; McArdle & Hamagami, 2001; Molenaar & Raijmakers, 1998). Having a more clearly articulated framework for translating theories of positive psychology into testable mathematical or statistical models is a critical first step toward achieving this goal.

## Concluding Remarks

Emotions research and positive psychology are poised to have deep and lasting mutual influence as these two intertwined specialty areas move forward in the coming decade. Indeed, tests of basic theory within emotions research—especially the long-range consequence of frequent experiences of certain emotions—can kick up promising positive psychology interventions. For instance, Fredrickson and colleagues' recent experimental tests of the build effect of positive emotions (Fredrickson et al., 2008; Cohn & Fredrickson, in press) reveal that mind-training exercises can set people on positive trajectories of growth that lastingly increase well-being. Likewise, tests of positive psychology interventions can kick up intriguing questions for basic emotions researchers to address. Why, for instance, does redesigning one's daily life to better utilize character strengths (e.g., Seligman et al., 2005) produce lasting changes in well-being? What emotional processes account for those effects?

As we researchers collectively embark on exploring these and other new frontiers, we wish to make two final notes of encouragement: First, be willing to leave the pack, think outside the box, all the while attending to the subtle yet recurrent patterns whispered by your data. Keep in mind that advances often represent bold and risky departures from current understanding. They may well be more likely if you adopt a different vantage point than do others working in similar areas. Zoom in to examine a given emotional process in greater detail than prior researchers have examined it. Or zoom out to see it in a larger temporal or social context than before. Second, be open to capitalize on the rapid advances in measurement tools and mathematical and statistical models. Armed with these new advances, while maintaining empirical and meth-odological rigor, emotion scientists working in positive psychology will be better equipped than ever before to find practical answers to age-old questions about what makes life good. We look forward to taking stock, a decade from now, of the breakthroughs you've made.

## Notes

1. The first two authors contributed equally to this chapter and author order was decided alphabetically.

2. A review of the studies shows that amusement is often used as a comparison condition only, and we therefore know much about what amusement does *not* do, relative to other positive emotions, but we know very little about what it *does* do. We take up comment on the study of amusement again later in the chapter.

3. Other research has called out individual positive emotions (with no emotion comparison) or has compared a positive to a negative, but this is just the list of publications that is amassing in which the focus of at least one study was to test the effects of at least two different positive emotional states on the same outcome measures in the same studies. The list is thorough, but probably not quite comprehensive.

*References*

Aaker, J. L., & Williams, P. (1998). Empathy versus pride: The influence of emotional appeals across cultures. *Journal of Consumer Research, 25,* 241–261.

Agrawal, N., Menon, G., & Aaker, J. L. (2007). Getting emotional about health. *Journal of Marketing Research, 44,* 100–113.

Algoe, S. B., Gable, S. L., & Maisel, N. (2010). It's the little things: Everyday gratitude as a booster shot for romantic relationships. *Personal Relationships, 17,* 217–233.

Algoe, S. B., & Haidt, J. (2009). Witnessing excellence in action: The "other-praising" emotions of elevation, gratitude, and admiration. *Journal of Positive Psychology, 4,* 105–127.

Algoe, S. B., Haidt, J., & Gable, S. L., (2008). Beyond reciprocity: Gratitude and relationships in everyday life. *Emotion, 8,* 425–429.

Algoe, S. B., Kurtz, L., & Fredrickson, B. L. (2010). Shared laughter and interpersonal closeness. *Unpublished data, University of North Carolina at Chapel Hill.*

Argyle, M., & Crossland, J. (1987). The dimensions of positive emotions. *British Journal of Social Psychology, 26,* 127–137.

Bachorowski, J-A., & Owren, M. J. (2001). Not all laughs are alike: Voiced but not unvoiced laughter readily elicits positive affect. *Psychological Science, 12,* 252–257.

Bartlett, M. Y., & DeSteno, D. (2005). Gratitude and prosocial behavior: Helping when it costs you. *Psychological Science, 17,* 319–325.

Baumeister, R. F., Bratslavsky, E., Finkenauer, C., & Vohs, K. D. (2001). Bad is stronger than good. *Review of General Psychology, 5,* 323–370.

Boker, S. M., Neale, M. C., & Rausch, J. (2008). Latent differential equation modeling with multivariate multi-occasion indicators. In K. van Montfort, H. Oud, & A. Satorra (Eds.), *Recent developments on structural equation models: Theory and applications* (p. 151–174). Amsterdam: Kluwer.

Bower, J. E., Epel, E. S., & Moskowitz, J. T. (2009). Biological correlates: How psychological components of benefit finding may lead to physiological benefits. In C. Park, S. Lechner, A. L. Stanton, & M. H. Antoni (Eds.), *Medical illness and positive life change: Can crisis lead to personal transformation?* (pp. 155–172) Washington, DC: American Psychological Association.

Brown, S. L., Fredrickson, B. L., Wirth, M., Poulin, M., Meier, E. A., Heaphy, E., & Schultheiss, O. C. (2009). Social closeness increases salivary progesterone in humans. *Hormones and Behavior, 56,* 108–111.

Cacioppo, J. T., Gardner, W. L., & Berntson, G. G. (1999). The affect system has parallel and integrative processing components: Form follows function. *Journal of Personality and Social Psychology, 76,* 839–855.

Carstensen L. L., & Mikels, M. A. (2005). At the intersection of emotion and cognition: Aging and the positivity effect. *Current Directions in Psychological Science, 14,* 117–121.

Charles, S. T., & Carstensen, L. L. (2008). Unpleasant situations elicit different emotional responses in younger and older adults. *Psychology and Aging, 23,* 495–504.

Charles, S. T., Mather, M., & Carstensen, L. L. (2004). Aging and emotional memory: The forgettable nature of negative images for older adults. *Journal of Experimental Psychology: General, 132,* 310–324.

Chow, S-M., Ferrer, E., & Nesselroade, J. R. (2007). An unscented Kalman filter approach to the estimation of nonlinear dynamical systems models. *Multivariate Behavioral Research, 42,* 283–321.

Chow, S-M., Nesselroade, J. R., Shifren, K., & McArdle, J. J. (2004). Dynamic structure of emotions among individuals with Parkinson's disease. *Structural Equation Modeling, 11,* 560–582.

Chow, S-M., Ram, N., Boker, S. M., Fujita, F., & Clore, G. (2005). Emotion as thermostat: Representing emotion regulation using a damped oscillator model. *Emotion, 5,* 208–225.

Cohn, M. A., & Fredrickson, B. L. (in press). In search of durable positive psychology interventions: Predictors and consequences of long-term positive behavior change. *Journal of Positive Psychology.*

Cohn, M. A., Fredrickson, B. L., Brown, S. L., Mikels, J. A., & Conway, A. M. (2009). Happiness unpacked: Positive emotions increase life satisfaction by building resilience. *Emotion, 9,* 361–368.

Danner, D. D., Snowdon, D. A., & Freisen, W. V. (2001). Positive emotions in early life and longevity: Findings from the nun study. *Journal of Personality and Social Psychology, 80,* 804–813.

Davidson, R. J. (1998). Affective style and affective disorders: Perspectives from affective neuroscience. *Cognition and Emotion, 12,* 307–330.

Davidson, R. J., Kabat-Zinn, J., Schumacher, J., Rosenkranz, M., Muller, D., Santorelli, S. F., et al. (2003). Alterations in brain and immune function produced by mindfulness meditation. *Psychosomatic Medicine, 65,* 564–570.

de Rivera, J., Possell, L., Verette, J. A., & Weiner, B. (1989). Distinguishing elation, gladness, and joy. *Journal of Personality & Social Psychology, 57,* 1015–1023.

Diener, E., & Diener, C. (1996). Most people are happy. *Psychological Science, 7,* 181–185.

Diener, E., Suh, E. M., Lucas, R. E., & Smith, H. L. (1999). Subjective well-being: Three decades of progress. *Psychological Bulletin, 125,* 276–302.

Dutton, J. E., Worline, M. C., Frost, P. J., & Lilius, J. (2006). Explaining compassion organizing. *Administrative Science Quarterly, 51,* 59–96.

Ekman, P. (1992). An argument for basic emotions. *Cognition & Emotion, 6,* 169–200.

Ellsworth, P. C., & Smith, C. A. (1988). Shades of joy: Patterns of appraisal differentiating pleasant emotions. *Cognition & Emotion, 2,* 301–331.

Emmons, R. A., & McCullough, M. E. (2003). Counting blessings versus burdens: An experimental investigation of gratitude and subjective well-being in daily life. *Journal of Personality and Social Psychology, 84,* 377–389.

Erber, R., & Erber, M. W. (2000). Mysteries of mood regulation, part II: The case of the happy thermostat. *Psychological Inquiry, 11,* 210–213.

Epel, E. S. (2009). Telomeres in life-span perspective: A new "psychobiomarker"? *Current Directions in Psychological Science, 18,* 6–10.

Eyal, T., & Fishbach, A. (2006). Affect as a cue for goal conflict resolution. *Advances in Consumer Research, 34,* 484.

Feldman Barrett, L., & Russell, J. A. (1998). Independence and bipolarity in the structure of affect. *Journal of Personality and Social Psychology, 74,* 967–984.

Ford, D. H., & Lerner, R. M. (1992). *Developmental systems theory: An integrative approach.* Newbury Park, CA: Sage.

Fredrickson, B. L. (1998). What good are positive emotions? *Review of General Psychology, 2,* 300–319.

Fredrickson, B. L. (2009). *Positivity.* New York: Crown.

Fredrickson, B. L., & Carstensen, L. L. (1990). Choosing social partners: How old age and anticipated endings make people more selective. *Psychology & Aging, 5,* 335–347.

Fredrickson, B. L., & Cohn, M. A. (2008). Positive Emotions. In M. Lewis, J. Haviland-Jones, & L. F. Barrett (Eds.), *Handbook of emotions, 3rd Edition* (pp. 777–796). New York: Guilford Press.

Fredrickson, B. L., Cohn, M. A., Coffey, K. A., Pek, J., & Finkel, S. M. (2008). Open hearts build lives: Positive emotions, induced through lovingkindness meditation, build consequential personal resources. *Journal of Personality and Social Psychology, 95,* 1045–1062.

Fredrickson, B. L., & Losada, M. (2005). Positive emotions and the complex dynamics of human flourishing. *American Psychologist, 60,* 678–686.

Fredrickson, B. L., Mancuso, R. A., Branigan, C., & Tugade, M. M. (2000). The undoing effect of positive emotions. *Motivation and Emotion, 24,* 237–258.

Fredrickson, B. L., & Levenson, R. W. (1998). Positive emotions speed recovery from the cardiovascular sequelae of negative emotions. *Cognition and Emotion, 12,* 191–220.

Fredrickson, B. L., Tugade, M. M., Waugh, C. E., & Larkin, G. R. (2003). What good are positive emotions in crisis? A prospective study of resilience and emotions following the terrorist attacks on the United States on September 11th, 2001. *Journal of Personality & Social Psychology, 84,* 365–376.

Freeman, D., Aquino, K., & McFerran, B. (2008). Overcoming beneficiary race as an impediment to charitable donations: Social dominance orientation, the experience of moral elevation, and donation behavior. *Personality & Social Psychology Bulletin, 35*, 72–84.

Freitas, A., & Salovey, P. (2000). Regulating emotion in the short and long term. *Psychological Inquiry, 11*, 178–179.

Froh, J. J., Kashdan, T. B., Ozimkowski, K. M., & Miller, N. (2009). Who benefits the most from a gratitude intervention in children? Examining positive affect as a moderator. *Journal of Positive Psychology, 4(5)*, 408–422.

Gervais, M., & Wilson, D. S. (2005). The evolution and functions of laughter and humor: A synthetic approach. *Quarterly Review of Biology, 80*, 395–430.

Gilboa, E., & Revelle, W. (1994). Personality and the structure of affective responses. In S. Van Goozen, N. Van de Poll, & J. Sergeant (Eds.), *Emotions: Essays on emotion theory* (pp. 135–159). Philadelphia: Lawrence Erlbaum Associates.

Gonzaga, G. C., Turner, R. A., Keltner, D., Campos, B., & Altemus, M. (2006). Romantic love and sexual desire in close relationships. *Emotion, 6*, 163–179.

Gonzaga, G. C., Keltner, D., Londahl, E. A., & Smith, M. D. (2001). Love and the commitment problem in romantic relationships and friendship. *Journal of Personality & Social Psychology, 81*, 247–262.

Gottman, J. M. (1994). *What predicts divorce? The relationship between marital processes and marital outcomes.* Hillsdale, NJ: Erlbaum.

Graham, S. M., Huang, J. Y., Clark, M. S., & Helgeson, V. S. (2008). The positives of negative emotions: Willingness to express negative emotions promotes relationships. *Personality and Social Psychology Bulletin, 34*, 394–406.

Gunthert, K. C., Conner, T. S., Armeli, S., Tennen, H., Coyault, J., & Kranzler, H. R. (2007). Serotonin transporter gene polymorphism (5-HTTLPR) and anxiety reactivity in daily life: A daily process approach to gene-environment interaction. *Psychosomatic Medicine, 69*, 762–768.

Haidt, J. (2003). The moral emotions. In R. J. Davidson, K. R. Scherer, & H. H. Goldsmith (Eds.), *Handbook of Affective Sciences* (pp. 852–870). Oxford: Oxford University Press.

Haken, H. (1977/83). *Synergetics, and introduction: Non-equilibrium phase transitions and self-organization in physics, chemistry and biology.* Berlin: Springer–Verlag.

Holt-Lunstad, J., Birmingham, W. A., & Light, K. C. (2008). The influence of a "warm touch" support enhancement intervention among married couples on ambulatory blood pressure, oxytocin, alpha amylase and cortisol. *Psychosomatic Medicine, 70*, 976–985.

Isen, A. M. (2000). Some perspectives on positive affect and self-regulation. *Psychological Inquiry, 11*, 184–187.

Isen, A. M., & Levin, P. F. (1972). Effect of feeling good on helping: Cookies and kindness. *Journal of Personality & Social Psychology, 21*, 384–388.

Johnson, K. J., & Fredrickson, B. L. (2005). "We all look the same to me": Positive emotions eliminate the own-race bias in face recognition. *Psychological Science, 16*, 875–881.

Kabat-Zinn, J. (1982). An outpatient program in behavioral medicine for chronic pain patients based on the practice of mindfulness meditation: theoretical considerations and preliminary results. *General Hospital Psychiatry, 4*, 33–47.

Kahneman, D. (1999). Objective happiness. In, D. Kahneman, E. Diener, N. Schwarz (Eds.) [] Well-being: *Foundations of hedonic psychology* (pp. 3–25). Russell Sage Foundation: New York.

Kanov, J. M., Maitlis, S., Worline, M. C., Dutton, J. E., Frost, P. J., Lilius, J. M. (2004). Compassion in organizational life. *American Behavioral Scientist, 47*, 808–827.

Kashdan, T. B., Biswas-Diener, R., & King, L. A. (2008). Reconsidering happiness: The costs of distinguishing between hedonics and eudaimonia. *The Journal of Positive Psychology, 3*, 219–233.

Kashdan, T. B., Mishra, A., Breen, W. E., & Froh, J. J. (2009). Gender differences in gratitude: Examining appraisals, narratives, the willingness to express emotions, and changes in psychological needs. *Journal of Personality, 77*, 1–40.

Keltner, D., & Buswell, B. N. (1996). Evidence for the distinctness of embarrassment, shame, and guilt: A study of recalled antecedents and facial expressions of emotion. *Cognition & Emotion, 10*, 155–171.

Keltner, D., & Haidt, J. (1999). Social functions of emotions. *Cognition & Emotion. Special Issue: Functional Accounts of Emotion, 13*, 505–521.

Keyes, C. L. M., Shmotkin, D., & Ryff, C. D. (2002). Optimizing well-being: The empirical encounter of two traditions. *Journal of Personality and Social Psychology, 82*, 1007–1022.

Kimata, H. (2007). Laughter elevates the levels of breast-milk melatonin. *Journal of Psychosomatic Research, 62*, 699–702.

Kitayama, S., Mesquita, B., & Karasawa, M. (2006). Cultural affordances and emotional experience: Socially engaging and disengaging emotions in Japan and the United States. *Journal of Personality and Social Psychology, 91*, 890–903.

Kok, B. E., & Fredrickson, B. L. (in press). Upward spirals of the heart: Autonomic flexibility, as indexed by vagal tone, reciprocally and prospectively

predicts positive emotions and social connectedness. *Biological Psychiatry*.

Larsen, R. J. (2000). Toward a science of mood regulation. *Psychological Inquiry, 11(3)*, 129–141.

Larsen, R. J., & Prizmic, Z. (2008). Regulation of
emotional well-being: Overcoming the hedonic
treadmill. In M. Eid & R. J. Larsen (Eds.), *The science of subjective well-being* (pp. 258–289). New
York: Guildford Press.

Lerner, J. S., & Keltner, D. (2000). Beyond valence:
Toward a model of emotion-specific influences
on judgment and choice. *Cognition & Emotion,
14*, 473–493.

Lerner, J. S., & Keltner, D. (2001). Fear, anger, and
risk. *Journal of Personality & Social Psychology,
81*, 146–159.

Lerner, J. S., & Tiedens, L. Z. (2006). Portrait of the
angry decision maker: How appraisal tendencies
shape anger's influence on cognition. *Journal of
Behavioral Decision Making, 19*, 115–137.

Lilius, J. M., Worline, M. C., Maitlis, S., Kanov, J.,
Dutton, J. E., & Frost, P. (2008). The contours and
consequences of compassion at work. *Journal of
Organizational Behavior, 29*, 193–218.

Lorenz, E. N. (1963). Deterministic nonperiodic
flow. *Journal of Atmospheric Science, 20*,
130–141.

Losada, M., & Heaphy, E. (2004). The role of positivity and connectivity in the performance of
business teams. *American Behavioral Scientist,
47*, 740–765.

Lun, J., Kesebir, S., & Oishi, S. (2008). On feeling
understood and feeling well: The role of interdependence. *Journal of Research in Personality, 42*,
1623–1628.

Lyubomirsky, S., King, L., & Diener, E. (2005). The
benefits of frequent positive affect: Does happiness lead to success? *Psychological Bulletin, 131*,
803–855.

Lyubomirsky, S., Sheldon, K. M., & Schkade, D.
(2005). Pursuing happiness: The architecture
of sustainable change. *Review of General
Psychology, 9*, 111–131.

Mashek, D. J., & Aron, A. P. (Eds.) (2004). *Handbook
of Closeness and Intimacy*. Mahwah, NJ:
Lawrence Erlbaum Associates Publishers.

McArdle, J. J., & Hamagami, F. (2001). Latent difference score structural models for linear dynamic
analysis with incomplete longitudinal data. In L.
Collins & A. Sayer (Eds.), *New methods for the
analysis of change* (pp. 139–175). Washington,
D. C.: American Psychological Association.

Mesquita, B. (2001). Emotions in collectivist and
individualist contexts. *Journal of Personality and
Social Psychology, 80*, 68–74.

Molenaar, P. C. M., & Raijmakers, M. E. J. (1998).
Fitting nonlinear dynamical models directly to
observed time series. In K. M. Newell & P. C. M.
Molenaar (Eds.), *Applications of nonlinear
dynamics to developmental process modeling*
(pp. 269–297). Mahwah, NJ: Lawrence Erlbaum.

Moskowitz, J. T. (2003). Positive affect predicts
lower risk of AIDS mortality. *Psychosomatic
Medicine, 65*, 620–626.

Moskowitz, J. T., & Epel, E. S. (2006). Benefit finding
and diurnal cortisol slope in maternal caregivers:
A moderating role for positive emotions. *Journal
of Positive Psychology, 1*, 83–91.

Oishi, S., Diener, E., Choi, D-W., Kim-Prieto, C., &
Choi, I. (2007). The dynamics of daily events and
well-being across cultures: When less is more.
*Journal of Personality and Social Psychology,
93*, 685–698.

Otake, K., Shimai, S., Tanaka-Matsumi, J., Otsui, K.,
& Fredrickson, B. L. (2006). Happy people become
happier through kindness: A counting kindnesses
intervention. *Journal of Happiness Studies, 7*,
361–375.

Oveis, C. Horberg, E. J., & Keltner, D. (2010).
Compassion, pride, and social intuitions of self-
other similarity. *Journal of Personality & Social
Psychology, 98(4)*, 618–630.

Posner, J., Russell, J. A., Gerber, A., Gorman, D.,
Colibazzi, T., Yu, S., Wang, Z., Kangarlu, A., Zhu,
H., Peterson, B. S. (2008). The neurophysiological
bases of emotion: An fMRI study of the affective
circumplex using emotion-denoting words.
*Human Brain Mapping, 30*, 883–895.

Pressman, S. D., & Cohen, S. (2005). Does positive
affect influence health? *Psychological Bulletin,
131*, 925–971.

Repetti, R. L. (1989). Effects of daily workload on
subsequent behavior during marital interaction:
The roles of social withdrawal and spouse support. *Journal of Personality and Social
Psychology, 57*, 651–659.

Reis, H., Clark, M. S., & Holmes, J. G. (2004).
Perceived partner responsiveness as an organizing construct in the study of intimacy and closeness. In D. J. Mashek & A. P. Aron (Eds.), *Handbook
of closeness and intimacy* (pp. 201–225). Mahwah,
NJ: Lawrence Erlbaum Associates Publishers.

Richman, L. S., Kubzansky, L., Maselko, J., Kawachi,
I., Choo, P., & Bauer, M. (2005). Positive emotion
and health: Going beyond the negative. *Health
Psychology, 24*, 422–429.

Roberts, L. M., Dutton, J. E., Spreitzer, G. M.,
Heaphy, E. D., & Quinn, R. E. (2005).
Composing the reflected best self portrait:
Building pathways for becoming extraordinary

in work organizations. *Academy of Management Review, 30,* 712–736.

Robles, T. F., Brooks, K. P., Pressman, S. D. (2009). Trait positive affect buffers the effects of acute stress on skin barrier recovery. *Health Psychology, 28,* 373–378.

Rozin, P., & Royzman, E. B. (2001). Negativity bias, negativity dominance, and contagion. *Personality and Social Psychology Review, 5,* 296–320.

Russell, J. A. (1980). A circumplex model of affect. *Journal of Personality and Social Psychology, 39,* 1161–1178.

Ryan, R. M., & Deci, E. L. (2001). On happiness and human potentials: A review of research on hedonic and eudaimonic well-being. *Annual Review of Psychology, 52,* 141–166.

Ryff, C. D., & Singer, B. H. (1998). The contours of positive human health. *Psychological Inquiry, 9,* 1–28.

Schmitz, T. W., De Rosa, E., & Anderson, A. K. (2009). Opposing influences of affective state valence on visual cortical encoding. *Journal of Neuroscience, 29,* 7199–7207.

Schwartz, R. M. (1997). Consider the simple screw: Cognitive science, quality improvement, and psychotherapy. *Journal of Consulting and Clinical Psychology, 65,* 970–983.

Seligman, M. E. P., Steen, T., Park, N., & Peterson, C. (2005). Positive psychology progress: Empirical validations of interventions. *American Psychologist, 60,* 410–421.

Shiota, M. N., Keltner, D., & Mossman, A. (2007). The nature of awe: Elicitors, appraisals, and effects on self concept. *Cognition & Emotion, 21,* 944–963.

Silvers, J. A., & Haidt, J. (2008). Moral elevation can induce nursing. *Emotion, 8,* 291–295.

Silvia, P. J. (2005). What is interesting? Exploring the appraisal structure of interest. *Emotion, 5,* 89–102.

Smoski, M., & Bachorowski, J-A. (2003). Antiphonal laughter between friends and strangers. *Cognition and Emotion, 17,* 327–340.

Soto, D., Funes, M. J., Guzman-Garcia, A., Warbrick, T., Rotshtein, P., & Humphreys, G. W. (2009). Pleasant music overcomes the loss of awareness in patients with visual neglect. *Proceedings of the U.S. National Academy of Sciences, 106(4),* 6011–6016

Takahashi, H., Matsuura, M., Koeda, M., Yahata, N., Suhara, T., Kato, M., & Okubo, Y. (2008). Brain activations during judgments of positive self-conscious emotion and positive basic emotion: Pride and joy. *Cerebral cortex, 18,* 898–903.

Teasdale, J. D., Segal, Z. V., Williams, J. M. G., Ridgeway, V. A., Soulsby, J. M., & Lau, M. A. (2000).

Prevention of relapse/recurrence in major depression by mindfulness-based cognitive therapy. *Journal of Consulting and Clinical Psychology, 68,* 615–623.

Thelen, E. (1989). Self-organization in developmental processes: Can systems approaches work? In M. R. Gunnar & E. Thelen (Eds.), *Systems and development* (pp. 77–117). Hillsdale, NJ: Lawrence Erlbaum Associates.

Tooby, J., & Cosmides, L. (1990). The past explains the present: Emotional adaptations and the structure of ancestral environments. *Ethology & Sociobiology, 11,* 375–424.

Tracy, J. L., & Robins, R. W. (2004). Show your pride: Evidence for a discrete emotion expression. *Psychological Science, 15,* 194–197.

Tracy, J. L., & Robins, R. W. (2008). The nonverbal expression of pride: Evidence for cross-cultural recognition. *Journal of Personality & Social Psychology, 94,* 516–530.

Tsai, J. L., (2007). Ideal affect: Cultural causes and behavioral consequences. *Perspectives on Psychological Science, 2,* 242–259.

Tsai, J. L., Knutson, B., & Fung, H. H. (2006). Cultural variation in affect valuation. *Journal of Personality & Social Psychology, 90,* 288–307.

Tsai, J. L., Miao, M. F., & Seppala, E. (2007). Good feelings in Christianity and Buddhism: Religious differences in ideal affect. *Personality & Social Psychology Bulletin, 33,* 409–421.

Tsang, J. (2006). Gratitude and prosocial behavior: An experimental test of gratitude. *Cognition & Emotion, 20,* 138–148.

Uchida, Y., Kitayama, S., Mesquita, B., Reyes, J. A. S., & Morling, B. (2008). Is perceived emotional support beneficial? Well-being and health in independent and interdependent cultures. *Personality and Social Psychology Bulletin, 34,* 741–754.

Vallacher, R. R., & Nowak, A. (Eds.) (1994). *Dynamical systems in social psychology.* SanDiego, CA: Academic Press.

Vangelisti, A. L., & Perlman, D. (Eds.) (2006). *The Cambridge handbook of personal relationships.* New York, NY: Cambridge University Press.

Watson, D. (2000). Basic problems in positive mood regulation. *Psychological Inquiry, 11,* 205–209.

Watson, D., Lee, A. C., & Tellegen, A. (1988). Development and validation of brief measures of positive and negative affect: The PANAS scale. *Journal of Personality and Social Psychology, 54,* 1063–1070.

Watson, D., Lee, A., & Tellegen, A. (1988). Development and validation of brief measures of positive and negative affect: The PANAS scales.

*Journal of Personality and Social Psychology, 54(6),* 1063–1070.

Watson, D., & Tellegen, A. (1985). Toward a consensual structure of mood. *Psychological Bulletin, 98,* 219–235.

Waugh, C. E., Dearing, K. F., Joormann, J., & Gotlib, I. H. (2009). Association between the COMT val158-met polymorphism, perceived social acceptance in adolescent girls. *Journal of Child & Adolescent Psychopharmacology, 19(4),* 395–401.

Waugh, C. E., & Fredrickson, B. L. (2006). Nice to know you: Positive emotions, self-other overlap, and complex understanding in the formation of a new relationship. *The Journal of Positive Psychology, 1,* 93–106.

Williams, L. A., & DeSteno, D. (2008). Pride: Adaptive social emotion or seventh sin? *Psychological Science, 20,* 284–288.

# IV

## Social-Cognitive Perspectives

# 9

# The Role of Hypo-egoic Self-Processes in Optimal Functioning and Subjective Well-Being

*Mark R.Leary and Jennifer Guadagno*

The emergence of self-awareness was an important turning point in the psychological development of the human species. Before the hominids became capable of conscious, self-relevant thought, they lived much like other mammals, responding emotionally and behaviorally to the immediate demands of their physical and social environments with little or no forethought or introspection. However, once self-awareness permitted them to think consciously about who they were and what they were doing, our prehuman ancestors became able to regulate their behavior partly on the basis of their long-term goals and abstract conceptualizations of themselves. Theorists disagree regarding precisely when and why the human capacity for self-awareness evolved (e.g., Gallup; 1997; Humphrey, 1982; Jaynes, 1976; Leary & Buttermore, 2003; Sedikides & Skowronski, 2000), but evidence suggests that human beings certainly possessed the capacity for self-awareness of modern people by at least 60,000 years ago at the time of the "cultural big bang" (Leary & Buttermore, 2003).

Self-awareness involves cognitive skills that are essential for many of the unique features of human life, at both the personal and societal level.

The central skill may involve the ability to represent oneself cognitively in abstract and symbolic ways. Being able to think consciously about oneself, and particularly being able to create a mental analogue of oneself in one's mind, is centrally involved in thinking about and planning for the future (Jaynes, 1976; Leary, Estrada, & Allen 2009). By imagining themselves in the future, people can anticipate future events, set goals, imagine the consequences of various courses of action, and mentally practice future behaviors, thereby allowing them to self-regulate on the basis of conscious goals and strategies that they conjure in their minds. Of course, the mental futures that people imagine are not always accurate, but the ability to self-reflect allows people the possibility of consciously controlling their own responses.

Despite the myriad benefits that self-awareness provides human beings over animals that lack a self, self-reflection came with some costs that undermined people's well-being (for a review, see Leary, 2004). Among other things, the capacity for self-reflection creates a great deal of personal suffering in the form of depression, anxiety, anger, envy, and other negative emotions by allowing people to ruminate about the past or imagine what might happen to them in the future. The self also distorts people's perceptions of the world in self-serving ways, leading them to make bad decisions based on biased views of themselves. Furthermore, the tendency to think about oneself and the world in egocentric and egotistical ways blinds people to their own shortcomings and undermines their relationships with others. The ability to self-reflect also underlies a great deal of social conflict by leading people to separate themselves into ingroups and outgroups on the basis of arbitrary self-conceptualizations and then to behave selfishly in line with their own and their groups' narrow interests.

### Taking Stock

Clearly, the capacity for self-awareness has strong and pervasive implications for the quality of people's lives, and people have long recognized that certain ways of thinking about oneself in relation to the world promote subjective well-being and prosocial behavior, whereas other ways compromise well-being and lead to dysfunctional actions. The idea that the self can be a source of personal and interpersonal difficulties (and that positive states are more likely when people are less self-absorbed) can be traced to a number of ancient philosophical and spiritual traditions. Vedanta, Hinduism, Taoism, Buddhism, Zen, and most mystical traditions share the belief that excessive self-focus undermines the quality of people's lives, and that quieting the self promotes adaptive functioning and well-being in numerous ways.

Yet, although contemporary psychologists recognize some of the problems that are associated with an excessive focus on oneself (Baumeister, 1991; Leary, 2004), little attention has been paid to the role of self-processes in positive experience, optimal functioning, and behaviors that allow people to thrive. This neglect is surprising both because the connection between self-awareness and optimal experience has been discussed for millennia and because social and personality psychologists have devoted a great deal of attention to the self in recent years (see Baumeister, 1999; Baumeister & Vohs, 2004; Leary & Tangney, 2003; Vohs & Finkel, 2006).

The central theme of this chapter is that many phenomena of interest to positive psychology share a common feature that involves a particular pattern of self-relevant cognitive activity. This hypo-egoic state is responsible both for the sense of well-being that tends to accompany many positive psychological experiences (such as flow, meditation, and transcendence) and for prosocial beliefs and actions in which people behave in ways that benefit other people, sometimes at cost to themselves. After describing the hypo-egoic state, we discuss the role of self-process in five phenomena—humility, positive emotions, other-oriented states (such as compassion, altruism, and love), wisdom, and transcendence.

### Hypo-egoic States and Positive Psychological Functioning

We use the term *hypo-egoic* to refer to psychological states that are characterized by relatively little involvement of the self. In their initial description of hypo-egoic states, Leary, Adams, and Tate (2006; in press) suggested that hypo-egoic states are characterized by two primary features—a low (as opposed to high) degree of self-awareness and highly concrete (as opposed to abstract) self-relevant thoughts. When self-awareness is low and whatever self-relevant thoughts that arise are concrete and present-centered, people's responses are minimally influenced by their self-relevant thoughts and they can be said to be functioning hypo-egoically.

We elaborate on this model to suggest that the degree to which people are operating in a hypo-egoic mode in a particular situation is an inverse function of three factors: (1) the proportion of time that the person is self-aware vs. functioning automatically and nonconsciously, (2) the degree to which the person's phenomenal self is individuated (i.e., the person conceives him- or herself as similar and connected to rather than distinct and separate from other people), and (3) the degree to which the person is personally invested (or ego-involved) in the outcome of a particular situation. Thus, a hypo-egoic state is one in which self-awareness is low, the phenomenal self is not highly individuated, and the person is not ego-involved. In contrast, an *egoic* state is characterized by high self-awareness, a highly abstract and individuated phenomenal self, and a high level of ego-involvement. We briefly describe each of these features of egoic and hypo-egoic states in the following sections.

### Low Self-Awareness

Although modern human beings are able to think consciously about themselves in ways that their prehistoric ancestors could not, they are, in fact, self-aware only a portion of the time. Many "dual-process" theories suggest that people possess two distinct psychological systems that process and respond to information (Bargh, 1997; Epstein, 1994). One system deliberately and systematically uses conscious thought to weigh important considerations, plan in advance how to respond, intentionally search for relevant information (instead of responding to whatever is there), and intentionally override unwanted impulses and emotions. These conscious or controlled processes, which typically involve self-awareness, occur relatively slowly, process information serially, and require considerable attentional and cognitive resources.

The second system processes information nonconsciously and automatically without intentional effort or self-awareness (Bargh & Chartrand, 1999). In cases in which behavior is effectively controlled by evolved dispositions, cognitive scripts, or habits, people can process information and respond behaviorally with little or no conscious self-thought. Nonconscious processing is much faster than conscious thinking, and it can process many pieces of information simultaneously using fewer cognitive resources. However, nonconscious processing does not allow the systematic and careful consideration of information, rarely considers the long-term implications of one's actions, and may cause people to respond mindlessly to external cues without considering important features of the situation (Langer, 1989).

Both modes of information-processing are essential. People do not have the cognitive resources to reflect consciously on all of their choices, but neither can they rely entirely on automatic, nonconscious processes because conscious, self-focused deliberation is sometimes needed. People alternate between conscious and nonconscious processing more or less continuously, perhaps thousands of times each day. At times, however, they temporarily become "stuck" in one mode or the other—processing information consciously that ought to be processed nonconsciously or responding automatically to situations that should be considered deliberately. Although people switch back and forth between modes, within a given span of time, the proportion of time that people are thinking consciously about themselves versus responding automatically and nonconsciously varies greatly. Hypo-egoic states are more likely when the proportion of time that a person is self-aware is low.

In many ways, the hypo-egoic state resembles the state of "cognitive deconstruction" that arises when people eliminate or severely reduce self-awareness. According to Baumeister (1991), this deconstructed state is characterized by a focus on the present moment, attention to one's movements and sensations rather than emotions and higher-level thinking, and reliance on immediate rather than long-term goals. These features are consistent with a hypo-egoic state in which people are not highly self-aware nor consciously thinking about or regulating their thoughts and behaviors.

## Nonindividuated Phenomenal Self

A person's phenomenal self (Rhodewalt, 1986)—sometimes called the spontaneous or working self-concept (Markus & Wurf, 1987; McGuire & McGuire, 1981)—is that aspect of his or her conceptualization of him- or herself of which the person is aware at a particular time. A person's overall identity is quite vast, containing self-relevant beliefs, descriptions, roles, autobiographical information, and other self-relevant representations that, if asked, the person would endorse as true of him- or herself. Yet, at any given moment, people can think about only a very small portion of their total self-identity. Thus, in a given situation, a person may be thinking only about his or her intellectual ability, physical appearance, membership in a particular group, or ability to tell interesting stories. The particular aspect of the person's identity of which the person is currently aware is his or her phenomenal self.

The attributes that constitute people's identities (and thus their phenomenal selves) vary in many ways, but two are central to the distinction between egoic and hypo-egoic states. First, aspects of people's self-identities differ in abstractness versus concreteness. A student thinking about her math ability may be thinking broadly about how good she is at math in general (a rather abstract conceptualization) or whether she has the ability to solve a specific math problem (which is more specific). In general, hypo-egoic states tend to involve specific rather than abstract self-relevant thoughts.

Second, elements of the phenomenal self differ in the degree to which they reflect features that make one unusual and different from other people (individuated) versus features that reflect one's similarities and connections with others (nonindividuated; McGuire, McGuire, Child, & Fujioka, 1978). A member of a minority group at a professional meeting may think about himself with respect to his minority status (an individuating feature of his phenomenal self at that moment) or as a member of the professional organization (a less individuating feature). The self-relevant thoughts of people in a hypo-egoic state tend to be less individuating than those of people in a highly egoic state.

### Ego-involvement

As used here, ego-involvement refers to the degree to which people desire a situation to transpire in a particular way. People are sometimes highly invested in the outcome of a particular situation (including the behavior of other people), whereas at other times they are less invested in how the situation turns out. When people are ego-involved, they are focused narrowly on the implications of an event for themselves and do not take a broader perspective on how the event might also affect other people or even on its wider implications for themselves in the long run. Ego-involvement is characterized by an egocentric insistence that events should occur the way that the person desires and other considerations be damned.

Hypo-egoic states are characterized by a low level of ego-involvement. Although people in a hypo-egoic state certainly prefer certain outcomes rather than others, they do not harbor the belief that the situation should transpire the way they personally desire. Low ego-involvement involves a balanced perspective that considers one's own desires alongside other considerations, including the desires of other people.

In the remainder of the chapter, we examine five phenomena of interest to positive psychology—humility, positive emotions, other-oriented states (such as compassion, altruism, and love), wisdom, and transcendence—that appear to share hypo-egoic states as a common basis. In each instance, people appear more likely to experience the state in question (to be humble or other-oriented, for example) when self-awareness is low, their phenomenal self is not highly individuated, and they are not ego-involved in the outcome of the situation.

### Humility

Most people view humility as a positive trait (if not a virtue), perceive humble people positively, and believe that humility has beneficial outcomes in many aspects of life (Exline & Geyer, 2004; Rowatt et al., 2006; Vera & Rodriguz-Lopez, 2004). Contrary to some connotations of the word, humility does not mean that one has a low opinion of oneself or regards oneself as inferior to other people (Tangney, 2000). Rather, humility seems to involve having an accurate assessment of one's characteristics and abilities, which necessarily includes a willingness to acknowledge one's limitations (Exline et al., 2004; Tangney, 2000). Perhaps most importantly, although humble people perceive their positive characteristics accurately, they keep them in perspective and do not believe that their positive characteristics and accomplishments entitle them to special treatment by other people. Thus, they are not necessarily "modest" in the sense of denigrating themselves but rather downplay the importance of their strengths and accomplishments. Humility also involves open-mindedness to new ideas, advice, and perspectives that are contrary to one's own. Humble people do not believe that they have an inside route to the truth, nor do they have the arrogance that they are wiser than other people. This tentativeness of one's own beliefs helps to keep the humble person's own abilities, achievements, and place in the world in perspective. One interesting feature of humility is a lack of awareness of or attention to one's own humbleness. Humble people rarely appear to know that they are humble.

Although little empirical evidence exists regarding the correlates, causes, and effects of humility (for reviews of the meager research, see Exline, 2008, Tangney, 2000, 2002), limited writing and speculation on the topic strongly suggest that humility operates hypo-egoically. Theorists have described humility as a "relative lack of self-focus or self-preoccupation" and as a process of becoming "unselved" (Tangney, 2000). Exline (2008) explicitly suggested that humble people have a "quiet ego" that is characterized by the realization that one is, in the large scheme of things, no better and no worse than other people. Similarly, Tangney (2000) posited that a "person who has gained a sense of humility is no longer phenomenologically at the center of his or her world" (p. 72). Thus, humility is clearly characterized by hypo-egoic features of low self-awareness and a low degree of individuation.

Although this hypothesis has not been tested, we believe that humble people are also less likely to feel personally invested or ego-involved in the outcomes of specific situations. Humble people are certainly committed to certain outcomes, sometimes deeply, but those outcomes tend to be communal rather than individual. Furthermore, because they acknowledge their weaknesses and see their place in the world, humble people do not always anticipate success or expect the world to conform to their wishes.

Some theorists have suggested that humility fosters a prosocial perspective, positive interpersonal relationships, and a greater sense of connection to other people and the larger world (Exline, 2008, Tangney, 2000). In our view, however, these positive outcomes may not be so much consequences of humility as co-effects of having a hypo-egoic perspective. When people operate hypo-egoically, they are naturally more humble but also more capable of recognizing the worth, importance, and potential of other people.

### Positive Emotions

Traditionally, positive emotions have been conceptualized as reactions to cognitive appraisals indicating the presence of environmental benefits or opportunities (Smith & Lazarus, 1993). Although such appraisals underlie certain positive emotions, such as happiness, not all positive emotions are evoked by events with clear implications for well-being. For example, the positive experiences associated with flow, awe, joy, amusement, interest, and certain meditative and mystical states are less clearly associated with appraisals involving obvious benefits and opportunities.

Many such positive experiences appear to occur primarily, if not exclusively, during hypo-egoic states. In the case of flow, awe, meditation, and mysticism, for example, the individual is in a cognitive state in which self-awareness is minimal and whatever self-thoughts do occur tend to focus on concrete aspects of the individual. A person entranced by a magnificent sunset, a meditator focused on her breathing, and a mystic in a blissful transcendent experience are each in a hypo-egoic state. Their self-awareness is minimal (if they have any self-relevant thoughts at all), they have lost a sense of having an individuated phenomenal self (and, in fact, often feel that they are part of the event that they are experiencing), and they are so non-ego-involved that they could be said to have no goals, engaging in the action for its own intrinsic experience.

## Reducing Negative Emotion

One reason that hypo-egoic states are linked to positive affect is that a great deal of emotional distress is generated by self-relevant thoughts (Leary, 2004). Even when things are objectively going well at the time, people often think themselves into negative emotions. Although self-relevant thoughts can induce any negative emotion, anxiety is perhaps the most common. In a historical look at anxiety among human beings, Martin (1999; Martin & Shirk, 2008) suggested that the problem of self-induced anxiety became particularly pronounced at the time of the agricultural revolution about 10,000 years ago. Prior to the emergence of agriculture, people lived in nomadic bands of hunter-gatherer-scavengers, living off the land on a day-to-day basis. In such an environment, people had little reason to plan more than a few days ahead or to think about long-term goals or future events. However, after they turned to farming, people began to worry about the distal future because they exerted much of their daily effort on tasks that had uncertain outcomes, such as planting and tending crops. In addition, as they established permanent settlements and began to accumulate property, people had more reason to worry about their personal homes and belongings than when, as nomads, they carried their meager possessions with them at all times. According to Martin's analysis, the source of a great deal of self-induced anxiety lies in mismatch between aspects of human psychology that evolved to deal with living in an immediate-return environment and the delayed-return nature of modern life.

Given that self-related thoughts can induce negative emotion, events that decrease self-awareness, and particularly those that create hypo-egoic states, naturally lower dysphoria (Leary, 2004). In the case of flow, for example, people are so intensely focused on and involved in what they are doing in the present moment that they do not engage in the kinds of self-relevant thoughts that cause anxiety and other unpleasant emotions (Nakamura & Csikszentmihalyi, 2002). Deeply concentrating on what one is doing leaves little room for self-awareness and, thus, worries about one's own problems or concerns. (Indeed, when people are preoccupied with their own worries, flow is unlikely to occur.) Furthermore, when people are in flow, they are intrinsically motivated by what they are doing and not invested or ego-involved in the outcome. Activities that induce flow are inherently rewarding and the outcome or end product is "just an excuse for the process" (Nakamura & Csikszentmihalyi, 2002, p. 90). When nothing is to be gained from an activity except the experience itself, it is difficult to be invested in the outcome.

Because excessive self-thought is often troubling, people often seek experiences that lower self-awareness. Some ways of escaping the self—such as meditation, becoming "lost" in nature or a good book, and seeking flow experiences—are probably beneficial diversions. Other escapes—such as alcohol and drug abuse—create problems of their own (Baumeister, 1991). Whether ultimately adaptive or maladaptive, hypo-egoic states often bring relief from self-induced negative emotions.

## Broadening and Building

Fredrickson (1998) has proposed that positive emotions are associated with psychological states that increase people's cognitive and behavioral capacities. Whereas negative emotions tend to be associated with specific action tendencies (such as fear being associated with avoiding or escaping feared stimuli), Fredrickson's broaden-and-build theory suggests that positive emotions broaden people's immediate repertoire of cognitive and behavioral options (so that more possible responses come to mind) and build their personal resources (e.g., skills, knowledge, social contacts) for the future.

The link between the broaden-and-build process and hypo-egoic states is straightforward. People are most likely to be highly egoic (that is, demonstrate high self-awareness, individuation, and ego-involvement) when they perceive physical or social threats to their well-being. When under threat, people focus on their own concerns and on how to minimize specific negative outcomes and, thus, are highly self-focused, individuated, and ego-involved. However, when people feel safe and negative emotions abate, they tend to become less self-focused, individuated, and ego-involved. As a result, positive emotions may be associated with a tendency to broaden-and-build because positive emotions arise in situations in which people are less focused on themselves. Put differently, similar situations lead to hypo-egoic functioning and to positive emotions that promote broadening and building.

## Prosocial Orientations: Compassion, Altruism, and Love

Some theorists maintain that true compassion, altruism, and love do not exist because helping

and loving behaviors are always beneficial to the helper in some way. In most instances, people gain social or self-administered rewards for doing what is right, avoid social or self-punishments from failing to help, or eliminate aversive arousal or stress by helping. However, other writers have suggested that, although people certainly gain personal benefits from helping, these benefits are often unintended consequences of reducing others' needs or distress, leaving open the possibility that the person acted in a selfless way in response to another's need (Batson, Ahmad, Lishner, & Tsang, 2002). These two positions on the nature of altruistic action have been hotly debated, and we will not enter the fray here. Rather, we will simply note that, whatever their initial impetus, positive other-oriented actions are more likely when people are in a hypo-egoic state.

People find it difficult to be genuinely interested and invested in other people while at the same time being preoccupied with their personal goals, concerns, feelings, and sense of self. Thus, other-oriented phenomena that involve an interest in and commitment to the happiness, well-being, and welfare of other people occur most frequently and strongly when people are in a hypo-egoic state. Compassion, empathy, kindness, forgiveness, and prosocial behaviors more generally require that people be minimally focused on themselves, see themselves as connected to others, and have a low level of ego-involvement in the outcome of the situation. When a young man had a seizure and fell between the tracks of a subway in New York City, a stranger jumped down to save him from an oncoming train. We suspect that the moment that this person jumped down onto the tracks, his preoccupation with his own concerns and safety were largely supplanted by a hypo-egoic perspective in which his own self-thoughts and desires were muted, leading him to respond in a prosocial manner at great risk to himself. As many theorists have suggested, a primary impediment to helping other people are the myriad costs and risks that people consider when facing another in need (see Latane & Darley, 1970). Thus, quieting the self can increase prosocial action.

Similar effects of hypo-egoic states may be seen in the nature of people's close relationships. Crocker and Canevello (2008) examined the implications of adopting self-image goals versus compassionate goals in close friendships. Self-image goals are associated with defending and promoting images of oneself that enable people to obtain rewards for themselves. Compassionate goals, on the other hand, are associated with supporting and looking out for the well-being of others without the explicit intention to gain something for oneself. Although self-image and compassionate goals differ in a number of ways, people who enact compassionate goals appear to be less egoic than those who enact self-image goals. For example, people who enact compassionate goals score lower in public self-consciousness—the tendency to think about publicly observable aspects of oneself—than people who enact self-image goals. Compassionate goal-oriented individuals also appear to have a less individuated identity, reporting greater feelings of connection and closeness with other people. Compassionate goals are also linked to a lower sense of entitlement and feeling that one deserves more than others, which may be related to low ego-involvement and less preoccupation with the personal implications of outcomes.

Love has been an incredibly difficult construct to define, partly because it seems to manifest in many different ways. Yet every definition of love suggests that one person has some degree of concern for the well-being of another; it would be difficult to say that one individual truly loved another yet had no interest whatsoever in his or her welfare. Yet that interest need not be total, and it need not be motivated by selfless concern. Although specific instances of love differ in many ways (see Fehr & Broughton, 2001), one important difference among them may involve the degree to which the person is operating egoically vs. hypo-egoically. The more hypo-egoic one's love—that is, the less self-aware, individuated, and ego-involved the lover—the more it is focused on and motivated by a concern for the other's well-being. People in hypo-egoic love are more agapic and selfless as they focus on the significant other and take into account the partner's needs, desires, feelings, and thoughts (Hendrick & Hendrick, 1988). Hyper-egoic forms of love, in contrast, are characterized by excessive self-focus, individuation, and ego-involvement. Thus, although the hyper-egoic person does care about the other, that care is rooted in the degree to which the other serves the person's personal goals.

The degree to which people treat *themselves* kindly vs. harshly is also related to hypo-egoic functioning. At times people are critical and self-punishing, whereas at other times they are kind and self-forgiving. Recent research on

self-compassion—the tendency to treat oneself with kindness and compassion in the face of loss, failure, rejection, and other distressing events—shows that self-compassion is associated with indices of well-being and adaptive functioning (Leary, Tate, Adams, Allen, & Hancock, 2007; Neff, Hsieh, & Dejitthirat, 2005). Although it has not previously been discussed in this way, a key feature of self-compassion is a hypo-egoic perspective that is associated with not taking oneself too seriously. In particular, a main component of self-compassion is the recognition that one's problems, hardships, and traumas are not unique. Self-compassionate people understand the shared nature of the human condition and that everyone suffers (Neff, 2008), which reflects a nonindividuated sense of identity. Not only does this recognition promote a sense of closeness and connectedness with others, but it also leads people to be less judgmental of themselves and less invested in personal outcomes (Neff, 2008). Self-compassionate individuals also tend to be mindful in the sense that they observe events and their own reactions in a balanced manner without excessive judgment or overidentification, and without getting caught up and swept away by negative events (Neff, 2008). This self-compassionate mindset is clearly facilitated by low levels of self-awareness, individuation, and ego-involvement.

Some readers may have realized that the hypo-egoic state bears a resemblance to deindividuation, which has been associated with antisocial rather than prosocial behaviors. Although several models of deindividuation have been proposed, most suggest that low self-awareness (often created by anonymity and the presence of arousing situations) and a decrease in individual identity are key elements (Mullen, Migdal, & Rozell, 2003). Low self-awareness and a deindividuated identity appear to increase people's responsivity to situational cues and promote a loss of normal inhibition of anti-normative behavior (see, however, Postmes & Spears, 1998). Although hypo-egoic and deindividuated states both involve changes in self-awareness and phenomenal self, they differ in that deindividuation seems to involve the loss of a phenomenal self (i.e., people stop thinking about themselves as people and devote their attention to the immediate situation), whereas hypo-egoic state appears to involve a nonindividuated phenomenal self. In addition, people in a deindividuated state appear to be more focused on their goals or outcomes than those in a hypo-egoic state.

## Wisdom, Perspective, and Open-Mindedness

Wise people have been revered throughout history, and wisdom ranks among the highest virtues in every culture today (Takahashi & Bordia, 2000). Although wisdom has been conceptualized in a number of ways, most definitions include the ability to take a broad, open, and non-egocentric perspective on problems and their solutions (Baltes, Glück, & Kunzmann, 2002). Maintaining a broad perspective that incorporates as many considerations as possible requires people to move beyond their own egocentric vantage point, override normal biases that distort their interpretations of events in self-serving ways, and suspend egoistic motivations to reach solutions that benefit them personally. In other words, wisdom requires a hypo-egoic state that is characterized by low self-awareness, a nonindividuated phenomenal self, and a low level of ego-involvement.

Several writers have explicitly suggested that wisdom involves the ability to transcend one's narrow perspectives and self-interests. For example, Pascual-Leone (1990) suggested that wisdom requires self-transcendence in which people move beyond ingrained, conditioned ways of thinking. Likewise, Ardelt (2003) suggested that one feature of wisdom is the ability to look at the world from many points of view with minimum intrusion by self-centeredness, subjectivity, and projections of one's own beliefs onto one's perceptions. In her words, "wise individuals are also *selfless*; that is, they have transcended the egotistical self and feel more part of the ocean instead of an individual wave" (Ardelt, 2008, pp. 221–222, italics in original). Similarly, Webster (2003) suggested that one of five central features of wisdom involves openness to ideas, values, and experiences, "particularly those which may be different from one's own," and Levenson and his colleagues conceptualized wisdom as a developmental process involving self-transcendence (Levenson, Aldwin, & Cupertino, 2001; Levenson & Crumpler, 1996). In this context, Le and Levenson (2005) defined self-transcendence as the "ability to move beyond self-centered consciousness and to see things as they are with clear awareness of human nature and human problems . . . ." (p. 444).

In two studies, Le and Levenson (2005) examined the correlations between self-transcendence, as measured by the Adult Self-Transcendence Inventory (ASTI; Levenson et al., in press), and other attributes that characterize wisdom. Results showed that self-transcendence predicted low endorsement of the tendencies to view oneself as unique and autonomous as well as a de-emphasis on competition, status, and inequality in social relationships. Although this finding supports our conceptualization of wisdom as involving low individuation and ego-involvement, inspection of items on the ASTI reveals that they do not clearly assess self-transcendence. Instead, items appear to measure the degree to which respondents are less emotional, materialistic, contemplative, and concerned with other people's impressions than they were five years ago, all of which may reflect processes other than self-transcendence; only three of the 10 items appear directly related to self-transcendence (e.g., "I feel like my individual life is part of a larger whole"). Thus, the Le and Levenson studies do not reflect directly on the link between the self and aspects of wisdom, and research is needed that examines the hypo-egoic nature of wisdom more clearly and directly.

## Transcendence and Spirituality

Most religious and spiritual traditions throughout history have suggested that egoism and self-centeredness interfere with moral behavior and spiritual realization, and encourage people to avoid selfishness and to treat others as they wish to be treated. To our knowledge, no major religious or spiritual tradition explicitly admonishes its followers to be self-centered, egotistical, selfish, and ego-involved.

The fact that all religious and spiritual traditions encourage people to be hypo-egoic may suggest some universal wisdom regarding the role of the self in human immorality and misbehavior. Philosophers and spiritual teachers have suggested that a great deal of human suffering arises from selfish and self-centered actions and that counteracting such tendencies makes people "good." Eastern religions (such as Taoism, Hinduism, and Buddhism) tend to counteract self-centeredness and selfishness through practices that quiet the self, such as meditation and chanting, whereas the Western religions (such as Judaism, Christianity, and Islam) typically use explicit teachings to urge their followers to control selfishness and resist temptation through a combination of willpower and divine guidance (see Leary, 2004, for a comparison of Eastern and Western approaches to counteracting the problems of the self). In either case, the goal is to enhance moral behavior by reducing or overriding people's natural inclination to be selfish.

Human nature being what it is, mere religious teachings often do little to quiet the self. Indeed, many people who claim to be devout are, in fact, highly egoic, and many traditions warn their adherents that piety may become another vehicle for self-promotion. For example, Buddhist writings hold up as negative example tales of competitive self-seeking among monks, and the Christian scriptures have stories about the apostles arguing among themselves about who was the best. Religions may promote group-based egocentrism and egotism by teaching that their religion is the only correct one and that their adherents are inherently better than the misguided devotees of other groups. Believing that one is particularly special in the eyes of God likely promotes an egoic mindset that includes a sense of superiority and entitlement.

Many spiritual traditions also teach that the self stands in the way of transcendent experiences in which people perceive connections to God, the universe, spiritual beings, or other planes of existence (Peterson & Seligman, 2004). For example, St. John of the Cross urged spiritual seekers to "lose the radical self-centered awareness of our being, for it is our own self than stands in the way of God." Likewise, Taoist teachings suggest that people who "live inside their egos" cannot perceive the oneness of all things, and Hindu teachings suggest that egotism is like a veil that creates illusion.

Whether one accepts the veridicality of transcendent experiences, there is little doubt that they are related to hypo-egoic states. People in a hypo-egoic state are probably more likely to have a transcendent experience; indeed, transcendence is often conceptualized as a loss of self-awareness (Maslow, 1971). For this reason, many traditions offer ways of quieting the self so as to enhance spiritual experiences, such as meditation, chanting, drumming, or dancing. Reciprocally, transcendent experiences also appear to make people less egoic. Perceiving a transcendent reality is often associated with changes in people's beliefs about the ultimate meanings of life, meanings that typically involve goodness, selflessness, and/or the oneness of all things, features that reflect a hypo-egoic mindset (Peterson & Seligman, 2004).

## Moving Forward: Implications for Positive Psychology

As we have seen, many positive psychological states appear to arise when people are in a hypo-egoic state characterized by low self-awareness, a nonindividuated phenomenal self, and a low degree of ego-involvement. Not only are such states generally subjectively pleasant, but they are also associated with prosocial behaviors and can sometimes cause long-term positive changes. Given the connection between hypo-egoic states and such experiences, positive psychology would benefit from greater attention to the nature of hypo-egoic functioning. In this concluding section, we offer four directions for future work.

First, the concept of hypo-egoic processes provides an integrative framework for thinking about many seemingly disparate phenomena in positive psychology. As suggested, something about lower levels of self-awareness, individuation, and ego-involvement appear to promote aspects of well-being. Hypo-egoic phenomena include not only those discussed in this chapter but others as well, including forgiveness and mercy, open-mindedness, authenticity, prudence, gratitude, awe, and elation. Not all positive experiences entail hypo-egoic functioning, and not all hypo-egoic states lead to positive experiences, but our review suggests a strong link that deserves attention. Given that the hypo-egoic state may be involved in an array of positive experiences, strengths, and virtues, studying the common psychological features of these diverse phenomena may shed light on them all.

Second, the nature of the hypo-egoic state has been only broadly described and requires additional conceptual and empirical work to understand its features. Precisely what common attentional and cognitive elements underlie the positive states discussed here? How and why are low self-awareness, a nonindividuated phenomenal self, and low ego-involvement related to each other? Are any of these components more important than others, and can changes in one be compensated for by changes in another? (For example, might high self-awareness sustain a hypo-egoic state if people are nonindividuated and non-ego-involved?) To what extent are the phenomena associated with hypo-egoic states due to the psychological features of the state that we have described as opposed to beliefs that may help to induce those states? (For example, does believing in the importance of gratitude help to facilitate both a hypo-egoic mindset and the experience of gratitude?)

Third, the hypo-egoic construct may be used to understand both state-like experiences in a particular situation (e.g., forgiveness, altruistic behaviors, awe, transcendence) as well as the trait-like personal characteristics that have been described as character strengths (e.g., humility, open-mindedness, wisdom; Peterson & Seligman, 2004). As in most psychological phenomena, optimal experience is a function of both the characteristics of the person and the features of the present situation (Funder, 2006), and research is needed to investigate the individual and combined effects of both sets of influences.

Finally, using the hypo-egoic concept as an integrative heuristic provides novel ideas regarding possible ways of promoting well-being and optimal functioning at individual, group, and community levels. For example, efforts to build hypo-egoic character strengths (e.g., humility, wisdom, forgiveness) will be enhanced by focusing specifically on ways to promote people's ability to function hypo-egoically. More remediatively, efforts to ameliorate nonoptimal states—of selfishness, entitlement, prejudice, closed-mindedness, injustice, grudge-holding, hostility, and so on—may benefit from techniques that promote hypo-egoic responding.

In concluding, we should stress that we are not suggesting that people should spend their lives in hypo-egoic states. In some circumstances, a high level of self-awareness may be beneficial, pondering how one is different and separate from other people may be advantageous, and ego-involvement is appropriate. The self presumably evolved to facilitate decisions and actions that require deliberation, and we would not wish to turn it off permanently. However, a cursory look at human behavior suggests that people tend to err in the direction of egoic responding in which they are self-aware, individuated, and ego-involved even in situations in which an egoic mindset is unnecessary or, worse, dysfunctional. Put differently, people are more likely to be unnecessarily hyper-egoic than hypo-egoic. People are rarely less self-conscious, individuated, or ego-involved than they ought to be, whereas excessive self-awareness, individuation, and ego-involvement are common. Understanding how hypo-egoic processes relate to well-being and optimal functioning is an important goal for the next phase of positive psychology.

*References*

Ardelt, M. (2003). Empirical assessment of a three-dimensional wisdom scale. *Research on Aging, 25*, 275–324.

Ardelt, M. (2008). Self-development through self-lessness: The paradoxical process of growing wiser. In H. A., Wayment, & J. J. Bauer (Eds.), *Transcending self-interest: Psychological explorations of the quiet ego* (pp. 221–233). Washington, DC: American Psychological Association.

Baltes, P., Glück, J., & Kunzmann, U. (2002). Wisdom: Its structure and function in regulating successful life span development. In C. R. Synder & S. J. Lopez (Eds.), *Handbook of positive psychology* (pp. 327–347). New York, NY: Oxford University Press.

Bargh, J. A. (1997). The automaticity of everyday life. In R. S. Wyer, Jr. (Ed.), *The automaticity of everyday life: Advances in social cognition* (vol. 10, pp. 1–61). Mahwah, NJ: Erlbaum.

Bargh, J. A., & Chartrand, T. L. (1999). The unbearable automaticity of being. *American Psychologist, 54*, 462–479.

Batson, C. D., Ahmad, N., Lishner, D. A., & Tsang, J. (2002). Empathy and altruism. In C. R. Synder & S. J. Lopez (Eds.), *Handbook of positive psychology* (pp. 485–498). New York: Oxford University Press.

Baumeister, R. F. (1991). *Escaping the self.* New York: Basic Books.

Baumeister, R. F. (Ed.) (1999). *The self in social psychology.* Philadelphia: Taylor and Francis.

Baumeister, R. F., & Vohs, K. D. (Eds.) (2004). *Handbook of self-regulation.* New York: Guilford.

Crocker, J., & Canevello, A. (2008). Creating and undermining social support in communal relationships: The role of compassionate and self-image goals. *Journal of Personality and Social Psychology, 95*, 555–575.

Epstein, S. (1994). Integration of the cognitive and the psychodynamic unconscious. *American Psychologist, 49*, 709–724.

Exline, J. J. (2008). Taming the wild ego: The challenge of humility. In H. A. Wayment & J. J. Bauer (Eds.), *Transcending self-interest: Psychological explorations of the quite ego* (pp. 53–62). Washington, DC: American Psychological Association.

Exline, J. J., Campbell, W. K., Baumeister, R. F., Joiner, T., & Krueger, J. (2004). Humility and modesty. In C. Peterson & M. Seligman (Eds.), *The Values In Action (VIA) classification of strengths* (pp. 461–475). Cincinnati, OH: Values in Action Institute.

Exline, J. J., & Geyer, A. L. (2004). Perceptions of humility: A preliminary study. *Self and Identity, 3*, 95–114.

Fehr, B., & Broughton, R. (2001). Gender and personality differences in conceptions of love: An interpersonal theory analysis. *Personal Relationships, 8*, 115–136.

Fredrickson, B. L. (1998). What good are positive emotions? *Review of General Psychology, 2,* 300–319.

Funder, D. C. (2006). Towards a resolution of the personality triad: Persons, situations, and behaviors, *Journal of Research in Personality, 40,* 21–34.

Gallup, G. G., Jr. (*1997*). On the rise and fall of self-conception in primates. *Annals of the New York Academy of Sciences, 818,* 73–84.

Hendrick, C., & Hendrick, S. (1988). Lovers wear rose colored glasses. *Journal of Social and Personal Relationships, 5,* 161–183.

Humphrey, N. (*1982*). Consciousness: A just-so story. *New Scientist, 95,* 473–477.

Jaynes, J. (1976). *The origin of consciousness in the breakdown of the bicameral mind.* Boston: Houghton-Mifflin.

Langer, E. J. (1989). *Mindfulness.* Reading, MA: Addison-Wesley.

Latane, B., & Darley, J. (1970). *The unresponsive bystander: Why doesn't he help?* New York: Appleton-Century-Crofts.

Le, T., & Levenson, M. (2005). Wisdom as self-transcendence: What's love (& individualism) got to do with it? *Journal of Research in Personality, 39,* 443–457.

Leary, M. R. (2004). *The curse of the self: Self-awareness, egotism, and the quality of human life.* New York: Oxford University Press.

Leary, M. R., Adams, C. E., & Tate, E. B. (2006). Hypo-egoic self-regulation: Exercising self-control by diminishing the influence of the self. *Journal of Personality, 74,* 1803–1831.

Leary, M. R., Adams, C. E., & Tate, E. B. (in press). Hypo-egoic self-regulation. In R. Hoyle (Ed.), *Handbook of personality and self-regulation.* New York: Guilford.

Leary, M., & Buttermore, N. (2003). The evolution of the human self: Tracing the natural history of self-awareness. *Journal for the Theory of Social Behaviour, 33,* 365–404.

Leary, M. R., Estrada, M., & Allen, A. B. (2009). The analogue-I and the analogue-me: The avatars of the self. *Self and Identity, 2-3,* 147–161.

Leary, M. R., & Tangney, J. P. (Eds.) (2003). *Handbook of self and identity.* New York: Guilford.

Leary, M. R., Tate, E. B., Adams, C. E., Allen, A. B., & Hancock, J. (2007). Self-compassion and reactions to unpleasant self-relevant events: The implications of treating oneself kindly. *Journal of Personality and Social Psychology, 92,* 887–904.

Levenson, M. R., Akdwin, C. M., & Cupertino, A. P. (2001). Transcending the self: Towards a liberative model of adult development. In A. L. Neri (Ed.), *Maturidade & Velhice: Um enfoque multidisciplinar* (pp. 99–116). Sao Paulo, BR: Papirus.

Levenson, M., & Crumpler, C. (1996). Three models of adult development. *Human Development, 39,* 135–149.

Markus, H., & Wurf, E. (1987). The dynamic self-concept: A social psychological perspective. *Annual Review of Psychology, 38,* 299–337.

Martin, L. L. (1999). I-D compensation theory: Some implications of trying to satisfy immediate-return needs in a delayed-return culture. *Psychological Inquiry, 10,* 195–209.

Martin, L., & Shirk, S. (2008). Immediate-return societies: What can they tell us about the self and social relationships in our society? In J. V. Wood, A. Tesser, & J. G. Holmes (Eds.), *The self and social relationships* (pp. 161–182). New York: Psychology Press.

Maslow, A. (1971). *The farther reaches of human nature.* New York: Viking.

McGuire, W. J., & McGuire, C. V. (1981). The spontaneous self-concept as affected by personal distinctiveness. In M. D. Lynch, A. A. Norem-Hebeisen, & K. Gergen (Eds.), *Self-concept: Advances in theory and research* (pp. 147–172). Cambridge, MA: Ballinger.

McGuire, W. J., McGuire, C. V., Child, P., & Fujioka, T. (1978). Salience of ethnicity in the spontaneous self-concept as a function of one's ethnic distinctiveness in the social environment. *Journal of Personality and Social Psychology, 36,* 77–90.

Mullen, B., Migdal, M., & Rozell, D. (2003). Self-awareness, deindividuation, and social identity: Unraveling theoretical paradoxes by filling empirical lacunae. *Personality and Social Psychology Bulletin, 29,* 1071–1081.

Nakamura, J., & Csikszentmihalyi, M. (2002). The concept of flow. In C.R. Synder & S.J. Lopez (Eds.), *Handbook of positive psychology* (pp. 89–105). New York, NY: Oxford University Press.

Neff, K. D. (2008). Self-compassion: Moving beyond the pitfalls of a separate self-concept. In H. A. Wayment & J. J. Bauer (Eds.) *Transcending self-interest: Psychological explorations of the quiet ego* (pp. 95–106). Washington, DC: American Psychological Association.

Neff, K., Hsieh, Y., & Dejitterat, K. (2005). Self-compassion, achievement goals, and coping with academic failure. *Self and Identity, 4,* 263–287.

Pascual-Leone, J. (1990). An essay on wisdom: Toward organismic processes that make it possible. In R. J. Sternberg (Ed.), *Wisdom, its nature, origins, and development* (pp.244–278). Cambridge, England: Cambridge University Press.

Peterson, C., & Seligman, M. E. P. (2004). *Character strengths and virtues: A classification and handbook*. Washington, DC: APA Books.

Postmes, T., & Spears, R. (1998). Deindividuation and antinormative behavior: A meta-analysis. *Psychological Bulletin, 123,* 238–259.

Rhodewalt, F. T. (1986). Self-presentation and the phenomenal self: On the stability and malleability of self-conceptions. In R. F. Baumeister (Ed.), *Public self and private self* (pp. 115–142). New York: Springer-Verlag.

Rowatt, W. C., Powers, C., Targhetta, V., Comer, J., Kennedy, S., & Labouff, J. (2006). Development and initial validation of an implicit measure of humility relative to arrogance. *The Journal of Positive Psychology, 1,* 198–211.

Sedikides, C., & Skowronski, J. (2000). On the evolutionary functions of the symbolic self: The emergence of self-evaluation motives. In A. Tesser, R. B. Felson, & J. M. Suls (Eds.), *Psychological perspectives on self and identity* (pp. 91–117). Washington, DC: American Psychological Association.

Smith, C. A., & Lazarus, R. S. (1993). Appraisal components, core relational themes, and the emotions. *Cognition and Emotion, 7,* 233–269.

Takahashi, M., & Bordia, P. (2000). The concept of wisdom: A cross-cultural comparison. *International Journal of Psychology, 35,* 1–9.

Tangney, J. P. (2000). Humility: Theoretical perspectives, empirical findings and directions for future research. *Journal of Social and Clinical Psychology, 19,* 70–82.

Tangney, J. P. (2002). Humility. In C. R. Synder & S. J. Lopez (Eds.), *Handbook of positive psychology* (pp. 411–419). New York, NY: Oxford University Press.

Vera, D., & Rodriguez-Lopez, A. (2004). Strategic virtues: Humility as a source of competitive advantage. *Organizational Dynamics, 33,* 393–408.

Vohs, K. D., & Finkel, E. J. (Eds.). (2006). *Self and relationships*. New York: Guilford.

Webster, J. D. (2003). An exploratory analysis of a self-assessed wisdom scale. *Journal of Adult Development, 10,* 13–22.

# 10

# Experiential Processing and the Integration of Bright and Dark Sides of the Human Psyche

*Kirk Warren Brown and Melissa Holt*

"... just learning to switch thoughts from negative to positive is not enough, helpful though it may be for the time being. A direct insight is needed into the moment-to-moment inner drama taking place in thought and image." (Packer, 2007)

## Inviting the Dark Side of the Human Psyche into Positive Psychology Research

Positive psychology research has made considerable progress in describing the terrain of virtues, strengths, and resiliency factors (Peterson & Seligman, 2004) and has begun to show how simple exercises and interventions to enhance gratitude (e.g., Emmons & McCullough, 2003), forgiveness (e.g., Reed & Enright, 2006), and other strengths and virtues can enhance positive subjective experience and behavior. As an empirical science, the field of positive psychology is still young, and much remains to be done in explaining the beneficial effects of positive states and traits, and translating such knowledge into validated change programs.

Perhaps even more challenging for the field—and the topic of the present chapter—will be to integrate our knowledge of the adaptive and maladaptive sides of human nature into a holistic understanding that will better promote human welfare. From the beginning, positive psychology carved out an identity to balance the pathology- and disease prevention-focused historic mainstream of psychology (Seligman & Csikszentmihalyi, 2000), and positive psychologists have succeeded in demonstrating that there is more to the human psyche than a propensity toward pain and suffering. Achieving the promise of full-functioning, optimal well-being and other goals of positive psychology is a daunting but invigorating task, and efforts are progressing well along multiple fronts, as this volume attests. Yet we will argue that the field of positive psychology will benefit by expanding beyond a focus on positive states and traits, for the fundamental reason that the human mind has a basic, ongoing vulnerability to suffering. In this chapter we present an approach to positive psychology that is founded upon an accounting of the full range of human cognitive and emotional experience. In doing so, we attempt to reframe a primary goal of positive psychology, namely shifting psychological experience from negative to positive, and instead attempt to show that the fundamental human capacity to see how mental states of all sorts arise, how they are experienced, and how they influence self and others, can enable an integration of psychological experience and behavior that helps to provide a stable platform for well-being (Brown, Ryan, & Creswell, 2007; Ekman, Davidson, Ricard, & Wallace, 2005). We hope to demonstrate that this approach can open up fresh lines of inquiry on positive psychology theory and practice.

## Positive Psychology and Human Vulnerability to Suffering

An ultimate goal of most research in positive psychology is the formulation of theory and methods to enhance positive experience and behavior. Many positive psychological change efforts take the approach long advocated in cognitive behavioral and other traditions, which concerns the restructuring of thoughts about, and evaluations of, self, psychological experience, and behavior. Research on positive psychological change is still at a nascent stage, but this structuring approach has demonstrated some effectiveness (see reviews by Seligman, Steen, Park, & Peterson, 2005; Sin & Lyubomirsky, 2009). However, there are reasons to suggest that efforts to lessen human suffering will be limited by a focus on restructuring thoughts, appraisals, and behaviors, or by simply shifting attention from negative to positive states of mind. These reasons concern inherited human tendencies for both pleasant and unpleasant subjective states and behaviors, a propensity for cognitive and emotional biases toward negativity, and, finally, the fundamental influence of self-awareness in creating both positive and negative psychological experience.

Evolutionary psychologists have argued that a variety of human psychological states and behaviors—both so-called "positive" and "negative"—evolved for adaptive purposes. While research continues to investigate the specific purposes served by such diverse emotions as joy and anger, and behaviors as disparate as altruism and jealousy, evolutionary theorists are in little doubt that states of anger, fear, sadness, and other common forms of human suffering can serve adaptive ends in appropriate contexts. Such theorizing has raised questions about

whether people should strive to be happier than they are if a mix of positive and negative emotions has adaptive value (Diener, 2008).

Human evolution also appears to have encoded psychological biases toward negative perceptions and emotions. Baumeister, Bratslavsky, Finkenauer, and Vohs (2001) and Rozin and Royzman (2001) argue that people place greater importance on negative thoughts, emotions, and events than their positive counterparts because over evolutionary time they have offered greater value in adapting to various physical and social circumstances. Negativity biases have been demonstrated in attention and information processing, learning, and memories of non-self-relevant events and behaviors (memory tends to be biased positively for self-relevant events). Negativity biases have also been demonstrated in individuals' social lives, such as in the formation of attitudes and impressions (e.g., Shook, Fazio, & Vasey, 2007; Peeters & Czapinski, 1990), and close relationships. One testament to the power of negativity biases in relationships comes from research indicating that positive interactions should outnumber negative interactions at a ratio of five to one for romantic relationships to succeed (Gottman, 1994). The way people interpret social support and threat also appears to be biased negatively. Research has shown that people perceive larger implications in negative social support, such as yelling or criticizing, than in positive support, such as complimenting or expressing interest (Manne, Taylor, Dougherty et al., 1997). Leary, Tambor, Terdal, and Downs (1995) found that while positive or no feedback led to no significant changes in self-esteem, rejection or negative feedback led to significantly lower self-esteem.

For the remainder of this discussion, we focus on a third evolved propensity to regularly experience both positive and negative psychological states that is rooted in what is arguably the very capacity that makes us human: an advanced capacity for self-awareness. Leary (e.g., 2004; 2007a) notes that what we typically call the self can be deconstructed into several distinct cognitive processes: the extended self, which permits humans to reflect on themselves over psychological time; the private self, which allows us to think and emote about subjective states of mind (memories, intentions, emotions, and so on); and the conceptual self, which permits the creation of abstract self-characterizations and evaluations of those characterizations. As Leary (2004) describes, all three forms of self-relevant thought and emotion have proven invaluable for self-regulation and other adaptive purposes, but they have also contributed to the propensity for humans to experience both pleasure and pain, both joy and suffering. For example, thinking about one's positive characteristics or behavior and the self-affirming reasons for them (e.g., effort) can induce happiness or contentment, while thinking about one's negative traits or actions and self-denigrating causes for them (e.g., lack of ability) can lead to a variety of aversive emotions. The range of emotions associated with the operation of personal identity is also seen when people symbolically identify themselves with the vicissitudes of their relationships and social groups.

These functional aspects of self-awareness that make up the ego identity are fundamental to the pursuit of happiness. Most lay and scientific approaches to psychological change are focused on self-improvement—that is, on regulating cognitions, emotions, and behaviors that the capacities for self-awareness permit a person to determine are desirable and undesirable, allowing the formulation of images of a "better person" toward which he or she can strive. Following the historic lead of mainstream psychology, the approach to optimal well-being taken by researchers and clinicians informed by positive psychology is one in which success in the pursuit of happiness is defined as the relative preponderance of desirable thoughts, emotions, and behaviors over undesirable ones. However, we suggest that there is another layer to the question of optimal well-being, one that does not depend on finding the best mix of thoughts, emotions, or behaviors, or on the need to regularly rebalance them to accommodate the ever-changing imperatives of evolution or circumstances that can impact a sense of well-being.

In accord with Hayes et al. (1999) and others (e.g., Segal, Teasdale, & Williams, 2002), we suggest that focusing well-being efforts upon mental content—particular thoughts, emotions, and so on—is inherently problematic because it implies a perpetual polarity between desirable and undesirable, or positive and negative experience, and the necessary ongoing shoring up, defense, and extension of the self and its experience that follows from this polarization of experience. That is, when rooted in self-striving, in which there are psychological experiences to gain, to maintain, and to be rid of, the individual has an inherent vulnerability to discontent, anxiety, sadness, and other forms of suffering. For example, stress frequently accompanies ego-involved goal striving (e.g., Deci & Ryan, 2000), and sadness, frustration, and other forms of unhappiness often result from failing to attain a desirable state of mind or life circumstances (e.g., Carver & Scheier, 1998). Even more fundamental, Hayes et al. (1999) argue, is the fact that identification with "positive" experience implies the threat of "negative" experience. So, for example, when a person identifies him/herself as happy, the possibility of unhappiness, and a sense of unease that accompanies it, always lurks in the background. Further, the polarization of "good" and "bad" thoughts, emotions, memories, and so on can lead to a psychological battle of good against bad mental content, a battle that is, of course, fought against oneself in the service of self-image.

## Experiential Processing and the Contextualization of the Ego Identity

If investment in ego identity is a problematic basis for happiness, what is the alternative? The proposition may appear quixotic, given the deeply entrenched, pervasively influential nature of identity. But there are two reasons to entertain the possibility. First, the common perception of the ego identity as a real, substantial phenomenon is, from a scientific perspective, an illusion and is rather a mental model that appears to be an emergent property of the mind/brain (Metzinger, 2003), formed from ongoing life experiences and cognitive elaborations on those experiences, and inseparable from the larger social and cultural contexts in which it is formed and continually operates (even in individualistic societies) (e.g., Waldron, 2003). The second reason to question the hegemony of the ego identity is that the human mind appears able to dissociate from the self-focused, narrative processing of the ego identity—that is, to observe and thereby contextualize its functioning, so that well-being conducive choices can be made from a wider perspective than identity-based functioning allows.

Theorists informed by both Buddhist and organismic psychologies (e.g., Hayes et al., 1999; Leary, 2004; Ryan, 1993) argue that through this capacity to be aware of thought patterns, emotional reactions, desires, and behavioral tendencies, the automatic flow of self-representations can be interrupted, their constructed nature seen more clearly, and responses can be made more volitionally rather than in reaction to identity-based productions (Rabinowitz, 2006). This view argues for the value of an observant stance on our experience—a *self-as-knower*, not as an agent of reflexive cognition, in which attention simply informs thought about the self (e.g., Duval & Wickland, 1972), but rather as an inner witness or observing self (Deikman, 1982). In this observant or experiential mode of processing (e.g., Teasdale, 1999), attention is focused on the concrete facts themselves, and the contents of consciousness—including self-relevant thoughts, images, and identities—and one's overt behavior are on display. By prolonging bare, or non-reflexive attention to phenomena, experiential processing permits the individual to "be present" to sensory or subjective phenomena as they are, rather than to process them through conceptual filters that derive self-relevant meaning from those phenomena. In this mode, even the usual psychological reactions that can occur when attention is engaged—thoughts, images, verbalizations, emotions, impulses to act, and so on—are observed as part of the ongoing stream of consciousness.

One conceptualization of this mode of processing is *mindfulness*, a receptive attention to internal and external stimuli in the present (e.g., Brown & Ryan, 2003). In an experiential-mindful mode of processing, internal and external events and occurrences are simply "seen" as phenomena, "rather than as the objects of a conceptually constructed world" (Olendzki, 2005, p. 253). Bringing such open, receptive attention to bear on experience may permit a clearer recognition that self-representations are simply mental concepts; that is, in observing that thoughts and emotions come and go, memories arise and replace each other, desires emerge, develop, change, and vanish, and so on, the ego and its striving after "more, better, different" may become less substantial and engrossing, allowing for dis-identification with it. In other words, when the functioning of the egoic self can be observed, then one is clearly not limited to its functioning.

Evidence for this disentangling of experiential and self-focused processing comes from recent brain imaging research. Researchers have identified neural regions, particularly in the medial prefrontal cortex (mPFC), associated with self-focused processing (Gusnard, Akbudak, Shulman, & Raichle, 2001; Lieberman, 2010). Way, Creswell, Eissenberg, and Lieberman (2010) found that individuals higher in dispositional mindfulness showed lower levels of activation in these regions at rest, suggesting a lower self-identification of thoughts and emotions in these individuals. Farb et al. (2007) further showed that individuals trained in mindfulness showed pervasive reductions in mPFC regions associated with self-focused processing, as well as increased engagement of neural regions (e.g., insula) associated with present-oriented, experiential processing. One theorized implication of such experiential-mindful processing is an immediacy of contact with events as they occur, without the dominance of self-focused evaluations, desires, and demands. Here, consciousness takes on a clarity and freshness that reduces reactivity and permits more fully informed responses that can subserve well-being. Evidence for this claim is discussed in the following sections.

## Mindfulness and Positive Cognitive and Emotional Relations

There are several reasons why the receptive attention that characterizes mindfulness should foster well-being, all of which center on the experiential nature of this manner of processing. First, because mindfulness involves a disengagement from habitually evaluative conceptual processing, mindfulness should conduce to more balanced affective states. That is, it should be related to less unpleasant affect and perhaps less pleasant affect as well, although a freshness and immediacy of contact with experience may in some circumstances add a pleasant affective overlay to it (Brown & Ryan, 2003; Csikszentmihalyi, 1990; Deci & Ryan, 1985). Second, with the clearer, objective perception that mindfulness is thought to afford, potentially challenging or threatening events and experiences are less likely to be distorted by cognitive biases or misinterpretations that can generate unpleasant emotional responses. So, for example, the instance of a friend turning away from one can simply be "seen" as is, rather than anxiously construed as rejection. A selfish or uncaring thought can be observed as it is—a thought—rather than taken as depressing evidence of one's self-improvement failure (cf., Claxton, 1999). Thus, this movement of the "cursor of consciousness" (Claxton, 1999) back to a more immediate, less elaborated state should not only help to diminish unpleasant affective experience but also inhibit emotional reactivity to self-discordant or otherwise threatening stimuli. Third, quality of attention is known to influence emotion regulatory outcomes (e.g., Gross & Thompson, 2007). Because mindfulness concerns a sustained, open attentiveness to internal and external phenomena as they are, it should discourage maladaptive emotion regulatory tendencies like rumination and thought suppression—which involve cognitive entanglement—and also encourage a voluntary exposure to unpleasant or threatening events and experiences that has been shown to promote adaptive emotion regulation and well-being (e.g., Felder, Zvolensky, Eifert, & Spira, 2003; Levitt et al., 2004; Sloan, 2004).

More broadly, a receptive attention to both pleasant and unpleasant experience is thought to facilitate a more deeply informed selection of behaviors that are consistent with one's needs, values, and interests that can subserve well-being (Brown & Ryan, 2003; Deci & Ryan, 1980). Consistent with this view, cognitive theorists have long highlighted the importance of open attention to the self and its habits, propensities, and concerns as a means to gather objective information on behavior and subjective experience as a first step in making health- and well-being enhancing behavior changes (e.g., Martin, 1997; Safran & Segal, 1990).

The empirical evidence that mindfulness supports well-being comes from the use of both correlational (cross-sectional, experience-sampling) and experimental (laboratory inductions, clinical intervention) methods. There are recent reviews of this evidence (Brown & Cordon, 2009; Brown et al., 2007), so it will be treated briefly here. We then focus on evidence that mindfulness can act as a resilience factor, helping to counter the inherent vulnerability to suffering that arises when the ego identity is under threat.

Dispositional, self-report measures of mindfulness, which generally reflect a tendency to abide in mindful states over time, have been associated with higher pleasant affect, lower unpleasant affect, and lower levels of emotional disturbance (e.g., depressive symptoms, anxiety, and stress), along with other, related mental health indicators including satisfaction with life and eudaimonic well-being (e.g., vitality, self-actualization) (e.g., Brown & Ryan, 2003). Mindfulness has also been associated with higher extroversion and lower neuroticism, global personality traits that support subjective well-being (Diener, Suh, Lucas, & Smith, 1999). Both trait-based and state-based research using experience-sampling and other longitudinal methods (e.g., Brown & Ryan, 2003; Weinstein, Brown, & Ryan, 2009) indicate that those higher in dispositional and state mindfulness experience higher

pleasant affect and significantly less unpleasant affective experience on a day-to-day basis.

Experimental research using mindfulness induction exercises has also been conducted to examine effects on well-being relevant outcomes. Such inductions are designed to facilitate an observant stance toward ongoing events and experience so that present realities can be seen clearly and without cognitive interference. These inductions typically guide individuals through instructions designed to bring attention to, and deepen awareness of, moment-to-moment physical, emotional, and cognitive experiences. Such research has found that when in an induced mindful state, individuals report more positive motivational and emotional responses to a task, relative to those in distraction and control conditions (Brown, 2006), and have been found to react less intensely to emotionally provocative stimuli (Arch & Craske, 2006). Corroborating this evidence outside the laboratory, Michalak, Heidenreich, Meibert, and Schulte (2008) found that dispositional mindfulness, assessed by the Mindful Attention Awareness Scale (MAAS; Brown & Ryan, 2003) served as a protective factor against forms of emotional provocation that could trigger relapse in those with major depressive disorder.

Mindfulness and mindfulness-related skills have also been associated with more adaptive emotion regulation, reflected in less frequent use of thought suppression, rumination, impulsivity, and passivity, all maladaptive forms of regulation linked with poorer mental health (e.g., Brown & Ryan, 2003; Chambers, Lo, & Allen, 2008; McKee, Zvolensky, Solomon, Bernstein, & Leen-Feldner, 2007; Shapiro, Brown, & Biegel, 2007; Wupperman, Neumann, & Axelrod, 2008). Conversely, mindfulness has been positively associated with adaptive regulatory strategies, including acceptance and letting go of negative thoughts (e.g., Brown & Ryan, 2003; Frewen, Evans, Maraj, Dozois, & Partridge, 2008). The adaptive nature of acceptance is consistent with the notion that it is sometimes more adaptive to experience or express an emotion than to alter its trajectory (Barrett & Gross, 2001). There is also indication that induced mindful states promote quicker recovery from emotional upsets (sadness) relative to distraction and rumination (Broderick, 2005; Brown, Broderick, & Williams, 2007). The lower reactivity found by Arch and Craske (2006), combined with evidence for quicker recovery from sad moods, suggests that mindfulness promotes more effective emotion regulation, which may help to explain the more positive emotional states associated with mindfulness. In turn, this research also offers support for a variety of theories emphasizing the importance of attentional sensitivity to psychological and other cues for self-regulated functioning (e.g., Baumeister, Heatherton & Tice, 1994; Carver & Scheier, 1998; Deci & Ryan, 1985).

In sum, a growing body of research suggests that mindfulness is associated with a variety of affective and cognitive indicators of well-being, while also helping to foster well-being supportive forms of emotion regulation. However, we have argued that a fully informed positive psychology will be one that points to capacities for wholeness that are not dependent on desirable experiences and circumstances. A primary means to test the efficacy of such capacities is to examine responses to challenging or threatening experiences. Responses to such experiences are often shaped by inborn and conditioned patterns reflected in automatic, habitual, or impulsive reactions that may, but do not always, serve adaptive ends. For example, few would argue that angry shouting in response to a perceived insult is adaptive. With some exceptions, as in work on forgiveness (e.g., Root & McCullough, 2007), self-compassion (Leary, Tate, Adams, Batts Allen, & Hancock, 2007; Neff & Vonk, 2009), and attachment quality (Mikulincer & Florian, 2000), positive psychology theory and research has yet to address adaptive responses to aversive events and experiences that threaten the self, and in particular the ego identity. We and others have theorized that the fuller awareness afforded by mindfulness facilitates more flexible, adaptive responses to such threats and helps to minimize automatic, habitual, or impulsive reactions (Bishop et al., 2004; Brown et al., 2007; Ryan & Deci, 2004).

## Mindfulness and Adaptive Responses to Ego Threats

To date, evidence for the adaptive nature of mindfulness in response to ego threats comes from research on social interactions. It is common that in real or imagined interactions, self-related thoughts and feelings are engaged and then feed back to influence how individuals behave. In this way, social exchanges can be viewed as interactions between the self-representations of those individuals, in which each person's perceptions, reactions, and responses to the other are filtered through and mediated by his or her internalized views of self and other (Leary, 2002). Also common is that when the self is threatened in social exchanges, people respond in defensive ways.

We have proposed (Brown et al., 2008) that the sustained, receptive attention characterizing mindfulness may facilitate non-defensive processing of threatening experience, leading to desensitization and a reduction in emotional reactivity, a greater tolerance of unpleasant states and, consequently, more adaptive responding in social and other situations where self-representations are under threat. Mindfulness is also thought to foster acceptance, not in the form of passive resignation, but as a willingness to face cognitively or emotionally challenging events and experiences as they are, without seeking to escape or avoid them. Thus, more mindful individuals should show lower levels of anger, anxiety, and other emotional responses in social threat situations that represent a disengagement from the "urgencies of risk assessment" (Allen & Knight, 2005, p. 250) and should manifest cognitive and behavioral responses reflecting greater tolerance, less judgment (including censorship, condemnation, and exclusion), and generally less concern for the status of personal identity in social threat contexts. In the remainder of this chapter, we review nascent evidence that mindfulness supports non-defensive processing in three spheres of social interactions where identity is commonly threatened: romantic relationship conflict, social evaluative threat, and worldview rejection by out-group members.

*Romantic relationship conflict.* A primary basis for identity is a presumed dichotomy between self and not-self that, at the interpersonal level, is reflected in images of self, other, and the relationship, developed from learning experiences and memories of how one was viewed and treated by the other, how one adjusted one's behavior to maximize reward and minimize punishment, and so on (Rabinowitz, 2006). These mental representations of self and other can color the perception and interpretation of past events and present interactions (Leary, 2002), perhaps most strongly when images of self and "my" relationship are threatened by conflict. In such circumstances, self-protective strategies, including avoidance, withdrawal, or aggression, may be invoked to minimize personal hurt, threats to self-esteem, and loss of power (Epstein & Baucom, 2003). When the identity is engaged in this way, direct, unmediated contact with the other is inhibited.

Romantic relationships are a primary arena in which the engagement of images of self and other can have detrimental effects. The investment of self in the partner and the relationship, coupled with an attachment to seeing the relationship unfold in particular ways, represents psychological tinder for couple conflict. However, mindfulness may have value in couple conflict situations through processes that reflect an abeyance of the ego. For example, the receptive attentiveness that defines mindfulness may promote a greater ability or willingness to take interest in a partner's thoughts, emotions, and welfare, and thereby to be less invested in one's own reactions. Boorstein (1996) has argued that mindfulness promotes an ability to witness thoughts and emotions so as not to react impulsively and destructively to them. Through a willingness to contact experience directly rather than defend against it, mindfulness may promote attunement, connection, and closeness in relationships (e.g., Welwood, 1996).

Barnes, Brown, Krusemark, Campbell, and Rogge (2007) conducted two studies to examine the role of mindfulness in romantic relationship functioning, with a particular interest in examining how this quality of consciousness could affect responses to relationship stress. In an initial, 10-week longitudinal study with dating college students, the authors found that higher mindfulness, as assessed with the MAAS, predicted more accommodation, a self-reported willingness to inhibit tendencies to act destructively, and instead to respond constructively, when the romantic partner had acted in a way that was potentially destructive to the relationship (Rusbult, Verette, Whitney, Slovik & Lipkus, 1991).

In a second study, Barnes et al. (2007) tested whether mindfulness would predict more adaptive cognitive, affective, and behavioral responses in the heat of a relationship conflict. Using a conflict discussion paradigm (Gottman, Coan, Carrere, & Swanson, 1998), steadily dating heterosexual partners discussed the top one or two most conflictual issues in their relationship. For both members of the couple, dispositional MAAS scores predicted lower emotional stress reactions—hostility and anxiety—to the conflict, and these effects were explained by lower hostility and anxiety, respectively, measured upon entry into the discussion. These results showed that rather than simply buffering the effects of emotional reactions during conflict, mindfulness helped to inoculate individuals against the arising of those reactions. The capacity of mindfulness to inhibit

reactivity to conflict was also evident in the cognitive judgments that each partner made; those higher in trait mindfulness showed a more positive (or less negative) pre-post conflict change in their perception of the partner and the relationship. Finally, the study also supported the importance of a mindful state in challenging exchanges, in that higher reported mindfulness during the conflict discussion was related to several indicators of better communication quality, as assessed by objective raters.

These studies lend support to the notion that mindfulness can enhance adaptive functioning in romantic relationships (cf., Carson, Carson, Gil, & Baucom, 2004) and suggest that one means by which it does so is by facilitating a greater willingness to be experientially present to a partner when challenged in ways that could provoke identity defense.

*Social exclusion.* Another interpersonal situation that presents significant identity challenges is social exclusion. As social creatures, humans have an inherent need to belong (e.g., Deci & Ryan, 1991) and are highly motivated to avoid social demotions and exclusions (e.g., Allen & Knight, 2005; Leary, 2004). The perception that one has been rejected, even by strangers, can quickly provoke psychological distress (e.g., Leary, 2004). Identity, as already noted, is strongly influenced by the opinions and reactions of others, and negative evaluative reactions to rejection occur because the individual's sense of self-worth is invested in, or contingent upon, validation by others. However, with the capacity to recognize the identity as a construction, events like rejection that impinge upon it may be less likely to be destabilizing because a deeper sense of self that is grounded in awareness is operational (Ryan & Brown, 2003).

Creswell, Eisenberger, and Lieberman (2007) tested aspects of this argument, specifically by examining the proposition that with consciousness more firmly rooted in mindful awareness, individuals are less likely to experience distress when excluded by members of a group. In line with our proposition that mindfulness promotes more open, non-defensive processing of challenging events, Creswell et al.'s (2007) study also examined whether the more mindful person's greater equanimity in the face of exclusion was due to reduced reactivity to this form of social threat, measured by functional Magnetic Resonance Imaging (fMRI) of neural regions known to be implicated in the experience of social pain and distress.

College students in this study engaged in a ball-tossing game ("Cyberball"), ostensibly with two other student participants situated in nearby fMRI scanners. In fact, each participant was interacting with a computer. In the first part of the game, each participant was included in the ball-tossing game by the "other players"; then, in a second block of trials, the participant was excluded from the game. Results showed that mindfulness, assessed via the MAAS upon entry into the study, predicted lower self-reported social distress after the exclusion experience. Mindfulness also predicted reduced activation of the dorsal anterior cingulate cortex (dACC) during the exclusion task relative to the inclusion task; the dACC is a neural region associated with reports of physical and social pain (Eisenberger, Lieberman, & Williams, 2003). Analyses also showed that the reduced dACC activation partially mediated, or helped to explain the relation between mindfulness and lower social distress. Finally, mindfulness was positively associated with activation in the medial prefrontal cortex (mPFC), which in turn was negatively associated with dACC activation. Interestingly, the mPFC may be associated with the monitoring of one's emotions (Amodio & Frith, 2006), suggesting that more mindful individuals may pay more attention to their emotional responses during social exclusion; this mindful monitoring may help to downregulate feelings of social distress.

The findings of this study are conceptually consistent with the romantic couple conflict findings described already in suggesting that mindfulness predicts a more subdued response to social threat, in this case, apparent rejection by peers, and that this attenuated response is due, in part, to reduced evaluative reactivity to that threat (see also Creswell, Way, Eisenberger, & Lieberman, 2007).

*Worldview defense.* The social embeddedness of the individual is reflected not only in intimate relationships and peer groups, but also in broader social or cultural groups defined by their shared worldviews. These worldviews, reflecting values, ideals, or beliefs about the world and the place of the individual or group in it, provide a sense of shared meaning and order that acts to affirm personal and group identity (e.g., Kosloff, Landau, Sullivan, & Greenberg, 2008; Solomon, Greenberg & Pyszczynski, 2004). Tajfel (1981) defined social or group identity as "that part of the individual's self-concept which derives from his [or her] knowledge of membership of a social

group (or groups) together with the value and emotional significance attached to that membership" (p. 255). Paralleling romantic relationship conflict, investment in a relational identity, in this case an in-group identity, can lead to conflict and antagonism when that identity ("us" and "ours") is threatened by an out-group, or representative thereof ("them" and "theirs"). As contemporary world events and the historical record suggest, people will often act as strongly to ward off threats to their social identities as they do to defend their own persons against attack.

Terror Management Theory (TMT; Solomon et al., 2004) argues that a key trigger for social identity defense is the threat of death. According to TMT, the knowledge of one's inevitable demise creates an omnipresent potential for anxiety that is managed by affirming or defending cultural worldviews. A common way in which this is manifest is by upholding in-group worldviews and by derogating out-group members whose views are counter to those of the in-group. In so doing, people are enabled to view themselves as valuable members of a permanent reality. Such action affirms the features of the ontological self—in this case, the social self—noted early in this chapter: as real, substantial, and independent. As noted earlier, however, such affirmation is directly contrary to a scientific understanding of the nature of the self.

If, as we have argued, more mindful people are less invested in identity, will they show less worldview defense, particularly when, as TMT argues, their sense of self is threatened by a confrontation with their own mortality? Niemiec et al. (2010) addressed this question in a series of studies. We first assessed mindfulness among American citizens, then asked them to either write about their death (mortality salience condition) or about TV watching or dental pain (control condition). After a brief delay, they then read a pro-U.S. essay and an anti-U.S. essay purportedly written by foreign students in the U.S. The outcome in these studies was a series of evaluations of the authors and their opinions. The studies showed that those with lower MAAS mindfulness scores receiving an existential threat (mortality salience) evidenced worldview defense, as reflected in stronger derogation of the anti-U.S. (out-group) author and higher favoritism toward the pro-U.S. (in-group) author. In contrast, the ratings of those higher in mindfulness showed no worldview defense. In an effort to explain these findings, Niemiec et al. (2010) found that when confronting their death, more mindful individuals spent more time writing about it and evidenced less suppression of death thoughts, suggesting a greater openness to processing this threatening potentiality. In turn, analyses showed that this more receptive processing of mortality helped to explain the association between mindfulness and lack of worldview defense.

The findings of these various studies on mindful responses to ego threats—in romantic relationships, peer relationships, and when confronting social out-groups—suggest that when a deeper sense of self that is grounded in experiential awareness is operational, events like conflict and rejection that impinge upon the self-concept are less threatening, and less likely to destabilize personal and relational well-being than they otherwise might.

## Integration and Conclusions

### Rethinking the Positive and Negative in Human Psychology

In this chapter we have outlined research showing that mindfulness is associated with a variety of cognitive and emotional indicators of well-being. Remarkable about the body of findings as a whole is the fact that mindfulness appears to have a wide range of relations with positive psychological outcomes. We drew special attention to evidence showing that mindfulness helps to foster adaptive responses to ego-based threats, primarily to support an argument that as an experiential mode of processing, mindfulness operates as a witness on mental content, rather than as an agent to change mental content from one form to another (negative emotion to positive emotion, for example). This mindful contextualization of mental content affords a key advantage to well-being enhancement: When positive experience is based on an identification with mental content, well-being is contingent and likely to fluctuate because positive mental content (e.g., pleasant thoughts and emotions) is always relative to negative mental content; that is, positive experience depends on the relative absence of negative experience at any given time. In contrast, awareness depends on nothing. Experiential modes of processing such as mindfulness involve a capacity to decouple from or observe mental content. The observant stance of mindfulness opens a gap between self and the vicissitudes of mental content, much of which,

we have argued, is rooted in ego-based perspectives and interpretations. When no longer ego-involved in this way, a wider perspective on life has room to emerge and guide experience and behavior.

To be sure, pleasant thoughts, emotions, and other positive mental contents are more desirable than unpleasant ones. But circumstances change, pleasant emotions give way to neutral or unpleasant ones, and mental states continuously recombine into forms that we have learned to label in positive and negative terms. As discussed earlier, the human mind appears to have fundamental propensities toward both pleasant and unpleasant states of mind. Where many individuals suffer, we and others suggest, is in selectively identifying with these states, positively appraising and seeking after pleasant mental content, negatively appraising and seeking to escape or avoid unpleasant thoughts and emotions, and defining well-being success in terms of desirable mental content. In disengaging from striving after happiness, mindfulness ironically enough appears to prepare the ground for happiness to arise.

### Integrating Positive and Pathological Psychologies

Our discussion of differing modes of processing and their consequences suggests a rethinking of what is "positive" in positive psychology and also offers a route by which to integrate positive and pathology-oriented psychologies. There are several processes through which the integrative potential of mindfulness may occur, including insight, exposure, and nonattachment (see Brown et al., 2007). Perhaps most fundamentally, mindfulness operates through a disengagement from self-concern—the perceptions, appraisals, beliefs, and feelings people have about themselves, others, and the wider social world that tend to channel and filter contact with reality in self-limited ways (Ryan & Brown, 2003; Leary, 2004; 2005). As an experiential mode of processing, mindfulness involves a capacity to contextualize the conceptual operations that fuel such egoic functioning (cf., Hayes et al., 1999). Importantly, mindfulness is not a form of escape that results in passivity or disconnection from life; rather, it is thought to bring one into closer contact with life by helping to circumvent the self-generated accounts *about* life that act to pull one away from it. Inherent in mindfulness is an acceptance of or willingness to experience what is, in contrast to states of mind that involve avoidance, control, and the investment of personal well-being in altering circumstances or attaining goals. Mindfulness may facilitate a balance of mind reflecting a stable experience of well-being— a noncontingent happiness—that is not dependent on positively appraised circumstances, behaviors, or experiences (cf., Ekman et al., 2005; McIntosh, 1997). When no longer caught up in the ever-changing drama of ego-involvement, a psychological "center of gravity" that is grounded in awareness has room to guide experience and behavior.

## Note

Portions of this chapter were drawn from Brown and Cordon (2009), Brown, Ryan, and Creswell (2007), and Brown, Ryan, Creswell, and Niemiec (2008).

*References*

Allen, N. B., & Knight, W. (2005). Mindfulness, compassion for self, and compassion for others. In P. Gilbert (Ed.), *Compassion: Conceptualizations, research, and use in psychotherapy* (pp. 239–262). New York: Routledge.

Amodio, D. M., & Frith, C. D. (2006). Meeting of minds: The medial frontal cortex and social cognition. *Nature Reviews Neuroscience, 7(4),* 268–277.

Arch, J. J., & Craske, M. G. (2006). Mechanisms of mindfulness: Emotion regulation following a focused breathing induction. *Behaviour Research and Therapy, 44(12),* 1849–1858.

Barnes, S., Brown, K. W., Krusemark, E., Campbell, W. K., & Rogge, R. D. (2007). The role of mindfulness in romantic relationship satisfaction and responses to relationship stress. *Journal of Marital & Family Therapy, 33(4),* 482–500.

Barrett, L. F., & Gross, J. J. (2001). Emotion representation and regulation: A process model of emotional intelligence. In T. Mayne & G. Bonnano (Eds.), *Emotion: Current issues and future directions* (pp. 286–310). New York: Guilford.

Baumeister, R. F., Bratslavsky, E., Finkenauer, C., & Vohs, K. D. (2001). Bad is stronger than good. *Review of General Psychology, 5(4),* 323–370.

Baumeister, R. F., Heatherton, T. F., & Tice, D. M. (1994). *Losing control: How and why people fail at self-regulation.* San Diego, CA: Academic Press.

Bishop, S. R., Lau, M., Shapiro, S., Carlson, L., Anderson, N. D., Carmody, J., et al. (2004). Mindfulness: A proposed operational definition. *Clinical Psychology: Science & Practice, 11,* 230–241.

Boorstein, S. (1996). *Transpersonal psychotherapy.* Albany, NY: State University of New York Press.

Broderick, P. C. (2005). Mindfulness and coping with dysphoric mood: Contrasts with rumination and distraction. *Cognitive Therapy and Research, 29,* 501–510.

Brown, K. W. (November, 2006). *The effect of induced mindfulness on task engagement, performance, and subjective experience.* Paper presented at the 40th Annual Convention of the Association for Behavioral and Cognitive Therapies, Chicago, IL.

Brown, K. W., Broderick, P., & Williams, J. M.G. (November, 2007). *The comparative efficacy of mindfulness, mindfulness + acceptance, rumination, and distraction on the regulation of induced sadness.* Paper presented at the 41st Annual Convention of the Association for Behavioral and Cognitive Therapies, Philadelphia, PA.

Brown, K. W., & Cordon, S. L. (2009). The phenomenological nature and emotional correlates of mindfulness. In F. Didonna (Ed.), *Clinical handbook of mindfulness.* New York, NY: Springer.

Brown, K. W., & Ryan, R. M. (2003). The benefits of being present: Mindfulness and its role in psychological well-being. *Journal of Personality and Social Psychology, 84(4),* 822–848.

Brown, K. W., Ryan, R. M., & Creswell, J. D. (2007). Mindfulness: Theoretical foundations and evidence for its salutary effects. *Psychological Inquiry, 18 (4),* 211–237.

Brown, K. W., Ryan, R. M., Creswell, J. D., & Niemiec, C. P. (2008). Beyond me: Mindful responses to social threat. In H. A. Wayment & J. J. Bauer (Eds.), *Transcending self-interest: Psychological explorations of the quiet ego.* (pp. 75–84). Washington, DC: American Psychological Association.

Carson, J. W., Carson, K. M., Gil, K. M., & Baucom, D. H. (2004). Mindfulness-based relationship enhancement. *Behavior Therapy, 35,* 471–494.

Carver, C. S., & Scheier, M. F. (1998). *On the self-regulation of behavior.* New York: Cambridge University Press.

Chambers, R., Lo, B. C. Y., & Allen, N. B. (2008). The impact of intensive mindfulness training on attentional control, cognitive style, and affect. *Cognitive Therapy and Research, 32,* 303–322.

Claxton, G. (1999). Moving the cursor of consciousness: Cognitive science and human welfare. In F. J. Varela & J. Shear (Eds.), *The view from within: First-person approaches to the study of consciousness* (pp. 219–222). Bowling Green, OH: Imprint Academic.

Creswell, J. D., Eisenberger, N. I., & Lieberman, M. D. (2007). Neurobehavioral correlates of mindfulness during social exclusion. Unpublished manuscript, University of California, Los Angeles.

Creswell, J. D., Way, B. M., Eisenberger, N. I., & Lieberman, M. D. (2007). Neural correlates of dispositional mindfulness during affect labeling. *Psychosomatic Medicine, 69,* 560–565.

Csikszentmihalyi, M. (1990). *Flow: The psychology of optimal experience.* New York: Harper/Collins.

Deci, E. L., & Ryan, R. M. (1980). Self-determination theory: When mind mediates behavior. *The Journal of Mind and Behavior, 1,* 33–43.

Deci, E. L., & Ryan, R. M. (1985). *Intrinsic motivation and self-determination in human behavior.* New York: Planum.

Deci, E. L., & Ryan, R. M. (1991). A motivational approach to self: Integration in personality. In R. Dienstbier (Ed.), *Nebraska symposium on motivation* (vol. 38, pp. 237–288). Lincoln, NE: University of Nebraska Press.

Deci, E. L., & Ryan, R. M. (2000). The "what" and "why" of goal pursuits: Human needs and the self-determination of behavior. *Psychological Inquiry, 11,* 227–268.

Deikman, A. J. (1982). *The observing self.* Boston, MA: Beacon Press.

Diener, E. (2008). Myths in the science of happiness, and directions for future research. In M. Eid & R. J. Larsen (Eds.), *The science of subjective well-being* (pp. 493–514). New York: Guilford Press.

Diener, E., Suh, E. M., Lucas, R. E., & Smith, H. L. (1999). Subjective well-being: Three decades of progress. *Psychological Bulletin, 2,* 276–302.

Duval, S., & Wicklund, R. A. (1972). *A theory of objective self-consciousness.* New York: Academic.

Eisenberger, N. I., Lieberman, M. D., & Williams, K. D. (2003). Does rejection hurt? An fMRI study of social exclusion. *Science, 302(5643),* 290–292.

Ekman, P., Davidson, R. J., Ricard, M., & Wallace, B. A. (2005). Buddhist and psychological perspectives on emotions and well-being. *Current Directions in Psychological Science, 11,* 59–63.

Emmons, R. A., & McCullough, M. E. (2003). Counting blessings versus burdens: An experimental investigation of gratitude and subjective well-being in daily life. *Journal of Personality and Social Psychology, 84(2),* 377–389.

Epstein, N. B., & Baucom, D. H. (2003). Couple therapy. In R.L. Leahy (Ed.), *Roadblocks in cognitive-behavioral therapy* (pp. 217–235). NY: Guilford.

Farb, N. A. S., Segal, Z. V., Mayberg, H., Bean, J., McKeon, D., Fatima, Z., et al. (2007). Attending to the present: Mindfulness meditation reveals distinct neural modes of self-reference. *Social Cognitive and Affective Neuroscience, 2,* 313–322.

Felder, M. T., Zvolensky, M. J., Eifert, G. H., & Spira, A. P. (2003). Emotional avoidance: An experimental test of individual differences and response suppression using biological challenge. *Behaviour Research and Therapy, 41,* 403–411.

Frewen, P. A., Evans, E. M., Maraj, N., Dozois, D., & Partridge, K. (2008). Letting go: Mindfulness and negative automatic thinking. *Cognitive Therapy Research, 32,* 758–774.

Gottman, J. M. (1994). *What predicts divorce? The relationship between marital processes and marital outcomes.* Hillsdale, NJ: Lawrence Erlbaum.

Gottman, J. M., Coan, J., Carrere, S., & Swanson, C. (1998). Predicting marital happiness and stability from newlywed interactions. *Journal of Marriage and the Family, 60,* 5–22.

Gross, J. J., & Thompson, R. A. (2007). Emotion regulation: Conceptual foundations. In J. J. Gross (Ed.), *Handbook of emotion regulation* (pp. 3–24). New York: Guilford.

Gusnard, D. A., Akbudak, E., Shulman, G. L., & Raichle, M. E. (2001). Medial prefrontal cortex and self-referential mental activity: relation to a default mode of brain function. *Proceedings of the National Academy of Sciences USA, 98,* 4259–4264.

Hayes, S. C., Strosahl, K., & Wilson, K. G. (1999). *Acceptance and commitment therapy: An experiential approach to behavior change.* New York, NY: Guilford Press.

Kosloff, S., Landau, M. J., Sullivan, D., & Greenberg, J. (2008). A terror management perspective on the quiet ego and the loud ego: Implications of ego volume control for personal and social well-being. In H.A. Wayment & J. J. Bauer (Eds.), *Transcending self-interest: Psychological explorations of the quiet ego* (pp. 33–42). Washington, DC US: American Psychological Association.

Leary, M. R. (2002). When selves collide: The nature of the self and the dynamics of interpersonal relationships. In A. Tesser, D. A. Stepel, & J. V. Wood (Eds.), *Self and motivation* (pp. 119–145). Washington, DC: American Psychological Association.

Leary, M. R. (2004). *The curse of the self: Self-awareness, egotism, and the quality of human life.* New York, NY US: Oxford University Press.

Leary, M. R. (2005). Nuggets of social psychological wisdom. *Psychological Inquiry, 16,* 176–179.

Leary, M. R. (2007a). How the self became involved in affective experience: Three sources of self-reflective emotions. In J. L. Tracy, R. W. Robins, &

J. P. Tangney (Eds.), *The self-conscious emotions: Theory and research.* (pp. 38–52). New York, NY: Guilford Press.

Leary, M. R. (2007b). Motivational and emotional aspects of the self. *Annual Review of Psychology, 58,* 317–344.

Leary, M. R., Tambor, E. S., Terdal, S. K., & Downs, D. L. (1995). Self-esteem as an interpersonal monitor: The sociometer hypothesis. *Journal of Personality and Social Psychology, 68*(3), 518–530.

Leary, M. R., Tate, E. B., Adams, C. E., Batts Allen, A., & Hancock, J. (2007). Self-compassion and reactions to unpleasant self-relevant events: The implications of treating oneself kindly. *Journal of Personality and Social Psychology, 92*(5), 887–904.

Levitt, J. T., Brown, T. A., Orsillo, S. M., & Barlow, D. H. (2004). The effects of acceptance versus suppression of emotion on subjective and psychophysiological response to carbon dioxide challenge in patients with panic disorder. *Behavior Therapy, 35,* 747–766.

Lieberman, M. D. (2010). Social cognitive neuroscience. In S. T. Fiske, D. T. Gilbert, & G. Lindzey (Eds.), *Handbook of social psychology* (pp. 143–193). New York, NY: McGraw-Hill.

Manne, S. L., Taylor, K. L., Dougherty, J., & Kemeny, N. (1997). Supportive and negative responses in the partner relationship: Their association with psychological adjustment among individuals with cancer. *Journal of Behavioral Medicine, 20,* 101–125.

Martin, J. R. (1997). Mindfulness: A proposed common factor. *Journal of Psychotherapy Integration, 7,* 291–312.

McIntosh, W. D. (1997). East meets West: Parallels between Zen Buddhism and social psychology. *International Journal for the Psychology of Religion, 7,* 37–52.

McKee, L., Zvolensky, M. J., Solomon, S. E., Bernstein, A., & Leen-Feldner, E. (2007). Emotional vulnerability and mindfulness: A preliminary test of associations among negative affectivity, anxiety sensitivity, and mindfulness skills. *Cognitive Behaviour Therapy, 36,* 91–100.

Metzinger, T. (2003). *Being no one: The self-model theory of subjectivity.* Cambridge, Massachusetts: MIT Press.

Michalak, J., Heidenreich, T., Meibert, P., & Schulte, D. (2008). Mindfulness predicts relapse/recurrence in major depressive disorder after mindfulness-based cognitive therapy. *Journal of Nervous and Mental Disease, 196,* 630–633.

Mikulincer, M., & Florian, V. (2000). Exploring individual differences in reactions to mortality salience: Does attachment style regulate terror management mechanisms? *Journal of Personality and Social Psychology, 79,* 260–273.

Neff, K. D., & Vonk, R. (2009). Self-compassion versus global self-esteem: Two different ways of relating to oneself. *Journal of Personality, 77,* 23–50.

Niemiec, C. P., Brown, K. W., Kashdan, T., Cozzolino, P. J., Breen, W., Levesque, C., & Ryan, R. M. (2010). Being present in the face of existential threat: The role of mindfulness in ameliorating worldview defense. *Journal of Personality and Social Psychology, 99,* 344–365.

Olendzki, A. (2005). The roots of mindfulness. In C. K. Germer, R. D. Siegel, & P. R. Fulton (Eds.), *Mindfulness and psychotherapy* (pp. 241–261). New York: Guilford.

Packer, T. (2007). *The silent question: Meditating in the stillness of not knowing.* Boston, MA: Shambhala.

Peeters, G., & Czapinski, J. (1990). Positive-negative asymmetry in evaluations: The distinction between affective and informational negativity effects. *European Review of Social Psychology, 1,* 33–60.

Peterson, C., & Seligman, M. E. (2004). *Character strengths and virtues: A handbook and classification.* Washington, DC: American Psychological Association.

Rabinowitz, J. (2006). *Cultivating presence.* Unpublished manuscript, Jewish Family Services.

Reed, G. L., & Enright, R. D. (2006). The effects of forgiveness therapy on depression, anxiety, and posttraumatic stress for women after spousal emotional abuse. *Journal of Consulting and Clinical Psychology, 74,* 920–929.

Root, L. M., & McCullough, M. E. (2007). Low-cost interventions for promoting forgiveness. In L. L'Abate (Ed.), *Low-cost approaches to promote physical and mental health: Theory, research, and practice.* (pp. 415–434). New York, NY: Springer Science + Business Media.

Rozin, P., & Royzman, E. B. (2001). Negativity bias, negativity dominance, and contagion. *Personality and Social Psychology Review, 5,* 296–320.

Rusbult, C. E., Verette, J., Whitney, G. A., Slovik, L. F., & Lipkus, I. (1991). Accommodation processes in close relationships. *Journal of Personality and Social Psychology, 60,* 53–78.

Ryan, R. M. (1993). Agency and organization: Intrinsic motivation, autonomy and the self in psychological development. In J. Jacobs (Ed.), *Nebraska symposium on motivation* (vol. 40, pp. 1–56). Lincoln, NE: University of Nebraska Press.

Ryan, R. M., & Brown, K. W. (2003). Why we don't need self-esteem: Basic needs, mindfulness, and the authentic self. *Psychological Inquiry, 14,* 71–76.

Ryan, R. M. & Deci, E. L. (2004). Autonomy is no illusion: Self-determination theory and the empirical study of authenticity, awareness, and will. In J. Greenberg, S. L. Koole, & T. Pyszcynski (Eds.), *Handbook of experimental existential psychology* (pp. 449–479). New York: Guilford.

Safran, J. D., & Segal, Z. V. (1990). *Interpersonal process in cognitive therapy.* New York: Basic.

Segal, Z. V., Williams, J. M. G., & Teasdale, J. D. (2002). *Mindfulness-based cognitive therapy for depression: A new approach to preventing relapse.* New York: Guilford Press.

Seligman, M. E. P., & Csikszentmihalyi, M. (2000). Positive psychology: An introduction. *American Psychologist, 55,* 5–14.

Seligman, M. E. P., Steen, T. A., Park, N., & Peterson, C. (2005). Positive psychology progress: Empirical validation of interventions. *American Psychologist, 60,* 410–421.

Shapiro, S. L., Brown, K. W. & Biegel, G. (2007). Teaching self-care to caregivers: The effects of mindfulness-based stress reduction on the mental health of therapists in training. *Training and Education in Professional Psychology, 1,* 105–115.

Shook, N. J., Fazio, R. H., & Vasey, M. W. (2007). Negativity bias in attitude learning: A possible indicator of vulnerability to emotional disorders? *Journal of Behavior Therapy and Experimental Psychiatry, 38,* 144–155.

Sin, N. L., & Lyubomirsky, S. (2009). Enhancing well-being and alleviating depressive symptoms with positive psychology interventions: A practice-friendly meta-analysis. *Journal of Clinical Psychology, 65,* 467–487.

Sloan, D. M. (2004). Emotion regulation in action: Emotional reactivity in experiential avoidance. *Behaviour Research and Therapy, 42,* 1257–1270.

Solomon, S., Greenberg, J., & Pyszczynski, T. (2004). The cultural animal: Twenty years of terror management theory and research. In J. Greenberg, S. L. Koole, & T. Pyszczynski (Eds.), *Handbook of experimental existential psychology* (pp. 13–34). NY: Guilford.

Tajfel, H. (1981). *Humans and social categories.* London: Cambridge University Press.

Teasdale, J. D. (1999). Emotional processing, three modes of mind and the prevention of relapse in depression. *Behaviour Research and Therapy, 37,* 53–77.

Waldron, W. S. (2003). Common ground, common cause: Buddhism and science on the afflictions of identity. In B. A. Wallace (Ed.), *Buddhism and science* (pp. 145–191). New York: Columbia University Press.

Way, B. M., Creswell, J. D., Eisenberger, N. I., & Lieberman, M. D. (2010). Dispositional mindfulness and depressive symptomatology: Correlations with limbic and self-referential neural activity during rest. *Emotion, 10,* 12–24.

Weinstein, N., Brown, K. W., & Ryan, R. M. (2009). A multi-method examination of the effects of mindfulness on stress attribution, coping, and emotional well-being. *Journal of Research in Personality, 43,* 374–385.

Welwood, J. (1996). *Love and awakening.* New York: HarperCollins.

Wupperman, P., Neumann, C. S., & Axelrod, S. R. (2008). Do deficits in mindfulness underlie borderline personality features and core difficulties? *Journal of Personality Disorders, 22,* 466–482.

# 11

# A Task-Focused Mind Is a Happy and Productive Mind: A Processing Perspective

*Michael D. Robinson and Maya Tamir*

## Taking Stock

Positive psychology can be defined as a set of topics, an agenda, and/or a scientific enterprise. As a set of topics, the field of positive psychology studies a heterogeneous set, including (but certainly not limited to) character and virtue, subjective well-being, optimal social functioning, intrinsic motivation, curiosity, forgiveness, wisdom, meaning in life, educational practices, counseling practices, and indeed the optimal society (Seligman & Csikszentmihalyi, 2000). As an agenda, positive psychology represents an attempt to move and shape the psychology field in a particular direction favoring positive outcomes (Seligman & Csikszentmihalyi; Sheldon & King, 2001). As a scientific enterprise, positive psychology reflects the study of a variety of desirable psychological outcomes (e.g., happiness) using rigorous research methods (Gable & Haidt, 2005) and the development of scientifically proven intervention efforts (Seligman, Steen, Park, & Peterson, 2005).

In our view, defining positive psychology as a set of topics could, at some point, pose problems to the field as a whole. This is so because it is an open question whether the positive psychology movement would be able to hold together an increasingly diverse set of topics over time. As any body of findings increases, psychologists tend to gravitate toward specialization (Mayer, 2005; Posner & Rothbart, 2007). Such specialization, if it occurs, would make it even more difficult for topics to remain linked together under the umbrella of positive psychology.

Of more concern to us are the views of positive psychology as an agenda and science. Agendas are ideological and guided by convictions. Science, on the other hand, is empirical and data-driven. Agendas can inspire and stimulate science, and positive psychology has definitely served this purpose (Bacon, 2005; Gable & Haidt, 2005). Nevertheless, pairing an agenda with a science may sometimes result in compromises to the science involved. There are risks for at least some versions of positive psychology to overstep empirical facts in favor of ideological viewpoints (Lazarus, 2003). Therefore, it is important to keep an open mind when considering the evidence

(Oishi, Diener, & Lucas, 2007; Steger, Kashdan, Sullivan, & Lorentz, 2008).

One example of the tension between agenda and science involves the identification of certain individual difference variables as positive ones (Peterson & Seligman, 2004). Such lists can be arbitrary when not governed by psychometric evidence or by unambiguous guidelines as to what qualifies as a personal strength. Even if such taxonomic issues can be solved, there is still the problem of identifying how and why such individual difference variables function as they do. An important issue in this respect, and one germane to our chapter, is the distinction between traits and processes. This distinction is mirrored in the personality literature by the contrast of taxonomic and process-based approaches to personality, which Cervone (1997; Cervone & Shoda, 1999) has suggested may not be reconcilable. Although we have been more optimistic concerning the possible reconciliation of these disparate approaches to personality (Robinson, 2007a; Tamir & Robinson, 2004), much work remains to be done (Matthews & Gilliland, 1999; Robinson, 2007b).

We are still far from understanding the processes associated with positive psychological functioning. For example, taken to the extreme, each of the 24 taxonomy-based personal strengths identified by Peterson and Seligman (2004) might be associated with distinct and non-overlapping processes. If so, an overwhelming task lies ahead. In contrast, a process-oriented approach could identify larger dynamics that might underlie multiple positive psychological attributes. In this chapter, we take such a process-oriented approach and make the case for a particular distinction between two modes of processing that appear to be associated with a wide range of positive psychological outcomes. By doing so, we hope to highlight the potential interrelations between these outcomes and point to the mechanisms that might be involved.

A major portion of the chapter will seek to make the point that positive psychological functioning can be viewed in terms of task-focused rather than self-focused processing. We will make a strong case for this idea and link it to multiple and diverse sources of evidence. Subsequently, however, multiple questions concerning the model will be discussed. Such questions include relations of our dual-process model to other dual-process models, potential boundary conditions, and directions for future research.

## Two Modes of Processing: Task-Focused and Self-Focused

Central to our framework is a distinction between two modes of processing. Task-focused processing is externally oriented and is concerned with maximizing goal-directed behavioral outcomes. Self-focused processing, on the other hand, is internally oriented and concerned with epistemic questions related to the phenomenological self. Task-focused processing can therefore be viewed in terms of engagement with the environment, whereas self-focused processing can be viewed in terms of some degree of preoccupation with the self. Because attention is limited (James, 1890; Pashler, 1998), these two modes of processing should be inversely related. That is, to the extent that one is task-focused, self-focus should be inhibited and vice versa. There are data in support of this tradeoff of task- and self-focused processing modes, reviewed below.

Seminal theories in social psychology have made a case for the benefits for a self-focused mode of processing (Carver & Scheier, 1981; Duval & Wicklund, 1972). However, we believe that such benefits have been overstated and in fact make a case for the opposite point, namely that a task-focused mode of processing is generally more conducive to positive affect, mental health, and desirable behavioral outcomes. In this respect, our analysis is consistent with modern thinking on the self, which generally views preoccupation with the self as a source of problems rather than benefits (Crocker & Wolfe, 2001; Leary, 2004). The integrative potential of our dual-process model is first highlighted. Subsequently, we marshal multiple sources of evidence in support of the psychological benefits of a task-focused mode of processing.

### Integrative Potential

The modes of processing highlighted appear to have considerable integrative potential in relation to prominent constructs in the positive psychology literature. For example, task-focused processing may underlie states of curiosity and interest. Curiosity is defined in terms of an open-minded desire to seek knowledge and involves full engagement with the environment (Kashdan, Rose, & Fincham, 2004). Interest is similarly defined as a desire to learn new information (Silvia, 2006). Curiosity and interest, therefore, likely reflect a state of task-focused processing.

Ryan and Deci (2000; 2001) have long argued for the benefits of intrinsic motivation, characterized by the desire to engage in an activity for its own sake rather than for the purpose of obtaining external rewards. Intrinsic motivation has been characterized in terms of high engagement with the task environment and low levels of self-focus (Ryan, 1982). Indeed, Plant and Ryan (1985) found that an induction of self-focus undermined intrinsic motivation. This result is consistent with our view that task-focus and self-focus are distinct modes of processing that inhibit each other. More broadly, we suggest a potentially close link of intrinsic motivation to a task-focused mode of processing, though this issue will be revisited.

Csikszentmihalyi has often conceptualized optimal states in terms of those that produce high levels of *flow* (Csikszentmihalyi, Abuhamdeh, & Nakamura, 2005). Flow is a state in which one is engaged with the task at hand and perceives a high level of challenge but also a high level of skill to meet that challenge. States of flow are associated with higher levels of task achievement and lower levels of self-consciousness (Hektner, Schmidt, & Csikszentmihalyi, 2007). Similar to intrinsic motivation, therefore, a state of flow likely involves higher levels of task-focused processing and lower levels of self-focused processing.

In a literature of relevance to positive psychology, approach motivation is often characterized in terms of assertive, goal-directed interactions with the environment (Depue & Collins, 1999). Avoidance motivation, on the other hand, has been viewed as defensive in nature, self-protective, and inhibited (Carver, Sutton, & Scheier, 2000). Of importance to our process-related analysis, we suggest that a task-focused mode of processing is likely to support and underlie higher levels of approach motivation, whereas a self-focused mode of processing is likely to support and underlie higher levels of avoidance motivation. Such relations may not be isomorphic, though, and we will thus revisit approach and avoidance later in the chapter.

Our integrative analysis thus far makes two important points. The first is that multiple motivational perspectives on positive psychological functioning—whether related to curiosity, flow, intrinsic motivation, or approach motivation—appear to overlap in nature. The second is that the overlap involved appears to support a common processing perspective. Specifically, task-focused processing, relative to self-focused

processing, appears more conducive to positive psychological functioning. We seek to make this point in the sections that follow. Subsequently, we consider issues of discriminant validity and boundary conditions.

## Modes of Processing, Correlates, and Consequences

There are good reasons for thinking that a task-focused mode of processing inhibits a self-focused mode of processing and vice versa. Relevant evidence comes from the coping literature, which has documented inverse relations between action-oriented versus state-oriented responses to threat or challenge (Kuhl, 2000), problem-focused versus emotion-focused coping (Lazarus & Folkman, 1991), and primary (i.e., attempts to change the situation) versus secondary (i.e., attempts to change the self) control strategies (Morling & Evered, 2006). Other evidence suggests that these modes of processing are likely to be reliant on regions of the brain that are mutually inhibitory (Lieberman & Eisenberger, 2005). Such considerations are reflected in Figure 11.1, which depicts an inhibitory relation between these distinct modes of processing.

As further depicted in Figure 11.1, we suggest that a predominantly task-focused mode of processing is conducive to positive affect, mental health, and behavioral success, all important outcomes in positive psychology (Seligman, & Csikszentmihalyi, 2000). By contrast, Figure 11.1 suggests that a predominantly self-focused mode of processing contributes to negative affect, psychopathology, and lesser success in behavioral terms, all constructs inimical to optimal functioning (Widiger, Verheul, & van den Brink, 1999). If so, a strong potential case could be made for the relevance of our processing distinction to positive psychology.

*Emotional experiences.* Curiosity (Kashdan et al., 2004), interest (Silvia, 2006), and inspiration (Thrash & Elliot, 2004) have all been shown to be predictive of higher levels of positive emotional experience. The common core to such constructs, we suggest, involves a greater degree of engagement with the task environment. In other words, to the extent that one is task-focused rather than self-focused, processing is likely to be inherently more rewarding. This suggestion fits with strong sources of data linking cross-temporal variations in positive affect to cross-temporal variations in behavioral striving and

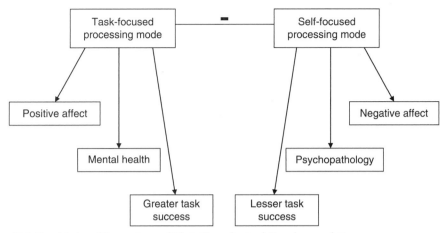

Figure 11.1 Two Modes of Processing and Their Hypothesized Correlates and Consequences.

attempts at task-mastery (e.g., Kashdan, Biswas-Diener, & King, 2009). For example, individuals report higher levels of positive affect when they are active (Watson, 2000) and diurnal variations in activity and positive affect are strongly correlated (Watson, Wiese, Vaidya, & Tellegen, 1999).

Duval and Wicklund (1972) suggested that self-focused attention is somewhat necessarily aversive and therefore should contribute to negative emotional states, at least in the short term. This point was disputed by Carver and Scheier (1981), who suggested that self-focused attention is likely to be associated with negative emotional experiences only when the individual views it as difficult if not impossible to rectify a perceived self-discrepancy. Current thinking on self-focus and/or consciousness of the self is more consistent with the initial perspective of Duval and Wicklund. For example, Baumeister (1987) contends that self-focus can be linked to existential problems in functioning and to negative emotional experiences, a perspective increasingly echoed by modern self-scholars (Crocker & Knight, 2005; Leary, 2004).

In support of such ideas, a recent meta-analysis convincingly established a robust relationship between self-focused states and negative (but not positive) emotional experiences (Mor & Winquist, 2002). Similarly, although dispositional variations in private self-consciousness were initially viewed in emotion-neutral terms (Carver & Scheier, 1981), this no longer appears to be the case. Specifically, Trapnell and Campbell (1999) convincingly established that a major component of private self-consciousness involves tendencies toward rumination and negative

affect. Although further developments in this literature are likely (e.g., Kross, Ayduk, & Mischel, 2005), we conclude that the preponderance of evidence favors the idea that a task-focused mode of processing, relative to a self-focused mode of processing, appears more conducive to higher levels of hedonic balance (i.e., the relative balance of positive to negative emotional experiences).

*Psychopathology.* Multiple theories of depression link it to low levels of engagement with the environment. For example, Lewinsohn and Libet (1972) viewed depression in terms of deficits in obtaining pleasure from daily activities. Tomarken and Keener (1998) summarize a body of evidence linking depression to hypoactivation of the left prefrontal cortex, a structure known to mediate proactive attempts to shape the environment according to one's goals (Davidson, 1999). Mogg and Bradley (1998) link depression to the withdrawal of active coping resources from interactions with the environment. Rottenberg, Gross, and Gotlib (2005) provide physiological sources of evidence for the idea that depressed individuals appear to be disengaged and non-responsive to environmental sources of stimulation. We note that there are also sources of data linking schizophrenia to low task-focused efforts (Bellak, Hurvich, & Gediman, 1973) and to diminished task monitoring in neurocognitive terms (van Veen & Carter, 2006).

We have suggested that high levels of self-focus may exacerbate psychopathological symptoms, and there are multiple sources of support for this idea. Ingram's (1990) review led him to conclude that high levels of self-focus appear endemic to multiple mood and anxiety disorders.

This suggestion has been substantiated in a quantitative meta-analytic review (Mor & Winquist, 2002). Higher levels of self-consciousness have been linked not only to depression but also to anxiety, obsessive-compulsive disorders, and phobias. For example, Gehring, Himle, and Nisenson (2000) suggested that obsessive-compulsive individuals suffer from an overactive self-critical monitor (also see Paulus, Feinstein, Simmons, & Stein, 2004). It is further worth noting that high levels of self-focus have been implicated in individual differences in shyness (Henderson & Zimbardo, 2001), social anxiety (Rodebaugh, 2009), and behavioral inhibition among children and adolescents (Kagan & Snidman, 2004). Finally, Pennebaker (2000) reviews evidence for the point that self-focus leads to exaggerated symptom perception and reporting.

Clinical psychologists generally operate under the assumption that distinct diagnoses and symptoms are mediated by distinct underlying mechanisms. However, the comorbidity of the mood and anxiety disorders (Clark, Watson, & Mineka, 1994) and the personality disorders (Widiger & Trull, 2007) suggests that there may be important common factors that generally predispose one to disordered symptomology. We suggest that our distinction of two processing modes may have significant value to such an integrative view of mental functioning. To the extent that task-focus is low, poorer coping with environmental stressors would somewhat naturally occur (Monroe & Simons, 1991). To the extent that self-focus is high, problematic symptoms would be more salient and therefore consequential (Ingram, 1990). The combination of low task-focus and high self-focus would be particularly problematic.

*Task performance.* The majority of life tasks that individuals view as important are those that necessarily rely on some degree of task-focused effort (Cantor, 1990; Gollwitzer, 1999). For example, studying hard for an exam, resisting temptations, and overcoming procrastination cannot be accomplished passively (Baumeister, Heatherton, & Tice, 1994). Instead, all such endeavors appear to rely on a common resource that has been termed effortful control (Rothbart, Ahadi, & Evans, 2000), ego control (Baumeister, Muraven, & Tice, 2000), or executive attention (Posner & Rothbart, 2007).

In reviewing such literature, we (Robinson, Schmeichel, & Inzlicht, 2010) have suggested that effort is nothing more than task-focus (Sarter & Gehring, 2006). That is, individuals fail

to achieve their difficult goals precisely because they fail to maintain such goals when significant distractions or obstacles occur (Fishbach & Zhang, 2008; Miller & Cohen, 2001). Robinson et al. (2009a) reviewed multiple sources of evidence for this idea across cognitive (e.g., Duncan et al., 2008), social cognitive (e.g., Muraven & Slessareva, 2003), and neurocognitive (e.g., Inzlicht & Gutsell, 2007) lines of investigation. Self-regulation failures, from this perspective, are synonymous with tendencies to lose task-focus in the face of threats or challenges (Koole & Jostmann, 2004; Kuhl, 2000).

Further, it stands to reason that higher levels of task-focus would promote goal-success. We have suggested that intrinsic motivation can be viewed (at least in part) in terms of task-focus, and it is therefore informative that higher levels of intrinsic motivation have been shown to promote better performance, learning, and task persistence (Ryan & Deci, 2001). Similarly, the state of flow (i.e., absorption in a task) has been linked to higher levels of task-achievement (Hektner et al., 2007). Curiosity and interest, which we also suggest are reliant on a task-focused mode of processing, also lead to higher levels of learning and achievement over time (Silvia, 2006).

By contrast, higher levels of self-focus often appear to be problematic to performance. Preoccupation with the self has been shown to undermine performance in the stereotype threat literature (Steele, 1997), the test-anxiety literature (Sarason, Sarason, & Pierce, 1990), the literature on trait anxiety (Eysenck, Derakshan, Santos, & Calvo, 2007), and in the context of high levels of neuroticism (Fetterman, Robinson, Ode, & Gordon, 2010). From one perspective, self-focus can be viewed in terms of a processing load that reduces the central executive's capacity (Clark & Rhyno, 2005). From another (though related) perspective, operating in a self-focused mode would inhibit task-focus according to our model and others (Dijksterhuis, Bargh, & Miedema, 2000; Eisenberger, Lieberman, & Satpute, 2005; Morling & Evered, 2006).

## Cognitive Underpinnings

We have suggested that higher levels of task-focus (relative to self-focus) are conducive to optimal functioning. We provided support for such ideas, yet in a manner that was necessarily reliant on some degree of inference concerning the processes involved. The purpose of the present section is both to understand task-focus from cognitive and neurocognitive perspectives and to provide additional support for its benefits, thus defined.

*Task-focus as response speed.* To the extent that task-focus is high, reaction time performance should be faster. This suggestion is consistent with results showing that reaction time performance is slower when individuals are tired, distracted, or stressed, all factors that would interfere with full attention to the task (Sanders, 1998). It is therefore informative that slow reaction time performance, as an individual difference variable, predicts problematic outcomes such as delinquency and crime (Jensen, 1998), health problems (Gottfredson & Deary, 2004), and even earlier deaths (Deary & Der, 2005). By contrast, faster processing speed in the same studies can be viewed as health-protective and promoting.

In individual difference terms, faster processing speed has been shown to be a robust correlate of general intelligence or the "g" factor (Jensen, 1998). This does not mitigate the potential of processing speed measures as indices of task-focus, as general intelligence has been viewed in terms of greater levels of task-focus (Duncan et al., 2000). On the other hand, slow processing speed could be reflective of other variables aside from task-focus, such as premorbid brain damage (Deary & Der, 2005). It may therefore be useful to control for baseline processing speed in understanding the purported benefits of a task-focused mode of processing.

One of the classic behavioral markers of high levels of motivational engagement is better performance following practice (McClelland, 1987). In reaction time tasks, processes of this type can be examined by assessing the extent to which individuals speed up across trials (Ackerman, 1988; Pashler, 1998). In a recent set of studies, we (Robinson, Meier, Tamir, Wilkowski, & Ode, 2009b) administered a number of basic choice categorization tasks, following which we quantified processing speed early in such tasks versus later. To then quantify individual differences in task-focus or engagement, we created residual scores such that they assessed the extent to which individuals "got into" the tasks across time.

Consistent with hypotheses, we (Robinson et al., 2009) found that this implicit processing measure of task-focus predicted positive affect and depressive symptoms in three studies and did so across diverse protocols such as those

involving informant reports or experience-sampling procedures. Specifically, task-focused individuals (i.e., those whose performance improved to a greater extent across time) experienced and displayed higher levels of positive emotion and were also less prone to depressive symptoms. Such results not only reinforce the value of implicit assessments of personality (Robinson & Neighbors, 2006), but do so in support of the idea that higher levels of task-engagement are hedonically beneficial.

In what we view to be a conceptually related study, Pronin and Wegner (2006) randomly assigned individuals to one of two processing speed conditions. One condition required individuals to be maximally task-focused in that they had to read sentences aloud at a faster rate than they would otherwise do so. The comparison condition allowed individuals to read the same sentences at a more leisurely pace. Pronin and Wegner found that individuals assigned to the fast processing condition subsequently reported higher levels of positive affect and lower levels of depressive symptomology, both in state-related terms. Thus, there is experimental support for the idea that faster processing speed, which we suggest is closely related to task-engagement, improves one's mood states.

*Task-focus as activation of the dorsolateral prefrontal cortex.* The strategic control of cognitive and emotional processes is reliant on frontal lobe brain structures (Zelazo & Cunningham, 2007). Yet an important division of labor contrasts lateral and medial portions of the frontal lobe, which are differentially involved in task-focused efforts versus emotional processing, respectively (Lieberman, 2007). When individuals control outcomes through the investment of working memory and task-focused effort, the dorsolateral portion of the prefrontal cortex (dlPFC) is differentially activated (Knight & Stuss, 2002). By contrast, when individuals determine the emotional significance of stimuli, the ventromedial portion of the prefrontal cortex (vmPFC) is differentially activated (Tranel, 2002).

This distinction is important because lesions to the vmPFC result in subtle deficits in social behavior and decision-making, but not to anhedonia (Wallis, 2007). On the other hand, lesions to the dlPFC result not only in poor cognitive performance but also in symptoms that are central features of major depression such as lethargy, catastrophic thinking, and prolonged states of negative affect (Saint-Cyr, Bronstein,

& Cummings, 2002; also see Gotlib & Hamilton, 2008). Further, McClure, and colleagues (e.g., McClure, Laibson, Loewenstein, & Cohen, 2004) demonstrated that activation of the vmPFC led individuals to make non-optimal choices in decision-making and specifically those that favored a myopic focus on short-term rewards. By contrast, activation of the dlPFC led individuals to make more rational choices favoring long-term outcomes over short-term gains.

A study of Eisenberger et al. (2005) is particularly important in the present context. These authors examined brain activation in response to unexpected stimuli requiring a response. They found that higher levels of extraversion, which have been linked to higher task-focused processing in previous cognitive studies (Lieberman, 2000), predicted greater dlPFC activation during the task. On the other hand, private self-consciousness (related to self-focus: Carver & Scheier, 1981) predicted greater vmPFC activation during the task. Levels of vmPFC and dlPFC activation were also inversely correlated across participants, suggesting that self-focus inhibits task-focus and vice versa according to this neurocognitive model.

The dlPFC has been characterized as the one structure of the brain that mediates task-focused processing to the greatest extent (Miller & Cohen, 2001). It is therefore informative that lesions to this brain structure are problematic in multiple ways—emotionally, behaviorally, and in terms of clinically significant symptoms (Knight & Stuss, 2002; Saint-Cyr et al., 2002). We accordingly suggest that what is viewed in terms of optimal human functioning in the positive psychology literature may be profitably thought of in terms of using the task-focused resources of the dlPFC (e.g., goal-maintenance, the inhibition of inappropriate processing routines, etc.) to support greater adaptation to the environment. On the basis of such considerations, we encourage further integration efforts linking dlPFC functioning to the sorts of strengths and virtues emphasized by the positive psychology movement.

*Task-focus as dopamine availability.* There are multiple reasons for thinking that higher levels of task-focus can be viewed in terms of greater dopamine availability. Arnsten and Robbins (2002) reviewed multiple sources of relevant data from animal models and concluded that greater availability of dopamine shifts processing such that it favors task-focus over passive reactions to environmental input. Lesion studies

of this type have shown that damage to dopamine-generating regions of the brain result in passive behavior and a striking absence of goal-directed action (Berridge, 1999). By contrast, artificially increasing dopamine availability by drugs results in more vigorous motor behavior and the greater pursuit of potentially rewarding stimuli (e.g., food, drugs, water, sex: Berridge).

This animal literature on dopamine availability has entertained a number of specific hypotheses, though. One theory of dopamine availability links it to superior learning (Schultz, 2004), another links it to increased motor output (Ashby, Alfonso-Reese, Turken & Waldron, 1998), and another links it to increased reward sensitivity (Berridge, 1999). Dopamine availability has also been viewed in terms of pleasure (Shizgal, 1999) or positive affect (Ashby, Isen, & Turken, 1999). Readers should consult a special issue of *Psychopharmacology* (e.g., Berridge, 2007) for a nuanced consideration of such subtly different views.

What we suggest, instead, is that many of the diverse correlates and consequences of dopamine availability appear to converge on its link to greater levels of task-focus. For example, dopamine availability would facilitate learning because of increased task-involvement (e.g., Ackerman, 1988), would facilitate motor activity because of its link to active coping (e.g., Arnsten & Robbins, 2002), and would facilitate pleasure because of the hedonic benefits of completing a task successfully (e.g., Carver et al., 2000). The bottom line, then, is that viewing task-focus and its multiple benefits in terms of dopamine availability appears to have considerable value (Knutson & Wimmer, 2007).

## Moving Forward

Science progresses both through integration efforts and through making distinctions. Our focus thus far has been on integration efforts. In this connection, we highlighted the apparent benefits of task-focus (relative to self-focus) to emotion and behavior as well as to greater freedom from psychopathology. We reviewed sources of evidence as diverse as those from personality, social, clinical, cognitive, and neuroscience literatures. Viewing optimal functioning from a task-focused perspective thus appears to have considerable integrative value. Distinctions are important too, however. Accordingly, and to better flesh out relations between the present two-process model and others, we discuss points of overlap and non-overlap.

We first point to frameworks that appear to be non-overlapping with ours. The implicit-explicit processing distinction (Fazio & Olson, 2003) is orthogonal to our distinction between task-focus and self-focus because we conceptualize both processing modes as implicit in nature and operation. The automatic-controlled processing distinction (Schneider & Shiffrin, 1977) is also not germane to the present framework. Instead, we conceptualize both self-focus and task-focus in terms of controlled processing, albeit in relation to different goals and objectives (Eisenberger et al., 2005). The private-public self-consciousness distinction (Carver & Scheier, 1981) is also not relevant, as task-focus cannot be equated with public self-consciousness (Csikszentmihalyi et al., 2005). Finally, our distinction should not be equated with that between mastery and performance goals, as both such goals seem best characterized in terms of task-focus rather than self-focus (Senko, Durik, & Harackiewicz, 2008).

Issues of overlap are less certain in relation to other models. Gollwitzer (e.g., 1999) contrasts two mindsets, one that is deliberative in nature (i.e., concerned with which course of action to pursue) and another that is implemental in nature (i.e., concerned with instantiating a particular course of action, once chosen). Viewing deliberative mindsets in terms of self-focused processing appears to have some value, as does viewing implemental mindsets in terms of task-focused processing. From another perspective, though, deliberative and implemental mindsets may be both characterized as task-focused, as both relate to the control of action. Thus, it is uncertain whether self-focus is represented in Gollwitzer's model.

A prominent meta-theory of optimal functioning views it in terms of higher levels of intrinsic relative to extrinsic motivation (Ryan & Deci, 2000; 2001). Intrinsic motivation can be viewed in terms of performing behaviors because one wants to do them, whereas extrinsic motivation can be viewed in terms of performing behaviors because such actions are expected to produce rewards, whether monetary or social. Above, we suggested that there should be some relationship between intrinsic motivation and a task-focused mode of processing, particularly because intrinsic (relative to extrinsic) motivation is thought to energize behavior to a greater extent (Ryan & Deci, 2008). On the other hand, we concede that this relationship may not be especially tight.

For example, the prospect of a good grade can be highly motivating to some individuals (Senko et al., 2008), and extensive efforts may sometimes support primarily self-focused endeavors such as updating a personal diary (Kaufman, Grigorenko, & Sternberg, 2009). For such reasons, the present distinction between task- and self-focused processing should not be equated with that between intrinsic and extrinsic motivation.

Prominent motivational theories of personality link positive affect to approach motivation and negative affect to avoidance motivation (Carver et al., 2000; Elliot & Thrash, 2002; Zelenski & Larsen, 1999). Although it seems somewhat intuitive to link approach motivation to task-focus and avoidance motivation to self-focus, such links again do not appear particularly strong. Avoidance motivation can lead to high levels of task-focused effort, a point perhaps best supported in literature linking individual differences in anxiety and related constructs to higher levels of vigilance for threatening stimuli (Mogg & Bradley, 1998), greater apparent levels of cognitive effort (Eysenck et al., 2007), and higher levels of performance in certain particular circumstances (Carver & Scheier, 1981; Eysenck & Eysenck, 1985). Such considerations suggest that the present distinction between task- and self-focused processing modes cannot be equated with the distinction between approach and avoidance motivation.

Instead, we emphasize the overlap of the present processes with those highlighted in the stress-coping literature. Rothbaum, Weisz, and Snyder (1982) contrasted modes of processing involving primary (i.e., changing the situation) versus secondary (i.e., changing the self) control. Lazarus and Folkman (1991) made a similar distinction between problem-focused versus emotion-focused coping. Kuhl (2000) has contrasted action-oriented versus state-oriented responses to stress. We suggest that a task-focused mode of processing would facilitate primary control and problem-focused coping and would be reflective of an action-oriented response to environmental stressors. Beyond such models, though, we suggest that individuals differ in their reliance on task-focused versus self-focused modes of processing quite independent of their responses to environmental stressors. If so, the present processing model is more general that those highlighted in the stress-coping literature.

Carver and Scheier (1981) suggested that self-focused processing may be adaptive. Yet they also reviewed sources of evidence for the idea that self-focus (a) makes individuals aware of discrepancies that often cannot be rectified (e.g., Gibbons & Wicklund, 1976), (b) is associated with aversive experiences in such contexts (e.g., Carver, Blaney, & Scheier, 1979), and (c) leads individuals to withdraw their task-focused efforts in a manner that can be ultimately problematic (e.g., Lewin, 1935). The test anxiety literature substantiates the latter point quite consistently: To the extent that one is self-focused in a performance context, self-doubts occur that can be quite detrimental to optimal performance (e.g., Sarason et al., 1990).

The work of Carver and Scheier (1981) is seminal, yet their suggestion that self-focus promotes optimal functioning now appears problematic. Quite the opposite appears to be the case. Effective self-regulation does not require self-focus (Robinson et al., 2009a), and self-focus often undermines effective self-regulation (Baumeister et al., 1994; Clark & Rhyno, 2005). This point can be made with reference to literature linking self-focus to psychopathology (Ingram, 1990), bulimic symptoms (Cooley & Toray, 2001), alcohol abuse (Sayette, 1999), and self-harm or suicide attempts (Tassava & Ruderman, 1999). Indeed, it is striking that both preoccupation with the self, in the form of narcissism (Twenge, Konrath, Foster, Campbell, & Bushman, 2008), and neuroticism (Twenge, 2000), have increased in parallel from the 1950s to today. Thus, self-focus appears to be a problematic rather than functional tendency according to modern literature on the self (Baumeister & Boden, 1994; Leary, 2004).

Can self-focus co-occur with significant achievements and therefore magnify their hedonic impact? Langston (1994) suggested so on the basis of his results, which primarily involved asking individuals to savor aspects of their lives. In the absence of such manipulations, though, we are somewhat convinced that people rarely employ self-focus in this affect-enhancing manner. Rather, there is somewhat convincing evidence that self-focus typically results from the recognition of failing to meet important self-standards (Higgins, 1987; Wicklund, 1979). Thus, although recruiting self-focus to bask in one's successes could well serve a mood-enhancing function, self-focus does not appear to naturally operate this way.

The reader may be thinking that there are some positive psychology constructs—such as mindfulness—that appear to support the idea that at least certain forms of self-focus may be beneficial. Mindfulness is quite distinct from self-focus, however. Self-focus often occurs in the context of lack of insight into the self (Trapnell & Campbell, 1999), and the benefits of mindfulness cannot be explained in terms of either private or public self-consciousness (Brown & Ryan, 2003). Finally, a quick perusal of the items of Brown and Ryan's mindfulness scale reveals that many of the items suggest lack of awareness of the environment, not the self (e.g., "I forget a person's name almost as soon as I've been told it"). In summary, mindfulness should not be equated with self-focus.

The implications of the current analysis for positive psychological interventions are several. First, it is important to identify individuals' task-focused goals. When individuals do not know what they want to accomplish, positive psychology counseling (Joseph & Linley, 2005) may be particularly helpful. Second, to the extent that such incentives can be identified, individuals should generally be encouraged to pursue them full-heartedly (Brown & Dutton, 1995; Csikszentmihalyi, 1990). Third, there appear to be hedonic and performance benefits to quieting the self-conscious mind, a point repeatedly emphasized in this chapter. We further suggest that the easiest way to lessen self-focus is to adopt a task-focused approach to daily activities (Kuhl, 2000: McClelland, 1987). With repeated practice in doing rather than doubting, we suspect that the task-focused mode of processing can be reinforced, just as nearly any mode of processing becomes habitual with sufficient practice (Bargh & Chartrand, 1999; James, 1890).

## Final Considerations

Self-focus can be viewed in terms of a "stop" signal that may be adaptive under certain conditions (Dijksterhuis et al., 2000). Therefore, individuals lacking any self-focus might be generally more effective in their behaviors, but at a potential cost when circumstances favor a change in processing strategies (Fazio, Ledbetter, & Towles-Schwen, 2000). From another perspective, though, the task-focused resources of the dlPFC appear exquisitely sensitive to such requirements to change processing strategies across trials and over time (Kerns et al., 2004; van Veen & Carter, 2006). For this reason, we suggest that theories equating self-focus with self-regulation potential (Carver & Scheier, 1981; Wicklund, 1979) appear to be contradicted by modern thinking on how the brain recruits and instantiates self-control (Lieberman & Eisenberger, 2005; Robinson et al., 2009a).

Does our perspective suggest that impulsive responding can be generally favored? No. Impulsive responding, defined in terms of fast responding at the expense of accurate responding, would not generally serve the self (Dickman & Meyer, 1988). On the other hand, there is no necessary tradeoff of processing speed and accuracy (Sanders, 1998). To the extent that processing speed is entrained to task-focused goals, multiple benefits to the self are likely to accrue. This was a major theme of the chapter and one that was well substantiated.

In more general terms, we suggest that positive psychology must increasingly establish itself as an empirical science rather than a set of topics or an agenda. To facilitate this transition, questions of process and mechanism are likely to be increasingly important in subsequent years and decades. The present chapter can be viewed as supporting the idea that a basic distinction between task- and self-focused modes of processing appears to have considerable leverage and scope. Task-focused processing, we suggest, captures an important source of variance (though not the only one) in understanding the fully functioning individual.

*References*

Ackerman, P. L. (*1988*). Determinants of individual differences during skill acquisition: Cognitive abilities and information processing. *Journal of Experimental Psychology: General, 117,* 288–318.

Arnsten, A. F. T., & Robbins, T. W. (2002). Neurochemical modulation of prefrontal cortical function in humans and animals. In D. T. Stuss & R. T. Knight (Eds.), *Principles of frontal lobe function* (pp. 51–84). New York: Oxford University Press.

Ashby, F. G., Alfonso-Reese, L. A., Turken, A. U., & Waldron, E. M. (1998). A neuropsychological theory of multiple systems in category learning. *Psychological Review, 105,* 442–481.

Ashby, F. G., Isen, A. M., & Turken, A. U. (1999). A neuropsychological theory of positive affect and its influence on cognition. *Psychological Review, 106,* 529–550.

Bacon, S. F. (2005). Positive psychology's two cultures. *Review of General Psychology, 9,* 181–192.

Bargh, J. A., & Chartrand, T. L. (1999). The unbearable automaticity of being. *American Psychologist, 54,* 462–479.

Baumeister, R. F. (1987). How the self became a problem: A psychological review of historical research. *Journal of Personality and Social Psychology, 52,* 163–176.

Baumeister, R. F., & Boden, J. M. (1994). Shrinking the self. In T. M. Brinthaupt & R. P. Lipka (Eds.), *Changing the self: Philosophies, techniques, and experiences* (pp. 143–173). Albany, NY: State University of New York Press.

Baumeister, R. F., Heatherton, T. F., & Tice, D. M. (1994). *Losing control: How and why people fail at self-regulation.* San Diego, CA: Academic Press.

Baumeister, R. F., Muraven, M., & Tice, D. M. (2000). Ego depletion: A resource model of volition, self-regulation, and controlled processing. *Social Cognition, 18,* 130–150.

Bellak, L., Hurvich, M., & Gediman, H. (1973). *Ego functions in schizophrenics, neurotics, and normals.* New York: John Wiley & Sons.

Berridge, K. C. (1999). Pleasure, pain, desire, and dread: Hidden core processes of emotion. In D. Kahneman, E. Diener, & N. Schwarz (Eds.), *Well-being: The foundations of hedonic psychology* (pp. 525–557). New York: Russell Sage Foundation.

Berridge, K. C. (2007). The debate over dopamine's role in reward: The case for incentive salience. *Psychopharmacology, 191,* 391–431.

Brown, J. D., & Dutton, K. A. (1995). Truth and consequences: The costs and benefits of accurate self-knowledge. *Personality and Social Psychology Bulletin, 21,* 1288–1296.

Brown, K. W., & Ryan, R. M. (2003). The benefits of being present: Mindfulness and its role in psychological well-being. *Journal of Personality and Social Psychology, 84,* 822–848.

Cantor, N. (1990). From thought to behavior: "Having" and "doing" in the study of personality and cognition. *American Psychologist, 45,* 735–750.

Carver, C. S., Blaney, P. H., & Scheier, M. F. (1979). Focus of attention, chronic expectancy, and responses to a feared stimulus. *Journal of Personality and Social Psychology, 37,* 1186–1195.

Carver, C. S., & Scheier, M. F. (1981). *Attention and self-regulation: A control-theory approach to human behavior.* New York: Springer-Verlag.

Carver, C. S., Sutton, S. K., & Scheier, M. F. (2000). Action, emotion, and personality: Emerging conceptual integration. *Personality and Social Psychology Bulletin, 26,* 741–751.

Cervone, D. (1997). Social-cognitive mechanisms and personality coherence: Self-knowledge, situational beliefs and cross-situational coherence in perceived self-efficacy. *Psychological Science, 8,* 43–50.

Cervone, D., & Shoda, Y. (1999). Beyond traits in the study of personality coherence. *Current Directions in Psychological Science, 8,* 27–32.

Clark, D. A., & Rhyno, S. (2005). Unwanted intrusive thoughts in nonclinical individuals: Implications for clinical disorders. In D. A. Clark (Ed.), *Intrusive thoughts in clinical disorders: Theory, research, and treatment* (pp. 1–29). New York: Guilford Press.

Clark, L. A., Watson, D., & Mineka, S. (1994). Temperament, personality, and the mood and anxiety disorders. *Journal of Abnormal Psychology, 103,* 103–116.

Cooley, E., & Toray, T. (2001). Body image and personality predictors of eating disorder symptoms during the college years. *International Journal of Eating Disorders, 30,* 28–36.

Crocker, J., & Knight, K. M. (2005). Contingencies of self-worth. *Current Directions in Psychological Science, 14,* 200–203.

Crocker, J., & Wolfe, C. T. (2001). Contingencies of self-worth. *Psychological Review, 108,* 593–623.

Csikszentmihalyi, M. (1990). *Flow: The psychology of optimal experience.* New York: Harper & Row.

Csikszentmihalyi, M., Abuhamdeh, S., & Nakamura, J. (2005). Flow. In A. J. Elliot & C. S. Dweck (Eds.), *Handbook of competence and motivation* (pp. 598–608). New York: Guilford Publications.

Davidson, R. J. (1999). Neuropsychological perspectives on affective styles and their cognitive consequences. In T. Dalgleish & M. Power (Eds.), *Handbook of cognition and emotion* (pp. 103–123). Chichester, England: John Wiley & Sons.

Deary, I. J., & Der, G. (2005). Reaction time explains IQ's association with death. *Psychological Science, 16,* 64–69.

Depue, R. A., & Collins, P. F. (1999). Neurobiology of the structure of personality: Dopamine, facilitation of incentive motivation, and extraversion. *Behavioral and Brain Sciences, 22,* 491–569.

Dickman, S. J., & Meyer, D. E. (1988). Impulsivity and speed-accuracy tradeoffs in information processing. *Journal of Personality and Social Psychology, 54,* 274–290.

Dijksterhuis, A., Bargh, J. A., & Miedema, J. (2000). Of men and mackerels: Attention, subjective experience, and automatic social behavior. In H. Bless & J. P. Forgas (Eds.), *The message within: The role of subjective experience in social cognition and behavior* (pp. 37–51). New York: Psychology Press.

Duncan, J., Parr, A., Woolgar, A., Thompson, R., Bright, P., Cox, S., et al. (2008). Goal neglect and Spearman's g: Competing parts of a complex task. *Journal of Experimental Psychology: General, 137,* 131–148.

Duncan, J., Seitz, R. J., Kolodny, J., Bor, D., Herzog, H., Ahmed, A., et al. (2000). A neural basis for general intelligence. *Science, 289,* 457–460.

Duval, S., & Wicklund, R. A. (1972). *A theory of objective self-awareness.* New York: Academic Press.

Eisenberger, N. I., Lieberman, M. D., & Satpute, A. B. (2005). Personality from a controlled processing perspective: An fMRI study of neuroticism, extraversion, and self-consciousness. *Cognitive, Affective and Behavioral Neuroscience, 5,* 169–181.

Elliot, A. J., & Thrash, T. M. (2002). Approach-avoidance motivation in personality: Approach and avoidance temperaments and goals. *Journal of Personality and Social Psychology, 82,* 804–818.

Eysenck, M. W., Derakshan, N., Santos, R., & Calvo, M. G. (2007). Anxiety and cognitive performance: Attentional control theory. *Emotion, 7,* 336–353.

Eysenck, H. J., & Eysenck, M. W. (1985). *Personality and individual differences: A natural science approach.* New York: Plenum.

Fazio, R. H., Ledbetter, J. E., & Towles-Schwen, T. (2000). On the costs of accessible attitudes: Detecting that the attitude object has changed. *Journal of Personality and Social Psychology, 78,* 197–210.

Fazio, R. H., & Olson, M. A. (2003). Implicit measures in social cognition research: Their meaning and uses. *Annual Review of Psychology, 54,* 297–327.

Fetterman, A. K., Robinson, M. D., Ode, S., & Gordon, K. H. (2010). Neuroticism as a risk factor for behavioral dysregulation: A mindfulness-mediation perspective. *Journal of Social and Clinical Psychology, 29,* 301–321.

Fishbach, A., & Zhang, Y. (2008). Together or apart: When goals and temptations complement versus compete. *Journal of Personality and Social Psychology, 94,* 547–559.

Gable, S. L., & Haidt, J. (2005). What (and why) is positive psychology? *Review of General Psychology, 9,* 103–110.

Gehring, W. J., Himle, J., & Nisenson, L. G. (2000). Action-monitoring dysfunction in obsessive-compulsive disorder. *Psychological Science, 11,* 1–6.

Gibbons, F. X., & Wicklund, R. A. (1976). Selective exposure to self. *Journal of Research in Personality, 10,* 98–106.

Gollwitzer, P. M. (1999). Implemental intentions: Strong effects of simple plans. *American Psychologist, 54,* 493–503.

Gotlib, I. H., & Hamilton, J. P. (2008). Neuroimaging and depression: Current status and unresolved issues. *Current Directions in Psychological Science, 17,* 159–163.

Gottfredson, L. S., & Deary, I. J. (2004). Intelligence predicts health and longevity, but why? *Current Directions in Psychological Science, 13,* 1–4.

Hektner, J. M., Schmidt, J. A., & Csikszentmihalyi, M. (2007). *Experience sampling method: Measuring the quality of everyday life.* Thousand Oaks, CA: Sage Publications.

Henderson, L., & Zimbardo, P. (2001). Shyness, social anxiety, and social phobia. In S. G. Hofmann & P. M. DiBartolo (Eds.), *From social anxiety to social phobia: Multiple perspectives* (pp. 46–85). Needham Heights, MA: Allyn & Bacon.

Higgins, E. T. (1987). Self-discrepancy: A theory relating self and affect. *Psychological Review, 94,* 319–340.

Ingram, R. E. (1990). Self-focused attention in clinical disorders: Review and a conceptual model. *Psychological Bulletin, 107,* 156–176.

Inzlicht, M., & Gutsell, J. N. (2007). Running on empty: Neural signals for self-control failure. *Psychological Science, 18,* 933–937.

James, W. (1890). *The principles of psychology.* New York: Henry Holt and Company.

Jensen, A. R. (1998). *The g factor: The science of mental ability.* Westport, CT: Praeger Publishers.

Joseph, S., & Linley, P. A. (2005). Positive psychological approaches to therapy. *Counseling and Psychotherapy Research, 5,* 5–10.

Kagan, J., & Snidman, N. (2004). *The long shadow of temperament.* Cambridge, MA: Harvard University Press.

Kashdan, T. B., Biswas-Diener, R., & King, L. A. (2009). Reconsidering happiness: The costs of distinguishing between hedonics and eudaimonia. *Journal of Positive Psychology, 3,* 219–233.

Kashdan, T. B., Rose, P., & Fincham, F. D. (2004). Curiosity and exploration: Facilitating positive subjective experiences and personal growth opportunities. *Journal of Personality Assessment, 82,* 291–305.

Kaufman, J. C., Grigorenko, E. L., & Sternberg, R. J. (2009). *The essential Sternberg: Essays on intelligence, psychology, and education.* New York: Springer Publishing Co.

Kerns, J. G., Cohen, J. D., MacDonald, A. W., Cho, R. Y., Stenger, V. A., & Carter, C. S. (2004). Anterior cingulate conflict monitoring and adjustments in control. *Science, 303,* 1023–1026.

Knight, R. T., & Stuss, D. T. (2002). Prefrontal cortex: The present and the future. In D. T. Stuss & R. T. Knight (Eds.), *Principles of frontal lobe function* (pp. 573–597). New York: Oxford University Press.

Knutson, B., & Wimmer, G. E. (2007). Reward: Neural circuitry for social valuation. In E. Harmon-Jones & P. Winkielman (Eds.), *Social neuroscience: Integrating biological and psychological explanations of social behavior* (pp. 157–175). New York: Guilford Press.

Koole, S. L., & Jostmann, N. B. (2004). Getting a grip on your feelings: Effects of action orientation and external demands on intuitive action regulation. *Journal of Personality and Social Psychology, 87,* 974–990.

Kross, E., Ayduk, O., & Mischel, W. (2005). When asking "why" does not hurt: Distinguishing rumination from reflective processing of negative emotions. *Psychological Science, 16,* 709–715.

Kuhl, J. (2000). A functional-design approach to motivation and self-regulation: The dynamics of personality systems and interactions. In M. Boekaerts, P. R. Pintrich, & M. Zeidner (Eds.), *Handbook of self-regulation* (pp. 111–169). San Diego, CA: Academic Press.

Langston, C. A. (1994). Capitalizing on and coping with daily-life events: Expressive responses to positive events. *Journal of Personality and Social Psychology, 67,* 1112–1125.

Lazarus, R. S. (2003). Does the positive psychology movement have legs? *Psychological Inquiry, 14,* 93–109.

Lazarus, R. S., & Folkman, S. (1991). The concept of coping. In A. Monat & R. S. Lazarus (Eds.), *Stress and coping: An anthology* (3rd ed., pp. 189–206). New York: Columbia University Press.

Leary, M. R. (2004). *The curse of the self: Self-awareness, egotism, and the quality of human life.* New York: Oxford University Press.

Lewin, K. (1935). *A dynamic theory of personality.* New York: McGraw-Hill.

Lewinsohn, P., & Libet, J. (1972). Pleasant events, activity schedules, and depressions. *Journal of Abnormal Psychology, 79,* 291–295.

Lieberman, M. D. (2000). Introversion and working memory: Central executive differences. *Personality and Individual Differences, 28,* 479–486.

Lieberman, M. D. (2007). Social cognitive neuroscience: A review of core processes. *Annual Review of Psychology, 58,* 259–289.

Lieberman, M. D., & Eisenberger, N. I. (2005). Conflict and habit: A social cognitive neuroscience approach to the self. In A. Tesser, J. V. Wood, & D. A. Stapel (Eds.), *On building, defending and regulating the self: A psychological perspective* (pp. 77–102). New York: Psychology Press.

Matthews, G., & Gilliland, K. (1999). The personality theories of H. J. Eysenck and J. A. Gray: A comparative review. *Personality and Individual Differences, 26*, 583–626.

Mayer, J. D. (2005). A tale of two visions: Can a new view of personality help integrate psychology? *American Psychologist, 60*, 294–307.

McClelland, D. C. (1987). *Human motivation.* New York: Cambridge University Press.

McClure, S. M., Laibson, D. I., Loewenstein, G., & Cohen, J. D. (2004). Separate neural systems value immediate and delayed monetary rewards. *Science, 306*, 503–507.

Miller, E. K., & Cohen, J. D. (2001). An integrative theory of prefrontal cortex function. *Annual Review of Neuroscience, 24*, 167–202.

Mogg, K., & Bradley, B. P. (1998). A cognitive-motivational analysis of anxiety. *Behaviour Research and Therapy, 36*, 809–848.

Monroe, S. M., & Simons, A. D. (1991). Diathesis-stress theories in the context of life stress research: Implications for the depressive disorders. *Psychological Bulletin, 110*, 406–425.

Mor, N., & Winquist, J. (2002). Self-focused attention and negative affect: A meta-analysis. *Psychological Bulletin, 128*, 638–662.

Morling, B., & Evered, S. (2006). Secondary control reviewed and defined. *Psychological Bulletin, 132*, 269–296.

Muraven, M., & Slessareva, E. (2003). Mechanisms of self-control failure: Motivation and limited resources. *Personality and Social Psychology Bulletin, 29*, 894–906.

Oishi, S., Diener, E., & Lucas, R. E. (2007). The optimum level of well-being: Can people be too happy? *Perspectives on Psychological Science, 2*, 346–360.

Pashler, H. (1998). *Attention.* Hove, England: Psychology Press.

Paulus, M. P., Feinstein, J. S., Simmons, A., & Stein, M. B. (2004). Anterior cingulate activation in high trait anxious subjects is related to altered error processing during decision making. *Biological Psychiatry, 55*, 1179–1187.

Pennebaker, J. W. (2000). Psychological factors influencing the reporting of physical symptoms. In A. A. Stone, J. S. Turkkan, C. A. Bachrach, J. B. Jobe, & H. S. Kurtzman (Eds.), *The science of self-report: Implications for research and practice* (pp. 299–315). Mahwah, NJ: Lawrence Erlbaum Associates.

Peterson, C., & Seligman, M. E. P. (2004). *Character strengths and virtues: A handbook and classification.* New York: Oxford University Press.

Plant, R. W., & Ryan, R. M. (1985). Intrinsic motivation and the effects of self-consciousness, self-awareness, and ego-involvement: An investigation of internally controlling styles. *Journal of Personality, 53*, 435–449.

Posner, M. I., & Rothbart, M. K. (2007). Research on attention networks as a model for the integration of psychological science. *Annual Review of Psychology, 58*, 1–23.

Pronin, E., & Wegner, D. M. (2006). Manic thinking: Independent effects of thought speed and thought content on mood. *Psychological Science, 17*, 807–813.

Robinson, M. D. (2007a). Personality, affective processing, and self-regulation: Toward process-based views of extraversion, neuroticism, and agreeableness. *Social and Personality Psychology Compass, 1*, 223–225.

Robinson, M. D. (2007b). Lives lived in milliseconds: Using cognitive methods in personality research. In R. W. Robins, R. C. Fraley, & R. Krueger (Eds.), *Handbook of research methods in personality* (pp. 345–359). New York: Guilford Press.

Robinson, M. D., Meier, B. P., Tamir, M., Wilkowski, B. M., & Ode, S. (2009b). Behavioral facilitation: A cognitive model of individual differences in approach motivation. *Emotion, 9*, 70–82.

Robinson, M. D., & Neighbors, C. (2006). Catching the mind in action: Implicit methods in personality research and assessment. In M. Eid & E. Diener (Eds.), *Handbook of multimethod measurement in psychology* (pp. 115–125). Washington, DC: American Psychological Association.

Robinson, M. D., Schmeichel, B. J., & Inzlicht, M. (2009a). How does the self control itself? Questions and considerations from a cognitive control perspective. *Manuscript submitted for publication.*

Robinson, M. D., Schmeichel, B. J., & Inzlicht, M. (2010). A cognitive control perspective of self-control strength and its depletion. *Social and Personality Psychology Compass, 4*, 189–200.

Rodebaugh, T. L. (2009). Hiding the self and social anxiety: The core extrusion schema measure. *Cognitive Therapy and Research, 33*, 90–109.

Rothbart, M. K., Ahadi, S. A., & Evans, D. E. (2000). Temperament and personality: Origins and outcomes. *Journal of Personality and Social Psychology, 78*, 122–135.

Rothbaum, F., Weisz, J. R., & Snyder, S. S. (1982). Changing the world and changing the self: A two-process model of perceived control. *Journal of Personality and Social Psychology, 42*, 5–27.

Rottenberg, J., Gross, J. J., & Gotlib, I. H. (2005). Emotion context insensitivity in major depressive disorder. *Journal of Abnormal Psychology, 114,* 627–639.

Ryan, R. M. (1982). Control and information in the intrapersonal sphere: An extension of cognitive evaluation theory. *Journal of Personality and Social Psychology, 43,* 450–461.

Ryan, R. M., & Deci, E. L. (2000). Self-determination theory and the facilitation of intrinsic motivation, social development, and well-being. *American Psychologist, 55,* 68–78.

Ryan, R. M., & Deci, E. L. (2001). On happiness and human potential: A review of research on hedonic and eudaimonic well-being. *Annual Review of Psychology, 52,* 141–166.

Ryan, R. M., & Deci, E. L. (2008). From ego depletion to vitality: Theory and findings concerning the facilitation of energy available to the self. *Social and Personality Psychology Compass, 2,* 702–717.

Saint-Cyr, J. A., Bronstein, Y. L., & Cummings, J. L. (2002). Neurobehavioral consequences of neurosurgical treatments and focal lesions of frontal-subcortical circuits. In D. T. Stuss & R. T. Knight (Eds.), *Principles of frontal lobe function* (pp. 408–427). New York: Oxford University Press.

Sanders, A. F. (1998). *Elements of human performance.* Mahwah, NJ: Erlbaum.

Sarason, I. G., Sarason, B. R., & Pierce, G. R. (1990). Anxiety, cognitive interference, and performance. *Journal of Social Behavior and Personality, 5,* 1–18.

Sarter, M., & Gehring, W. J. (2006). More attention must be paid: The neurobiology of attentional effort. *Brain Research Reviews, 51,* 145–160.

Sayette, M. A. (1999). Does drinking reduce stress? *Alcohol Research and Health, 23.* 250–255.

Schneider, W., & Shiffrin, R. M. (1977). Controlled and automatic human information processing: I. Detection, search, and attention. *Psychological Review, 84,* 1–66.

Schultz, W. (2004). Neural coding of basic reward terms of animal learning theory, game theory, microeconomics and behavioural ecology. *Current Opinion in Neurobiology, 14,* 139–147.

Seligman, M. E. P., & Csikszentmihalyi, M. (2000). Positive psychology: An introduction. *American Psychologist, 55,* 5–14.

Seligman, M. E. P., Steen, T. A., Park, N., & Peterson, C. (2005). Positive psychology progress: Empirical validation of interventions. *American Psychologist, 60,* 410–421.

Senko, C., Durik, A. M., & Harackiewicz, J. M. (2008). Historical perspectives and new directions in achievement goal theory: Understanding the effects of mastery and performance-approach goals. In J. Y. Shah & W. L. Gardner (Eds.), *Handbook of motivational science* (pp. 100–113). New York: Guilford Press.

Sheldon, K. M., & King, L. (2001). Why positive psychology is necessary. *American Psychologist, 56,* 216–217.

Shizgal, P. (1999). On the neural computation of utility: Implications from studies of brain stimulation reward. In D. Kahneman, E. Diener, & N. Schwarz (Eds.), *Well-being: The foundation of hedonic psychology* (pp. 500–524). New York: Russell Sage Foundation.

Silvia, P. J. (2006). *Exploring the psychology of interest.* New York: Oxford University Press.

Steele, C. M. (1997). A threat in the air: How stereotypes shape intellectual identity and performance. *American Psychologist, 52,* 613–629.

Steger, M. F., Kashdan, T. B., Sullivan, B. A., & Lorentz, D. (2008). Understanding the search for meaning in life: Personality, cognitive style, and the dynamic between seeking and experiencing meaning. *Journal of Personality, 76,* 199–228.

Tamir, M., & Robinson, M. D. (2004). Knowing good from bad: The paradox of neuroticism, negative affect, and evaluative processing. *Journal of Personality and Social Psychology, 87,* 913–925.

Tassava, S. H., & Ruderman, A. J. (1999). Application of escape theory to binge eating and suicidality in college women. *Journal of Social and Clinical Psychology, 18,* 450–466.

Thrash, T. M., & Elliot, A. J. (2004). Inspiration: Core characteristics, component processes, antecedents, and function. *Journal of Personality and Social Psychology, 87,* 957–973.

Tomarken, A. J., & Keener, A. D. (1998). Frontal brain asymmetry and depression: A self-regulatory perspective. *Cognition and Emotion, 12,* 387–420.

Tranel, D. (2002). Emotion, decision making, and the ventromedial prefrontal cortex. In D. T. Stuss & R. T. Knight (Eds.), *Principles of frontal lobe function* (pp. 338–353). New York: Oxford University Press.

Trapnell, P. D., & Campbell, J. D. (1999). Private self-consciousness and the five-factor model of personality: Distinguishing rumination from reflection. *Journal of Personality and Social Psychology, 76,* 284–304.

Twenge, J. M. (2000). The age of anxiety? The birth cohort change in anxiety and neuroticism, 1952–1993. *Journal of Personality and Social Psychology, 79,* 1007–1021.

Twenge, J. M., Konrath, S., Foster, J. D., Campbell, W. K., & Bushman, B. J. (2008). Egos inflating over time: A cross-temporal meta-analysis of the Narcissistic Personality Inventory. *Journal of Personality, 76*, 875–902.

van Veen, V., & Carter, C. S. (2006). Conflict and cognitive control in the brain. *Current Directions in Psychological Science, 15*, 237–240.

Wallis, J. D. (2007). Neuronal mechanisms in prefrontal cortex underlying adaptive choice behavior. In G., Schoenbaum, J. A. Gottfried, E. A. Murray, & S. J. Ramus (Eds.), *Linking affect to action: Critical contributions of the orbitofrontal cortex* (pp. 447–460). Malden, MA: Blackwell Publishing.

Watson, D. (2000). *Mood and temperament.* New York: Guilford Press.

Watson, D., Wiese, D., Vaidya, J., & Tellegen, A. (1999). The two general activation systems of affect: Structural findings, evolutionary considerations, and psychobiological evidence. *Journal of Personality and Social Psychology, 76*, 820–838.

Wicklund, R. A. (1979). The influence of self-awareness on human behavior. *American Scientist, 67*, 187–193.

Widiger, T. A., & Trull, T. J. (2007). Plate tectonics in the classification of personality disorder: Shifting to a dimensional model. *American Psychologist, 62*, 71–83.

Widiger, T. A., Verheul, R., & van den Brink, W. (1999). Personality and psychopathology. In L. A. Pervin & O. P. John (Eds.), *Handbook of personality: Theory and research* (2nd ed., pp. 347–366). New York: Guilford Press.

Zelazo, P. D., & Cunningham, W. A. (2007). Executive function: Mechanisms underlying emotion regulation. In J. J. Gross (Ed.), *Handbook of emotion regulation* (pp. 135–158). New York: Guilford Press.

Zelenski, J. M., & Larsen, R. J. (1999). Susceptibility to affect: A comparison of three personality taxonomies. *Journal of Personality, 67*, 761–791.

# 12

# Finding Positive Value in Human Consciousness: Conscious Thought Serves Participation in Society and Culture

*E. J. Masicampo and Roy F. Baumeister*

Humans spend much of their lives thinking about people, places, and events that transcend the immediate physical environment. They eagerly anticipate (or else worry uncontrollably about!) imagined futures. They are keenly interested in the experiences of those around them, often gossiping about friends and strangers alike, trading stories with each other as if exchanging some valuable commodity. Together, people create and share whole nonphysical realities, such as those described by religions, philosophical doctrines, and the constitutions of nations. Thoughts and ideas figure prominently in human experience and behavior. It is around them that people plan their lives, and the ability to process them is a (if not *the*) uniquely human trait (Tulving, 2005; Suddendorf, 2006).

The current chapter highlights the importance of researching this unique capacity, which we refer to as conscious thought. We argue that conscious thought enables the processing of information outside of the immediate environment so as to help people adapt to society and culture. To understand this aspect of human cognition is essential for realizing not only how humans function but also how they can function optimally.

Moreover, we think that the widespread neglect and skepticism about consciousness that has become influential in recent decades presents an unbalanced picture of human life and, in particular, a major opportunity for positive psychology. If positive psychologists can begin to elucidate what consciousness can do and what beneficial, adaptive functions it serves in human life, they will help to furnish a better and more complete understanding of human nature than the negatively biased discussions of recent decades have furnished.

At present, much of the work in social psychology emphasizes unconscious, automatic, and effortless mental processes. First, we take stock of these programs of research, including evidence that shows the unconscious mind is capable of guiding a wide range of complex behaviors. One consequence of this work has been that the long-standing and naïve view of the conscious self as being in charge of behavior has come under criticism. We acknowledge that conscious thought may not be necessary for the direct control of action. However, in the spirit of positive psychology, we propose looking for some positive value in what conscious thought does. Evidence suggests that the contribution of conscious thought is to allow individuals to experience and thus respond to actions and events that transcend the immediate physical environment (Schacter & Addis, 2007; Suddendorf, 2006). To be able to process information in such a unique manner must have afforded people new and adaptive ways of responding.

We suggest that conscious thought evolved to enable the human animal to navigate complex social and cultural (rather than physical) environments. Human consciousness enables one to participate in telling and understanding narratives (stories), counterfactual thinking, fantasy play, economic systems, religion, plan making, and fiction. In the present chapter, we propose that the purposes of these and other consciously communicated phenomena are to enable people to learn from others, coordinate their behaviors within large groups, and operate by shared rules and standards. We also remark on how conscious thought operates, which is through simulations of non-present information that can reprogram automatic associations and thus affect later behavior. Last, we suggest future directions for work in social and positive psychology. To understand conscious thought (and hence human nature), we suggest looking between people rather than within individual minds or brains.

Ultimately, a well-informed positive psychology must include a thorough understanding of how conscious thought enables humans to function within their natural, cultural environment. The widespread skepticism about whether consciousness does anything useful amounts to trashing one of humankind's noblest and most distinctive attributes. We think the future of positive psychology should include efforts to rehabilitate human consciousness and recognize that it confers remarkable powers, even if it does not do everything that it was once thought to do.

*Conscious thought and other types of consciousness.* Conscious thought, as the term is used in this chapter, is distinguished from at least one other major category of conscious phenomena. Academics from numerous disciplines acknowledge two major levels of consciousness (Damasio, 1999; Edelman, 2004; Mendl & Paul, 2004; Panksepp, 2005). The first level describes the conscious awareness that deals primarily in feelings and sensations. The general view is that this lower level of consciousness is much older in phylogeny and is present in many if not all

animals (Mendl & Paul, 2004; Panksepp, 2005). The second level of consciousness involves the ability to think rationally, imagine, and reflect on one's experiences. Researchers have argued that this level of consciousness is unique to humans (Damasio, 1999; Edelman, 2004) and that it is characterized most centrally by an ability to extend one's self-awareness beyond the here and now as through mental time travel (Suddendorf, 2006). This chapter is concerned with the higher (second) level of consciousness that is unique to humans, which we will refer to as conscious thought. To understand this ability is crucial for understanding those behaviors for which humans are uniquely designed, most prominently participation in complex, meaningful social systems and culture.

## Taking Stock: The Unconscious and Conscious Thought in Social Psychology

Research on automatic and unconscious processes has flourished in recent decades. Below, we review findings that suggest the unconscious mind is capable of controlling a wide range of effortful processes, including the regulation of social interactions (Dijksterhuis & Bargh, 2001), the initiation and guidance of goal pursuit (Bargh, Gollwitzer, Lee-Chai, Barndollar, & Trötschel, 2001), and complex decision making (Dijksterhuis & Nordgren, 2006). We also review numerous lines of work that have brought the naïve view of conscious thought as controller of behavior under criticism (e.g., Libet, 1985; Wegner, 2002). Together, these lines of work have been taken as indications that human consciousness is an epiphenomenon, that is, an idle and ineffective aspect of psychological functioning. To us, and we hope to many positive psychologists, these lines of work serve as a call to rethink and re-characterize the role of conscious thought in the human psyche.

We then review various theories and findings that together seem to open the door for a new understanding of conscious thought and its function. In particular, recent theories suggest conscious thought may be helpful for simulating sequences of events away from the here and now (Suddendorf, 2006; Schacter & Addis, 2007). Such a process may be the mind's way of making input into itself so as to recalibrate automatic responses and to alter future behavior based on information from the social and cultural environment.

## The Unconscious Mind

The notion that the unconscious mind causes and guides much of human behavior has become the prevailing view based on the previous three decades of psychological research (Bargh, 2006). This notion is both surprising and counterintuitive given that everyday experience instills in one a sense of consciously causing one's moment-to-moment behaviors. A food is encountered, one deliberates about what to do, and a decision to eat or not to eat is made, whereupon the person acts to implement that decision. Yet where perceptions instill one with the sense of conscious control, psychological science has uncovered repeatedly the invisible hand of the unconscious, pushing and pulling every step of the way. Apparently, most actions are triggered automatically in response to incoming cues from the external environment. Thus, behavior tends to follow directly from perception (the so-called perception-behavior link; Bargh, Chen, & Burrows, 1996; Dijksterhuis & Bargh, 2001). For conscious processes to intervene causally between perception of a stimulus and one's behavioral response to it is presumably the rare exception, rather than the usual way of doing things.

Much of the research on unconscious influences on behavior has been conducted by John Bargh and his colleagues (for a review, see Bargh, 2006; Bargh & Chartrand, 1999). Their work has shown that numerous social behaviors are initiated automatically in response to subtle, environmental cues (Bargh et al., 1996). Merely priming people with some social category (e.g., the elderly) can cause them to behave in ways that are stereotypic of the category (e.g., walking slowly). Likewise, priming people with the concept of being rude can increase their willingness to interrupt a conversation. While initial work in this area primed social concepts through exposure to verbal cues, later work indicated that numerous kinds of information can automatically trigger changes in social behavior. People automatically imitate the behaviors of those around them (Chartrand & Bargh, 1999), adopt other peoples' motivations (Aarts, Gollwitzer, & Hassin, 2004), and act in line with the expectations of close others when reminded of their presence (Shah, 2003a; 2003b). The implication is that the regulation of behavior can occur quite automatically in response to various external cues. People modify their behaviors according to changing social environments, all without the conscious intention to do so.

Full-blown goal pursuit can also be initiated outside of conscious awareness. A number of environmental cues, including words related to the goal (Bargh et al., 2001), exposure to means for attaining the goal (Shah & Kruglanski, 2003), and even subtle suggestions that a goal's end state is desirable (Custers & Aarts, 2005), can automatically induce pursuit of the goal. Moreover, goals initiated outside of one's awareness have many of the same features as consciously initiated goals. These include increased effort toward achieving the goal, resumption of the goal after interruption, and goal persistence in the face of obstacles (Bargh et al., 2001). Even motivational states and flexible goal striving may follow directly from encounters with goal-appropriate environments.

The reach of the unconscious mind has also been extended into complex reasoning and decision making (Dijksterhuis & Nordgren, 2006). Decisions reached through the unconscious processing of information are sometimes as good as or even better than choices made through conscious deliberation. In research on unconscious thought, people are given a complex choice that involves tradeoffs on as many as a dozen different dimensions. For example, participants may be asked to consider which of a number of homes one would like to purchase, in which case one must consider the number of bathrooms, yard size, distance from work, neighborhood demographics, and so forth. Each participant in the study is asked to review the multiple options and to choose whichever one he or she thinks is best. In a control condition, participants are forced to choose immediately upon reviewing the options. In a conscious thought condition, participants are told to deliberate for some period of time and then to choose whichever option is best. In an unconscious thought condition, participants read through the multiple options but are then distracted for some period of time, after which they are immediately told to make a choice. The surprising finding is that participants in the unconscious thought condition usually outperform participants in both the control condition and the conscious thought condition, reaching decisions that are both objectively and subjectively better. Apparently, even complex and difficult choices are handled well by unconscious processes (though for recent criticisms of this work, see Acker, 2008; Payne, Samper, Bettman, & Luce, 2008).

Freud argued long ago that the most important causes of behavior originate outside of conscious awareness. Social psychological research has kept this idea alive and well. According to a quickly growing body of work, the unconscious is capable of initiating and guiding some of the most complex of behaviors and decisions. The dynamic unconscious is apparently capable of handling much of what people do.

## Questioning the Function of Conscious Thought

While the number of functions attributable to the unconscious continues to grow, so do the reasons to doubt that conscious thought has direct access to or control over one's decisions and behaviors. Here we review a number of critiques against conscious thought that suggest it may not be useful for the control of action.

One major problem for the notion of consciously willed action is that thoughts are too delayed to initiate behavior. Libet (1985) studied the link between conscious thoughts and actions by measuring the temporal onset of both. In his studies, he asked individuals to perform a movement (e.g., a flick of the wrist) and to indicate the precise moment at which the decision to perform it was made. He found that people's conscious decisions to act occurred a substantial portion of a second after the unconscious mind had already set the action into motion. According to this work, the conscious self perceives an action after it has already started to occur, and thus it operates too slowly to lay claim to having initiated the process.

Conscious reports about one's decisions and behaviors also apparently show no reliable connection to some of their true causes. Nisbett and Wilson (1977) found that people will behave in some way and then explain that behavior to others in a manner that is demonstrably false or inaccurate. (That is, they explained the basis of their decision in a way that omitted one important factor, of which they were unaware.) Apparently, people explain their behaviors based on what is plausible or commonly expected rather than what actually took place. Thus, conscious thought does not have access to some of the inner processes that influence decisions and guide behavior.

Other work has emphasized the illusory nature of conscious will. Wegner (2002) has argued that people come to believe that they cause their behaviors because of a natural tendency to infer causation when one event precedes another. Usually, a thought occurs, and a behavior consistent with that thought follows closely after. Naturally, then, people perceive that the thought caused the behavior. However, Wegner showed repeatedly that people can be led to perceive conscious will over events that were caused subtly—or even quite loudly (Wegner, Sparrow, & Winerman, 2004)—by the hands of someone else. Thus, the perception of conscious will is not a result of any real link between conscious thought and action. Instead, conscious will is an illusion that occurs as a by-product of other processes.

Everyday experience suggests that actions are guided by thoughts, but extant research has suggested that thoughts are too slow to directly guide muscle movements, that the conscious self is often mistaken about what caused them, and that conscious will is sometimes an illusion (and an easily manipulated one at that). Together, these lines of work cast serious doubt on conscious efficacy, so much so that some have wondered out loud whether there is any function to conscious thought at all (Bargh, 1997; Pockett, 2004).

## Toward Understanding the Conscious Mind

Although we accept the possible correctness of research favoring unconscious control and questioning a direct link between conscious thought and behavior, we emphasize that these lines of work point not to the uselessness of conscious thought but to the need to redefine how and what it does. Thus, in the spirit of positive psychology, we propose looking for some positive function of human consciousness. If conscious thought is not for the direct control of present actions, then its influence may lie elsewhere.

There are many important reasons to be skeptical of the idea that conscious thought is a feckless by-product of other processes. Conscious processes are psychologically effortful and biologically expensive, and they seem to have appeared very recently in evolution. From an evolutionary standpoint, such an expensive capacity would not have survived or become so widespread in the species unless it conferred some benefit to outweigh the costs of having it. Conscious thought is also fairly unique to humans. No other animal has the ability to engage in conscious thought in the manner that humans do (Suddendorf, 2006). Presumably, this unique mental process allows for some useful, unique aspects of human life, and understanding those may be essential for understanding human nature.

Other animals navigate their physical environments and execute quite complex actions within them without requiring consciousness in the human sense. Conscious thought, then, is perhaps better suited to dealing with social and cultural environments. Indeed, evidence converges on the idea that the human brain inherited its complexity, including the capacity for conscious thought, in order to adapt to an increasingly complex social life (Dunbar, 1995; Tomasello, 1999). This section starts by describing the idea that conscious thought enables a person to process meaningful sequences of events and to simulate experiences away from the here and now (e.g., Baars, 1998; Suddendorf, 2006), and we suggest this ability is best understood as serving social and cultural purposes. These ideas are the seeds of what we think may be fruitful areas of research. Moreover, we view this functional approach to conscious thought as essential for providing positive psychology with a more complete picture of human thinking and being.

*What conscious thought is.* To define human consciousness has proven to be an unsolvable task for just about every field of philosophy and science. It has been made difficult in part by the large number of seemingly disparate, conscious abilities that separate humans from other animals. Human consciousness is closely associated with language, episodic memory, reasoning, theory of mind, and self-awareness, among others. The goal to define conscious thought has become in part the goal to determine which of the uniquely human cognitive capacities came first and thus allowed for the rest. Rather than try to resolve that debate here, we consider the multiple aspects of human consciousness together and consider what features they have in common, and how they might work together to confer on people adaptive social and cultural benefits.

We emphasize two major characteristics of conscious thought. First, conscious thought is characterized as the construction of meaningful sequences of events. This notion is consistent with numerous dual-process theories that equate the conscious, controlled system with the ability to reason, follow rules, and otherwise engage in serial information processing (Epstein, 1994; Evans, 2003; Kahneman, 2003; Sloman, 1996). An entire suite of uniquely human cognitive abilities falls under this umbrella. Humans can think logically, combine words and sentences into meaningful language, and engage in narrative storytelling. Each of these involves the capacity to process sequences of events in a meaningful manner.

Another defining aspect of conscious thought is that it allows people to experience, process, and simulate non-present events (Hesslow, 2005; Suddendorf, 2006). To think in sequences implies the manipulation of information through time, and this is precisely what conscious thought enables the human animal to do. Most animals are stuck in the present (Roberts, 2002), but humans have the ability to think of themselves, other people, and their needs and motivations as existing and changing through time (Schacter & Addis, 2007; Suddendorf, 2006; Tulving, 2005).

*Conscious thought enables sharing of social and cultural information.* We propose that conscious thought processes are for social and cultural functioning. It has become axiomatic in social psychology to describe humans as social animals (Aronson, 1972), but humans have adapted to a social structure that is much more complex than those of other animals, namely culture. To share information and to rely on others on such a large scale is a new and much more advanced way of being social. This section focuses on the various ways that conscious thought serves as the interface between the human animal and culture.

The most obvious means by which people share information with others is through language, for which conscious thought is crucial. Everything people say passes through consciousness. The unconscious, automatic system seems capable of responding only to single words (Baars, 2002; Greenwald & Liu, 1985). In contrast, conscious thought can combine words in order to create and derive meaning from the interactions between them. Full-fledged language beyond single words and ideas is crucial for transmitting information across individuals.

A common form of information that relies in large part on language is structured narrative. Narratives have been described as the fundamental constituent of human thought and communication (Bruner, 2002; Schank & Abelson, 1995), and conscious rehearsal plays a crucial role in developing and processing them (Wegner, Quillian, & Houston, 1996). Moreover, structure narratives are crucial for learning from social events (Costabile & Klein, 2008), and they are perhaps the most common means for transmitting information about social life (e.g., Baumeister, Zhang, & Vohs, 2004; Mar & Oatley, 2008).

Another major form of information exchange involves the sharing of systems of rules. Some of these systems are relatively hard and fast, as in the areas of logical reasoning, math, and science. These rules are (presumably) objectively true, but most people learn them from the social and cultural environment. In addition, use of these rules greatly facilitates participation in cultural life. Planning, coordinating behavior within large groups, and managing large amounts of resources all benefit immensely from counting and quantification. Also, many social interactions and exchanges operate on the assumption that all parties are relying on the same system of rules and numbers (Basu & Waymire, 2006). To understand and use these systems of rules requires the capacity for conscious thought (De Neys, 2006; DeWall, Baumeister, & Masicampo, 2008). Indeed, logical reasoning is one of the greatest powers of the human psyche. Our own experiments have shown that the unconscious is not able to reason effectively, try as it might (DeWall et al., 2008; see also Lieberman, Gaunt, Gilbert & Trope, 2002). Libet's demonstrations that conscious thought may be dispensable in initiating wrist movements seem trivial in comparison to its capacity for logical reasoning.

Other systems of rules include governments, religions, and economic markets. These socially shared realities influence individuals in ways that physical reality does not. The rules by which the physical world operates do not constrain one's ability to grab any item in a store and walk out without paying, but the rules by which most social environments (including governments, religions, and economies) operate do not allow such behavior to occur. If it does occur, serious negative repercussions follow.

Conscious thought enables individuals to learn about, live by, and enforce social rules for behavior. Indeed, human thought processes may be best suited to evaluating adherence to social rules, as evidenced by the ease with which people can spot cheaters (Cosmides, 1989). Moreover, social psychological research has begun to show that enforcement of these consciously learned and processed rules promotes social functions. Both the productivity and cohesiveness of large groups suffer when their members cheat, freeload, or otherwise game the structure as through social loafing (e.g., Latané, Williams, & Harkins, 1979). Honor codes, however, which are promoted in many social systems, can greatly decrease if not eliminate the natural tendency to cheat (Mazar & Ariely, 2006). When groups implement the punishment of cheaters, prosocial behavior increases and this benefits both individuals and the group as a whole in the long run (Gachter, Renner, & Sefton, 2008). Moreover, even unconscious reminders of social systems can promote prosociality. Subliminal reminders of god have been shown to increase the amount of money allocated to anonymous strangers in an economic game (Shariff & Norenzayan, 2007). Among American college students, exposure to subliminal images of the United States flag has been shown to increase egalitarian thinking and decrease hostile attitudes toward a stigmatized outgroup (Butz, Plant, & Doerr, 2007). In these latter examples, the most proximal causes of the prosocial responses were unconscious. However, the manipulations could almost certainly not have had such an effect without some prior conscious processing of religious and national ideals and at least some endorsement of their meaning. To participate in social systems involves learning to live by rules, expectations, and potential consequences (e.g., arrest or eternal damnation) that are never directly observed or experienced. Yet the conscious sharing and processing of these ideas ensure that they can have a profound impact on individuals' behaviors.

Conscious thought enables people to share information of numerous forms, including through language, narratives, logical reasoning, and larger social realities like nations and religions. These forms of input differ considerably from the moment-to-moment environmental cues that trigger the unconscious, automatic system. While external cues are sufficient to enable action initiation and behavioral guidance, conscious processing of information enables social and cultural functioning.

*Conscious thought affects behavior indirectly.* People obtain information from the cultural environment, but how does that information influence behavior? Consciously processed information affects behavior indirectly by providing feedback to the unconscious systems that guide behavior. Conscious thought helps to reprogram attitudes and automatic responses, and those changes in turn manifest as altered future behavior.

Conscious thought recalibrates the automatic system (e.g, Cosmides & Tooby, 2000; Tooby & Cosmides, 2005). One way it does this is by causing novel responses to be formed toward simulated objects and events. Mentally simulated experience mimics actual experience, and it does so well enough to elicit many of the same perceptual responses as actual experience (Hesslow, 2002). As a result, one can simulate an experience and learn from it as if it were real. The phenomenon of phobias is a good illustration of this process (e.g., Bogels & Zigterman, 2000; Ottaviani & Beck, 1987). Phobics engage in undesirable thought patterns, such as repeatedly imagining some unlikely but tragic series of events. A spider phobic may have the habit of simulating negative experiences with spiders, including being bitten or injured in some dramatic manner. Even if no actual negative experience with a spider occurs, repeated simulations are sufficient for solidifying the novel aversion (toward spiders) and the accompanying automatic response (to flee when a spider is near).

The way people plan is also evidence of the recalibration process in action. The likelihood of performing some desired future action is greatly increased simply by committing to an implementation intention, or a specific plan of action in the form of an if-then statement (e.g., if $x$ happens, then I will do $y$; Gollwitzer, 1999; Gollwitzer & Schaal, 1998). Formation of an implementation intention works by allowing a person to pass control of the desired action to the automatic system, or else to the specified external cue. Once the cue is encountered, the behavior is executed. Apparently, by committing to the plan, one internalizes the novel automatic link from perception to behavior. Indeed, such plans to act are successful even when the person is consciously distracted at the moment the critical cue is encountered (Brandstätter, Lengfelder, & Gollwitzer, 2001), suggesting that conscious thought is essential for making the plan (i.e., reprogramming the automatic response) but not for initiating the action.

Information from others can be used to recalibrate automatic, physiological responses. Telling someone that a tone will be followed by a shock is sufficient to cause the person to exhibit increases in skin conductance in response to the tone (Cook & Harris, 1937). Likewise, a learned skin conductance response (e.g., aversion to a tone that has been paired many times over with a shock) can be greatly reduced by telling a person that the usual consequence will no longer occur (Colgan, 1970). Thus, conscious thought via language enables people to acquire information from others that can be used to form new ways of responding.

These numerous lines of work show how conscious thought can influence behavior in an indirect but nevertheless impactful way. The notion that conscious thought provides input to automatic responses rather than exerts direct control over behavior helps to address the problem that conscious thought is too slow to guide action (Libet, 1985). Automatic associations may drive behavior, but conscious thought can influence behavior by reprogramming those associations. Thus, conscious thought processes social and cultural information (in the form of meaningful, sequential thought) and uses that information (through plans, mental simulations, etc.) so that the unconscious system can respond appropriately.

## Moving Forward: Conscious Thought at the Animal–Culture Interface

Numerous theories and findings have paved a wide road for moving toward a science of conscious thought. As reviewed above, ample work in social psychology has focused on automatic processes, often with the conclusion that the unconscious mind is capable of directing much if not all of human behavior (e.g., Bargh, 2006). But the scope of this work is limited only to those processes that occur within the individual, that are old in phylogeny, and that are likely to be homologous with most other animals. There has been some work on unconscious social behaviors, but it has mostly employed subtle reminders of others (e.g., Shah, 2003a; 2003b) in place of verbal communication, information exchange, and other everyday cultural phenomena. Future work ought to look to these latter processes, which require conscious forms of thinking and sharing. Conscious thought is a defining component of human life, even if its influence on behavior is indirect. To seek a more thorough understanding of how conscious thought functions is crucial for understanding human nature.

Conscious thought and most of what it does is a phenomenon of complex society and culture. This includes imagining, mathematical problem solving, role playing, reasoning logically, reading fiction, participating in religion, and investing in the stock market. To understand conscious thought, future work will need to look between the individuals in culture as well as within them. First, we review potential areas of inquiry into the intrapersonal aspects of culture, including how cultural information is processed by individuals and what effects those processes have on behavior. Then, we review potential areas of inquiry into the more interpersonal processes involved in culture, including research into the kinds of information people share and how that information is shared between them.

## Intrapersonal Aspects of Conscious Thought and Culture

How do individuals process and ultimately become affected by culturally transmitted information? One challenge in this area will be to understand the functioning of imagination, mental simulations, and planning, which all play a crucial role in translating cultural information into the appropriate behavioral responses. A second challenge will be to understand the role of shared realities and systems of rules, including nation states, mathematical concepts, and even fictional environments, in the regulation of everyday behavior.

How does simulated information translate into changes in automatic responding? A large body of work has already started to address this question, as reviewed previously in this chapter. Research on implementation intentions (Gollwitzer, 1999) has shown that commitment to simple but specific plans can alter automatic responses. Other lines of work have suggested that verbal communication from others can alter automatic responses (Cook & Harris, 1937; Colgan, 1970) and that novel responses may be altered via affective responses to mental simulations (Cosmides & Tooby, 2000; see also Baumeister, Vohs, DeWall, & Zhang, 2007). The relationship between these various means for altering automatic responses is one area for future inquiry. One possibility is that they each involve a single mechanism. If so, mental simulation is a likely candidate. Thus, implementation intentions may rely on a person's ability to envision the future behavior. Moreover, other aspects of simulations (e.g., vividness, perspective) may determine whether conscious thoughts can translate into changes in behavior.

Future work may also examine when simulations take place. Simulation is a key component of behavior change, but the antecedents of simulation are not yet understood. One possibility is that conscious thoughts and rumination occur in response to negative feedback (e.g., goal failure; Bongers & Dijksterhuis, 2009; Martin & Tesser, 1989) or motivational conflict (Morsella, 2005). Future work must address more specifically when and how information enters into the stream of conscious thought. This question is particularly important given the vast amount of information from the external environment that is processed unconsciously from moment to moment. Some processes presumably filter and monitor these vast amounts of input so as to consciously process only the most necessary parts.

A related issue is whether and when information from others (e.g., in everyday conversation) is translated into full-blown mental simulation. Extant research suggests that all language comprehension involves some degree of mental simulation (e.g., Glenberg & Kaschak, 2002; Kaschak & Glenberg, 2000), yet presumably not all language processing requires the full-blown simulation. It is important to distinguish between shallow processing and full simulation insofar as information is more likely to influence one's behavior when one is asked to imagine and simulate that information in full (Gregory, Cialdini, & Carpenter, 1982). Numerous features of communication may influence the extent to which information is simulated, including the nature of the information shared, the motivational state of the person receiving that information, and the traits of the person who is offering it.

What different forms do simulations take? One variable is the perspective of the simulation, which can be in either first- or third-person. Recent work has found that third-person simulations are better than first-person simulations for growing beyond one's past self (Libby, Eibach, & Gilovich, 2005) and for realizing simulated future behaviors (Libby, Shaeffer, Eibach, & Slemmer, 2007). Future work may determine what causes a person to simulate from one perspective instead of another, and how these simulations affect other forms of thinking (e.g., consumption of fiction). In addition, there may be other features of simulations that determine how they exert their influence. The type of content that simulations seek out may be variable. Recent research distinguishes between process-oriented simulations, which focus on possible paths of action, and outcome-oriented simulations, which focus on possible end results (e.g., Escalas & Luce, 2004). Individual differences in simulation vividness have been documented as well (Marks, 1973), and these can have a profound impact on how conscious thought operates. In addition, some simulations may favor certain modalities. Simulated experience can presumably mean simulated sight, simulated sound, or a combination of both (Baddeley & Hitch, 1974). These factors and numerous others may alter the influence of simulations.

Introspection is the ability to access one's inner states, including perhaps one's responses to both real and simulated experience. Research on introspection has spent considerable time in the proverbial closet (Locke, 2009), yet everyone accesses inner processes every day and communicates them with others. Introspective efficacy has been criticized in the past, but a more sympathetic approach to introspection ought to note that only some aspects of introspection are demonstrably inaccurate. Introspective efficacy may falter when it is judged by its grasp of specific details such as the causes for one's behavior (Nisbett & Wilson, 1977), but that may be an unfair standard by which to judge introspective usefulness. One area where access to inner states is perhaps more accurate is in simple approach or avoidance judgments, as in reports of whether one likes or dislikes a person, object, or event. If someone dislikes a person, there is presumably a good reason for the opinion regardless of whether she can pinpoint its cause. Such a judgment is not information rich, yet it could nonetheless be immensely adaptive, particularly if communicated for the benefit of close others, such as friends and family. Future research on introspection may focus on these and other simple judgments, as well as the sharing of these judgments with others.

While a specific mental simulation can work to alter a single, automatic response, thoughts and simulations over months and years may weave entire systems of rules into new ways of behaving. What are the characteristics of these systems and what purpose do they serve? One crucial issue is whether and how each system's various rules influence behavior so as to benefit the individuals and groups. One may expect that systems tend to promote rules that foster group functioning. Research on perceptions of free will is consistent with this idea. Many belief systems work to instill their members with a sense of free will and volition, and recent work has suggested that such perceptions promote prosocial behavior. Manipulating disbelief in free will has been shown to lead to an increase in cheating and stealing (Vohs & Schooler, 2008). Other work has found that similar procedures can increase aggression and decrease helping (Baumeister, Masicampo, & DeWall, 2009). Thus, free will beliefs seem hugely beneficial for group functioning. Other shared rules, such as punishment for violations of group norms, have been shown to increase prosocial behavior in the short term and both individual and group gains in the long term (Gachter et al., 2008). Future work is needed to continue to examine cultural rules and beliefs and the social functions that they serve.

Another issue regarding systems of rules and beliefs concerns the boundary between endorsement of an idea and understanding of it. One view of understanding is that it cannot be entirely objective, so that one must at some level also believe and accept it so as to grasp its full meaning. If this view were true, one implication would hold that mere knowledge of rules (rather than conscious endorsement of them) could influence behavior. Indeed, recent work has shown that priming of god concepts can increase prosocial behavior regardless of individual differences in religiosity (Shariff & Norenzayan, 2007). Presumably, the knowledge of religious ideals alone is sufficient for causing one's behavior to conform to them in certain contexts. This phenomenon, if common to other concepts and ideas, may have important implications for the sharing of information in culture.

Other cultural systems dictate rules for thinking and managing information rather than for regulating behavior. These include the relatively objective systems of math and logic. Unlike nations or religious institutions, these systems do not specify what social behaviors one can or cannot do. But they are still crucial for social functioning. Mostly, these systems behave as a shared means for organizing behavior, as when using money, calendars, clocks, maps, and other implementations of math, science, and technology. How these phenomena help to regulate behavior is one important issue. Another important and more elusive issue is how these apparently objective systems interface with other systems of rules. How does knowledge of science interact with religious beliefs? Some theories attribute supernatural thinking (e.g., the belief in spirits, souls, and ghosts) to incompatibilities in multiple systems of rules, namely between physical rules and psychological ones (Bloom, 2004). People deal with countless different systems of rules and beliefs, so an understanding of how those interact is necessary for understanding how people operate within their cultural environments.

This list of future directions is by no means exhaustive, but its contents have been chosen to illustrate that beyond the direct control of action remains a wide array of means through which conscious thought may serve positive functions. We propose that to operate within complex social systems may be the purpose of most uniquely human cognitive capacities, including conscious thought. Indeed, multiple perspectives have argued that thinking is for social doing (Cosmides, 1989; Haidt, 2007). Thus, how people think and how they translate such thoughts into doing remains an important area of inquiry for positive psychology.

## Interpersonal Aspects of Conscious Thought and Culture

To appreciate that conscious thought is for simulating experiences and processing information means also appreciating that culture is about sharing these experiences and information with others. As conscious thought is not merely a by-product of other mental processes, so culture is not merely a by-product of other ways of being social. Rather, culture is a new way of being social that entails benefits over and above the other types. Thus, future research ought to examine what happens between people to create culture, including what kinds of information people share, how that information is shared between them, and the individual processes that cause people to share them.

Participation in culture requires a set of social cognitive skills for obtaining information from others, and future work may begin to examine these. To whom do people look for information, and to whom are people willing to listen? One obstacle for navigation of information-rich environments is figuring out who has the right information. Many cultures seem designed to facilitate this. Most societies use systems for marking expertise, such as by conferring degrees, honors, and titles. An appreciation for the psychology of these systems is important, and future research ought also to look into the more natural ways that prestige, skill, and knowledge are marked and perceived in cultural circles (e.g., Reyes-Garcia et al., 2008). Leadership is a related phenomenon, inasmuch as individuals are more likely to consider leading figures as reliable sources for information (Berger, Cohen, & Zelditch, 1972). Trust may also be a key factor when communicating with others (White, 2005) or when engaging in economic exchange (Lynch, Kent, & Srinivasan, 2001). Perception of such qualities in others is likely to be an essential skill for living in culture, and thus for living in the natural human environment.

Another issue pertains to the kinds of information people seek from others. Much of the information exchanged between individuals may serve basic, pragmatic functions, such as to help one find a meal or make one's way home. Yet much of the information that people actively consume is purely fictional. Recent theories suggest that the function of fiction is to enable

social learning (Mar & Oatley, 2008). This is consistent with theories of fantasy play as crucial for social learning in children (Singer & Singer, 1990) and of gossip as a tool for cultural learning (Baumeister et al., 2004). However, future work may consider whether all forms of media consumption serve a similar learning function, or whether they also serve as a proxy for other needs and desires (e.g., the need to belong; see Epley, Waytz, & Cacioppo, 2007).

Other animals exchange and share food, protection, and shelter. However, humans, as cultural animals, must share much more than that. What inner processes motivate participation in culture? One possibility is that, as members of large social and cultural networks, people have a fundamental motivation to contribute resources to their group. If so, the ability to contribute may partly determine one's happiness and well-being. Work has shown that volunteering and helping others can be beneficial to one's self-esteem and well-being (Midlarsky, Fagin-Jones, & Nemeroff, 2006; Thoits & Hewitt, 2001), and more recent work has shown that giving gifts to others can increase positive feelings (Dunn, Aknin, & Norton, 2008). Thus, contributing physical resources is beneficial, and perhaps contributing to culture (e.g., via skill or information sharing) is also important. People may derive well-being out of providing informational support to others (e.g., as in transactive memory systems; Wegner, Erber, & Raymond, 1991) and by feeling like active participants in their individual social and cultural circles. Indeed, people expend considerable time and resources into gaining prestige, or else they will go to great lengths, often hindering close others, so as to appear competent in domains that do not overlap with the skill areas of those around them (Tesser, 1988). The need to contribute uniquely to culture, if proven to be a real, motivating force in the human psyche, may provide a new lens with which to view a number of social phenomena. People need to belong, but they may also want to be useful to those around them.

To participate in culture, one must be able to process information from that culture as well as participate in information sharing within the culture. In this section, we have reviewed numerous aspects of intrapersonal functioning that may be involved in simulating cultural information so that behaviors may be altered in response to the cultural environment. We also reviewed numerous aspects of sharing within the culture, including the skills and motivations that may be needed for contributing information and for efficiently obtaining information from others. Future work will be needed to examine these capacities and understand how they are acquired and honed throughout the lifetime.

## Conclusion

*Happiness is conscious too, after all.* We have proposed that an understanding of consciousness and conscious processes holds considerable promise for positive psychology. Such an understanding would overcome the prevailing, negative tendencies to dismiss one of the most powerful and remarkable capacities of the human psyche as a feckless epiphenomon. Indeed, elucidating the value of consciousness would enable positive psychology to make a contribution to one of the greatest problems in Western intellectual history, namely what consciousness does and how it fits into the human mind.

Before closing, we want to point out that an understanding of consciousness seems a natural direction for positive psychology to take. One of the great contributions positive psychology has already made is to raise the dignity and importance of studying happiness. Happiness is, in the final analysis, a state of consciousness. It makes no sense to speak of making people happy in a way that would elude their consciousness so that they do not realize they are happy and continue to think they are no different from before. Change in conscious experience is the *sine qua non* of happiness.

We think that is just the beginning. All human experience is by definition conscious; what never enters consciousness is not experienced (though it may have other consequences, as we have reviewed). To the extent that positive psychology aims to improve human experience, its goals lie within the province of consciousness.

For these reasons also, then, we urge positive psychologists to take up the study of consciousness. Understanding what it is and how it works will inform most aspects of the positive psychology enterprise. Plus, as we have said, understanding consciousness is a grand end in itself, and any contribution positive psychology can make will echo through multiple disciplines. In short, advances in understanding consciousness will enable positive psychology to make a lasting mark in intellectual history.

*Concluding remarks.* Positive psychology must begin to examine conscious thought in order to gain a more complete understanding of human functioning. By doing so, it can advance its purview, improve its practice, and make lasting contributions to intellectual history. Recent work on unconscious, automatic processes has brought the importance of conscious thought into question (e.g., Bargh, 2006; Dijksterhuis & Nordgren, 2006; Libet, 1985; Wegner, 2002), in the best tradition of negative psychology! Apparently, conscious thought is not the controller of behavior, as naïve views have held. Rather, unconscious processes appear to guide most of what people do. Yet to treat individuals as automata that respond only to the immediate physical environment seems immensely incomplete and inaccurate. Unconscious automata do not drool over the memory of yesterday's breakfast, fear invisible gods, or play cops and robbers. These and similar thought processes are a ubiquitous feature of the human experience. A complete psychology must account for their presence.

We have suggested that conscious thought exerts a powerful albeit indirect influence on human behavior. Numerous perspectives are converging on the notion that conscious thought is designed for processing information, constructing sequences of events, and simulating experiences away from the here and now (Suddendorf, 2006; Tulving, 2005; Schacter & Addis, 2007). Such a process may be indispensable for participating in complex social systems such as culture. Reframing conscious thought as a tool for adapting the human animal to cultural life can serve as a helpful framework for future research. In this chapter, we have outlined some of the processes through which conscious thought may influence human behavior indirectly, including through planning and mental simulation. These are the mechanisms that enable an individual to play an active role in cultural practices and institutions. Thus, to examine these and the other psychological processes that enable and motivate cultural sharing and learning is essential for understanding human nature.

## References

Aarts, H., Gollwitzer, P. M., & Hassin, R. R. (2004). Goal contagion: Perceiving is for pursuing. *Journal of Personality and Social Psychology, 87*(1), 23–37.

Acker, F. (2008). New findings on unconscious versus conscious thought in decision making: Additional empirical data and meta-analysis. *Judgment and Decision Making, 3*(4), 292–303.

Aronson, E. (1972). *The social animal.* Oxford, England: Viking Press.

Baars, B. J. (1998). Metaphors of consciousness and attention in the brain. *Trends in Neurosciences, 21*(2), 58–62.

Baars, B. J. (2002). The conscious access hypothesis: Origins and recent evidence. *Trends in Cognitive Sciences, 6*(1), 47–52.

Baddeley, A. D., & Hitch, G. (1974). Working memory. In G.H. Bower (Ed.), *The psychology of learning and motivation: Advances in research and theory* (vol. 8, pp. 47–89). New York: Academic Press.

Bargh, J. A. (1997). The automaticity of everyday life. In R. S. Wyer, Jr. (Ed.), *The automaticity of everyday life: Advances in social cognition* (vol. 10, pp. 1–61). Mahwah, NJ: Erlbaum.

Bargh, J. A. (2006). What have we been priming all these years? On the development, mechanisms, and ecology of nonconscious social behavior. *European Journal of Social Psychology, 36,* 147–168.

Bargh, J. A., & Chartrand, T. L. (1999). The unbearable automaticity of being. *American Psychologist, 54,* 462–479.

Bargh, J. A., Chen, M., & Burrows, L. (1996). Automaticity of social behavior: Direct effects of trait construct and stereotype activation on action. *Journal of Personality and Social Psychology, 71*(2), 230–244.

Bargh, J. A., Gollwitzer, P. M., Lee-Chai, A. Y., Barndollar, K., & Trötschel, R. (2001). The automated will: Nonconscious activation and pursuit of behavioral goals. *Journal of Personality and Social Psychology, 81,* 1014–1027.

Basu, S., & Waymire. G. B. (2006). Recordkeeping and human evolution. *Accounting Horizons, 20,* 201–229.

Baumeister, R. F., Masicampo, E. J., & DeWall, C. N. (2009). Prosocial benefits of feeling free: Disbelief in free will increases aggression and reduces helpfulness. *Personality and Social Psychology Bulletin, 35,* 260–268.

Baumeister, R. F., Vohs, K. D., DeWall, C. N., & Zhang, L. (2007). How emotion shapes behavior: Feedback, anticipation, and reflection, rather than direct causation. *Personality and Social Psychology Review, 11*(2), 167–203.

Baumeister, R. F., Zhang, L., & Vohs, K. D. (2004). Gossip as cultural learning. *Review of General Psychology, 8,* 111–121.

Berger, J., Cohen, B. P., & Zelditch, M. (1972). Status characteristics and social interaction. *American Sociological Review, 37*(3), 241–255.

Bloom, P. (2004). *Descartes' baby: How the science of child development explains what makes us human.* New York, NY, US: Basic Books, 271.

Bogels, S. M., & Zigterman, D. (2000). Dysfunctional cognitions in children with social phobia, separation anxiety, and generalized anxiety disorder. *Journal of Abnormal Child Psychology, 28,* 205–211.

Bongers, K.C.A., & Dijksterhuis, A. (2009). Consciousness as a trouble shooting device? The role of consciousness in goal-pursuit. In E. Morsella, J.A. Bargh, & P. Gollwitzer (Eds.), *The Oxford handbook of human action,* 589–604. New York: Oxford University Press, Inc.

Brandstätter, V., Lengfelder, A., & Gollwitzer, P. M. (2001). Implementation intentions and efficient action initiation. *Journal of Personality and Social Psychology, 81,* 946–960.

Bruner, J. S. (2002). *Making stories: Law, literature, life.* Cambridge, MA: Harvard University Press.

Butz, D. A., Plant, E. A., & Doerr, C. E. (2007). Liberty and justice for all? Implications of exposure to the U.S. flag for intergroup relations. *Personality and Social Psychology Bulletin, 33*(3), 396–408.

Chartrand, T. L., & Bargh, J. A. (1999). The chameleon effect: The perception-behavior link and social interaction. *Journal of Personality and Social Psychology, 76*(6), 893–910.

Colgan, D. M. (1970). Effects of instructions on the skin resistance response. *Journal of Experimental Psychology, 86*(1), 108–112.

Cook, S. W., & Harris, R. E. (1937). The verbal conditioning of the galvanic skin reflex. *Journal of Experimental Psychology, 21*(2), 202–210.

Cosmides, L. (1989). The logic of social exchange: Has natural selection shaped how humans reason? Studies with the Wason selection task. *Cognition, 31*(3), 187–276.

Cosmides, L., & Tooby, J. (2000). Consider the source: The evolution of adaptations for decoupling and metarepresentation. In D. Sperber (Ed.), *Metarepresentations: A multidisciplinary perspective* (pp. 53–115). Vancouver Studies in Cognitive Science. NY: Oxford University Press.

Costabile, K. A., & Klein, S. B. (2008). Understanding and predicting social events: The effects of narrative construction on inference generation. *Social Cognition, 26*(4), 420–437.

Custers, R., & Aarts, H. (2005). Positive affect as implicit motivator: On the nonconscious operation of behavioral goals. *Journal of Personality and Social Psychology, 89*(2), 129–142.

Damasio, A. R. (1999). *The feeling of what happens: Body and emotion in the making of consciousness.* New York, NY: Harcourt Brace.

De Neys, W. (2006). Dual processing in reasoning: Two systems but one reasoner. *Psychological Science, 17(5),* 428–433.

DeWall, C. N., Baumeister, R. F., & Masicampo, E. J. (2008). Evidence that logical reasoning depends on conscious processing. *Consciousness and Cognition: An International Journal, 17(3),* 628–645.

Dijksterhuis, A., & Bargh, J. A. (2001). The perception-behavior expressway: Automatic effects of social perception on social behavior. In M. P. Zanna (Ed.), *Advances in experimental social psychology* (vol. 33, pp. 1–40). San Diego: Academic Press.

Dijksterhuis, A., & Nordgren, L. F. (2006). A theory of unconscious thought. *Perspectives on Psychological Science, 1(2),* 95–109.

Dunbar, R. I. M. (1995). Neocortex size and group size in primates: A test of the hypothesis. *Journal of Human Evolution, 28,* 287–296.

Dunn, E. W., Aknin, L. B., & Norton, M. I. (2008). Spending money on others promotes happiness. *Science, 319(5870),* 1687–1688.

Edelman, G. M. (2004). *Wider than the sky: The phenomenal gift of consciousness.* New Haven, CT: Yale University Press.

Epley, N., Waytz, A., & Cacioppo, J. T. (2007). On seeing human: A three-factor theory of anthropomorphism. *Psychological Review, 114(4),* 864–886.

Epstein, S. (1994). Integration of the cognitive and the psychodynamic unconscious. *American Psychologist, 49(8),* 709–724.

Escalas, J. E., & Luce, M. F. (2004). Understanding the effects of process-focused versus outcome-focused thought in response to advertising. *Journal of Consumer Research, 31(2),* 274–285.

Evans, J. S. B. T. (2003). In two minds: Dual-process accounts of reasoning. *Trends in Cognitive Sciences, 7(10),* 454–459.

Gachter, S., Renner, E., & Sefton, M. (2008). The long-run benefits of punishment. *Science, 322(5907),* 1510.

Glenberg, A. M., & Kaschak, M. P. (2002). Grounding language in action. *Psychonomic Bulletin and Review, 9,* 558–565.

Gollwitzer, P. M. (1999). Implementation intentions: Strong effects of simple plans. *American Psychologist, 54,* 493–503.

Gollwitzer, P. M., & Schaal, B. (1998). Metacognition in action: The importance of implementation intentions. *Personality and Social Psychology Review, 2,* 124–136.

Greenwald, A. G., & Liu, T. J. (1985). Limited unconscious processing of meaning. *Bulletin of the Psychonomic Society, 23,* 292–313.

Gregory, W. L., Cialdini, R. B., & Carpenter, K. M. (1982). Self-relevant scenarios as mediators of likelihood estimates and compliance: Does imagining make it so? *Journal of Personality and Social Psychology, 43(1),* 89–99.

Haidt, J. (2007). The new synthesis in moral psychology. *Science, 316,* 998–1002.

Hesslow, G. (2002). Conscious thought as simulation of behavior and perception. *Trends in Cognitive Sciences, 6,* 242–247.

Kahneman, D. (2003). A perspective on judgment and choice: Mapping bounded rationality. *American Psychologist, 58(9),* 697–720.

Kaschak, M. P., & Glenberg, A. M. (2000). Constructing meaning: The role of affordances and grammatical construction in sentence comprehension. *Journal of Memory and Language, 43,* 508–529.

Latané, B., Williams, K., & Harkins, S. (1979). Many hands make light the work: The causes and consequences of social loafing. *Journal of Personality and Social Psychology, 37(6),* 822–832.

Libby, L. K., Eibach, R. P., & Gilovich, T. (2005). Here's looking at me: The effect of memory perspective on assessments of personal change. *Journal of Personality and Social Psychology, 88(1),* 50–62.

Libby, L. K., Shaeffer, E. M., Eibach, R. P., & Slemmer, J. A. (2007). Picture yourself at the polls: Visual perspective in mental imagery affects self-perception and behavior. *Psychological Science, 18(3),* 199–203.

Libet, B. (1985). Unconscious cerebral initiative and the role of conscious will in voluntary action. *Behavioral and Brain Sciences, 8,* 529–566.

Lieberman, M. D., Gaunt, R., Gilbert, D. T., & Trope, Y. (2002). Reflexion and reflection: A social cognitive neuroscience approach to attributional inference. In M. P. Zanna (Ed.), *Advances in experimental social psychology* (pp. 199–249). San Diego, CA: Academic Press.

Locke, E. A. (2009). It's time we brought introspection out of the closet. *Perspectives on Psychological Science, 4(1),* 24–25.

Lynch, P. D., Kent, R. J., & Srinivasan, S. S. (2001). The global Internet shopper: Evidence from shopping tasks in twelve countries. *Journal of Advertising Research, 41(3),* 15–23.

Mar, R. A., & Oatley, K. (2008). The function of fiction is the abstraction and simulation of social experience. *Perspectives on Psychological Science, 3*, 173–192.

Marks, D. F. (1973). Visual imagery differences in the recall of pictures. *British Journal of Psychology, 64(1)*, 17–24.

Martin, L. L., & Tesser, A. (1989). Toward a motivational and structural theory of ruminative thought. In J. S. Uleman & J. A. Bargh (Eds.), *Unintended thought* (pp. 306–326). New York: Guilford Press.

Mazar, N., & Ariely, D. (2006). Dishonesty in everyday life and its policy implications. *Journal of Public Policy & Marketing. Special Issue: Helping consumers help themselves: Improving the quality of judgments and choices, 25(1)*, 117–126.

Mendl, M., & Paul, E. S. (2004). Consciousness, emotion, and animal welfare: Insights from cognitive science. *Animal Welfare, 13*, 17–25.

Midlarsky, E., Fagin-Jones, S., Nemeroff, R. K. (2006). Heroic rescue during the Holocaust: Empirical, methodological perspectives. In R. Bootzin & P. McKnight (Eds.), *Strengthening research methodology* (pp. 29–45). Washington, DC: American Psychological Association.

Morsella, E. (2005). The function of phenomenal states: Supramodular interaction theory. *Psychological Review, 112*, 1000–1021.

Nisbett, R. E., & Wilson, T. D. (1977). Telling more than we can know: Verbal reports on mental processes. *Psychological Review, 84*, 231–259.

Ottaviani, R., & Beck, A. T. (1987). Cognitive aspects of panic disorders. *Journal of Anxiety Disorders, 1*, 15–28.

Panksepp, J. (2005). Affective consciousness: Core emotional feelings in animals and humans. *Consciousness and Cognition, 14*, 30–80.

Payne, J. W., Samper, A., Bettman, J. R., & Luce, M. F. (2008). Boundary conditions on unconscious thought in complex decision making. *Psychological Science, 19*, 1118–1123.

Pocket, S. (2004). Does consciousness cause behavior? *Journal of Consciousness Studies, 11*, 23–40.

Reyes-Garcia, V., Molina, J. L., Broesch, J., Calvet, L., Huanca, T., Saus, J., et al. (2008). Do the aged and knowledgeable men enjoy more prestige? A test of predictions from the prestige-bias model of cultural transmission. *Evolution and Human Behavior, 29(4)*, 275–281.

Roberts, W. A. (2002). Are animals stuck in time? *Psychological Bulletin, 128(3)*, 473–489.

Schacter, D. L., & Addis, D. R. (2007). The ghosts of past and future: A memory that works by piecing together bits of the past may be better suited to simulating future events than one that is a store of perfect records. *Nature, 445*, 27.

Schank, R. C., & Abelson, R. P. (1995). Knowledge and memory: The real story. In R. S. Wyer (Ed.), *Advances in Social Cognition*, VIII (pp. 1–95). Hillsdale, New Jersey: Lawrence Erlbaum Associates, Publishers.

Shah, J. (2003a). Automatic for the people: How representations of significant others implicitly affect goal pursuit. *Journal of Personality and Social Psychology, 84(4)*, 661–681.

Shah, J. (2003b). The motivational looking glass: How significant others implicitly affect goal appraisals. *Journal of Personality and Social Psychology, 85(3)*, 424–439.

Shah, J. Y., & Kruglanski, A. W. (2003). When opportunity knocks: Bottom-up priming of goals by means and its effects on self-regulation. *Journal of Personality and Social Psychology, 84(6)*, 1109–1122.

Shariff, A. F., & Norenzayan, A. (2007). God is watching you: Priming God concepts increases prosocial behavior in an anonymous economic game. *Psychological Science, 18(9)*, 803–809.

Singer, D. G., & Singer, J. L. (1990). *The house of make-believe: Children's play and the developing imagination.* Cambridge, MA: Harvard University Press.

Sloman, S. A. (1996). The empirical case for two systems of reasoning. *Psychological Bulletin, 119(1)*, 3–22.

Suddendorf, T. (2006). Behavior: Foresight and evolution of the human mind. *Science, 312*, 1006–1007.

Tesser, A. (1988). Toward a self-evaluation maintenance model of social behavior. *Berkowitz, Leonard, 21*, 181–227.

Thoits, P. A., & Hewitt, L. N. (2001). Volunteer work and well-being. *Journal of Health and Social Behavior, 42(2)*, 115–131.

Tomasello, M. (1999). *The cultural origins of human cognition.* Cambridge, MA, US: Harvard University Press, 248.

Tooby, J., & Cosmides, L. (2005). Conceptual foundations of evolutionary psychology. In D. Buss (Ed.), *The handbook of evolutionary psychology* (pp. 5–67). Hoboken, NJ: Wiley.

Tulving, E. (2005). Episodic memory and autonoesis: Uniquely human? In H. S. Terrace & J. Metcalfe (Eds.), *The missing link in cognition: Origins of self-reflective consciousness* (pp. 3–56). New York: Oxford University Press.

Vohs, K. D., & Schooler, J. W. (2008). The value of believing in free will: Encouraging a belief in determinism increases cheating. *Psychological Science, 19(1)*, 49–54.

Wegner, D. M. (2002). *The illusion of conscious will.* Cambridge, MA: MIT Press.

Wegner, D. M., Erber, R., & Raymond, P. (1991). Transactive memory in close relationships. *Journal of Personality and Social Psychology, 61(6)*, 923–929.

Wegner, D. M., Quillian, F., & Houston, C. E. (1996). Memories out of order: Thought suppression and the disturbance of sequence memory. *Journal of Personality and Social Psychology, 71*, 680–691.

Wegner, D. M., Sparrow, B., & Winerman, L. (2004). Vicarious agency: Experiencing control over the movements of others. *Journal of Personality and Social Psychology, 86(6)*, 838–848.

White, T. B. (2005). Consumer trust and advice acceptance: The moderating roles of benevolence, expertise, and negative emotions. *Journal of Consumer Psychology, 15(2)*, 141–148.

# V

# Personality Perspectives

# 13

# Personality Traits and the Potential of Positive Psychology

*Robert R. McCrae*

As an undergraduate at the end of the 1960s, I devised a grandiose scheme for saving the world that I called *cultural therapy*[1]: "the deliberate and cooperative effort to remold our culture to fit intrinsic human needs, through an understanding of the nature of culture and man [*sic*]." I argued (correctly, I think) that we needed to change more than simply the economic or political system in order to reform society, and I assumed (incorrectly, I fear) that humanistic psychologists like Fromm, Maslow, and Rogers had identified clear paths toward ideal psychological development. If we created a culture that provided freedom, insight, and unconditional positive regard, succeeding generations would be blessed with courage, creativity, and love.

In retrospect, the saving grace of my naïve proposal was that it was intended to be fundamentally empirical: We should try social experiments and see what worked. Positive psychologists, who share many ideals with the earlier humanistic psychologists, are also wisely devoted to empiricism (e.g., Ong & Van Dulmen, 2007; Seligman, Steen, Park, & Peterson, 2005) and open to the kind of criticism that is seen in this volume. My contribution is to argue that the

understanding of culture and human nature essential for positive psychology includes the perspective of trait psychology.

## Taking Stock

At the end of the 1970s, Paul Costa and I examined data from the longitudinal Normative Aging Study and came to two conclusions: Psychological well-being is strongly influenced by personality traits, and traits themselves are quite stable over long periods of time (Costa & McCrae, 1980a, 1980b). Both of these broad generalizations have been supported by subsequent research (Roberts & DelVecchio, 2000; Steel, Schmidt, & Shultz, 2008; Terracciano, Costa, & McCrae, 2006). Together, these findings seem to imply that psychological well-being must, in the long run, also be stable: Happiness is not so much a matter of what we have or what we do; it is a matter of who we are. Add to these findings the oft-replicated observation that personality traits are substantially inherited (Riemann, Angleitner, & Strelau, 1997), and the resulting picture appears to be one of psychological fatalism: Some people are born to be happy, others are destined to lives of unhappiness (Lykken & Tellegen, 1996). Worse yet, the same logic applies to many other attributes that are associated with stable, heritable personality traits, including hope, humor, wisdom, gratitude, and personal growth (e.g., Schmutte & Ryff, 1997; Staudinger, Maciel, Smith, & Baltes, 1998). Given the centrality of all these constructs to the enterprise of positive psychology, traits seem to set formidable barriers to its success.

Many positive psychologists are aware of these challenges (e.g., Lyubomirsky, Sheldon, & Schkade, 2005), but they may be less familiar with the more heartening lessons of trait psychology. A careful consideration of the data shows that the inferential leap from observed trait stability to ironclad destiny is unwarranted. Traits and their stability are in many respects desirable. Persistence of individual differences does not preclude group-level changes, and most data show that normative trait development leads to greater maturity. Theoretically, traits can be distinguished from acquired characteristic adaptations, and the latter offer greater opportunities for intervention. In this chapter I hope to offer a more nuanced picture of the implications of traits for the goals of positive psychology.

## Traits and Positive Psychology

### Proper Inferences

The syllogism *happiness depends on traits, traits are stable, ergo happiness is fixed* can be faulted on both logical and empirical grounds. Trait psychology is based on statistical associations, and correlations need not imply causality. Further, associations are probabilistic, leaving a good deal of room for deviations from any presumed destiny. The facts seem to be these:

1. Rank-order consistency of personality increases with age and decreases over longer retest intervals (Roberts & DelVecchio, 2000). By the 30s, however, observed 10-year retest correlations for the five broad personality factors—Neuroticism, Extraversion, Openness, Agreeableness, and Conscientiousness—are about .80; retest reliabilities are near .90 (Terracciano et al., 2006). By disattenuating, we can estimate that about .80/.90 = 89% of the true score variance is stable over this interval. Stability declines over longer intervals but seems to

approach a non-zero asymptote, so that perhaps as much as 80% of true trait variance is stable across the full adult lifespan (Terracciano et al., 2006). This is remarkable stability, but it leaves at least 20% of the variance in true scores free to vary over time.

2. The longitudinal studies from which stability estimates are obtained are observational; they tell us what happened to a particular cohort assessed at a particular time. Enough studies have been conducted with different instruments, populations, and times of measurement to be fairly confident that trait stability is high under most of the conditions in which modern humans live. The kinds of events that people routinely encounter do not tend to have a net effect that markedly changes trait levels. But this does not mean that specific interventions might not have such effects. Religious conversions, traumatic events, or effective psychotherapy might in principle make dramatic and lasting changes. Such dramatic changes have not yet been documented, but they cannot be ruled out.

3. Estimates of heritability vary with the study design. In a family study in Sardinia (Pilia et al., 2006), additive (narrow) heritability estimates from self-report data ranged from .20 for C to .32 for O. Twin studies of self-reports typically report broad heritabilities (including dominance effects) close to .50 for all factors (Jang, McCrae, Angleitner, Riemann, & Livesley, 1998). Using structural modeling on self- and peer-reports of the five factors, Riemann, Angleitner, and Strelau (1997) reported heritabilities of estimated true scores ranging from .66 to .79. This upper-bound estimate implies that as much as a third of trait variance is not heritable. It might be attributed to other biological influences such as disease or diet, but it might also be due to purely psychological experience.

4. The effect of personality traits on subjective well-being at any given time is large compared to other predictors such as age, race, education, and income (Costa & McCrae, 1984), but generally modest to moderate in an absolute sense. Steel, Schmidt, and Shultz (2008) provided the largest estimated effect—63%—by disattenuating a multiple correlation of personality traits with subjective well-being.

Even here at least a third of well-being at any given time is unrelated to personality. The same is likely to be true for other personality correlates, such as wisdom or gratitude, and all unaccounted variance points to a potential for interventions.

5. Multi-wave longitudinal studies of life satisfaction show strong short-term stability (about two-thirds of the variance is stable over one year) and modest to moderate long-term stability (about one-third of the variance), with the rest of the variance attributed to state changes in life satisfaction and error (Lucas & Donnellan, 2007). As these authors note, "there is room for change" (p. 1097).

These data justify cautious optimism about the prospects for increasing well-being and other desirable psychological outcomes. Traits are not immutable, and they are not the sole determinant of well-being. Caution is still needed, however, because it cannot be assumed that all non-trait sources of variance are controllable. Accidents, disease, war, and injustice are part of the human condition, and they also may limit the impact that psychological interventions can have on well-being (see Lucas, 2007).

## A Positive Spin on Traits

Given the important, though not determinative, role of traits in human life, it is useful for positive psychologists to understand that many of the findings of trait psychology can be considered good news. The first of these is the fact of stability itself (McCrae, Terracciano, & Khoury, 2007). Although some may view stability as stagnation, for most people it is instead a source of predictability and security. Crafting a satisfying life structure requires long-term planning, and a reasonably stable identity is essential. Why would one go to graduate school if one's intellectual interests were likely to disappear in a few years? How could one decide between an exciting urban environment and a secluded rural home if Extraversion varied as much as fashion? People make plans for the future based on what appeals to them now; these plans would be useless without continuity of personality.

Stability is equally important in our dealings with others. Employers select applicants they presume will continue to show enthusiasm, initiative, or responsibility. Presidential candidates are chosen in part based on perceptions of

character, with the implicit understanding that their behavior as president can be predicted from their past actions and reactions. People sometime marry a partner whose habits, attitudes, and dispositions they hope to change, but judging from letters to advice columnists, this is ill-advised.

Most people acknowledge traits as an authentic part of their identity (cf. Sheldon, Ryan, Rawsthorne, & Ilardi, 1997) and recognize that their trait profile is relatively stable (Herbst, McCrae, Costa, Feaganes, & Siegler, 2000). They can do so with relative equanimity because most traits are either beneficial or neutral. Half the population is above average in cheerfulness, altruism, industriousness, and aesthetic appreciation; for this lucky half, the prospect that they are likely to be happy, giving, productive, and responsive to beauty for years to come must be very pleasing. Although controversy persists over whether the dimensions of the Five-Factor Model of personality traits (FFM; Digman, 1990) are truly orthogonal (McCrae et al., 2008), they are at least approximately independent. If, therefore, we assign each of the five factors a desirable and an undesirable pole and divide the population at the median of each, then half the people have at least three desirable traits, and 97% (31 of 32 possible profiles) have at least one desirable trait. At the more differentiated facet level, virtually everyone can boast of a few personality strengths.

In fact, the situation is even better than this because some traits that are generally considered undesirable by psychologists may be valued by those who have them (Konstabel, 2007). Antagonistic people take pride in their skepticism and toughness. Closed individuals staunchly defend their traditionalism; they do not feel deprived because they lack refined feelings or intellectual curiosity. Those low in Conscientiousness may covet the rewards of hard work but are happy to pass on the work itself. Introverts value the solitude they seek (Burger, 1995). Only high Neuroticism is perhaps without redeeming attractions, which may explain why abnormal psychology for so long had priority over positive psychology.

Finally, personality stability, interpreted as rank-order consistency of scores, is not inconsistent with mean level change. In adulthood there are continuing changes in trait levels, albeit at a very gradual rate (Costa & McCrae, 2006; Roberts, Walton, & Viechtbauer, 2006). Both cross-sectional and longitudinal studies have shown these changes (Terracciano, McCrae,

Brant, & Costa, 2005), and most of them have been seen in cultures around the world (McCrae et al., 1999; McCrae, Terracciano, & 78 Members of the Personality Profiles of Cultures Project, 2005a). It was once believed that adaptive personality traits must decline with age, as physical health and mental speed do, and that old age would be characterized by depression, rigidity, and social alienation. We now know that most personality changes are positive in nature. As they age, individuals increase in Agreeableness and Conscientiousness and decline in Neuroticism (Donnellan, Conger, & Burzette, 2007), although some of these trends reverse a bit in extreme old age (Terracciano et al., 2005). These normative changes are reflected in changing rates of psychopathology, where the prevalence of conditions such as Borderline and Antisocial Personality Disorder decline from early adulthood on (American Psychiatric Association, 1994). However, it must also be noted that there are normative declines across the lifespan in Positive Emotions and in Openness to Fantasy that might well be considered losses. As individuals age, they find life is less exciting but more deeply satisfying.

## Descriptive Psychology

The goals of science are often summarized as understanding, prediction, and control, and there is no doubt that trait psychology is more useful for the first two goals than for the last. For decades, clinicians have turned to trait measures to help them understand their clients. Should an episode of depression be seen as a response to a recent stressor, or a reflection of longstanding difficulties in adjustment? Is a troubled relationship due to miscommunication or fundamental distrust of others? Is antisocial behavior a reflection of poor impulse control, or of rebellion against authority? Are clients ready to commit to the work of psychotherapy, or will they give up after a few sessions? Instruments like the Minnesota Multiphasic Personality Inventory (MMPI; Hathaway & McKinley, 1983) and the Personality Assessment Inventory (PAI; Morey, 1991) were designed specifically to answer such questions; their constructs are closely related to a subset of personality traits (Costa & McCrae, 1992a; McCrae, 1991).

But clinicians have also periodically called for assessment measures that reflect the strengths as well as the weaknesses of clients. For this purpose, general trait assessment is particularly

useful. The FFM was the culmination of a decades-long search for an adequate taxonomy of personality traits (Norman, 1963); it summarizes almost all the personality variables found in lay terminology and in scientific theories of personality. In contrast to most clinical models of personality, the FFM includes such positive traits as imagination, generosity, joyfulness, and self-control.

Positive traits are of particular interest to positive psychologists. Peterson and Seligman (2004) identified 24 strengths (e.g., fairness, prudence) categorized into six virtues (e.g., justice, temperance), deriving their list from a review of philosophical and psychological treatments of positive characteristics. Another set of desirable traits recently in vogue is associated with emotional intelligence. This construct was introduced as a form of cognitive ability, and at least one cognitive measure has been developed and validated (Mayer, Salovey, & Caruso, 2002). But other popular measures conceive of emotional intelligence as a set of personality-like traits, such as stress tolerance, optimism, flexibility, empathy, and social responsibility (Bar-On, 1997). Ryff's (1989) Psychological Well-Being scales, which include autonomy and self-acceptance, also might be considered trait measures, although they were designed as outcome variables. Cloninger and colleagues (Cloninger, Przybeck, Svrakic, & Wetzel, 1994) attempted to go beyond biologically based variables when they added character scales such as self-transcendence and cooperativeness to their earlier temperament inventory. All these efforts represent new attention paid to adaptive, constructive, and growth-oriented aspects of personality.

But because the FFM is intended to be a comprehensive model of personality traits, all these positive traits ought to be closely related to one or more of the factors, and there is evidence that they are. Peterson and Seligman (2004) explicitly acknowledged this, both in their conceptualization of virtues (Chapter 3) and in their report of early factor analyses of the Values in Action Inventory of Strengths (VIA-IS; Chapter 28). Cawley, Martin, and Johnson (2000) had already shown empirical correspondences between a list of virtues and the five factors, especially Agreeableness and Conscientiousness; and Haslam, Bain, and Neal (2004) demonstrated substantial correspondences in the implicit (judged) associations of VIA-IS and FFM variables.[2] Overlap between FFM dimensions and emotional intelligence measures (McCrae, 2000) was demonstrated by Saklofske, Austin, and Minski (2003). Schmutte and Ryff (1997) showed strong correlations between their measures of Psychological Well-Being and FFM measures, even when self-reports of personality were related to spouse ratings of well-being. Cloninger's character dimensions cannot be clearly separated from the temperament dimensions (Farmer & Goldberg, 2008), and both fall within the limits of the FFM (McCrae, Herbst, & Costa, 2001). From such findings, Haslam and colleagues concluded that "it seems inappropriate to conceptualize strengths as psychologically distinct constructs from traits and values" (pp. 539–540).

If in fact many of the qualities positive psychologists hope to promote are familiar traits in a new guise, then a great deal is already known about them. Evidence of consensual validation for traits—especially those defining the Agreeableness and Conscientiousness factors—strongly suggests that character strengths are not mere artifacts of social desirability (McCrae & Costa, 1987). Because traits are universal (McCrae & Costa, 1997), research on moral virtues may be widely generalizable across cultures (cf. Schwartz, 1992). Positive psychologists may not be as pleased to realize that moral traits are also likely to be stable and heritable, perhaps as difficult to mold or reform as temperamental traits are.

For the enterprise of descriptive psychology, however, the newfound interest in positive personality traits is surely welcome. Historically, much more attention has been paid to traits like anxiety and aggression than to gratitude, bravery, or prudence. We have much to learn about such strengths and how they affect life outcomes (e.g., Ames & Bianchi, 2008). Even if there are stringent limitations on the degree to which virtues can be taught, positive psychology can help society understand how best to utilize naturally occurring virtues. Traits have long been used to select individuals for particular positions: Assertiveness is desirable in leaders, empathy in clinicians, emotional stability in hostage negotiators. A fuller understanding of positive traits might help vocational counselors and I/O psychologists steer individuals into their most rewarding and productive roles. Again, a focus on personality strengths might provide a useful guide to finding friends, spouses, or life partners.

Whatever their roles or relationships, people bring their traits with them, and an understanding of their strengths may help optimize fit.

Clinicians, for example, might profitably try nontraditional therapies if they know their clients are especially high in Openness to Experience, and thus willing to experiment (Miller, 1991). Teachers could choose extraverts to head learning teams. Religious leaders could channel the generosity of their followers to help society's neediest. According to Five-Factor Theory (McCrae & Costa, 2008), people naturally gravitate toward behavior that expresses their traits; positive psychology can facilitate the expression of positive traits.

## Traits in Theoretical Perspective

To know how best to optimize human psychological functioning, it is helpful to have a broad theoretical perspective; Five-Factor Theory (FFT) provides one. FFT uses a systems theoretical approach to make sense of findings from trait research (McCrae & Costa, 1996, 2008). The basic model, shown in Figure 13.1, makes a crucial distinction between *basic tendencies* (including personality traits) and *characteristic adaptations* (including habits, attitudes, roles, relationships, and the *self-concept*, given its own box in the figure). In FFT, traits are exclusively biologically based; they are insulated from direct input from the social environment. This radical postulate is based on well-established findings that (a) traits have a genetic basis but are not influenced by the shared environment (including shared parenting, schools, and neighborhoods; Bouchard & Loehlin, 2001); (b) the same traits, with the same structure, are found in widely different cultures (McCrae et al., 2005a); (c) the events of history seem to have little lasting impact on trait levels (Terracciano et al., 2005; Yang, McCrae, & Costa, 1998); and (d) traits are highly stable across long periods in adulthood, despite the vicissitudes of life circumstances.

According to FFT, traits have a pervasive influence on characteristic adaptations and, through them, on behavior and experience, but they are themselves not amenable to the usual interventions practiced by psychologists—and there's the rub with regard to positive psychology. It is, of course, possible that FFT is simply wrong. But the findings listed above are quite robust, and they require some kind of theoretical explanation. It is more reasonable to argue that FFT is not wrong, but it is oversimplified, and there are special circumstances in which it does not

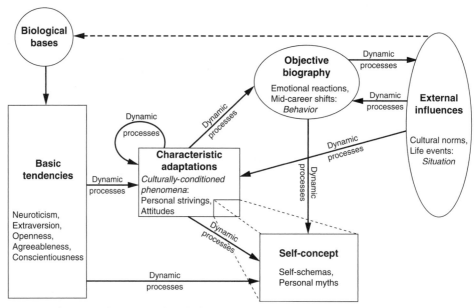

Figure 13.1 The personality system described by Five-Factor Theory. Boxes indicate core components, ellipses are peripheral components, and arrows show the direction of causal processes. Adapted from McCrae & Costa, 2008.

apply. Find those circumstances, and you will have a point of entry for optimizing human functioning.

If personality consisted of nothing but traits, changing traits would be the only option for intervention. But personality is far more complex than that. Most psychologists study variables that fall in the category of characteristic adaptations, and most are concerned with behavior and experience as outcomes. As Figure 13.1 shows, both characteristic adaptations and the *objective biography* are influenced by more than traits, and one lesson from FFT is that positive psychologists may be well advised to focus on these other components of the system.

## Changing Traits

That traits can change is not disputed. Conscientiousness increases as people age and declines when they develop Alzheimer's disease (Siegler et al., 1991). Costa, Bagby, Herbst, and McCrae (2005) showed that Neuroticism declines and Extraversion, Openness, and Conscientiousness increase when depressed patients respond to antidepressant medication.

These all arguably operate by changing the biological bases of traits, as FFT predicts. But can traits change as the result of purely psychological interventions? Perhaps. Piedmont (2001) reported changes in personality in a drug-abusing population following intensive outpatient counseling (although some of the change might have been a biological effect due to reduced drug use). Acculturation in Canada appeared to modify mean trait levels in a group of immigrants from Hong Kong (McCrae, Yik, Trapnell, Bond, & Paulhus, 1998). Roberts, Helson, and Klohnen (2002) found that divorce resulted in personality change in women, as did Costa, McCrae, Herbst, and Siegler (2000)—although the two studies apparently differed in the direction of the change (McCrae & Costa, 2008). Baumeister and colleagues (e.g., Muraven, Baumeister, & Tice, 1999) have argued that the exercise of self-control (a trait related chiefly to Conscientiousness; McCrae & Löckenhoff, 2010) can develop it, just as physical exercise can develop muscles; there are as yet no long-term studies of this hypothesis.

It is fair to say that at this point we do not really know how to change traits, or how much they can be changed, or how long changes will endure. Even small changes in a beneficial direction would be worth targeting if they last a long time, or if they move the individual across some critical threshold—for example, if chronic depressive affect is reduced below the level at which suicide is a danger.

## Changing Characteristic Adaptations

From the perspective of FFT, a far more promising approach to modifying behavior and experience—as indicators of optimal psychological functioning—is to change the acquired habits, attitudes, and goals that lead to them. Harkness and McNulty (2002) have made this idea a guide to psychotherapy, advising clinicians to "explore options for the development of new characteristic adaptations that are consonant with the patient's personality" (p. 399) but that are more effective responses to the patient's life circumstances. A similar strategy is implicit in the work of many positive psychologists. Lyubomirsky and colleagues (2005), in discussing the pursuit of happiness, refer to this as changing *intentional activities*, which may be behavioral, cognitive, or volitional. In the short run, these changes affect only behavior (the objective biography in Figure 13.1), but sustained change would require people to adopt new cognitive perspectives, new patterns of acting, new projects and goals—in short, new characteristic adaptations.

This strategy requires that psychologists identify the right habits and attitudes (which may vary across persons) and have a feasible method of instilling them. It also assumes that the targeted individual has the resources to implement and sustain them. Trait psychology is instructive here.

What kinds of thoughts, behaviors, and goals are conducive to psychological well-being? Headey (2008) analyzed national survey data and concluded that family-oriented and altruistic goals were associated with well-being, whereas economic success goals were not. Using daily diary methods, Steger, Kashdan, and Oishi (2007) found that eudaimonic activities including "gave money to a person in need" and "volunteered my time" were related to well-being, whereas hedonic behaviors such as "got drunk" and "went to a big party" were not. Fredrickson, Cohn, Coffey, Pek, and Finkel (2008) showed that the practice of loving-kindness meditation increased positive emotions and life satisfaction and decreased symptoms of depression. All these studies show links between well-being and

behaviors associated with the personality factor of Agreeableness; Agreeableness itself is known to be a predictor of well-being (McCrae & Costa, 1991).

Conscientiousness is also known to be associated with life satisfaction, and behaviors linked to that factor have also been shown to enhance well-being. Fordyce's (1983) 14 fundamentals of happiness included keeping busy, being productive, and getting organized. Steger and colleagues (2008) listed writing out goals and persevering in the face of obstacles as eudaimonic behaviors. Sheldon (2008) assessed goal-attainment as an indicator of the success of intentional activity intended to promote well-being. In his seminal contribution to the assessment of well-being, Bradburn (1969) included the item "pleased about having accomplished something" to measure positive affect.

The success of interventions related to Agreeableness and Conscientiousness might be explained by a hypothesis offered by McCrae and Costa (1991). They argued that Extraversion and Neuroticism provided a *temperamental* explanation of well-being: Extraverts are, by nature, cheerful people; regardless of what they do, extraverts tend to be happier than introverts (see Lucas & Baird, 2004). Similarly, those high in Neuroticism will be gloomy under any circumstances. By contrast, McCrae and Costa argued that the mechanisms linking Agreeableness and Conscientiousness to well-being may be *instrumental*, mediated by the benevolent and productive activities high scorers engage in. They noted that such activities could provide a continuing source of gratification: "it appears that individuals do not adapt to the satisfactions of love and work . . . . providing opportunities for the expression of Agreeableness and Conscientiousness may be the best way to increase well-being" (p. 231).

Trait theories thus appear to be consistent with interventions to promote well-being, but they also suggest that there are likely to be specific conditions that affect the success of such interventions:

1. It is likely that well-being can be increased only within limits (cf. Zinbarg, Uliaszek, & Adler, 2008). For example, an individual very high in Neuroticism may be somewhat happier when instructed to focus on achieving goals but may still be relatively unhappy on balance. Such people are disposed to undercut their own

successes—for example, by setting unrealistic and perfectionistic standards they cannot reach and by discounting as unimportant the goals they can reach (cf. Ellis, 1987).

2. According to the hypothesis, it is only the active expression of Agreeableness and Conscientiousness that raises levels of well-being. Those prevented by circumstances from exercising these tendencies—perhaps prisoners or nursing home residents—would benefit from opportunities to do so. Young adults (who tend to be relatively low in Agreeableness and Conscientiousness) may not have adequately considered the rewards of altruism and organization and might benefit from hedonic education in this regard. But it seems likely that most adults will have come to understand by trial and error that they feel better when they do a good deed or accomplish a task, and they are probably already utilizing these strategies. Thus, the benefits of these interventions may already have reached a ceiling.

3. Not everyone is likely to benefit from these interventions, and part of the reason probably has to do with personality traits. Very antagonistic individuals will scoff at the idea that they would be happier if they meditated on loving-kindness, and rightly so: For such people, charity is not intrinsically rewarding. People low in Conscientiousness are probably less motivated by achievement goals because they feel little pride in what they do accomplish. Lyubomirsky and colleagues (2005) emphasized the need to match the activity to the person, but the activities proposed above are a poor fit for disagreeable and disorganized people.

4. Low Conscientiousness in particular presents a further obstacle. As Lyubomirski and colleagues (2005) pointed out, initiating and sustaining a prescribed activity "requires considerable self-discipline and will-power," which they acknowledge may be a limited resource. People low in Conscientiousness will fail to follow through not only on recommendations to set and achieve goals, but also on advice to do good deeds or count their blessings or appreciate beauty. Clinicians complain that such patients are difficult to work with, even when they should be motivated by intense suffering (Mutén, 1991); it seems even less likely that they would be good candidates for optimizing psychological functioning.

## Changing External Influences

These reflections indicate the extent to which traits can sabotage interventions, even those aimed at characteristic adaptations—that is how adaptations continue to be characteristic of the person. An obvious counter is to design interventions that modify the environment and thus affect people's behavior and experience, willy-nilly. Positive psychologists are concerned with changes not only to individuals but also to organizations, communities, and societies (e.g., Diener, Lucas, & Scollon, 2006), so such macro-interventions are not beyond their scope. Public health practitioners have found that some of the most effective ways to stop cigarette smoking are by raising taxes and enforcing smoking bans at the workplace. Are there similar societal or cultural interventions that could further optimal psychological development?

Such a question is perhaps more meaningful if we expand the scope of positive psychology to move beyond subjective well-being to the broader and largely independent construct of quality of life. As long ago as 1977, Rosow argued that morale (a form of subjective well-being) is irrelevant to the quality of life and should not be used to assess the value of social policies. Most people would admit that ending hunger is a worthwhile goal, even if well-fed people continue to complain about other aspects of their lives. Unfortunately, beyond such basics, a consensus on the elements of life quality may be more difficult. Few people are opposed to beautifying highways, but they differ greatly on how high a social priority that should be. Some would argue that society should eliminate institutionalized homophobia, whereas others would contend that we should restore traditional family values. If positive psychologists cling to subjective well-being as a touchstone for optimal psychological functioning, they must face the limitations imposed by trait psychology; if they abandon this criterion, they need to devise and justify alternative criteria of psychological health.

## Moving Forward

When stress and coping research was ascendant in the 1970s and 1980s, traits were out of fashion, and its relatively disappointing achievements (Somerfield & McCrae, 2000) were due in part to the neglect of traits. Contemporary positive psychologists are certainly not ignorant of trait perspectives, but there are still ways in which trait psychology can inform better research designs.

*Correlational studies.* Given the centrality of traits to many of the constructs of positive psychology, the inclusion of trait measures ought to be routine. Do constructs like hope, forgiveness, or self-control add incrementally to what traits can explain? A number of studies in this area (e.g., Schnitker & Emmons, 2007) have included assessments of the five factors. Exline, Baumeister, Bushman, and Finkel (2004) showed that dispositional forgiveness was strongly related to the Big Five (as assessed by the Big Five Inventory; John, Donahue, & Kentle, 1991), especially Agreeableness ($r = .65$, $N = 241$, $p < .001$). However, designs that assess only the five broad factors leave open the possibility that additional variance might be accounted for by some of the specific facets that define the traits. Wood, Joseph, and Maltby (2008) assessed both factors and facets using the Revised NEO Personality Inventory (Costa & McCrae, 1992b) and found that gratitude uniquely predicted life satisfaction even after controlling for 30 facet scales (including Warmth, Positive Emotions, Trust, and Tender-Mindedness, its strongest correlates).

Trait psychology offers another important lesson for positive psychology: the need for multimethod assessment. In general, self-reports of traits show agreement with ratings made by knowledgeable informants (spouses, parents, friends; e.g., Funder, Kolar, & Blackman, 1995). However, agreement is by no means perfect. For example, Watson and Humrichouse (2006) identified patterns of personality development in self-reports from young married couples but failed to confirm these changes using spouse ratings. Cross-method replication (e.g., Sheldon & Houser-Marko, 2001) greatly strengthens research findings. In some contexts, observer ratings offer distinct advantages (McCrae & Weiss, 2007). For example, Lucas (2007) pointed out that studies of subjective well-being may be influenced by demand characteristics. Participants in a study designed to show the benefits of meditation might feel obliged to claim improvements in well-being simply because they were invested in the study; ratings by roommates or spouses could provide a more objective assessment of any changes. Ideally, both baseline personality

traits and outcome measures would be assessed by multiple sources.

*Experimental studies.* Experimental designs are essential for truly informative intervention studies, and, fortunately, they have been widely adopted by positive psychologists (e.g., Fordyce, 1983; Fredrickson et al., 2008). Trait measures may prove useful here as covariates, controlling for baseline differences in traits that may be strongly related to the outcomes of interest. To date, the major limitation of experimental studies is that their long-term effects have not been assessed. Sheldon (2008) provided a four-year follow-up of successful intentional activity (in this case, goal striving), but this was not a true experimental design: There was no control group, and the predictor variable was the participant's appraisal of success in achieving goals, which might well reflect Conscientiousness (an unmeasured variable in that study).

Longitudinal studies are not experiments but can often be analyzed as quasi-experimental designs. Lucas (2007) and others have used longitudinal data to address the functioning of a postulated happiness set-point. Such studies show, for example, that bereaved individuals return to near-baseline levels of happiness, but that full recovery requires as long as seven years. Inclusion of personality data (assessed, ideally, at baseline) could help understand the process of adaptation: Individuals high in Neuroticism will presumably show lower pre-event levels of well-being; do they also show more marked declines after the event, or slower rates of recovery? Do individuals high in Extraversion show greater increases in well-being after positive events? If experimental interventions (say, coping skills or gratitude sensitization) are introduced after naturally occurring events, is their success moderated by personality traits like Conscientiousness?

*Tailoring interventions.* Lyubomirsky and colleagues (2005) argued that effective interventions must be tailored both to the individual and to the (presumably universal) process of hedonic adaptation. For example, they point out that if an individual's goal is to practice the piano, that person should choose a style of music he or she enjoys as a way of sustaining interest. Lybomirski and colleagues also argued that the timing of intentional activities may be crucial so that the activity remains "fresh, meaningful, and positive for a particular person" (p. 120).

Traits do not offer much guidance about the timing of activities, but they are clearly relevant to the person/intervention fit, as clinicians have long noted (Miller, 1991). Extraverts may flourish when their activities are given a social context; introverts may prefer to act alone. Variety is important for those high in Openness, whereas routines may be more comfortable for those who are low. The instrumental model of trait/well-being relations (McCrae & Costa, 1991) suggests that individuals high in Agreeableness will benefit most from interventions that express this trait (e.g., loving-kindness meditation)—unless those participants are already at ceiling. Perhaps, instead, Agreeableness-related interventions would be most helpful for those initially lowest in Agreeableness. This would appear to be an interesting empirical question that could be easily addressed in future studies.

Ryff (1989) and others have argued that psychological well-being is not a unidimensional construct, and it is possible that certain forms of optimal psychological functioning may be more appropriate for some individuals. Because Conscientiousness is strongly related to Environmental Mastery but weakly related to Personal Growth (Schmutte & Ryff, 1997), it may be more realistic for people low in Conscientiousness to strive for Personal Growth. By the same logic, people low in Openness may have more luck cultivating Self-Acceptance than Personal Growth. Trait psychologists understand that people have different strengths; positive psychologists may wish to capitalize on these.

## Notes

1. The term *cultural therapy* is indexed in PsycINFO fewer than 100 times and refers mainly to forms of psychotherapy that take cultural differences into account (Van Dusen & Sherman, 1974) or to educational interventions that raise consciousness about culture (Spindler & Spindler, 1994), but see Kagan (1972) for usage similar to mine. My intention was to treat cultures themselves, though I recognized that "in all likelihood, no one will ever be hired as a cultural therapist per se—where is the society enlightened enough to admit it needs one?"

2. There does not seem to be a direct comparison of the VIA-IS with NEO-PI-R facet scales at the individual level. But Park, Peterson, and Seligman (2006) reported mean scores on their measures of character strengths in 54 nations, and one might hope for convergence with aggregate NEO-PI-R measures (McCrae, Terracciano, & 79 Members of the Personality Profiles of Cultures Project, 2005b). In fact, comparisons across 32 cultures common to the two projects showed little systematic agreement. For example,

VIA-IS Self-Regulation was positively (and predictably) related to aggregated NEO-PI-R Self-Discipline ($r = .43$, $p < .05$), but VIA-IS Modesty was inversely related to NEO-PI-R Modesty ($r = -.38$, $p < .05$). One possible explanation is that, at least at the culture level, the character strength scores show poor discriminant validity, all loading strongly on a single general factor (loadings = .54 to .88, $N = 54$). This, in turn, is perhaps due to the fact that most items in each scale are positively keyed (Peterson & Seligman, 2004): There are systematic cultural differences in acquiescent responding (Smith, 2004). Cultural differences in socially desirable responding might also help account for a general factor.

## References

American Psychiatric Association. (1994). *Diagnostic and statistical manual of mental disorders* (4th ed.). Washington, DC: Author.

Ames, D. R., & Bianchi, E. C. (2008). The Agreeableness asymmetry in first impressions: Perceivers' impulse to (mis)judge Agreeableness and how it is moderated by power. *Personality and Social Psychology Bulletin, 34,* 1719–1736.

Bar-On, R. (1997). *The Emotional Quotient Inventory (EQ-i): Technical manual.* Toronto: Multi-Health Systems.

Bouchard, T. J., & Loehlin, J. C. (2001). Genes, evolution, and personality. *Behavior Genetics, 31,* 243–273.

Bradburn, N. M. (1969). *The structure of psychological well-being.* Chicago: Aldine.

Burger, J. M. (1995). Individual differences in preference for solitude. *Journal of Research in Personality, 29,* 85–108.

Cawley, M. J., III, Martin, J. E., & Johnson, J. A. (2000). A virtues approach to personality. *Personality and Individual Differences, 28,* 997–1013.

Cloninger, C. R., Przybeck, T. R., Svrakic, D. M., & Wetzel, R. D. (1994). *The Temperament and Character Inventory (TCI): A guide to its development and use.* St. Louis, MO: Author.

Costa, P. T., Jr., Bagby, R. M., Herbst, J. H., & McCrae, R. R. (2005). Personality self-reports are concurrently reliable and valid during acute depressive episodes. *Journal of Affective Disorders, 89,* 45–55.

Costa, P. T., Jr., Herbst, J. H., McCrae, R. R., & Siegler, I. C. (2000). Personality at midlife: Stability, intrinsic maturation, and response to life events. *Assessment, 7,* 365–378.

Costa, P. T., Jr., & McCrae, R. R. (1980a). Influence of Extraversion and Neuroticism on subjective well-being: Happy and unhappy people. *Journal of Personality and Social Psychology, 38,* 668–678.

Costa, P. T., Jr., & McCrae, R. R. (1980b). Still stable after all these years: Personality as a key to some issues in adulthood and old age. In P. B. Baltes & O. G. Brim Jr. (Eds.), *Life span development and behavior* (vol. 3, pp. 65–102). New York: Academic Press.

Costa, P. T., Jr., & McCrae, R. R. (1984). Personality as a lifelong determinant of well-being. In C. Malatesta & C. Izard (Eds.), *Affective processes in adult development and aging* (pp. 141–157). Beverly Hills, CA: Sage.

Costa, P. T., Jr., & McCrae, R. R. (1992a). Normal personality assessment in clinical practice: The NEO Personality Inventory. *Psychological Assessment, 4,* 5–13.

Costa, P. T., Jr., & McCrae, R. R. (1992b). *Revised NEO Personality Inventory (NEO-PI-R) and NEO Five-Factor Inventory (NEO-FFI) professional manual.* Odessa, FL: Psychological Assessment Resources.

Costa, P. T., Jr., & McCrae, R. R. (2006). Age changes in personality and their origins: Comment on Roberts, Walton, & Viechtbauer (2006). *Psychological Bulletin, 132,* 26–28.

Diener, E., Lucas, R. E., & Scollon, C. N. (2006). Beyond the hedonic treadmill: Revising the adaptation theory of well-being. *American Psychologist, 61,* 305–314.

Digman, J. M. (1990). Personality structure: Emergence of the Five-Factor Model. *Annual Review of Psychology, 41,* 417–440.

Donnellan, M. B., Conger, R. D., & Burzette, R. G. (2007). Personality development from late adolescence to young adulthood: Differential stability, normative maturity, and evidence for the maturity-stability hypothesis. *Journal of Personality, 75,* 237–263.

Ellis, A. (1987). The impossibility of achieving consistently good mental health. *American Psychologist, 42,* 364–375.

Exline, J. J., Baumeister, R. F., Bushman, B. J., & Campbell, W. K. (2004). Too proud to let go: Narcissistic entitlement as a barrier to forgiveness. *Journal of Personality and Social Psychology, 87,* 894–912.

Farmer, R. F., & Goldberg, L. R. (2008). Brain modules, personality layers, planes of being, spiral structures, and the equally implausible distinction between TCI-R "Temperament" and "Character" scales: Reply to Cloninger (2008). *Psychological Assessment, 20,* 300–304.

Fordyce, M. W. (1983). A program to increase happiness: Further studies. *Journal of Counseling Psychology, 30,* 483–498.

Fredrickson, B. L., Cohn, M. A., Coffey, K. A., Pek, J., & Finkel, S. M. (2008). Open hearts build lives: Positive emotions, induced through loving-kindness meditation, build consequential personal resources. *Journal of Personality and Social Psychology, 95,* 1045–1062.

Funder, D. C., Kolar, D. C., & Blackman, M. C. (1995). Agreement among judges of personality: Interpersonal relations, similarity, and acquaintanceship. *Journal of Personality and Social Psychology, 69,* 656–672.

Harkness, A. R., & McNulty, J. L. (2002). Implications of personality individual differences science for clinical work on personality disorders. In P. T. Costa, Jr., & T. A. Widiger (Eds.), *Personality disorders and the Five-Factor Model of personality* (2nd ed., pp. 391–403). Washington, DC: American Psychological Association.

Haslam, N., Bain, P., & Neal, D. (2004). The implicit structure of positive characteristics. *Personality and Social Psychology Bulletin, 30,* 529–541.

Hathaway, S. R., & McKinley, J. C. (1983). *The Minnesota Multiphasic Personality Inventory manual.* New York: Psychological Corporation.

Headey, B. (2008). Life goals matter to happiness: A revision set-point theory. *Social Indicators Research, 86,* 213–231.

Herbst, J. H., McCrae, R. R., Costa, P. T., Jr., Feaganes, J. R., & Siegler, I. C. (2000). Self-perceptions of stability and change in personality at midlife: The UNC Alumni Heart Study. *Assessment, 7,* 379–388.

Jang, K. L., McCrae, R. R., Angleitner, A., Riemann, R., & Livesley, W. J. (1998). Heritability of facet-level traits in a cross-cultural twin sample: Support for a hierarchical model of personality. *Journal of Personality and Social Psychology, 74,* 1556–1565.

John, O. P., Donahue, E. M., & Kentle, R. L. (1991). *The "Big Five" Inventory—Versions 4a and 54.* Berkeley: University of California, Berkeley, Institute of Personality and Social Research.

Kagan, S. (1972). *Ethics and concepts of cultural therapy.* Retrieved from ERIC database. (ED069379)

Konstabel, K. (2007). *"The more like me, the better": Individual differences in social desirability ratings of personality items.* Unpublished manuscript, University of Tartu, Estonia.

Lucas, R. E. (2007). Adaptation and the set-point model of subjective well-being: Does happiness change after major life events? *Current Directions in Psychological Science, 16*, 75–79.

Lucas, R. E., & Baird, B. M. (2004). Extraversion and emotional reactivity. *Journal of Personality and Social Psychology, 86*, 473–485.

Lucas, R. E., & Donnellan, M. B. (2007). How stable is happiness? Using the STARTS model to estimate the stability of life satisfaction. *Journal of Research in Personality, 41*, 1091–1098.

Lykken, D., & Tellegen, A. (1996). Happiness is a stochastic phenomenon. *Psychological Science, 7*, 186–189.

Lyubomirsky, S., Sheldon, K. M., & Schkade, D. (2005). Pursuing happiness: The architecture of sustainable change. *Review of General Psychology, 9*, 111–131.

Mayer, J. D., Salovey, P., & Caruso, D. R. (2002). *Mayer-Salovey-Caruso Emotional Intelligence Test (MSCEIT) user's manual.* North Tonawanda, NY: Multi-Health Systems.

McCrae, R. R. (1991). The Five-Factor Model and its assessment in clinical settings. *Journal of Personality Assessment, 57*, 399–414.

McCrae, R. R. (2000). Emotional intelligence from the perspective of the Five-Factor Model of personality. In R. Bar-On & J. D. A. Parker (Eds.), *The handbook of emotional intelligence* (pp. 263–276). San Francisco: Jossey-Bass.

McCrae, R. R., & Costa, P. T., Jr. (1987). Validation of the Five-Factor Model of personality across instruments and observers. *Journal of Personality and Social Psychology, 52*, 81–90.

McCrae, R. R., & Costa, P. T., Jr. (1991). Adding *Liebe und Arbeit:* The full Five-Factor Model and well-being. *Personality and Social Psychology Bulletin, 17*, 227–232.

McCrae, R. R., & Costa, P. T., Jr. (1996). Toward a new generation of personality theories: Theoretical contexts for the Five-Factor Model. In J. S. Wiggins (Ed.), *The Five-Factor Model of personality: Theoretical perspectives* (pp. 51–87). New York: Guilford.

McCrae, R. R., & Costa, P. T., Jr. (1997). Personality trait structure as a human universal. *American Psychologist, 52*, 509–516.

McCrae, R. R., & Costa, P. T., Jr. (2008). The Five-Factor Theory of personality. In O. P. John, R. W. Robins & L. A. Pervin (Eds.), *Handbook of personality: Theory and research* (3rd ed., pp. 159–181). New York: Guilford.

McCrae, R. R., Costa, P. T., Jr., Lima, M. P., Simões, A., Ostendorf, F., Angleitner, A., et al. (1999). Age differences in personality across the adult life span: Parallels in five cultures. *Developmental Psychology, 35*, 466–477.

McCrae, R. R., Herbst, J. H., & Costa, P. T., Jr. (2001). Effects of acquiescence on personality factor structures. In R. Riemann, F. Ostendorf, & F. Spinath (Eds.), *Personality and temperament: Genetics, evolution, and structure* (pp. 217–231). Berlin: Pabst Science Publishers.

McCrae, R. R., & Löckenhoff, C. E. (2010). Self-regulation and the Five-Factor Model of personality traits. In R. H. Hoyle (Ed.), *The handbook of self-regulation and personality* (pp. 145–168). Oxford: Blackwell Publishing.

McCrae, R. R., Terracciano, A., & 78 Members of the Personality Profiles of Cultures Project. (2005a). Universal features of personality traits from the observer's perspective: Data from 50 cultures. *Journal of Personality and Social Psychology, 88*, 547–561.

McCrae, R. R., Terracciano, A., & 79 Members of the Personality Profiles of Cultures Project. (2005b). Personality profiles of cultures: Aggregate personality traits. *Journal of Personality and Social Psychology, 89*, 407–425.

McCrae, R. R., Terracciano, A., & Khoury, B. (2007). *Dolce far niente*: The positive psychology of personality stability and invariance. In A. Ong & M. Van Dulmen (Eds.), *Handbook of methods in positive psychology* (pp. 176–188). New York: Oxford University Press.

McCrae, R. R., & Weiss, A. (2007). Observer ratings of personality. In R. W. Robins, R. C. Fraley, & R. F. Krueger (Eds.), *Handbook of research methods in personality psychology* (pp. 259–272). New York: Guilford Publications.

McCrae, R. R., Yamagata, S., Jang, K. L., Riemann, R., Ando, J., Ono, Y., et al. (2008). Substance and artifact in the higher-order factors of the Big Five. *Journal of Personality and Social Psychology, 95*, 442–455.

McCrae, R. R., Yik, M. S. M., Trapnell, P. D., Bond, M. H., & Paulhus, D. L. (1998). Interpreting personality profiles across cultures: Bilingual, acculturation, and peer rating studies of Chinese undergraduates. *Journal of Personality and Social Psychology, 74*, 1041–1055.

Miller, T. (1991). The psychotherapeutic utility of the Five-Factor Model of personality: A clinician's experience. *Journal of Personality Assessment, 57*, 415–433.

Morey, L. (1991). *Personality Assessment Inventory: Professional manual.* Odessa, FL: Psychological Assessment Resources.

Muraven, M., Baumeister, R. F., & Tice, D. M. (1999). Longitudinal improvement of self-regulation through practice: Building self-control strength through repeated exercise. *Journal of Social Psychology, 139,* 446–457.

Mutén, E. (1991). Self-reports, spouse ratings, and psychophysiological assessment in a behavioral medicine program: An application of the Five-Factor Model. *Journal of Personality Assessment, 57,* 449–464.

Norman, W. T. (1963). Toward an adequate taxonomy of personality attributes: Replicated factor structure in peer nomination personality ratings. *Journal of Abnormal and Social Psychology, 66,* 574–583.

Ong, A., & Van Dulmen, M. (Eds.) (2007). *Handbook of methods in positive psychology.* New York: Oxford University Press.

Park, N., Peterson, C., & Seligman, M. E. P. (2006). Character strengths in fifty-four nations and the fifty US states. *Journal of Positive Psychology, 1,* 118–129.

Peterson, C., & Seligman, M. E. P. (2004). *Character strengths and virtues: A handbook and classification.* Washington, DC: American Psychological Association.

Piedmont, R. L. (2001). Cracking the plaster cast: Big Five personality change during intensive outpatient counseling. *Journal of Research in Personality, 35,* 500–520.

Pilia, G., Chen, W-M., Scuteri, A., Orrú, M., Albai, G., Deo, M., et al. (2006). Heritability of cardiovascular and personality traits in 6,148 Sardinians. *PLoS Genetics, 2,* 1207–1223.

Riemann, R., Angleitner, A., & Strelau, J. (1997). Genetic and environmental influences on personality: A study of twins reared together using the self- and peer report NEO-FFI scales. *Journal of Personality, 65,* 449–475.

Roberts, B. W., & DelVecchio, W. F. (2000). The rank-order consistency of personality traits from childhood to old age: A quantitative review of longitudinal studies. *Psychological Bulletin, 126,* 3–25.

Roberts, B. W., Helson, R., & Klohnen, E. C. (2002). Personality development and growth in women across 30 years: Three perspectives. *Journal of Personality, 70,* 79–102.

Roberts, B. W., Walton, K. E., & Viechtbauer, W. (2006). Patterns of mean-level change in personality traits across the life course: A meta-analysis of longitudinal studies. *Psychological Bulletin, 132,* 3–25.

Rosow, I. (1977). Morale: Concept and measurement. In C. N. Nydegger (Ed.), *Measuring morale: A guide to effective assessment* (pp. 39–45). Washington, DC: The Gerontological Society.

Ryff, C. D. (1989). Happiness is everything, or is it? Explorations on the meaning of psychological well-being. *Journal of Personality and Social Psychology, 57,* 1069–1081.

Saklofske, D. H., Austin, E., & Minski, P. S. (2003). Factor structure and validity of a trait emotional intelligence measure. *Personality and Individual Differences, 34,* 707–721.

Schmutte, P. S., & Ryff, C. D. (1997). Personality and well-being: Reexamining methods and meanings. *Journal of Personality and Social Psychology, 73,* 549–559.

Schnitker, S. A., & Emmons, R. A. (2007). Patience as a virtue: Religious and psychological perspectives. *Research in the Social Scientific Study of Religion, 18,* 177–207.

Schwartz, S. H. (1992). Universals in the content and structure of values: Theoretical advances and empirical tests in 20 countries. In M. P. Zanna (Ed.), *Advances in experimental social psychology* (vol. 25, pp. 1–65). New York: Academic Press.

Seligman, M. E. P., Steen, T. A., Park, N., & Peterson, C. (2005). Positive psychology progress: Empirical validation of interventions. *American Psychology, 60,* 410–421.

Sheldon, K. M. (2008). Assessing the sustainability of goal-based changes in adjustment over a four-year period. *Journal of Research in Personality, 42,* 223–229.

Sheldon, K. M., & Houser-Marko, L. (2001). Self-concordance, goal-attainment, and the pursuit of happiness: Can there be an upward spiral? *Journal of Personality and Social Psychology, 80,* 152–165.

Sheldon, K. M., Ryan, R. M., Rawsthorne, L. J., & Ilardi, B. (1997). Trait self and true self: Cross-role variation in the Big Five personality traits and its relations with psychological authenticity and subjective well-being. *Journal of Personality and Social Psychology, 73,* 1380–1393.

Siegler, I. C., Welsh, K. A., Dawson, D. V., Fillenbaum, G. G., Earl, N. L., Kaplan, E. B., et al. (1991). Ratings of personality change in patients being evaluated for memory disorders. *Alzheimer Disease and Associated Disorders, 5,* 240–250.

Smith, P. B. (2004). Acquiescent response bias as an aspect of cross-cultural communication style. *Journal of Cross-Cultural Psychology, 35,* 50–61.

Somerfield, M. R., & McCrae, R. R. (2000). Stress and coping research: Methodological challenges, theoretical advances, and clinical applications. *American Psychologist, 55,* 620–625.

Spindler, G., & Spindler, L. (Eds.). (1994). *Pathways to cultural awareness: Cultural therapy with teachers and students*. Thousand Oaks, CA: Corwin Press.

Staudinger, U. M., Maciel, A. G., Smith, J., & Baltes, P. B. (1998). What predicts wisdom-related performance? A first look at personality, intelligence, and facilitative contexts. *European Journal of Personality, 12,* 1–17.

Steel, P., Schmidt, J., & Shultz, J. (2008). Refining the relationship between personality and subjective well-being. *Psychological Bulletin, 134,* 138–161.

Steger, M. F., Kashdan, T. B., & Oishi, S. (2007). Being good by doing good: Daily eudaimonic activity and well-being. *Journal of Research in Personality, 42,* 22–42.

Terracciano, A., Costa, P. T., Jr., & McCrae, R. R. (2006). Personality plasticity after age 30. *Personality and Social Psychology Bulletin, 32,* 999–1009.

Terracciano, A., McCrae, R. R., Brant, L. J., & Costa, P. T., Jr. (2005). Hierarchical linear modeling analyses of NEO-PI-R scales in the Baltimore Longitudinal Study of Aging. *Psychology and Aging, 20,* 493–506.

Van Dusen, W., & Sherman, S. L. (1974). Cultural therapy: A new conception of treatment. *Drug Forum, 4,* 65–72.

Watson, D., & Humrichouse, J. (2006). Personality development in emerging adulthood: Integrating evidence from self-ratings and spouse ratings. *Journal of Personality and Social Psychology, 91,* 959–974.

Wood, A. M., Joseph, S., & Maltby, J. (2008). Gratitude uniquely predicts satisfaction with life: Incremental validity about the domains and facets of the Five-Factor Model. *Personality and Individual Differences, 45,* 49–54.

Yang, J., McCrae, R. R., & Costa, P. T., Jr. (1998). Adult age differences in personality traits in the United States and the People's Republic of China. *Journal of Gerontology: Psychological Sciences, 53B,* P375–P383.

Zinbarg, R. E., Uliaszek, A. A., & Adler, J. M. (2008). The role of personality in psychotherapy for anxiety and depression. *Journal of Personality, 76,* 1649–1688.

# 14

## Character and Personality: Connections between Positive Psychology and Personality Psychology

*Erik E. Noftle, Sarah A. Schnitker, and Richard W. Robins*

### Personality and Positive Psychology

In the late 1990s, the field of positive psychology emerged to correct mainstream psychology's emphasis on human error, irrationality, misbehavior, and pathology. A plan was laid out to investigate three domains of human strength and flourishing: positive subjective experience, positive character traits, and positive institutions and communities (Seligman & Csikszentmihalyi, 2000). To catalogue the second domain, Peterson and Seligman (2004) proposed a broad taxonomy of character strengths—the Values in Action (VIA) classification—which has served as an agenda for future research on positive traits. The purpose of the current chapter is to examine critically this proposed set of character strengths, applying some lessons learned from nearly a century of research on personality.

Personality psychology is a remarkably diverse field concerned with at least four overlapping but separable research agendas: studying the whole person; identifying the enduring patterns of thoughts, feelings, and behaviors that make people different from each other; revealing the processes underlying those patterns; and charting how people's personalities develop and change over time. These four agendas are likely to have interesting and important links with the three domains of positive psychology. Most notably, the study of enduring patterns of thoughts, feelings, and behaviors, or personality traits, seems to have a direct analog in the positive psychology domain of character strengths.

Character strengths are conceptually quite similar to personality traits. Park, Peterson, and Seligman (2004) define character strengths as "positive traits reflected in thoughts, feelings, and behaviors. They exist in degrees and can be measured as individual differences (p. 603)." Indeed, in *Character Strengths and Virtues*, Peterson and Seligman (2004) explicitly place the development of their VIA taxonomy in the tradition of personality psychology's trait theory. However, they attempt to differentiate character strengths from the trait tradition (especially the Big Five approach; John, Naumann, & Soto, 2008) in four ways, all four of which we attempt to refute:

- The study of character strengths is concerned with the causes and consequences of the constructs, whereas trait psychology has been largely concerned with the content of traits.

- The study of character strengths is concerned with a narrower level of analysis, whereas trait psychology has focused on traits at broader levels such as the Big Five.
- The study of character strengths uniquely identifies attributes that are morally valued in their own right.
- Finally, and perhaps most importantly, the study of character strengths focuses exclusively on the *positive* rather than the negative endpoint of trait continua, that is, on compassion rather than cruelty, originality rather than conventionality, bravery rather than timidity, and so on.

First, Peterson and Seligman critique the Big Five approach as a tradition in which "classification per se seems to be the goal, not an understanding of the causes or consequences of the classification's entries" (Peterson & Seligman, 2004, p. 68). However, trait theorists going back to Gordon Allport (1937) have emphasized the importance of understanding the underlying mechanisms or, in Allport's terms, the "neuropsychic entities," that cause personality differences. The trait literature is replete with studies investigating the origins of traits, including the underlying cognitive, affective, neural, and genetic mechanisms, as well as the processes through which these mechanisms interact with situational factors to produce individual differences in behavior. Similarly, there is a vast body of literature exploring the consequences of personality traits (Ozer & Benet-Martinez, 2006; Roberts et al., 2007), as well as a multimillion-dollar personality testing industry in which personality questionnaires are used to predict real-world outcomes such as job performance (Hogan, Hogan, & Roberts, 1996).

Second, Peterson and Seligman characterize the Big Five as overly broad "and unlikely to capture the meaning of a more nuanced individual difference" (Peterson & Seligman, 2004, p. 69), contrasting them with the more specific character strengths. However, the Big Five have always been conceptualized as the broadest level of a hierarchical personality taxonomy that subsumes more specific traits, the latter of which have been frequently studied in their own right (e.g., Costa & McCrae, 1992; De Young, Quilty, & Peterson, 2007; Saucier & Ostendorf, 1999).

Third, Peterson and Seligman stipulate that character strengths are morally valued in their own right, regardless of the specific outcomes they produce. However, as we describe below, this emphasis does not represent a significant departure from historic conceptions of personality.

Fourth, the entire mission of positive psychology is predicated on the assumption that psychology has neglected the study of positive characteristics. We argue below that although this may be true of many areas of psychology, it is not generally true of personality psychology and is specifically false when it comes to trait psychology.

This chapter has three central aims. First, we examine the validity of the claim that mainstream psychology has neglected the study of positive character traits and argue that the field of personality psychology has actually led to important advances in the understanding of character traits and their outcomes. Second, we critically evaluate the VIA classification of character strengths and summarize research testing its empirical structure, assessing its overlap with the Big Five trait dimensions and comparing its predictive validity to the Big Five (Noftle, Schnitker & Robins, 2010). Third, we suggest ways in which the field of positive psychology can move forward, applying the lessons of nearly a century of personality psychology. We argue that future research needs to address validity concerns, forge links between the character strengths and underlying processes, and pursue large-scale longitudinal studies examining normative development, the efficacy of interventions, and long-term real-world outcomes.

## Has Personality Psychology Neglected Positive Traits?

Peterson and Seligman (2004) place the origins of positive psychology in the humanistic movement of the 1950s, particularly the personality theories of Carl Rogers and Abraham Maslow. However, Peterson and Seligman argue that humanistic approaches ultimately failed due in part to their nearly exclusive reliance on qualitative rather than quantitative methods; thus the discipline was deemed unscientific and never led to an accumulation of empirical knowledge (although see Taylor, 2001). Another likely contribution to the downfall of humanistic psychology was that the approach did not yield a set of core constructs that could be precisely defined and easily assessed in samples of individuals. To address this limitation of humanistic psychology, Seligman, Csikszentmihalyi, and their colleagues advanced the newly minted field of positive psychology to be "about positive individual traits: the capacity for love and vocation, courage, interpersonal skill, aesthetic sensibility, perseverance, forgiveness, originality, future mindedness, spirituality, high talent, and wisdom" (Seligman & Csikszentmihalyi, 2000, p. 5). The VIA classification system, and associated measures, were developed to explicitly define and operationalize these core constructs and render them amenable to systematic empirical studies.

Yet this new perspective did not emerge de novo. Although the humanistic psychologists failed to develop an empirically based taxonomic system of character traits, personality researchers dating back to the turn of the 20th century have been seeking scientifically valid ways to classify and assess trait constructs. And, although clinical psychologists emphasized human weakness and pathology and social psychologists focused on people's proneness to error and misbehavior (e.g., Krueger & Funder, 2004), personality psychologists have long studied positive characteristics and their beneficial effects on the lives of individuals (e.g., see Ryff, 2003, pp. 156–157). For example, Ozer and Benet-Martinez (2006) reviewed research documenting the influence of the Big Five traits on a wide range of positive life outcomes, including subjective well-being, longevity, successful coping, relationship satisfaction, job performance, acceptance by peers, and volunteerism.

The study of positive traits has a long and venerable history in personality psychology. In 1949, when the humanistic movement was first emerging, the Institute of Personality Assessment and Research (IPAR) was founded at the University of California, Berkeley, by Donald MacKinnon and Nevitt Sanford. The overarching goal of IPAR was to produce scientific knowledge about the personality traits associated with adaptive human functioning and to develop psychometrically sound measures of these traits (Gough, 1988). Over the past several decades, and continuing to the present, researchers at IPAR (now called the Institute for Personality and Social Research, or IPSR) conducted systematic scientific studies of many different aspects of human potential including creativity, leadership, maturity, resilience, aesthetic experiences, and other traits related to the character strengths of the positive psychology movement. Harrison Gough, a former director of IPAR, developed one of the first comprehensive, multidimensional measures of "normal" (i.e., non-clinical) personality characteristics, the California Psychological Inventory

(CPI; Gough, 1957; 1987). The CPI assessed people's everyday "folk concepts" of personality, with scales devoted to self-control, well-being, tolerance, empathy, achievement, and other human strengths and virtues.

Although the field of personality has always included positive traits as part of its purview, as exemplified by the IPAR research tradition, trait approaches have tended to focus on the descriptive rather than evaluative aspects of personality (Cawley, Martin, & Johnson, 2000; McCullough & Snyder, 2000; Nicholson, 1998). Evaluation can have several meanings, and it is important to differentiate between two meanings here. First is the idea of judgment, whether a person is good or bad, without explicit reference to the behavior or qualities that precipitate that judgment. Second is the idea of desirability, whether or not a person's specific characteristics are of social or moral value, with fairly explicit reference to the content of those characteristics.

In their pioneering studies of the personality lexicon, Allport and Odbert (1936) excluded from consideration purely judgmental terms (e.g., "average," "superior," "worthy," "likeable"), which lack any descriptive meaning and are thus irrelevant to personality differences (e.g., it is unclear whether the person is "superior" because she is kind, creative, responsible, etc., just that the person is being *judged*). Allport (1937) argued that personality traits, but not the aforementioned purely evaluative judgments, should be the focus of the science. In contrast, terms that were highly evaluative but contained descriptive content (e.g., sociable, aggressive) were retained in the "trait" list and thus influenced the categories formed by Allport and Odbert.

In addition to excluding purely evaluative terms, Allport argued for constraining personality to the study of descriptive traits in another way. Allport wished to move personality specifically away from the study of moral characteristics that might be defined in terms of "conventional meanings" that were historically contextualized, and thus less scientific (Allport, 1931). Allport and Odbert (1936) bemoaned "the tendency of each social epoch to characterize human qualities in the light of standards and interests peculiar to the times" (p. 2). Allport's conclusion, stated in his still-influential personality textbook, was that "Character is personality evaluated, and personality is character devaluated" (Allport, 1937, p. 52). In studying personality, Allport wanted to identify and analyze descriptive differences that were as free of desirability or undesirability as possible. However, in Allport's differentiation of personality and character, it is clear that the content under study could actually be the same, but how it is considered (whether it is evaluated or not) would be starkly different.

Allport's notion that character was a proper subject of study for ethics, but not psychology, certainly influenced the field. First, personality psychologists largely abandoned the term "character." Perhaps reflecting this shift in terminology, in 1945, the journal *Character and Personality* changed its name to the *Journal of Personality* because, as then-editor Zener (1945) put it, "[t]he psychological aspects of character are regarded as included within the broader field of personality (p. 1)." Second, the purely evaluative judgments that Allport and Odbert distinguished from personality traits tended to receive little attention and were largely relegated to the fringes of the discipline (but see Benet & Waller, 1995). The lexical approach to personality, which traces its roots to Allport and Odbert's (1936) seminal work, continues to strongly influence the study of personality (Goldberg, 1993; John & Robins, 1993a).

However, the field has not stayed true to Allport's focus on traits as "devaluated." For almost as long as traits have been studied, their positive and negative consequences have been theorized about and assessed. Not only has this approach supported the validity of traits—they are not just figments of the mind; they predict important outcomes—but it has also implicitly (and sometimes explicitly) led to evaluation of whether it is desirable or undesirable to have a specific trait. Consequently, the field of personality has not neglected positive characteristics, and, as the next section reveals, several important aspects of character have been studied for decades.

## The Big Five Personality Traits

The Big Five is a hierarchical taxonomy of traits, which attempts to organize all of the ways in which people differ from one another. At the basic level it includes the five relatively independent, broad traits of Extraversion (talkative, sociable, assertive), Agreeableness (kind, cooperative, altruistic), Conscientiousness (organized, responsible, industrious), Emotional Stability (calm, even-tempered, imperturbable), and Openness to Experience (creative, intellectual, reflective). The traits included within the Big Five Taxonomy have their origins in Allport and Odbert's (1936) list of trait terms (John et al., 2008), but agreement

about the Big Five structure as a consensually accepted taxonomy of traits emerged in the early 1990s (Goldberg, 1993; McCrae & John, 1992). After decades of research, there is now a great deal of support for the cross-cultural universality, heritability, judgability, temporal stability, and predictive validity of the Big Five (John et al., 2008).

Although the Big Five includes content that is descriptive of a person's personality traits, it clearly also includes evaluative content related to character. The traits of Extraversion, Agreeableness, Conscientiousness, Emotional Stability, and Openness are all socially desirable, albeit to varying degrees (Agreeableness is the most socially desirable and Extraversion the least; John & Robins, 1993b). Supporting the social desirability of the Big Five, individuals who have greater self-worth tend to be higher on all of the Big Five dimensions, particularly Emotional Stability, Extraversion, and Conscientiousness (Robins, Tracy, Trzesniewski, Potter, & Gosling, 2001). According to the sociometer theory of self-esteem (Leary, Tambor, Terdal, & Downs, 1995), this suggests that individuals who display more of these traits believe they are accepted by and living up to the standards of society.

A second piece of evidence has to do with the beneficial outcomes of being higher on the Big Five traits. Although "niche" models have been proposed for the low pole of each dimension having adaptive or beneficial qualities (Nettle, 2006), so far most findings for Big Five prediction suggest that it is better on average to be higher on the traits rather than lower on them. Ozer and Benet-Martinez (2006) conducted a literature review of real-world outcomes of the Big Five and found that higher trait levels were positively related to good outcomes at the individual, interpersonal, and societal levels.

A third piece of evidence stems from a recent study (Cawley et al., 2000) that sought to examine virtue as an aspect of personality and employed the lexical approach with the purpose of creating a virtues scale. Cawley and his colleagues searched the dictionary for words that displayed qualities that one ought to embody or display (i.e., virtues), wrote items related to these qualities, and then factor-analyzed the resulting set of 140 items. They identified four factors: empathy, order, resourcefulness, and serenity. Interestingly, these virtue dimensions corresponded moderately to highly with the Big Five dimensions, with correlations ranging from .45 to .63. These sizable correlations further suggest that the Big

Five might actually capture many aspects of character.

In sum, most people would consider an individual who is sociable, cooperative, responsible, even-tempered, and reflective—that is, higher on all the Big Five traits—to be a person of good character. The next question is: is anything missing? Does the Big Five taxonomy miss important character traits that have been revealed by the positive psychology movement? More specifically, does the VIA character strengths inventory include personality content that is not captured by the Big Five?

## Critical Evaluation of VIA Character Strengths

### The VIA Classification of Character Strengths

The VIA is a taxonomy of 24 character strengths organized under six umbrella virtues. Developed to serve as a "manual of the sanities," or a classification of mental health and flourishing comparable to the Diagnostic and Statistical Manual of Mental Disorders (American Psychiatric Association, 1994), the VIA seeks to delineate individual differences in the complex nuances of character. In this classification system, virtues are defined as the core characteristics valued by moral philosophers and religious thinkers across time and cultures. These virtues are construed as broad universals, rooted in biology, that have been evolutionarily selected. Character strengths fall under these "high six" broad virtues and are conceptualized as the psychological processes and mechanisms by which virtue may be achieved. For example, a person may display the virtue of transcendence through a variety of routes: gratitude, hope, humor, spirituality, or appreciation of beauty. Although theoretically compelling, the validity of the VIA taxonomy has received relatively little empirical attention. Only a few published studies have examined its factor structure or its correspondence with other taxonomic models such as the Big Five.

To further examine the validity of the VIA, we conducted two studies to (a) evaluate the theoretical structure of the VIA and test the fit of alternative structural models; (b) examine the degree of correspondence between the VIA and the Big Five dimensions; and (c) examine whether the VIA has incremental validity beyond the Big Five in predicting measures of well-being and adjustment (Noftle, Schnitker, & Robins, 2010). The participants in Study 1 included 324 undergraduate students who completed the VIA-IS (Peterson & Seligman, 2004), the BFI (John, Naumann, & Soto, 2008), and several measures of well-being. The participants in Study 2 included 607 members of the Eugene-Springfield community sample (ESCS; Goldberg, 2008), aged 18–83 years, who completed the NEO-PI-R (Costa & McCrae, 1992) and an IPIP measure of the VIA[1] (Goldberg et al., 2006), as well as two measures of well-being.

### Evaluating the Structure of VIA Character Strengths

The first question we consider in evaluating the VIA is its structure. Whereas the VIA has served a substantial catalytic function for research on character and virtue, the classification system has received criticism for its proposed theoretical structure, which subsumes 24 character strengths under six broad virtues. Although Peterson and Seligman explain that their hierarchy was theoretically (and not empirically) derived, an empirical evaluation of the structure of the classification system seems necessary to establish its scientific validity. Previous research has failed to replicate the theoretical structure of character strengths (e.g., Haslam, Bain, & Neal, 2004; MacDonald, Bore, & Munro, 2008). Indeed, even Peterson and Seligman's (2004) own exploratory factor analysis of the VIA identified five, not six, broad factors, which they labeled strengths of restraint, intellectual strengths, interpersonal strengths, emotional strengths, and teleological strengths. MacDonald et al. (2008) analyzed the IPIP version of the 24 character strengths and found that a four-factor solution provided the best fit: positivity, intellect, conscientiousness, and niceness.[2] This structure differs from the theoretical structure of six virtues proposed by Peterson and Seligman, as well as from their empirically-derived five-factor solution. Using cluster analysis, Haslam et al. (2004) found six clusters of strengths that had only a modest correspondence with Peterson and Seligman's theoretical structure. Clearly, given the lack of agreement apparent in previous findings, more work needs to be done to establish the structure of character strengths.

Previous attempts to verify the theoretical structure of the VIA have used exploratory factor analysis or cluster analysis; however, confirmatory factor analysis (CFA) is the most appropriate technique in this context. Noftle, Schnitker, and Robins (2010) used CFA to compare the fit of several proposed structural models. Our analyses failed to confirm Peterson and Seligman's (2004) theoretically-derived six-factor structure ($X^2$= 1437.65, df= 237, AIC = 963.64, RMSEA =.125), which groups the 24 character strengths under six broad virtues. In addition, poor fit was found for several alternative models, including Peterson and Seligman's (2004) empirically-derived five-factor structure ($X^2$= 2414.70, df= 247, AIC = 1920.70, RMSEA =.165); Macdonald, Bore, and Munro's (2008) empirically-derived four-factor structure identified by ($X^2$= 1558.80, df= 246, AIC = 1066.80, RMSEA =.129); and a single factor model ($X^2$= 1736.85, df= 252, AIC = 1232.86, RMSEA =.135).

These confirmatory analyses suggest that none of the models proposed to represent the structure of character strengths provides a good fit to the data. Consequently, the field of positive psychology does not have an empirically viable overarching framework for classifying and organizing its primary theoretical constructs. Although it is possible that an alternative model that was not tested could capture the structure of the VIA scales, it seems more likely that the VIA simply does not have a clear hierarchical structure. Researchers may consider the inclusion of new strengths (or perhaps the exclusion of certain strengths like modesty) to clarify the structure of character.

Why does the VIA seem not to have a replicable hierarchical structure? It is possible that there are strong situational factors affecting responses to the items that shift the structure in various ways from study to study and from context to context. However, this does not seem especially likely given the high test-retest reliabilities of the scale (Peterson & Seligman, 2004). A second possibility is that the measure consists of some problematic items that are obscuring the structure. For example, if items are worded in such a way that the understood meaning varies from participant to participant, the items might cluster differently depending on the sample studied. One possibly problematic aspect of the VIA-IS is that there are a substantial number of "always" or "never" items (e.g., "I always admit when I am wrong," "I never quit a task before it is done," "I always go out of my way to visit museums."), which might be answered quite differently by different participants depending on how absolutely the item is interpreted. For example, a person who likes to go to museums but does not literally "always" go out of her way to do so may rate herself at the midpoint of the scale, whereas a person who does not interpret the item quite as literally may rate himself very highly yet be equally likely to attend museums as the first person. Another problematic aspect of the VIA is that several items ask participants to rate themselves on characteristics that may be difficult to gauge or that may be highly evaluative. For example, people may not have a great amount of insight into such things as "I always know what makes someone tick," "Others trust me to keep their secrets," "I have never steered a friend wrong by giving bad advice," or "I have a great sense of humor." Research has demonstrated that the self may have less insight into highly evaluative attributes than others who know a person well (John & Robins, 1993b; Vazire, 2010). Another problem is that several items may have a restricted range of accurate responses, at least strictly speaking, for most people. It is the rare person who is able to strongly agree with the previously mentioned item about museums or with the items "I read all of the time" or "I always allow others to leave their mistakes in the past and make a fresh start." All of these problematic aspects of the VIA may contribute to obscuring its structure.

## Correspondence Between VIA Character Strengths and Personality Traits

The degree of correspondence between the 24 character strengths and the Big Five personality traits is an important question for at least three reasons. First, by mapping the character strengths onto the Big Five, we will gain a deeper conceptual understanding of each strength and the nomological network surrounding it, allowing us to generate hypotheses about the correlates and consequences of the strengths. Second, we will be able to determine whether the character strengths are truly assessing something unique or whether they are empirically reducible to the Big Five. Third, understanding how character strengths map onto personality traits will suggest which traits may be helpful in fostering development of particular character strengths, as well as revealing more about the overall personalities of virtuous individuals.

Despite its importance, only three previous studies have examined how the VIA character strengths are linked to broad personality dimensions. Peterson and Park (2006a) reported that correlations between the Big Five and the VIA-Youth measure of character strengths ranged from the .40s to the .50s but did not provide more specific details of the precise relations between the sets of variables. Steger, Hicks, Kashdan, Krueger, and Bouchard (2007) investigated how the VIA scales were related to the Multidimensional Personality Questionnaire (MPQ; Tellegen, 1982), which assesses 11 subscales representing the broad traits of Positive Emotionality, Negative Emotionality, and Constraint. Steger et al. found that the MPQ subscales accounted for 8% to 26% of the total variance in each of the character strength scores. MacDonald et al. (2008) investigated how the VIA scales were related to the Big Five, using IPIP measures of the VIA and the Big Five (Goldberg, 1999). MacDonald et al. conducted a factor analysis of the 24 IPIP-VIA character strength scales and identified four interpretable factors. The highest correlations between the Big Five and the four VIA factors were .71 between Extraversion and the "positivity" factor (top loading: citizenship/teamwork), .68 between Openness and the "intellect" factor (top loading: originality/ creativity), .71 between Conscientiousness and the "conscientiousness" factor (top loading: self-regulation/self-control), and .57 between Agreeableness and the "niceness" factor (top loading: modesty/humility). These correlations are almost as high as one would expect between two different measures of the same construct and suggest a substantial amount of overlap between the VIA and the Big Five.

One limitation of previous research is that only the broad Big Five dimensions were assessed, and not the specific facets of each dimension. Peterson and Seligman argue that the breadth of the Big Five makes it unlikely that any of them will be closely tied to a particular character strength (which are theoretically much narrower constructs), because of a mismatch in breadth. The results of Steger et al. and MacDonald et al. suggest that this may not be the case: some character strengths were highly related to individual Big Five dimensions. However, moving to the narrower facet level of Big Five assessment may reveal specific aspects of the Big Five that are even more strongly related to the character strengths.

Noftle et al. (2010) extended previous findings on associations between character strengths and personality traits in two studies. In Study 1, we attempted to replicate MacDonald's findings, examining the relations between the VIA and a commonlyused Big Five measure, the Big Five Inventory (BFI; John, Naumann, & Soto, 2008). In Study 2, we examined the relations between

the IPIP-VIA and a Big Five measure that includes facet scales: the NEO-PI-R (Costa & McCrae, 1992).

In Study 1, the percentage of variance in character strengths explained by the Big Five domains (BFI) ranged from 14% (spirituality) to 46% (persistence) with a mean percentage of 33% of the variance explained by the Big Five across the 24 strengths. With the exception of spirituality, the Big Five predicted more than 20% of the variance for each of the individual strengths.

In Study 2, to examine whether facet-level analyses allowed for more predictability of the character strengths, we regressed all 30 NEO-PI-R facets on each character strength (see Table 14.1). For the NEO-PI-R facets, the percentage of variance in character strengths explained by the Big Five ranged from 30% (fairness) to 50% (persistence) with a mean of 40% for the 24 strengths. Thus, although the facets added to the predictability of the VIA character strengths over the global five factors, the character strengths were not completely redundant with, or reducible to, the facets of the Big Five. In Table 14.1, we present the highest facet correlate for each of the character strengths, as well as the second-highest correlate if the magnitude of the correlation is similar. Aside from the correlations for spirituality and fairness that were more modest in magnitude, all other correlates were moderate to large in magnitude, ranging from .42 (gratitude and creativity) to .63 (persistence).

Overall, these findings suggest that the VIA dimensions are associated with a broad range of personality traits. For some of the virtues, it appears as if there is a common thread of personality attributes underlying the character strengths that comprise the virtue: Openness and Conscientiousness for Wisdom, Conscientiousness and Extraversion for Courage, Agreeableness and Extraversion for Humanity and for Justice, and Agreeableness for Temperance. However, there does not seem to be a core set of personality traits underlying Transcendence. Although it is not clear how to interpret these relations, it is possible that personality dimensions facilitate the development of certain virtues and perhaps channel the way in which they are expressed in everyday behaviors. For example, if a person wants to cultivate wisdom, it would be helpful to be open to ideas or to act with deliberation or competence. If this interpretation is true, it would partly support Peterson and Seligman's theory that the different character strengths related to a

TABLE 14.1    Predicting the VIA Character Strengths from the NEO-PI-R Big Five Facets
(Noftle, Schnitker, & Robins, 2010, Study 2)

| VIA character strength | R | Strongest correlate(s) | |
|---|---|---|---|
| | | NEO-PI-R facet scale | r (corrected r) |
| *Wisdom and Knowledge* | | | |
| Creativity | .63 | O5: Openness to Ideas | .42 (.50) |
| Curiosity | .65 | O5: Openness to Ideas | .44 (.55) |
| Judgment | .61 | C6: Deliberation | .45 (.60) |
| Love of Learning | .64 | O5: Openness to Ideas | .50 (.63) |
| Perspective | .62 | C1: Competence | .44 (.61) |
| *Courage* | | | |
| Bravery | .67 | E3: Assertiveness | .48 (.62) |
| Integrity | .63 | C3: Dutifulness | .44 (.63) |
| Persistence | .70 | C5: Self-Discipline | .63 (.78) |
| Zest | .63 | E4: Activity | .41 (.55) |
| *Humanity* | | | |
| Love | .59 | E1: Warmth | .46 (.61) |
| Kindness | .61 | A3: Altruism; E1: Warmth | .47 (.65); .46 (.62) |
| Social Intelligence | .61 | E1: Warmth | .46 (.59) |
| *Justice* | | | |
| Citizenship | .58 | E1: Warmth | .45 (.57) |
| Fairness | .55 | A3: Altruism | .36 (.51) |
| Leadership | .69 | E3: Assertiveness | .56 (.71) |
| *Temperance* | | | |
| Forgiveness | .62 | A4: Compliance | .50 (.67) |
| Modesty | .67 | A5: Modesty | .53 (.73) |
| Prudence | .68 | C6: Deliberation | .52 (.73) |
| Self-Regulation | .68 | N5: Impulsiveness; C5: Self-Discipline | −.54 (−.72); .53 (.68) |
| *Transcendence* | | | |
| Appreciation of Beauty | .66 | O2: Aesthetics | .62 (.77) |
| Gratitude | .59 | E1: Warmth; A3: Altruism | .42 (.53); .40 (.56) |
| Hope | .65 | E6: Positive Emotions; N3: Depression | .46 (.60); −.45 (−.58) |
| Humor | .60 | E6: Positive Emotions | .53 (.64) |
| Spirituality | .66 | A6: Tender-Mindedness | .27 (.36) |
| *Mean:* | *.63* | | *.47 (.65)* |
| *Range:* | *.55 – .70* | | *.27 – .63 (.36 – .78)* |

*Note.* N=607. More than one NEO-PI-R facet is listed for a character strength if the size of the correlation was within .02 of the strongest correlate. "Corrected r" (shown in parentheses) refers to correlations corrected for measurement error in the VIA and NEO-PI-R scales.

particular virtue may reflect different ways to pursue that virtue.

## Predicting Well-being from VIA Character Strengths and Personality Traits

Both character strengths and the Big Five dimensions have been linked to a wide range of measures of health and well-being, and other indicators of the "good life" (Peterson & Seligman, 2004; Hampson & Friedman, 2008; Ozer & Benet-Martinez, 2006; Roberts et al., 2007). Thus, in the quest to disentangle the relationships between character strengths and personality, Noftle et al. (2010) examined the degree to which the VIA scales predict well-being above and beyond the Big Five personality dimensions, and vice versa. In Study 1, we assessed three "proxy" indicators of well-being: *time perspective* reflects an individual's propensity to use five theoretically autonomous time orientations, which are strongly related to a plethora of health and well-being outcomes (Zimbardo & Boyd, 1999); proneness to *regret* negatively correlates with life satisfaction and happiness and positively correlates with depression (Schwartz et al., 2002); and *mindfulness* (Brown & Ryan, 2003) correlates with decreased anxiety and depression, increased subjective and eudaimonic well-being, and fewer physical symptoms and doctor visits. In Study 2, we assessed two direct measures of well-being: the Satisfaction with Life scale (Pavot & Diener, 1993) and a single-item measure of physical health (DeSalvo et al., 2006).

We performed a series of hierarchical linear regressions on each of the direct and proxy well-being variables. For each variable, we entered the character strengths at Step 1 and the Big Five dimensions at Step 2, and then repeated the analysis in the opposite order. In all analyses, the set of variables entered at Step 1 (either character strengths or the Big Five) significantly predicted the outcome (see Table 14.2). In a few cases, character strengths and the Big Five incrementally predicted well-being at Step 2 (i.e., independently of the other set of variables). Specifically, character strengths had independent effects on past-positive time perspective, regret, life satisfaction, and general health, whereas the Big Five had independent effects on past-negative time perspective, future time perspective, mindfulness, life satisfaction, and general health.

Overall, character strengths and personality traits had relatively similar predictive abilities for both direct and proxy measures of well-being.

However, the two sets of variables did not completely overlap in their predictive abilities and, in some cases, had predictive power over and above the other set of variables. Certainly, character strengths do predict different aspects of well-being, but they do not predict well-being substantially better than personality traits do. These analyses constitute a critical test of a basic tenet of positive psychology, that moral character engenders well-being and other positive subjective experiences independently of basic personality traits.

In summary, our evaluation of character strengths leads to three conclusions. First, the empirical structure of character strengths has yet to be replicated, in our own analyses or those of other researchers. Future studies, especially those utilizing large samples, are needed to clarify the structure of the VIA. Second, character strengths appear to share a good deal of conceptual and empirical overlap with personality traits, and future work will be needed to conceptually clarify the distinction between the two sets of constructs and empirically demonstrate the degree to which they are separable. Third, character strengths are predictive of emotional and physical well-being, but their predictive power is sometimes entirely redundant with the Big Five; future research will be required to demonstrate the incremental validity of character strengths above basic personality traits.

## Moving Forward in the Study of Character Strengths

In this final section, we describe several directions for future research on character strengths and their relations with personality traits. Our suggestions are based on lessons learned from more than a century of research on personality. We argue that future research needs to clarify the conceptualization of the core constructs—character strengths—and differentiate them from personality traits; provide stronger evidence for the construct validity of the VIA and the theorized hierarchical structure of character strengths and virtues; clarify the cognitive and affective processes underlying the character strengths; and pursue large-scale longitudinal studies examining the normative development of character strengths and the efficacy of interventions aimed at improving moral character and establishing the prospective influence of character strengths on real-world outcomes.

TABLE 14.2 Predicting Direct and Indirect Measures of Well-Being from the VIA Character Strengths and the Big Five Dimensions (Noftle, Schnitker, & Robins, 2010, Studies 1 and 2)

| DV | Order | Step 1 $\Delta R^2$ | Step 2 $\Delta R^2$ | Total $R^2$ |
|---|---|---|---|---|
| Life Satisfaction | VIA, NEO-PI-R | .409** | .055** | .465 |
| | NEO-PI-R, VIA | .287** | .178** | |
| General Health | VIA, NEO-PI-R | .233** | .088** | .320 |
| | NEO-PI-R, VIA | .185** | .136** | |
| Time Perspective | | | | |
| *Future* | VIA, BFI | .560** | .051* | .611 |
| | BFI, VIA | .451** | .160 | |
| *Present-Fatalistic* | VIA, BFI | .308** | .073 | .381 |
| | BFI, VIA | .164** | .217 | |
| *Present-Hedonistic* | VIA, BFI | .424** | .057 | .480 |
| | BFI, VIA | .289** | .192 | |
| *Past-Positive* | VIA, BFI | .368** | .039 | .407 |
| | BFI, VIA | .142** | .265* | |
| *Past-Negative* | VIA, BFI | .333** | .102** | .464 |
| | BFI, VIA | .286** | .178 | |
| Regret | VIA, BFI | .330** | .040 | .370 |
| | BFI, VIA | .063** | .307* | |
| Mindfulness | VIA, BFI | .268** | .115** | .383 |
| | BFI, VIA | .194** | .188 | |

$* p < .05 ** p < .01$. Life Satisfaction and General Health were assessed in Study 2.
Time Perspective, Regret, and Mindfulness were assessed in Study 1.

## Conceptual Concerns

Peterson and Seligman (2004; Park, Peterson, & Seligman, 2004) outlined 12 criteria for a character strength to be included in their taxonomy. According to their criteria, character strengths: (1) are cross-culturally universal, (2) contribute to positive aspects of life and life outcomes, (3) are valued as ends and not just as means, (4) elevate others who witness their display, (5) are not directly contrasted with weaknesses, (6) are trait-like and manifested in behavior, (7) are measureable, (8) are distinctive and not reducible to existing strengths in the taxonomy, (9) are embodied in paragons, (10) can be found in prodigies, (11) are absent in other individuals, and (12) are supported by societal institutions and shared social rituals.

In our view, these criteria are not sufficiently distinct from the way personality traits are conceptualized to merit differentiating the two sets of constructs. Consider the trait of conscientiousness. Conscientiousness: (1) has been identified as a major personality characteristic across many cultures, using both etic and emic approaches (Saucier, 2009; Schmidtt, Allik, McCrae, & Benet-Martinez, 2007); (2) has been linked to higher college GPAs, greater family satisfaction, and better job performance (Noftle & Robins, 2007; Ozer & Benet-Martinez, 2006); (3) is commonly considered to be morally valued; (4) when displayed in work and achievement contexts often makes others contagiously more responsible; (5) could be conceptually contrasted with being either lazy or flexible; (6) is highly stable across time (Roberts & DelVecchio, 2000) and is obviously manifested in behavior (Bogg & Roberts, 2004; Fleeson & Gallagher, 2009); (7) has been measured successfully using numerous scales and inventories; (8) is distinct from and not reducible to Extraversion, Agreeableness, Neuroticism, or Openness (Goldberg, 1990); (9) is embodied in paragons like social leaders; (10) can be found in extremely disciplined children like musical prodigies; (11) is largely absent in individuals like psychopaths; and (12) is supported by social institutions and rituals like savings accounts, day planners, and awards. Although some of these examples may be debatable, not all of the character strengths identified by Peterson and Seligman meet all of their criteria either, which the authors acknowledge. Given that the VIA classification of strengths originates "in the spirit of personality psychology, and specifically that of trait theory" (Peterson & Seligman, 2004; p. 10), and given the high amount of overlap revealed by our empirical studies, it will be important to clearly define and measure character strengths in ways that do not both conceptually and empirically resemble established trait systems.

Furthermore, several of the criteria may not be scientifically falsifiable. For example, the criteria of being able to identify paragons and prodigies to represent specific character strengths seems to resemble literary criteria rather than scientific ones; specifically, it is not clear on what grounds one would determine whether a particular exemplar is, or is not, a paragon or prodigy. Additionally, the current data, which shows some fairly strong negative correlations between character strengths and facets of personality, suggests that the criterion that remains agnostic about character weaknesses may be flawed. For example, out of all of the personality facets examined, the character strength of self-regulation was most strongly correlated, and negatively, with the Impulsiveness facet of Neuroticism ($r=-.54$). Obviously, each character strength may be opposed with at least one weakness, but as Peterson and Seligman proposed, there may exist several unrelated weaknesses. Alternately, Aristotle's formulation of a virtue as a mean between two extremes of vice, reflecting an excess and deficiency (Rorty, 1980), may be supported. It seems like a realistic and important scientific goal to identify such weaknesses.

Other questions remain about the inherent positivity of strengths. Are strengths always good in all situations, or are there some situations in which having a lower level of a strength might have a more beneficial effect? Should strengths be displayed in some situations and not others? Is their goodness contingent on certain conditions being met? Certainly one can imagine times when it is better to be prudent and times when it is better to be zestful. A considerable amount of theorizing has been applied to

understanding the benefits and drawbacks of being high or low on different traits (e.g., Nettle, 2006). Surely this could also be true of strengths?

A related question concerns Peterson and Seligman's (2004) interesting, but somewhat underdeveloped, notion of "situational themes," which are "specific habits that lead people to manifest given character strengths in given situations" (p. 14). Unfortunately, analysis of character strengths at this "behavioral" or "state" level has not been pursued, at least not that we were able to determine. A debate that plagued personality psychology for many years was the person-situation debate, for which two major points of contention were whether personality was consistent and whether traits predicted behavior at any kind of reasonable level (Donnellan, Lucas, & Fleeson, 2009; Kenrick & Funder, 1988; Mischel, 1968). One outcome of the debate was the realization that there were several different kinds of consistency (Ozer, 1986) and that traits may be highly consistent in some ways but not in others (Fleeson & Noftle, 2008). Another outcome of the debate was the insight that traits did seem to be good predictors of behavior in several circumstances but not in others (Epstein, 1979; Fleeson & Gallagher, 2009; Mischel & Shoda, 1995). If positive psychologists are interested in pursuing the (important, we believe) study of how and when character strengths are manifested in behavior, and whether character strengths are situationally consistent or are contingent on situational themes (e.g., Fleeson, 2007; Heller, Komar, & Lee, 2007), they would do well to learn from the complex conclusions taken from the person-situation debate.

Another question concerns how individual strengths are related to one another. In general, the strengths tend to be weakly to moderately positively intercorrelated. But from a conceptual standpoint, could any of the strengths be at odds with one another? From a measurement perspective, the influence of response styles such as socially desirable responding can lead to positive intercorrelations among self-report scales even when the latent constructs are negatively correlated. Does being high in one strength make it more difficult to attain high levels of another strength? For example, as conceptualized in the VIA, "open-mindedness" and "persistence" seem to point in different directions; open-mindedness is defined as "examining them [things] from all sides; *not* jumping to conclusions" (emphasis in original), whereas persistence involves "persisting in a course of action in spite of obstacles; 'getting it out the door'" (Peterson & Seligman, 2004, p. 29). The Big Five were designed and theorized to be orthogonal to one another, which was not an aim pursued for the character strengths. However, in measurement, some Big Five facets are moderately negatively correlated with other facets. For example, the assertiveness and activity facets of Extraversion are negatively correlated, between −.18 and −.34, with the compliance and modesty facets of Agreeableness (e.g., Costa & McCrae, 1992). People who are assertive and active are less compliant and modest, which makes sense. Surely the same thing could be true of strengths.

A final concern that we have is the apparent plethora of terms for some of the character strengths. Peterson and Seligman (2004) referred to their approach in identifying the character strengths as "one of *piling on synonyms*" (emphasis in the original; p. 16) to denote the quite reasonable idea that each strength includes a group of related traits with a family resemblance. However, perusing the publications on character strengths from the last few years, we note that different publications (even those from the same laboratory!) do not consistently refer to the strengths but use several different synonyms. In some circumstances the differences are minor and easy to reconcile (e.g., Beauty vs. Appreciation of Beauty), but in others the terms are numerous and rather confusing (e.g., Open-mindedness vs. Judgment; Integrity vs. Honesty vs. Authenticity; Citizenship vs. Teamwork). Certainly, the Big Five literature has also dealt with different terms for the same traits over the years (Surgency vs. Extraversion, Openness vs. Intellect vs. Culture), but with only five broad traits (instead of 24), these have been relatively easy to assimilate. It would be very useful for the study of character strengths to standardize the referent terms.

## Validity Concerns

John and Soto (2007) outlined five key aspects of construct validity: generalizability, content validity, structural validity, external validity, and substantive validity. We evaluate the VIA-IS on each of these criteria and suggest future recommendations. Peterson and Seligman (2004) and subsequent researchers (including ourselves) have attempted to validate the VIA character strengths. However, there are several aspects of construct validity that have been neglected and others for

which the VIA does not meet traditional psychometric standards. Below we briefly summarize the validity evidence for the VIA and note areas that merit further exploration.

## Generalizability

Generalizability refers to whether scores and their interpretations generalize across contexts, occasions, and raters. It appears as though this aspect of validity has been most thoroughly explored. For example, individuals' self-nominations of strengths are typically correlated with their VIA scale scores. The 24-character strength scales also demonstrate adequate internal reliability (alphas typically above .70) and reasonable test-retest reliability across four months, although stability across longer time periods will need to be examined to see if the character strengths are truly trait-like, as commonly claimed, and whether the degree of stability is comparable to that found for personality traits.

Studies of the VIA have also been conducted in nations around the globe. For example, a web study of 54 nations was conducted using the VIA inventory (Park, Peterson, & Seligman, 2006), which revealed that profiles of most versus least common strengths were similar across the nations studied (although the researchers did not examine whether the differential social desirability of the items could explain this finding). However, the researchers did not examine whether the structure of the VIA generalized across nations, an important aspect of generalizability that is related to structural validity, which we discuss below. Furthermore, a crucial weakness of the study was that the VIA was offered only in English, which placed a severe limitation on who could participate in the study. Future studies will need to replicate the results with translated measures, using an "etic" approach (e.g., Benet & Waller, 1995), such as two studies that have employed the VIA after it was translated into Japanese (Otake et al., 2005; Shimai et al., 2006).

Peterson and Seligman (2004) have thoughtfully surveyed the world literature to develop a classification of virtues that does not simply reflect the characteristics "valued at the turn of the new century by upper-middle-class agnostic European American academic males" (p. 20). Generally, the VIA measure itself also appears to stand by this credo. However, direct translations of the VIA items into the languages of some cultures, such as pre-industrialized non-Westernized cultures, may pose a problem. Inspection of the content of specific scales, such as "Love of Learning," reveals items such as "I rarely read non-fiction books for fun" (reverse-scored) and "If I want to know something, I immediately go to the library or the Internet and look it up," which seem needlessly constrained to middle-class concerns and opportunities. Similarly, some items on the "Love" scale seem to reflect an individualistic notion of love rather than a collectivistic one, including "I am always willing to take risks to establish a relationship" and "I am the most important person in someone else's life." Allport's (1931) concern about characteristics representing the conventional meanings of a specific time and place seems relevant here.

Finally, the VIA character strengths have been investigated largely through self-report methods, to the neglect of other types of data, such as informant reports (e.g., peer, romantic partner, teacher, and parent reports), behavioral observations, standardized laboratory tasks, and life history data. In one study, Peterson and Seligman (2004) report that peer reports reveal self-other agreement for some character strengths, but the evidence is neither strong nor extensive. Especially for measurement of character strengths such as integrity (e.g., honesty), evidence that generalizes beyond self-reports will be important (e.g., a standardized laboratory task that allows for honesty vs. dissembling or teacher reports of student helping and other aspects of moral conduct). A VIA structured interview has been developed, and it will be important to examine the convergence between that measure and the VIA-IS. Like all individual difference measures, a multi-method nomological network must be established before the field accepts the validity of the VIA-IS.

## Content Validity

Content validity refers to the relevance, coverage, and quality of the measurement strategy in reference to the construct being studied. One aspect of content validity is face validity. The VIA-IS clearly has face validity because the vast majority of items are transparent (e.g., the item "I am always curious about the world" is on the Curiosity character strengths scale). It is more difficult to establish the degree to which a measure comprehensively covers the full content of the construct, or set of constructs, being assessed. In surveying world literature and philosophy for themes of virtue and character that were common across cultures (Dahlsgaard et al., 2005),

Peterson and Seligman surely have attended to this aspect of validity more so than for the average personality questionnaire. However, researchers continue to debate whether all important aspects of virtue have been incorporated into the VIA, and Peterson and Seligman (2004) note that several proposals have been made for the inclusion of other strengths, for example patience (Schnitker & Emmons, 2007). In addition, there is little evidence that each character strength scale covers the full content of the construct or just certain aspects. One way to examine this question would be to ask a separate group of experts, independent from the set who collaborated in developing the VIA, to evaluate the content validity of the scales. Similarly, there is little evidence that the character strengths theorized to constitute each virtue actually cover all aspects of that virtue.

## Structural Validity

Structural validity refers to whether the factor structure of a measure is consistent with the hypothesized structure of the construct. In our recent research (Noftle et al., 2010), we found little evidence for the structural validity of the VIA. The conceptual structure proposed by Peterson and Seligman (2004), organizing the 24 strengths under six broad virtues, was not empirically supported, which replicates past failures to model the conceptual structure (e.g., MacDonald et al., 2008). We also found that other previously identified empirical structures of the VIA were not replicated, but that possible factor structures for the 24 character strengths tended to resemble the Big Five domains. Thus, we propose that the VIA-IS be modified so that its empirical structure more closely corresponds to the theorized structure; alternatively, the theoretical conception of the hierarchical structure of strengths and virtues needs to be revised. Once the empirical structure maps onto the theoretical structure, further research is needed to establish the cross-cultural generalizability of the structure, just as the Big Five structure has been replicated across a wide range of cultures.

## External Validity

External validity refers to whether a measure relates to other measures and types of data in a theoretically consistent manner. A large component of external validity is establishing convergent and discriminant validity: does a scale correlate with measures of theoretically related constructs (convergent validity), and does it not correlate with measures of theoretically unrelated constructs (discriminant validity)?

The Noftle et al. study addressed the discriminant validity of the VIA. Character strengths are theorized to be conceptually and empirically distinct from personality traits. However, in some cases, we found very strong relations between the two sets of constructs, particularly for the character strengths of persistence (correlated .63 with NEO-PI-R self-discipline), appreciation of beauty (correlated .62 with NEO-PI-R openness to aesthetics), modesty (correlated .53 with NEO-PI-R modesty), and prudence (correlated .52 with NEO-PI-R deliberation). When these correlations were corrected for measurement error, the relations between the two sets of constructs ranged from .73 to .78. Thus, several character strengths, as measured by the VIA, are almost identical to certain personality traits. In fact, when corrected for unreliability, 15 of the 24 character strengths were correlated at least .60 with specific facets from the NEO-PI-R, suggesting considerable overlap. This is remarkable because the NEO-PI-R was administered approximately 10 years before the IPIP-VIA; for example, despite the time interval, the self-discipline facet of the NEO-PI-R prospectively predicted the character strength of persistence 10 years later with a disattenuated correlation of .78. In addition, these estimations of the overlap between character strengths and personality represent only the amount of overlap between the character strengths and the individual facets that are most highly correlated with them. When multiple personality facets are considered together, the amount of overlap increases substantially.

Together, these results suggest that much of the reliable variance in several character strengths is essentially redundant with existing, well-validated personality scales. Although one would expect some amount of overlap between personality traits and character strengths, and some overlap would actually be indicative of convergent validity, the strong correspondence observed in Noftle et al. is problematic, raising concerns about the external validity of the VIA character strength scales.

Another key aspect of external validity is convergent validity. Almost all of the character strengths proposed by Peterson and Seligman have been studied individually by researchers before the development of the VIA. However, extensive mapping of the VIA character strength scales onto these previously developed measures

within a nomological net has not been done. This seems necessary for the rich pre-VIA literature on such qualities to inform and shape efforts stemming from the VIA approach.

## Substantive Validity: Happiness and Well-Being

Substantive validity refers to the process of linking a measure to theoretically expected underlying processes. Some progress has been made in this aspect of validation. One central question concerns how character strengths are related to happiness and well-being, broadly construed. The last decade of research on character strengths has focused on this particular outcome. For example, Park, Peterson, and Seligman (2004) demonstrated, using data from multiple studies, that life satisfaction was positively related to the great majority of the character strengths, from those that had modest associations in the .15 to .20 range (judgment, prudence, and fairness) to those that had moderate to strong associations in the .40 to .60 range (hope, zest, and gratitude). In another study with a large Internet sample of over 12,000 respondents from the U.S., Peterson, Ruch, Beermann, Park, and Seligman (2007) replicated the life satisfaction findings and showed that the character strengths were modestly to moderately positively associated with three different happiness orientations, one focused on pleasure, one on engagement, and one on meaning in life. Similar results were also found in the same study for a sample of German-speaking Swiss adults and in a separate study by Brdar and Kashdan (2010) of Croatian students.

However, life satisfaction and other aspects of happiness have also been shown to be modestly to moderately associated with personality traits such as the Big Five (DeNeve & Cooper, 1998; Diener, Oishi, & Lucas, 2003). It is possible that the associations between character strengths and happiness and well-being can be explained by their overlap with personality. In Noftle et al., we attempted to extend this aspect of the nomological network by directly comparing the predictive validity of VIA character strengths and the Big Five personality traits. The relative predictive power of the two types of measures was essentially equivalent, although the VIA strengths were stronger in some instances. Admittedly, the analyses were exploratory, and some of the measures were proxy measures rather than direct assessments of happiness and well-being. It will be important to determine whether the VIA scales outpredict personality traits when outcomes theoretically central to character strengths are considered, such as aspects of well-being related to pleasure, engagement, and meaning in life (e.g., Peterson, Ruch, Beerman, Park, & Seligman, 2007). Conversely, the Big Five dimensions may do a better job predicting outcomes other than well-being (e.g., relationship, work, and health outcomes), given that the VIA scales were specifically developed to predict positive subjective experiences.

Other questions related to substantive validity are important. To what extent are the character strengths related to "the good life"? Obviously subjective well-being (SWB) is a central aspect, and focus on this aspect of the good life is theoretically compelling. However, the problem with reliance on SWB is that it shares method variance with the central method of measuring the character strengths, namely self-report. It will be important to examine whether the relation between VIA strengths and SWB holds when the strengths are measured using non-self-report methods and for non-subjective aspects of the "good life" such as living up to one's potential and making positive contributions to society.

Intervention research in positive psychology helps to address concerns about method variance inflating correlations between character strengths and self-report-based outcomes as well as helping to establish the causal influence of character strengths. Seligman, Steen, Park, and Peterson (2005) described a set of intervention studies to improve happiness. Three of the studies involved manipulations related to one or more of the 24 character strengths. In one intervention study, participants completed the VIA and were given feedback about their five highest strengths. They were then asked to use one of their five highest character strengths in a novel way for the next seven days. Compared with a control group, participants from the experimental group were happier and less depressed when tested up to six months later. Such studies suggest that happiness interventions may produce more than just transient change, but whether they have long-term positive effects is currently not known.

## Substantive Validity: Three Domain-Specific Areas of Functioning

We propose three important domains that should be investigated to examine the effects of character strengths. Freud famously invoked the importance of love and work to humanity; to this small set we add health. A few studies have been conducted in these areas, but this work has taken a backseat to the main research focus in the positive psychology movement on overall happiness.

*Health.* Health is an obvious next step in examining the benefits of strengths beyond happiness. Researchers should consider not only the direct effects of character strengths on general health but also how strengths affect the way a person responds to and copes with physical and mental health concerns and troubles, as the vast literature on personality and health has demonstrated for personality traits (Hampson & Friedman, 2008). At least three studies have begun to investigate these issues. Peterson, Park, and Seligman (2006) found a buffering effect of specific character strengths on life satisfaction for those with a history of physical illness and those with a history of mental illness. Peterson et al. (2008) found that the number of traumatic events experienced by individuals were positively associated with higher levels of character strengths and greater growth following recovery. Finally, Peterson and Park (2006a) found that teenagers who had higher levels of character strengths tended to list fewer internalizing and externalizing problems on a behavioral checklist.

*Love.* One surprising area of neglect in the character strength literature is close relationships. Personality traits have important implications for romantic relationships. Both one's traits, and the traits of one's partner, influence relationship satisfaction both concurrently and longitudinally (Karney & Bradbury, 1995; Robins, Caspi, & Moffitt, 2000; 2002; Watson, Hubbard, & Wiese, 2000). Having a romantic partner who is higher in certain character strengths seems likely to have beneficial effects on one's relationship. Many questions could be asked, such as: How do character strengths impact relationship satisfaction? Which strengths are most strongly related to having a stable relationship? Is there assortative mating on some of the character strengths? In regard to the last question, one of the interesting, but surprising, findings in personality is that there is little evidence of assortative mating in personality traits on average (Luo & Klohnen, 2005; Watson, Klohnen, Casillas, Simms, Haig, & Berry, 2004), but that the assortative mating within couples that does occur does appear to be related to higher relationship satisfaction, at least in some samples (e.g., Luo & Klohnen, 2005). It will be interesting to see whether character strengths also show low levels of assortative mating and what relation, if any, couple similarity in strengths has to satisfaction.

*Work.* Another area of inquiry should continue to be educational and work settings. The importance of personality traits to academic and work settings has been clearly demonstrated (Barrick & Mount, 1991; Hogan, Hogan, & Roberts, 1996; Noftle & Robins, 2007; Roberts et al., 2007). Peterson and Park (2006a) have shown that some of the character strengths are correlated with academic achievement, peer-rated popularity, and self-rated social skills in young adults. Park, Peterson, and Seligman (2004) found that work satisfaction in a variety of domains is correlated with higher levels of certain character strengths, but there have been no intervention or longitudinal studies to help tease apart the causal direction. Peterson and Park (2006b) describe several findings related to work performance, but some of these findings have not yet been reported in empirical articles and thus are difficult to evaluate. In order to build a cumulative set of findings on character strengths and work (rather than ending up with a hodge-podge of disparate findings), future researchers are advised to draw from models of organizational behavior developed by personality psychologists. For example, Roberts (2006) proposed a model to explain and organize a full set of transactions between personality and work experiences across time, including processes of attraction, selection, transformation, manipulation, and attrition. Using this framework, positive psychologists could explore how strengths feed into successful organizations and, in turn, how organizations may foster strengths in their employees. This would also help to fulfill the promise of studying positive institutions, the relatively neglected third pillar of positive psychology.

Work and love are just two specific, albeit important, instances from the respective broader agentic and communal domains (Wiggins, 2003). One thing that will be intriguing in future research on character strengths is their relative benefits within these two broad domains. Interestingly, although virtue is often conceptualized in terms of its benefits to others, most research so far has examined only the benefits of character strengths to the individual. Future research should explore benefits of character strengths to close others and the group, and demonstrate the importance of character strengths to the self beyond that of happiness and health. Certainly hypotheses may be easily formed to match strengths appropriately to each domain. For example, the strengths of fairness, kindness, forgiveness, and love might have benefits within communal domains, as they all could function to build harmony and acceptance among group members. On the other hand, the strengths of leadership, bravery, vitality, and love of learning might have benefits within agentic domains, since they could function to build status for the individual. Will character strengths facilitate both getting along and getting ahead as (positive) personality traits do? Only future research will tell.

Overall, there are some promising directions of research examining substantive validity. However, many of the associations revealed so far tend to hinge on a handful of strengths in ways that are not always theoretically obvious. For example, why should hope, zest, and leadership be related to fewer self-reported internalizing problems rather than spirituality, gratitude, and humor (Peterson & Park, 2006a)? Why should persistence, prudence, love, and authenticity be related to fewer externalizing problems rather than self-regulation, forgiveness, and kindness? Future findings need to be organized within, and guided by, a more carefully constructed theoretical framework.

Furthermore, more studies should examine mediators and moderators of the connection between VIA character strengths and outcomes. Which variables moderate the persistence of a character strength-related intervention on happiness over time? If character strengths are linked with satisfaction in romantic relationships, what types of behaviors do partners with good character engage in that make their relationships more satisfying? How do these partners act toward and react to their significant other?

## Development

Positive psychology will benefit from studying how the character strengths grow and develop across the lifespan. Large cross-sectional studies, such as the one of Linley et al. (2007), are useful to begin to understand normative age differences in character strengths. However, longitudinal studies will provide greater insight into the processes and outcomes of character strength development (Lazarus, 2003). It may be the case that levels of some character strengths are higher in some periods of life than other periods. We can already hypothesize how certain strengths might change with age, based on the substantial body of research documenting age-related changes in the Big Five dimensions (Roberts, Walton, & Viechtbauer, 2006). Zest, associated with the

Social Vitality aspect of Extraversion, is likely to peak early in life, whereas persistence and prudence, associated with Conscientiousness, are likely to peak later in life. Longitudinal studies will also reveal the stability of character strengths over long periods of life and the degree to which strengths exhibit trait-like consistencies over time. Longitudinal studies can also be used to examine the factors that predict within-person changes in character strengths; for example, which life experiences predict whether a person increases or decreases in wisdom during the transition from young adulthood to midlife? Finally, longitudinal studies will reveal how much of a buffering effect character strengths provide in response to both acute and chronic negative life events.

## Conclusions

The positive psychology approach to studying character strengths has numerous benefits over past approaches investigating moral character. First, it has utilized scientifically suitable research designs and methods (e.g., Ong & Van Dulmen, 2006). Second, it attempts to study character strengths outside a particular cultural perspective and focus on universal virtues. Third, it has set a lofty goal to study character strengths comprehensively rather than in a piecemeal fashion.

However, the study of character strengths poses several problems. First, it is unclear both conceptually and empirically that the VIA character strengths do not simply represent normal dimensions of personality traits that have been reconfigured (i.e., different mixes of the same domain of content) and re-labeled. We believe that the main distinctions made by Peterson and Seligman between character strengths and traits do not hold up to close scrutiny. Second, the structure of character strengths has not been clearly identified, has not been tested extensively in other cultures and linguistic groups, and does not conform to theoretically-derived broad virtue dimensions. Third, validity evidence for character strengths, especially demonstrating what they add beyond existing personality taxonomies, is lacking. This is not surprising in a field that is so new, but the future success of the field depends on establishing the validity of character strengths. At present, the evidence for positive psychology's constructs at the individual trait level of analysis is not strong and thus is at risk for the same attacks that were levied against

humanistic psychology decades ago. To avoid the decline that befell their predecessors and move the field forward, positive psychologists would do well to address the existing validity concerns with stronger empirical evidence.

*Acknowledgments*   We wish to thank Lew Goldberg, Maureen Barckley, and the Oregon Research Institute for providing us with the Eugene-Springfield Community Sample data.

## Notes

1. The IPIP version of the VIA was constructed somewhat differently than most IPIP measures, in that most of the items were newly-written specifically for developing the inventory. The 240 items from Peterson and Seligman's VIA were rephrased into IPIP style items, but the content remained the same. Thirty-nine of these items were subsequently removed and replaced with 12 new items that were thematically related but not simply reworded; thus the total scale consisted of 213 items.

2. This solution is quite similar to the results of a study by Brdar and Kashdan (2010) of Croatian college students, using a translated version of the VIA-IS, which emerged as this chapter was going to press.

*References*

Allport, G. W. (1931). What is a trait of personality? *Journal of Abnormal and Social Psychology, 25,* 368–372.

Allport, G. W. (1937). *Personality: A psychological interpretation.* New York: Holt.

Allport, G. W., & Odbert, H. S. (1936). Trait-names: A psycho-lexical study. *Psychological Monographs, 47,* 211.

American Psychiatric Association (1994). *Diagnostic and statistical manual of mental disorders* (4thed.). Washington, DC.

Barrick, M. R., & Mount, M. K. (1991). The Big Five personality dimensions and job performance: A meta-analysis. *Personnel Psychology, 44,* 1–26.

Benet, V., & Waller, N. G. (1995). The big seven factor model of personality description: Evidence for its cross-cultural generality in a Spanish sample. *Journal of Personality and Social Psychology, 69,* 701–718.

Bogg, T., & Roberts, B. W. (2004). Conscientiousness and health behaviors: A meta-analysis. *Psychological Bulletin, 130,* 887–919.

Brdar, I., & Kashdan, T.B. (2010). Character strengths and well-being in Croatia: An empirical investigation of structure and correlates. *Journal of Research in Personality, 44,* 151–154.

Brown, K.W., & Ryan, R.M. (2003). The benefits of being present: Mindfulness and its role in psychological well-being. *Journal of Personality and Social Psychology, 84,* 822–848.

Cawley, M.J., Martin, J.E., & Johnson, J.A. (2000). A virtues approach to personality. *Personality and Individual Differences, 28,* 997–1013.

Costa, P. T., Jr., & McCrae, R. R. (1992). *NEO PI-R and NEO-FFI professional manual.* Odessa, FL: Psychological Assessment Resources.

Dahlsgaard, K., Peterson, C., & Seligman, M. (2005). Shared virtue: The convergence of valued human strengths across culture and history. *Review of General Psychology, 9,* 203–213.

DeNeve, K. M., & Cooper, H. (1998). The happy personality: A meta-analysis of 137 personality traits and subjective well-being. *Psychological Bulletin, 124,* 197–229.

DeSalvo, K. B., Fisher, W. B., Tran, K., Bloser, N., Merrill, W., & Peabody, J. (2006). Assessing measurement properties of two single-item general health measures. *Quality of Life Research, 15,* 191–201.

DeYoung, C. G., Quilty, L. C., & Peterson, J. B. (2007). Between facets and domains: 10 aspects of the Big Five. *Journal of Personality and Social Psychology, 93,* 880–896.

Diener, E., Oishi, S., & Lucas, R. E. (2003). Personality, culture, and subjective well-being: Emotional and cognitive evaluations of life. *Annual Review of Psychology, 54,* 403–425.

Donnellan, M. B., Lucas, R. E., & Fleeson, W. (2009). Introduction to personality and assessment at age 40: Reflections on the legacy of the person–situation debate and the future of person–situation integration. *Journal of Research in Personality, 43,* 117–119.

Epstein, S. (1979). The stability of behavior: I. On predicting most of the people much of the time. *Journal of Personality and Social Psychology, 37,* 1097–1126.

Fleeson, W. (2007). Situation-based contingencies underlying trait-content manifestation in behavior. *Journal of Personality, 75,* 825–861.

Fleeson, W., & Gallagher, P. (2009). The implications of Big Five standing for the distribution of trait manifestation in behavior: Fifteen experience-sampling studies and a meta-analysis. *Journal of Personality and Social Psychology, 97,* 1097–1114.

Fleeson, W., & Noftle, E. E. (2008). Where does personality have its influence? A supermatrix of consistency concepts. *Journal of Personality, 76,* 1355–1385.

Goldberg, L. R. (1990). An alternative "description of personality": The Big-Five factor structure. *Journal of Personality and Social Psychology, 59,* 1216–1229.

Goldberg, L. R. (1993). The structure of phenotypic personality traits. *American Psychologist, 48,* 26–34.

Goldberg, L. R. (1999). A broad-bandwidth, public domain, personality inventory measuring the lower-level facets of several five-factor models. In I. Mervielde, I. Deary, F. De Fruyt, & F. Ostendorf (Eds.), *Personality Psychology in Europe, Vol. 7* (pp. 7–28). Tilburg, The Netherlands: Tilburg University Press.

Goldberg, L. R. (2008). The Eugene-Springfield community sample: Information available from the research participants. Oregon Research Institute Technical Report (Vol. 48, No. 1).

Goldberg, L. R., Johnson, J. A., Eber, H. W., Hogan, R., Ashton, M. C., Cloninger, C. R., & Gough, H. C. (2006). The International Personality Item Pool and the future of public-domain personality measures. *Journal of Research in Personality, 40,* 84–96.

Gough, H. G. (1957). *Manual for the California Personality Inventory.* Palo Alto, CA: Consulting Psychologists Press.

Gough, H. G. (1987). *California Personality Inventory administrator's guide.* Palo Alto, CA: Consulting Psychologists Press.

Gough, H. G. (1988). Along the way: Recollections of some major contributors to personality assessment. *Journal of Personality Assessment, 52,* 5–29.

Hampson, S., & Friedman, H. S. (2008). Personality and health: A life span perspective. In O. P. John, R. W. Robins, & L. Pervin (Eds.), *The Handbook of Personality* (3rd ed.). New York: Guilford, pp. 770–794.

Haslam, N., Bain, P., & Neal, D. (2004). The implicit structure of positive characteristics. *Personality and Social Psychology Bulletin, 30,* 529–541.

Heller, D., Komar, J., & Lee, W. B. (2007). The dynamics of personality states, goals, and well-being. *Personality and Social Psychology Bulletin, 33,* 898–910.

Hogan, R., Hogan, J., & Roberts, B. W. (1996). Personality measurement and employment decisions: Questions and answers. *American Psychologist, 51,* 469–477.

John, O. P., Naumann, L. P., & Soto, C. J. (2008). Paradigm shift to the integrative Big-Five trait taxonomy: History, measurement, and conceptual issues. In O. P. John, R. W. Robins, & L. A. Pervin (Eds.), *Handbook of personality: Theory and research* (pp. 114–158). New York, NY: Guilford Press.

John, O. P., & Robins, R. W. (1993a). Gordon Allport: Father and critic of the Five-Factor Model. In K. H. Craik, R. T. Hogan, & R. N. Wolfe (Eds.), *Fifty years of personality research* (pp. 215–236). New York: Plenum.

John, O. P., & Robins, R. W. (1993b). Determinants of interjudge agreement on personality traits: The Big Five domains,observability, evaluativeness, and the unique perspective of the self. *Journal of Personality, 61*, 521–551.

John, O. P., & Soto, C. J. (2007). The importance of being valid: Reliability and the process of construct validation. In R. W. Robins, R. C. Fraley, & R. F. Krueger (Eds.), *Handbook of research methods in personality psychology* (pp. 461–494). New York: Guilford.

Karney, B. R., & Bradbury, T. N. (1995). The longitudinal course of marital quality and stability: A review of theory, method, and research. *Psychological Bulletin, 118*, 3–34.

Kenrick, D. T., & Funder, D. C. (1988). Profiting from controversy: Lessons from the person-situation debate.*American Psychologist, 43*, 23–34.

Krueger, J. I., & Funder, D. C. (2004). Towards a balanced social psychology: Causes, consequences and cures for the problem-seeking approach to social behavior and cognition. *Behavioral and Brain Sciences, 27*, 313–327.

Leary, M., Tambor, E., Terdal, S., & Downs, D. (1995). Self-esteem as an interpersonal monitor: The sociometer hypothesis. *Journal of Personality and Social Psychology, 68*, 518–530.

Lazarus, R. J. (2003). Does the positive psychology movement have legs? *Psychological Inquiry, 14*, 93–109.

Linley, P. A., Maltby, J., Wood, A. M., Joseph, S., Harrington, S., Peterson, C., et al. (2007). Character strengths in the United Kingdom: The VIA Inventory of Strengths. *Personality and Individual Differences, 43*, 341–351.

Luo, S., & Klohnen, E. C. (2005). Assortative mating and marital quality in newlyweds: A couple-centered approach. *Journal of Personality and Social Psychology, 88*, 304–326.

MacDonald, C., Bore, M.R., & Munro, D. (2008). Values in action scale and the Big 5: An empirical indication of structure. *Journal of Research in Personality, 42*, 787–799.

McCrae, R. R., & John, O. P. (1992). An introduction to the Five-Factor Model and its applications. *Journal of Personality, 60*, 174–214.

McCullough, M. E., & Snyder, C. R. (2000). Classical sources of human strength: Revisiting an old home and building a new one. *Journal of Social and Clinical Psychology, 19*, 1–10.

Mischel, W. (1968). *Personality and Assessment.* New York, NY: Wiley.

Mischel, W., & Shoda, Y. (1995). A cognitive-affective system theory of personality: Reconceptualizing situations, dispositions, dynamics, and invariance in personality structure. *Psychological Review, 102*, 246–268.

Nettle, D. (2006). The evolution of personality variation in humans and other animals. *American Psychologist, 61*, 622–631.

Nicholson, I. A. M. (1998). Gordon Allport, character, and the "culture of personality," 1897–1937. *History of Psychology, 1*, 52–68.

Noftle, E. E., & Robins, R. W. (2007). Personality predictors of academic outcomes: Big Five correlates of GPA and SAT scores. *Journal of Personality and Social Psychology, 93*, 116–130.

Noftle, E. E., Schnitker, S. A., & Robins, R. W. (2010). The VIA character strengths, personality traits, and well-being. Manuscript in preparation.

Ong, A. D., & van Dulmen, M. H. M. (2006). *Handbook of methods in positive psychology.* New York, NY: Oxford University Press.

Otake, K., Shimai, S., Ikemi, A., Utsuki, N., Peterson, C., & Seligman, M. E. P. (2005). Development of the Japanese version of the Value in Action Inventory of Strengths (VIA-IS). *The Japanese Journal of Psychology, 76*, 461–467.

Ozer, D. J. (1986). *Consistency in personality: A methodological framework.* Berlin, Germany: Springer-Verlag.

Ozer, D.J., & Benet-Martinez, V. (2006). Personality and the prediction of consequential outcomes. *Annual Review of Psychology, 57*, 401–421.

Park, N., Peterson, C., & Seligman, M. (2004). Strengths of character and well-being. *Journal of Social and Clinical Psychology, 23*, 603–619.

Park, N., Peterson, C., & Seligman, M. (2006). Character strengths in fifty-four nations and the fifty US states.*Journal of Positive Psychology, 1*, 118–129.

Pavot, W., & Diener, E. (1993). Review of the Satisfaction with Life Scale. *Psychological Assessment, 5*, 164–172.

Peterson, C., & Park, N. (2006a). Moral competence and character strengths among adolescents: The development and validation of the Values in

Action Inventory of Strengths for Youth. *Journal of Adolescence, 29,* 891–909.

Peterson, C., & Park, N. (2006b). Character strengths in organizations. *Journal of Organizational Behavior, 27,* 1149–1154.

Peterson, C., Park, N., Pole, N., D'Andrea, W. & Seligman, M. E. P. (2008). Strengths of character and posttraumatic growth. *Journal of Traumatic Stress, 21,* 214–217.

Peterson, C., Park, N., & Seligman, M. E. P. (2006). Greater strengths of character and recovery from illness. *Journal of Positive Psychology, 1,* 17–26.

Peterson, C., Ruch, W., Beermann, U., Park, N., & Seligman, M. E. P. (2007). Strengths of character, orientations to happiness, and life satisfaction. *Journal of Positive Psychology, 2,* 149–156.

Peterson, C., & Seligman, M. E. P. (2004). *Character strengths and virtues: A handbook of classification.* Washington, DC: American Psychological Association; New York: Oxford University Press.

Roberts, B. W. (2006). Personality development and organizational behavior. In B. M. Staw (Ed.), *Research on organizational behavior* (pp. 1–41). Elsevier Science/JAI Press.

Roberts, B. W., & DelVecchio, W. F. (2000). The rank-order consistency of personality from childhood to old age: A quantitative review of longitudinal studies. *Psychological Bulletin, 126,* 3–25.

Roberts, B. W., Kuncel, N. R., Shiner, R., Caspi, A., & Goldberg, L. R. (2007). The power of personality: The comparative validity of personality traits, socioeconomic status, and cognitive ability for predicting important life outcomes. *Perspectives in Psychological Science, 2,* 313–345.

Roberts, B. W., Walton, K. E., & Viechtbauer, W. (2006). Patterns of mean-level change in personality traits across the life course: A meta-analysis of longitudinal studies. *Psychological Bulletin, 132,* 1–25.

Robins, R. W., Caspi, A., & Moffitt, T. E. (2000). Two personalities, one relationship: Both partners' personality traits shape the quality of their relationship. *Journal of Personality and Social Psychology, 79,* 251–259.

Robins, R. W., Caspi, A., & Moffitt, T. E. (2002). It's not just who you're with but who you are: Personality and relationship experiences across multiple relationships. *Journal of Personality, 70,* 925–960.

Robins, R. W., Tracy, J. L., Trzesniewski, K. H., Potter, J., & Gosling, S. D. (2001). Personality correlates of self-esteem. *Journal of Research in Personality, 35,* 463–482.

Rorty, A. (1980). *Essays on Aristotle's ethics.* Berkeley, CA: University of California Press.

Ryff, C. D. (2003). Corners of myopia in the positive psychology parade. *Psychological Inquiry, 14,* 153–159.

Saucier, G. (2009). What are the most important dimensions of personality? Evidence from studies of descriptors in diverse languages. *Social and Personality Psychology Compass 3/4,* 620–637.

Saucier, G., & Ostendorf, F. (1999). Hierarchical subcomponents of the Big Five personality factors: A cross-language replication. *Journal of Personality and Social Psychology, 76,* 613–627.

Schmitt, D. P., Allik, J., McCrae, R. R., & Benet-Martínez, V. (2007). The geographic distribution of Big Five personality traits: Patterns and profiles of human self-description across 56 nations. *Journal of Cross-Cultural Psychology, 38,* 173–212.

Schnitker, S. A., & Emmons, R. A. (2007). Patience as a virtue: Religious and psychological perspectives. *Research in the Social Scientific Study of Religion, 18,* 177–207.

Schwartz, B., Ward, A., Monterosso, J., Lyubomirsky, S., White, K., & Lehman, D. R. (2002). Maximizing versus satisficing: Happiness is a matter of choice. *Journal of Personality and Social Psychology, 83,* 1178–1197.

Seligman, M. E. P., & Csikszentmihalyi, M. (2000). Positive psychology [Special issue]. *American Psychologist, 55,* 5–14.

Seligman, M. E. P., Steen, T., Park, N., & Peterson, C. (2005). Positive psychology progress: Empirical validation of interventions. *American Psychologist, 60,* 410–421.

Shimai, S., Otake, K., Park, N., Peterson, C., & Seligman, M. E. P. (2006). Convergence of character strengths in American and Japanese young adults. *Journal of Happiness Studies, 7,* 311–322.

Steger, M. F., Hicks, B. M., Kashdan, T. B., Krueger, R. F., & Bouchard, T. J., Jr. (2007). Genetic and environmental influences on the positive traits of the Values in Action classification, and biometric covariance with normal personality. *Journal of Research in Personality, 41,* 524–539.

Taylor, E. (2001). Positive psychology and humanistic psychology: A reply to Seligman. *Journal of Humanistic Psychology, 41,* 13–29.

Tellegen, A. (1982). *Brief manual of the Multidimensional Personality Questionnaire.* Unpublished manuscript. Minneapolis: University of Minnesota.

Vazire, S. (2010). Who knows what about a person? The self–other knowledge asymmetry (SOKA) model. *Journal of Personality and Social Psychology, 98,* 281–300.

Watson, D., Hubbard, B., & Wiese, D. (2000). General traits of personality and affectivity as predictors of satisfaction in intimate relationships: Evidence from self- and partner-ratings. *Journal of Personality, 68,* 413–449.

Watson, D., Klohnen, E. C., Casillas, A., Simms, E. N., Haig, J., & Berry, D. S. (2004). Match makers and deal breakers: Analyses of assortative mating in newlywed couples. *Journal of Personality, 72,* 1029–1068.

Wiggins, J. S. (2003). *Paradigms of personality assessment.* New York: Guilford.

Zener, K. (1945). A note concerning editorial reorientation. *Journal of Personality, 14,* 1–2.

Zimbardo, P.G., & Boyd, N.J. (1999). Putting time in perspective: A valid, reliable individual-differences metric. *Journal of Personality and Social Psychology, 77,* 1271–1288.

# 15

# Personality Science and the Northern Tilt: As Positive as Possible Under the Circumstances

*Brian R. Little*

## Introduction: Positive Psychology and Personality Science

Positive psychology and personality science emerged virtually simultaneously as the new millennium appeared on our horizon. The aspirations and research agendas of these two intellectual movements overlap, yet their core tasks differ.[1] The central concern of positive psychology is to *reorient* psychology to positive features of human conduct that have been understudied in conventional psychology, such as hope, happiness, exceptional accomplishment, virtuous action, and human flourishing (Sheldon, Frederickson, Rathunde, Csikszentmihalyi, & Haidt, 2000.) In exploring these topics, positive psychology is concerned with aspects of human thought, feeling, and action that are, in Peterson's (2006) terms, "north of neutral." Personality science, the hub of which is an invigorated and expanded personality psychology, aims to explore and *integrate* the full range of diverse influences on personality, drawing on disciplines ranging from molecular genetics to narrative theory (Cervone & Mischel, 2002a; Little, 2005, 2006). Its explorations extend both north and south of neutral.

I suggest that the geographic center of personality science is essentially equatorial.

My goal for this chapter is to reflect on how these two movements have co-evolved and how they may continue to do so. The key substantive question I explore is this: to what extent and in what ways are positive emotions, orientations, and actions critical for human well-being? Drawing on research in personality science, I will make the case that for some individuals, under certain circumstances, adopting what I will call a *northern tilt* will be highly adaptive. Under other circumstances, however, an upward-bound approach to life might be less adaptive. At its worst, unmitigated positivity might catch us unawares and bring us to our knees.

I begin by taking stock of some shared themes in positive psychology and the study of personality. I start with the most important common concern—the conceptual and empirical analysis of human well-being and the diverse forms it may take. I then discuss three major sources of influence on human well-being: stable features of persons such as traits and basic orientations, volitional action such as personal projects, and influences within the social ecology where traits are expressed and projects are pursued. After taking stock, I will then propose three areas for future exploration that blend the aspirations of both of these vital fields of inquiry.

## Taking Stock: Four Conjoint Themes in Personality Science and Positive Psychology

### Human Well-Being: The Complexity and Contestability of the Good

Concern with human happiness, well-being, and flourishing is a constitutive and defining feature of positive psychology. In formulating theories of the life well led, positive psychology has drawn from a diversity of fields within and outside of psychology.[2] Personality psychology has been one of the most stimulating of these sources. A frequently invoked link has been with theories of personality arising out of humanistic psychology, which reached its zenith in the middle of the 20th century. However, many positive psychologists have been wary of identifying too strongly with this tradition because of the perceived antimeasurement bias in much of humanistic psychology (Little, 1972a, Peterson, 2006).

If the rhetorical passion of positive psychology emanated from 1950s humanistic psychology, its rigorous empirical groundwork originated elsewhere. During the 1970s and '80s, a group of largely independent research programs emerged in personality, social, and individual differences psychology that were explicitly concerned with positive features of human functioning. It is notable that some of these research programs arose concomitantly with the person-situation debate in personality psychology and in certain respects were the beneficiaries of the challenges and changes incurred during that fractious period. The resolution of the person-situation debate was found in perspectives positing the joint impact of person and situational factors on human action. Although sharing common assumptions, they adopted diverse names such as person-environment psychology, transactional and social ecological perspectives in personality (Little, 1987b). These research programs brought to the fore diverse measures of human functioning, many of which would become incorporated into positive psychology, including subjective well-being and life satisfaction (Diener, 1984), individual and institutional factors influencing physical and emotional health (Moos & Insel, 1974), and

specialized orientations, competencies, and intelligences (Cantor & Kihlstrom, 1987; Gardner, 1983; Little, 1976). In short, rigorous analyses of the causes and complexities of positive human functioning were well underway three decades before the official launch of positive psychology, and perspectives that would stimulate the rise of personality science were prominent among them.

Despite the theoretical elegance of a unified concept of flourishing, and despite a generally positive manifold of correlations between diverse measures of positive functioning, several research programs advanced the proposition that the good life is a complex and multifaceted phenomenon. Evidence began to accrue that hedonistic well-being may be independent of eudaimonic well-being, or more simply, that being happy may be independent of having a sense of meaning in one's life (McGregor & Little, 1998; Ryan & Deci, 2000; Ryff, 1989; Waterman, 1993).[3] Also, if one examines human flourishing as exemplified in high-level achievement such as notable creativity, there has been substantial evidence that such achievement might be accompanied by the frequent experience of both positive *and* negative affect (see MacKinnon, 1962; Sheldon, 1995). Indeed, since antiquity and in particular historic periods, such as the 19th-century romantic literary tradition, it was widely speculated that joyful happiness is conceivable only against a backdrop of melancholy (Wilson, 2008).

Positive psychology has stimulated consideration of the complexities that arise when we try to specify the nature of the life well lived. By inviting to the table philosophers, both ancient and modern, who have reflected deeply on such issues, positive psychologists enliven discussion about foundational concerns such as the *contestability* of the good. For example, the audacious pursuit of core projects may simultaneously enhance the well-being of the project pursuer, create problems for a partner, and yet redound to the benefit of the larger community: Gauguin's journey to artistic fulfillment was achieved at a cost to his family and a gain to Western culture. Similarly, the initial positive effects of optimism may be based on a misreading of one's circumstances and the ensuing action becomes unsustainable. In short, sometimes the well-being of individuals might be achieved at the cost of their social ecology. Focusing attention on human well-being in its diverse forms is at the very core of positive psychology. By drawing on and pulling together insights gleaned from diverse intellectual traditions, including that of personality psychology, positive psychology exposes human well-being to be complex, contestable, and, as a capstone of an emerging discipline, of compelling interest.

## Positive Dispositions: Northern Tilt as Natural Inclination

The search for relatively stable factors that predispose individuals to experience happiness and engage in a rich and satisfying life is a robust and growing area of research. Is there a set of dispositions that would naturally tilt in the northerly direction? I will consider two different categories of dispositions: traits and basic orientations. The former is a dominant focus of contemporary research in both personality and positive psychology; the latter has been all but ignored.[4]

### Traits and Well-Being: Beyond Stable Extraversion

After a period of turbulence during the great trait debate, the study of stable dispositions has gone through a period of steady, sustained growth. There is a broad consensus that human personality comprises five major factors: Openness to Experience, Conscientiousness, Extraversion, Agreeableness, and Neuroticism.[5]

One of the most reliable and robust findings regarding traits and well-being is that two of the Big Five dimensions of personality are very strongly linked to measures of well-being—Extraversion (positively) and Neuroticism (negatively) (Costa & McCrae, 1980). Indeed, the formulaic title, "Happiness is a thing called stable extraversion" (Francis, 1998) does not seem particularly contentious. Extraversion is associated with states of positive affect and longer-term happiness in part because of the sensitivity of extraverts to reward cues in the environment. Extraverts have low thresholds for the detection of such cues and are particularly likely to find positive stimulation in social encounters (Argyle & Lu, 1990; Lucas, Le, & Dyrenforth, 2008). Neurotic individuals are highly sensitive to punishment cues, in contrast with stable individuals who are less sensitive to such cues (Gray, 1982). Consequently, stable extraverts have a decidedly northern tilt to their perceptions of the environment, which in turn promotes their active engagement with a world of positive opportunities. Neurotic introverts,

in contrast, are more likely to have a southern discomfort to their world views, which in turn promotes disengagement from a world of threat and potential danger.

If we move beyond happiness and examine the exercise of competencies and talents as aspects of human flourishing, traits beyond Extraversion and Neuroticism play a key role. For example, Conscientiousness and Openness to Experience are predictors of conventional and creative achievements, respectively (e.g., Chamorro-Premuzic, 2006). Once again, however, there are subtleties in terms of the specific domains in which stable traits predict success. In meta-analytic studies, Conscientiousness is consistently found to be a robust predictor of occupational success (e.g., Barrick & Mount, 1991), but there are some occupational exceptions. Hogan and Hogan (1993) demonstrated this in a group of Tulsa jazz musicians, among whom the least conscientious were the most effective. Why do conscientious jazz musicians strike a discordant note among their peers? Possibly they may adopt a highly focused style that actually inhibits the detection of pitch changes or tempo shifts spontaneously initiated by others during a jam session. Contemporary work organizations, in many respects, seem to be more like jam sessions than the classical hierarchies that conventional organization charts imply. So, even though stable traits may well predict positive outcomes in achievement and other domains, our joint research enterprise requires constant checking on and updating of the nature of the job, task, or project requirements that define such success. Yesterday's northward tilting traits might tomorrow point due south.

Are the Big Five dispositions "natural" in the sense that there is a biological substratum, of genetic origin, underlying them? The evidence suggests an affirmative answer: Each of the major dimensions of personality has a moderately high level of heritability (e.g., Jang, Livesley, & Vernon, 1996). There is also evidence that happiness, itself, has a high degree of heritability (Lykken & Tellegen, 1996). This evidence led the authors to suggest that happiness is essentially luck in the genetic lottery and wanting to be happy for an adult was as futile as wanting to be taller, a claim that Lykken (2000) subsequently reconsidered and disavowed. Recent developments in trait theory are consistent with the postulate that there may be a biological base to positive traits. DeYoung, Peterson, and Higgins (2002) propose that the Big Five dimensions of personality can be subsumed by two higher-order factors of *plasticity*, subsuming Extraversion and Openness, and *stability*, subsuming Agreeableness, Conscientiousness, and (negatively) Neuroticism. They postulate that plasticity is related to chronic levels of dopaminergic activity and that stability is related to chronic levels of serotonergic activity. The joint capacity to maintain order while being open to change in the environment is particularly likely to be adaptive.

One of the most interesting intersections of personality science and positive psychology has been explorations on whether we can change levels of happiness by having individuals simulate one of the Big Five traits associated with happiness, such as Extraversion. Fleeson and his colleagues (Fleeson, Malanos, & Achille, 2002) found that introverts who acted in an extraverted fashion in a laboratory situation reported high levels of positive affect during those enactments. The boundary conditions on this intriguing finding remain to be discovered. Are such shifts in positive affect temporary, or might there even be "costs" of acting out of character, particularly if such behavior is engaged in over a protracted period of time (Little, 1996, 2000a; Little & Joseph, 2007)?

To summarize: Personality science provides increasing evidence that relatively stable traits of personality may contribute to a northern tilt of positive evaluations about and encounters with the environment. But to which features of the environment are such positive encounters directed? What is the terrain of the northern territories to which we tilt in our transactions with the environment? Traits get us only so far in answering these questions; something more is needed.

## Primary Orientations: Persons, Things, and Self

Positive psychology stimulates new inquiry, but it also invites us to revisit older research topics of potential relevance to human flourishing that appeared promising but that, for whatever reason, didn't flourish. In so doing, we may discover research domains that are worthy of resuscitation. One such broad domain is the study of interests and orientations (e.g., Peterson, 2006, Chapter 8). Like traits, basic orientations are relatively stable features of individuals. Although such positively tilting dispositions would be expected to be natural units of analysis for

personality psychology, their study has been primarily undertaken by vocational and counseling psychologists, and the research has been largely atheoretical. However, one program of research in personality, called specialization theory, had basic orientations as a core theoretical construct (Little, 1972a, 1976). For reasons that, quite naturally, I find difficult to understand, this research initiative was comprehensively ignored. By revisiting it through the lens of positive psychology, I want to make the case for resuscitation.[6]

Specialization theory (Little, 1972a) was proposed as a constructive alternative to Kelly's (1955) personal construct theory and to theories of personality based on humanistic psychology. Both of these theoretical orientations were precursors to positive psychology, although Kelly's theory has received far less attention among positive psychologists than Rogers, Maslow, and other humanistic psychologists. Kelly argued that all people, not just those with Ph.Ds, are essentially scientists—erecting and testing hypotheses about the world and revising them in the light of experience. Kellian theory was remarkably prescient in its systematic treatment of cognitive aspects of human endeavors. Humanistic psychology promoted a similarly uplifting view of personality. Individuals were attuned to values and experiences that challenged the image inherent in psychoanalytic and behavioral theories of the day. Both Kellian and humanistic perspectives were consistent with positive psychology's plea for an "open and appreciative" stance toward those whom they study (Sheldon & King, 2001, p.216). They both captured the propensity of people to tilt northwards.

Specialization theory took a related but somewhat different view. It argued that in their thoughts, feelings, and actions, individuals were *selectively* attuned to their environments: humans were essentially "specialists." Our theoretical job was to explore the nature of such specialized orientations and their implications for human adaptation, particularly for effective engagement in the world and with creativity (Little, 1976).

In retrospect, I think specialization theory was a kind of mitigated positive psychology. It shared with the Kellian and humanist perspectives, and therefore with contemporary positive psychology, a conviction that humans were audacious creatures actively engaged with the world and its objects. But specialization means that some domains will be necessarily ignored. We may be astute Kellian scientists in some areas of our lives and utterly inept and disinterested in others. More subtly, specialization entails errors of omission *and* commission. Specialization may stimulate hyperdevelopment of particular interests. Positive orientation, through positive feedback loops, can drift into dysfunction.[7]

The first theoretical challenge was to inquire into the nature of human environments to which individuals might tilt. Here the work of the analytic philosopher Strawson (1959) in descriptive metaphysics was foundational. Strawson's concern was to determine what he called the "primary particulars" of daily realities, and he posited that persons and material objects met his stringent criteria. Persons and things, in short, were foundational, ontologically primitive elements of human contexts. The notion of primary objects as the foci of differential orientation was compelling and suggested that *psychological* specialization might arise through individuals selectively orienting themselves toward these primary domains. Modes of thinking about more abstract concepts or about blends of persons and things might then be influenced by a person's primary orientation. It was also assumed that some individuals might tilt toward both persons and things, but that remained an open empirical question. These were the theoretical hunches that stimulated the empirical research program on primary orientations.

The research agenda of specialization theory was inspired by personality psychology's integrative challenge. It included the development of assessment tools tapping into the affective, cognitive, and behavioral aspects of differential orientation. The Thing-Person orientation scale (T-P scale) was constructed to examine primary orientation—the affective component of specialization (Little, 1972b). By having separate measures of person orientation and thing orientation, it was possible to test whether there is a general tendency to have positive orientations toward the environment or whether person and thing orientation were, as some vocational theorists had argued, contrary orientations. Neither assumption was supported. Person orientation and thing orientation were shown to be internally consistent and orthogonal dimensions (Little, 1972b).

Research with the T-P scale suggested that primary orientation toward a domain created a "specialization loop" in which affective, cognitive, and behavioral processes became mutually reinforcing (Little, 1976). For example, thing specialists (those scoring high on T and low on P) experienced more positive affect toward a diversity of physical objects; they were more cognitively complex regarding things and engaged in greater frequency of encounters with them. Similarly, person specialists (high on P, low on T) enjoyed being with diverse people, construed them more complexly, and spent more time in interaction with them (Little, 1972b).[8]

The orthogonality of person and thing orientation means that, along with person and thing specialists, we can identify equal numbers of individuals scoring high on both dimensions and those scoring low. The former we called generalists. They were shown to have a broad range of competencies and scored particularly highly on measures of creativity. The latter we called non-specialists and were the least engaged of the four groups. When we studied the way in which the four groups construed their daily environments, specifically a diversity of neighborhoods with which they were familiar, the orientations of all four quadrants became clearer. As expected, person specialists focused on the human elements of their environments (e.g., "lots of kids"); thing specialists focused on the material and technical aspects (e.g., "cobblestone streets"). Generalists noticed emergent features of the milieu (e.g., "exciting atmosphere"). Non-specialists were more likely to construe in terms of the relevance of the particular settings to their own needs (e.g., "close to where I live")— suggesting that they might be more appropriately called *self*-specialists (Little, 1972b).[9]

Are primary orientations, like traits, "natural" features of individuals? Again an affirmative answer seems warranted. There is evidence for moderately high heritability coefficients for vocational interests that are essentially measures of person and thing orientation (Schermer & Vernon, 2008). There are also substantial and consequential sex differences in primary orientations, with women showing considerably higher levels of orientation toward persons (Little, 1972b, Lippa, 1998). Graziano and his colleagues (e.g., Graziano, Habashi, Evangelou, and Ngambeki, 2009) have been exploring the implications of person-thing orientation for attraction to and retention in engineering, physical science, and related fields, where women are seriously underrepresented. Thing orientation, particularly for women, is a very strong predictor of entry into and retention in these fields.

There are several implications of this line of inquiry for positive psychology. First, primary orientations are associated with greater efficacy, enjoyment, and engagement in two fundamental domains relevant to the quality of lives—our commerce with the social world and the world of material objects. Second, the notion of specialization loops provides a perspective on how positive orientations can both advance human effectiveness and compromise it. In terms of adaptive competencies, generalists, those equally engaged with persons and things, seem able to adopt both agentic and communal orientations toward their environmental encounters. Third, specialization theory by exploring human orientation to the non-human environment highlights an area that is radically understudied in psychological research on well-being (Little, 1972a; Searles, 1960).[10] Specialization theory shifts the adaptive landscape considered relevant to personality and well-being to include the physical objects, both natural and constructed, which are too often obscured by the overwhelming presence of other people as the analytic focus of our psychological theories of well-being. When we tilt toward the environment to explore and be audacious, it is a world full of both material objects and social actors. I suggest that, as personality scientists and positive psychologists, our theories are rich in detail about the role of other persons in enhancing the well-being of our respondents. But the material world of mountain landscapes and four-stroke engines also needs our attention. We need to theorize about *things* more clearly.

## The Happiness of Pursuit: Northern Tilt as Personal Action

A major area of common concern to positive psychology and personality science is that of personal action constructs (PAC). PAC units include the study of current concerns, personal strivings, personal projects, and life tasks (Little, 1999a, 1999b). In contrast with broader-based motivational theories, PAC units are middle-level and contextually embedded analytic concepts that provide a fine-grained analysis of the motivational dynamics of daily lives (Little, 1989).

## Emergence of PAC Units: Internal and External Dynamics of Daily Lives

Two influential PAC units emerged independently during the 1970s: current concerns and personal projects. Klinger's (1977) work on current concerns arose out of the fields of motivational and clinical psychology. Current concerns are conceived to be processes stimulated by a person's commitments, and these processes

remained active until the concern is consummated or abandoned. A rich array of internal processes was shown to be influenced by current concerns, including effects upon fantasy and dreaming (Klinger, 1987).

Personal projects arose out of the field of personality and environmental psychology (Little, 1972a, 1976, 1979, 1983) and comprise extended sets of personally salient action in context. Personal projects lie at the intersection of internal, self-regulatory processes and external, social ecological affordances and constraints. The earliest published empirical research with personal projects was explicitly focused on how such pursuits might influence well-being (Palys & Little, 1983). Subsequent research revealed that well-being was enhanced to the extent that people are engaged in personal projects that are meaningful, efficacious, structured, supported by others, and not unduly stressful (Little, 1989). Although arising out of different theoretical lineages, current concerns and personal projects methods have increasingly been integrated, particularly in the domain of motivational counseling (Cox & Klinger, 2004; Little & Chambers, 2004).

During the 1980s, research with PAC units flourished, and this research, conjoined with the study of personal goals, continues to this day.[11] Two particularly generative research programs were those on personal strivings (Emmons, 1986) and life tasks (Cantor, Norem, Niedenthal, Langston, & Brower, 1987). Personal strivings comprise pursuits that reflect what a person is *typically* trying to achieve. Like other PAC units, appraisals of personal strivings display strong and theoretically compelling links with measures of well-being (Emmons, 1986, 1999). For example, conflict between personal strivings has been linked to compromised physical and emotional health (Emmons & King, 1988).

Life tasks comprised socially mandated and age-graded norms about what one was expected to be doing. For example, students in transition through the first year of university could readily categorize their daily pursuits into life task categories such as "do well in my studies," "make new friends," or "get independent of my parents." Successful transitions were associated with the skills and strategies that students used in pursuing their life tasks, and contrasting styles such as "defensive pessimism" and "illusory glow optimism" were identified as alternative routes to successful transitions (Cantor & Norem, 1989).

PAC units can be considered to form a continuum ranging from internally generated sources of action to externally generated sources of action. Current concerns and personal strivings are primarily focused on internal factors. Life tasks, arising as they do out of cultural expectations, are more attuned to the external sources of daily pursuits. Personal projects, as mentioned, have a focus primarily at the interactional cusp of internal and external sources of personal action. Indeed, when we ask individuals to list their everyday personal projects, the lists include pursuits that span the full spectrum from current concerns and strivings through to life tasks and imposed social roles (Little & Gee, 2007).

PAC units and personal goal research have now generated a substantial body of research literature, much of which straddles the boundary between personality science and positive psychology. In the following sections I will focus on personal projects as representative of this research, primarily because the project analytic perspective was developed explicitly as a way of providing both the integration required in personality science and a focus on well-being consistent with the aspirations of positive psychology.

## Personal Project Pursuit and Well-Being: Major Themes

Studies of individuals' appraisals of their personal projects have consistently demonstrated substantial relations with diverse measures of well-being (Little, 1989; Little, Salmela-Aro & Phillips, 2007; Palys & Little, 1983). Although dozens of appraisal dimensions have been studied, depending on the particular group or ecosystem under investigation, contemporary research reveals these to be subsumable under five major factors: project meaning, manageability, support, positive affect, and negative affect. It seems reasonable to postulate that human well-being will be positively related to pursuing personal projects that are appraised as meaningful, manageable, supported, and as generating greater positive than negative affect.[12] As we shall see, as reasonable as such a postulate might appear, the cumulative data suggest that the links between project pursuit and well-being are more subtle, but no less interesting. I will briefly and selectively discuss each of these factors, noting some of the major findings as well as some of the complexities that arise when we explore how project pursuit influences the quality of lives.

## Meaning: A Predictive Paradox of Meaningful Project Pursuit?

Of considerable relevance to the theme of the current volume is that there is a definite northern tilt to people's appraisals of their personal projects. If we regard meaningful pursuit to subsume both the hedonic and more value-laden aspects of daily activity, there is clear evidence for the prevalence of meaningful projects in our daily lives. Relative to the midpoints of scales (from 0 to 10) individuals rate their projects to be consistent with their core values (M = 7.67), important (M = 7.54), self-expressive (M = 6.81), absorbing (M = 6.16.), and enjoyable (M = 6.07). When we examine only dimensions that tap into the affect experienced during pursuit of a project, the northerly tilt is even more apparent, with ratings on positive affect dimensions being considerably higher than ratings on negative affect dimensions (for example, experiencing feelings of happiness (M = 5.90) versus sadness (M = 2.12).

When we examine the types of projects individuals are pursuing, several categories are particularly likely to bring pleasure to individuals. Both interpersonal and recreational pursuits are especially likely to be appraised positively, suggesting that leisure and love contribute importantly to individuals' well-being. Academic work for students and occupational projects for working individuals are consistently rated as less enjoyable and more onerous.

One particularly interesting category of personal project is that of intrapersonal projects, which are essentially self-focused. These include pursuits such as "try to be more outgoing" or "be less hard on myself." Such projects have been reliably associated with the experience of depressive affect (Salmela-Aro, 1992). However, they also have interesting links with creativity (Little, 1989). Creative individuals appraise their intrapersonal projects as highly self-expressive, whereas depressed individuals do not. It is of both theoretical and practical significance to ask what might tip an intrapersonal project in the direction of being a creative pursuit rather than one that cascades down into depression. One potential answer, consistent with self-determination theory (e.g., Ryan & Deci, 2000), relates to the origin of the intrapersonal project. If the project has been extrinsically imposed upon an individual ("you had better try to be more outgoing if you're going to keep your job") rather than intrinsically generated ("I might actually enjoy being a bit more outgoing"), it is likely that the affect experienced will be more negative. Such projects have an additional significance: they induce individuals to act in ways that run counter to their current dispositions. As mentioned above, in the context of relatively stable dispositions, free traits may be engaged to advance other projects. From a personality science perspective, this means that there may be a disjunction between genotypic and phenotypic aspects of trait-like behavior. From a positive psychology perspective, this means that individuals may be promoting well-being by advancing core projects, but simultaneously compromising it by acting in ways that might extract a physiological cost (Little, 2008).

If people generally have high levels of meaningful projects, and if certain categories of project reliably differ in their meaning, it seems reasonable to predict that individuals engaged in projects relatively high in meaning will experience a higher quality of life. However, if we look at the strength of relation between project meaning dimensions and indices of well-being, a predictive paradox occurs: Of the five major project factors, meaning has the lowest degree of linkage with measures of well-being. Indeed, in meta-analytic studies, only project enjoyment, among the meaning dimensions, is reliably and significantly associated with measures of life satisfaction (Wilson, 1990). I first noted and explored this paradox in a volume dedicated to the "human quest for meaning" (Wong & Fry, 1998), where I had originally intended to summarize the importance of project meaning in predicting outcome measures of well-being. The lack of strong relations between project meaning and well-being seemed rather ironic.

But the paradox turned out to be only an apparent one. Two sets of studies helped clarify a rather more subtle role of meaning in project pursuit that emerged only when more sophisticated research designs were employed (Little, 1998). One problem with studies that suggested well-being was unrelated to project meaning was that the outcome measures were heavily weighted toward the more hedonic aspects of well-being. However, when measures that tapped into life purposes and a sense of coherence were used, the more value-laden dimensions of project meaning were indeed related to these measures and were unrelated to the more hedonic outcome measures (McGregor & Little, 1998). Another set of findings, to be discussed below, raised the pivotal issue of the joint importance of meaning and manageability in goal pursuit for the promotion of well-being (Sheldon & Kasser, 1998).

## Manageability: Initiation, Efficacy, and Control

We may be pursuing deeply meaningful personal projects, but they may be so chaotically organized that they detract from, rather than enhance, our sense of well-being. The Manageability factor in PPA includes dimensions such as initiation, efficacy, and control. As with the meaning dimensions, there is a northerly tilt to the Manageability dimensions with mean scores (from 0–10) well beyond the scale midpoint (initiation M = 7.11, efficacy (M = 7.18, control M = 7.29). Moreover, meta-analytic studies have shown that factors related to manageability, such as efficacy and control in project pursuit, have consistently been the strongest positive predictors of a diversity of well-being measures, stronger even than dimensions of enjoyment or those more focused on meaning (Wilson, 1990).

The appraisal dimension of initiation asks respondents to rate the extent to which the original impetus for each project lies primarily with them (high scores) or with external sources. As noted above, mean scores on this were definitely tilted in the direction of self-generated projects. However, in a study of mainland Chinese students it was found that initiation scores were considerably lower and significantly different from a comparable group of Canadian students. It turned out that the reason for this was that the cadre or group to which an individual belonged was more likely to generate everyday projects, a state of affairs consistent with the communitarian, indeed, communistic society within which these individuals lived out their days. Interestingly, the Chinese group's projects were also rated as more enjoyable than those of Canadian students (Little, Xiao, & Watkinson, 1985). We regard project initiation as a key aspect of managing one's projects, on the assumption that we are more likely to have ascertained the viability of a self-initiated project than one thrust upon us. But the concept of initiation is theoretically similar to the notion of intrinsically (versus externally) regulated behavior in self-determination theory (Deci & Ryan, 1985; Ryan & Deci, 2000), which is arguably more related to the meaning factor. It can be suggested that, at least in Western culture, to initiate one's projects is likely to enhance both their meaning and their manageability.

Efficacy is assessed by asking respondents to rate the degree of progress on their personal projects as well as their likelihood of success. Project efficacy is very strongly linked to measures of life satisfaction across a broad array of samples and ages. In meta-analyses, among the projects dimensions it has consistently been the single best positive predictor of life satisfaction (Wilson, 1990). However, Sheldon & Kasser (1998) demonstrated that mere efficacy, at least in terms of progress made in pursuing personal goals, is insufficient for predicting well-being. Only efficacy as experienced in self-determined goal pursuits had an impact on well-being. Because most of the projects generated in personal projects methodology are highly meaningful and primarily self-initiated, our finding that efficacy is a very strong predictor of well-being is consistent with Sheldon and Kasser's findings. However, their results serve as a warning that the efficacious completion of truly trivial pursuits is not going to yield a dividend in human happiness and quality of life.

Control is a ubiquitous concept in research in personality and positive psychology. Since its inception, PPA has included a measure of the extent to which individuals feel they are in control of their projects. Generally, the degree of perceived control is significantly correlated with measures of well-being. Once again, however, there are important issues that need to be taken into account before postulating that perceived control is an unmitigated positive factor in enhancing well-being. A central tenet of our social ecological perspective is that a sense of control is adaptive to the extent that it is based on an "accurate reading of ecosystem constraints and resources" (Little, 1979, p.12). In some projects, particularly those involving work settings, both actual and perceived control may be comparatively low. Acting upon expectations of high levels of control in such projects may not be adaptive (Little, 1987b).

### Support: With a Little Help (and Hindrance) from Our Friends

One's personal projects may be both meaningful and manageable, but other people may accord them little significance, may provide no help in bringing them to fruition, or may even actively conspire to thwart them. Our earliest research attempted to tap into this aspect of project pursuit by the use of two dimensions—project visibility and the respondent's perception of the importance

other people attached to the project. These dimensions are consistently highly correlated and defined what we called the "community" factor— the extent to which a project was embedded in and valued by others in the surrounding social ecology. In more recent studies we have added another dimension, project support, that loads on the same factor and which we have now taken as the name for that factor. We expected that Support would be a key predictor of well-being and related measures. However, unlike some of the Manageability dimensions, visibility and perceived importance by others had only marginal direct relationships with measures of well-being. Even in studies that developed more differentiated measures of support, including measures of both support and hindrance, the impact of such measures were statistically swamped by the dominating effects of the other major factors, particularly the dimensions of efficacy and stress (James, 2001; Ruehlman & Wolchik, 1988).

Should we simply conclude, then, that well-being is unrelated to the level of support we receive in the projects we pursue? Not quite. Although support may be relatively unimportant for many everyday projects, we have evidence that in *core* projects, those that are particularly central and important to a person's life, support is not just a significant factor, but it may also be a particularly important one. McKeen (1984) examined the factors that predicted both subjective and "hard" indicators of successful pregnancy. Spousal support was a key factor in such success. Dowden (2004) explored the personal projects of entrepreneurs, also using subjective and hard indicators, such as annual revenue, as outcome measures. Once again, support of partners was a highly significant predictor of success. These studies suggest that some of the factors that play only a marginal role in daily projects display themselves, in different circumstances, to be important sources enhancing the quality of lives. When we find ourselves pregnant or delivering an entrepreneurial project that is very much "our baby," the positive role of perceived support is vital.

### Positive Affect and Negative Affect in Project Pursuit

Just as affective processes have become a central focus of positive psychology, they also rose in prominence in personality research and now are among the most prolific areas of research in both fields. Once again the modular nature of project analytic methods enables us to address theoretical developments in the field by creating dimensions that expanded and refined the study of affect and emotion as they played out in the project pursuits of daily lives. It will be recalled that in earlier studies with personal projects, only two dimensions could be regarded as heavily affective in nature—enjoyment and stress—the rest being "cooler" cognitive appraisal dimensions. Enjoyment typically loaded on the Meaning factor while the Stress dimension, together with Difficulty and Challenge, reliably and robustly formed a separate factor also labeled Stress. However, when we began to explore an expanded set of affective dimensions, the original five factors of PPA, not surprisingly, changed, and in ways that made theoretical sense.

Little, Pedrosa-Lima, & Whelan (2006) explored the relation between "hot" affective dimensions and the "cooler" cognitive appraisal dimensions. Although some dimensions, such as challenge, can be seen as a blend (indeed this is the only project dimension to have double loadings on meaning and stress), most dimensions can be differentiated in terms of whether or not they are affectively charged. We used a set of dimensions that had emerged in response to open-ended accounts of feelings experienced during project pursuit (Goodine, 2000). The positive dimensions included feelings of love, happiness, and hopefulness; the negative dimensions included feelings of sadness, fear, anger, stress, and depression. We also included ambivalence, which we felt, somewhat ambivalently, could be appraised as either a positive or negative emotion, or both. In order to get rough numerical equivalence between cognitive appraisals and affective ones, we explored the relations between representative dimensions of the cognitive factors of the original five-factor model and an expanded set of affective dimensions.

Two key issues were explored. First, is there evidence that the "hot" affective dimensions are independent of the "cooler" cognitive appraisal dimensions? Second, if affective dimensions emerge as independent, do they form one bipolar or two orthogonal factors? To broaden the generalizability of the study, we examined groups in Canada and Portugal. The results were clear and held across both countries. The affective dimensions were, indeed, independent of the cognitive dimensions, and they formed two coherent, unambiguous factors of positive and negative affect. All three positive affect appraisal dimensions appeared on a single factor, with "feelings

of love" having the highest loading. All five negative affect dimensions appeared on a single factor, with "depression" having the highest loading. Interestingly, ambivalence clearly loaded on the negative affect factor, with no cross-loadings (cf. Emmons & King, 1988). Even though the structure of affective appraisals was virtually identical in Canadian and Portuguese samples, there were strong mean differences in the affect experienced in daily project pursuit. The Portuguese sample displayed considerably more affective involvement in their projects, including significantly higher ratings on the dimensions of depression and ambivalence but also on happiness and hopefulness. An exceptional difference was found on the dimension of "feelings of love" experienced in project pursuit (Portuguese M = 6.89; Canadian M = 3.69).

The study of affect in project pursuit feeds into the research agendas of both personality science and positive psychology. It also raises an important question about the types of research design that will best advance our knowledge of the interplay of affect and action and their impact on human well-being. PPA dimensions have most frequently been used as predictor variables for diverse measures of well-being. However, they have also been employed as outcome measures themselves—as ways of accessing the thick textures of meaningful lives (Little, 2007; McGregor, 2007; Omodei & Wearing, 1990). The modular nature of PPA and related methodologies allows us to test differential hypotheses about the happiness of pursuit. These can be explored at the level of the individual, while also allowing us to lift data up to a normative level for use in more conventional designs. The implications for applied positive psychology are noteworthy. Instead of examining only *inter*-individual differences with normative scales such as locus of control, stress, and positive emotion, personal projects and related methodologies allow us to explore *intra*-individual relations between the same variables as assessed *within* the action systems of singular individuals. A strong case can be made for the primacy of such intra-individual measurement in personality science (Cervone & Mischel, 2002b); Little, 2005, 2006).

## The Social Ecology of Project Pursuit: Connections and Affordances

Individuals are embedded in a social ecology that can stimulate, shape, and sustain the personal projects they pursue. Positive psychology's concern with "enabling institutions" (e.g., Peterson, 2006) acknowledges this contextual influence on human pursuits and on a life well lived. Within personality science, social ecological frameworks have long been concerned with how the outer realities of social, physical, and institutional influences co-constitute, with inner dispositions, the shape of a human life (Little, 1979, 2007; Little & Ryan, 1979).

## Social Influences and the Project Community: From Support to Connecting

Earlier we discussed the key role of other people's support of our projects in enhancing the quality of lives. However, well-being is enhanced not only by the support we get in our own project pursuits but also by the positive impact we have on others. We can conceive of the project community as a set of social influences ranging from our intimate romantic relationships to the more impersonal exchanges we have with others in our daily pursuits. Several research findings converge on the proposition that having a positive impact on others has a salutary effect on the project pursuer. When we explored the categories of project pursuit that were most meaningful to teenagers, the highest appraisals were in categories such as team sports, intimate relations with others, and, highest of all, community volunteering (Little, 1987a). What seems to be common to these is not just feeling supported in one's own pursuits but a sense of *connection* with others in theirs. Studies of intimate relationships and relational satisfaction provide further evidence of the vital role of connection in project pursuit (Frost, 2009; Hwang, 2004). Hwang (2004) studied relationship satisfaction among a group of romantically involved couples and found that the number of joint projects they were pursuing as a couple was a key predictor of satisfaction with that relationship. It is likely that there are sex differences in the linkage between the sense of connection in project pursuit and well-being. For example, in studies of the factors in the work environment that were most important to men and women in senior positions in governmental agencies and private-sector companies, the sense of community and connectedness associated with one's personal projects was particularly important for women. For men, a sense of connectedness did not predict job satisfaction or well-being. In fact, other people seemed to frustrate rather than

facilitate their project pursuit. For senior male executives, connection was far less important than having other people simply get out of the way while the executives could pursue their projects unimpeded (Phillips, Little, & Goodine, 1997).

## Physical Influences and Affordance: Persons, Projects, and Places

As a construct designed to integrate the domains of personality and environmental psychology, personal projects are particularly suited to explore the physical circumstances of our daily pursuits and the places within which they are enacted (Little, 1979, 1983; Wallenius, 1999, 2004). The extent to which a particular environment provides affordances for, rather than barriers to, project pursuit is critical in promoting well-being (Heft, 1997; Little, 1987b). Wallenius (1999) has shown that the perceived supportiveness of the physical environment is related to both physical and emotional well-being. She has also shown that noise stress in daily environments interacts with project stress to predict physical health status independent of trait neuroticism (Wallenius, 2004).

Places may be examined not only in terms of their physical affordances but also in terms of the modal personality characteristics of their residents (Florida, 2008; Rentfrow, Gosling & Potter, 2008). These researchers have literally mapped the Big Five traits for different states in the U.S., and the results provide some intriguing hints about the best degree of fit between persons and places. For example, North Dakota has the highest state scores on both Extraversion and Agreeableness, but a very low aggregate score on Openness to Experience (Rentfrow, Gosling, & Potter, 2008). It is an interesting and open question whether or not there may be a Fargo factor that inclines happy agreeable people to flourish in North Dakota (particularly if they are closed minded). And it is also an interesting and open question as to whether state level measures of flourishing, such as productivity and creativity, may be related to diversity rather than homogeneity of personalities. In terms of mediating influences that might attract and sustain migration to different places, it could be suggested that the kind of projects that places inspire and support, be they conventional, communal, or creative, might be pivotal. The study of the interplay between persons, projects, and places promises to be a rich vein for exploration.

## Macro-level Influences: Don't Even Think About It

Organizational, institutional, and other macro-level factors can play both subtle and powerful roles in determining the kinds of projects individuals feel free to pursue and the likelihood that such pursuits will be sustainable. Explicit roles and rules and implicit norms of conduct may lead individuals to forego engaging in some projects that could advance their well-being. Once again we find sex or gender differences playing an important role. For example, in studies of the impact of office culture on personal project pursuit in senior managers, we found that there were extremely strong differences between men and women in terms of the degree of perceived linkage between features of the environment and appraisals of personal projects (Phillips, Little, & Goodine, 1997). Woman were far more likely to see strong linkages than were men and were more sensitively attuned to features of the everyday work environment that prescribed or proscribed what could and what could not be undertaken. The organizational climate may, intentionally or not, promote project affordances for some and send out "don't even think about it" message to others.

The same forces can be discerned at the level of political culture. Frost (2009) carried out an exemplary study of the impact of macro-level factors on *intimacy* projects, those characterized by sexual and romantic concerns. Frost was particularly interested in intimacy projects as pursued by lesbian, gay, and bisexual (LGB) individuals. Using a Web-based research strategy, he was able to sample widely from diverse geographical locations and political jurisdictions. These places varied in the degree to which there are explicit barriers against same sex marriage and, more subtly, in the norms guiding the expression of intimacy in daily activities. From a positive psychology perspective, his findings are instructive. First, intimacy projects were fully as meaningful to LGB couples as to heterosexual couples, a finding Frost attributes to the expression of a fundamental human need for intimacy regardless of sexual orientation (Baumeister & Leary, 1995; Deci & Ryan, 2008; Ryan, Huta, & Deci, 2008). However, LGB individuals, in pursuing their intimacy projects, experienced greater barriers than heterosexuals. These stigma-related processes arose from both interpersonal and macro-level sources. Of particular note was the fact that the macro-level influences were specific to the intimacy domain. Personal projects related to job and career showed no differences between the LGB and heterosexual groups. In short, the likelihood of successfully pursuing projects that may enhance well-being can be compromised by the social ecology within which the incipient projects are embedded. Current research shows these forces to be both strong and subtle. Whether a core project is successfully pursued depends on who is engaging in what specific project in which locations and, as Frost's research underscores, with whom.

## Moving Forward: Advancing Personality Science and Positive Psychology

Each of the four themes that bridge personality science and positive psychology is rich in possibility for theoretical, methodological, and empirical development. I will propose a research agenda for each of these and then examine some overarching issues whose exploration would advance both fields.

## The Varieties of Well-Being: Goodness and the Happiness of Pursuit

As a foundational concept in positive psychology and a major research focus in personality science, the question of the nature of human well-being is vital to the research agendas of both fields. Recently, there has been a spirited debate about whether eudaimonic and hedonic happiness are qualitatively distinct or are better seen as interlinked phenomena (Kashdan, Biswas-Diener, & King, 2008; Ryan & Huta, 2009). The debate turns, in part, on discerning whether virtue and enjoyment are independent, antagonistic, or mutually facilitative phenomena. The empirical examination of this issue typically involves examining correlations between measures of value or purpose in life (eudaimonic happiness) and measures tapping into enjoyment and pleasure (hedonic happiness). The assessment devices are most often normative scales that measure differences in orientation *between* individuals. I want to endorse a different approach and propose its further development as a way of adjudicating the relative merits of plausible conceptual alternatives about the varieties of well-being.

As will be anticipated from the earlier sections of this chapter, the approach I advocate is to examine how eudaimonic and hedonic themes play out in the personal projects that individuals are pursuing. This can be done by getting individuals to appraise their projects on dimensions relevant to the theoretical debate. In fact, we have been gathering relevant data on this issue for many years, but it is only in the light of the current theoretical controversy in positive psychology that the relevance of these data became clear.

Consider, for example, the dimensions of enjoyment, value congruency, and self-identity in personal projects analysis (Little & Gee, 2007). Enjoyment is a clear hedonic appraisal dimension. Value congruency, the extent to which individuals believe the project is consistent with their core values, is clearly more eudaimonic, as is self-identity, the extent to which the project is self-expressive. What is the relation between these dimensions? During the early years of our research, we consistently found that these three dimensions loaded on a single factor we called project meaning, a finding consistent with those who see the pursuit of the good and the enjoyable as compatible. However, the methodology is modular and flexible, so that as new theoretical constructs emerge in various research literatures they can be incorporated into the assessment matrix. When we began to add affective dimensions such as fun and feelings of love, the factor structure changed and enjoyment joined the positive affect dimensions on a separate factor from the more eudaimonic dimensions. It should be noted that these factor analytic studies were carried out by averaging an individual's appraisals across all his or her projects and then carrying out essentially a normative analysis between individuals. However, PPA and related methodologies allow us to examine within the single case. Adopting this option, researchers may find individuals for whom hedonic and eudaimonic pursuits are highly related and others for whom they are independent or even negatively correlated. By inductively aggregating individuals into groups based on the similarity of their idiographic profile, we can then discern different varieties of well-being and their causes, correlates, and consequences.

## Traits and Orientations: Freeing Traits, Expanding Orientations

The study of traits will continue to be a major research area in personality science, particularly in the areas of neurophysiology and molecular genetics, and that research will inform positive psychologists about the relatively stable "fixed" traits that are conducive to living well. However, more fluid aspects of dispositions should be of particular interest to positive psychology. For example, free traits (Little, 2000a) are patterns of phenotypic behavior that simulate genotypic traits but are enacted in the service of core projects or compelling roles. A biogenically introverted mother acts as an extravert at her daughter's party, or a highly disagreeable grouch is uncharacteristically sweet when attending to his ailing mother. Such behavior can be regarded as "acting out of character" in the sense that it is acting away from what one typically does, but it is also acting out of character in another sense—it is acting so as to achieve one's sense of what is right and to advance one's core projects.

Positive psychology's reintroduction of the concept of character into the empirical mainstream is a notable achievement, and the study of the costs and benefits of free traits is relevant to exploring how character plays out in our daily lives. Those who act out of character, as mentioned earlier, enhance their well-being by advancing their core projects. But they also run the risk of burning out if they protractedly act in ways that run counter to their "natural" traits. Having restorative niches, where their first natures may be indulged, might mitigate the cost of acting out of character (Little & Joseph, 2007). The research agenda here is wide open. Although the early empirical findings are encouraging, they are still preliminary and have been restricted to examining the dimension of Extraversion. Which Big Five traits are easiest to enact in a free-traited manner? Is it easier for a highly agreeable person to act disagreeably when pursuing a project of redressing a grievance, and does the end justify the meanness? What are the costs of a testy and disagreeable person acting pleasantly when engaged in the life task of "finding a mate"? Positive psychologists can bring theoretical skills to bear on the question of authenticity in such free trait behavior. Is acting "out of character" simply disingenuous? Is fidelity to one's natural dispositions more conducive to the good life than fidelity to one's core projects and most cherished roles? An exceptionally rich array of questions tumble out when we begin to think of traits as freely constructed courses of action as well as deeply rooted propensities.

Our discussion of primary orientation called for the resuscitation of specialization theory and of the recognition of person and thing orientation as a major dimension of individual differences relevant to positive psychology. Within personality science, studies on the molecular genetics of primary orientations would be valuable as well as studies on early developmental patterns of selective orientation toward persons and things. Within positive psychology, explorations of the consequences of differential orientation for creative achievement could be exceptionally informative, particularly as they bear upon issues of sex and gender differences in pathways to educational and professional achievement.

In both personality and positive psychology, I proposed that there has been an imbalance in the kinds of objects that we are theorizing about. They tend to be objects that have warm bodies and first names. But things, physical objects, the material world all are matters that have meaning in our lives. What might be the practical implications of taking this proposition seriously? I believe it could lead to important advances in our understanding of basic human dispositions. Imagine a series of studies in which we augmented the standard Big Five measures with measures of environmental dispositions of the sort that were studied in the early days of environmental psychology (Little, 1987a) so that both the person and thing domains (natural and constructed) were included. What would be the major dimensions of individual differences that would emerge from a Cultural Orientation Inventory in which we sampled from both the social and material worlds? Would primary orientations toward persons and thing emerge, or would we be more likely to see blends of interests clustering together? The construction of such an inventory (which would also include items about new technologies, to which so many of us are constantly tilting) would be best carried out in interdisciplinary collaboration. Sheldon (2004 has made a strong case for the relevance of diverse fields of study in explaining the course and contexts of human lives: I think encouraging practitioners from these disparate disciplines to collaborate in developing a taxonomy of orientations would be salutary for all.

## Personal Projects: Core, Change, and Sustainability

When considering the role of personal projects in people's lives, it is important to differentiate between fairly peripheral projects and those that we have called "core projects" (Little, 2007; see also Williams, 1981). These are the projects that hold other projects together—were one to lose a core project, we theorized, the system as a whole would be compromised. The measurement of core projects can be approached in a variety of ways. The most theoretically relevant and sophisticated approach is to ask individuals to directly evaluate their resistance to changing each of their projects and, separately, to look at the degree of connectedness among personal projects. The empirical results strongly confirmed that core projects are the most deeply connected ones (MacDiarmid, 1990). Similarly, Sheldon's self-concordance model of personal goals (e.g., Sheldon & Elliot, 1999; Sheldon & Houser-Marko, 2001) demonstrates the importance of pursuing personal goals that are concordant with core values. But here is where a theoretically interesting and practically important issue arises. A very strong case has been made that of all of the factors that influence human well-being, it is the daily actions—projects and goal pursuits— that offer the greatest traction for change (Little, 2007; Sheldon & Lyubomirsky, 2009. As one's core projects are those that are most resistant to change, attempts to enhance well-being by leveraging core projects need to be handled very sensitively. Research on both the theory and practice of core project change would be extremely important to both personality science and to positive psychology.

A key proposition that also requires considerably more empirical exploration is that well-being is enhanced to the extent that an individual is engaged in the *sustainable* pursuit of core projects.[13] What are the reasons why a core project may not be sustainable? The person may lack the self-regulatory skills to manage the project successfully or may lack the social ecological awareness and capacity to move the project along through the thickets of daily life. The project may, as a consequence, lose both meaning and manageability (Little, 2007; Weick, 2004). Here, flexibility is critical, both in terms of personal dispositions and of being able to reformulate one's core projects without compromising their essence.

## Social Ecology and Well-Being: Positive Tilting, Fortuity, and Circumstantial Evidence

The circumstances of our lives influence whether our core projects can be pursued and sustained. Human well-being, therefore, is partly shaped by the material, social, economic, and political contexts of the day. I wish to make some observations about these social ecological conditions within which lives are lead for better or for worse. To do so I need to allude, finally, to the rather obscure title of this chapter. It requires a brief story. A beloved radio personality in Canada, Peter Gzowski, once held a contest in which he asked listeners to provide an answer to the following question—"What is the Canadian equivalent of the phrase 'As American as apple pie'?" I assume a lot of ice and hockey suggestions came in. But the winner, sent in by a young woman from White Rock, B.C., was splendidly insightful—"As Canadian as possible under the circumstances." The circumstances included, of course, living next door to the most powerful country on Earth—a reality that generates both audacious aspirations and strategic diffidence. I want to invoke the same sentiment in framing my final comments on the research agenda ahead for those committed to both personality science and positive psychology.

What are the circumstances that influence our possibilities? Is northern tilting an unmitigated good? Are there bounds to positive thinking? Any good positive psychologist would recognize a straw person lurking about here. Of course there are boundaries and mitigating circumstances, they would say, but positive tilting and the study of the northern territories are both estimable activities. I would agree with them. However, the personality scientist in me wants to take a somewhat more equatorial stance. As the chapter has shown, I hope, there are constraining and potentiating influences on well-being ranging from stable dispositions to chaotic economies. A positive orientation is adaptive, we might say, to the extent that it is based on an accurate reading of these constraints. The theoretical point might be conceded, but the practical implications are challenging. As suggested earlier regarding perceived control, basing the launching of a course of action on an accurate reading of the circumstances does not mean that we need to be restricted by it. We just need to show some alacrity and avoid getting gobsmacked by reality in the form of subprime mortgages or spurious self-worth.

Finally, I wish to say something about fortuity and the impact of chance on the shape of a life. Although I am a keen proponent of individuals shaping their lives through project pursuit, it is important to acknowledge that random events and chance encounters can play havoc with a life plan. But far more subtly, the very idea of living our lives and enhancing our well-being through following a life plan may be missing something critical (Larmore, 1999). By assiduously following life plans, or resolutely pursuing our personal goals, we may inadvertently blind ourselves to the good luck and happy circumstances that fall outside our focal vision. For human flourishing to be enhanced, we need both the tenacity to craft lives through projects that matter as well as keen peripheral vision and the flexibility to look up. Under these circumstances, a positive tilt can reveal delightful surprises and our lives can be enriched.

## Notes

1. Seligman's (1998, 1999) vision for psychology during his presidency of APA is often taken as the official launching of the field of positive psychology (e.g., Peterson, 2006, p. 4). It was followed rapidly by conferences, featured editions in major journals (e.g., Sheldon & King, 2001), and by the Akumal Manifesto (Sheldon, Frederickson, Rathunda, Csikszentmihalyi, & Haidt, 199, 2000), which codified an ambitious agenda of both scientific and institutional development for the new field. Also in the late nineties, a conference at Dartmouth brought together a small group of researchers with a commitment to expanding the science of personality. The group comprised equal numbers of self-defined personality psychologists and others outside the field who were convinced of the increasing relevance of personality research. That meeting led to the creation of the Association for Research in Personality (ARP) in 2002. Unlike the broad base and revolutionary nature of positive psychology, the emergence of personality science was a gradual evolutionary development in the scope of traditional personality psychology. The rapid growth of ARP reflected the fact that personality psychology had been taking on a major new identity as a hub specialty within a hub science (Little, 2005).

2. For expositional clarity, I will use the generic term well-being to refer to the diverse forms of the human good, or good life, that concern both positive psychology and personality science. When appropriate, other terms like enjoyment, happiness, life satisfaction, flourishing, and quality of life will be used. An early and influential clarification of the relation among terms capturing aspects of well-being is found in Diener (1985). A more recent treatment and comprehensive treatment is found in Kahneman, Diener, & Schwartz (1999).

3. It is important to note that even this consensus is now regarded as contestable. Kashdan, Biswas-Diener, & King (2008) make the case that a too-stringent distinction between eudaimonic and hedonic well-being is fundamentally misleading. This has prompted rejoinders by those who contend that the distinction is important (e.g., Ryan & Huta, 2009).

4. As explained in a later section, the fields of vocational and counseling psychology are exceptions here, but personality psychologists have been considerably more interested in traits than in interests and orientations.

5. Plausible cases have been made for six-factor models (e.g., Ashton & Lee, 2007) and even a single-factor model (Musek, 2007; Rushton, Bons, & Hur, 2008), but for present purposes I will accept the current consensus and simply note that much creative non-consensual research is currently underway.

6. I should note that a major reason for its moribund status was that I abandoned it for what seemed at the time a more promising line of inquiry on people's personal projects.

7. Although it goes beyond the scope of this chapter, the form of this dysfunction can be briefly noted. Those who displayed high levels of specialized orientation to persons had tightly linked construct systems that facilitated rapid inference when construing other people. However, this frequently resulted in inferential leaps that were well beyond the relevant information available and could be seriously maladaptive. It is intriguing, therefore, to see contemporary research in psychopathology postulating a similar process as critical in differentiating between the autism-spectrum and psychotic-spectrum disorders (Crespi & Badcock, 2008).

8. Another component of specialization loops was discovered: Person specialists both generated a larger number of expressive nonverbal cues when engaged in interaction and were more receptive to the expression of such cues than did their more thing-oriented peers. Person specialists' positive orientation toward others was readily detectable in their nonverbal behavior, and it stimulated others to interact with them (Little, 1976).

9. There is also evidence that self-specialists overestimate walking distances in neighborhood environments, suggesting further that they may have lower levels of energy for investment in daily pursuits (Little, 1976).

10. It should be noted, though, that Csikszentmihalyi, as usual, was way ahead of the curve in this area. See Csikszentmihalyi & Rochberg-Halton, 1981) for a compelling analysis of the cultural and personal significance of physical objects.

11. Although the study of personal goals had a rather different history and was deeply influenced by European psychology, PAC units and personal goal units are now seen as essentially interchangeable. My own view is that these units of analysis differ in important ways (Little, 2007, pp. 36–38).

12. Our earlier research, as mentioned above, was organized around a slightly different five-factor framework. The modular nature of personal projects methodology means that as new dimensions are added, both the theoretical framework and empirical factor solutions change. The current five-factor model reflects the addition of several affective dimensions.

13. It is interesting to consider the similarities and differences between the concept of core project sustainability and the "sustainable happiness" concept in positive psychology (Lyubomirsky, Sheldon, & Schkade, 2005). The similarities are clear: both internal and external factors can militate against sustainable core projects and sustainable happiness. However, by focusing on sustainable core projects, I am not claiming that such a condition is necessarily conducive to happiness. I claim that core projects are deeply significant and meaningful to individuals. If they are fun and joyful as well, that is a marvelous bonus in daily living. As mentioned earlier, the exploration of such felicitous outcomes and the factors influencing them is an open empirical question well worth pursuing.

## References

Argyle, M., & Lu., L. (1990). The happiness of extraverts. *Personality and Individual Differences. 11*, 1011–1017.

Ashton, M. C., & Lee, K. (2007). Empirical, theoretical and practical advantages of the HEXACO model of personality structure. *Personality and Social Psychology Review, 11*, 150–166.

Barrick, M. R., & Mount, M. K. (1991). The Big Five personality dimensions and job performance: A meta-analysis. *Personnel Psychology, 44*, 1–26.

Baumeister, R., & Leary, M. (1995). The need to belong: Desire for interpersonal attachments as a fundamental human motivation. *Psychological Bulletin, 117*, 497–529.

Cantor, N., & Kihlstrom, J. F. (1987). *Personality and social intelligence.* New York: Prentice Hall.

Cantor, N., & Norem, J. K. (1989). Defensive pessimism and stress and coping. *Social Cognition, 7*, 92–112.

Cantor, N., Norem, J. K., Niedenthal, P. M., Langston, C. A., & Brower, A. M. (1987). Life-tasks, self-concept ideals, and cognitive strategies in a life transition. *Journal of Personality and Social Psychology, 53*, 1178–1191.

Cervone, D., & Mischel, W. (Eds.) (2002a). *Advances in personality science.* New York: Guilford.

Cervone, D., & Mischel, W. (2002b). Personality science. In D. Cervone & W. Mischel (Eds.), *Advances in personality science* (pp. 1–26). New York: Guilford Press.

Chamorro-Premuzic, T. (2006). Creativity versus conscientiousness: Which is a better predictor of student performance? *Applied Cognitive Psychology, 20*, 521–531.

Costa, P. T., Jr., & McCrae, R. R. (1980). Influence of extraversion and neuroticism on subjective well-being: happy and unhappy people. *Journal of Personality and Social Psychology, 38*, 668–678.

Cox, W. M., & Klinger, E. (2004). Measuring motivation: The Motivational Structure Questionnaire and Personal Concerns Inventory (pp. 141–176). In W. M. Cox & E. Klinger (Eds.), *Handbook of motivational counselling: Concepts, approaches, and assessment.* Chichester: Wiley.

Crespi, B., & Badcock, C. (2008). Psychosis and autism as diametrical disorders of the social brain. *Behavioral and Brain Sciences,* 31, 241–320.

Deci, E. L. & Ryan, R. M. (1985). *Intrinsic motivation and self-determination in human behavior.* New York: Plenum.

Deci, E., & Ryan, R. (2008). Self-determination theory: A macrotheory of human motivation, development, and health. *Canadian Psychology/ Psychologie Canadienne,* 49, 182–185.

DeYoung, C. G., Peterson, J. B., & Higgins, D. M. (2002). Higher order factors of the Big Five predict conformity: Are there neuroses of health? *Personality and Individual Differences,* 33, 533–552.

Diener, E. (1984). Subjective well-being. *Psychological Bulletin,* 95, 542–575.

Dowden, C. E. (2004). Managing to be "free": Personality, personal projects and well-being in entrepreneurs. Unpublished doctoral dissertation, Carleton University, Ottawa, ON, Canada.

Emmons, R, A. (1986). Personal strivings: An approach to personality and subjective well-being. *Journal of Personality and Social Psychology,* 51, 1058–1068.

Emmons, R. A. (1999). *The psychology of ultimate concerns: Motivation and spirituality in personality.* New York: Guilford Press.

Emmons, R. A., & King, L. A. (1988). Conflict among personal strivings: Immediate and long-term implications for psychological and physical well-being. *Journal of Personality and Social Psychology,* 54, 1040–1048.

Fleeson, W., Malanos, A., & Achille, N. (2002). An intra-individual, process approach to the relationship between extraversion and positive affect: Is acting extraverted as "good" as being extraverted? *Journal of Personality and Social Psychology,* 83, 1409–1422.

Florida, R. (2008). *Who's your city? How the creative economy is making where to live the most important decision of your life.* Toronto: Random House Canada.

Francis, L. J. (1998). Happiness is a thing called stable extraversion: A further examination of the relationship between the Oxford Happiness Inventory and Eysenck's dimensional model of personality and gender. *Personality and Individual Differences,* 26, 1, 5–11.

Frost, D. M. (2009). Stigma, intimacy, and well-being: A personality and social structures approach. Doctoral dissertation. New York: Graduate School of the City University of New York.

Gardner, H. (1983). *Frames of Mind: The theory of multiple intelligences,* New York: Basic Books.

Goodine, L. A. (2000). An analysis of personal project commitment. Doctoral dissertation, Ottawa: Carleton University, *Dissertation Abstracts International,* 61 (4-B), 2260.

Graziano, W. G., Habashi, M. M., Evangelou, D. & Ngambeki, I. (2009). Preferences, choices and sex differences in STEM: Do interests in people undermine interest in things? Unpublished manuscript. School of Engineering Education, Purdue University, West Lafeyette Indiana.

Gray, J. A. (1982). *The neuropsychology of anxiety: An enquiry into the functions of the septo-hippocampal system.* New York: Oxford University Press.

Heft, H. (1997). Affordances and the body: An intentional analysis of Gibson's ecological approach to visual perception. *Journal for the Theory of Social Behaviour,* 19, 1–30.

Hogan, J., & Hogan, R. (1993, May). Ambiguities of conscientiousness. Paper presented at the Eighth Annual Conference of the Society for Industrial and Organizational Psychology, Inc. San Francisco.

Hwang, A. A. (2004). Yours, mine, ours: The role of joint personal projects in close relationships. Unpublished doctoral dissertation. Harvard University, Cambridge, MA.

James, D. (2001). The nature of the self and well-being: A relational analysis using personal projects. (Doctoral dissertation, Carleton University, 2000). Dissertations Abstracts International, Ottawa, Ontario 61, 4475.

Jang, K. L., Livesley, W. J., & Vernon, P. A. (1996). Heritability of the Big Five personality dimensions and their facets: A twin study. *Journal of Personality,* 64, 577–592.

Kahneman, D., Diener, E., & Schwartz, N (1999). *Well-being: The foundations of hedonic psychology.* New York: Russell Sage.

Kashdan, T. B., Biswas-Diener, R., & King, L. A. (2008). Reconsidering happiness: The costs of distinguishing between hedonics and eudaimonia. *Journal of Positive Psychology,* 3, 219–233.

Kelly, G. A. (1955). *The psychology of personal constructs.* New York: W. W. Norton.

Klinger, E. (1977). *Meaning and void: Inner experiences and the incentives in people's lives.* Minneapolis: University of Minnesota Press.

Klinger, E. (1987). Current concerns and disengagement from incentives. In F. Halisch & J. Kuhl (Eds.), *Motivation, intention, and volition* (pp. 337–347). Berlin: Springer-Verlag.

Larmore, C. (1999). The idea of a life plan. In E. E. Paul, F. Miller Jr., & J. Paul (Eds.), *Human flourishing* (pp. 96–112). New York: Cambridge University Press.

Lippa, R. (1998). Gender-related individual differences and the structure of vocational interests: The Importance of the people-things dimension. *Journal of Personality and Social Psychology 1998, 74,* 996–1009.

Little, B. R. (1972a). Psychological man as scientist, humanist and specialist. *Journal of Experimental Research in Personality, 6,* 95–118.

Little, B. R. (1972b). *Person–Thing orientation: A provisional manual for the T-P Scale.* Department of Experimental Psychology, Oxford University, Oxford, UK.

Little, B. R. (1976). Specialization and the varieties of environmental experience: Empirical studies within the personality paradigm. In S. Wapner, S. B. Cohen, & B. Kaplan (Eds.), *Experiencing the environment* (pp. 81–116). New York: Plenum.

Little, B. R. (1979). *The social ecology of children's nothings.* Paris: UNESCO.

Little, B. R. (1983). Personal projects: A rationale and method for investigation. *Environment and Behavior, 15,* 273–309.

Little, B. R. (1987a). Personal projects and fuzzy selves: Aspects of self-identity in adolescence. In T. Honess & K. Yardley (Eds.), *Self and identity: Perspectives across the life span* (pp. 230–245). Lond: Routledge & Kegan Paul.

Little, B. R. (1987b). Personality and the environment. In D. Stokols & I. Altman (Eds.), *Handbook of environmental psychology* (pp. 205–244). New York: Wiley.

Little, B. R. (1989). Personal projects analysis: Trivial pursuits, magnificent obsessions, and the search for coherence. In D. Buss & N. Cantor (Eds.), *Personality psychology: Recent trends and emerging directions* (pp. 15–31). New York: Springer-Verlag.

Little, B. R. (1996). Free traits, personal projects and idio-tapes: Three tiers for personality psychology. *Psychological Inquiry, 7,* 340–344.

Little, B. R. (1998). Personal project pursuit: Dimensions and dynamics of personal meaning. In P. T. P. Wong & P. S. Fry (Eds.), *The human question for meaning: A handbook of psychological research and clinical applications* (pp. 197–221). Thousand Oaks, CA: Sage.

Little, B. R. (1999a). Personal projects and social ecology: Themes and variation across the life span. In J. Brandtstadter & R. M. Lerner (Eds.), *Action & self-development: Theory and research through the life span* (pp. 197–221). Thousand Oaks, CA: Sage.

Little, B. R. (1999b). Personality and motivation: Personal action and the conative evolution. In L. A. Pervin & O. P. John (Eds.), *Handbook of Personality Theory and Research* (2nd ed., pp. 501–524). New York: Guilford.

Little, B. R. (2000a). Free traits and personal contexts: Expanding a social ecological model of well-being. In W. B. Walsh, K. H. Craik, & R. Price (Eds.), *Person environment psychology* (2nd ed.) (pp. 87–116). New York: Guilford.

Little, B. R. (2005). Personality science and personal projects: Six impossible things before breakfast. *Journal of Research in Personality, 39,* 4–21.

Little, B. R. (2006). Personality science and self-regulation: Personal projects as integrative units. *Applied Psychology: An International Review, 55,* 419–427.

Little, B. R. (2007). Prompt and circumstance: The generative contexts of personal projects analysis. In B. R. Little, K. Salmela-Aro, & S. D. Phillips (Eds.), *Personal project pursuit: Goals, action and human flourishing* (pp. 3–49). Mahwah, NJ: Lawrence Erlbaum Associates.

Little, B. R. (2008). Personal projects and free traits: Personality and motivation reconsidered. *Social and Personality Psychology Compass, 2,* 1235–1254.

Little, B. R., & Chambers, N. C. (2004). Personal project pursuit: On human doings and well beings. In M. Cox & E. Klinger (Eds.), *Handbook of motivational counseling: Concepts, approaches and assessment* (pp. 65–82). Chichester, UK: Wiley.

Little, B. R., & Gee, T. L. (2007). The methodology of personal projects analysis: Four modules and a funnel. In B. R. Little, K. Salmela-Aro, & S. D. Phillips (Eds.), *Personal project pursuit: Goals, action and human flourishing* (pp. 51–93). Mahwah, NJ: Lawrence Erlbaum Associates.

Little, B. R., & Joseph, M. F. (2007). Personal projects and free traits: Mutable selves and well beings. In B. R. Little, K. Salmela-Aro, & S. D. Phillips (Eds.), *Personal project pursuit: Goals, action and human flourishing* (pp. 375–400). Mahwah, NJ: Lawrence Erlbaum Associates.

Little, B. R., Pedrosa de Lima, M., & Whelan, D. C. (2006, January). Positive and negative affect in personal projects: Exploring hot pursuits in ortugal and Canada. Presented at Association for Research in Personality, Palm Springs, CA.

Little, B. R., & Ryan, T. J. (1979). A social ecological model of development. In K. Ishwaran (Ed.), *Childhood and Adolescence in Canada* (pp. 273–301). Toronto, ON, Canada: McGraw-Hill Ryerson.

Little, B. R., Salmela-Aro, K., & Phillips, S. D. (Eds.). (2007). *Personal project pursuit: Goals, action and human flourishing.* Mahwah, NJ: Lawrence Erlbaum Associates.

Little, B. R., Xiao, B. L. & Watkinson, B. (1985). Personal projects of Canadian and Chinese students. Unpublished manuscript, Social Ecology Laboratory, Department of Psychology, Carleton University, Ottawa, ON,

Lucas, R. E., Le, K., & Dyrenforth, P. E. (2008). Explaining the extraversion/positive affect relation: Sociability cannot account for extraverts' greater happiness. *Journal of Personality, 76,* 385–414.

Lykken, D. T. (2000). *Happiness: The nature and nurture of joy and contentment.* New York: St. Martin's.

Lykken, D. T., & Tellegen, A. (1996). Happiness is a stochastic phenomenon. *Psychological Science, 7,* 186–189.

MacDiarmid, E. W. (1990). Level of molarity, project cross impact, and resistance to change in personal project systems. Unpublished master's thesis, Carleton University, Ottawa, ON, Canada.

MacKinnon, D. W. (1962). The nature and nurture of creative talent. *American Psychologist, 17,* 484–495.

McGregor, I. (2007). Personal projects as compensatory convictions: Passionate pursuit and the fugitive self. In B. R. Little, K. Salmela-Aro, & S. D. Phillips (Eds.), *Personal project pursuit: Goals, action and human flourishing* (pp. 171–195). Mahwah, NJ: Lawrence Erlbaum Associates.

McGregor, I., & Little, B. R. (1998). Personal projects, happiness, and meaning: On doing well and being yourself. *Journal of Personality and Social Psychology, 74,* 494–512.

McKeen, N.A. (1984). The personal projects of pregnant women. Unpublished bachelor's thesis, Carleton University, Ottawa, ON, Canada.

Moos, R. & Insel, P. (Eds.), (1974). *Issues in social ecology: Human Milieus.* Palo Alto, Ca: National Press Books.

Musek, J. (2007). A general factor of personality: Evidence for the Big One in the five-factor model. *Journal of Research in Personality, 41,* 1213–1233.

Omodei, M. M., & Wearing, A. J. (1990). Need satisfaction and involvement in personal projects: Toward an integrative model of well-being. *Journal of Personality and Social Psychology, 59,* 762–769.

Palys, T.S., & Little, B. R. (1983). Perceived life satisfaction and the organization of personal project systems. *Journal of Personality and Social Psychology, 44,* 1221–1230.

Peterson, C. (2006). *A primer in positive psychology.* New York: Oxford University Press.

Phillips, S. D., Little, B. R., & Goodine, L. A. (1997). Reconsidering gender and public administration: Five steps beyond conventional research. *Canadian Journal of Public Administration, 40,* 563–581.

Rentfrow, P. J., Gosling, S. D., & Potter, J. (2008). A theory of the emergence, persistence, and expression of geographic variation in psychological characteristics. *Perspectives on Psychological Science, 3,* 339–369.

Ruehlman, L. S., & Wolchik, S. A. (1988). Personal goals and interpersonal support and hindrance as factors in psychological distress and well-being. *Journal of Personality and Social psychology, 55,* 293–301.

Rushton, J. P., Bons, T. A., & Hur, Y-M. (2008). The genetics and evolution of a general factor of personality. *Journal of Research in Personality, 42,* 1173–1185.

Ryan, R. M., & Deci, E. L. (2000). On happiness and human potentials: A review of research on hedonic and eudaimonic well-being. *Annual Review of Psychology, 52.* 141–166.

Ryan, R. M., Huta, V., & Deci, E. (2008). Living well: A self-determination theory perspective on eudaimonia. *Journal of Happiness Studies, 9(1),* 139–170.

Ryan, R. M., & Huta, V. (2009). Wellness as healthy functioning or wellness as happiness: The importance of eudaimonic thinking. *Journal of Positive Psychology, 4,* 202–204.

Ryff, C. D. (1989). Happiness is everything, or is it? Explorations of the meaning of psychological well-being. *Journal of Personality and Social Psychology, 57,* 1069–1081.

Salmela-Aro, K. (1992). Struggling with self: The personal projects of students seeking psychological counselling. *Scandinavian Journal of Psychology, 33,* 330–338.

Schermer, J. A., & Vernon, P. A. (2008). A behavior genetic analysis of vocational interests using a modified version of the Jackson Vocational Interest Survey. *Personality and Individual Differences, 45,* 103–109.

Searles, H. F. (1960). *The non-human environment in normal development and in schizophrenia.* New York: International Universities Press.

Seligman, M. E. P. (1998). Positive social science. *APA Monitor Online, 29* (4). Document available at http://www.apa.org/monitor/apr98/pres.html. Accessed May 1, 2009.

Seligman, M. E. P. (1999). The president's address. *American Psychologist, 54,* 559–562.

Sheldon, K. M. (1995). Creativity and goal conflict. *Creativity Research Journal, 8,* 299–306.

Sheldon, K. M. (2004). *Optimal human being: Towards integration within the person and between the human sciences.* Mahwah, NJ: Erlbaum.

Sheldon, K. M., & Elliot, A. J. (1999). Goal striving, need satisfaction, and longitudinal well-being: The self-concordance model. *Journal of Personality and Social Psychology, 76,* 482–497.

Sheldon, K., Frederickson, B., Rathunde, K. Csikszentmihalyi, M., & Haidt, J. (2000). Akumal manifesto on positive psychology.

Sheldon, K. M., & Houser-Marko, L. (2001). Self-concordance, goal attainment, and the pursuit of happiness: Can there be an upward spiral? *Journal of Personality and Social Psychology, 80,* 152–165.

Sheldon, K. M., & Kasser, T. (1998). Pursuing personal goals: Skills enable progress, but not all progress is beneficial. *Personality and Social Psychology Bulletin, 24,* 1319–1331.

Sheldon, K. M., & King, L. (2001). Why positive psychology is necessary. *American Psychologist, 56,* 216–217.

Sheldon, K. M., & Lyubomirsky, S. (2009). Change your actions, not your circumstances: An experimental test of the Sustainable Happiness model.

In A. K. Dutt & B. Radcliff (Eds.), *Happiness, economics, and politics: Towards a multi-disciplinary approach* (pp. 324–342). Cheltenham, UK: Edward Elgar.

Strawson, P. (1959). *Individuals: An essay in descriptive metaphysics.* London: Methuen.

Wallenius, M. (1999). Personal projects in everyday places: Perceived supportiveness of the environment and psychological well-being. *Journal of Environmental Psychology, 19,* 131–143.

Wallenius, M. (2004). The interaction of noise stress and personal project stress on subjective health. *Journal of Environmental Psychology, 24,* 167–177.

Waterman, A. S. (1993). Two conceptions of happiness; Contrasts of personal expressiveness (eudaimonia) and hedonic enjoyment. *Journal of Personality and Social Psychology, 64,* 678–691.

Weick, K. E. (2004). How projects lose meaning: The dynamics of renewal. In R. Stablein & P. Frost (Eds.), *Renewing Research Practice.* Stanford, CA: Stanford.

Williams, B. (1981). *Moral luck.* Cambridge, UK: Cambridge University Press.

Wilson, D. A. (1990). Personal project dimensions and perceived life satisfaction: A quantitative synthesis. Unpublished master's thesis, Carleton University, Ottawa, ON, Canada.

Wilson, E. G. (2008). *Against happiness: In praise of melancholy.* New York: Farrar, Straus and Giroux.

Wong, P. T. P., & Fry, P. S. (Eds.), (1998). *The human quest for meaning: A handbook of psychological research and clinical applications.* Mahwah, NJ: Lawrence Erlbaum Associates.

# 16

## Why Gratitude Enhances Well-Being: What We Know, What We Need to Know

*Robert A. Emmons and Anjali Mishra*

Gratitude is held in high esteem by virtually everyone, at all times, in all places. From ancient religious scriptures through modern social science research, gratitude is advanced as a desirable human characteristic with the capacity for making life better for oneself and for others. Though gratitude is associated with pleasantness and highly desirable life outcomes, it is certainly not an easy or automatic response to life situations. Resentment and entitlement often seem to come naturally. Individual personality flaws such as neuroticism or narcissism make it difficult to recognize the positive contributions of others. The very fact that gratitude is a virtue suggests that it must be deliberately cultivated. Like any virtue, it must be taught, or at least modeled, and practiced regularly, until it becomes, in an Aristotelian sense, a habit of character. A grateful person is one who is prone to react to the goodness of others in a benevolent and receptive fashion, reciprocating kindness when opportunities arise. The grateful person has been able to overcome tendencies to take things for granted, to feel entitled to the benefits they have received, and to take sole credit for all of their advantages in life. They are able to gladly recognize the

contributions that others have made to their well-being. Further, they are able to discern when it is appropriate to express gratitude and are not overly concerned with exacting gratitude from those whom *they* benefit.

What have we learned about gratitude and the grateful personality? First, a definition: Gratitude is an acknowledgment that we have received something of value from others. It arises from a posture of openness to others, where we are able to gladly recognize their benevolence. Societies through the ages have long extolled the benefits of gratitude, and classical writings have deemed it the "greatest of the virtues." But only recently has psychological theory and research on gratitude begun to catch up with philosophical commendations. In the first part of this chapter, we review research on gratitude and positive human functioning. First, we briefly consider the research on gratitude and well-being. After a consideration of this evidence, we explore the mechanisms by which gratitude enhances well-being. We consider several explanations and evaluate the empirical evidence for each. In the latter part of the chapter, we establish an agenda for the future by considering some ways in

which the scientific field of gratitude can be advanced.

## Gratitude and Well-Being: Taking Stock

Gratitude is foundational to well-being and mental health throughout the lifespan. From childhood to old age, accumulating evidence documents the wide array of psychological, physical, and relational benefits associated with gratitude. In the past few years, there has been an accumulation of scientific evidence showing the contribution of gratitude to psychological and social well-being (Emmons & McCullough, 2003; McCullough, Kilpatrick, Emmons, & Larson, 2001; Wood, Froh, & Geraghty, 2010). Gratitude has been shown to contribute to not only an increase in positive affect and other desirable life outcomes but also to a decrease in negative affect and problematic functioning as demonstrated in diverse samples such as among patients with neuromuscular disease, college students, hypertensives, and early adolescents (Emmons & McCullough, 2003; Froh, Sefick, & Emmons, 2008; Shipon, 2007).

Based on Rosenberg's (1998) hierarchical levels of affective experience, gratitude has been identified as a trait, emotion, and mood. The grateful disposition can be defined as a stable affective trait that would lower the threshold of experiencing gratitude. As an emotion, gratitude can be understood as an acute, intense, and relatively brief psychophysiological reaction to being the recipient of a benefit from an other. Lastly, as a stable mood, gratitude has also been identified to have a subtle, broad, and longer-duration impact on consciousness (McCullough, Tsang, & Emmons, 2004). Both state and dispositional gratitude have been shown to enhance overall psychological, social, and physical well-being. Gratitude promotes optimal functioning at multiple levels of analysis—biological, experiential, personal, relational, familial, institutional, and even cultural (Emmons & McCullough, 2004).

Two main measures have been administered to assess dispositional gratitude: the six-item Gratitude Questionnaire (GQ-6; McCullough, Emmons, & Tsang, 2002), and the 44-item Gratitude Resentment and Appreciation Test or the GRAT (Watkins, Grimm, & Hailu, 1998). The GQ-6 measures dispositional gratitude as a generalized tendency to recognize and emotionally respond with thankfulness, after attributing benefits received to an external moral agent (Emmons, McCullough, & Tsang, 2003). The 44-item GRAT form measures three dimensions of gratitude: resentment, simple appreciation, and appreciation of others (Watkins et al., 1998). Beyond these scales to assess gratitude, other measures include personal interviews (Liamputtong, Yimyam, Parisunyakul, Baosoung, & Sansiriphun, 2004), rating scales (Saucier & Goldberg, 1998), and other self-report measures such as free response (Sommers & Kosmitzki, 1988) and personal narratives (Kashdan, Mishra, Breen, & Froh, 2009).

Dispositional gratitude has been shown to uniquely and incrementally contribute to subjective well-being (McCullough et al., 2004; Watkins, Woodward, Stone, & Kolts, 2003; Wood, Joseph, & Maltby, 2008) and to benefits above and beyond general positive affect (Bartlett & DeSteno, 2006). Dispositional gratitude has also been found to be positively associated with prosocial traits such as empathy, forgiveness, and willingness to help others (McCullough et al., 2002). People who rate themselves as having a grateful disposition perceived themselves as having more prosocial characteristics, expressed by their empathetic behavior, and emotional support for friends within the last month. Similar associations have been found between state gratitude and social well-being (Emmons & McCullough, 2003).

While gratitude has been studied as a trait, it has also been studied as a state—feeling grateful and equivalent states (appreciation, thankfulness) at the moment. State gratitude has been experimentally activated through the self-guided exercise of journaling. In the first study examining the benefits of experimentally induced grateful thoughts on psychological well-being in daily life, a gratitude induction was compared to a hassles and a neutral life events condition (Emmons & McCullough, 2003). The cultivation of grateful affect through daily and weekly journaling led to overall improved well-being, including fewer health complaints and a more positive outlook toward life. Participants in the gratitude condition also reported more exercise and appraised their life more positively compared to participants in the hassles and neutral conditions. Furthermore, in a study examining the contribution of gratitude in daily mood over 21 days, gratitude was strongly associated with spiritual transcendence and other positive affective traits (e.g., extraversion) (McCullough et al., 2004). In the past few years, a number of laboratory and research-based intervention studies have also been examining the positive impact of gratitude-induced activities (e.g., the gratitude visit, gratitude letter) on psychological well-being, including happiness, depression, and materialism (Bono, Emmons, & McCullough, 2004; Lyubomirsky, Sheldon, & Schkade, 2005; McCullough et al., 2004; Seligman, Steen, Park, & Peterson; 2005; Watkins, 2000).

Given the emerging strong association between gratitude and well-being, an important step becomes exploring the reasons for this relationship. What are the mechanisms responsible for why gratitude promotes well-being? A number of possible explanations have been suggested; however, not all of them have been fully investigated. In the next section, we examine several explanations for the relation between gratitude and well-being, some of which stem from new research from our laboratory that is relevant to these hypotheses.

## Hypothesis 1: Gratitude Facilitates Coping with Stress

Pondering the circumstances in one's life for which one is grateful appears to be a common way of coping with both acute and chronic stressful life events. Our first hypothesis is that gratitude improves well-being by providing useful coping skills for dealing with losses. These include building a supply of more positive thoughts, increasing the focus on benefits in life and on others, and reducing the maladaptive focus on losses (Fredrickson, 2004; Watkins, 2000). For example, gratitude has been associated with distinct coping styles of seeking social support, positive reframing, approach-oriented problem solving, and active coping (Wood, Joseph, & Linley, 2007). The coping styles linked with gratitude might be based on the recognition of benefits, stronger social bonds, prosocial motivation, and the evolutionary adaptation of gratitude as an emotion for regulating reciprocal altruism (McCullough et al., 2001; McCullough, Kimeldorf, & Cohen, 2008; Trivers, 1971). In the past few years there has been growing empirical evidence for gratitude's association with coping and post-traumatic growth (Peterson, Park, Pole, D'Andrea, & Seligman, 2008).

One of the first studies examining the benefits of psychological strengths on well-being in combat veterans found that, compared to veterans with Post-Traumatic Stress Disorder (PTSD), veterans without PTSD reported more dispositional gratitude on the GQ-6 (Kashdan, Uswatte, & Julian, 2006). Gratitude also emerged as one of

the strongest themes for quality of life (toward the donor, their families, and the renal team) in a sample of kidney transplant recipients, followed by long-lasting psychosocial effects on the recipients (Orr, Willis, Holmes, Britton, & Orr, 2007). In a prospective study examining college students in the aftermath of the September 11 terrorist attacks, gratitude emerged as one of the primary themes and contributed to resilience and post-crisis coping (Fredrickson, Tugade, Waugh, & Larkin, 2003). Lastly, a recent study including undergraduate women with trauma history showed strong associations between gratitude (measured by a four-item post-trauma gratitude scale including the items "fortunate," "grateful," "appreciated life," and "relieved") and emotional growth ($r = .43$, $p < .001$). Most importantly, gratitude after trauma was negatively associated with PTSD symptom levels ($r = -.18$, $p < .05$) (Vernon, Dillon, & Steiner, 2009). Therefore, the evidence strongly supports the supposition that gratitude promotes adaptive coping and personal growth.

## Hypothesis 2: Gratitude Reduces Toxic Emotions Resulting from Self and Social Comparisons

Another possible explanation for the relation between gratitude and well-being is that grateful individuals are less likely to engage in upward social comparisons that can result in envy or resentment, or self-comparisons with alternative outcomes in one's own life that can result in regret. Either type of these invidious comparisons can cause people to feel that they lack something important that either others have or that they desire for themselves. Envy is a negative emotional state characterized by resentment, inferiority, longing, and frustration about other people's material and non-material successes (Parrott & Smith, 1993). Considerable research has shown that envy creates unhappiness and is associated with a host of negative mental health indicators (Smith & Kim, 2007). As gratitude is a focus on the benevolence of others, it is incompatible with envy and resentment, as the grateful person appreciates positive qualities in others and is able to feel happy over the good fortune that happens to others (Smith, Turner, Leach, Garonzik, Urch-Druskat, & Weston, 1996). Grateful people, who tend to focus on the positive contributions of others to their well-being, probably devote less attention to comparing their outcomes with those of other people and thus experience less envy as a result. Using Smith, Parrott, Diener, Hoyle, & Kim's (1999) measure of dispositional envy and the envy subscale of Belk's materialism scale (Ger & Belk, 1996; McCullough et al., 2002) reported moderate negative correlations (ranging from −.34 to −.40) between gratitude and envy. Furthermore, the correlations between trait gratitude and envy remained significant after controlling for positive affect, negative affect, and agreeableness. Grateful people do experience less frustration and resentment over the achievements and possessions of other people, and the overlap between gratitude and envy is not produced by their common bond with trait affect.

Regret is a counterfactual emotion produced by perceptions of what might have been. In regret, some action, event, or state of affairs is construed as "unfortunate" and contrasted with some more propitious alternative that "might have been" (Roberts, 2004). In that it is a form of welling on the negative, regret generates related unpleasant states of anxiety, unhappiness, and even depression (Isenberg, 2008; Landman, 1993). There is no empirical evidence that directly tests the hypothesized linkage between regret and gratitude, though the opposing causal attributions that give rise to gratitude versus regret have been well-established (Weiner, 2007). It is likely that the dispositionally grateful have a firewall of protection against incapacitating regrets because they are inclined to dwell on the favorable, rather than the regrettable, in life (Roberts, 2004). By appreciating the gifts of the moment, gratitude offers freedom from past regrets. While a promising hypothesis, more research is needed before we can draw definitive conclusions concerning this hypothesis.

## Hypothesis 3: Gratitude Reduces Materialistic Strivings

Gratitude and materialism represent opposing motivational goals. Gratitude may aid well-being by motivating people to fulfill basic needs of personal growth, relationships, and community— motives that are incompatible with materialism (Polak & McCullough, 2006). As a route to the bolstering of well-being, gratitude may block materialistic pursuits. Materialism is damaging to subjective well-being. Materialistic adults tend to exhibit life dissatisfaction (Richins & Dawson, 1992); unhappiness (Belk, 1985; Kasser & Kanner, 2004); low self-esteem (Kasser, 2003); less concern with the welfare of others

(Sheldon & Kasser, 1995); less relatedness, autonomy, competence, and meaning in life (Kashdan & Breen, 2007), and higher levels of depressive symptoms (Kasser & Ryan, 1993) and envy (Belk, 1985). Materialistic adults are less satisfied with their standards of living, family lives, and the amount of fun and enjoyment they experience (Richins & Dawson, 1992).

Gratitude is most closely related to the values of *benevolence*, an orientation characterized by "the preservation and enhancement of the welfare of people with whom one is in frequent personal contact" (Bilsky & Schwartz, 1994, p. 167) and *universalism*, defined as "understanding, appreciation, tolerance, and protection for the welfare of all people and for nature" (Bilsky & Schwartz, 1994, p. 167). Furthermore, in the Values-in-Action taxonomy of human strengths (Peterson & Seligman, 2004), gratitude is one of the five strengths that falls under the broader virtue of *transcendence*. These value orientations are diametrically opposed to *power* ("social status and prestige, control or dominance over people and resources") (p. 167) and *hedonism* (pleasure and sensuous gratification for oneself") (p. 167), which likely are the two values in this theory most aligned with materialism. Values theory would therefore predict a negative correlation between gratitude and materialism on the grounds that they represent opposing value systems.

Evidence suggests that gratitude can reduce the pernicious effects of materialism on well-being. Grateful people report themselves as being less materialistic and are less likely to define personal success in terms of material accomplishments and possessions (McCullough et al., 2002). In particular, grateful people report being more willing to part with their possessions, more generous with them, less envious of the material wealth of others, less committed to the idea that material wealth is linked with success in life, and less convinced of the idea that material wealth brings happiness. Using structural equation modeling, Froh, Emmons, Card, Bono, & Wilson (in press) found that gratitude mediates the relation between materialism and well-being. Apparently, material success is not a very important factor in the happiness of highly grateful people, so this hypothesis has received considerable support.

## Hypothesis 4: Gratitude Improves Self-Esteem

Self-esteem has emerged as a powerful correlate of happiness (e.g., Denny & Steiner, 2009;

Lyubomirsky, Tkach, & DiMatteo, 2006; Walker & Schimmack, 2008). Gratitude might be important because focusing on receiving benefits from benefactors might enhance self-esteem and self-respect. This hypothesis has not been extensively tested, but the data that do exist are supportive. For example, grateful youth report high levels of self-esteem (Froh, Wajsblat, & Ubertini, 2008). They also report high levels of self-satisfaction concurrently (Froh et al., 2008, 2008; Froh, Yurkewicz, & Kashdan, 2009) and three and six months later (Froh et al., 2008). Grateful people, in focusing on how their lives are supported and sustained by others, might feel more secure and are therefore less likely to seek material goods to strengthen their self-image. Grateful people may also have more stable self-esteem that is less contingent upon transient success and failure experiences, contributing to their ability to cope with stress, as discussed in Hypothesis 1. We do not yet know, however, the direction of the relation. It may be that high self-esteem leads to more feelings of gratitude because it makes it more likely that the person will respond positively to the benevolence of others. Conversely, it may be that feelings of gratitude produce more positive self-construals. Future research will have to decide this sequence.

## Hypothesis 5: Gratitude Enhances Accessibility to Positive Memories

Gratitude has also been shown to contribute to well-being by boosting the retrieval of positive autobiographical memories. Grateful people are characterized by a positive memory bias (Watkins, Grimm, & Kolts, 2004). This positivity bias extends to both intentional and intrusive positive memories. These findings were reliably replicated in a subsequent study by the authors after controlling for depression. In a more recent study by Watkins, Cruz, Holben, & Kolts (2008), the reappraising benefit of gratitude on memory was shown to promote successful closure of unpleasant open memories, ultimately contributing to happiness. Therefore, gratitude enhances the retrievability of positive experiences by increasing elaboration of positive information. The positive impact of gratitude on memory was further confirmed in a study by Watkins et al. (2008). The grateful reappraisal of upsetting memories was shown to promote better emotional processing and closure of the upsetting open memories.

Future research could examine the influence of gratitude on the construction of self-construals. These construals might subsequently impact appraisals of autobiographical memories. According to Ross (1989), implicit theories of personal attributes can influence the retrieval of self-construal and facilitate biased recall. Furthermore, the perception of self can change (or remain relatively stable) over time (Ross, 1989). The role of gratitude in influencing construal of life histories might be tested both for state and trait gratitude. People high on trait gratitude may be better able to retrieve more positive personal life experiences compared to less grateful individuals. The effect of experimentally induced gratitude on the quality of autobiographical memories (e.g., positive-negative valence of the memories, perception of negative life events) could also be investigated.

## Hypothesis 6: Gratitude Builds Social Resources

Gratitude may contribute to overall well-being by enhancing social relationships. Gratitude has been linked in a variety of ways to positive interpersonal functioning. Gratitude facilitates the building of social resources by broadening the thought action repertoire (i.e., via initiation of friendships or consideration of a wide range of strategies by the beneficiary as a form of repayment) (Fredrickson, 2004, pp. 150). Moreover, besides building new bonds, gratitude also helps strengthen and maintain existing relationships (Algoe, Haidt, & Gable, 2008) and fosters trust (Gino & Schweitzer, 2008). Grateful people possess a number of resources that make them desirable friends and romantic partners. They are extraverted, agreeable, empathic, emotionally stable, forgiving, trusting, and generous (McCullough et al., 2002; Wood et al., 2008). Further, gratitude is a strength of character that is highly desired in romantic partners (Steen, Kachorek, & Peterson, 2003).

From an attachment perspective, gratitude has been shown to promote social bonds since it is closely associated with attachment security. In a sample of Israeli undergraduates, attachment security uniquely contributed to the grateful disposition over and beyond the association of attachment security with self-esteem or trust (Mikulincer, Shaver, & Slav, 2006). In a subsequent study the link between trait gratitude and attachment security was examined in context of new marital relationships. For both husband and wife, the perceived positive behavior of the partner was strongly associated with greater gratitude toward the partner on a particular day (Mikulincer et al., 2006, pp. 203). The link is not limited to newlyweds. In a sample of older adults, greater social support from adult children was found to be related with a higher sense of gratitude (Dahua, Yan, & Liqing, 2004).

The social benefits of gratitude can also be construed in terms of the affect theory of social exchange proposed by Lawler (2001). This theory proposes that positive emotions generated by social exchange partners lead to social cohesion and strengthening of social networks. Therefore, by promoting prosocial behavior, building social resources, fostering trust, attachment security, and social exchange, gratitude is a vital interpersonal emotion, the absence of which undermines social harmony.

## Hypothesis 7: Gratitude Motivates Moral Behavior

Gratitude is an essential part of creating and sustaining positive social relations. One way that gratitude sustains personal relationships is that it motivates moral behavior—action that is undertaken in order to benefit another. McCullough et al. (2001) proposed that gratitude possesses three psychological features that are relevant to processing and responding to prosocial behavior: It is a benefit detector as well as both a reinforcer and motivator of prosocial behavior. In this functional account, gratitude is more than a pleasant feeling. Gratitude is also motivating and energizing. It is a positive state of mind that gives rise to the "passing on of the gift" through positive action. As such, gratitude serves as a key link in the dynamic between receiving and giving. While a response to kindnesses received, gratitude drives future benevolent actions on the part of the recipient. In the language of evolutionary dynamics, gratitude leads to "upstream reciprocity" (Nowak & Roch, 2007), the passing on of a benefit to a person uninvolved in the initial exchange. Part of gratitude's magnetic appeal lies in its power to evoke a focus by the recipient on the benevolence of others, thereby ensuring a perception that kindness has been offered, and its beneficial consequences that frequently are the motive to respond favorably toward another. The idea that the capacity to receive and be grateful fosters the desire to return goodness is theoretically compelling and empirically viable.

Recent experimental evidence indicates that gratitude is a unique facilitator of reciprocity (Bartlett & DeSteno, 2006; Watkins, Schneer, Ovnicek & Kolts, 2006). After appraising the evidence that gratitude fosters moral behavior, McCullough, Kimeldorf, and Cohen (2008) propose that gratitude evolved to facilitate social exchange. Compelling evidence suggests that gratitude evolved to stimulate not only direct reciprocal altruism but also upstream reciprocity (Nowak & Roch, 2007).

## Hypothesis 8: Grateful People Are Spiritually Minded

Several studies have found a relationship between religion, spirituality, and gratitude (Adler & Fagley, 2005; Emmons & Kneezel, 2005; McCullough et al., 2002; Watkins et al., 2003). People with stronger dispositions toward gratitude tend to be more spiritually and religiously minded. Not only do they score higher on measures of traditional religiousness, but they also scored higher on non-sectarian measures of spirituality that assess spiritual experiences (e.g., sense of contact with a divine power) and sentiments (e.g., beliefs that all living things are interconnected) independent of specific theological orientation. All measures of public and private religiousness in the Emmons and Kneezel (2005) study were significantly associated with both dispositional gratitude and grateful feelings assessed on a daily basis. Although these correlations were not large (ranging from $r = .28$ to $r = .52$), they suggest that spiritually or religiously inclined people have a stronger disposition to experience gratitude than do their less spiritual/religious counterparts. Research is also beginning to examine gratitude toward God. Krause (2006) found that gratitude felt toward God reduced the effect of stress on health in late-life adults and deteriorated neighborhood. The stress-buffering effect of theocentric gratitude was more pronounced among the women compared to the men in Krause's (2006) study.

Many world religions commend gratitude as a desirable human trait (see Carman & Streng, 1989; Emmons & Crumpler, 2000), which may cause spiritual or religious people to adopt a grateful outlook. Religion also provides texts, teachings, and traditions that encourage gratitude. When contemplating a positive circumstance that cannot be attributed to intentional human effort, such as a miraculous healing or the gift of life itself, spiritually inclined people may attribute these positive outcomes to a non-human agent (viz., God or a higher power) and thus experience more gratitude. Third, spiritually inclined people also tend to attribute positive outcomes to God's intervention, but not negative ones (Lupfer, De Paola, Brock, & Clement, 1994; Lupfer, Tolliver, & Jackson, 1996). As a result, many positive life events that are not due to the actions of another person (e.g., pleasant weather, avoiding an automobile accident) may be perceived as occasions for gratitude to God, although negative events (e.g., a long winter, an automobile accident) would likely *not* be attributed to God. This attributional style, then, is likely to magnify the positive emotional effects of pleasant life events.

## Hypothesis 9: Gratitude Facilitates Goal Attainment

The possession of and progression toward important life goals are essential for long-term well-being (Emmons, 1999). Goal attainment is a major benchmark for the experience of well-being. Quality of life therapy (Frisch, 2006) advocates the importance of revising goals, standards, and priorities as a strategy for boosting life happiness and satisfaction. Yet goal striving and gratitude or the grateful disposition have not been explicitly linked. In one experimental study on gratitude and well-being, we asked participants at the beginning of the gratitude journaling study to provide a short list of goals they wished to accomplish over the next two months. As these were students, most goals fell into the interpersonal or academic domains. Participants in the gratitude condition, relative to the control and hassles conditions, reported making more progress toward their goals over the 10-week period. The results of this study stand in strong opposition to an empirically undocumented but widely held assumption that gratitude promotes passivity and complacency. On the contrary, gratitude enhances effortful goal striving. Much more future research could examine the goal correlates of gratitude, as well as grateful affect as an emotional regulator of goal-directed action.

## Hypothesis 10: Gratitude Promotes Physical Health

Gratitude is a mindful awareness of the benefits in one's life. Dwelling on goodness may promote more efficient physical functioning, through either inhibiting unhealthy attitudes and emotions or facilitating more health-promoting inner states. A small number of studies have reported physical health benefits of gratitude, and these relations have been largely independent of trait negative affect (Wood, Joseph, Lloyd, & Atkins, 2008). Gratitude interventions have been shown to reduce the bodily complaints, increase sleep duration and efficiency, and promote exercise (Emmons & McCullough, 2003; Wood et al., 2008). Experimental research suggests that discrete experiences of gratitude and appreciation may cause increases in parasympathetic myocardial control (McCraty & Childre, 2004), lower systolic blood pressure (Shipon, 2007), as well as improvements in more molar aspects of physical health such as everyday symptoms and physician visits (Emmons & McCullough, 2003). McCraty and colleagues found that appreciation increased parasympathetic activity, a change thought to be beneficial in controlling stress and hypertension, as well as "coherence" or entrainment across various autonomic response channels. Therefore, there might be some direct physiological benefits to frequently experiencing grateful emotions. This line of research conducted by McCraty demonstrates a link between positive emotions and increased physiological efficiency, which may partly explain the growing number of correlations documented between positive emotions, improved health, and increased longevity.

## Moving Forward: Future Directions

As the evidence we reviewed earlier in the chapter indicates, gratitude interventions in adults consistently produce positive benefits, many of which appear to endure over reasonably lengthy periods of time. Gratitude interventions lead to greater gratitude, life satisfaction, optimism, prosocial behavior (Emmons & McCullough, 2003), positive affect (Emmons & McCullough, 2003; Watkins et al., 2003, Study 4), and well-being (Lyubomirsky et al., 2005; Seligman et al., 2005), as well as decreased negative affect (Emmons & McCullough, 2003; Seligman et al., 2005; Watkins et al., 2003, Study 3) compared with controls for up to six months. Similar findings, over shorter follow-up periods, have been documented in youth (Froh et al., 2008). Despite these encouraging results, much remains unknown. We have several suggestions for future research involving gratitude interventions.

*Mechanisms.* What are the active ingredients in gratitude interventions? It is not known whether the effects of these activities are relatively specific (e.g., increases in happiness alone) or are more general (e.g., increases in perceived physical health and decreases in negative mood). In addition, no research has attempted to examine the effects of these activities in the context of participants' levels of dispositional gratitude, an established individual difference that may modulate the positive effects of activities aimed at increasing gratitude in one's life (McCullough et al., 2002). The active ingredients may relate to processes of reflecting on things for which one is grateful, or recording these in some way, or expressing them. Until it is known which of these is essential, we cannot state why these exercises work and it is difficult to make informed recommendations about how they might be used. Future research must employ increasingly sophisticated designs using statistical tests of mediating and moderating effects.

*Comparison groups.* What is the most appropriate condition to contrast with gratitude? Nearly one-half of the studies that have been published to date found support for gratitude interventions when making contrasts with techniques that induce negative affect (e.g., record your daily hassles). Gratitude interventions have shown limited benefits, if any, over control conditions. Thus, there is a need to better understand whether gratitude interventions are beyond a control condition and if there exists a subset of people who benefit. Perhaps gratitude interventions are differentially effective for groups of people with varying backgrounds. Sample characteristics themselves might show differences. People who are actively seeking positive psychology interventions may have greater expectations for their efficacy compared to college students participating for extra credit or to fulfill a course requirement.

*Trait moderators.* A moderating effect might be found if pre-existing trait characteristics of people affect their ability to profit from gratitude interventions. Several dispositional factors may moderate the effectiveness of gratitude interventions. Of these, trait affect and dispositional gratitude are obvious candidates for consideration. It seems a reasonable prediction that persons high in positive affect (PA) may have reached an "emotional ceiling" and thus are less susceptible to experiencing gains in well-being. People lower in PA, however, may need more positive events—like expressing gratitude to a benefactor—to

"catch up" to the positive experiences of their peers. Froh, Kashdan, Ozimkowski, and Miller (2009) examined whether individuals differences in positive affective style moderated the effects of a gratitude intervention where youth were instructed to write a letter to someone to whom they were grateful and deliver it to them in person. Eighty-nine children and adolescents were randomly assigned to the gratitude intervention or a control condition. Findings indicated that youth low in PA in the gratitude condition, compared with youth writing about daily events, reported greater gratitude and PA at post-treatment and greater PA at the two-month follow-up. Children and adolescents low in PA in the gratitude condition, compared with the control group, reported more gratitude and PA at two later time points, at three-week and two-month follow-ups. This is an important study because it is the first known randomized controlled trial of a gratitude intervention study in children and adolescents and the first paper to reinterpret the gratitude intervention literature arguing to carefully consider controls groups when concluding the efficacy of gratitude interventions. Furthermore, when considering both youth and adult populations, it is also the first known attempt at investigating positive affect as a moderator.

Then there is dispositional gratitude. Can we expect gratitude inductions to be more effective in increasing the well-being of grateful individuals or less grateful persons? Grateful individuals would be more susceptible to recognizing when others are being kind to them, and more open to perceiving benefits more generally. One could even postulate a gratitude schema (Wood et al., 2008) as an interpretive bias on the part of dispositionally grateful individuals prone to making benevolent appraisals. Alternatively, gratitude interventions might also be more efficacious for individuals low on trait gratitude since they may have more room for improvement on the gratitude dimension. No published studies have examined dispositional gratitude as a moderator of state gratitude interventions.

Trait gratitude might also interact with trait affect. Froh et al. (2009) found that, compared to the control group, individuals in the gratitude group who were low on positive affect benefited the most from the gratitude intervention. Given the recent evidence on the contribution of positive affect as a moderator, it might also be reasonable to examine the possibility of a curvilinear relationship between trait gratitude and well-being. For example, individuals at the extreme ends of the gratitude distribution might extract the least benefits from gratitude interventions.

*The effect of instructional set.* The instructions that participants in the gratitude condition are given appear to be essential. The counting blessings gratitude intervention guides participants to reflect on and record benefits in their lives. Participants generally focus on the presence of good things in their lives that they currently enjoy. Yet a recent study found that people's affective states improve more after mentally subtracting positive events from their lives than after thinking about the presence of those events (Koo, Algoe, Wilson & Gilbert, 2008). People wrote about why a positive event might never have happened and why it was surprising or why it was certain to be part of their lives and was not at all surprising. The results showed that the way in which people think about positive life events is critical, namely whether they think about the presence of the events (e.g., "I'm grateful that I was in Professor Wiseman's class") or the absence of the events (e.g., "imagine I had never met Professor Wiseman!"). The latter impacted positive affect more than did the former. Inasmuch as most previous studies adopted the former approach, asking participants to think about the presence of positive events, the effects of gratitude on well-being may well have been underestimated. Koo et al. adduce that thinking about how events might have not happened triggers surprise, and it is surprise that amplifies the event's positivity. Along these lines, another recent study (Bar-Anan, Wilson, & Gilbert, 2009) found that the uncertainty of an event intensifies felt reaction, such that outcomes that are uncertain produce greater emotional reactions. Another recent study found that focusing on an experience's ending could enhance one's present evaluation of it (Kurtz, 2008). Future gratitude interventions could capitalize on these three studies by giving participants explicit instructions to include in their journals events or circumstances that might not have happened, have turned out otherwise, where the initial outcome may have been uncertain, or increasing an awareness that the experience is soon ending.

*Dose-Effect Relationship.* More than two decades ago, an influential psychotherapy review article reported that by eight sessions of psychotherapy, approximately one-half of patients show a measureable outcome improvement, and that by 26 sessions, this number increases to 75% (Howard, Kopta, Krause, & Orlinksy, 1986).

Is there an equivalent dose-response relationship for gratitude interventions? Interventions have asked people to keep gratitude journals every day to a few times a week to once a week for 10 weeks. While some differences have been reported across these studies, an insufficient number of trials have yet to be conducted such that recommendations could be made with confidence. The definition of a dose itself is up for debate. Should a dose be considered a single session of writing in a gratitude journal? Should a minimum time be set for participants to write in their journals each session? We would expect that the greater the degree of elaboration over a simple listing or counting of blessings, the greater would be the potential payoff. But a systematic comparison of the relevant variables that "gratitude dosages" vary on has yet to be conducted.

*Gender.* Gender may be another critical individual factor affecting the outcomes of intervention studies. Given the interpersonal correlates and interdependent nature of gratitude, women might have an edge over men in extracting benefits from gratitude interventions. In fact, recent studies have demonstrated significant gender differences in gratitude (Kashdan et al., 2009; Watkins et al., 2003). However, in another recent study by Froh et al. (2009), the usual trend of gender differences couldn't be captured in an adolescent sample. Even though adolescent girls reported more gratitude, adolescent boys appeared to derive more social benefits from gratitude for whom a stronger relationship between gratitude and family support was found.

As an extension of possible gender differences in gratitude, it would be compelling to examine the contribution of gratitude in romantic relationships. Dyadic interventions involving grateful activities might foster higher-quality relationships. For example, a recent study examined the influence of attachment orientations on gratitude in new marital relationships over a period of 21 days (Mikulincer et al., 2006). Daily feelings of gratitude for the partner were related to appraisals of partner's behavior (i.e., the higher the level of partner's perceived positive behavior, the greater the gratitude). For both partners, perceived positive behavior by the partner toward the self on one day was significantly associated with greater gratitude toward the partner on that same day. Moreover, in the same study, attachment avoidance was found to be associated with lower feelings of gratitude for the partner across the 21 days. However, most interestingly, only the husband's avoidance orientation moderated the relationship between the perceived partner's behavior and feelings of gratitude (i.e., avoidant husbands reported lower gratitude even on days when they appraised their wife's behaviors to be highly positive). As an extension of these findings, future studies can examine if and why gratitude has the potential of contributing more to the relationship quality for women, compared to men. Given the interdependent and interpersonal nature of gratitude, women might be more susceptible toward perceiving a partner's positive behaviors as gifts and extract more benefits from gratitude in their romantic relationships. Women are expected to expand their caretaking and relational roles, whereas men are expected to focus their emotional expression on the expansion and pursuit of power and status (Brody, 1997, 1999; Stoppard & Gruchy, 1993). Therefore, seeking more of a "provider's" role in marital relationships, gratitude may trigger feelings of vulnerability and weakness for men, which they may perceive to be harmful to their masculinity and social standing (Levant & Kopecky, 1995). As a result, men might extract fewer benefits from gratitude to enhance their relationship quality.

*Enhancing retention in self-guided programs.* Gratitude interventions may increase compliance with and the possible success of self-guided therapies in the realms of health management. Given that grateful people tend to take better care of their health, would an intervention to increase gratitude lead a person to stick with their commitments say to reduce weight, eat more nutritionally, exercise, or reduce smoking? Attrition is a major problem, especially in Internet interventions (Christensen, Griffiths, Mackinnon, & Brittliffe, 2006). A recent study found that retention in a two-week intervention for depressed persons was significantly higher for those who completed gratitude journals compared to recording automatic thoughts (Geraghty, Wood, & Hyland, 2010).

Gratitude was effective in both reducing dropout and lowering depression scores, and increased retention by 12% over those recording daily thoughts.

## The Uniqueness of Gratitude Interventions

An important issue to be addressed in future research concerns the unique contributions that gratitude interventions make to well-being outcomes that distinguish them, say from related positive psychology interventions. The uniqueness of these interventions could be compared with other positive psychological constructs such as forgiveness and hope, both of which have been shown to contribute to well-being (Bono, McCullough, & Root, 2008; Snyder, Rand, & Sigmon, 2002). What is different about gratitude? First, the underlying prosocial and relational nature of gratitude, subsequently leading to strengthened social bonds, might facilitate unique pathways to well-being. Second, gratitude has a fulfillment aspect to it, unlike hope, that might facilitate extraction of benefits via mindful appreciation of both present and past received benefits. For example, given that hope is a positive motivational state driven by goal-directed energy and planning toward reaching future goal(s) (Snyder, 2000), it probably reaches its fruition only in a prospective fashion in the *absence* of a desired goal—a goal that may or may not be attained. Gratitude has also been shown to be activated strongly by first focusing on absence of benefits (Koo et al., 2008). However, unlike hope, gratitude is almost always felt in retrospection, thereby facilitating a positive cognitive framework toward an already present benefit. Furthermore, gratitude may be extracted from immediate or present life circumstances (e.g., "I am grateful for all the benefits that I received today"), and also from the past (e.g., "I am grateful for the love and support that I received when I was sick two years back"), promoting more expanded positive emotional experience. Besides the retrospective recognition of benefits, gratitude also drives future prosocial motivations (e.g., "I want to return benefits to others who have helped me").

Forgiveness is a motivational and emotional transformation whereby a person relinquishes feelings of past hurts and engages in constructive thoughts and possibly conciliatory actions toward the person who has hurt him or her (McCullough, Worthington, & Rachal, 1997). Given the psychological hurdles preceding forgiveness, such as overcoming past hurts, psychological well-being via forgiveness might be attained more gradually compared to gratitude.

In our laboratory, we recently compared gratitude with these two other positive psychological interventions and a control condition. Online interventions for gratitude, forgiveness, and hope were developed and implemented daily over a two-week period. Participants were randomly assigned to one of four conditions—the gratitude, forgiveness, hope, or control conditions.

In the gratitude condition, participants were asked to focus and engage grateful thoughts and feelings toward multiple gifts received each day. In the forgiveness condition the participants were asked to engage in benefit finding and forgiving thoughts toward an offender each day. In the hope condition, participants were asked each day to write about a goal that they hope to pursue in the future. The control group was asked to list activities attended each day over the two weeks. The four groups also reported their daily emotions and a daily checklist of spiritual, materialistic, prosocial, and grateful activities.

Compared to men, women in all three intervention conditions reported greater levels of both trait and state gratitude. More specifically, for the gratitude composite variable (i.e., appreciative, thankful, grateful) across the 14 days, gender differences were observed most strongly in the gratitude intervention condition. Women had higher levels of grateful emotions in the gratitude condition, indicating that women were more sensitive to the gratitude intervention. Women also reported higher levels of positive affect in the gratitude condition, compared to men (Mishra & Emmons, 2009). These findings resonate well with the gender differences findings revealed in recent studies (see Kashdan et al 2009; Watkins et al., 2003). As discussed earlier, the gender differences in gratitude may be explained by the greater susceptibility of women to extract benefits from gratitude because of its utility as an interpersonal emotion. Examining gender differences in gratitude may also lead to further insight into the possibility of gender-specific gratitude interventions that may applied in future studies.

## Conclusion

The science of gratitude is young. Even so, considerable progress has already been made in understanding how both state and trait gratitude are conducive to well-being. Of the 10 hypotheses advanced in this chapter, considerable empirical support was found for the majority of them. Some of these have been the object of more research than others, so it may be premature to suggest that a comprehensive evaluation of each has been accomplished. One conclusion that we can draw with confidence is that relation between gratitude and well-being is multiply determined. In particular, we found considerable evidence that gratitude builds social resources by

strengthening relationships and promoting prosocial actions. It is also likely that these 10 hypotheses do not exhaust the possible ways in which gratitude impacts well-being, and future research will undoubtedly uncover additional mechanisms. Toward that end, we offered some suggestions for the design of future studies that will hopefully continue to illuminate the richness and complexity of this social emotion and optimize the practice of gratitude for promoting harmonious intrapsychic and interpersonal functioning.

*References*

Adler, M. G., & Fagley, N. S. (2005). Appreciation: Individual differences in finding value and meaning as a unique predictor of subjective well-being. *Journal of Personality, 73,* 79–114.

Algoe, S. B., Haidt, J., & Gable, S. L. (2008). Beyond reciprocity: Gratitude and relationships in everyday life. *Emotion, 8,* 425–429.

Bar-Anan, Wilson, T. D., & Gilbert D. T. (2009). The feeling of uncertainty intensifies affective reactions. *Emotion, 9,* 123–127.

Bartlett, M.Y., & DeSteno, D. (2006). Gratitude and prosocial behavior: Helping when it costs you. *Psychological Science, 17,* 319–325.

Belk, R. W. (1985). Materialism: Trait aspects of living in the material world. *Journal of Consumer Research, 12,* 265–280.

Bilsky, W., & Schwartz, S. H. (1994). Values and personality. *European Journal of Personality, 8,* 163–181.

Bono, G., Emmons, R. A., & McCullough, M. E. (2004). Gratitude in practice and the practice of gratitude. In P. A. Linley and S. Joseph (Eds.), *Positive psychology in practice* (pp. 464–481). New York: Wiley.

Bono, G., McCullough, M. E., & Root, L. M. (2008). Forgiveness, feeling connected to others, and well-being: Two longitudinal studies. *Personality and Social Psychology Bulletin, 34,* 182–195.

Brody, L. R. (1999). *Gender, emotion, and the family.* Cambridge: Harvard University Press.

Brody, L. R. (1997). Gender and emotion: Beyond stereotypes. *Journal of Social Issues, 53,* 369–394.

Carman, J. B., & Streng, F. J. (Eds.) (1989). *Spoken and unspoken thanks: Some comparative soundings.* Cambridge, MA: Harvard University Press.

Christensen, H., Griffiths, K. M., Mackinnon, A. J., & Brittliffe, K. (2006). Online randomized controlled trial of brief and full cognitive behaviour therapy for depression. *Psychological Medicine, 36*, 1737–1746.

Dahua, W., Yan, T., & Liqing, Z. (2004). Inner-mechanisms between intergenerational social support and subjective well-being of the elderly. *Acta Psychologica Sinica, 36*, 78–82.

Denny, K. G., & Steiner, H. (2009). External and internal factors influencing happiness in elite collegiate athletes. *Child Psychiatry and Human Development, 40*, 55–72.

Emmons, R. A. (1999). Religion in the psychology of personality: An introduction. *Journal of Personality, 67*, 873–888.

Emmons, R. A., & Crumpler, C. A. (2000). Gratitude as a human strength: Appraising the evidence. *Journal of Social and Clinical Psychology, 19*, 56–67.

Emmons, R. A., & Kneezel, T. E. (2005). Giving thanks: Spiritual and religious correlates of gratitude. *Journal of Psychology and Christianity, 24*, 140–148.

Emmons, R. A., & McCullough, M. E. (Eds.). (2004) *The psychology of gratitude*. New York: Oxford University Press.

Emmons, R. A., & McCullough, M. E. (2003). Counting blessings versus burdens: An experimental investigation of gratitude and subjective well-being in daily life. *Journal of Personality and Social Psychology, 84*, 377–389.

Emmons, R. A., McCullough, M. E., & Tsang, J. (2003). The assessment of gratitude. In S. J. Lopez & C. R. Snyder (Eds.), *Positive psychological assessment: A handbook of models and measures* (pp. 327–341). Washington, DC: American Psychological Association.

Fredrickson, B. L. (2004). Gratitude like other positive emotions, broaden and builds. In R. A. Emmons & M. E. McCullough (Eds.), *The psychology of gratitude* (pp. 145–166). New York: Oxford University Press.

Fredrickson, B. L, Tugade, M. M., Waugh, C. E., & Larkin, G. R. (2003). What good are positive emotions in crisis? A prospective study of resilience and emotions following the terrorist attacks on the United States on September 11th, 2001. *Journal of Personality and Social Psychology, 84*, 365–376.

Frisch, M. B. (2006). *Quality of life therapy: Applying a life satisfaction approach to positive psychology and cognitive therapy*. New York: Wiley.

Froh, J. J., Emmons, R. A., Card, N. A., Bono, G., & Wilson, J. A. (in press). Gratitude and the reduced costs of materialism in adolescents. *Journal of Happiness Studies*.

Froh, J. J., Kashdan, T. B., Ozimkowski, K. M., & Miller, N. (2009). Who benefits the most from a gratitude intervention in children and adolescents? Examining positive affect as a moderator. *The Journal of Positive Psychology.4*, 408–422.

Froh, J. J., Sefick, W. J., & Emmons, R. A. (2008). Counting blessings in early adolescents: An experimental study of gratitude and subjective well-being. *Journal of School Psychology, 46*, 213–233.

Froh, J. J., Wajsblat, L., & Ubertini, L. (2008, November). Gratitude's role in promoting flourishing and inhibiting languishing: Using positive psychology to complement clinical practice. Poster session presented at the Association for Behavioral and Cognitive Therapies Annual Convention, Orlando, FL.

Froh, J. J., Yurkewicz, C., & Kashdan, T. B. (2009). Gratitude and subjective well-being in early adolescence: Examining gender differences. *Journal of Adolescence, 32*, 633–650.

Ger, G., & Belk, R. W. (1996). Cross-cultural differences in materialism. *Journal of Economic Psychology, 17*, 55–77.

Geraghty, A.W.A., Wood, A.M., & Hyland, M.E. (2010). Attrition from self-directed interventions: Investigating the relationship between psychological predictors, intervention content, and dropout from a body dissatisfaction intervention. *Social Science and Medicine, 71*, 30–37.

Gino, F., & Schweitzer, M. (2008). Blinded by anger or feeling the love: How emotions influence advice taking. *Journal of Applied Psychology, 93*, 1165–1173.

Howard, K. I., Kopta, S. M., Krause, S. M., & Orlinsky, D. E. (1986). The dose-effect relationship in psychotherapy. *American Psychologist, 41*, 159–164.

Isenberg, C. (2008). An examination of regret as expressed in the life reflections of older adults: Predictors of regret intensity and frequency, and association with well-being. *Dissertation Abstracts International, 69*, 4–B, 2653.

Kashdan, T. B., & Breen, W. E. (2007). Materialism and diminished well-being: Experiential avoidance as a mediating mechanism. *Journal of Social and Clinical Psychology, 26*, 521–539.

Kashdan, T. B., Mishra, A., Breen, W. E., & Froh, J. J. (2009). Gender differences in gratitude: Examining appraisals, narratives, the willingness to express emotions, and changes in psychological needs. *Journal of Personality, 77*, 691–730.

Kashdan, T. B., Uswatte, G., & Julian, T. (2006). Gratitude and hedonic and eudaimonic well-being in Vietnam War veterans. *Behavior Research and Therapy, 44,* 177–199.

Kasser, T. (2002). *The high price of materialism.* Cambridge, MA: MIT Press.

Kasser, T., & Kanner, A. D. (Eds.) (2003). *Psychology and consumer culture: The struggle for a good life in a materialistic world.* Washington DC: American Psychological Association.

Kasser, T., & Ryan, R. M. (1993). A dark side of the American dream: Correlates of financial success as a central life aspiration. *Journal of Personality and Social Psychology, 65,* 410–422.

Koo, M., Algoe, S. B., Wilson, T. D., & Gilbert, D. T. (2008). It's a wonderful life: Mentally subtracting positive events improves people's affective states, contrary to their affective forecasts. *Journal of Personality and Social Psychology, 95,* 1217–1224.

Krause, N. (2006). Gratitude toward God, stress, and health in late life. *Research on Aging, 28,* 163–183.

Kurtz, J. L. (2008). Looking to the future to appreciate the present: The benefits of perceived temporal scarcity. *Psychological Science, 19,* 1238–1241.

Landman, J. (1993). *Regret: The persistence of the possible.* New York: Oxford University Press.

Lawler, E. J. (2001). An affect theory of social exchange. *American Journal of Sociology, 107,* 321–352.

Levant, R. F., & Kopecky, G. (1995). *Masculinity, reconstructed.* New York: Dutton.

Liamputtong, P., Yimyam, S., Parisunyakul, S., Baosoung, C., & Sansiriphun, N. (2004). When I become a mother! Discourses of motherhood among northern Thai women. *Women's Studies International Forum, 27,* 589–601.

Lupfer, M. B., De Paola, S. J., Brock, K. F., & Clement, L. (1994). Making secular and religious attributions: The availability hypothesis revisited. *Journal for the Scientific Study of Religion, 33,* 162–171.

Lupfer, M. B., Tolliver, D., & Jackson, M. (1996). Explaining life-altering occurrences: A test of the "god-of-the-gaps" hypothesis. *Journal for the Scientific Study of Religion, 35,* 379–391.

Lyubomirsky, S., Sheldon, K. M., & Schkade, D. (2005). Pursuing happiness: The architecture of sustainable change. *Review of General Psychology, 9,* 111–131.

Lyubomirsky, S. Tkach, C., & DiMatteo, R. M. (2006). What are the differences between happiness and self-esteem. *Social Indicators Research, 78,* 363–404.

McCraty, R., & Childre, D. (2004). The grateful heart: The psychophysiology of appreciation.

In R. A. Emmons & M. E. McCullough (Eds.), *The psychology of gratitude* (pp. 230–255). New York: Oxford University Press.

McCullough, M. E., Emmons, R. A., & Tsang, Jo-Ann (2002). The grateful disposition: A conceptual and empirical topography. *Journal of Personality and Social Psychology, 82,* 112–127.

McCullough, M. E., Kilpatrick, S. D., Emmons, R. A., & Larson, D. B. (2001). Is gratitude a moral affect? *Psychological Bulletin, 127,* 249–266.

McCullough, M. E., Kimeldorf, M. B., & Cohen, A. D. (2008). An adaptation for altruism? The social causes, social effects, and social evolution of gratitude. *Current Directions in Psychological Science, 17,* 281–285.

McCullough, M. E., Tsang, J., & Emmons, R. A. (2004). Gratitude in intermediate affective terrain: Links of grateful moods to individual differences and daily emotional experience. *Journal of Personality and Social Psychology, 86,* 295–309.

McCullough, M. E., Worthington, E. L., & Rachal, K. C. (1997). Interpersonal forgiving in close relationships. *Journal of Personality and Social Psychology, 73,* 321–336.

Mikulincer, M., Shaver, P. R., & Slav, K. (2006). Attachment, mental representations of others, and interpersonal gratitude and forgiveness within romantic relationships. In M. Mikulincer & G. S. Goodman (Eds.), *Dynamics of romantic love* (pp. 191–215). New York: Guilford.

Mishra, A., & Emmons, R. A. (2009, June). Sex differences in positive psychology interventions: Comparing gratitude, forgiveness, hope. Poster presented at the First World Congress on Positive Psychology, Philadelphia, PA.

Nowak, M. A., & Roch, S. (2007). Upstream reciprocity and the evolution of gratitude. *Proceedings of the Royal Society B: Biological Sciences, 274,* 605–610.

Orr, A., Willis, S., Holmes, M., Britton, P., & Orr, D. (2007). Living with a kidney transplant. *Journal of Health Psychology, 12,* 653–662.

Parrott, W. G., & Smith, R. H. (1993). Distinguishing the experiences of envy and jealousy. *Journal of Personality and Social Psychology, 64,* 906–920.

Peterson, C., Park, N., Pole, N., D'Andrea, W., & Seligman, M. E. P. (2008). Strengths of character and posttraumatic growth. *Journal of Traumatic Stress, 21,* 214–217.

Peterson, C., & Seligman, M. E. P. (Eds.) (2004). *Character strengths and virtues: A handbook of classification.* Washington DC: American Psychological Association. New York: Oxford University Press.

Polak, E., & McCullough, M. E. (2006). Is gratitude an alternative to materialism? *Journal of Happiness Studies, 7,* 343–360.

Richins, M. L., & Dawson, S. (1992). A consumer values orientation for materialism and its measurement: Scale development and validation. *Journal of Consumer Research, 19,* 303–316.

Roberts, R. C. (2004). The blessings of gratitude: A conceptual analysis. In R. A. Emmons & M. E. McCullough (Eds.), *The psychology of gratitude* (pp. 58–78). New York: Oxford University Press.

Rosenberg, E. L. (1998). Levels of analysis and the organization of affect. *Review of General Psychology, 2,* 247–270.

Ross, M. (1989). Relation of implicit theories to the construction of personal histories. *Psychological Review, 96,* 341–357.

Saucier, G., & Goldberg, L. R. (1998). What is beyond the Big Five? *Journal of Personality, 66,* 495–524.

Seligman, M. E. P., Steen, T. A., Park, N., & Peterson, C. (2005). Positive psychology progress: Empirical validation of interventions. *American Psychologist, 60,* 410–421.

Sheldon, K. M., & Kasser, T. (1995). Coherence and congruence: Two aspects of personality integration. *Journal of Personality and Social Psychology, 68,* 531 543.

Shipon, R. W. (2007). Gratitude: Effect on perspectives and blood pressure of inner-city African-American hypertensive patients. *Dissertation Abstracts International: Section B: The Sciences and Engineering, 68*(3–B), 1977.

Smith R. H., & Kim S. H. (2007). Comprehending envy. *Psychological Bulletin, 133,* 46–64.

Smith, R. H., Parrott, W. G, Diener, E., Hoyle, R. H., & Kim, S. H. (1999). Dispositional envy. *Personality and Social Psychology Bulletin, 25,* 1007–1020.

Smith, R. H., Turner, T., Leach, C., Garonzik, R., Urch-Druskat, V., & Weston, C. M. (1996). Envy and schadenfreude. *Personality and Social Psychology Bulletin, 22,* 158–168.

Snyder, C. R. (2000). Hypothesis: There is hope. In C. R. Snyder (Ed.), *Handbook of hope: Theories, measures, and applications* (pp. 3–21). Orlando, FL: Academic Press.

Snyder, C. R., Rand, K. L., & Sigmon, D. R. (2002). Hope theory: A member of the positive psychology family. *Handbook of positive psychology* (pp. 257–276). New York: Oxford University Press.

Sommers, S., & Kosmitzki, C. (1988). Emotion and social context: An American–German comparison. *British Journal of Social Psychology, 27,* 35–49.

Steen, T. A., Kachorek, L. V., & Peterson, C. (2003). Character strengths among youth. *Journal of Youth and Adolescence, 32,* 5–16.

Stoppard, J. M., & Gruchy, C. (1993). Gender, context, and expression of positive emotion. *Personality and Social Psychology Bulletin, 19,* 143–150.

Trivers, R. L. (1971). The evolution of reciprocal altruism. *The Quarterly Review of Biology, 46,* 35–57.

Vernon, L. L., Dillon, J. M., & Steiner, A. R. W. (2009). Proactive coping, gratitude, and posttraumatic stress disorder in college women. *Anxiety, Stress, & Coping, 22,* 117–127.

Walker, S. S., & Schimmack, U. (2008). Validity of a happiness implicit association test as a measure of subjective wellbeing. *Journal of Research in Personality, 42,* 490–497.

Watkins, P. C. (2000, August). Gratitude and depression: How a human strength might mitigate human adversity. Paper presented at the 109th Annual Convention of the American Psychological Association, San Francisco, CA.

Watkins, P. C., Cruz, L., Holben, H., & Kolts, R. L. (2008). Taking care of business? Grateful processing of unpleasant memories. *The Journal of Positive Psychology, 3,* 87–99.

Watkins, P. C., Grimm, D. L., & Hailu, L. (1998, June). Counting your blessings: Grateful individuals recall more positive memories. Presented at the 11th Annual Convention of the American Psychological Society, Denver, CO.

Watkins, P. C., Grimm, D. L., & Kolts, R. (2004). Counting your blessings: Positive memories among grateful persons. *Current Psychology, 23,* 52–67.

Watkins, P. C., Scheer, J., Ovnicek, M., & Kolts, R. (2006). The debt of gratitude: Dissociating gratitude and indebtedness. *Cognition and Emotion, 20,* 217–241.

Watkins, P. C., Woodward, K., Stone, T., & Kolts, R. L. (2003). Gratitude and happiness: Development of a measure of gratitude, and relationships with subjective well-being. *Social Behavior and Personality, 31,* 431–452.

Weiner, B. (2007). *Social motivation, justice, and the moral emotions.* Mahwah, NJ: Lawrence Erlbaum Associates.

Wood, A.M., Froh, J.J., & Geraghty, A.W.A. (2010). Gratitude and well-being: A review and theoretical orientation. *Clinical Psychology Review, 30,* 890–905.

Wood, A. M., Joseph, S., & Linley, P. A. (2007). Coping style as a psychological resource of grateful people. *Journal of Social & Clinical Psychology, 26,* 1076–1093.

Wood, A. M., Joseph, S., Lloyd, J., & Atkins, S. (2009). Gratitude influences sleep through the mechanism of pre-sleep cognitions. *Journal of Psychosomatic Research, 66,* 43–48.

Wood, A. M., Joseph, S., & Maltby, J. (2008). Gratitude uniquely predicts satisfaction with life: Incremental validity above the domains and facets of the five factor model. *Personality and Individual Differences, 45,* 49–54.

# VI

**Relationship Perspectives**

# 17

# The Positive Side of Close Relationships

*Shelly L. Gable and Courtney L. Gosnell*

Research from several sources has unequivocally shown that close relationships are strongly linked to health and well-being. For example, in terms of physical health, large-scale epidemiological studies have demonstrated that social isolation is associated with a substantial increase in all-cause mortality risk (e.g., Berkman & Syme, 1979; House, Landis, Umberson, 1988). Studies focused on specific physiological systems have found that poor-quality relationships or a lack of social ties are associated with poorer functioning cardiovascular, immune, and endocrine systems (see Uchino, Cacioppo, & Keicolt-Glaser, 1996, for review). In terms of well-being, it has been well-established that positive close relationships are closely tied to happiness and satisfaction with life (e.g., Berscheid & Reis, 1998; Diener & Seligman, 2002). These links do not exist solely on the pages of empirical journals; they are clearly recognized by the public. For example, people routinely cite their close relationships as their most significant or meaningful areas of life (e.g., Little, 1989; Sears, 1977). In short, both the empirical data and common experience support the idea that forming and maintaining stable and positive close relationships is a critical component of health and well-being. Moreover, the human condition cannot be understood without a careful understanding of close relationships (e.g., Baumeister & Leary, 1995) and how the mind evolved to develop and maintain these ties.

Even though the field of close relationships is a relatively young science, scholars have made considerable progress in understanding processes that unfold in close relationships. The lion's share of this research has focused on processes that undermine close relationships and the links between poor-quality social relationships or social isolation and negative outcomes. However, over the years there have been several notable exceptions to the focus on negative relationship processes, and recently researchers have begun to pay closer attention to positive processes in relationships. In this chapter, we first take stock of work that has focused on processes that promote high-quality relationships and the role that these processes play in health and well-being. We then discuss areas that we see as ripe for future research on positive processes in close relationships that are likely to shed light on important links to health and well-being.

## Taking Stock

## Social Support

Tangible and emotional support from other people during times of stress has long been thought to be a major pathway through which social ties are linked to health and well-being. The way in which social support has been defined and measured has varied both across disciplines (e.g., psychology, epidemiology) and within disciplines (Vangelisti, 2009). Three major conceptualizations of support have been used in the literature. Structural support refers to the number of social ties or the interconnectedness of those ties (often called density) that a person reports. Enacted or received support refers to specific support transactions or support that is actually given or received in response to a stressor. Finally, perceived support (or perceived availability of support) is the perception that others will come to one's aide if needed (Vangelisti, 2009).

### Correlates of Support

The outcomes associated with social support depend largely on which conceptualization of support is employed. One puzzling aspect of the social support literature is that there appear to be differences between what researchers refer to as perceived social support (the perception that one has supportive others who would be available in times of need) and enacted social support (the actual transaction of tangible or emotional support from a support provider). Perceived support is consistently associated with positive health and well-being (Kaul & Lakey, 2003; Lakey & Cassady, 1990). For example, perceived availability of support has been associated with a reduction of anxiety and depression during stressful times (Fleming, Baum, Gisriel, & Gatchel, 1982;), more positive adjustment to diseases (Holahan, Moos, Holahan, & Brennan, 1997; Stone, Mezzacappa, Donatone, & Gonder, 1999), and reduced heart rate and blood pressure response during a stressful speech task (Smith, Ruiz, & Uchino, 2004). However, enacted support has often been unrelated to outcomes, or in some cases, associated with negative outcomes (Dunkel-Schetter & Bennett, 1990; Bolger, Kessler, & Zuckerman, 2000). Why is it that thinking that support will be available to you (regardless of the veracity of that belief) is better than actually receiving that support?

Researchers have hypothesized that receiving support from others can carry costs such as lowering self-esteem, drawing attention to the problem, making the recipient feel incompetent, or lead the recipient to feel indebted (Bolger, Zuckerman, & Kessler, 2000; Shrout, Herman, & Bolger, 2006). Thus, the potential costs of enacted support may mask their potential benefits such as practical help and emotional comfort (see Sarason, Sarason, & Gurung, 1997). Supporting the notion that enacted support may carry costs, Bolger and colleagues (2000) conducted a study examining the effects of actual support interactions. They found that stressed individuals reported the better outcomes (e.g., lower anxiety) on days that their partner reported providing support, but they did not report receiving support themselves (which the researchers called invisible support) compared to days the stressed recipient reported receiving support from the partner (called visible support).

Other researchers have argued that one of the reasons that actual support has been only tenuously linked to outcomes is that the support received may not be very skilled or can be perceived as unhelpful (Dunkel-Schetter & Bennett, 1990). Thus, it seems it is imperative that researchers investigating enacted social support recognize the close relationship context in which support transactions take place (e.g., Collins & Feeney, 2000). In particular, the construct of perceived responsiveness is likely a critical factor regarding whether or not the support transaction is beneficial. Perceived responsiveness is the idea that the relationship partner understands, validates, and cares for "core . . . features of the self" (Reis, Clark, & Holmes, 2004, p.203). Many theoretical approaches to relationships (e.g., attachment theory, communal relationships theory) regard perceived responsiveness as a central aspect of satisfying relationships (Murray, Holmes, & Collins, 2007), and researchers have specifically conceptualized effective social support as "responsiveness to another's needs and . . . as acts that communicate caring; that validate the other's worth, feelings, or actions" (Cutrona, 1996, p. 10).

A recent study by Maisel and Gable (2009) examined enacted support transactions in terms of perceived responsiveness. They found that received support, both visible and invisible, was associated with positive outcomes for the recipient when it was intended to be or perceived to be responsive—understanding, validating, and caring. Conversely, when support was low in responsiveness, it was associated with no benefits or even negative outcomes. Moreover, the outcomes were not limited to the support recipient per se (e.g., decreased anxiety) but also extended to the recipient's perceptions of the relationship with the support provider (e.g., increased connection). This study illustrates the potential insights to be gained by examining social support in the context of close relationship processes and identifying the theoretically predicted key components of successful support transactions.

## Mechanisms

Although several studies have documented important outcomes associated with social support, fewer have focused on the question of how or through what mechanisms social support is linked to outcomes. This research has shown that different mechanisms may link support to outcomes. Again however, different mechanisms have been associated with the different conceptualizations of support. For example, Cohen and Wills (1985) reviewed a series of studies connecting social support with well-being and found support for two separate models, the main effects model and the buffering model. The main effects model argues that effective social support has a direct affect on well-being. Cohen and Wills (1985) found that the direct effects model was most clearly supported in studies where support is measured through degree of social integration in a large social network. Thus, the direct effect model finds that people who report having more social ties also report greater well-being than those with fewer ties, even when no stressors are present. The buffering model argues that effective support protects an individual from the negative effects of stressful events when they do occur. Cohen and Wills (1985) found that the buffering model was supported when social support was measured through the perceived availability of interpersonal resources.

Similarly, Bolger and Zuckerman (1995) described two processes through which personality factors can interact with stress to affect outcomes: an exposure process (how often the individual encounters the stressor) and a reactivity process (the extent to which a person shows an emotional or physical reaction to a stressor). Social support may be involved in both the exposure and reactivity processes such that high levels of social support decrease the number of stressors (or perceived stressors) in life and attenuate reactions to stressors. There is evidence for both of these processes in the literature.

Social support may have a direct impact on positive outcomes because supportive others can alter the perception of everyday events so that they are not perceived as threats or stressors. For example, a study by Schnall, Harber, Stefanucci, and Proffitt (2008) found that the presence of a friend (real or in one's thoughts) led observers to perceive a hill that they were told they would have to climb to be less steep. Moreover, once stressors do occur, having close ties with supportive others helps people cope more effectively with them; this is true for both major life events and smaller, everyday hassles (e.g., Bolger & Eckenrode, 1991; Harlow & Cantor, 1995). In short, there is good evidence that social support operates both through reducing the number of stressors in one's life (direct effect) as well as by equipping individuals to better handle stressors (buffering). However, even outside of the context of stressful life events, social support is associated with an increased sense of self-efficacy and personal goal fulfillment, as was shown by Brunstein, Dangelmayer and Schultheiss (1996), who found that social support was predictive of personal goal enactment (findings that are consistent with Cohen & Wills' direct effects model reviewed above).

In short, although much has been learned about social support processes, more research is needed to fully understand the role that social support plays in health and well-being. We believe there are three topics ripe for further inquiry. First, researchers need to more fully understand the dyadic nature of these transactions—that is, support transactions and, presumably, the role they play in close relationship formation and maintenance, and the impact that these transactions have on the support provider.

## Capitalization

Although it seems inevitable that at least a little rain must fall in everyone's life, good things happen too. In fact, in everyday life, positive events outpace negative events at a ratio of at least three to one (Gable & Haidt, 2005). And just as the social support literature has shown that people turn to others to cope with negative events, recent research has also shown that people often turn to others to share their good news. This process was termed *capitalization* by Langston (1994) because it refers to the act of making the most out of, or capitalizing on, positive events. Capitalization research has investigated the consequences of the act of telling others about a positive event, as well as the effect of the response of the person with whom the event was disclosed (e.g., Gable, Reis, Impett, & Asher, 2004; Gable, Gonzaga, & Strachman, 2006; Langston, 1994). In addition, empirical studies have focused on both intrapersonal and interpersonal outcomes (e.g., Gable et al., 2006, Reis et al., 2009).

This work began with a pair of daily experience studies by Langston (1994). He found that when people shared the news of a positive event with others, they experienced positive affect above and beyond the positive event itself. In subsequent studies, we replicated and expanded on these original findings (e.g., Gable et al., 2004; 2006; Reis et al., 2009). One surprising finding in our work is that capitalization is quite common. For example, in one daily experience study, people told at least one other person about the best thing that happened to them over the course of the day between 70% and 80% of the time (e.g., Gable et al., 2004). This high frequency of sharing was also found by studies using very different methods. For example, Algoe and Haidt (2009) found that when participants recalled and described a time when they got something, they spontaneously mentioned having told or having wanted to tell other people about it more than 80% of the time. Not surprisingly, we have also found that people are more likely to tell other people about important positive events than less important events (the correlation between event importance and sharing is low to moderate, e.g., r = .26; Gable et al., 2004, Study 1). In addition, the likelihood of sharing events with others was not correlated with attributing the event to luck or effort.

Also, replicating and extending Langston's (1994) original findings, we have found that when people share positive events with others, they experienced more positive affect, well-being, self-esteem, and less loneliness than is attributable to the events themselves. In addition, the more people with whom they shared the event, the better their outcomes (Gable et al., 2004; Reis et al., 2009). Our next step in this research was to identify the people with whom positive events are shared. We found that positive events were shared almost exclusively with close relationship partners. For example, in one study we found that nearly all (97%) of the people with whom the positive event was shared

were close relationship partners, such as friends, siblings, parents, roommates, or romantic partners; only 3% of events were shared with non-close others, such as coworkers and acquaintances.

Our findings regarding the near-exclusive involvement of close others in capitalization disclosures suggested that in addition to being an intrapersonal process, capitalization is also an interpersonal process. Specifically, we hypothesized two things. First, the reaction of the person to whom the event was disclosed accounts for the majority of capitalization of the observed effects. Second, we hypothesized that capitalization interactions provide a crucial opportunity for relationship partners to cultivate closeness and intimacy. That is, a supportive response to a close relationship partner's positive event disclosure builds intimacy, likely without the potential pitfalls associated with enacted social support for a negative event (see above for discussion), and contributes to the perceived availability of support. What, exactly, is a supportive, positive response to a capitalization attempt?

To answer this question, we created a measure of perceptions of how a relationship partner responds when a positive event has been shared (Gable et al, 2004). This measure, the Perceived Responses to Capitalization Attempts (PRCA), employed an adaptation of Rusbult and colleagues' typology of responses to a partner's negative behavior, such as criticisms, snapping, and other relationship transgressions (Rusbult, Zembrodt, & Gunn, 1982)—called accommodation responses. This empirically validated model describes responses to a partner's potentially destructive behavior along two independent dimensions: constructive-destructive and active-passive. Thus, there are four types of reactions to problematic behavior: active-constructive (e.g., talking about the problem), passive-constructive (e.g., giving the partner the benefit of the doubt), active-destructive (e.g., considering ending the relationship), or passive-destructive (e.g., avoiding the partner for a while). In their research on accommodation process, Rusbult and colleagues have found that both types of constructive responses are positively associated with relationship well-being, whereas both active and passive types of destructive responses are natively associated with relationship well-being (Rusbult, Verette, Whitney, Slovic, & Lipkus, 1991). The PRCA was based on the accommodation framework and also characterized positive event disclosures along these two dimensions. The four types of responses to capitalization attempts are as follows: active-constructive responses (e.g., "He/she reacts to my good fortune enthusiastically"), passive-constructive responses (e.g., He/she is silently supportive of the good things that occur to me"), active-destructive responses (e.g., "He/she points out the potential problems or down sides of the good event"), and passive-destructive responses (e.g., "My partner doesn't pay much attention to me").

To elaborate on the four types, *active-constructive* responding entails the expression of excitement or enthusiasm about the positive event and active involvement in the exchange. The responder often asks questions about the event, elaborates on the event's implications for the discloser, and reflects on the meaning of the event to the discloser in particular. Interest, happiness, and pride are commonly expressed emotions in this response. *Passive-constructive* responding conveys a positive reaction to the event, but this reaction is subdued as the responder says little or is silent about the event. The responder may provide a pleasant but short exchange. This response differs from the active-constructive response primarily in the responder's level of involvement (i.e., no questions posed or elaborations or implications presented).

*Active-destructive* responding is similar to active-constructive responding in terms of its level of involvement on the part of the responder. However, with an active-destructive response, the feedback is negative. The responder often points out possible negative implications of the event, interprets the event less favorably than the discloser did, or minimizes the significance of the event. Finally, the *passive-destructive* response simply fails to acknowledge the event at all. The responder either changes the subject to discuss something completely different or directs the conversation to an event that occurred to him or her.

Consider the following example. Deborah rushes home from her job at a law firm to tell her husband Rich that the senior partners just assigned her to be the lead attorney for the firm's biggest client. If Rich provides an active-constructive response, it would sound something like this: "This is great news! You will be a wonderful lead attorney; you have a sharp legal mind and you are a born leader. The partners have recognized your talents! I know you worked hard, and I am proud of you. Can you talk about the case?" A passive-constructive response would sound something like this: "How nice, dear." If Rich provides an active-destructive response,

it would sound something like this: "That sounds like a lot of work. Are you ready to take on such a big client? Will you have to work even longer hours? I am surprised they didn't give it to someone with more experience than you." Finally, a passive-destructive response would sound something like "What do you want to have for dinner tonight?" or "Wait until you hear what happened to me at work today."

We conducted a series of studies on the association between the perceived typical responses to capitalization attempts in established relationships (using the PRCA measure) and relationship quality outcomes, using samples of dating couples and married couples. For example, in the study of dating couples, we found that when participants reported that their partners typically responded in an active-constructive manner, they reported greater relationship satisfaction, trust, and intimacy (this was true for both men and women). However, reporting that one's partner typically responds in a passive-constructive, active-destructive, or passive-destructive manner was consistently negatively correlated with these outcomes (Gable et al., 2004; Study 2). These results remained robust when controlling for reports of how a partner typically responds to one's negative behavior (i.e., accommodation; Rusbult, Verette, Whitney, Slovic, & Lipkus, 1991). We found similar results in the married sample, using outcomes collected on a daily basis (e.g., daily relationship quality, reports of conflict), and controlling for overall relationship satisfaction.[1]

It is particularly interesting that passive-constructive responses were negatively predictive of relationship quality because in Rusbult and colleagues' (1991) accommodation work, passive-constructive responses to a partner's transgressions are typically positively associated with outcomes (or sometimes uncorrelated with outcomes). However, this pattern was replicated in experimental work and with previously unacquainted dyads. For example, Reis and colleagues (2009; Study 3) conducted an experiment in which they had confederates interview participants about an important positive event that occurred in their lives. The confederate responded in either an active-constructive manner or a passive-constructive manner. Participants felt closer to their interviewers when in the active-constructive condition than in the passive-constructive condition, both right after the exchange and at a follow-up assessment one week later.

At first it may seem that pleasant but quiet reactions to the disclosure of positive events would not be bad; however, these quiet exchanges are predictive of poorer relationship quality. Thus, passive-constructive responses show a pattern quite similar to active-destructive and passive-destructive responses in terms of the impact they have on relationship quality. We also assessed how a response affects the *discloser*. That is, do the personal benefits of sharing positive events that we reported above fluctuate in accordance with the response of the other person? To answer this question, we examined the intrapersonal consequences of the reaction of the responder to capitalization attempts using measures adapted from the PRCA.

We found that receiving active-constructive responses was associated with increased positive affect and subjective well-being. The effects of the response to capitalization attempts on the discloser were above and beyond his or her rated importance of the event in the first place. However, passive or destructive responses were associated with either no increase in positive affect and well-being associated with the event or, in several instances, decreases in these outcomes (Gable et al., 2004; Study 4; Gable, 2008; Reis et al., 2009, Study 2). In an experimental study aimed at delineating mechanisms of capitalization, Reis and colleagues (2009, Study 2) found that after participants received an active-constructive response from a confederate while discussing a recent positive event, they increased their ratings of the importance of that event. This augmentation of the event's importance did not occur if they were randomly assigned to receive passive feedback.

*Capitalization reactions and perceived responsiveness to the self.* In our work on capitalization, we hypothesized that one very important ingredient in reactions to capitalization disclosures is the perception of responsiveness to the self (see above section for discussion). When an interaction partner provides an active-constructive response to a capitalization disclosure, recognition of the importance of that event to the discloser *in particular* is conveyed. This demonstrates understanding (or a desire to understand) of what is significant to the discloser. Second, enthusiastically supportive reactions, questions about the event, and expressions of joy convey that the responder agrees that the event itself is or will be significant. This conveys validation to the discloser. Finally, when the responder exhibits emotion in his or her reaction, it conveys

affective investment, or a sense of caring. In short, an active-constructive response conveys the three critical elements of perceived responsiveness. On the other hand, a passive or destructive response does not convey understanding, validation, or caring, and may convey their opposites.

In order to test the idea that active-constructive responses convey perceived responsiveness, we conducted an observational study of dating couples. Dating couples came into the laboratory and engaged in a series of discussions in the laboratory that were videotaped (Gable et al., 2006). Prior to these interactions, they independently completed several measures, including how their partner typically responds to their positive event disclosures (the PRCA measure). During the videotape portion, they took turns sharing a recent positive event with one another (capitalization) and sharing a recent negative event with one another (traditional social support). After they shared their events, they rated how understood, validated, and cared for their partners made them feel (perceived responsiveness).

In support of the idea that active-constructive reactions convey perceived responsiveness, we found that the more participants reported that their partners typically responded in an active-constructive manner (and not an active or destructive manner), the greater perceived responsiveness they reported after the positive event discussion in the laboratory. However, the PRCA did not predict how much perceived responsiveness the partner conveyed during the negative event discussion. In addition to providing the first evidence that active-constructive responding conveys responsiveness, these results showed that responding well to a partner's good fortune does not necessarily indicate that the partner will respond effectively in times of stress because PRCA scores did not predict feelings responded to after negative event disclosures.

In addition to looking at the link between typical reactions to capitalization attempts and perceived responsiveness, in this study we examined the actual behavior during the videotaped capitalization exchange. Specifically, we trained raters to code the reactions of partners to participants' capitalization attempts on the active-passive dimension and the constructive-destructive dimension. We found that the more active and constructive the coders rated partners' responses, the higher participants rated their partners on perceived responsiveness. These results provided strong support for our prediction that active and constructive responding increases feelings of responsiveness, while passive or destructive responding undermines feelings of responsiveness.

Moreover, this study provided evidence regarding the critical nature of perceived responsiveness in healthy relationships. Specifically, couples were contacted after the study to complete a follow-up survey on their relationship status and quality (e.g., satisfaction, commitment). For both men and women, perceived responsiveness ratings following the positive event disclosure predicted relationship health at the follow-up. Moreover, perceived responsiveness to positive event disclosures may be particularly important because responsiveness ratings after the negative event disclosure did not predict relationship health at the follow-up. Many other studies have found strong links between perceived responsiveness and intimacy (e.g., Laurenceau, Barrett, & Pietromonaco, 1998; Manne, Ostroff et al., 2004), thus capitalization responses may play a crucial role in the growth or stagnation of intimacy and closeness in relationships.

In summary, the research on capitalization has shown the important role that close others can play in capitalizing on positive events. Disclosing positive events and having close interaction partners who are good at responding when things go right has benefits for both the individual and the relationship. Despite the research progress to date, more work needs to be conducted to understand the processes that link capitalization to outcomes. For example, how do expectations of a partner's response affect the choice to disclose a positive event? Are some partners more or less likely to be the targets of capitalization attempts? On a related note, are there individual differences or contextual factors that contribute to one's ability to respond effectively to a capitalization attempt? Perhaps attachment styles (Bowlby, 1982) moderate capitalization responses; or it may be difficult to respond effectively when the positive event has implications for the responder's own self-concept (e.g., Tesser, 1988). Another area we know little about is the role that capitalization plays in parent-child relationships and the formation of the child's self-concept. Finally, little is known about how responding to others' positive event disclosures affects the responder. That is, providing a capitalization response may have direct affects on the responder that are distinct from his or her relationship with the discloser.

## Close Relationships, Motivation, and Emotion

### Pursuit of the Ideal Self

Close relationship partners are often active participants in each other's personal development and goal pursuit. In this vein, research on what is known as *the Michelangelo phenomenon* (e.g., Drigotas, Rusbult, Weiselquist, & Whitton, 1999, Drigotas, 2002; Rusbult, Kumashiro, Kubacka, & Finkel, 2009) has provided excellent evidence for the process through which close partners can promote (or hinder) one's pursuit of the ideal self. The term Michelangelo phenomenon is eloquently derived from Michelangelo Buonarroti's description of the sculptor's job as releasing an ideal figure from a block of stone (Rusbult et al., 2009). In the case of people, the ideal figure inside the stone is the ideal self (e.g., Higgins, 1987). A person's pursuit of his or her ideal self may be represented as an explicit, clearly defined set of goals, or the ideal self can be vaguer, such as a collection of dreams or aspirations.

Research on the Michelangelo phenomenon has found evidence for how partners influence movement toward each one other's ideal selves. Primarily, partners do this through perceptual or behavioral affirmation, known collectively as partner affirmations. Specifically, the degree to which one's cognitive representation of the partner is consistent with his or her ideal self is perceptual affirmation, and the degree to which the partner treats the target in a manner that is consistent with his or her ideal self is behavioral affirmation (e.g., Drigotas et al, 1999). Of course, perceptual affirmation is closely associated with behavioral affirmation (people tend to behave toward their partners in ways consistent with their cognitive representations of their partners), and behavioral affirmation (which is actually displayed to the partner) is more directly related to movement toward the ideal self than perceptual affirmation.

The influence that partners have on one another stems from the nature of their interdependent relationship. Interdependent relationships are by definition those in which partners influence one another's outcomes (e.g., rewards, costs, well-being) through the course of their interactions (Kelley et al., 2003). Over the course of the many coordinated activities partners engage in with one another, they can affirm (or conversely, disaffirm) each other's pursuit toward the ideal self. That is, partner affirmations elicit aspects of the ideal self through these interactions, and this can be done in an automatic or intentional manner (Rusbult et al., 2009). Partner affirmations, in turn, are strongly associated with perceptions of similarity to the ideal self, and changes in perceptions of similarity to the ideal self over time (Drigotas et al., 1999; Rusbult et al., 2009). Moreover, partner affirmations are also strongly associated with personal well-being and relationship quality (Drigotas, 2002; Drigotas et al., 1999; Rusbult et al., 2009). Conceptually, partner affirmations are similar to Deci and Ryan's (2000) construct of autonomy support, which they define as support for *self-ascribed* goals, values, and needs.

## Motivation to Expand the Self

Another area of research that has focused on the role of close relationships in the development of the self is Arthur Aron and colleagues' research on the self-expansion model (Aron, Aron, Tudor, & Nelson, 1991; see also Aron et al., 2004 for review). The self-expansion model posits that people are *motivated* to increase the bounds of their self-concept by incorporating the resources, perspectives, and identities of close others into their own self-concept. This model has been supported by extensive empirical evidence. In close relationships, mental models of the self and other are linked and overlap; the closer the relationship, the greater this degree of overlap. Thus, the partner's personal qualities and resources are less distinguishable from one's own.

Aron and colleagues have argued that the motivation to expand the self is a central motivation, and the desire for self-expansion drives us to seek, enter, and deepen close relationships. Moreover, they argue that the act of self-expansion, or including the other in the self, is rewarding and creates positive affect. Hence the rapid expansion of the self that occurs at the beginning of relationships at least partially accounts for the euphoric feelings attributed to falling in love (Aron et al., 1991). Of course, the theory speaks largely to incorporating the positive qualities, attributes, and resources of the other person. Thus, a straightforward future direction would be to investigate the inclusion of other in the self from a strength-based perspective (Peterson & Park, 2009).

Interestingly, very recent research has shown that the idea that motivation to expand the self can lead people to draw closer to another can actually occur in the reverse order. Specifically, Slotter and Gardner (2009) have found that the

motivation to be close to someone can lead to self-expansion. In an impressive series of studies, these researchers showed that when individuals anticipate or desire to be close to another, they are motivated to integrate aspects of the other into their self-concept. For example, in one study participants were told their interaction partner possessed an attribute of which they had been previously unaware. Participants incorporated this novel attribute into their self-concept only when motivated to be closer (i.e., the effect was observed only when romantic partners were the interaction partner, not when a stranger was the interaction partner; Slotter & Garder, 2009; Study 2). In another study, participants incorporated attributes of a new person into their self-concepts only when the other person was presented as a potential dating partner (not when presented as a potential job applicant; Slotter & Gardner, 2009; Study 3). The authors discuss their results in terms of the functions of self-other integration. In established relationships, self-other integration likely leads to pro-relationship thoughts and behavior (e.g., Agnew, 2006). In addition, perceived similarity to the self is a central tenet of attraction (Byrne, 1971).

## Gratitude

Although research on emotions in close relationships has tended to focus on negative emotions, such as jealously, anger, anxiety, and grief, recent work on gratitude in close relationships is an exception. The emotion of gratitude has been studied largely as an intrapersonal phenomenon; studies have tended to focus on the attributions associated with and the personal consequences of gratitude (see McCullough et al., 2001 for review). Recently, however, Algoe and colleagues (Algoe & Haidt, 2009; Algoe, Haidt, & Gable, 2008; Algoe, Gable, & Maisel, in press) have examined gratitude in the context of interpersonal relationships. This work is grounded in a social-functional model of emotions (e.g., Keltner & Haidt, 1999) and examines what function gratitude serves for the benefactor and recipient and the relationship between them.

Specifically, Algoe and colleagues have argued that gratitude functions to promote relationship formation and maintenance and have offered evidence for this in several studies employing different methods and involving diverse samples. For example, Algoe and Haidt (2009) had participants recall events that had happened to them, either when another person evoked feelings of gratitude or happiness. Participants who were in the gratitude condition were more likely to report noticing new positive qualities about their benefactors and that they would be more willing to spend time with their benefactors in the future than those in the happiness condition (note in both conditions the emotions was caused by the actions of the other person).

This relational function of the gratitude emotion has been empirically studied in both newly formed relationships and stable dating relationships. Specifically, in a study of emerging friendships in college sororities, Algoe and colleagues (2008) examined the role of gratitude during a week of gift-giving from older members to new members. They asked the new sorority members (the gift recipients) to record their reactions to the benefits received from the older member assigned to be their anonymous gift-giver during this special week. They found that that the more the benefit conveyed perceived responsiveness to the self (i.e., understanding, validation, and caring), the more gratitude the recipient reported. This effect controlled for the cost of the benefit and the liking for the benefit. Moreover, the emotion of gratitude positively predicted future relationship outcomes (e.g., closeness, liking).

In a subsequent study of cohabiting couples, both members of the dyad reported on their emotions and behaviors in a daily experience study (Algoe, Gable, & Maisel, 2010). They found that the receipt of thoughtful benefits predicted gratitude in both men and women. Moreover, participants' gratitude predicted increases in relationship connection and satisfaction the following day, for both them and their partners (i.e., both the recipient and benefactor reported greater relationship quality). The results of these studies suggest that gratitude is associated with noticing the benefactor's positive qualities and relationship-enhancement, a process that Algoe and colleagues (2008) refer to as *find, remind, and bind*. Although the work on gratitude in interpersonal relationships is very recent, it can serve as a model for investigating how other positive emotions function in close relationships. In the next section, we speculate on a few of the areas in close relationships that we see as in need of increased empirical and theoretical attention.

## Love

Love has always been a popular topic; historically poets, philosophers, and playwrights have had a corner on the market. Prominent psychologists long ago recognized the importance of love in human behavior. John Bowlby (1969) proposed that maternal love, attachment bonds, and caregiving were central processes in human behavior. Others such as Harry Harlow (1958) demonstrated that maternal love was not the result of secondary reinforcement (e.g., providing food) in his famous cloth and wire monkey experiments. Despite these early insights, love as the topic of scientific study has not been universally embraced. The quintessential illustration of the public's skepticism of psychologists' ability to empirically investigate love come in 1975 when Senator Proxmire awarded one of his "Golden Fleece" awards to two social psychologists who had a National Science Foundation grant to study love (see Hatfield, 2006). Proxmire thought this topic was not a meritorious use of taxpayers' money. Ironically, this contradicts everything we know about the critical role that close relationships play in health and well-being. Despite these historical trends, researchers have made important strides in understanding the positive emotion of love.

Several researchers distinguish between two kinds of love: passionate love and companionate love (Bercheid & Walster; 1978; Sternberg, 1986). Passionate love is the intense excitement and attraction one has for someone else, and companionate love is the affection and liking we feel for someone else. Both types of love are important in close relationships. From an evolutionary perspective, the function of passionate love and desire is to foster attraction and relationship initiation. Relationship initiation involves finding a partner and disrupting current activities to direct energies to build the new relationship. The function of companionate love, in contrast, is to foster commitment to maintaining an existing relationship to gain evolutionary benefits from the partnership (e.g. Gonzaga et al., 2001).

Aron and colleagues have been particularly interested in the phenomena of intense passionate love, such as that experienced in the beginning of a new relationship (e.g., Aron, Fisher, & Strong, 2006). The emotion of intense passionate love is also associated with noted changes in the self-concept and self-esteem (Aron, Paris, & Aron, 1995) and has been described as consuming and euphoric. The largely positive feelings associated with the experience of passionate love are supported by functional magnetic resonance imaging studies. This work using fMRI techniques has found that passionate love is associated with activity in phylogenically old reward and motivation systems (Aron et al., 2005)

Whereas passionate love has been primarily associated with arousal and reward motivation, companionate love has been associated with bonding and intimacy (Reis & Aron, 2008). Companionate love is a defining feature of communal relationships—relationships characterized by mutual expectations that each will respond to the other's needs (Clark & Mills, 1993). Companionate love has also been described as an attachment or bond with another and is highly predictive of long-term romantic relationship satisfaction and maintenance (e.g., Huston & Evangelisti, 1991). In summary, although research on love has not always enjoyed a prominent place in either the public or scientific community, psychologists have made great strides in understanding love (see Aron et al., 2006 for a comprehensive review).

## Future Directions

### Biological Underpinnings

As we stated in the beginning of this chapter, many studies have found strong links between interpersonal relationships and physical health (e.g., House et al., 1988). However, investigations of the mediators of these links are not as common. Specifically, there would be a great deal gained from studies that pinpoint the physiological systems affected by close relationships. Specifically, these studies could focus on the biological processes associated with affiliation and close relationships and the role that close relationships play in enhancing and protecting health.

Research on the role that hormones play in affiliative behavior in humans has already proven fruitful. For example, Bartz and Hollander (2006) found that the hormone oxytocin reduces anxiety and increases trust in others. And, in addition to the stress-attenuating affects of oxytocin, Taylor (2006) suggests that oxytocin is biomarker of social distress such that it is released during strains or problems in social relationships and provides momentum to connect or reconnect with others. Another example of the potential of research on the biological underpinnings of close relationship processes is a study that examined the brain activity of people under the threat of electric shock (Coan, Schaeffer, & Davidson, 2006). Participants either held the hand of their

husband, a male stranger (experimenter), or no hand. The results showed attenuated activation in the response to threat at the neural level in the condition in which women held their husband's hands. Most interestingly, those with the highest-quality marriages showed the most attenuation. Even holding the stranger's hand had some benefit. Similarly, Master and colleagues (2009) recently found that the presence of a loved one reduced the perception of physical pain in response to a painful stimulation, and even viewing a photo of a loved one showed the same effect.

In short, there are many possible mechanisms linking close relationships to health and psychological well-being. Future research can pinpoint how close relationships might have a direct affect on health, perhaps by building or strengthening certain biological systems. In turn, like the work on oxytocin and trust (Taylor, 2006), researchers can focus on how fluctuations in these systems influence close relationship formation and maintenance. In addition, future research can try to understand how close relationships buffer (or exacerbate) the negative impact of stress or environmental assaults, similar to the work on the neural response attenuation associated with human touch (Coan et al., 2006).

### Other Positive Emotions

Although we reviewed recent literature on the emotions of love and gratitude here, the role of other positive emotions in close relationships remains an open question. For example, we see great potential in understanding how interest and contentment function in close relationships, which were described by Fredrickson (1998) as examples of positive emotions in her original broaden-and-build paper. She and other emotion theorists tended to focus on the individual antecedents and consequences of these two emotions, and we would like to consider the relational functions of these two emotions.

Interest[2] has been described as a feeling of wanting to investigate and become involved with the target of interest (Fredrickson, 1998). Although much of the work on interest has been outside the context of close relationships (e.g., Kashdan & Silvia, 2009; Silvia & Kashdan, 2009), it seems like this emotion may be at the heart of an important relationship process known as "minding" the relationship (Harvey and Omarzu; 1997). Minding involves attending to and responding to a partner in a manner that signifies esteem, and it contributes to a sense of closeness and satisfaction. Harvey and Omarzu (1997) argue that minding the relationship is associated with empathy, shared positive affect, and a supportive perspective (all important relational resources, which is consistent with Fredrickson's functional model). In addition to the role that interest may play in relationship maintenance, it likely plays an equally large role in relationship formation and initial attraction, perhaps through the self-expansion processes (Aron et al., 1991) described above.

Contentment is seen as an emotion that arises when one is certain of safety, and Fredrickson (1998) has argued that it leads to savoring and an integration of recent achievements into the self-concept. In the context of a close relationship, this seems particularly important to understand in terms of how interactions with the partner are integrated into one's overall representation of the relationship. In addition, the role of the feeling of safety in the experience of contentment calls out for an understanding of links between contentment and the attachment system. Although it is beyond the scope of this chapter to thoroughly review attachment theory, a central tenet of Bowlby's original theory is that confident exploration of the environment occurs only when attachment needs (i.e., safety and security) have been satisfied (Bowlby, 1969). Thus contentment may be a signal that attachment needs have been met and exploration of the environment is prudent.

## Close Relationships and Other Domains of Life

Research on close relationships clearly shows that domains of life that lie outside of close relationships influence what happens in close relationships. Work by Repetti and colleagues has shown for example how daily stressors outside of the home (e.g., at work) have both immediate and long-term effects on family relationships (Repetti, Wang, Saxbe, 2009). We suggest that the final future direction to consider is the flipside of this; that is the role of close relationships in other life domains of interest to positive psychology. Close relationship researchers have largely been interested in interpersonal outcomes, such as relationship commitment and satisfaction. And researchers interested in other processes have not incorporated close relationships into their thinking. There are, however, excellent examples of these cross-domain studies

in the literature that hint at their potential contribution to the understanding of close relationships and these other processes. One example comes from a recent study by Cavallo, Fitzsimons, & Holmes (2009). They found that when individuals' close relationships are threatened, it changes the way they make decisions regarding risk in non-social domains (e.g., bungee jumping, white-water rafting). Another example is the work by Feeney (2004) on the role of close relationships in individual goal attainment. Specifically, in both observational and experimental work, Feeney (2004) found that supportive responses from close others for disclosure of personal goals predicted increases in the likelihood of goal attainment.

Finally, ongoing work by Fitzsimons and colleagues (e.g., Fitzsimons & Bargh, 2003) on automatic processes associated with close others has shown that priming the thought of a significant other brings to mind interpersonal goals that are linked to that significant other (e.g., doing well in school to make my mom proud). These goals are then pursued nonconsciously. Conversely, the degree to which others help us or hinder us in our goal pursuit influences our perception of them such that those who are instrumental to the pursuit of our personal goals are seen more positively, but primarily only when we are actively pursuing those goals or are reminded of them (e.g., Fiztsimons & Shah, 2008). Thus, we feel that the role of close relationships in processes such as creativity, flow, and intergroup cooperation is an open question and ripe for future research.

## Concluding Comments

The majority of research on close relationships has emphasized the contexts and consequences of negative processes, such as conflict, criticism, betrayal, stress, rejection, social isolation, jealousy, loneliness, and hostility. We do not intend to suggest that these areas are not important; they are important. However, our review has hopefully demonstrated the potential impact of studying the positive side of close relationships. Moreover, a complete understanding of close relationships cannot be achieved without an understanding of positive processes like capitalization, social support, and self-expansion. To achieve this goal, however, there is much work to be done.

## Notes

1. Few meaningful gender differences have been found in the research on capitalization, thus gender is not discussed in the current article.

2. Other emotions in the emotion family of interest include excitement, curiosity, and wonder.

*References*

Agnew, C. R. (2006). Cognitive interdependence: Considering self-in relationship. In K. D. Vohs & E. J. Finkel (Eds.), *Self and relationships: Connecting intrapersonal and interpersonal processes* (pp. 274–293). New York: Guilford Press.

Algoe, S., Gable, S. L., & Maisel, N. C. (2010). It's the little things: Everyday gratitude as a booster shot for romantic relationships. *Personal Relationships, 17(2)*, 217–233.

Algoe, S. B., & Haidt, J. D. (2009). Witnessing excellence in action: The "other-praising" emotions of elevation, gratitude, and admiration. *Journal of Positive Psychology, 4*, 105–127.

Algoe, S., Haidt, J., & Gable, S. L. (2008). Beyond reciprocity: Gratitude and relationships in everyday life. *Emotion, 8*, 425–429.

Aron, A., & Aron, E. (1997). Self-expansion motivation and including other in the self. In S. Duck (Ed.), *Handbook of personal relationships: Theory, research and interventions, 2nd Ed.* (pp. 251–270). Hoboken, NJ, US: John Wiley & Sons Inc.

Aron, A., Aron, E. N., Tudor, M., & Nelson, G. (1991). Close relationships as including other in the self. *Journal of Personality and Social Psychology, 60(2)*, 241–253.

Aron, A., Fisher, H., Mashek, D. J., Strong, G., Li, H., & Brown, L. L. (2005). Reward, motivation, and emotion systems associated with early-stage intense romantic love. *Journal of Neurophysiology, 94(1)*, 327–337.

Aron, A., Fisher, H., Strong, G. (2006). Love. In D. Perlman & A. Evangelisti (Eds.), *Cambridge Handbook of Personal Relationships* (pp. 595–614). New York: Cambridge University Press.

Aron, A., McLaughlin-Volpe, T., Mashek, D., Lewandowski, G., Wright, S. C., & Aron, E. N., (2004). Including others in the self. *European Review of Social Psychology, 15*, 101–132.

Aron, A., Norman, C. C., Aron, E. N., McKenna, C., & Heyman, R. E. (2000). Couples' shared participation in novel and arousing activities and experienced relationship quality. *Journal of Personality & Social Psychology, 78*, 273–284.

Aron, A., Paris, M., & Aron, E. N. (1995). Falling in love: Prospective studies of self-concept change. *Journal of Personality and Social Psychology, 69(6)*, 1102–1112.

Baumeister, R.F. & Leary, M.R. (1995). The need to belong: Desire for interpersonal attachments as a fundamental human motivation. *Psychological Bulletin, 117*, 497–529.

Bartz, J. A., & Hollander, E. (2006). The neuroscience of affiliation: Forging links between basic and clinical research on neuropeptides and social behavior. *Hormones and Behavior, 50(4)*, 518–528.

Berkman, L. F.,Syme, S. L. (1979). Social networks, host-resistance, and mortality—9-year follow-up-study of alameda county residents. *American Journal of Epidemiology, 109 (2)*, 186–204.

Berscheid, E., & Reis, H. T. (1998). Attraction and close relationships. In D. T. Gilbert, S. T. Fiske, & G. Lindzey (Eds.), *The handbook of social psychology* (4th ed., vol. 2, pp. 193–281). New York: McGraw-Hill.

Hatfield, E. & Walster, G. W. (1978). A new look at love. Lanham, MD: University Press of America.

Bolger, N., & Eckenrode, J. (1991). Social relationships, personality, and anxiety during a major stressful event. *Journal of Personality & Social Psychology, 61(3)*, 440–449.

Bolger, N., & Zuckerman, A. (1995). A framework for studying personality in the stress process. *Journal of Personality and Social Psychology, 69(5)*, 890–902.

Bolger, N., Zuckerman, A., & Kessler, R.C. (2000). Invisible support and adjustment to stress. *Journal of Personality and Social Psychology, 79*, 953–961.

Bowlby, J. (1969/1982). *Attachment and loss: Vol. 1.* Attachment (2nd ed.). New York: Basic Books.

Brunstein, J. C., Dangelmayer, G., & Shultheiss, O.C. (1996). Personal goals and social support in close relationships: Effects on relationship mood and marital satisfaction. *Journal of Personality and Social Psychology, 71(5)*, 1006–1019.

Byrne, D. (1971). *The attraction paradigm.* New York: Academic Press.

Cavallo, J.V., Fitzsimmons, G.M., & Holmes, J.G. (2009). Taking chances in the face of threat: Romantic risk regulation and approach motivation. *Personality and Social Psychology Bulletin, 35(6)*, 737–751.

Coan, J. A., Schaefer, H. S., & Davidson, R. J. (2006). Lending a hand. Social regulation of the neural response to threat. *Psychological Science, 17*, 1032–1039.

Cohen, S., & Wills, T.A. (1985). Stress, social support, and the buffering hypothesis. *Psychological Bulletin, 98(2)*, 310–357.

Collins, N. L., & Feeney, B. C. (2000). A safe haven: An attachment theory perspective on support seeking and caregiving in intimate relationships. *Journal of Personality and Social Psychology, 78(6)*, 1053–1073.

Cutrona, C. E. (1996). Social support in couples; Marriage as a resource in times of stress. Thousand Oaks, CA: Sage.

Deci, E. L., & Ryan, R. M. (2000). The "what" and "why" of goal pursuits: Human needs and the self-determination of behavior. *Psychological Inquiry, 11*, 227–268.

Diener, E., & Seligman, M. E. P. (2002). Very happy people. *Psychological Science, 13(1)*, 81–84.

Drigotas, S. M. (2002). The Michelangelo phenomenon and personal well-being. *Journal of Personality, 70*, 59–77.

Drigotas, S. M., Rusbult, C. E., Wieselquist, J., & Whitton, S. (1999). Close partner as sculptor of the ideal self: Behavioral affirmation and the Michelangelo phenomenon. *Journal of Personality and Social Psychology, 77*, 293–323.

Dunkel-Schetter, C., & Bennett, T.L. (1990). Differentiating the cognitive and behavioral aspects of social support. In B.R. Sarason, I.G. Sarason, & G.R. Pierce (Eds.). *Social support: An interactional view* (pp. 267–296). New York: Wiley.

Feeney, B. C. (2004). A secure base: Responsive support of goal strivings and exploration in adult intimate relationships. *Journal of Personality and Social Psychology, 87*, 631–648.

Fitzsimons, G. M., & Shah, J. Y. (2008). How goal instrumentality shapes relationship evaluations. *Journal of Personality and Social Psychology, 95(2)*, 319–337.

Fitzsimons, G. M., & Bargh, J. A. (2003). Thinking of you: Nonconscious pursuit of interpersonal goals associated with relationship partners. *Journal of Personality and Social Psychology, 84(1)*, 148–163.

Fleming, R., Baum, A., Gisriel, M.M., Gatchel, R.J. (1982). Mediating influences of social support on stress at Three Mile Island. *Journal of Human Stress, 8(3)*, 14–22.

Fraley, B., & Aron, A. (2004). The effect of a shared humorous experience on closeness in initial encounters. *Personal Relationships, 11(1)*, 61–78.

Fredrickson, B. L. (1998). What good are positive emotions? *Review of General Psychology, 2(3)*, 300–319.

Gable, S., Gonzaga, G., & Strachman, A. (2006). Will you be there for me when things go right? supportive responses to positive event disclosures. *Journal of Personality and Social Psychology, 91*, 904–917.

Gable, S. L., & Haidt, J. (2005). What (and why) is positive psychology? *Review of General Psychology, 9*, 103–110.

Gable, S. L., & Maisel, N. C. (2008). Perceived responsiveness to positive event disclosures. Unpublished data. University of California, Santa Barbara.

Gable, S. L., & Reis, H. T. (2001). Appetitive and aversive social interaction. In J. H. Harvey & A. E. Wenzel (Eds.), *Close romantic relationship maintenance and enhancement* (pp. 169–194). Mahwah, NJ: Erlbaum.

Gable, S. L., & Reis, H. T. (2006). Intimacy and the self: An iterative model of the self and close relationships. In P. Noller & J. A. Feeney (Eds.), *Close relationships: Functions, forms and processes* (pp. 211–225). New York: Psychology Press.

Gable, S. L., Reis, H. T., Impett, E., & Asher, E. R. (2004). What do you do when things go right? The intrapersonal and interpersonal benefits of sharing positive events. *Journal of Personality and Social Psychology, 87*, 228–245.

Gonzaga, G. C., Keltner, D., Londahl, E. A., & Smith, M. D. (2001). Love and the commitment problem in romantic relations and friends. *Journal of Personality and Social Psychology, 81*, 247–262.

Harlow, R.E., & Cantor, N. (1995). To whom do people turn when things go poorly? Task orientation and functional social contacts. *Journal of Personality and Social Psychology, 69(2)*, 329–340.

Harvey, J. H., & Omarzu, J. (1997). Minding the close relationship. *Personality and Social Psychology Review, 1*, 224–240.

Hatfield, E. (2006). The Golden Fleece Award: Loves labors (almost) lost. *Observer, 19*, 6.

House, J. S., Landis, K. R., & Umberson, D. (1988). Social relationships and health. *Science, 241(4865)*, 540–545.

Kashdan, T.B., & Silvia, P.J. (2009). Curiosity and interest: The benefits of thriving on novelty and challenge. In S.J. Lopez & C. R. Snyder (Eds.), *Oxford handbook of positive psychology (2nd ed.)* (pp. 367–374). New York, NY, US: Oxford University Press.

Kaul, M., & Lakey, B. (2003). Where is the support in perceived support? The role of generic relationship satisfaction and enacted support in perceived support's relation to low distress. *Journal of Social & Clinical Psychology, 22(1)*, 59–78.

Keltner, D., & Haidt, J. (1999). Social functions of emotions at four levels of analysis. *Cognition and Emotion, 13(5),* 505–521.

Kelley, H. H., Holmes, J. G. Kerr, H. L., Reis, H. T., Van Lange, P. A. M. (2003). *An atlas of interpersonal situation.* New York: Cambridge University Press.

Lakey, B., & Cassady, P. B. (1990). Cognitive processes in perceived social support. *Journal of Personality and Social Psychology, 59(2),* 337–343.

Langston, C.A. (1994). Capitalizing on and coping with daily-life events: Expressive responses to positive events. *Journal of Personality and Social Psychology, 67,* 1112–1125.

Holahan, C. J., Moos, R. H., Holahan, C. K., & Brennan, P. L. (1997). Social context, coping strategies, and depressive symptoms: An expanded model with cardiac patients. *Journal of Personality and Social Psychology, 72(4),* 918–928.

House, J. S., Landis, K. R., & Umberson, D. (1988). Social relationships and health. *Science, 241(4865),* 540–545.

Huston, T. L., & Vangelisti, A. L. (1991). Socioemotional behavior and satisfaction in marital relationships: A longitudinal study. *Journal of Personality and Social Psychology, 61,* 721–733.

Laurenceau, J. P., Barrett, L. F., & Pietromonaco, P. (1998). Intimacy as an interpersonal process: The importance of self-disclosure, partner disclosure, and perceived partner responsiveness in interpersonal exchanges. *Journal of Personality and Social Psychology, 74,* 1238–1251.

Little, B. R. (1989). Personal projects analysis: Trivial pursuits, magnificent obsessions and the search for coherence. In D. M. Buss and N. Cantor (Eds.), *Personality psychology: Recent trends and emerging directions* (pp. 15–31). New York: Springer-Verlag.

Maisel, N.C., & Gable, S.L. (2009). The paradox of received social support: The importance of responsiveness. *Psychological Science, 20(8),* 928–932.

Manne, S., Ostroff, J., Rini, C., Fox, K., Goldstein, L., & Grana, G. (2004). The interpersonal process model of intimacy: The role of self-disclosure, partner disclosure, and partner responsiveness in interactions between breast cancer patients and their partners. *Journal of Family Psychology, 18(4),* 589–599.

Master, S. L., Eisenberger, N. I., Taylor, S. E., Naliboff, B. D., Shirinyan, D., & Lieberman, M. D. (2009). A picture's worth: Partner photographs reduce experimentally induced pain. *Psychological Science, 20(11),* 1316–1318.

McCullough, M. E., Kilpatrick, S. D., Emmons, R. A., & Larson, D. B. (2001). Is gratitude a moral affect? *Psychological Bulletin, 127,* 249–266

Murray, S. L., Holmes, J. G., & Collins, N. L. (2006). Optimizing assurance: The risk regulation system in relationships. *Psychological Bulletin, 132(5),* 641–666.

Peterson, C., & Park, N. (2009). Classifying and measuring strengths of character. In S. Lopez & C. R. Snyder (Eds.), *Oxford handbook of positive psychology* (2nd ed.) (pp. 25–33). New York, NY, US: Oxford University Press.

Reis, H. T., Clark, M. S., & Holmes, J. G. (2004). *Perceived partner responsiveness as an organizing construct in the study of intimacy and closeness.* Mahwah, NJ, US: Lawrence Erlbaum Associates Publishers.

Reis, H. T., & Aron, A. (2008). Love: What is it, why does it matter, and how does it operate? *Perspectives on Psychological Science, 3,* 80–86.

Reis, H. T., Smith, S. M., Carmichael, C. L., et al. (1997). Close personal relationships and health outcomes: A key to the role of social support. In S. Duck (Ed.), *Handbook of personal relationships* (2nd ed.) (pp. 547–573).

Schnall, S., Harber, K. D., Stefanucci, J. K., Proffitt, D. R. (2008). Social support and the perception of geographical slant. *Journal of Experimental Social Psychology, 44,* 1246–1255.

Slotter, E.B., & Gardner, W.L. (2009). Where do you end and I begin? Evidence for anticipatory, motivated self-other integration between relationship partners. *Journal of Personality and Social Psychology, 96(6),* 1137–1151.

Sternberg, R.J. (1986). A triangular theory of love. *Psychological Review, 93(2),* 119–135.

Repetti, R., Wang, S., & Saxbe, D. (2009). Bringing it all back home: How outside stressors shape families' everyday lives. *Current Directions in Psychological Science, 18(2),* 106–111.

Rusbult, C. E., Kumashiro, M., Kubacka, K. E., & Finkel, E. J. (2009). "The part of me that you bring out": Ideal similarity and the Michelangelo phenomenon. *Journal of Personality and Social Psychology, 96(1),* 61–82.

Rusbult, C. E., Kumashiro, M., Stocker, S. L., & Wolf, S. T. (2005). The Michelangelo phenomenon in close relationships. In A. Tesser, J. V. Wood, & D. A. Stapel (Eds.), *On building, defending and regulating the self: A psychological perspective* (pp. 1–29). New York: Psychology Press.

Rusbult, C. E., Verette, J., Whitney, G. A., Slovik, L. F., & Lipkus, I. (1991). Accommodation processes in close relationships: Theory and preliminary empirical evidence. *Journal of Personality and Social Psychology, 60,* 53–78.

Rusbult, C. E., Zembrodt, I. M., & Gunn L. K. (1982). Exit, voice, loyalty, and neglect: Responses to dissatisfaction in romantic involvements. *Journal of Personality and Social Psychology, 43,* 1230–1242.

Sears, R. R. (1977). Sources of life satisfactions of the Terman gifted men. *American Psychologist, 32,* 119–128.

Shrout, P. E., Herman, C. M., & Bolger, N. (2006). The costs and benefits of practical and emotional support on adjustment: A daily diary study of couples experiencing acute stress. *Personal Relationships, 13,* 115–134.

Smith, T. W., Ruiz, J. M., Uchino, B. N. (2004). Mental activation of supportive ties, hostility, and cardiovascular reactivity to laboratory stress in young men and women. *Health Psychology, 23*(5), 476–485.

Stone, A. A., Mezzacappa, E. S., Donatone, B. A., & Gonder, M. (1999). Psychosocial stress and social support are associated with prostate-specific antigen levels in men: Results from a community screening program. *Health Psychology, 18*(5), 482–486.

Taylor, S. E. (2006). Tend and befriend: Biobehavioral bases of affiliation under stress. *Current Directions in Psychological Science, 15*(6), 273–277.

Uchino, B. N., Cacioppo, J. T., & Kiecolt-Glaser, J. K. (1996). The relationship between social support and physiological processes: A review with emphasis on underlying mechanisms and implications for health. *Psychological Bulletin, 119,* 488–531.

Vangelisti, A. L. (2009). Challenges in conceptualizing social support. *Journal of Social and Personal Relationships, 26,* 39–51.

# 18

# Positive Relationship Science: A New Frontier for Positive Psychology?

*Nathaniel M. Lambert, Frank D. Fincham, A. Marlea Gwinn, and Christine A. Ajayi*

## Relationship Science: A New Frontier for Positive Psychology?

When an idea is independently noted by multiple scholars, it is usually quite apparent that its time has come. Such is the case regarding the marriage of close relationships and positive psychology research. The important role of close relationships for personal well-being has long been documented in the broader psychological literature (e.g., Bloom, Asher, & White, 1978; Argyle, 1987; Proulx, Helms, & Buehler, 2007), a circumstance that the field of positive psychology has also recognized. The centrality of relationships to individual well-being has been acknowledged repeatedly in the positive psychology literature with many texts in the field (e.g., Carr, 2004; Ong & van Dulmen, 2007; Snyder & Lopez, 2007) openly acknowledging that "close relationships are essential to well-being" (Diener & Oishi, 2005, p. 162). Indeed, in his positive psychology textbook, Peterson (2006) states simply that there is a "three-word summary of positive psychology: *Other people matter*" (p. 249, italics in original).

It would therefore seem that the marriage between research on close relationships and positive psychology has long been consummated, a view that is endorsed by at least some in the field (e.g., Caughlin & Huston, in press). However, this consummation is more apparent than real as the focus in positive psychology tends to be on "experience, engagement, and personal feelings of well-being. Rather than a focus on relationships per se, there is typically only a recognition that relationships contribute to these goals" (Beach & Fincham, 2010). As a result, most of the material on relationships in positive psychology is usually that found in standard textbooks of social psychology. As Maniaci & Reis (2010) so aptly note, "positive psychologists have paid relatively little attention to how strengths, well-being, and human flourishing may be embedded in relational contexts."

In light of the above observations, it is not surprising that explicit attempts to develop a positive psychology of close relationships are relatively recent (e.g., Fincham & Beach, 2010; Reis & Gable, 2003). Indeed, these efforts have culminated in the call for establishing close relationships to constitute the fourth pillar of positive psychology (Fincham & Beach, in press), a sentiment well-received by the field as evidenced by

Seligman's endorsement of this view at the first World Congress on Positive Psychology.

Yet some researchers have found that negative life experiences tend to bear more weight than positive experiences (Baumeister, Bratslavsky, Finkenauer, & Vohs, 2001), and the study of negative relationship processes, especially destructive conflict, has dominated the literature on prototypic close relationships such as marriage (see Bradbury, Fincham, & Beach, 2000). Why then advocate for positive relationship processes to be emphasized? Although negative experiences may be more salient, positive experiences occur much more frequently. More specifically, estimates from studies of daily experiences conservatively place the ratio at about three positive to every negative event (Gable & Haidt, 2005). Moreover, positive and negative affect have been conceptualized as different dimensions, and each appears to have distinct neural processes (e.g., the amygdala in negative affect, Irwin et al., 1996; the dopaminergic pathways in positive affect, Hoebel, Rada, Mark & Pothos, 1999). It is therefore not surprising to find evidence that positive affect can be seen as critical to individual and relationship flourishing (Frederickson & Losada, 2005, identify positivity ratios above about 3 to 1 and below about 11 to 1 as ones that humans need to flourish). For example, Gable, Gonzaga, and Strachman (2006) showed that responses to positive rather than negative events tend to be better predictors of relationship well-being. Thus, a complete picture of the role of close relationships in human functioning cannot emerge from the study of negative relationship processes alone (for more complete discussion, see Fincham & Beach, in press).

The current chapter thus joins an ongoing effort to establish a positive relationship science (PRS). It has a twofold objective: (1) to capture the current status of research on the proposed fourth pillar by briefly reviewing research on positive constructs likely to facilitate relationship flourishing and (2) to make specific recommendations for improving the quality of research in this realm and in positive psychology more generally.

## Current Status of Research: Can We Bank on It?

Early on, psychologists studying marital behavior found that distressed couples contingently exchanged behavior but that "lack of reciprocity in the context of high positive exchange" (Gottman et al., 1976, p. 21) characterized happily married couples. That is, happy spouses functioned in accordance with a bank account model. In a popular book, *Seven Habits of Highly Effective People,* Covey (1989) compared human relationships to bank accounts, positing that we are constantly making deposits or withdrawals from each relationship account. He argued that keeping a positive reserve by making regular deposits helped buffer negative behavior in the relationship. This metaphor of emotional capital is helpful in thinking about a positive psychology of relationships and hence we use it to highlight constructs that contribute to such capital.

## Why Daily Relationship Deposits Matter

As noted earlier, there are approximately three positive experiences to every negative experience (Gable & Haidt, 2005). This would suggest that—in stark contrast to actual bank accounts that are fraught with frequent withdrawals—there are typically far more deposits (or at least opportunities for deposits) in relationship bank accounts than there are withdrawals. Thus, the study of how daily relationship deposits are made and under what circumstances these deposits are most valued is an important priority for positive psychology researchers.

Although they may seem mundane, the opportunities to make regular positive deposits through daily interactions are abundant. Daily positive interactions have important implications for positive affect, intimacy, and health symptoms. For example, participants had higher levels of positive affect not only if they disclosed a positive daily event but also if their partner disclosed a mundane positive event (Hicks & Diamond, 2008). Additionally, self-disclosure and perceived partner responsiveness in daily social interactions play a role in intimacy (Lin & Huang, 2006). People are also happier and experience fewer negative health symptoms when they feel understood in daily social interactions (Lun, Kesebir, & Oishi, 2008). Finally, accumulated positive deposits should provide a buffer against later withdrawals that are inherent in every relationship.

An individual's perception of his or her partner is largely contingent on specific interactions. These daily interactions provide many opportunities for deposits or withdrawals. To illustrate further the potential influence of daily interaction deposits on relationships, we will describe research that has been done on intimacy, capitalization, gratitude, and forgiveness. Then we will discuss some evidence on how an accumulation of such daily relationship deposits seems to provide a buffer against the impact of conflict.

## Intimacy

Daily deposits are critical for building intimacy. Intimacy has been positively correlated with individual need fulfillment (Prager & Buhrmester, 1998), marital satisfaction (Patrick, Sells, Giordano & Tollerud, 2007), and well-being (e.g., Waltz & Badura, 1987; Prager & Buhrmester, 1998). Conversely, deficiencies in marital intimacy are correlated with a higher severity of depression (Waring & Patton, 1984).

With regard to intimacy, disclosure and responsiveness in daily interactions are paramount. In fact, using daily diary methods, Laurenceau, Rovine, and Barrett (2005) found that the relationship between partner disclosure and intimacy seems to be mediated by perceived partner response. Enthusiastic positive responses (which will be expanded upon in a later section) are positively correlated with levels of intimacy (Gable, Reis, Impett, & Asher, 2004). This effect of partner response on intimacy goes beyond the response itself. Specifically, responses that were perceived by the participants to be intentionally hurtful had more of a distancing effect on their relationship than responses that were unintentionally hurtful (Vangelisti & Young, 2000). Another study suggests that males' disclosure and empathetic responses predicted their feelings of intimacy, while women's feelings of intimacy were predicted by their partners' displays of these actions (Mitchell, Castellani, Herrington, Joseph, Doss, & Snyder, 2008). These studies imply that daily interactions can provide a means of daily deposits that contribute specifically to intimacy and the relationship bank account as a whole.

## Capitalization

There is evidence that between 60 and 80 percent of the time, people disclose their most positive daily experience (Gable, Reis, Impett, & Asher, 2004; Gable & Maisel, 2008). Thus, responding in an appropriate manner to a relationship partner's good news could be one of the most prevalent opportunities to make a deposit in a relationship bank account; therefore, most people are presented the chance to enhance or dampen

levels of relationship satisfaction almost every day. In fact, even though past research has focused on the importance of partners' responses to negative events, responses to positive events tend to be better predictors of relationship well-being (Gable & Gonzaga, 2006).

A person's desire to share his/her good news with others has been termed capitalization, and the most effective response is an active-constructive one (e.g., "enthusiastic support"), which has been found to be positively correlated with commitment, satisfaction, intimacy, and trust (Gable, Reis, Impett, & Asher, 2004). Conversely, active-destructive ("quashing the event") and passive-destructive ("ignoring the event") responses as well as passive-construction ("quiet, understated support") responses have been related to negative relationship outcomes. The research on capitalization demonstrates the need for humans to feel genuinely cared about and supported by their partner during daily interactions (Gable, Reis, Impett, & Asher, 2004). Assessment of how individuals respond to the good news of their partner can tell us a lot about the daily deposits and withdrawals that are being made to and from the relationship bank account.

## Gratitude

Gratitude is a construct that has received considerable attention from positive psychologists (e.g., Emmons & Crumpler, 2000). Building on this work, relationship researchers have now recognized that expressing gratitude on a regular basis is another means by which positive deposits may be made into relationship bank accounts. In a recent study, participants were randomly assigned to write about daily events, express gratitude to a partner, discuss a positive memory with a partner, or think grateful thoughts about a partner twice a week for three weeks. At the end of the three weeks, those assigned to the expression of gratitude in relationships condition reported higher positive regard for their partner (a friend) and more comfort voicing relationship concerns than did those in the other conditions, even when controlling for the baseline scores of these variables and frequency of participation in the intervention. In addition, positive regard mediated the relationship between condition and comfort in voicing relationship concerns (Lambert & Fincham, 2009). Furthermore, those assigned to express gratitude to a friend reported greater perceived communal strength (e.g., caring, willingness to sacrifice, etc.)

than participants in all control conditions (Lambert, Clark, Durtschi, Fincham, & Graham, in press). These studies indicate that expressing gratitude to a partner is an important way by which individuals make positive relationship deposits.

## Forgiveness

Potentially more controversial is forgiving a partner's transgression as a means of making deposits in the relationship bank account. This is because forgiveness has a potential dark side. For example, among newlyweds, McNulty (2008) found frequency of partner negative behavior moderated the effect of forgiveness: more forgiveness led to a lower decline in satisfaction, but only for spouses married to partners who infrequently engaged in negative behavior and that among spouses married to partners who frequently engaged in negative behavior, increased forgiveness appeared to be harmful over time. In a similar vein, forgiving domestic violence is potentially dangerous because women in domestic violence shelters who were more forgiving were more likely to form an intention to return to their partner (Gordon, Burton & Porter, 2004). Our view of such findings is that they result largely from laypersons confusing forgiveness with condoning and/or reconciliation (see Kearns & Fincham, 2005).

When properly understood, forgiveness is robustly and positively related to core relationship constructs such as relationship satisfaction (e.g., Fincham, 2000; Paleari, Regalia, & Fincham, 2003) and commitment (e.g., Finkel, Rusbult, Kumashiro, & Hannon, 2002; Karremans & VanLange, 2008). In each case, there are data to suggest that the association may be bidirectional (e.g., Fincham & Beach, 2007; Tsang, McCullough, and Fincham, 2006).

Unresolved conflict provides a potential mechanism that links forgiveness and relationship satisfaction. Specifically, it can be argued that transgressions that are not forgiven may spill over into future conflicts and, in turn, impede their resolution, thereby putting the couple at risk of developing the negative cycle of interaction that characterizes distressed relationships. Supporting this line of reasoning, lack of forgiveness is linked to ineffective conflict resolution (Fincham, Beach, & Davila, 2004). Moreover, for wives, forgiveness predicted husbands' reports of better conflict resolution 12 months later, controlling for initial levels of conflict resolution and degree of hurt (Fincham, Beach, & Davila, 2007).

It is telling that the search for a mechanism linking forgiveness to relationship satisfaction involves the negative. This is because an explicit link to positive psychology has not been made, an omission that this chapter seeks to rectify. Making such a link immediately draws attention to constructs such as empathy and humility as potential mediators. In any event, forgiveness appears to be a powerful means of building emotional capital in the relationship.

## Accumulated Positive Deposits and Conflict Management

The level of positive deposits in the relationship account should affect conflict management and how much of a withdrawal is made during an argument. There is evidence to support this suggestion. Some research indicates that a husband's level of enthusiasm in everyday marital interactions were correlated with his wife's affection in the midst of conflict, and that the husband's playful bids during a neutral interaction predicts couple's humor during conflict (Driver & Gottman, 2004). Another study found that positive behavior during conflict is important for predicting changes in satisfaction attributable to negative behavior (Johnson, Cohan, & Davila et al., 2005). Furthermore, in an earlier study, Gottman and Levinson (1992) found that couples rated as having higher positive affect (compared with couples displaying lower positive affect) reported (a) marital problems as less severe (at Time 1); (b) higher marital satisfaction (Time 1 and Time 2); (c) better physical health (Time 2); (d) less negative ratings for interactions; (e) less negative emotional expression; (f) more positive emotional expression; (g) less stubbornness and withdrawal from interaction; (h) less defensiveness; and (i) less risk for marital dissolution (lower marital satisfaction and higher incidence of consideration of dissolution and of actual separation). Finally, Janicki et al. (2006) showed that the intensity of contemporaneously recorded, everyday conflictual interactions with the spouse predicted marital satisfaction but did not do so when positive partner interactions were also considered (conflict frequency was unrelated to marital satisfaction). Thus, positive partner behaviors and a store of positive deposits seem to affect the degree to which withdrawals are made during a conflict, which would contribute to the overall level of emotional capital.

The positive relationship bank likely matters so much because in intimate relationships we voluntarily make ourselves most vulnerable to another human being. We do so by linking the realization of our needs, aspirations, and hopes to the goodwill of a relationship partner. Rendering ourselves vulnerable in this way is a double-edged sword. It makes possible the profound sense of well-being that can be experienced in close relationships. At the same time, the imperfection of any partner means that hurt or injury is inevitable, and when it occurs, the hurt is particularly poignant precisely because we have made ourselves vulnerable. It is therefore perhaps not surprising that ongoing injury (e.g., chronic conflict) takes a toll physiologically and is related to general responses (e.g., immunological down-regulation and pro-inflammatory responding, Kiecolt-Glaser et al., 2005) as well as specific disorders (e.g., congestive heart failure, Coyne et al., 2001).

*Critique.* In this critique we offer an answer to the question posed in the section heading. No, we cannot bank on building a Positive Relationship Science (PRS) by simply continuing with research like that reviewed thus far. The above review is far from complete, but it suffices to illustrate some serious conceptual problems. One critical issue concerns the boundary between the positive and the negative. Any PRS must necessarily define the positive, a more difficult task than it first appears to be. As Maniaci and Reis (in press) point out, nearly all relational activities (e.g., forgiveness, social support, conflict) can lead to positive or negative outcomes depending on how they unfold and the context in which they do so. As a consequence, these authors question the wisdom of defining processes in terms of whether they are beneficial or harmful to the relationship. This critique applies more generally to positive psychology, as accepted virtues such as generosity are not inexorably positive and can manifest in ways that are harmful to the individual.

For example, a study by McNulty, O'Mara, & Karney (2008) well illustrates this point. The process of benevolent cognitions (making positive attributions or disengaging global evaluations of the relationship from negative experiences) might be expected to have very positive effects on a relationship. Indeed, at Time 1 benevolent cognitions were positively related to relationship satisfaction, and such a strategy continued to benefit healthier marriages four years later. However, benevolent cognitions predicted steeper declines in satisfaction among more troubled marriages, as spouses allowed

problems to worsen over time. The authors suggest that this highly touted strategy for improving relationships may be harmful for some, as it could decrease their motivation to address problems directly. Thus, context matters. What may be helpful for certain types of couples may be harmful for others.

On a related note, oftentimes the tendency of researchers is to empirically measure and analyze positive and negative variables as if they are two points on one continuum. Eagly and Chaiken (1993) suggested that "social scientists typically assess people's attitudes by placing them on a bipolar evaluative continuum" (p. 90). In fact, attitudes "are largely treated as unidimensional summary statements" even though they are often considered to be multidimensional (Thompson, Zanna, & Griffin, 1995, p. 362). In the realm of relationships, Fincham and Linfield (1997) provided evidence that the common conception of relationship satisfaction as a bipolar construct is incomplete. They used confirmatory factor analysis to demonstrate that separate positive and negative dimensions exist, which they then used to define a two-dimensional space. The authors then identified ambivalent (high positive and high negative) as well as indifferent (low-positive and low-negative) relationship types and showed that even though they were indistinguishable in (bipolar) marital satisfaction, they differed in important ways. Mattson, Paldino, and Johnson (2007), using the two-dimensional measure developed by Fincham and Linfield (1997), found that it captured well the relationship quality of engaged couples and accounted for unique variability in observed behavior and attributions. Thus, researchers in positive psychology should avoid the temptation to treat positive or negative constructs as two points on one continuum. The research evidence points to much greater complexity.

A final, important concern is that a collection of positively valenced constructs does not a positive relationship science (PRS) make, no matter how intensively they are studied. A general criticism of positive psychology is that it lacks a set of organizing principles, and the same can be said of the emerging PRS. If it is to avoid this criticism, PRS needs to develop in a more integrative, theory-driven manner than hitherto. Attachment theory has had a profound impact on relationship research, so it is not surprising that Lopez (2009) builds on Mikulincer and Shaver's (2005) suggestion that attachment security become "a theoretical foundation for a positive social psychology"

(p. 233) by identifying it as "the relational scaffolding of positive psychology" (Lopez, 2009, p. 405). Certainly there is much merit to such a view, though other candidates such as self-expansion theory (Aron, Aron, Tudor, & Nelson, 1991) and Reis and Gable's (2003) analysis of appetitive and avoidance motivational systems in relationships should not be overlooked.

## The Future: Rigor and Diversity

Added to the knotty conceptual problems identified are critical methodological issues that have important implications for our understanding of positive processes in relationships. These also need to be attended to in building a viable PRS. The majority of past research on relationships has focused exclusively on only one member of the dyad, which provides an incomplete picture of what is going on in the relationship. Increased use of appropriate dyadic data analysis procedures would greatly enhance what is known about positive relationship deposits. Also, overreliance on cross-sectional designs, or experimental designs with weak controls, plagues past research. We make several specific suggestions for improving the rigor of study designs. Finally, past research has relied almost entirely on self-report data, so we provide examples of using implicit measures and observational data.

### Rigor in Analysis

The vast majority of the studies on positive relationship processes have focused exclusively on one member of the relationship. To analyze the interactions between individuals nested within couples, the Actor-Partner Interdependence Model (APIM) uses the dyad as the unit of analysis (Kenny, 1990, 1996; Kenny & Cook, 1999; Kenny, Kashy, Cook, & Simpson, 2006). This type of statistical procedure is important because most frequently only one partner's responses has been taken into consideration and the other partner's responses are either left out or are not analyzed appropriately. To truly understand dyadic relationships, these types of procedures need to be used more regularly. APIM is a mixed-models approach in which data from two dyad members are treated as nested scores within the same group. This model suggests that a participant's independent variable score affects both his or her own dependent variable score (actor effect) as well as the dependent variable of his or her partner (partner effect). The APIM analysis is an important advance, as traditional methods do not take into account both actor and partner effects on dependent variables. This information is obviously critical for an accurate assessment of the relationship bank account.

Use of the APIM is fast becoming routine in relationship research and provides a healthy corrective to past practices in which interdependency in relationship data was not recognized, was ignored (both can lead to inaccurate estimates of standard errors, incorrect degrees of freedom, and improper effect sizes), or was dealt with in non-optimal ways (e.g., use of couple average scores, which due to the extreme score of one member may not be an accurate reflection of the couple). Positive psychologists who wish to contribute to the "fourth pillar" will thus have to add the APIM to their skill set. A useful introduction full of practical ("how to") advice is provided by Ackerman, Donnellan & Kashy (in press). However, this will not be sufficient, for besides including the partner in an appropriate analysis strategy, there are several other things that need to be done to improve rigor so that we may find out more about what activities make a contribution to positive daily deposits.

### Rigor in Study Designs

Much of the research done in positive psychology has utilized a cross-sectional design, which is not particularly useful if trying to assess the relationship bank account, as tracking the accumulation of daily deposits over time is central to understanding the current emotional capital in the relationship. Also, these types of designs do little to expand knowledge about the interrelationship between variables, as they reflect only one instance in time (limiting knowledge about the direction of effects), do not allow for causal inferences to be drawn (because of the lack of experimental design), and there is often no examination of why the variables are related (through mediators) or for whom and under what conditions they are related (using moderators).

Longitudinal designs provide stronger information about the direction of effects and help us to begin to understand the effects of the accumulated deposits over time. Such designs should be used more frequently in positive psychology. Of course, there is also a need for more studies using experimental designs. However, in several cases, even when an experimental design is used, it may not be particularly informative if rigorous control conditions are absent. For example, if a researcher is attempting to demonstrate the effect of gratitude journaling on depression and the control condition is to write about daily news reports (which are predominantly negative), then it may not be surprising nor informative that gratitude journaling had an effect on depression when compared to such a control condition. Positive psychologists should consider designs that control for other *positive* alternative explanations to the phenomenon of interest as well as mood.

For example, in a recent study (Lambert et al., in press) we wanted to test whether expressing gratitude to a relationship partner increased the expresser's sense of communal strength, defined as the degree of felt responsibility for a partner's welfare (Mills, Clark, Ford, & Johnson, 2004). We proposed that simply thinking grateful thoughts about a partner would not have the same effect as expressing gratitude to a partner. In order to rigorously test the hypothesis, we used a four-condition journal study design, collecting pre- and post-test reports of participants' communal strength. We found that even when controlling for baseline scores of communal strength, those who had expressed gratitude to their partner reported higher perceived communal strength than those who (a) wrote about daily activities, (b) wrote about grateful thoughts, or (c) had positive interactions with their partner.

In this study we were attempting to demonstrate how one positive construct—gratitude—may build upon another positive construct—perceived communal strength. Including a truly neutral referent condition can aid in providing a comparison group necessary to demonstrate the effect of the target variable. Including positive control conditions, however, such as the grateful thoughts condition and the positive interaction condition, helped rule out the potential confound that naturally occurring covariance between positive constructs was producing an artificial or inflated result. Also, such rigorous controls provide a test of whether the target independent variable has specific, unique effects on the target dependent variable.

Finally, there is a shortage of studies in positive psychology that include questions of "how" and "why" (through mediators) or that answer questions of "for whom" or "under what conditions" (through moderators). Once the main effect of one variable on another is demonstrated, further attempts should be made to determine why. For example, in the first study of our research on prayer (Lambert, Fincham, Stillman, Graham, & Beach, 2010), we established a link between praying for one's partner and forgiveness of that partner. Our next step was to provide data on mechanisms that could explain the connection between prayer and forgiveness. We hypothesized that praying for benefits for a specific individual increased one's general sense of selfless concern for others, and this increase in selfless concern mediated the effect of experimental condition on increased forgiveness. To test our hypothesis, we conducted a journal study in which the design very closely resembled the one described earlier in that it included two positive activities that might have served as confounds.

We found that praying for the well-being of a friend and being a positive aspect of the friend's life had an effect on forgiveness even when compared to the rigorous control conditions of undirected prayer and thinking positive thoughts about the friend. Praying for a friend also increased a general sense of selfless concern for others, which mediated the relationship between praying for a friend and forgiveness. Examining this mediator provided helpful information as to why praying for one's partner increases forgiveness. Identification of mechanisms accounting for phenomena should enhance the explanatory power of studies in positive psychology.

In sum, increased rigor points to the need for more longitudinal research (yielding information on duration and direction of effects), more positive control conditions to experiments (to test the unique contribution of a specific independent variable), and increased investigation of mediators and moderators (providing answers to questions like "why," "how," "for whom," and "under what conditions"). Although making such improvements will significantly raise the bar for research in positive psychology and should help us discover under what conditions positive deposits may be most helpful for a relationship, further steps should be taken to overcome the limitations of self-report data that are omnipresent in positive psychology.

## Diversity: Overcoming the Limitations of Self-Report Data

The limitations of self-report have been extensively documented (e.g., see Stone et al., 2000) and include impression management, motivated distortion, and the limits of self-awareness (Fincham & Rogge, in press). We focus on impression management, which is the tendency of individuals to present themselves in a favorable light or to respond in a socially desirable manner (Reynolds, 1982). This is a serious source of bias in any research, but especially for the field of positive psychology because all, or nearly all, of the constructs we study are socially desirable, and people want to portray themselves favorably. This results in an inflated covariance between variables due to the shared variance with social desirability.

In marital research, Edmonds (1967) created the Marital Conventionalization Scale, which contains items that describe the marriage in an impossibly positive light, portraying it as "perfect" and "meeting my every need." It correlates strongly (in the .50 to .73 range) with numerous measures of marital adjustment and satisfaction (Fowers & Applegate, 1996). Edmonds (1967) argued that the social desirability bias in responses to assessment of marital satisfaction was unconscious and unintended and therefore involved "fooling oneself rather than fooling others" (Edmonds, 1967, p. 682).

In our research on young adult romantic relationships, we noticed a ceiling effect in which most students report their relationship satisfaction at the high end of the scale. An average satisfaction score in our sample has often been a score of six on a seven-point scale. Of course we recognize that young adults likely are more satisfied with their romantic relationships than couples at other stages of life, due in part to the novelty of the relationship and lack of constraints (e.g., having to provide, the responsibility of caring for children, etc.). Nonetheless, there is some social pressure (e.g., Fowers & Applegate, 1996) to report a great deal of satisfaction in one's relationship, regardless of life stage.

Researchers in the field of positive psychology should, at a minimum, include measures of social desirability in their battery of measures and control for this tendency in analyses. However helpful including such measures may be, there are even better and more rigorous ways to overcome the limitations of self-report. We describe three alternatives to typical self-report measures and include examples of implementing such techniques in our own studies on relationships. These include the need for (1) implicit measures, (2) behavioral measures, and (3) observational methods.

## Need for Implicit Measures of Positive Relationships

Implicit measures aim to assess attitudes (or constructs) that respondents may not be willing to report directly, or of which they may not even be aware. Such measures provide an assessment of the construct of interest without having to ask directly for a verbal report, and they are therefore likely to be free of social desirability biases (Fincham & Rogge, in press).

Given the ceiling effect that we observed in self-reported relationship satisfaction, we saw the need to create an implicit measure of relationship satisfaction. Cognizant of Fazio and Olson's (2003, p. 303) observation that modern implicit measures that assess constructs without directly asking about them are, in this regard, no different from "earlier proposals regarding projective methods," we were prompted to think quite literally about projective techniques. As a result, we presented participants with a blank sheet of paper, some colored pencils, and the following instructions: "Please draw a picture with (a) a house, (b) a tree (c) a car, and (d) two people *who represent you and your partner*. You may draw them in any way you like, but you must include the above items. Please label the figure that represents you as 'me' and the one that represents your partner as 'partner.'" Research assistants then measured the distance between the necks of two depicted partners and recorded them in millimeters. One distinct advantage to the way this measure is administered is that there is no social pressure or apparent reason why individuals should draw themselves closer to or further from their partner. Also, participants remain unaware that we are measuring the distance between the necks and of course are not privy to any of the implications that we have found regarding distance between necks.

As it turns out, the distance between the necks is predictive of several important indicators of relationship well-being. Across three samples there was good evidence of convergent validity. For example, neck distance correlated significantly with relationship satisfaction, as well as with the likeability of the partner and commitment to him/her. The neck distance measure predicted a number of relevant variables four weeks later over and beyond relationship satisfaction and initial level of the variable predicted. The variables thus predicted included expression of appreciation, commitment to partner, likeability of partner, intimacy, mattering, perceived relationship maintenance efforts of the partner, and perceived commitment of partner. Finally, the "neck measure" may also foretell extradyadic sexual behavior and how safe a person feels in the relationship (p < .06 in each case). Other studies have demonstrated the validity of this measure, as neck distance has consistently been positively correlated with relationship satisfaction and other indicators of well-being. Using or developing such implicit measures to assess constructs important to positive psychologists is essential for future research.

## Need for Behavioral Measures

Our aforementioned journal studies utilized a longitudinal design, included rigorous controls, and tested for mechanisms. However, the studies were limited by exclusive use of self-report data. Thus, we perceived the need to obtain a behavioral measure of forgiveness that was free from some of the limitations of self-report data that we have previously discussed. To do so, we needed to create a transgression that would be the same across participants and then provide some type of quantifiable activity related to forgiveness that participants could engage in following the supposed "transgression." Having already collected the "neck measure," we decided to make further use of that activity. Thus, upon completion of their drawings, participants were told that the purpose of the task was to assess creativity and that their partner would rate their drawing on a scale of "1—not at all creative" to "5—extremely creative." The research assistant took each participant's drawing as if to give to the partner to rate.

A few minutes later, the research assistant returned with an envelope containing the supposed feedback rating of their partner and said, "I thought you might be interested to see how your partner rated your picture; it's here in this envelope. I'll let you go ahead and look at your partner's rating of your drawing, and then I need you to do a short task for a different study." All participants were then handed the false rating sheet with the number "1—not at all creative" circled, as if by their partner. They also received instructions for a three-minute activity that varied based on their condition, which they completed after having looked at the false rating supposedly by their partner. Then, depending on the group to which they were randomly assigned, participants either prayed for their partner or wrote a response to a philosophical religious question.

Following the manipulation, participants engaged in the prisoner dilemma game in which they believe they are playing a game with their partner and are required to decide to "cooperate with" or "antagonize" their partner for a specified amount of points. In actuality, the participants were playing against the computer, which simulates the partner by providing the same responses to all participants. The number of "cooperative" choices was summed, and, in this case, those participants who prayed for their partner demonstrated more cooperative responses during the game (Lambert et al., 2010). This is simply one example of a behavioral measure that could be implemented as part of a study design. This type of measure provides evidence that ought to be much less subject to social desirability and limits of self-awareness.

## Need for Observational Data

Numerous marital studies have utilized observation of couple interaction and analyzed observers' coding of positive affect (among other things). The rigor demonstrated by these methods needs to be extended to other areas of positive relationship research as well as to positive psychology in general. Furthermore, observational methods should be more frequently utilized in evaluating the efficacy of positive relationship interventions, as this level of rigor has rarely been applied to experimental tests of factors that positively affect relationships. To illustrate the potential usefulness of observational coding, we further describe some of our prayer research.

In a recent study (Fincham, Lambert & Beach, in press), we assigned one group of participants to say a daily prayer for their partner and another group to think positive thoughts about their partner for four weeks. At the conclusion of the four weeks, participants returned to the laboratory with their original partner, where they were seated with their partner in front of a video camera. The following question was posed to the study participants: "Please describe the short- or long-term future of your relationship with your partner." The videotaped responses to this question were coded by a group of five trained research assistants blind to study hypotheses. After watching the participants' response to this question, the research assistants coded their response based the on the question, "How would you rate the commitment that the participant demonstrated to the partner during this interaction?" on a scale from 1 = "Not at all committed" to 7 = "Extremely committed." Our hypothesis was supported as comparisons revealed higher objective reports of commitment for those in the prayer for partner condition than among those in the positive thought condition. These results indicate that the effect of praying for one's partner on commitment is apparent even to objective observers. Again, this is just one example illustrating the usefulness of observed behavior.

In sum, by increasing the use of implicit measures, behavioral measures, and observational methods, researchers of positive relationship processes may greatly improve the quality and contribution of their research. And use of such methods will provide a more objective understanding of a couple's relationship bank account.

## Conclusion

To summarize, relationships have now been acknowledged as the fourth pillar in positive psychology. As a result, there has been a recent uptick in the amount of research that has been done on positive relationship processes. To truly understand the nature and status of relationships and the accumulated emotional capital that exists, we need to examine the daily deposits and withdrawals into and out of the relationship bank account. To provide an accurate assessment of the accumulation of deposits and withdrawals, data from both partners in the relationship dyad need to be included in analysis. In addition, the quality of research in this area and in the realm of positive psychology generally could be improved by implementing more rigorous study designs and by going beyond traditional self-report data. As positive psychologists enter the field of close relationship research, there is the potential not only to enrich the relationship literature but also to enhance the credibility and scientific contribution of positive psychology research more generally.

*References*

Ackerman, R. A., Donnellan, M.B., & Kashy, D.A. (in press). Working with dyadic data in studies of emerging adulthood: Specific recommendations, general advice, and practical tips. In F. Fincham & M. Cui (Eds.), *Romantic Relationships in emerging adulthood*. New York: Cambridge University Press.

Argyle, M. (1987). *The psychology of happiness.* New York: Methuen.

Aron, A., Aron, E. N., Tudor, M., & Nelson, G. (1991). Close relationships as including other in the self. *Journal of Personality and Social Psychology, 60,* 241–253.

Baumeister, R. F., Bratslavsky, E., Finkenauer, C., & Vohs, K. D. (2001). Bad is stronger than good. *Review of General Psychology, 5,* 323–370.

Beach, S. R. H., & Fincham, F. D. (2010). Conflict can be constructive: Reflections on the dialectics of relationship science. *Journal of Family Theory and Review, 2,* 54–57.

Beach, S. R. H., Fincham, F. D., Hurt, T., McNair, L. M., & Stanley, S. M. (2008). Prayer and marital intervention: Toward an open empirically grounded dialogue. *Journal of Social and Clinical Psychology, 27,* 693–710.

Bloom, B. L., Asher, S. J., & White, S. W. (1978). Marital disruption as a stressor: A review and analysis. *Psychological Bulletin, 85,* 867–894.

Bradbury, T. N., Fincham, F. D., & Beach, S. R. H. (2000). Research on the nature and determinants of marital satisfaction: A decade in review. *Journal of Marriage and the Family, 62,* 964–980.

Carr, A. (2004). *Positive psychology: The science of happiness and human strengths.* New York: Brunner-Routledge.

Caughlin, J. P., & Huston, T. L. (in press). The flourishing literature on flourishing relationships. *Journal of Family Theory and Review.*

Covey, S. R. (1989). *The seven habits of highly effective people.* New York: Simon and Schuster.

Coyne, J. C, Rohrbaugh, M. J., Shoham, V., Sonnega, J. S., Nicklas, J. M., & Cranford, J. A. (2001). Prognostic importance of marital quality for survival of congestive heart failure. *The American Journal of Cardiology, 88:5,* 526–529.

Diener, E., & Oishi, S. (2005). The nonobvious social psychology of happiness. *Psychological Inquiry, 16,* 162–167.

Driver, J., & Gottman, J. (2004). Daily marital interactions and positive affect during marital conflict among newlywed couples. *Family Process, 43,* 301–314.

Eagly, A. H., & Chaiken, S. (1993). *The psychology of attitudes.* Orlando, FL: Harcourt Brace Jovanovich.

Edmonds, V. H. (1967). Marital conventionalization: Definition and measurement. *Journal of Marriage and the Family, 24,* 349–354.

Emmons, R. A., & Crumpler, C. A. (2000). Gratitude as a human strength: Appraising the evidence. *Journal of Social and Clinical Psychology, 19,* 56–69.

Fincham, F. D. (2000). The kiss of the porcupines: From attributing responsibility to forgiving. *Personal Relationships, 7*, 1–23.

Fincham, F. D., & Rogge, R. (in press). Understanding relationship satisfaction: Theoretical challenges and new tools for assessment.

Fincham, F. D., & Beach, S. R. H. (2007). Forgiveness and marital quality: Precursor or consequence in well-established relationships. *Journal of Positive Psychology, 2*, 260–268.

Fincham, F., Beach, S., & Davila, J. (2004). Conflict resolution in marriage and forgiveness. *Journal of Family Psychology, 18*, 72–81.

Fincham, F. D., Beach, S. R. H., & Davila, J. (2007). Longitudinal relations between forgiveness and conflict resolution in marriage. *Journal of Family Psychology, 21*, 542–545.

Fincham, F. D., & Linfield, K. J. (1997). A new look at marital quality: Can spouses feel positive and negative about their marriage? *Journal of Family Psychology, 11*, 489–502.

Fincham, F. D., Lambert, N. M., & Beach, S. R. H. (in press). Faith and unfaithfulness: Can praying for your partner reduce infidelity? *Journal of Personality and Social Psychology.*

Fincham, F. & Beach, S. R. H. (2010). Of memes and marriage: Towards a positive relationship science. *Journal of Family Theory and Review, 2*, 4–24.

Finkel, E. J., Rusbult, C. E., Kumashiro, M., & Hannon, P. A. (2002). Dealing with betrayal in close relationships: Does commitment promote forgiveness? *Journal of Personality and Social Psychology, 82*, 956–974.

Fowers, B. J., & Applegate, B. (1996). Marital satisfaction and conventionalization examined dyadically. *Current Psychology, 15*, 197–214.

Fredrickson, B. L., & Losada, M. F. (2005). Positive affect and the complex dynamics of human flourishing. *American Psychologist, 60*, 678–686.

Gable, S. L., Gonzaga, G., & Strachman, A. (2006). Will you be there for me when things go right? Social support for positive events. *Journal of Personality and Social Psychology, 91*, 904–917.

Gable, S. & Haidt, J. (2005). What (and why) is positive psychology? *Review of General Psychology, 9*, 103–110.

Gable, S., Reis, H., Impett, E., & Asher, E. (2004). What do you do when things go right? The intrapersonal and interpersonal benefits of sharing positive events. *Journal of Personality and Social Psychology, 87*, 228–245.

Gordon, K, Burton, S., & Porter, L. (2004). Predicting the intentions of women in domestic violence shelters to return to partners: Does forgiveness play a role? *Journal of Family Psychology, 18*, 331–338.

Gottman, J. M., & Levenson, R. W. (1992). Marital processes predictive of later dissolution: Behavior, physiology and health. *Journal of Personality and Social Psychology, 63*, 221–233.

Gottman, J. M., Notarius, C., Markman, H., Banks, S., Yoppi, B., & Rubin, M. E. (1976). Behavior exchange theory and marital decision making. *J. Personality and Social Psychology, 34*, 14–23.

Hoebel, B. G., Rada, P. V., Mark, G. P., & Pothos, E. N. (1999). Neural systems for reinforcement and inhibition of eating: Relevance to eating, addiction, and depression. In D. Kahneman, E. Diener, & N. Schwarz (Eds.), *Well-being: The foundations of hedonic psychology* (pp. 558–572). New York: Cambridge University Press.

Irwin, W., Davidson, R. J., Lowe, M. J., Mock, B. J., Sorenson, J. A., & Turski, P. A. (1996). Human amygdala activation detected with echoplanar functional magnetic resonance imaging. *Neuroreport, 7*, 1765–1769.

Janicki, D., Kamarck, T., Shiffman, S., & Gwaltney, C. (2006). Application of ecological momentary assessment to the study of marital adjustment and social Interactions during daily life. *Journal of Family Psychology, 20*, 168–172.

Johnson, M. D., Cohan, C. L., Davila, J., Lawrence, E., Rogge, R. D., Karney, B. R., Sullivan, K. T., & Bradbury, T. N. (2005). Problem-solving skills and affective expressions as predictors of change in marital satisfaction. *Journal of Consulting and Clinical Psychology, 73*, 15–27.

Karremans, J. C., & Van Lange, P. A. M. (2008). Forgiveness in interpersonal relationships: Its malleability and powerful consequences. *European Review of Social Psychology, 19*, 202–241.

Kearns, J. N., & Fincham, F. D. (2005). Victim and perpetrator accounts of interpersonal transgressions: Self-serving or relationship-serving biases? *Personality and Social Psychology Bulletin, 31*, 321–333.

Kenny, D. A. (1990). Design issues in dyadic research. In C. Hendrick & M. S. Clark (Eds.), *Review of personality and social psychology: Research methods in personality and social psychology* (pp. 164–184). Newbury Park, CA: Sage.

Kenny, D. A. (1996). Models of interdependence in dyadic research. *Journal of Social and Personal Relationships, 13*, 279–294.

Kenny, D. A., & Cook, W. (1999). Partner effects in relationship research: Conceptual issues, analytic and illustrations. *Personal Relationships, 6*, 433–448.

Kenny, D. A., Kashy, D. A., Cook, W. L., & Simpson, J. A. (2006). *Dyadic data analysis.* New York: Guilford Press.

Kiecolt-Glaser, J. K., Loving, T. J., Stowell, J. R., Malarkey, W. B., Lemeshow, S., Dickinson, S. L., et al. (2005). Hostile marital interactions, proinflammatory cytokine production, and wound healing. *Archives of General Psychiatry, 62,* 1377–1384.

Lambert, N. M., Clarke, M. S., Durtschi, J. A., Fincham, F. D., & Graham, S. M. (in press). Benefits of expressing gratitude: Expressing gratitude to a partner changes the expresser's view of the relationship. *Psychological Science.*

Lambert, N. M., Fincham, F. D., Stillman, T. F., Graham, S. M., & Beach, S. R. M. (2010). Motivating change in relationships: Can prayer increase forgiveness? *Psychological Science, 21,* 126–132.

Lambert, N. M., Fincham, F. D., DeWaal, N., & Beach, S. R. H. (2010). Can prayer change behavior? Prayer increases forgiving behavior toward relationship partners. Manuscript submitted for publication.

Laurenceau, J-P., Barrett, L. F., & Rovine, M. J. (2005). The interpersonal process model of intimacy in marriage: Daily-diary and multilevel modeling approach. *Journal of Family Psychology, 19,* 314–323.

Lopez, F. G. (2009). Adult attachment security: The relational scaffolding of positive psychology. In C. R. Snyder & S. J. Lopez (Eds.), *Oxford handbook of positive psychology* (2nd ed., pp. 405–416). New York: Oxford University Press.

Maniaci, M. R. & Reis, H. T. (in press). The marriage of positive psychology and relationship science: A reply to Fincham and Beach. *Journal of Family Theory and Review, 2,* 47–53.

Mattson, R. E., Paldino, D., & Johnson, M. D. (2007). The increased construct validity and clinical utility of assessing relationship quality using separate positive and negative dimensions. *Psychological Assessment, 19,* 146–151.

McNulty, J. K., O'Mara, E. M., & Karney, B. R. (2008). Benevolent cognitions as a strategy of relationship maintenance: "Don't sweat the small stuff"… but it is not all small stuff. *Journal of Personality and Social Psychology, 94,* 631–646.

McNulty, J. K. (2008). Forgiveness in marriage: Putting the benefits into context. *Journal of Family Psychology, 22,* 171–175.

Mikulincer, M., & Shaver, P. R. (2005). Mental representations of attachment security: Theoretical foundation for a positive social psychology.

In M. W. Baldwin (Ed.), *Interpersonal cognition* (pp. 233–266). New York: Guilford.

Mills, J., Clark, M. S., Ford, T. E., & Johnson, M. (2004). Measurement of communal strength. *Personal Relationships, 11,* 213–230.

Mitchell, A. E., Castellanie, A. M., Herrington, R. L., Joseph, J. I., Doss, B. D., & Snyder, D. K. (2008). Predictors of intimacy in couples' discussions of relationship injuries: An observational study. *Journal of Family Psychology, 22,* 21–29.

Ong, A. D., & van Dulmen, M. H. M. (Eds.) (2007). *Oxford handbook of methods in positive psychology.* New York: Oxford University Press.

Paleari, G., Regalia, C., & Fincham, F. D. (2003). Adolescents' willingness to forgive parents: An empirical model. *Parenting: Science and Practice, 3,* 155–174.

Patrick, S., Sells, J. N., Giordano, F. G., & Tollerud, T. R. (2007). Intimacy, differentiation, and personality variables as predictors of marital satisfaction. *The Family Journal, 15,* 359–367.

Peterson, C. (2006). *A primer in positive psychology.* New York: Oxford University Press.

Prager, K. J., & Buhrmester, D. (1998). Intimacy and need fulfillment in couple relationships. *Journal of Social & Personal Relationships, 15,* 435–469.

Proulx, C. M., Helms, H. M., & Buehler, C. (2007). Marital quality and personal well-being: A meta-analysis. *Journal of Marriage and Family, 69,* 576–593.

Reis, H. T., & Gable, S. L. (2003). Toward a positive psychology of relationships. In C. L. Keyes & J. Haidt (Eds.), *Flourishing: The positive person and the good life* (pp. 129–159). Washington, DC: American Psychological Association.

Reynolds, W. M. (1982). Development of reliable and valid short forms of the Marlowe-Crowne Social Desirability scale. *Journal of Clinical Psychology, 38,* 119–125.

Snyder, C. R., & Lopez, S. J. (2007). *Positive psychology: The scientific and practical explorations of human strengths.* Thousand Oaks, CA: Sage.

Stone, A. A., Turkan, J. S., Bachrach, C. A., Jobe, J. B., Kurtzman, H. S., & Cain, V. S. (2000). *The science of self-report: Implications for research and practice.* Mahwah, NJ: Lawrence Erbaum.

Thompson, M. M., Zanna, M. P., & Griffin, D. W. (1995). Let's not be indifferent about (attitudinal) ambivalence. In R. E. Petty & J. A. Drosnick (Eds.), *Attitude strength: Antecedents and consequences* (pp. 361–386). Hillsdale, NJ: Erlbaum.

Tsang, J., McCullough, M. Fincham, F. D. (2006). Forgiveness and the psychological dimension of reconciliation: A longitudinal analysis. *Journal of Social and Clinical Psychology, 25,* 404–428.

Vangelisti, A. L., & Young, S. L. (2000). When words hurt: The effects of perceived intentionality on interpersonal relationships. *Journal of Social and Personal Relationships, 17,* 393–424.

Waltz, M., & Badura, B. (1988). Subjective health, intimacy, and perceived self-efficacy after heart attack: Predicting life quality five years afterwards. *Social Indicators Research, 20,* 303–332.

Waring, E. M., & Patton, D. (1984). Marital intimacy and depression. *British Journal of Psychiatry, 145,* 641–644.

# 19

## Coaching and Positive Psychology

*Anthony M. Grant and Michael J. Cavanagh*

The past decade has seen the use of coaching in personal, health, workplace, and executive settings grow from being a novel and somewhat derided methodology to a mainstream activity in business organizations and health settings worldwide. Recently, the annual revenue expended on corporate coaching has been estimated to be at US$1.5 billion, with approximately 30,000 professional coaches globally (International Coach Federation, 2006). The UK Chartered Institute of Personnel and Development reports that 88% of UK organizations use coaching (Jarvis, Lane, & Fillery-Travis, 2005). In Australia, 64% of business leaders and 72% of senior managers report using coaches, with 96% rating the experience as beneficial (Leadership Management Australia, 2006). The use of health coaching in medical settings for helping patients recover from physical illness has also significantly grown (Newham-Kanas, Goreznski, Morrow, & Irwin, 2009), and personal coaching is being increasingly used as a means of enhancing psychological well-being in addition to goal attainment (Grant, 2007).

The recent growth of coaching and coaching psychology parallels the development of the positive psychology movement. The core principles and foci of interest of positive psychology are evidenced throughout the history of philosophy and psychology. However, it was only in the latter 1990s that psychologists and behavioral scientists explicitly articulated an agenda for a sub-discipline of psychology that focused attention on sources of psychological health, well-being, and the scientific study of the factors that enable individuals, organizations, and communities to flourish and thrive (see for example the Akumal Manifesto, 1999 and Seligman & Csikszentmihalyi, 2000). Similarly, although methodologies for helping individuals reach their goals and fulfill their personal potential had long been in existence in therapeutic and non-therapeutic domains, it was only during the latter 1990s that coaching began to emerge as a popular human change methodology. The emergence of coaching was propelled by many of the same socio-cultural factors that underpinned the positive psychology movement: dissatisfaction with traditional approaches to facilitating human change (Spence, 2007a) and a frustration with established psychological teaching, research, and practice (for a detailed history of the contemporary coaching movement, see Brock, 2008). Thus, coaching and positive psychology share common historical roots and interests and, potentially, a common future.

In this chapter, we draw on and extend our previous work (e.g, Grant, Passmore, Cavanagh, & Parker, 2010) and take stock of the current state in relation to coaching research and practice and then highlight how coaching could make important contributions to the future of positive psychology. In taking stock of the present state of play in coaching, we begin with definitions and delineations of coaching; we then report on the professional status of coaching and the bodies that seek to accredit and organize coaches. Research into the efficacy of coaching is briefly discussed. Moving forward, we present an overview of a future coaching-related research and practice agenda. We conclude by outlining some potentially fruitful lines of inquiry for future work in this emerging and exciting sub-field of psychological research.

## Taking Stock: What Is Coaching?

Coaching is a relationship formed between a coach and the coachee for the purpose of attaining valued professional or personal outcomes (for a recent discussion, see Spence & Grant, 2007). Hence, coaching is a goal-driven activity. This is true whether the coaching is focused on instilling skills, improving performance, or developmental growth. In most coaching engagements, the coaching process facilitates goal attainment and enhances well-being by helping individuals to (i) identify desired outcomes, (ii) establish specific goals, (iii) enhance motivation by identifying strengths and building self-efficacy, (iv) identify resources and formulate action plans, (v) monitor and evaluate progress, and (vi) modify action plans. The monitor-evaluate-modification steps of this process constitute a simple cycle of self-regulated behavior, and this is a key in creating intentional behavior change (Carver & Scheier, 1998). It requires some considerable skill on the part of the coach to properly facilitate this process, not least in assisting the coachee to keep focused on his or her goals over time and helping him or her to develop and implement innovative solutions to the ongoing challenges that invariably arise during the goal-striving process.

## Coaching and Coaching Psychology

Coaching psychology is "coaching" that draws on and develops established psychological approaches, and coaching psychology involves the systematic application of behavioral science to the enhancement of life experience, work performance, and well-being. It is important to note that, at this point in time, most coaches do not have explicit training in the behavioral sciences or in positive psychology, nor are they registered psychologists (Grant & Zackon, 2004).

Furthermore, most coaches tend not to use theoretically coherent approaches or scientifically validated techniques and measures (Grant and O'Hara, 2006). Interestingly, whilst the discipline of psychology would appear to be an ideal grounding for the practice of coaching, a psychology background has not been viewed as essential for coaching by the coaching industry (Coutu & Kauffman, 2009; Garman, Whiston, & Zlatoper, 2000).

We do not argue that a psychological education or training in positive psychology is essential for solid coaching practice. Indeed, many great coaches do not have a formal education in psychology, and the relevance of a psychological background will vary depending on the focus of the coaching engagement. However, we contend that, whilst non-psychology-based approaches to coaching have merit, utility, and a clear place in the human change enterprise, coaching psychology adds a depth and grounding to contemporary coaching practice, particularly where the coaching addresses personal or emotionally laden issues.

We do argue that both coaching psychology and positive psychology have much to offer the field of coaching. Many psychologists have a grounding in a scientist-practitioner or scholar-practitioner model. This is invaluable in the generation and validation of practical knowledge. Psychological education also builds critical thinking skills critical to understanding the dynamic link between theory and change methodologies. These skills, derived from a long-standing tradition of research and a broad base of tested theory, can bring much needed rigor to the coaching arena. (For a discussion of the application of the scientist practitioner model in coaching, see Cavanagh & Grant, 2006.)

Coaching has a broad remit and has been applied to many areas of human change, including: business coaching (Clegg, Rhodes, Kornberger,

& Stilin, 2005), dealing with workplace stress (Wright, 2007), learning how to work with difficult people, leadership and sales skills development (Wilson, 2004), career coaching (Scandura, 1992), team building (Cunha & Louro, 2000), coaching to improving sales performance (Rich, 1998), and coaching to improve job interview performance (Maurer, Solamon, & Troxtel, 1998).

While the above coaching activities address clearly substantive issues, some coaching applications seem trivial or even farcical. Seligman (2007) has observed that the scope of present coaching practice is almost without limits, with life coaches offering to coach you in arranging your closet, fighting dark thoughts, or organizing your memories in a scrap book! From such a perspective, it is hard to see that such activities bear the hallmark of a genuine helping profession.

**Credentialing, Professional Status, and Professional Bodies**

Indeed, when judged against the commonly accepted criteria for professional status, coaching presently fails to display the key hallmarks of a profession. There are no barriers to entry, no minimal educational process or training route, and no binding ethical or practice standards (Sherman & Freas, 2004). Anyone can call themselves a coach, and the practice of coaching is unregulated. In calling for a greater degree of scientific and professional rigor in coaching, Seligman (2007) has commented that:

*People who call themselves coaches and get paid for coaching have an enormous range of academic qualifications from none at all to bachelor's degrees in almost anything, to masters degrees in counselling, education, social work, or positive psychology, to doctorates in psychology, medicine, and philosophy… Some have taken face-to-face or telecourses in coaching, but many have not. Some are "accredited" by the self-appointed International Coach Federation… but most are not. The right to call oneself a coach is unregulated. And this is why a scientific and a theoretical backbone… (is essential)…"* (Seligman, 2007, p. 266).

The issue of the accreditation of coaches is somewhat controversial. In the recent past, much of the coach training industry appears to have been driven by a quest for quick credibility and status (Grant & Cavanagh 2007). Worldwide there is a veritable industry offering a range of "coach certifications." Indeed, some coach training organizations seem to be little more than credentialing mills where, following a few days training and payment of the appropriate fee, one can be awarded the title of "Professional Certified Master Coach" or the like (Grant & O'Hara, 2006). The value of these certifications is highly questionable. This is an important issue because the general public are not well-informed about the value of various genuine psychological qualifications, let alone coaching qualifications, and may rely on impressive-sounding titles to guide them in selecting a coach or coach training program.

However, there is growing recognition of the need for well-grounded and commonly accepted standards of accreditation. Some coaching organizations, like the European Mentoring and Coaching Council (EMCC; UK-based, has more than 3,000 members) and the International Coach Federation (ICF; U.S.-based, 15,000 members in nearly 90 countries), have put considerable effort into establishing credentialing processes and developing coaching competencies. The recent Dublin Declaration of the Global Coaching Convention (GCC, 2008) saw leaders and members of many international and national coaching bodies call for international collaboration on developing common frameworks of understanding around training, ethics, and accreditation. Some of these organizations (e.g., the EMMC and the ICF) are beginning to collaborate in the development of aligned ethical standards. Such efforts are important moves toward genuine professionalism.

The role of accreditation by such bodies is becoming more salient. Within both the U.S. and Australia, some commercial and government organizations are beginning to require that external coaches be accredited by different bodies as a condition of employment. This may reflect a search for some security on the part of organizations and government departments, in a market that is marked by variable service standards and a lack of clearly articulated alternative accreditation models. It may also reflect effective lobbying on the part of various industry bodies to be seen as the representatives of "professional" coaching. Such a development is likely to exacerbate the tension felt by some coaches who have many years of psychological training and who would argue that their training represents a superior preparation for the role of coach, both practically and academically.

## The Current Academic Status of Coaching

Psychology as a body of knowledge and as a professional practice has traditionally been slow to engage with the public's demand for personal and professional development, leaving the way open for other, possibly less qualified, individuals to dominate the market (Fox, 1996). Recognizing the importance of psychology's role in coaching, a number of professional psychological societies have now established formal coaching psychology groups, including the Australian and British Psychological Societies, the Danish Psychological Association, the Swedish Psychological Association, and the Federation of Swiss Psychologists. Many other groups around the world, such as the Society for Industrial and Organisational Psychology in South Africa (SIOPSA), are developing strong interests in coaching. Most recently (April, 2008), the Psychological Society of Ireland's Division of Work and Organisational Psychology established a Coaching Psychology Group to further develop coaching psychology as a psychological subdiscipline.

In addition, worldwide there are now a number of universities offering coaching degree programs. Since the commencement in 2000 of the first postgraduate degree in coaching psychology at Sydney University, Australia now has three universities offering master's-level coaching degrees and doctoral programs. In the UK there are several degree programs operating, with coaching psychology units now established at City University and the University of East London, and professional mentoring and coaching programs up to doctoral level at universities such as Oxford Brookes and Sheffield Hallam. The University of Copenhagen in Denmark has also recently established a coaching psychology unit. Between Australia and the UK, there are at least eight university-accredited master's degrees in coaching psychology. In the U.S., at least seven universities offer coaching degree programs, with a Coaching and Positive Psychology Initiative recently being established at Harvard University. It appears that coaching is becoming increasingly accepted within the academic sphere. We envisage that the increasing availability of specialist professional qualifications in coaching psychology, like those available in clinical, organizational, and forensic psychology, will do much to raise the bar for the coaching industry in general.

Of course both psychologists and non-psychologists have much to contribute to professional coaching. Indeed, most of the coaching degrees worldwide are offered by business or education faculties, rather than from within schools of psychology. The challenge for psychology is to engage with other sectors of the coaching industry in a way that brings the best of both to the fore and provides a solid educational grounding for professional coaching practice (Cavanagh & Palmer 2006).

Regardless of whether such programs are housed within schools of psychology or not (or indeed whether coaching is primarily conducted by psychologists or non-psychologists), the development of a professional approach to coaching is reliant on a rigorous and coherent body of coaching-specific research (Grant & Cavanagh, 2007). It is to this issue we now turn.

## Coaching Research: What Do We Know?

The first coaching citations listed in PsycINFO are Gorby's (1937) report of senior staff coaching junior employees on how to save waste and Bigelow's (1938) article on how best to implement a sales coaching program. Despite these early citations, research in the area of coaching is in its infancy. There has been significant growth in the coaching literature in recent years, and the bulk of the literature on coaching is less than 10 years old. As of February 2009, there were more than 520 published scholarly papers or dissertations on coaching cited in PsycINFO, yet in the 62 years between 1937 and 1999 only 93 papers were published (note that these figures include life (or personal coaching) and workplace and executive coaching, but exclude papers on less relevant applications such as sports coaching, clinical or therapeutic populations, educational coaching, or coaching for psychometric or educational tests).

There has been significant growth in the coaching literature in recent years. Between 2000 and February 2009, more than 360 peer-reviewed papers were published. However, of these papers, approximately 60% have been articles, opinion papers, descriptive articles, or theoretical discussions and about 30% empirical studies (20% of all these have been PhD dissertations). Many of the published empirical papers are surveys (e.g., Fanasheh, 2003) or descriptive studies into the nature of executive coaching or life coaching (e.g., Griffiths & Campbell, 2008; Schnell, 2005), investigations into organizations' use of coaching (e.g., Douglas & McCauley, 1999; Vloeberghs, Pepermans, & Thielemans, 2005; Wycherley & Cox, 2008), or examinations of different perceptions of coaching (e.g. Garman, Whiston & Zlatoper, 2000). That is, most of the empirical literature is contextual or survey-based research about coaching as a professional service activity or about the characteristics of coaches and coachees, rather than outcome research examining the efficacy of coaching as a means of creating individual or organizational change.

## Outcome Studies

The first published empirical outcome study on workplace coaching in psychology literature was Gershman's (1967) dissertation on the effects of specific factors of the supervisor-subordinate coaching climate upon improvement of attitude and performance of the subordinate. No other coaching outcome studies were published until Duffy's (1984) dissertation on the effectiveness of a feedback-coaching intervention in executive outplacement.

We located a total of 81 outcome studies that have examined the effectiveness of coaching since 1980. There have been a total of 27 case studies, 40 within-subject studies, and 15 between-subject studies.

Of course, single case designs can provide useful data-driven evaluations. However, many of the 27 case studies in the coaching literature are purely descriptive and emphasize issues related to practice rather than the development of theory or coaching outcomes (Kilburg, 2004). Very few of these case studies incorporated established and validated quantitative measures (one exception is Libri & Kemp, 2006). The 40 within-subject studies represent the largest single methodological approach to coaching outcome research. While within-subject studies can provide useful quantitative data and allow for the use of inferential statistics, provided that the studies are well-designed and use validated and reliable measures, randomized controlled studies are frequently held to represent best practice in researching the impact of specific interventions.

## Randomized Controlled Studies

Eleven of the 15 between-subject outcome studies used a randomized controlled design (Deviney

1994; Duijts, Kant, van den Brandt, & Swaen, 2008; Taylor, 1997; Grant, 2002; Miller, Yahne, Moyers, Martinez & Pirritano, 2004; Gattellari et al., 2005; Green, Oades & Grant, 2006; Green, Grant & Rynsaardt, 2007; Spence & Grant, 2007; Grant, Frith, and Burton, in press; Spence, Cavanagh, & Grant, 2008). Sue-Chan and Latham (2004) used random assignment to self, peer, or external coaching group but did not use a no-intervention or placebo intervention control group. Table 19.1 presents summaries of the 15 between-subject studies.

The 11 randomized controlled studies of coaching that have been conducted to date indicate that coaching can indeed improve performance in various ways.

Four of these 11 studies have been in the medical or health areas. Taylor (1997) found that solution-focused coaching fostered resilience in medical students. Gattellari et al. (2005) found that peer coaching by general practitioners improved coachees' ability to make informed decisions about prostate-specific antigen screening. Miller, Yahbe, Moyers, Martinez, & Pirritanol (2004) found that coaching with feedback was superior to training-only conditions, in a program designed to help clinicians learn motivational interviewing skills. Exploring the utility of mindfulness training when used within health coaching and comparing this to a health education seminar intervention, Spence, Cavanagh, & Grant (2008) found that the mindfulness/coaching intervention was superior to the health education seminar intervention.

Four outcome studies have been in the life (or personal) coaching domain with community samples and students. These have indicated that coaching can improve and indeed facilitate goal attainment and reduce anxiety and stress (Grant, 2003), enhance psychological and subjective well-being (Green, Oades, & Grant, 2006; Spence & Grant, 2007) and resilience, while reducing depression, stress, or anxiety (Green, Grant, & Rynsaardt, 2007).

There have been only three randomized controlled studies of coaching in the workplace. Deviney (1994) examined the efficacy of supervisors acting as internal workplace coaches, finding no changes in supervisors' feedback skills following a multiple-rater feedback intervention and coaching from their managers over nine weeks. Duijts, Kant, van den Brandt, & Swaen, (2008) examined the effectiveness of coaching as a means of reducing sick leave and found that although coaching did not reduce the amount of

TABLE 19.1   Summary Table of Between-Subjects Studies to 2009

| Study | Intervention Overview | Type of Study | Key Findings |
|---|---|---|---|
| Miller (1990) | 33 employees. Some received coaching by their managers over four weeks | Quasi-experimental field study (a) Coaching group; (b) Control group | No sig. differences pre-post for interpersonal communication skills |
| Deviney (1994)* | 45 line supervisors at a nuclear power plant. Some received feedback and coaching from their managers over nine weeks | Randomized controlled study (a) Feedback plus coaching; (b) Feedback with no coaching; (c) Control group | No sig. differences in pre-post feedback behavior |
| Taylor (1997)* | Participants undergoing a Medical College Admission Test preparation course | Randomized controlled study (a) Training only; (b) Coaching only; (c) Training plus coaching; (d) Control group | Coaching reduced stress more than training |
| Grant (2002)* | 62 trainee accountants received group coaching over one semester | Randomized controlled study (a) Cognitive coaching only; (b) Behavioral coaching only; (c) Combined cognitive and behavioral coaching; (d) Control groups for each condition | Combined cognitive and behavioral coaching most effective in increasing grade point average, study skills, self-regulation, and mental health. GPA gains maintained in 12 month follow-up |
| Miller, Yahne, Moyers, Martinez, & Pirritano (2004)* | 140 licensed substance abuse professionals learned Motivational Interviewing via a range of methods | Randomized controlled study (a) Workshop only; (b) Workshop plus feedback; (c) Workshop plus coaching; (d) Workshop, feedback, and coaching; or (e) Waitlist control group | Relative to controls, the 4 trained groups had gains in proficiency. Coaching and/or feedback increased post-training proficiency |
| Sue-Chan & Latham (2004) | 53 MBA students in two studies in Canada and Australia | Random assignment (a) External coach; (b) Peer coach; (c) Self-coached | Study 1: External coaching associated with higher team playing behavior than peer coaching; Study 2: External and self coaching associated with higher grades than peer coaching |
| Gattellari, M., N. Donnelly et al. (2005)* | 277 GPs in total. Some received two phone-based peer coaching sessions integrated with educational resources | Randomized controlled study (a) Peer coaching and educational resources; (b) Control group | Compared to controls, peer coaching increased GPs ability to make informed decisions about prostate-specific antigen screening |
| Gyllensten & Palmer (2005) | 31 participants from UK finance organization | Quasi-experimental field study (a) Coaching group; (b) Control group | Anxiety and stress decreased more in the coaching group compared to control group |

TABLE 19.1    (*continued*) Summary Table of Between-Subjects Studies to 2009

| Study | Intervention Overview | Type of Study | Key Findings |
|---|---|---|---|
| Evers, Brouwers, & Tomic (2006) | 60 managers of the federal government | Quasi-experimental field study (a) Coaching group; (b) Control group | Coaching increased outcome expectancies' and self-efficacy |
| Green, Oades, & Grant (2006)* | 56 adults (community sample) took part in SF-CB life coaching program | Randomized controlled study (a) Group-based life coaching; (b) Waitlist control | Coaching increased goal attainment, well-being, and hope. 30-week follow-up found gains were maintained |
| Green, Grant, & Rynsaardt (2007)* | 56 female high school students took part in SF-CB life coaching program for 10 individual coaching sessions over two school terms | Randomized controlled study (a) Coaching group; (b) Waitlist control group | Coaching increased cognitive hardiness, mental health, and hope |
| Spence & Grant (2007)* | 63 adults (community sample) took part in SF-CB life coaching program | Randomized controlled study (a) Professional coaching group; (b) Peer coaching group; (c) Waitlist control group | Professional coaching more effective in increasing goal commitment, goal attainment, and environmental mastery |
| Duijts, Kant, van den Brandt, & Swaen (2008)* | Dutch employees assessed for the effectiveness of a preventive coaching program on sickness absence due to psychosocial health complaints and on well-being outcomes | Randomized controlled study (a) 6-month course of preventive coaching; (b) Control group | Significant improvements in health, life satisfaction, burnout, psychological well-being, but no improvement in self-reported sickness absence |
| Spence, Cavanagh, & Grant (2008)* | 45 adults (community sample) took part in mindfulness-based health coaching over eight weeks | Randomized controlled study SF-CB coaching followed by mindfulness training (MT); (b) Mindfulness training followed by SF-CB coaching; (c) Health education only control group | Goal attainment greater in coaching than in the educative/directive format. No significant differences were found for goal attainment between the two MT/CB-SF conditions |
| Grant, Curtayne, & Burton, 2009 | 41 executives in a public health agency received 360-degree feedback and four SF-CB coaching sessions over 10-week period | Randomized controlled study (a) Coaching group; (b) Waitlist control group | Coaching enhanced goal attainment, resilience, and workplace well-being and reduced depression and stress and helped participants deal with organizational change |

Notes: SF-CB = Solution-focused cognitive behavioral; * = Randomized controlled study self-reported sick leave, the coaching intervention group reported statistically significant improvements in health, reduced psychological distress, lower rates of burnout, less need for recovery, and an increased satisfaction with life. Grant, Frith, & Burton (in press) found that short-term solution-focused, cognitive behavioral executive coaching consisting of four coaching sessions over 10 weeks increased resilience and workplace well-being, and reduced stress and depression. These studies indicate that coaching in the workplace can have a positive effect on general well-being of employees (for a recent review of coaching, see Joo, 2005; Passmore & Gibbes, 2007).

The lack of randomized controlled studies is a major shortcoming in the coaching literature. While there is debate over the practical utility of randomized controlled trials, they are currently held to be the "gold standard" in quantitative outcome research where interventions are used to produce specific outcomes. However, true randomized allocation to intervention or control is often extremely difficult in real-life field research. Thus, most coaching outcome studies have used single-group, pre-post within-subject designs (e.g., Grant 2003, Jones, Rafferty, & Griffn, 2006; Olivero, Bane, & Kipelman, 1997; Orenstein, 2006).

There have been some quasi-experimental studies with pretest and posttest comparisons and non-randomized allocation to an experimental or control group. Miller (1990) examined the impact of coaching on transfer of training skills, but the drawing of conclusions was restricted by a high rate of participant dropout: 91 participants began the study, but only 33 completed the final measures. Gyllensten and Palmer (2005) found that, compared with a no-coaching control group, coaching was associated with lower levels of anxiety and stress. Evers, Brouwers, and Tomic (2006) found that executive coaching enhanced participants' self-efficacy beliefs in personal goal setting, but they did not measure goal attainment itself. Barrett (2007) used a quasi-experimental, modified posttest-only control group design, finding that group coaching reduced burnout but did not improve productivity.

## Longitudinal Studies

Not surprisingly, the number of longitudinal studies conducted in coaching is small. The few follow-up studies that have been conducted indicate that coaching can indeed produce sustained change. Grant (2002) investigated the effects of

cognitive-only, behavioral-only, and combined cognitive and behavioral coaching and found that only the gains from the combined cognitive-behavioral coaching were maintained at a six-month follow-up. In a 12-month follow-up, Miller et al., (2004) found coaching with feedback was superior to training-only conditions in maintaining clinicians' interviewing skills. Green, Oades, & Grant, (2006) found that gains from participation in a 10-week solution-focused cognitive-behavioral life coaching were maintained at a 30-week follow-up. Libri & Kemp (2006) provide a refreshing example of a well-designed case study of cognitive-behavioral executive coaching. Using an A-B-A-B design with an 18-month follow-up, they found that cognitive-behavioral coaching enhanced the coachees' sales performance and core self-evaluations.

## Measuring Outcomes of Coaching

It appears that coaching outcome research, as a relatively new area of study, may be moving through the "natural" stages of research development, from case studies, through to within-subject studies, and on to quasi-experimental and randomized controlled between-subject designs. Indeed, the 55 within-subject or between-subjects outcome studies conducted to date are a useful foundation for knowledge about the effectiveness of coaching. Encouragingly, the amount of research is increasing over time.

However, a major problem in this body of work is lack of consistency between studies in the use of outcome measures, seriously limiting meaningful comparison between studies. The idiosyncratic use of measures means that it is difficult for a coherent body of knowledge to develop over time. Many researchers develop their own somewhat simplistic "satisfaction with coaching" surveys, and the validity and reliability of such measure is unknown.

Given that coaching is frequently promoted as being effective in enhancing goal attainment and well-being (e.g., Levine, Kase, & Vitale, 2006; Passmore & Gibbes, 2007), it is surprising that few studies to date have used well-validated measures of mental health and well-being, despite the fact that there are many such measures designed for use in non-clinical populations. For example, the Depression, Anxiety, and Stress Scale (Lovibond & Lovibond, 1995); the Psychological Well-being Scale (Ryff & Keyes, 1996); and the Cognitive Hardiness Scale (Nowack, 1990) fit such a description.

As a goal-focused change methodology, goal attainment is an important outcome measure in coaching. However, few outcome studies have measured the impact of coaching on goal attainment. Goal attainment scaling (GAS) techniques offer a useful means of measuring goal progression in relation to predetermined objective success benchmarks (see Fillery-Travis & Lane, 2006) and can provide a means of making comparisons between studies. Well-conducted GAS would also help address the serious limitations of the few studies that have examined return on investment in coaching using subjective post-coaching ratings of success (e.g., McGovern et al., 2001). See Spence (2007) for a comprehensive discussion of the use of GAS in coaching.

## Coaching and Therapy: Sorting out the Boundaries

Of particular importance for future research is the boundary between coaching and therapy. While often mentioned in the coaching literature, little by way of empirical research has been conducted into the prevalence of mental health issues in coaching populations. This area was given prominence by Berglas's (2002) somewhat controversial article on the potential danger of psychologically naïve coaches unwittingly reinforcing unhealthy patterns in those they coach. Until recently, much of the concern with mental health in the coaching community has focused on identifying depression in coaching. However, while important, a singular focus on depression is insufficient (Cavanagh 2005). It seems reasonable to suspect that Mental health is a major moderating factor for coaching effectiveness yet, to date, we have little empirical understanding of the nature and prevalence of mental health issues in personal or workplace coaching.

Some mental health-related data has been gathered in studies of life coaching clients. Green, Oades, and Grant (2006) and Spence & Grant (2007) found clinically significant levels of mental distress in 52% and 26% of participants seeking life coaching in their studies respectively. While it seems likely that those presenting for executive and workplace coaching will have a different profile than people presenting for free life coaching as part of a research study, little deliberate research has been conducted into the mental health of executive and workplace coaching clients. Our experience tells us that it is not a question of whether mental health issues are an important consideration in coaching, but the extent to which this is so. We would argue that research into the prevalence of the full range of mental health issues in coaching is both important and sorely needed (Cavanagh, 2005; Cavanagh and Grant, 2004)).

## Return on Investment: A Valid Outcome Measure for Coaching?

Return on investment (ROI) using metrics typically valued by organizations (e.g., growth in market share, profitability, sales, etc.) is often promoted as being the most important indicator of coaching success in organizational settings. Return on investment figures are frequently used by coaching and consulting organizations as sales or marketing tools in order to promote their coaching products. Return on investment figures of 788% (Kampa-Kokesch & Anderson, 2001) and 545% (McGovern et al., 2001a) are commonly reported as being "*the*" ROI for executive coaching.

Return on investment is essentially calculated by subtracting the value of the outcomes of coaching from the costs of coaching and then expressing this as a percentage (coaching benefits – costs of coaching/costs of coaching × 100%). There are a number of variations to this formula, for example, including factoring into the equation a rating of the coachee's level of confidence that all or some of the perceived benefits are in fact due to coaching, or deliberately undervaluing the benefits of coaching.

However, we argue that whilst ROI can provide some guidance as to the perceived impact of a coaching intervention, it has serious limitations as a benchmark outcome measure for coaching effectiveness. Reducing the benefits of coaching to a single financial amount may give the purchasers of coaching services a sense of comfort and some reassurance that their money has beenwell spent, but does it truly measure the impact of coaching? We think not.

The point here is that the ROI metric depends on two key variables: (1) the amount the coach charges and the costs of the coaching intervention, and (2) the financial benefit obtained. These are highly vague and contextually bound variables. What counts as costs? How are benefits assessed and what causal chain links the coaching to those benefits?

Even if there were some clearly accepted standard for measuring costs and benefits, making general claims about the effectiveness of coaching based on ROI data would remain extremely problematic. For example, company X employs a coach who charges $1,000 for the coaching engagement. The coach works with an executive who is working on a $10 million deal. The deal is done, and the executives estimates that 50% of the result is due to the coach (and let us assume that this estimate is fair and accurate). In this case, ROI is 49,000%. Can we now claim that the ROI for executive coaching is in the region of 50,000%? Of course not. At best, ROI can be indicative of only a single specific coaching engagement. In order to make any meaningful statement about ROI, and in order to compare ROI across different coaching studies, all facets of the coaching engagement, including coaching costs, benefits (and importantly, the opportunities available to the executive to derive benefits, must be accounted for and controlled across studies.

Cause and effect is an important issue in assessing the efficacy of coaching interventions. While organizations often seek to improve financial performance via coaching, such measures are typically not the direct focus of coaching interventions. It is often difficult to draw clear lines of causality between coaching and shifts in wider organizational metrics. Here coaching research has much to learn from research methodologies used in areas such as training, education, and organizational psychology. As more researchers move into the coaching arena, we expect to see increases in greater interpenetration with these more established fields of research, and an increased sophistication in the coaching literature around the measurement of coaching outcomes.

It is of note that all the ROI research that we could identify in researching for this chapter had been conducted by consultants and organizations that supply coaching services, and/or by the human resources professionals that employ them to provide coaching services to their organization. Thus, as is sometimes the case with practitioner research, there may well be some vested interests in demonstrating success and reporting value for money. This is not to imply misreporting of results. Rather, it suggests that these issues may unconsciously effect the way in which participants answer questions and the ways in which data is interpreted. For this reason, such research should be conducted and read with some caution.

Finally, as we will discuss in the "moving forward" section of this chapter, we believe that there are far more important, informative, and valuable outcome measures for coaching than a single ROI metric.

## Moving Forward: Game Plans for the Future

In discussing the future of coaching as an applied positive psychology, we want to focus on three key areas: (1) The use of coaching as an experimental methodology for investigating the psycho-mechanics of purposeful positive human change; (2) the use of coaching in organizational settings as a means of facilitating positive individual and organizational change; and (3) the role of coaching in catalysing systems change at local national and global levels.

### Coaching as an Experimental Methodology for Studying Positive Change

While coaching, and particularly coaching psychology, is connected to more than a century of psychological theory, research, and development, it often seems as if our understanding of what makes for effective positive human change is still in its infancy and that the potential research agenda is vast. We believe that coaching has a vital role to play in defining the research agenda and in assisting researchers in understanding the dynamics of positive human change.

In terms of the agenda for research, there is a clear need to focus on conducting large-scale efficacy studies of coaching. Multiple studies using randomized controlled designs are required to assess the efficacy of coaching within different populations and its suitability as an intervention for a range of different issues and goals. In other words, we are still largely ignorant, at a scientific level, as to what kinds of coaching interventions work best, for which change agendas, and for whom.

The problem here is that there is a serious bottleneck in our ability to conduct research. Although the coaching industry and the number of coaching practitioners are growing rapidly, the number of coaching researchers is small. Indeed, most coaching services providers are small businesses, employing between one and ten employees. Most do not have training in research methodologies, and the industry as a whole tends to use idiosyncratic outcome measures. In short, the scientist practitioner model used in psychology is largely unknown in coaching (Cavanagh & Grant, 2006).

One solution to this bottleneck would be to enable professional coaches who are not trained in conducting research to contribute to the body of knowledge in coaching. Here the establishment of a Web-based research platform such as that used by Seligman and Peterson to study the efficacy of PP interventions might be very helpful. This would enable coaches to assess the efficacy of their coaching interventions while providing a large-scale database of coaching outcomes. Variables could include standard outcome measures such as measures of mental health and stress as well as positive psychology measures of well-being, goal attainment, and assessment of the quality of the relationship between coach and coachee.

Coaching has also great potential to be used to explore the psycho-mechanics of human change. Coaching can be used as a means of manipulating or purposefully altering specific aspects of the change process. These might include goal formation, action planning, attentional focus, formulation, rehearsal, emotion, cognition, behavior, and contextual modification, to name but a few potential contributors to the change process. Such research would help to develop frameworks of case conceptualizations that will help integrate positive psychology theories such as Deci and Ryan's Self-Determination Theory, Csikszentmihalyi's concept of flow, and Fredrickson's broaden-and-build theory.

The use of positive psychology in coaching may also help to elucidate the boundary between coaching and therapy. As noted above, the boundary between coaching and therapy is often mentioned in the coaching literature. However, the tenor of this complex debate is often rather unidimensional and superficial. Coaching and therapy as often seen as either/or options the choice of which is determined by the presence of diagnosable mental illness. Even at this level, little by way of empirical research has been conducted into the prevalence of mental health issues in coaching populations. While the investigation of mental illness in coaching represents a significant and worthwhile research agenda in its own right, we believe that the debate on the boundary between coaching and therapy should be based on a more solid empirical footing—one that includes both mental illness and mental health. Indeed, both are present simultaneously to varying degrees over time. Hence, we would advocate that coaching research also investigate the way in which coaching methodologies promote resilience and human flourishing in the presence of mental health issues (Cavanagh & Grant 2004; Grant & Cavanagh 2004). Of course, ethical practice dictates that any such research needs to hold the safety and wellbeing of participants as paramount, and should not be seen as a license for unqualified coaches to practice beyond their skillset or knowledge.,

## Coaching as a Means of Effecting Organizational Change

The second major focus for future research and practice concerns the extended impact of coaching on organizations. Of course, this includes research into the return on investment (ROI) for coaching programs but goes beyond this to establish the nature and extent of the impact of coaching interventions on a range of workplace outcomes. This research also spans the impact of interventions, not just on the individuals, but on different groups, organizations, and indeed the wider community. In this way, coaching can be assessed as a developmental tool with the potential to create stronger, more resilient individuals, organizations, and communities. We believe that coaching will become increasingly used as a means of facilitating organization-wide change. Indeed, such interventions are being increasingly reported in the professional and trade media (e.g., Anderson, Anderson, & Mayo, 2008).

The needs of organizational change will continue to shape the type of research conducted in executive and workplace coaching. Hence, aside from research into ROI, we expect that there will be greater levels of research into the interplay between complex systems dynamics and coaching. Complexity theory has for some time been applied to organizations (Stacey, 2000; Waldrop, 1992; Wheatley, 1999) and has more recently been applied to coaching (Cavanagh, 2006). The emerging science of networking theory has clear application to coaching in organizations. This area of theoretical development considers the dynamics that shape connectivity in complex natural networks such as cells, organs, and ecosystems, and social networks such as organizations, professional networks, the Internet, and even terrorist groups (Kilduff, Crossland, Tsai, Krackhardt, 2008). Given that one of the major areas of coaching intervention is communication within and across networks, the application of both complexity and network theories would seem a fruitful avenue of research.

Over the last 20 years in psychology, we have seen a renewed interest in areas of psychological research that were hitherto viewed as somewhat peripheral and perhaps even scientifically marginal. For example, there is currently great interest in both the clinical and positive psychology literature on mindfulness meditation, or the intentional use of attention. We expect that the application of mindfulness and other metacognitive techniques in coaching will be an increasing area of focus. (For a fuller exploration of the use of metacognition and mindfulness to coaching, see Collard & Walsh, 2008; Passmore & Marianetti, 2007; Spence, Cavanagh, & Grant, 2006).

Coaching also has much to contribute to the emerging Positive Organizational Scholarship (POS) movement (Cameron, Dutton, & Quinn, 2003). The aims of POS is to focus on the dynamics in organizations that lead to developing human strengths, producing resilience, fostering vitality, and understanding how to enable human excellence in organizations and to facilitate positive human and organization welfare (Cameron & Caza, 2004). The focus on well-being, functionality, and performance articulated within the coaching agenda receives even greater explicit emphasis within POS, and we believe that a conjunction of the two will form an important future framework in organizational settings. Indeed, a number of papers have foreshadowed this development (e.g., Boyatzis, Smith, & Blaize, 2006; Luthans & Youssef, 2007). However, as in much of the positive psychology literature, the POS literature tends to report theoretical, cross-sectional, or correlational research rather than interventions designed to enhance workplace well-being and performance (e.g., Luthans, 2002; Muse, Harris, Giles, & Feild, 2008; Spreitzer, Sutcliffe, Dutton, Sonenshein, & Grant, 2005; Wright, 2003; Zhong, 2007). Coaching may well provide an applied methodology for implementing the insights developed in such research.

Coaching is increasingly seen as an applied arm of the rapidly developing positive psychology movement (Grant & Cavanagh 2007). As both coaching and positive psychology develop, it appears likely that there will be a greater cross-pollination of ideas, models of practice, and research between them. Indeed, both Seligman (2007) and Kauffman (2006) contend that research in the area of positive psychology can help to scientifically ground the field of coaching, claiming that that "positive psychology theory and research will provide the scientific legs upon which the field of coaching can firmly stand" (Kauffman, 2006; p.221). We would also contend

that coaching offers to positive psychology a valuable methodology for assessing the utility and adequacy of its theories.

## Coaching as a Means of Catalyzing Systems Change

While the youthfulness of coaching as an area of research presents challenges, it also presents exciting opportunities. Coaching is ideally placed to be a point of connection between disparate areas of research. The knowledge base of coaching remains an open question, and coaches can and do utilize multiple theories and models drawn from traditional psychology, positive psychology, and wider fields of endeavor such as management, medicine, biology, sociology, complexity and systems research, spirituality, education, and philosophy. While this certainly adds complexity to the work of coaches and researchers, it also makes coaching ideally suited as a means of catalyzing change in systems at the local, national regional, and global levels.

Our world is beset by major challenges, the likes of which we have never seen before: global warming, environmental degradation, increasing frequency of extreme weather events, energy and water shortage, economic upheaval, terrorism, and social dislocation. Scientists and thinkers and Nobel laureates from every field of endeavor have argued cogently that as a species we have reached a rapidly diminishing window of opportunity to make the choices needed to shape a sustainable future. If these people are correct, to date, it seems that not enough has been done to change our trajectory away from catastrophic and chaotic change at the hands of the systems forces our behavior has unbalanced, toward a new sustainable equilibrium.

According to some authors (see Lazlo, 2006) solutions for these problems are not primarily to be found in technology or even politics (though these need to be involved in the solution. Rather, they argue that the primary issue we face is one of consciousness. As Einstein so elegantly said, the significant problems we face cannot be solved with the same level of thinking we were at when we created them. The simple application of technology without a radical shift in the relationship we have with ourselves, our communities, and our planet will not lead to a new equilibrium. What is required is a new level of thinking—a new perspective upon ourselves, others, and the world. This is essentially a developmental shift in thinking toward a whole of systems understanding.

What role do coaching and positive psychology have to play in such large-scale events?

There is a growing awareness of the need for more holistic approaches. The current ascendency of positive psychology as a field of research reflects this. Reductionist and individualistic or atomistic approaches that focus on identifying linear chains of cause and effect are unable to grasp the unique and emergent dynamics of complex adaptive systems, whether at the level of the individual, dyad community, or planet. By taking wholeness seriously, positive psychology and coaching are in a position to support and catalyze a larger view capable of new approaches and solutions.

We are not suggesting that coaching and positive psychology should become some sort of medium through which a new social orthodoxy is to be imposed on our clients, either explicitly or implicitly. Indeed, such an approach would be merely another manifestation of a linear control mentality that has created the significant issues we face. Rather, we are suggesting that coaching is fundamentally about assisting clients to find new, more effective pathways via the art of dialogue and reflective practice. The coach's role is largely one of asking questions that open new possibilities for understanding, make new connections and new meanings and, ultimately, new patterns of action. It is clear that positive psychology can be valuable in informing this meaning making.

In order to be consistent with the emerging understanding of complex systems gleaned from the sciences and social research, the role of the developmental coach is not to impose solutions but to assist clients in noticing connections and engaging with the tensions and paradoxes inherent in any complex system. It is in the tensions and paradoxes on the edge of chaos that new understandings and creative possibilities emerge. While coaching and positive psychology may scaffold this process, they cannot control the outcome. This understanding of complexity leads to three main tasks in developmental coaching:

1. To assist clients in noticing and making connections on and between three levels: intrapersonal, interpersonal, and systemic.
2. to develop and support processes of communication that enable connectedness at the intrapersonal, interpersonal, and systemic levels, and sustain that connection long enough for new possibilities to emerge.

3. to assist clients to articulate goals and processes of action that are congruent with and respectful of the new understanding and connectedness that have emerged through the process.

As it is often currently practiced, coaching for skills acquisition and performance enhancement reverses the order of these three tasks. It begins by articulating a goal toward which the elements of the system are shaped (i.e., intrapersonal, interpersonal, and systemic elements). Patterns of communication are then developed to maximize the probability of goal attainment and the system monitored for impacts of these processes. This is a perfectly fine model if one is seeking to work within existing systems and frameworks in a way that maintains existing understandings and meaning making, but it is unlikely to produce the shift in thinking that is required to address the significant problems we face. It is a type of horizontal development, rather than the vertical development of reaching new understandings.

Both types of development are needed. The development of a new perspective often requires the acquisition of new skills, or the redeployment of old skills. The linear development of skills acquisition and performance enhancement helps to thicken up one's ability to function following the upheaval associated with a new way of seeing one's relationship to the self, to others, and to the wider world.

## Conclusion

As a young enterprise, coaching has all the problems and the promise associated with youth. It is in a process of formation but has the possibility to grow into more than its parent disciplines. It has the opportunity to gather knowledge and information from disparate and distant sources, and the flexibility to develop entirely new understandings and processes for developing understanding. This makes it ideally suited to engage with the challenges of our day.

The current interest in mindfulness, dialogue, wisdom, creativity, meaning, well-being, and wholeness we see in positive psychology is also a manifestation of the challenge of our time. From a systems perspective, the ongoing and increasing popularity of coaching as a process of change in organizations and individuals, and the emergence of positive psychology, are not random events, mere quirks of management or academic fashion. Positive psychology and the coaching approach have arisen and are developing in response to the growing forces of the systems in which we live. These forces seek new understandings and new approaches to engagement. In complexity terms, coaching and positive psychology are both being shaped by and shaping the attractors and phase space of the system. From this perspective, the task for us is to continue to develop in dialogue with each other and with the systems in which we live.

*References*

Anderson, M. C., Anderson, D. L., & Mayo, W. D. (2008). Team coaching helps a leadership team drive cultural change at Caterpillar. *Global Business & Organizational Excellence, 27*(4), 40–50.

Barrett, P. T. (2007). The effects of group coaching on executive health and team effectiveness: A quasi-experimental field study. *Dissertation Abstracts International Section A, 67,* 26–40.

Berglas, S. (2002). The very real dangers of executive coaching. *Harvard Business Review (June),* 87–92.

Bigelow, B. (1938). Building an effective training program for field salesmen. *Personnel, 14,* 142–150.

Boyatzis, R. E., Smith, M., L., & Blaize, N. (2006). Developing sustainable leaders through coaching and compassion. *Academy of Management Learning & Education, 5*(1), 8–24.

Brock, V. (2008). Grounded theory of the roots and emergence of coaching. Unpublished dissertation: International University of Professional Studies.

Cameron, K. S., & Caza, A. (2004). Contributions to the Discipline of Positive Organizational Scholarship. *American Behavioral Scientist, 47*(6), 731–739.

Cameron, K. S., Dutton, J. E., & Quinn, R. E. (Eds.) (2003). *Positive organizational scholarship: Foundations of a new discipline.* San Francisco: Berrett-Koehler.

Carver, C. S., & Scheier, M. F. (1998). *On the self-regulation of behavior.* Cambridge, UK: Cambridge University Press.

Cavanagh, M. (2005). Mental-health issues and challenging clients in executive coaching. In M. Cavanagh, A. M. Grant, & T. Kemp (Eds.), *Evidence-based coaching (vol. 1): Contributions from the behavioural sciences* (pp. 21–36). Qld: Australian Academic Press.

Cavanagh, M., & Grant, A. M. (2004) Executive Coaching in Organisations: The personal is the professional. *International Journal of coaching in Organizations 2,* 6–15.

Cavanagh, M., & Grant, A. M. (2006). Coaching psychology and the scientist-practitioner model. In S. Corrie & D. Lane (Eds.), *The modern scientist practitioner* (pp. 146–157). New York: Routledge.

Cavanagh, M., & Palmer, S. (2006). The theory, practice and research base of coaching psychology is developing at a fast pace. *International Coaching Psychology Review, 1*(2), 5–7.

Clegg, S., Rhodes, C., Kornberger, M., & Stilin, R. (2005). Business coaching: Challenges for an emerging industry. *Industrial and Commercial Training, 37*(5), 218–223.

Collard, P., & Walsh, J. (2008). Sensory awareness mindfulness training in coaching: Accepting life's challenges. *Journal of Rational-Emotive & Cognitive Behavior Therapy, 26*(1), 30–37.

Coutu, D., & Kauffman, C. (2009). *The Realities of Executive Coaching.* Cambridge, MA: Harvard Business Review Research Report.

Cunha, P. V., & Louro, M. J. (2000). Building teams that learn. *Academy of Management Executive, 14*(1), 152.

Deviney, D. E. (1994). The effects of coaching using multiple rater feedback to change supervisor behavior. *Dissertation Abstracts International Section A, 55,* 114.

Douglas, C. A., & McCauley, C. D. (1999). Formal developmental relationships: A survey of organizational practices. *Human Development Quarterly, 10*(3), 203–220.

Duffy, E. M. (1984). A feedback-coaching intervention and selected predictors in outplacement. *Dissertation Abstracts International Section B, 45,* 1611.

Duijts, S. F. A. P., Kant, I. P., van den Brandt, P. A. P., & Swaen, G. M. H. P. (2008). Effectiveness of a preventive coaching intervention for employees at risk for sickness absence due to psychosocial health complaints: Results of a randomized controlled trial. *Journal of Occupational & Environmental Medicine, 50*(7), 765–776.

Evers, W. J., Brouwers, A., & Tomic, W. (2006). A quasi-experimental study on management coaching effectiveness. *Consulting Psychology Journal: Practice & Research, 58,* 174–182.

Fanasheh, H. A. (2003). *The perception of executive coaching among CEOs of America's top 500 companies.* Los Angeles: Pepperdine University.

Fillery-Travis, A., & Lane, D. (2006). Does coaching work or are we asking the wrong question?

*International Coaching Psychology Review,* 1(1), 23–35.

Fox, R. E. (1996). Charlatanism, scientism, and psychology's social contract. *American Psychologist,* 51(8), 777–784.

Garman, A. N., Whiston, D. L., & Zlatoper, K. W. (2000). Media perceptions of executive coaching and the formal preparation of coaches. *Consulting Psychology Journal: Practice and Research,* 52(3), 201–205.

Gattellari, M., Donnelly, N., Taylor, N., Meerkin, M., Hirst, G., & Ward, J. (2005). Does peer coaching increase GP capacity to promote informed decision making about FSA screening? A cluster randomised trial. *Family Practice, 22,* 253–265.

Gershman, L. (1967). The effects of specific factors of the supervisor-subordinate coaching climate upon improvement of attitude and performance of the subordinate. *Dissertation Abstracts International Section B, 28,* 2122.

Gorby, C. B. (1937). Everyone gets a share of the profits. *Factory Management & Maintenance,* 95, 82–83.

Grant, A. M. (2002). Towards a psychology of coaching: The impact of coaching on metacognition, mental health and goal attainment. *Dissertation Abstracts International Section A: Humanities and Social Sciences, 63*(12), 6094.

Grant, A. M. (2003). The impact of life coaching on goal attainment, metacognition and mental health. *Social Behavior and Personality: An International Journal, 31*(3), 253–264.

Grant, A. M. (2007). A languishing-flourishing model of goal striving and mental health for coaching populations. *International Coaching Psychology Review, 2*(3), 250–264.

Grant, AM & Cavanagh, M. (2004), Toward a Profession of Coaching: Sixty five years of progress and challenges for the future. *International Journal of Evidence Based Coaching and Mentoring 2*: 8–21

Grant, A. M., Passmore, J., Cavanagh, M. J., & Parker, H. (2010). The State of Play in Coaching Today: A Comprehensive Review of the Field. *International Review of Industrial and Organisational Psychology 2010, 25,* 125–168.

Grant, A. M., & Cavanagh, M. J. (2007). Evidence-based coaching: Flourishing or languishing? *Australian Psychologist, 42*(4), 239–254.

Grant, A. M., Curtayne, L., & Burton, G. (2009). Executive coaching enhances goal attainment, resilience and workplace well-being: A randomised controlled study. *Journal of Positive Psychology, 4*(5), 396–407.

Grant, A. M., & O'Hara, B. (2006). The self-presentation of commercial Australian life coaching schools: Cause for concern? *International Coaching Psychology Review, 1*(2), 20–32.

Grant, A. M., & Zackon, R. (2004). Executive, workplace and life coaching: Findings from a large-scale survey of International Coach Federation members. *International Journal of Evidence-based Coaching and Mentoring, 2*(2), 1–15.

Green, L., Oades, L., & Grant, A. (2006). Cognitive-behavioral, solution-focused life coaching: Enhancing goal striving, well-being, and hope. *The Journal of Positive Psychology, 1*(3), 142–149.

Green, S., Grant, A., & Rynsaardt, J. (2007). Evidence-based life coaching for senior high school students: Building hardiness and hope. *International Coaching Psychology Review, 2,* 24–32.

Griffiths, K., & Campbell, M. A. (2008). Semantics or substance? Preliminary evidence in the debate between life coaching and counselling. *Coaching: An International Journal of Theory, Research and Practice, 1*(2), 164–175.

Gyllensten, K., & Palmer, S. (2005). Can coaching reduce workplace stress: A quasi-experimental study. *International Journal of Evidence Based Coaching and Mentoring, 3*(2), 75–85.

Federation International Coach (2006). Global coaching study. Retrieved October 20, 2008.

Jarvis, J., Lane, D., & Fillery-Travis, A. (2005). *Making the case for coaching: Does it work?* London: Chartered Institute of Personnel and Development.

Jones, R. A., Rafferty, A. E., & Griffn, M. A. (2006). The executive coaching trend: Towards more flexible executives. *Leadership and Organization Development Journal, 27,* 584–596.

Joo, B-K. (2005). Executive Coaching: A conceptual framework from an integrative review of practice and research. *Human Resource Development Review, 44,* 462–488.

Kampa-Kokesch, S., & Anderson, M. Z. (2001). Executive coaching: A comprehensive review of the literature. *Consulting Psychology Journal: Practice and Research, 53*(4), 205–228.

Kauffman, C. (2006). Positive psychology: The science at the heart of coaching. In D. R. Stober & A. M. Grant (Eds.), *Evidence based coaching handbook: Putting best practices to work for your clients* (pp. 219–253). Hoboken, NJ, US: John Wiley & Sons, Inc.

Kilburg, R. R. (2004). "Trudging Toward Dodoville: Conceptual Approaches and Case Studies in Executive Coaching." *Consulting Psychology Journal: Practice & Research 56*(4): 203–213.

Kilduff, M., Crossland, C., Tsai, W., & Krackhardt, D. (2008). Organizational network perceptions versus reality: A small world after all? *Organizational Behavior and Human Decision Processes, 107,* 15–28.

Lazlo, E. (2006). *The chaos point: The world at the crossroads.* Virginia: Hampton Roads.

Leadership Management Australia (2006). *The L.E.A.D. Survey 2005/6.* Melbourne: Leadership Management Australia

Levine, T., Kase, L., & Vitale, J. (2006). *The successful coach: Insider secrets to becoming a top coach.* New York, NY: John Wiley & Sons Ltd.

Libri, V., & Kemp, T. (2006). Assessing the efficacy of a cognitive behavioural executive coaching programme. *International Coaching Psychology Review, 1*(2), 9–18.

Lovibond, S. H., & Lovibond, P. F. (1995). *Manual for the Depression Anxiety Stress Scales.* Sydney: Psychology Foundation of Australia.

Luthans, F. (2002). The need for and meaning of positive organization behavior. *Journal of Organizational Behavior, 23*(6), 695–706.

Luthans, F., & Youssef, C. M. (2007). Emerging positive organizational behavior. *Journal of Management, 33*(3), 321–349.

Maurer, T., Solamon, J., & Troxtel, D. (1998). Relationship of coaching performance with performance in situational employment interviews. *Journal of Applied Psychology, 83*(1), 128–136.

McGovern, J., Lindermann, M., Vergara, M. A., Murphy, S., Barker, L., & Warrenfelz, R. (2001). Maximizing the impact of executive coaching: Behavioral change, organizational outcomes and return on investment. *The Manchester Review, 6*(1), 1–9.

Miller, D. J. (1990). The effect of managerial coaching on transfer of training. *Dissertation Abstracts International Section B, 50*(8–A) 2435.

Miller, W. R., Yahne, C. E., Moyers, T. B., Martinez, J., & Pirritano, M. (2004). A randomized trial of methods to help clinicians learn motivational interviewing. *Journal of Consulting & Clinical Psychology, 72*(6), 1050–1062.

Muse, L., Harris, S. G., Giles, W. F., & Feild, H. S. (2008). Work-life benefits and positive organizational behavior: Is there a connection. *Journal of Organizational Behavior, 29,* 171–192.

Newham-Kanas, C., Goreznski, P., Morrow, D., & Irwin, J. D. (2009). Annotated bibliography of life coaching and health research. *International Journal of Evidence Based Coaching and Mentoring, 7*(1), 39–103.

Nowack, K. M. (1990). Initial development of an inventory to assess stress and health. *American Journal of Health Promotion, 4,* 173–180.

Olivero, G., Bane, K., & Kipelman, R. E. (1997). Executive coaching as a transfer of training tool: Effects on productivity in a public agency. *Public Personnel Management, 26*(461–469).

Orenstein, R. L. (2006). Measuring executive coaching efficacy? The answer was right here all the time. *Consulting Psychology Journal: Practice & Research, 58*(106–116).

Passmore, J., & Gibbes, C. (2007). The state of executive coaching research: What does the current literature tell us and what's next for coaching research? *International Coaching Psychological Review, 2*(2), 116–128.

Passmore, J., & Marianetti, O. (2007). The role of mindfulness in coaching. *The Coaching Psychologist, 3*(3), 130–136.

Rich, G. A. (1998). Selling and sales management in action: The constructs of sales coaching: Supervisory feedback, role modeling and trust. *Journal of Personal Selling & Sales Management, 18*(1), 53–63.

Ryff, C., & Keyes, C. (1995). The structure of psychological well-being revisited. *Journal of Personality and Social Psychology, 69,* 719–727.

Scandura, T. (1992). Mentoring and career mobility: An empirical investigation. *Journal of Organizational Behavior, 13*(2), 169–174.

Schnell, E. R. (2005). A case study of executive coaching as a support mechanism during organizational growth and evolution. *Consulting Psychology Journal: Practice & Research, 57*(1), 41–56.

Seligman, M. E. (2007). Coaching and positive psychology. *Australian Psychologist, 42*(4), 266–267.

Seligman, M. E., & Csikszentmihalyi, M. (2000). Positive psychology: An introduction. *American Psychologist, 55*(1), 5–14.

Sherman, S., & Freas, A. (2004). The Wild West of executive coaching. *Harvard Business Review, 82*(11), 82–90.

Spence, G. B. (2007a). Further development of evidence-based coaching: Lessons from the rise and fall of the human potential movement. *Australian Psychologist, 42*(2), 255–265.

Spence, G. B. (2007). GAS powered coaching: Goal Attainment Scaling and its use in coaching research and practice. *International Coaching Psychology Review, 2,* 155–167.

Spence, G. B., Cavanagh, M., & Grant, A. M. (2006). Duty of care in an unregulated industry: Initial findings on the diversity and practice of Australian coaches. *International Coaching Psychology Review, 1*(1), 71–85.

Spence, G. B., Cavanagh, M. J., & Grant, A. M. (2008). The integration of mindfulness training and health coaching: an exploratory study. *Coaching: An International Journal of Theory, Research and Practice, 1*(2), 145–163.

Spence, G. B., & Grant, A. (2007). Professional and peer life coaching and the enhancement of goal striving and well-being: An exploratory study. *The Journal of Positive Psychology, 2*, 185–194.

Spreitzer, G., Sutcliffe, K., Dutton, J., Sonenshein, S., & Grant, A. M. (2005). A socially embedded model of thriving at work. *Organization Science, 16*(5), 537–549.

Stacey, R. D. (2000). *Strategic management and organizational dynamics (3 ed.).* Harlow, UK: Pearson Education.

Sue-Chan, C., & Latham, G. P. (2004). The relative effectiveness of expert, peer and self coaches. *Applied Psychology, 53*(2), 260–278.

Taylor, L. M. (1997). The relation between resilience, coaching, coping skills training, and perceived stress during a career-threatening milestone. *Dissertation Abstracts International Section B, 58*(05), 27.

Vloeberghs, D., Pepermans, R., & Thielemans, K. (2005). High-potential development policies: an empirical study among Belgian companies. *Journal of Management Development, 24*(6), 546–558.

Waldrop, M. (1992). *Complexity: The emerging science at the edge of order and chaos.* New York: Simon & Schuster.

Wheatley, M. (1999). *Leadership and the new science: Discovering order in a chaotic world.* San Francisco: Berrett-Koehler.

Wilson, C. (2004). Coaching and coach training in the workplace. *Industrial & Commercial Training, 36*(3), 96–98.

Wright, J. (2007). Stress in the workplace: A coaching approach. *Work: Journal of Prevention, Assessment & Rehabilitation, 28*, 279–284.

Wright, T. A. (2003). Positive organizational behavior: An idea whose time has truly come. *Journal of Organizational Behavior, 24*(4), 437–442.

Wycherley, I. M., & Cox, E. (2008). Factors in the selection and matching of executive coaches in organisations. *Coaching: An International Journal of Theory, Research and Practice, 1*(1), 39–53.

Zhong, L. (2007). Effects of psychological capital on employees' job performance, organizational commitment, and organizational citizenship behavior. *Acta Psychologica Sinica, 39*(2), 328–334.

# VII

# Clinical Perspectives

# The Dog Woman, Addie Bundren, and the Ninth Circle of Hell: Positive Psychology Should Be More Open to the Negative

*Jennifer L. Hames and Thomas E. Joiner Jr.*

*"As I lay dying the woman with dog's eyes would not close my eyelids for me as I descended into Hades."*
— *the ghostly Agamemnon to Odysseus in the Eleventh Book of the* Odyssey

*"My guide and I came on that hidden road to make our way back into the bright world; and with no care for any rest, we climbed—he first, I following—until I saw, through a round opening, some of those things of beauty heaven bears. It was from there that we emerged, to see—once more—the stars."*
— *Dante emerging from the ninth (and last) circle of hell in the* Inferno

On its surface, Faulkner's *As I Lay Dying* (the title of which was inspired by Agamemnon's comment in the *Odyssey*) is a hellish and tragic portrait of the avarice, pettiness, and vulgarity of the human spirit. In the novel, Anse Bundren's wife Addie dies, and the pathetic trip to bury her (with borrowed shovels) in her family's plot 40 miles away includes, among other things, the drowning of the family's mules in a doomed attempt to cross a river; the failure of the family's

daughter to secretly obtain an abortion; a son's injured leg, which is not only broken, but which also loses its skin as the cement incompetently applied to set the bone is cracked off with a hammer and flatiron; and the incarceration (for arson) of another son in the state insane asylum. As the trip proceeds in the July heat, buzzards accumulate, but Anse refuses to bury his wife anywhere but in her family's plot, ostensibly because "[He] gave her [his] promised word in the presence of the Lord," but really because a new, pre-arranged wife and a long-desired set of false teeth await him in the town near the burial site.

Against this hellish backdrop, however, the human virtues of compassion, pity, sacrifice, loyalty, and honor are fully illuminated, as illustrated, for example, by the character of Cash (whose leg is injured). Despite his injury, absurdly made worse by the cement treatment, and despite much else, Cash remains loyal and sacrificial, affably stating that his leg "don't bother none" and that he can last what becomes a six-day trip on a springless wagon over rutted roads, even as pain-induced "sweat big as marbles" runs down his face. Even humor emerges from the tragedy: After learning of the cement treatment, the doctor treating Cash says, ". . . why didn't Anse carry you to the nearest saw-mill and stick your leg in the saw? That would have cured it. Then you all could have stuck his head into the saw and cured a whole family." Instead of merely describing the countless negative events that occurred to the Bundren family, Faulkner took care to starkly accentuate the positive by letting virtues such as loyalty, sacrifice, and even humor shine through in their grotesque journey. The main point of the current chapter is that both positive psychology researchers and psychopathology researchers can learn from Faulkner and his Bundrens.

## Taking Stock

Without question, positive psychology researchers and psychopathology researchers have made important contributions to the study of human flourishing and human suffering, respectively. However, there is reason to believe that both positive psychology and experimental psychopathology boast missions that are too narrowly defined and executed. In this section, we review the implications of these narrowly defined missions and take stock of current research that is expanding these boundaries by attending to both the positive and the negative.

## Narrowly Defined Missions

On the surface, the missions of experimental psychopathology and positive psychology appear to be polar opposites, and understandably so. While the mission of experimental psychopathology is to investigate disorder (i.e., the negative), the mission of positive psychology is to study that factors that lead to human flourishing (i.e., the positive). Setting aside these surface generalizations, it becomes clear that a commonality exists between experimental psychopathology and positive psychology, and that commonality is that both boast narrowly defined missions.

Consider the case of positive psychology—here, the tendency to study the positive in and of itself (instead of also as a means to inform the negative) is quite logical. Certainly, it is intuitive to study the factors that lead to flourishing in individuals who are in fact flourishing. Similarly, consider the case of experimental

psychopathology—here, the tendency to study psychopathology in and of itself (instead of also as a means to study psychology generally) is both understandable and long-standing. It is understandable—indeed salutary—because investigating the nature, causes, and treatments of mental illnesses relieves human suffering. It is also long-standing in that early psychopathologists had already construed their purpose as investigating disorder per se, rather than investigating disorder per se *and* using it as a means to illuminate basic processes (e.g., Wells' [1914] paper, entitled, "Experimental Psychopathology"). It appears that experimental psychopathology's mission was narrowly defined all along, motivated by the press of human suffering.

While narrowly defined, wisps of a broader mission for psychopathologists waft through the literature from time to time, but with regrettably little impact. For example, in his description of Morton Prince, founder of the *Journal of Abnormal Psychology*, White (1992, p. 605) states, "He began to realize that it was impossible to think of abnormal psychology as a free-standing body of knowledge. Logically, it implied an accepted base as to what was normal in human life, from which base the different disorders were departures." Or, consider Shakow's (1978, p. 149) comment: "When I went up to Harvard in 1921, I was buttressed by William James's notion (and Freud's also, to some extent) of psychology being one. Because of my own high regard for James, I expected to have a fairly easy time of it in this respect. What did I find? A few thought as I did, but this thinking was far from universal." Here, and in other papers (Shakow, 1965, 1976), Shakow encourages a broad and unified approach but also notes resistance to it (as early as 1921). McFall's (1991) "Manifesto for a science of clinical psychology" sounds a similar note (see also Andreasen, 1997).

But even in the writings of Shakow and McFall, and in the description of Prince, the direction of inquiry is unidirectionally from the normal to the abnormal. That is, in the case of Prince, the endeavor is to use the normal as a base from which to understand the abnormal, rather than *also* using the abnormal to illuminate the normal; in the writings of Shakow and McFall, the emphasis is on taking the concepts and methods of general psychological science *to* psychopathology (which is absolutely necessary, as Shakow, McFall, and others persuasively show), rather than *also* bringing general psychological science *back from* psychopathology. It is precisely because of a scientific psychological (including neuroscientific) approach that psychopathology researchers have plumbed psychopathology's nine circles and thereby alleviated suffering. Indeed, it is the lack of bringing general psychological science back from psychopathology that is problematic. Therefore, in order to go beyond the ninth circle and to more generally promote a more comprehensive and rigorous approach to both psychopathology and positive psychology research, we must awaken the early calls of the field for a more unified approach to psychology, whereby the negative informs the positive, and the positive informs the negative.

Carrying such a narrowly defined mission is not without implications. For instance, in at least some positive psychology circles, there exists an inflexible insistence that only the positive be studied, and such a mentality risks at least three main dangers. One is that it neglects at least half of life (at least half because "bad is stronger than good"; Baumeister et al., 2001); another is that it decontextualizes the positive; and lastly, there are insights about the positive that are not possible without studying the negative. To be sure, a thoroughgoing understanding of the negative has greatly contributed to the field's understanding of the positive. Consider, for example, a study by Wood, Perunovic, and Lee (2009), which found that repeating positive self-statements actually led to a *decrease* in state self-esteem and mood for people with low self-esteem. In this study, Wood and colleagues recruited individuals with low and high self-esteem and then randomly assigned these participants to either use or not use positive self-statements. Following the manipulation, participants then filled out measures of state self-esteem and mood. Importantly, Wood and colleagues did not inflexibly insist that only the positive be studied; rather, they used relevant theories and evidence to make predictions about the efficacy of positive self-statements for individuals with high *and* low self-esteem. Surely, researchers could have conducted this study with their eyes gazing only toward the positive (i.e., not including individuals with low self-esteem), and they likely would have found that using positive self-statements led to a boost in self-esteem and mood. If this were the case, though, and this study had been designed without a thorough understanding of the negative, a vital insight about the potentially harmful effects of the positive would not have been illuminated.

Furthermore, maintaining an exclusive focus on the positive closes one's eyes to fact that there are many negative things that are inherently positive. One example of this is fear. Fear is traditionally studied as a symptom of psychopathology, and while fear can certainly be debilitating when considered in the context of anxiety disorders, it can be positive and adaptive when considered in other contexts. For instance, having a fear of death saves lives, and similarly, having a fear of snakes helps one avoid injury or death by means of a venomous bite. Another instance that brings to light the value of fear is the case of the Laweiplein-Drachten roundabout in Europe. This roundabout is located in the central part of town and at one point was cluttered with street signs directing drivers and pedestrians where to go. It is thus not surprising that this intersection experienced a great deal of congestion and a notoriously high number of traffic accidents. In hopes of improving the safety of this intersection, city authorities decided to remove all of the signs and advertisements located in the intersection, thus removing many of the drivers' visual distractions. Intriguingly, this intervention was successful at reducing the number of traffic accidents, likely because removing the traffic signs from the intersection not only reduced the amount of distractions (i.e., reduced drivers' cognitive load), but it also led to increased fear in drivers because there were no longer traffic signs directing them where to go. Therefore, the absence of traffic signs necessitated that drivers be more cautious and attentive, which resulted in a noticeable improvement in the safety of the intersection.

It is relatively easy to recognize how fear can be inherently positive in some contexts, but what about depressive symptoms—can insights about the positive shine through here too? Without question, depression is an extremely debilitating disorder that can affect many aspects of a person's life (e.g., mood, energy level, appetite, sleep, concentration). In fact, by the year 2020, depression is projected to be the second leading cause of disability worldwide (Murray & Lopez, 1997). Given its impairing nature, it is not surprising that psychopathology researchers have primarily focused on understanding the negative impact that this disorder has on people and society. Understandably so, it seems hardly intuitive to question the ways in which depression can have a positive impact on a person's life. Wrosch and Miller (2009), though, tackled this very question by conducting a longitudinal study of depressive symptoms and goal-disengagement capacities in adolescents. They found that adolescents who had high baseline levels of depressive symptomatology experienced an increase in goal-disengagement capacities over time (i.e., they were better able to adjust to unattainable goals), and they also found that this increase in goal-disengagement capacities predicted a later reduction in depressive symptoms. It is important to note that these findings are not meant to discount the debilitating nature of depressive symptoms; on the contrary, these findings act as a compelling example that there are insights about the positive that can be learned by looking at something that is traditionally conceptualized as negative in a different light.

Indeed, there is much that positive psychology researchers can learn by keeping their eyes open to the negative. In a sense, immersing oneself in an unfamiliar domain provides a new contextual environment whereby an individual can begin to see his or her own domain in a new light. While the venture of positive psychology researchers into the negative is undoubtedly important in and of itself, it is even more important for positive psychology researchers to use the insights they learned from the negative to inform their research on the positive. It is through this "double duty" of looking to both the positive and the negative that integration between the two domains begins to take place, and it is through such integration that science can be advanced.

This is not to let psychopathology researchers off the hook, though—they too are held accountable, as psychopathology researchers far too often remain submerged within their own domain. Like Faulkner—and like Dante and Agamemnon (the latter reluctantly, with the "dog woman's" help)—psychopathology researchers have amply and capably documented a kind of agony: psychopathology. That psychopathology is agonizing is hardly contestable (e.g., major depression is associated with more suffering and impairment than *any* medical condition save heart disease (Hays, Wells, Sherbourne, Rogers, & Spritzer, 1995); that psychopathology researchers have adequately "seen" it (i.e., theorized and scientized about psychopathology) is also difficult to dispute (e.g., workable treatments for several major disorders have emerged). Although successfully plumbing the depths of the negative, psychopathology researchers have nonetheless stopped short of their full mission and potential. In fervent hope of relieving human suffering, psychopathology researchers have far too often

not allowed the positive to inform their work. Therefore, just as Dante emerged blinking from the ninth and final circle of hell into the starry night, and just as Faulkner used the grotesque to point up the virtuous, so we suggest that psychopathology researchers should *both* study psychopathology *and simultaneously* draw out its general implications for human nature and mind, regardless of whether such implications relate to the disordered or to the normative.

We thus argue in this chapter that both positive psychology and psychopathology researchers need to emerge from the confines of their own domain and allow their work to be informed by *both* the positive *and* the negative. Just as positive psychology researchers should venture from the comfort of the starry night sky into the depths of the negative, so too should psychopathology researchers emerge from the "ninth circle" and allow the positive to inform their work. Therefore, we are advocating for a new "woman with dog's eyes," who props open researchers' eyelids to both the negative *and* the positive.

Subtle attempts *have* been made in the past to open researchers' eyes to both the negative and the positive, albeit rather unsuccessfully. In fact, the field of experimental psychopathology serves as a prime example of a domain where this goal of simultaneously addressing psychopathology *and* basic psychology has been occasionally mentioned as a part of the field's mission, but largely relegated or forgotten. Of course, there are exceptions, some of which we summarize, and from which we generalize principles that serve as heuristics to guide both psychopathology researchers and positive psychology researchers to simultaneously study mental disorder as well as general human nature. It is our sentiment that if both positive psychology researchers and psychopathology researchers take heed of these exceptions and begin to make them more of the rule in their respective domains, both parties will reap the benefits.

**Are We Stuck in These Narrowly Defined Missions?**

The editorial statement of the APA's lead psychopathology journal, the *Journal of Abnormal Psychology*, explicitly states that the study of normal processes (albeit in abnormal individuals) is within the journal's area of major focus. Even so, this acknowledgement gets trumped by the remainder of the statement: "...studies of patient populations, analyses of abnormal behavior and hypnotic phenomena, and theoretical papers of scholarly substance on deviant personality and emotional abnormality would all fall within the boundaries of the journal's interests. Each article should represent an addition to knowledge and understanding of abnormal behavior in either its etiology, description, or change." To reiterate: The study of psychopathology qua psychopathology is obviously commendable; our point is that it could be even more so. A similar note rings true in the realm of positive psychology. To be sure, the study of the positive qua the positive is also commendable, but it too could be even more so if positive psychology researchers submitted to journals such as the *Journal of Abnormal Psychology* and thus gleaned more insights about the positive from the negative.

Given the editorial policy, it is unsurprising that empirical articles have followed suit. It is difficult indeed to find a paper in the *Journal of Abnormal Psychology* that mentions, much less emphasizes, normal psychological processes. In other words, utilizing the abnormal to illuminate the normal, while an explicit (yet overshadowed) part of the APA's flagship psychopathology journal's mission, is rarely accomplished. Surely, past behavior is the best predictor of future behavior, but it's not the only predictor. For instance, in the realm of clinical psychology, therapeutic interventions hold the potential to enact significant changes in even the most stubborn symptoms and behaviors. So too, a change in the mindset and research practices of positive psychology researchers can help pave the way for this prominent psychopathology journal's mission to be fulfilled.

As a rule, experimental psychopathologists are preoccupied with psychopathology—and so they should remain (why wouldn't they be?). Additionally, positive psychologists are preoccupied with human flourishing—and so they should remain. However, for both positive psychologists and experimental psychopathologists, shuttling back and forth between the positive and the negative—with a "dog woman" preventing closed eyes as overseer—may produce compounded dividends. In fact, it already has.

## There Are Exceptions: Abnormal Conditions Illuminate the Nature of Normal Memory Functioning

Abnormalities of mental function have been crucial in illuminating basic cognitive processes, particularly the structures and functions of normal memory. Take, as just one obvious example, the famous case of H.M., whose mental functions became abnormal indeed. H.M.'s hippocampus (among other structures) was surgically removed (as treatment for severe epilepsy), leaving him with anterograde amnesia (e.g., H.M. was not able to remember people he had met since the operation) and leaving scientists aware that the hippocampus is a crucial anatomical structure for the functioning of normal memory. Here, the abnormal (hippocampal oblation) illuminated the normal (an anatomical seat of normal memory functioning).

Moreover, in addition to informing the neuroanatomy of memory, the study of amnesic patients also has shed light on the general cognitive structure of memory (Kihlstrom, 1987). That is, many amnesic patients can acquire some new cognitive and motor skills, as well as learn new vocabulary items and other facts. But they are generally not able to remember the episodes in which they acquired this new knowledge. The amnesic syndrome thus points up the distinction between procedural knowledge and semantic memory on the one hand (which is spared), and the encoding of new episodic memories on the other hand (which is impaired). Here, too, the abnormal (amnesic syndrome) informs the normal (the structure of memory).

Similarly, researchers studying hypnosis instill the abnormal in the normal by inducing hysteria-like states via hypnosis (cf. Kihlstrom, 1979, 1987). Following hypnotic suggestions, hypnotized people may not remember that which occurred while they were hypnotized. However, their amnesia may be reversed by a prearranged cue to cancel the amnesia suggestion, showing that posthypnotic amnesia involves an impairment of memory retrieval, rather than an impairment of encoding or of storage. Not only is the memory disruption specific to retrieval versus encoding and storage, the disruption is also specific regarding some but not other aspects of retrieval. That is, like amnesic patients, hypnotized people may still acquire procedural and semantic knowledge during hypnosis, but they do not remember the circumstances under which this knowledge was acquired (episodic memory is disrupted). Here, the abnormal (hypnotic amnesia) is used to "carve nature at its joints"; that is, as a sort of arbiter that divides up the components of normal memory.

The work of Ericsson and colleagues (see, e.g., Chase & Ericsson, 1982; Ericsson & Kintsch, 1995;

Ericsson & Lehmann, 1996), although not on psychopathology, also illustrates the principle of the abnormal illuminating the normal. These researchers trained normal undergraduates to be "abnormal"; more specifically, undergraduates selected to be of approximately average intelligence (e.g., average SAT scores) were trained to possess an abnormal intellectual attribute—the ability to recall a series of digits, with each digit stated at approximately one-second intervals, of more than 80 digits! Traditional models of short- and long-term memory have difficulty accounting for this and related phenomena. On the basis of this and other evidence, Ericsson and colleagues delineated a new memory mechanism, termed long-term working memory, which allows for cognitive products to be stored in long-term working memory and be kept selectively accessible by means of retrieval cues activated during ongoing thought processes. One implication of this view is that world-class performers (e.g., international chess masters) are not born with unusual capacities, but rather acquire (through years of particular forms of practice) the ability to rapidly encode relevant information in long-term memory in a way that it can be efficiently accessed with retrieval cues when needed. These researchers began with the normal, instilled the abnormal, and thereby learned about the process and structure of a new memory mechanism.

### It's Not Just Memory: Two Examples from Our Own Psychopathology Research Program on the Cusp of the "Ninth Circle"

#### Suicide, "Perceived Burdensomeness," and the Need to Contribute as a Fundamental Motive

According to the Interpersonal Theory of Suicide (Joiner, 2005; Van Orden et al., 2010), in order for an individual to make a lethal suicide attempt, he or she must have both the *desire* to die by suicide and the *ability* to do so. The theory posits that if individuals simultaneously hold the two specific psychological states of perceived burdensomeness and thwarted belongingness for a long enough time, they will develop a "desire for death." Having a desire for death, however, is not sufficient for a person to make a lethal suicide attempt. An individual must also have the *ability* to die by suicide, which is acquired through experiences that lead to increased physical pain tolerance and decreased fear of death.

While on the surface, the Interpersonal Theory of Suicide appears to be a theory geared toward understanding the psychopathology found at the deepest point of the "ninth circle," this appearance is deceiving, as valuable insights about the positive can be gleaned from this theoretical framework. For instance, this research illuminates the fact that the "need to contribute" (i.e., mattering) is strong—so strong, in fact, that someone may resort to ending his or her own life if the need is not satisfied. This insight about the positive can be gleaned by studying one of the theory's three primary components—perceived burdensomeness.

Patients with suicidal symptoms often believe that they are a burden on others—almost as if they are a heavy weight shackled to the ankles of the people in their lives. This feeling of burdensomeness tends to lead individuals with suicidal symptoms to believe that their death will be a relief for others in that the burden will be removed. Tragically, though, this perception that one is a burden is often just that—a mistaken perception of reality. While mistaken, the perception of burdensomeness is very real for those who experience it, as these individuals tend to make the mental calculation that their death would be worth more than their life to their family, friends, and/or society.

Indeed, there is a great deal of empirical support linking perceived burdensomeness to the desire for death and suicidal behavior. For instance, in a clinical sample of young adults, Joiner and colleagues (2009) found that the three-way interaction of thwarted belongingness, perceived burdensomeness, and acquired capability predicted whether or not participants' current suicidal crises involved suicide attempts above and beyond depression, hopelessness, and borderline personality disorder features. This study thus provides compelling evidence not only for the role of perceived burdensomeness in suicidal behavior but also for the Interpersonal Theory of Suicide more broadly. Additionally, a study looking at the content of suicide notes found that compared to the notes of non-lethal attempters, the notes of lethal attempters were more likely to be characterized by a perception of burdensomeness (Joiner, Pettit, Walker, Voelz, Cruz, Rudd et al., 2002).

Providing further support for the role of perceived burdensomeness in suicidal ideation and behavior, there is evidence that economic recessions are associated with increased suicide risk, but only those recessions that produce marked elevations in negative outcomes such as job losses and home foreclosures (American Association of Suicidology, 2009). What these negative outcomes have in common is that they have the potential to make a person feel as though he or she is a burden on his or her family, friends, and/or society. For instance, a man who loses his job may believe that he is a financial and emotional burden on his spouse and family, and people experiencing a home foreclosure may feel as though they are a burden on the family and friends with whom they are staying until they find another place to live. Similarly, Bastia and Kar (2009) conducted a psychological autopsy study of suicidal hanging and found that unemployment, prolonged illness, failure on examinations with long-term consequences, dowry disputes, and relationship and financial problems were most frequently associated with hanging. Again, a common thread of burdensomeness runs through the factors that were found to be most frequently associated with hanging.

Indeed, all of this seems quite awful on the surface, but we argue that this research on perceived burdensomeness and suicide goes beyond the "ninth circle" in that it points out that "the need to contribute" is so strong that when it is thwarted, one may develop a desire for death. Therefore, this research highlights the importance of fulfilling one's "need to contribute." Fulfilling this need may not seem so positive on the surface, but a closer look reveals that its fulfillment is a necessary foundation on which human flourishing can be built. For instance, how can people flourish if this thwarted need contributes to them ending their life? Thus, this research on perceived burdensomeness and suicide provides just one example of how positive psychology researchers can glean insights about the positive (i.e., the foundational nature of mattering in human flourishing) by looking to research on the negative. This example is also pertinent to psychopathology researchers in that it demonstrates the importance of presenting their findings in more general outlets so that others can glean insights from them.

## Self-Verification and Bulimic Symptoms: Do Bulimic Women Play a Role in Perpetuating Their Own Dissatisfaction and Symptoms?

Similar to our research on perceived burdensomeness and suicide, our research on self-verification and bulimic symptoms provides an additional example of how insights about the positive can be gleaned from the negative. Why are bulimic symptoms so persistent? Self-verification theory (e.g., Swann, Stein-Seroussi, & Giesler, 1992) provides one possible answer. An intriguing possibility is that bulimic women, in an effort to meet self-verification needs, solicit information from others that perpetuates their body dissatisfaction and low self-esteem, and thus their bulimic symptoms. Bulimic women clearly experience self-esteem problems—problems that involve physical appearance and body satisfaction, and also include other aspects of self-esteem. But is it possible that bulimic women structure interpersonal discourse such that these negative views—views that by all accounts are quite painful—are stabilized and perpetuated? Isn't this the *last* thing a bulimic woman would want (by all clinical accounts, it is)? With a goal of providing a preliminary answer to these questions, we conducted a study that looked at the relationship between interest in negative feedback, bulimic symptoms, and body dissatisfaction (Joiner, 1999).

There were three primary findings. First, results showed that interest in negative feedback from others (including but not limited to feedback regarding physical appearance) was correlated with bulimic symptoms and body dissatisfaction, thus suggesting that bulimic women—despite grave concerns about physical appearance—may preferentially solicit *negative* feedback from others. Second, it was found that women who expressed interest in negative feedback at one point in time were more vulnerable than other women to future increases in body dissatisfaction and bulimic symptoms, thus suggesting that negative feedback seeking is involved in instigating and perpetuating the occurrence of bulimic symptoms. Finally, it was found that the relation between interest in negative feedback and bulimic symptom increases was *mediated* by changes in body dissatisfaction.

Overall, these results show that bulimic women may get caught in a vicious cycle wherein they need the very interpersonal responses that serve to maintain or exacerbate their symptoms. An excruciating dilemma thus emerges: Either sacrifice self-confirmation needs and thus escape from bulimia, or meet self-confirmation needs at the price of bulimia. Why don't bulimic women choose the former option (i.e., sacrifice self-confirmation and escape bulimia)? According to Swann and colleagues (1992), the self-confirmation motive is extremely difficult to overcome because it serves fundamental human needs for predictability, certainty, and a consistent identity.

A main point of this study, then—and the reason it is relevant to this chapter—is that this study illuminates the fact that the desire for self-verification is so fundamental to human nature that bulimic women will seek the very feedback they dread in order to satisfy it. In the case of bulimic women, the act of seeking feedback consistent with their negative self-views perpetuates their bulimic symptoms. However, for individuals with a positive self-view, the act of seeking self-verification lays a foundation for human flourishing. In other words, without first fulfilling the need for self-verification, individuals would likely not be capable of developing the very strengths that positive psychology researchers study. Therefore, without looking to the negative to glean insights about the positive, it would be difficult to gain a comprehensive understanding of just how vital the desire for self-verification really is for people. Thus, our research on self-verification in bulimic women not only provides an example of the potential that exists for positive psychology researchers to glean insights about the positive from the negative, but it also highlights how important it is for psychopathology researchers to bring their own research findings back from the negative and into the positive.

### Moving Forward

As is evidenced by the research programs described above, it is clear that when researchers keep their eyes open to both the negative and the positive, new insights about both psychopathology and basic psychology have the potential to shine through. What steps, then, can be taken in order for more positive psychology researchers and psychopathology researchers to follow suit and keep their eyes open to the negative and the positive? Attention to the following principles may prop open researchers' eyes to the negative and the positive in their respective domains.

### Heuristic Principles: A Dog Woman for Psychopathology Researchers

1. *Psychopathology opens a window into what is normally obscure*. Indeed, there are insights about the general that would not have been possible without studying the negative. For instance, consider again the example of H. M., whereby the removal of the patient's hippocampus led to the localization of memory in the brain. Without awareness of the memory deficits that H. M. exhibited after his surgery, an insight such as this would have been very difficult to learn. Laurence Miller poignantly emphasized this point as well when he stated, "By the deficits, we may know the talents, by the exceptions, we may discern the rules, by studying pathology we may construct a model of health. And—most important—from this model may evolve the insights and tools we need to affect our own lives, mold our own destinies, change ourselves and our society in ways that, as yet, we can only imagine" (found in the introduction of Ramachandran and Blakeslee [1999]). It is important that both positive psychology researchers and psychopathology researchers alike take the words of Laurence Miller to heart when conducting research. Thus, positive psychology researchers should look to research on the negative, mindful of the fact that it can open up a window to what is normally obscure; similarly, psychopathology researchers must remember to bring their findings back from the negative and relate them to the positive.

2. *Psychopathology as test case for universality*. Scientific psychologists, particularly social psychologists, have proposed fundamental human motives that are *universal*. For example, Swann (1983) has argued that self-confirmation is a basic and universal motive, and similarly, Baumeister and Leary (1995) have argued that the need to belong is a fundamental human motive. If these motives are truly universal, then they should still be visible, even when they are placed in grave danger of refutation. One way of placing these motives in grave danger of refutation is to use psychopathology as a test case for universality. If such motives are visible within cases of severe psychopathology, then this bolsters their case for universality. The two examples we provided from our own research program have done just that—for instance, our lab's work on perceived burdensomeness and suicide has highlighted the universality of a person's need to contribute, and our lab's work on self-verification in bulimic women has

highlighted the universality of the need for self-confirmation. As this body of research has shown, these motives are so fundamental to humans that when they are thwarted, people are willing to subject themselves to undesirable feedback, and sometimes even death. If both positive psychology researchers and psychopathology researchers keep this heuristic in mind and use psychopathology as a test case for the universality of both positive and negative processes, new insights about the positive and the negative can be gleaned that will benefit the field as a whole.

3. *Psychopathology as exaggeration.* When considering different forms of psychopathology, insights about the general can be more easily gleaned by both positive psychology researchers and psychopathology researchers when psychopathology is conceptualized as an exaggeration of normal functioning. Consider the example of the panic disorder—a syndrome in which people experience terrifying episodes of anxiety from "out of the blue"—and the faulty suffocation alarm system (Klein, 1993). All people have a suffocation alarm system, but for most individuals, the alarm system is triggered only in instances of real danger. Panic disorder, however, shows us the possibility of an evolved or exaggerated suffocation alarm system that falsely alerts an individual of danger, thus inducing panic at random and unnecessary times. Similarly, fear shows us the possibility of an exaggerated physiological and psychological reaction to a stimulus, and depression shows us the possibility of an exaggerated negative mood response to stress. In each of these cases, it is considered normal to experience these reactions in well-defined situations (e.g., when one is truly suffocating, when the stimulus is truly harmful, or when grieving the loss of a loved one), but it is when these responses are exaggerated and misplaced that they begin to fall within the realm of psychopathology. Such examples provide evidence that it is important for both positive psychology researchers and psychopathology researchers to remain mindful of the fact that in some cases, psychopathology can be conceptualized as an exaggeration of normal processes. By keeping this heuristic in mind, a more solid path is paved for psychopathology researchers to relate their

work back to the general and for positive psychology researchers to trek into the "ninth circle" to glean insights about the positive from the negative.

## A Note on Limitations and Pragmatics

Even in light of the evidence provided above for the utility of translating findings from psychopathology to the general, it seems only natural for positive psychology researchers and psychopathology researchers alike to rebut that there are easier ways to study normal and extraordinary processes. Why study the abnormal to learn about the normal and the extraordinary when we could just learn about the normal directly from the source? Without question, a great deal can be learned by studying normal processes in normal individuals, but some pieces of the puzzle would likely still be missing if we limited ourselves to this single path of research. For instance, our hindsight bias tells us that we would have eventually localized the function of memory in the brain even if the case of H. M. had not come along, but when would that discovery have been made, and what if it hadn't been made at all? Surely, there's little guarantee that full understanding will come through path of least resistance, or through a single method. In order to create good science, it is crucial to test our hypotheses using multiple methods and types of samples. Therefore, by simply gleaning insights about the extraordinary from samples of flourishing individuals, we are not subjecting our research to a sufficient degree of scientific rigor, and we are allowing the field to fall short of its full potential.

In order for a solid, lasting change to occur in the field, a dog woman must pry open the eyes of both positive psychology researchers and experimental psychopathology researchers to the negative and the positive from the very beginning—starting with their training. Therefore, the practical implication for positive psychology researchers is that they be trained from the very beginning to glean insights about the positive from the negative. The practical implication for psychopathology researchers is that they be trained to be other types of psychologists first, *then* psychopathology researchers. Just as a horse must precede the cart that it tows, psychopathology researchers must begin to think of basic scientific psychology as the horse and psychopathology research as the cart.

The cart is placed before the horse when we dispute that psychopathology research or scientific clinical psychology is anything other than basic psychological science *as applied to* psychopathology. Logic tells us that putting the cart before the horse is a rather futile endeavor if one expects any progress to be made, so we too must reposition our cart and horse in psychology so that the field as a whole can progress onward and continue to advance science.

## Concluding Comment

Like Faulkner's Bundren family, positive psychology researchers and psychopathology researchers are embarking on their own separate journeys through the field of psychology. Positive psychology researchers are navigating through the starry night sky of the positive in one wagon, while psychopathology researchers are navigating through the "ninth circle" of psychopathology in a separate wagon. While a great deal has been learned about the positive and the negative from these predominately separate journeys thus far, we contend that the field as a whole would benefit if positive psychology researchers journeyed more frequently into the "ninth circle" to glean insights about the positive and, similarly, if psychopathology researchers emerged more frequently from the "ninth circle" and related their findings to basic psychological science.

Therefore, in order to create a more unified field of psychology, we can no longer shut our eyes to that which lies on the other side of our work. Just as psychopathology researchers cannot shut their eyes to the starry night of the positive that awaits them when they return from plumbing the depths of psychopathology, so, too, positive psychology researchers cannot inflexibly insist that only the positive be studied and thus shut their eyes to the negative. As researchers, we must not shut our eyes because in doing so, we limit ourselves and risk missing important insights that could prove to be invaluable to the advancement of our field as a whole. Therefore, our goal in this chapter was to advocate for a new "woman with dog's eyes" of sorts to open up researchers' eyes to both the negative and the positive. Indeed, keeping our eyes open to both the negative and the positive is no easy feat, but as researchers, we must begin to take on this "double duty" so that findings can be translated and integrated across domains. As Kihlstrom

(1979, p. 471) fittingly said, "To the extent that this integration is achieved, we will have edged much closer to the comprehensive scientific understanding of human behavior and experience that we all are seeking."

*References*

American Association of Suicidology (2009). AAS statement on the economy and suicide. Retrieved August 18, 2009, from http://www.suicidology.org/web/guest/current-research.

Andreasen, N. C. (1997). Linking mind and brain in the study of mental illnesses: A project for a scientific psychopathology. *Science, 275*, 1586–1593.

Bastia, B. K., & Kar, N. (2009). A psychological autopsy study of suicidal hanging from Cuttack, India: Focus on stressful life situations. *Archives of Suicide Research, 13*, 100–104.

Baumeister, R. F., Bratslavsky, E., Finkenauer, C., & Vohs, K. D. (2001). Bad is stronger than good. *Review of General Psychology, 5*, 323–370.

Baumeister, R. F., & Leary, M. R. (1995). The need to belong: Desire for interpersonal attachments as a fundamental human motivation. *Psychological Bulletin, 117*, 497–529.

Chase, W. G., & Ericsson, K. A. (1982). Skill and working memory. In G. H. Bower (Ed.), *The psychology of learning and motivation* (vol. 16, pp. 1–58). New York: Academic Press.

Ericsson, K. A., & Kintsch, W. (1995). Long-term working memory. *Psychological Review, 102*, 211–245.

Ericsson, K. A., & Lehmann, A. C. (1996). Expert and exceptional performance: Evidence of maximal adaptations to task constraints. *Annual Review of Psychology, 47*, 273–305.

Hays, R. D., Wells, K. B., Sherbourne, C. D., Rogers, W., & Spritzer, K. (1995). Functioning and well-being outcomes of patients with depression compared with chronic general medical illnesses. *Archives of General Psychiatry, 52*, 11–19.

Joiner, T. E., Jr. (1999). Self-verification and bulimic symptoms: Do bulimic women play a role in perpetuating their own dissatisfaction and symptoms? *International Journal of Eating Disorders, 26*, 145–151.

Joiner, T. E., Jr. (2005). *Why people die by suicide.* Cambridge, MA: Harvard University Press.

Joiner, T. E., Jr., Pettit, J. W., Walker, R. L., Voelz, Z. R., Cruz, J., Rudd, M. D., et al. (2002). Perceived burdensomeness and suicidality: Two studies on the suicide notes of those attempting and those completing suicide. *Journal of Social & Clinical Psychology, 21,* 531–545.

Joiner, T. E., Jr., Van Orden, K. A., Witte, T. K., Selby, E. A., Ribeiro, J. D., Lewis, R., et al. (2009). Main predictions of the interpersonal-psychological theory of suicidal behavior: Empirical tests in two samples of young adults. *Journal of Abnormal Psychology, 118,* 634–646.

Kihlstrom, J. F. (1979). Hypnosis and psychopathology: Retrospect and prospect. *Journal of Abnormal Psychology, 88,* 459–473.

Kihlstrom, J. F. (1987). The cognitive unconscious. *Science, 237,* 1445–1452.

Klein, D. F. (1993). False suffocation alarms, spontaneous panics, and related conditions: An integrated hypothesis. *Archives of General Psychiatry, 50,* 306–317.

McFall, R. (1991). Manifesto for a science of clinical psychology. *The Clinical Psychologist, 44,* 75–88.

Murray, C. J., & Lopez, A. D. (1997). *The global burden of disease.* Harvard University Press, Cambridge, MA.

Ramachandran, V. S., & Blakeslee, S. (1999). *Phantoms in the brain: Probing the mysteries of the human mind.* New York: Harper Perennial.

Shakow, D. (1965). Seventeen years later: Clinical psychology in the light of the 1947 committee on training in clinical psychology report. *American Psychologist, 20,* 353–362.

Shakow, D. (1976). What is clinical psychology? *American Psychologist, 31,* 553–560.

Shakow, D. (1978). Clinical psychology seen some 50 years later. *American Psychologist, 33,* 148–158.

Swann, W. B., Jr. (1983). Self-verification: Bringing social reality into harmony with the self. In J. Suls & A.G. Greenwald (Eds.), *Social psychological perspectives on the self* (vol. 2, pp. 33–66). Hillsdale, NJ: Erlbaum.

Swann, W. B., Jr., Stein-Seroussi, A., & Giesler, B. (1992). Why people self-verify. *Journal of Personality and Social Psychology, 62,* 392–401.

Van Orden, K. A., Witte, T. K., Cukrowicz, K. C., Braithwaite, S., Selby, E. A., & Joiner, T. E., Jr. (2010). The interpersonal theory of suicide. *Psychological Review, 117,* 575–600.

Wells, F. L. (1914). Experimental psychopathology. *Psychological Bulletin, 11,* 202–212.

White, R. W. (1992). Who was Morton Prince? *Journal of Abnormal Psychology, 101,* 604–606.

Wood, J. V., Perunovic, W. Q., & Lee, J. W. (2009). Positive self-statements: Power for some, peril for others. *Psychological Science, 20,* 860–866.

Wrosch, C., & Miller, G. E. (2009). Depressive symptoms can be useful: Self-regulatory and emotional benefits of dysphoric mood in adolescence. *Journal of Personality and Social Psychology, 96,* 1181–1190.

# 21

# Meaning and Growth within Positive Psychology: Toward a More Complete Understanding

*Crystal L. Park*

*Positive psychology is an umbrella term for the study of positive emotions, positive character traits, and enabling institutions. Research findings from positive psychology are intended to supplement, not remotely to replace, what is known about human suffering, weakness, and disorder. The intent is to have a more complete and balanced scientific understanding of the human experience—the peaks, the valleys, and everything in between. We believe that a complete science and a complete practice of psychology should include an understanding of suffering and happiness, as well as their interaction, and validated interventions that both relieve suffering and increase happiness—two separable endeavors* (Seligman, Steen, Park, & Peterson, 2005, p. 410)

Those promoting positive psychology note that their emphasis on the positive serves as a balance to the broader field of psychology's preoccupation with the broken, aversive, and pathological. Emphasizing the positive aspects of human existence, then, has been argued to be a needed corrective to the field. As reflected in this opening excerpt (Seligman et al., 2005), however, positive psychology aspires to provide a *more complete* understanding of human beings that encompasses both the highs and the lows. However, many of those writing about positive psychology have given mixed messages about what positive psychology is and how much room there truly is for integrating the full range of experiences (Lazarus, 2003; Seligman & Pawelski, 2003).

True, some researchers have made explicit efforts to locate the "negative" within positive psychology (e.g., Joseph & Linley, 2004) and have striven to show how positive psychological approaches can speak to both trauma and suffering (Joseph & Linley, 2005). In their lead article inaugurating the *Journal of Positive Psychology*, Linley and his colleagues highlighted this effort at integration (Linley, Joseph, Harrington, & Wood, 2006) by defining positive psychology as "the scientific study of optimal human functioning . . . it aims to redress the imbalance in psychological research and practice by calling attention to the positive aspects of human functioning and experience, and integrating them with our understanding of the negative aspects of human functioning and experience" (p. 3).

However, an underlying emphasis on the positive in isolation characterizes much of the positive psychology literature (e.g., Gable & Haidt, 2005). This lack of balance persists in spite of the oft-expressed desire of positive psychology enthusiasts to promote a view of the whole spectrum of human experiences as put forth by Seligman and his colleagues (2005). For example, there is an intensive focus on happiness (e.g., Peterson et al., 2005), flourishing (e.g., Keyes & Haidt, 2003), positive emotions (Fredrickson, 1998, Fredrickson et al., 2003), and gratitude (e.g., Emmons & McCullough, 2004). Further, writers from the positive psychology perspective argue that these positive aspects of experience are important in their own right, rather than only in contrast to, or as protection against, the negative aspects of life (Gable & Haidt, 2005). In spite of avowed interest in a more comprehensive understanding, and in spite of some positive psychologists' efforts at integration, most of the writings and research within positive psychology fail to include or even acknowledge the full range of experiences (Wong, 2007), perhaps because of positive psychologists' stated intention to emphasize the positive.

In this chapter, I assess the present state of integration within positive psychology regarding one particular aspect of human experience, meaning, which is central to human existence, regardless of the valence of that meaning. I examine the extent to which meaning is adequately captured in positive psychology perspectives and then describe what seems to be missing from this view at present. As a potential remedy, I propose the grounding of positive psychological inquiry into issues of meaning and meaning making in an existential spiritual framework. Such a framework could bridge the fairly extensive but distinct work being conducted on meaning and stress-related growth and that on positive psychology, benefitting both areas of inquiry. I conclude with ideas about how research on meaning, so framed, might move forward.

## Taking Stock

*Many well-intentioned positive psychologists have repeatedly tried to set me straight by telling me that suffering and negative emotions are beyond the parameters of positive psychology, which is a 'science of*

*positive subjective experiences, positive traits, and positive institutions' (Seligman & Csikszentmihalyi, 2000, p. 5). Resistance toward negative emotions and experiences comes from a narrow interpretation of . . . American positive psychology and a culture obsessed with personal happiness and success* (Wong, 2007, p. 236).

In this section, I take stock of the extent to which positive psychology approaches to meaning have incorporated the full range of human experience, particularly with reference to meaning. I first describe the current state of the literature within positive psychology on meaning, and identify the perspectives that positive psychology is currently missing. These missing perspectives include (1) *Breadth of focus:* In positive psychology approaches, the construct of meaning is typically operationalized using measures of "meaning in life" that essentially assess individuals' feeling or sense that their life has purpose or meaning. However, meaning encompasses much more than feelings. As will be discussed below, meaning also refers to individuals' understanding of the world and their place in it as well as their value systems and hierarchies of strivings and goals. (2) *Depth of focus*: Positive psychology research on meaning has not typically been grounded in underlying philosophies or worldviews. Most of these studies of meaning exclude or ignore the basis of meaning in the deeper givens or essential truths of human existence. This oversight of many of these studies renders the contribution to our understanding of this central aspect of human experience meager and superficial. (3) *Dynamic understanding*: Only by studying meaning systems in action, during highly stressful times, can the full functioning and impact of meaning become apparent. In addition, only by examining meaning making as a broad set of processes following a stressful experience can we understand stress-related or post-traumatic growth, the most commonly studied aspect of meaning making (Park, Edmondson, Fenster, & Blank, 2008) in context rather than in isolation.

## Current Positive Psychology Approaches to Meaning

Meaning in life has long been a topic of research interest among psychologists, and a great deal of research on various aspects of meaning in life has accumulated (see McNight & Kashdan, 2009; Steger, 2009, and Park, 2005 and 2010, for reviews).

Specifically within positive psychology, the focus on meaning has usually been in the context of happiness, contrasting eudemonia (the pursuit of happiness through meaning, the use of one's strengths and virtues toward achieving a greater good) with hedonism (the pursuit of happiness through pleasure) (Peterson, Park, & Seligman, 2005; Seligman, Parks, & Steen, 2004). In addition, some positive psychologists have examined meaning in terms of its pursuit and possession (e.g., Steger, Frazier, Oishi, & Kaler, 2006) and its associations with positive affect (e.g., King, Hicks, Krull, & Del Gaiso, 2006).

Meanwhile, a line of research outside of the positive psychology tradition focusing on meaning making has proliferated in recent years (see Park, 2010, for a review). Meaning making concerns the processes of coping with stressful circumstances by changing one's global beliefs and goals or one's appraisal of particular situations (Park, 2005), as will be detailed below. However, this topic has not been framed as a province of positive psychology nor been examined in the context of positive psychological functioning. The single exception to this separation of positive psychology and meaning making is research on stress-related growth, which has proliferated in the past 15 years (Helgeson, Reynolds, & Tomich, 2006; Park, 2009). Stress-related growth concerns the positive changes that people report experiencing following adverse events. Some research on growth has been framed from a positive psychology perspective, notably the work of Joseph and Linley and their colleagues. For example, Joseph and Linley (2005) used a theoretical construct, organismic valuing, to explain stress-related growth, positing that humans possess an inherent motivation toward growth.

## What's Missing in Current Positive Psychology Approaches to Meaning

Clearly, life is not all sunshine and happiness; struggle and suffering invariably constitute a significant portion of human experience. While positive psychologists do not deny these realities, they frequently ignore or overlook them in discussions of positive psychology. In general, these aspects of human experience that might be described as "negative" are poorly integrated with those aspects that are typically the focus of positive psychology. Absent is a serious and sustained effort to integrate both sides—positive human experience in the context of negative (or vice versa).

Although balance is often the stated goal of positive psychology (e.g., Linley et al., 2006), there is inherent tension or ambivalence about the role of struggle and suffering in this sub-discipline, reflected in Seligman et al.'s (2005) above-quoted description of positive psychology. The integration of the focus on the positive with stress and trauma is a lofty goal, but as Seligman intimates, in many ways they remain separate endeavors. It is rarely acknowledged that positive aspects of human experience (e.g., positive emotions, gratitude and appreciation, harmony) exist in a dialectical relationship with negative aspects (Wong, 2007). That is, positive states are especially—or even exclusively—positive in contrast to the alternative (i.e., felt more acutely when the possibility of their opposite is salient; Janoff-Bulman & Berger, 2000). This lack of integration is clearly seen in the ways that meaning is typically discussed within the context of positive psychology, as reviewed above. These three missing perspectives of meaning (breadth, depth, and dynamic understanding), detailed below, all stem from this lack of integration and all impede our understanding of meaning.

(1) *Breadth.* Meaning is often described as referring to a purposeful life (e.g., Poseck, Baquero, & Jiménez, 2006) or as being connected to causes greater than oneself (e.g., Peterson et al., 2005). Yet meaning comprises much more than a subjective feeling, although this is clearly one important aspect of meaning. As conceptualized by many writers outside of positive psychology, global meaning encompasses beliefs and goals as well as subjective feelings of purpose or meaning in life (Halama, 2002; Park & Folkman, 1997). These facets of meaning are clearly complex and interdependent, and all are important, yet current positive psychology approaches to meaning typically do not include any focus on broader *systems* of meaning.

(2) *Depth.* Even in research explicitly focusing on the subjective sense aspect of meaning, positive psychologists have not securely grounded this research in a deeper understanding of the roots of meaning. That is, very little research within positive psychology has examined the underlying sources of meaning or traced the philosophical or spiritual antecedents of meaning. Although some positive psychologists have reviewed the background in which a sense of meaning may be found (e.g., King et al., 2006; Steger & Frazier, 2005), the studies themselves rarely delve into the deeper aspects of meaning, but rather use meaning as a starting point for

work on other positive psychology topics, such as happiness and positive affect (e.g., King et al., 2006). Aside from a few notable exceptions (e.g., Steger & Frazier's 2005 study of religiousness as a precursor to meaning), very little work has delved into the underpinnings of meaning in life.

This lack of interest in meaning per se and the minimal grounding of work on meaning may, in part, be traced to positive psychology's general disinterest in spirituality. Although spirituality is listed as one of the 24 character strengths in the VIA Classification (http://www.viastrengths. org/VIAClassification/tabid/56/Default.aspx), there has been little discussion of spirituality in the positive psychology literature (cf., van Dierendonck & Mohan, 2006). An authentic understanding of meaning requires more sustained and intentional attention to its deeper sources including, perhaps, its wellspring in spiritual existence.

(3) *Dynamic understanding.* Although positive psychology topics are usually examined in a positive context, some positive psychologists have framed their areas of study within negative life events. For example, optimism has been studied extensively in the context of illness (e.g., Culver, Carver, & Scheier, 2003) and other stressful life events (e.g., Riolli, Savicki, & Cepani, 2002). Also, some work on positive emotions has examined their maintenance in the face of stressful life circumstances (e.g., Tugade & Fredrickson, 2004), and, by its nature, stress-related growth research is conducted within the context of aversive life events (Park, 2009). However, in the main, positive psychology has not been concerned with how positive psychological aspects function because of, in spite of, in the midst of, or in the aftermath of profoundly difficult and aversive life experiences.

Even those studies that examine positive psychology topics within the context of stress tend to overlook the true reality of both the positive and negative nature of the situation. For example, the vast majority of studies on stress-related growth, while giving a nod to the unfortunate circumstances that led to the positive life changes reported, rarely attend to the grievous suffering of the participants. Studies rarely simultaneously focus on both sides of the impact of a stressful experience. Zebrack and Cella (2005) captured this sentiment in discussing the paradox of cancer survivorship, which entails a great sense of sadness, physical losses, and anxiety along with a sense of gratitude and personal growth, all driven by the experience. Studies seem to come down on one side or the other but rarely capture the entirety of the experience.

This lack of deep inquiry into the ways that positive psychological aspects play out in the context of negative life events means that positive psychology misses the opportunity to understand the processes by which these positive aspects may make their greatest difference to people—in times of great difficulty or suffering. For example, work by Susan Folkman and her colleagues (e.g., Billings, Folkman, Acree, & Moskowitz, 2000) has shown how positive emotions often exist in the midst of giving care to one's partner dying of AIDS and can, in fact, sustain and nurture those caregivers. While understanding happiness in the abstract or in good times may be valuable, surely understanding happiness when the going gets rough is at least equally valuable. Further, the processes of adaptation that unfold within the context of such highly stressful situations provide invaluable information regarding how these positive aspects arise and change over time. This area of study, meaning making, involves the illumination of these processes (Park, 2010), which has not been a province of positive psychologists.

## Moving Forward: Toward a More Complete Understanding of Meaning

*Any perspective on life that elevates the rich possibilities of existence without reference to its limiting factors perpetuates a fantasy* (Bretherton & Orner, 2004, p. 420).

Adding these three identified missing perspectives on meaning to the current work within positive psychology yields a vision of a more complete psychological science. I use the remainder of this chapter to provide suggestions for restoring these three missing perspectives on meaning within positive psychology. It is important to note that many related ideas have been voiced over the years by humanistic psychologists and others, but to date have not been put into a rigorous scientific framework. Positive psychology now has the empirical tools to build a more complete science of meaning (Wong, 2007).

### Breadth

As noted above, meaning involves much more than simply a feeling or subjective sense. Human meaning systems are complex and involve a whole orienting system of beliefs and goals as well as feelings. Positive psychology should embrace the broader concept of meaning systems to better explore their role in optimal psychological functioning. The global beliefs aspect of meaning (also called "assumptive worlds," "personal theories," or "worldviews"; see Koltko-Rivera, 2004, for a review) comprises the core schemas through which people interpret their experiences. Global beliefs involve one's views on fairness, justice, luck, control, predictability, coherence, benevolence, identity, and personal vulnerability. The global goals aspect of meaning involves internal representations of one's desired long-term processes, events, or outcomes (Austin & Vancouver, 1996). Goals may be desired states that one already possesses and seeks to maintain or future states one hopes to attain (Klinger, 1998; Karoly, 1999). Common global goals include relationships, health, work, wealth, knowledge, and achievement (Emmons, 2003). The third aspect of global meaning, the subjective sense, refers to feelings of "meaningfulness," direction, or purpose in life (Klinger, 1977; Reker & Wong, 1988). A sense of meaningfulness derives from seeing one's actions as oriented toward or in the service of reaching a desired future state or goal (Wrosch, Scheier, Carver, & Schulz, 2003; cf. King et al., 2006).

## Depth

To add heft to positive psychology's take on meaning, I concur with Wong (2007), who argued that a mature positive psychology needs to incorporate suffering. Wong (2007) asserted that if positive psychology is to address the challenges and potential of human beings, it must embrace the paradoxical nature of an authentic life, with its potential for misery as well as joy. Such contrary experiences can coexist and, in fact, as noted above, may be dependent on one another to be fully experienced. Drawing on the work of Viktor Frankl (1963), Wong (2007) proposed the concept of "tragic optimism" as the key to integrating suffering into positive psychology. Tragic optimism is "a state where hope and despair can coexist and in which we can remain optimistic, no matter how helpless and hopeless we feel" (p. 238).

Pushing a little further along these lines, I propose that positive psychology would profit from a deeper grounding in spirituality, broadly defined.[1] Spirituality can be considered the search for understanding life's ultimate questions and the meaning and purpose of living, usually in the context of the transcendent or divine. This search often, but not always, leads to the development of rituals and a shared religious community (Larson, Swyers, & McCullough, 1997).

Thus, spirituality encompasses the existential perspective promoted by Wong (2007) and others (e.g., Frankl, 1963; Yalom, 1980). It also encompasses Eastern approaches such as Buddhism (Wray, 1986; Rothberg et al., 1998) as well as traditional Western approaches to religion (e.g., Zinnbauer & Pargament, 2005). Grounding the science of meaning in spirituality will add the depth missing from current approaches to meaning in positive psychology and will also facilitate the application of positive psychology topics into the study of suffering, thereby achieving the integration expressly desired by many positive psychologists (e.g., Seligman et al., 2005).

Grounding the study of meaning in an existential spirituality opens up many possible pathways for this exploration. Below I describe several spiritual approaches that offer potentially fruitful directions for deepening the study of the positive psychology of meaning. A grounding of meaning within existential spiritual perspectives allows integration of positive psychology perspectives on meaning with those of other areas of psychology. Tying the study of meaning to these deeper aspects of spirituality will enrich our understanding of the ways that meaning pervades human existence.

*Existential psychology.* Existential psychology starts with the existential fundamentals that humans are alone and mortal, that their lives have no inherent meaning, and that they have a terrible freedom and responsibility for their own lives (see Table 21.1). Equipped with such knowledge, people still manage to create meaning in their lives, or find belief systems that provide them with some of the answers to life's questions. They develop deeply significant relationships with others in spite of the ultimate gaps between any two humans. They make choices and take responsibility for the consequences of those choices. Positive psychology could greatly contribute to understanding how people forge ahead with the heavy knowledge of existence.

*Buddhist psychology.* Buddhist psychological perspectives also begin with some basic teachings regarding the nature of existence (Wray, 1986). The Buddha's Five Remembrances (Table 21.2) illustrate some of these nonnegotiable facts. Rather than comprising "negative thinking," Boccio (2008) argues that if people embrace and remain aware of these Remembrances, they

TABLE 21.1  Four Existential Givens

| | |
|---|---|
| 1. *Mortality* | All humans get a finite (and all too brief) existence and must live with the knowledge of their approaching demise. |
| 2. *Freedom/Responsibility* | Humans are given absolute freedom, and along with this freedom, total responsibility for the choices made. As two sides of the same coin, the terms freedom and responsibility are interchangeable. |
| 3. *Isolation* | Although human nature is essentially relational, we are ultimately alone. |
| 4. *Meaninglessness* | Humans are placed in the universe without any preordained system of ultimate meaning. Each person must create or discover life's meaning for himself or herself. |

TABLE 21.2  The Five Remembrances of the Buddha

I am of the nature to grow old. There is no way to escape growing old.

I am of the nature to have ill health. There is no way to escape ill health.

I am of the nature to die. There is no way to escape death.

All that is dear to me and everyone I love are of the nature to change. There is no way to escape being separated from them.

My actions are my only true belongings. I cannot escape the consequences of my actions. My actions are the ground upon which I stand.

*Note:* Adapted from Thich Nhat Hanh (1991).

will awaken from their denial. By reminding them of the temporary nature of their lives, these Remembrances help people to cultivate gratitude and appreciation and, ultimately, teach people about nonattachment and peace. Positive psychological perspectives to meaning could be informed by the role that Buddhist perspectives might play in deepening the sense of meaning people experience.

*Western religious perspectives.* Generalizations about Western religious perspectives are difficult to make, but the key tenets of specific religious perspectives make excellent taking-off points for examining how people imbue their lives with meaning and purpose (Joseph, Linley, & Maltby, 2006). For example, for adherents of specific religious traditions that hold that reaching a desirable afterlife is the ultimate goal of earthly existence (e.g., Clarke, Hayslip, Edmondson, & Guarnaccia, 2003), how does this base belief influence the ways that they structure their lives, the goals that they set, and the means by which they strive for those goals? Similar types of questions can be posed about other basic teachings.[2]

## Dynamic Understanding

If positive psychology embraced deeper philosophical and spiritual underpinnings, spirituality could then serve as the bridge between standard positive psychological approaches to meaning and the accumulating literature on meaning in the context of trauma and stress. As Wong (2007) noted, "The acid test of any model of positive psychology is how it fares in boundary situations of suffering. Positive psychology needs to work for the good and bad times" (p. 237). Applying this assertion to the issue of meaning, positive psychology would profit from embracing and contributing to the abundant literature on meaning making.

Park and her colleagues (e.g., Park, 2005; Park et al., 2008) described one framework characterizing meaning making (see Figure 21.1). This framework posits that when confronting a potential stressor, people assign a meaning to it. Events can be appraised on many dimensions, including the extent to which they pose a threat or a loss and the extent to which adequate coping resources are available as well as attributions for the cause

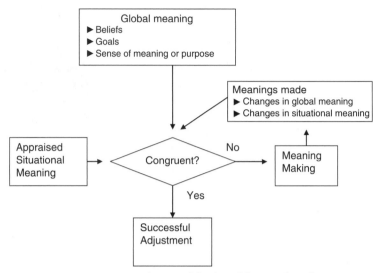

Figure 21.1  Meaning Making Model (adapted from Park et al., 2008).

of the occurrence. The appraised meaning of a situation may be incongruent with individuals' global meaning systems (i.e., violate their global beliefs about the world and themselves and their overarching goals). The distress generated by perceiving incongruence between people's appraisals of a particular situation and their global meaning initiates efforts to restore congruence within their meaning system. Congruence can be accomplished by meaning-making coping, which involves changing their way of understanding the stressor (assimilation) or by changing aspects of their global meaning (accommodation). The processes of meaning making can lead to various products, or meaning made, such as changes in one's appraisal of the stressful event (e.g., coming to see it as less damaging or even, perhaps, in some ways fortuitous), changes in one's global meaning (e.g., viewing oneself or God differently), and stress-related growth (e.g., reordering one's priorities or experiencing increased appreciation for life). Meaning making appears to lead to better adjustment, particularly if an adaptive meaning is made (see Gillies & Neimeyer, 2006, for a review).[3]

## Topics and Questions for Future Research

Incorporating these perspectives on meaning within positive psychology opens the door for a great deal of future inquiry that will vastly enrich our understanding of meaning with

knowledge that is solidly integrated within both positive and more traditional ("negative") approaches. Below, I outline some topics that would profitably serve as research foci and pose several questions relevant to each. However, these questions are merely a starting point for a positive psychology of meaning that has real breadth, depth, and a dynamic process orientation, and readers will likely come up with many other topics more specific to their own unique interests.

*Meaning Systems.* In spite of many years of psychological research on various aspects of global meaning, there is very little that we can confidently state about human meaning systems. Much work is needed to better understand global beliefs, goals, and a sense of meaning or purpose and how they influence the lives people live.

Koltko-Rivera (2004) expertly outlined 42 separate dimensions of global beliefs that, together, constitute individuals' belief systems. For many of these dimensions of belief, there is very little research. For example, we do not know much about how many of these beliefs develop and change over the lifespan. Other questions that should be addressed to provide a fuller understanding of global beliefs include: How much are individuals' beliefs based on an underlying spiritual or existential framework? How does adherence to various spiritual traditions inform individuals' global beliefs? Do individuals differ in the extent to which their global beliefs are coherent and consistent versus fragmented and contradictory? And what are the implications of consistency for well-being?

In terms of goals, research suggests that people whose behavior (e.g., in terms of expenditures of effort, time, and money) is better aligned with their expressed goals are psychologically better off than are those less closely aligned (e.g., Sheldon & Elliot, 1999; Mahoney et al., 2005). Yet many questions remain: How aware are individuals of their goals and purposes? How well do individuals' expressed goals match with enacted goal-directed behaviors? Are those with more consistency across beliefs and goals better off than those whose beliefs and goals conflict with one another (e.g., Emmons & King, 1988)?

Regarding the subjective sense of meaning or purpose, even though this aspect of meaning has received the lion's share of positive psychologists' research attention, much remains to be learned. For example, how do individuals find and sustain a sense that their life is meaningful in the face of an awareness of the vast suffering people inevitably experience—and are currently experiencing around the world (Wong, 2007)? How do people maintain a positive sense of meaning and significance in the face of existential givens such as their own mortality (see Tables 21.1 and 21.2)? Under what conditions does having knowledge and awareness of the inevitabilities of change and loss potentiate the living of a more authentic and deeply satisfying life? That is, why do people so often reach for defenses that protect them from this awareness (Yalom, 1980), and what enables some people to incorporate this awareness into being open to the fullness of their experience?

*Meanings made.* Stress-related growth (also called post-traumatic growth, adversarial growth, and benefit-finding; Park, 2010) is by far the most studied product of meaning making. Even though research has established a great deal about this topic, much remains to be learned. For example, how does growth arise? To what extent are the positive changes that people report accurate? Some evidence indicates that much self-reported growth is illusory (Frazier et al., 2009; Ransom, Sheldon, & Jacobsen, 2008), but when is it accurate and what determines accuracy of growth reports? In addition, a very important and poorly understood issue is what reports of growth mean in terms of well-being. It will be important to simultaneously examine the effects of perceived positive and negative effects in tandem, as research suggests that negative changes occur

frequently in the same domains as the positive and, further, reported negative changes have a much stronger association with negative outcomes than do positive changes (e.g., Bellizzi, Miller, Arora, & Rowland, 2007).

In addition to stress-related growth, there are other products of meaning making that have been neglected by positive psychology researchers as well as more traditional researchers. Other meanings made include changed global beliefs, changed global goals, and changed views of one's stressful situation. Many questions arise regarding these changes: What determines whether global meaning or the appraised meaning of the situation changes in the service of restoring congruence? What determines the specific types of changes that individuals make? How are these changes incorporated into a revised global meaning system? And what kinds of influences do pre-existing philosophical, religious, or spiritual meaning systems exert on these meanings made?

## Summary

Positive psychology has already advanced our understanding of meaning in many ways. However, this approach could be vastly improved by including greater depth and breadth in the treatment of meaning and taking a more dynamic view of the ways that meaning is formed and re-formed in the context of challenging and stressful life events. These elements will produce a much richer and more authentic psychology of meaning. If positive psychology is able to grow in these ways, the positive psychological perspective on meaning will cease to exist as distinct and rather be integrated into a fuller, richer integrated psychology (Linley et al., 2006; Seligman et al., 2005).

## Author note

Many thanks to Jeanne Slattery for comments on an earlier version of this chapter.

### Notes

1. Disagreements about the definition of spirituality and its relation to religion continue unabated in the psychology literature. Although far beyond the scope of the present chapter, interested readers are referred to Zinnbauer and Pargament (2005) and Hill, Pargament, Hood, McCullough, Swyers et al. (2000).

2. Clearly the effects of religiousness and spirituality are not all salubrious (e.g., Bushman, Ridge, Das, Key, & Busath, 2007). An important issue for future researchers is determining the circumstances under which religious and spiritual aspects are—and are not—related to health and well-being.

3. This is a brief overview of the meaning making model; readers are referred to Park (2005) and (2010) for in-depth explication of this model.

## References

Austin, J. T., & Vancouver, J. B. (1996). Goal constructs in psychology: Structure, process, and content. *Psychological Bulletin, 120,* 338–375.

Bellizzi, K. M., Miller, M. F., Arora, N. K., & Rowland, J. H. (2007). Positive and negative life changes experienced by survivors of non-Hodgkin's lymphoma. *Annals of Behavioral Medicine, 34,* 188–199.

Billings, D. W., Folkman, S., Acree, M., & Moskowitz, J. T. (2000). Coping, physical health during caregiving: The roles of positive and negative affect. *Journal of Personality and Social Psychology, 79,* 131–142.

Boccio, F. J. (2008). http://www.yogajournal.com/practice/1748 Retrieved 10/15/2008.

Bretherton, R., & Orner, R. J. (2004). Positive psychology and psychotherapy: An existential approach. In P. A. Linley & S. Joseph (Eds.), *Positive psychology in practice* (pp. 420–430). Hoboken, NJ: John Wiley & Sons.

Bushman, B. J., Ridge, R.D., Das, E., Key, C. W., Busath, G. L. (2007). When God sanctions killing: Effect of scriptural violence on aggression. *Psychological Science, 18,* 204–207.

Clarke, S. M., Hayslip, B. J., Edmondson, R., & Guarnaccia, C. A. (2003). Religiosity, afterlife beliefs, and bereavement adjustment in adulthood. *Journal of Religious Gerontology, 14,* 207–224.

Culver, J. L., Carver, C. S., & Scheier, M. F. (2003). Dispositional optimism as a moderator of the impact of health threats on coping and well-being. In R. Jacoby, G. Keinan, R. Jacoby, & G. Keinan (Eds.), *Between stress and hope: From a disease-centered to a health-centered perspective* (pp. 27–55). Westport, CT: Praeger Publishers/Greenwood Publishing Group.

Emmons, R. A. (2003). Personal goals, life meaning, and virtue: Wellsprings of a positive life. In C. L. M. Keyes & J. Haidt (Eds.), *Flourishing: Positive psychology and the life well-lived* (pp. 105–128). Washington, DC: American Psychological Association.

Emmons, R. A., & King, L. A. (1988). Conflict among personal strivings: Immediate and long-term implications for psychological and physical well-being. *Journal of Personality and Social Psychology, 54,* 1040–1048.

Emmons, R. A., & McCullough, M. E. (Eds.)(2004). *The psychology of gratitude.* New York: Oxford University Press.

Frankl, V. E. (1963). *Man's search for meaning: An introduction to logotherapy.* Oxford England: Washington Square Press.

Frazier, P., Tennen, H., Gavian, M., Park, C. L., Tomich, P., & Tashiro, T. (2009). Does self-reported post-traumatic growth reflect genuine positive change? *Psychological Science, 20,* 912–919.

Fredrickson, B. L. (1998). What good are positive emotions? *Review of General Psychology, 2,* 300–319.

Fredrickson, B. L., Tugade, M. M., Waugh, C. E., & Larkin, G. R. (2003). What good are positive emotions in crisis? A prospective study of resilience and emotions following the terrorist attacks on the United States on September 11th, 2001. *Journal of Personality and Social Psychology, 84,* 365–376.

Gable, S. L., & Haidt, J. (2005). What (and why) is positive psychology? *Review of General Psychology, 9,* 103–110.

Gillies, J., & Neimeyer, R. A. (2006). Loss, grief, and the search for significance: Toward a model of meaning reconstruction in bereavement. *Journal of Constructivist Psychology, 19,* 31–65.

Hanh, T. N. (1991). *The Plum Village chanting and recitation book.* Berkeley, CA: Parallax Press.

Halama, P. (2002). From establishing beliefs through pursuing goals to experiencing fulfillment: Examining the three-component model of personal meaning in life. *Studia Psychologica, 44,* 143–154.

Helgeson, V. S., Reynolds, K. A., & Tomich, P. L. (2006). A meta-analytic review of benefit finding and growth. *Journal of Consulting and Clinical Psychology, 74,* 797–816.

Hill, P. C., Pargament, K. I., Hood, R. W., McCullough, J. M., Swyers, J.P., Larson, D. B., & Zinnbauer, B. J. (2000). Conceptualizing religion and spirituality: Points of commonality, points of departure. *Journal for the Theory of Social Behaviour, 30,* 51–77.

Janoff-Bulman, R., & Berger, A. R. (2000). The other side of trauma: Towards a psychology of appreciation. In J. H. Harvey & E. D. Miller (Eds.), *Loss and trauma: General and close relationship perspectives* (pp. 29–44). New York: Brunner-Routledge.

Joseph, S., & Linley, P. A. (2004). Adversarial growth and positive change following trauma: Theory, research, and practice. *Ricerche Di Psicologia, 27,* 177–190.

Joseph, S., & Linley, P. A. (2005). Positive adjustment to threatening events: An organismic valuing theory of growth through adversity. *Review of General Psychology, 9,* 262–280.

Joseph, S., Linley, P. A., & Maltby, J. (2006). Editorial: Positive psychology, religion, and spirituality. *Mental Health, Religion & Culture, 9,* 209–212.

Karoly, P. (1999). A goal systems-self-regulatory perspective on personality, psychopathology, and change. *Review of General Psychology, 3,* 264–291.

Keyes, C. L. M., & Haidt, J. (2003). *Flourishing: Positive psychology and the life well-lived.* Washington, DC: American Psychological Association.

King, L. A., Hicks, J. A., Krull, J. L., & Del Gaiso, A. K. (2006). Positive affect and the experience of meaning in life. *Journal of Personality and Social Psychology, 90,* 179–196.

Klinger, E. (1977). *Meaning & void: Inner experience and the incentives in people's lives.* Oxford, England: U Minnesota Press.

Klinger, E. (1998). The search for meaning in evolutionary perspective and its clinical implications. In P. T. P. Wong & P. S. Fry (Eds.), *The human quest for meaning: A handbook of psychological research and clinical applications* (pp. 27–50). Mahwah, NJ: Lawrence Erlbaum.

Koltko-Rivera, M. E. (2004). The psychology of worldviews. *Review of General Psychology, 8,* 3–58.

Larson, D. B., Swyers, J. P., & McCullough, M. E. (1997). *Scientific research on spirituality and health: A consensus report.* Rockville, MD: National Institute for Healthcare Research.

Lazarus, R. S. (2003). The Lazarus manifesto for positive psychology and psychology in general. *Psychological Inquiry, 14,* 173–189.

Linley, P. A., Joseph, S., Harrington, S., & Wood, A. M. (2006). Positive psychology: Past, present, and (possible) future. *The Journal of Positive Psychology, 1,* 3–16.

Mahoney, A., Pargament, K. I., Cole, B., Jewell, T., Magyar, G. M., Tarakeshwar, N., et al. (2005). A higher purpose: The sanctification of strivings in a community sample. *International Journal for the Psychology of Religion, 15,* 239–262.

McKnight, P. E., & Kashdan, T. B. (2009). Purpose in life as a system that creates and sustains health and well-being: An integrative, testable theory. *Review of General Psychology, 13,* 242–251.

Park, C. L. (2005). Religion and meaning. In R. F. Paloutzian & C. L. Park (Eds.), *Handbook of the psychology of religion and spirituality* (pp. 295–314). New York: Guilford.

Park, C. L. (2009). Overview of theoretical perspectives. In C. L. Park, S. Lechner, M. H. Antoni, & A. Stanton (Eds.), *Positive life change in the context of medical illness: Can the experience of serious illness lead to transformation?* (pp. 11–30). Washington, DC: American Psychological Association.

Park, C. L. (2010). Making sense of the meaning literature: An integrative review of meaning making and its effects on adjustment to stressful life events. *Psychological Bulletin, 136,* 257–301.

Park, C. L., Edmondson, D., Fenster, J. R., & Blank, T. O. (2008). Meaning making and psychological adjustment following cancer: The mediating roles of growth, life meaning, and restored just-world beliefs. *Journal of Consulting and Clinical Psychology, 76,* 863–875.

Park, C. L., & Folkman, S. (1997). Meaning in the context of stress and coping. *Review of General Psychology, 1,* 115–144.

Peterson, C., Park, N., & Seligman, M. E. P. (2005). Orientations to happiness and life satisfaction: The full life versus the empty life. *Journal of Happiness Studies, 6,* 25–41.

Poseck, B. V., Baquero, B. C., & Jiménez, M. L. V. (2006). The traumatic experience from positive psychology: Resiliency and post-traumatic growth. *Papeles Del Psicólogo, 27,* 40–49.

Ransom, S., Sheldon, K. M., & Jacobsen, P. B. (2008). Actual change and inaccurate recall contribute to posttraumatic growth following radiotherapy. *Journal of Consulting and Clinical Psychology, 76,* 811–819.

Reker, G. T., & Wong, P. T. P. (1988). Aging as an individual process: Toward a theory of personal meaning. In J. E. Birren & V. L. Bengtson (Eds.), *Emergent theories of aging* (pp. 214–246). New York: Springer.

Riolli, L., Savicki, V., & Cepani, A. (2002). Resilience in the face of catastrophe: Optimism, personality and coping in the Kosovo crisis. *Journal of Applied Social Psychology, 32,* 1604–1627.

Rothberg, D. J., Goldstein, J., Kornfield, J., & McDonald-Smith, M. (1998). How straight is the spiritual path? Conversations with three Buddhist teachers. In D. J. Rothberg & S. M. Kelly (Eds.), *Ken Wilbur in dialogue: Conversations with leading transpersonal thinkers* (pp. 131–178). Wheaton, IL: Quest Books/The Theosophical Publishing House.

Seligman, M. E. P., Parks, A. C., & Steen, T. (2004). A balanced psychology and a full life. *Philosophical Transactions of the Royal Society of London. Series B, Biological Sciences, 359*, 1379–1381.

Seligman, M. E., & Csikszentmihalyi, M. (2000). Positive psychology: An introduction. *American Psychology, 55*, 5–14.

Seligman, M. E. P., & Pawelski, J. O. (2003). Positive psychology: FAQs. *Psychological Inquiry, 14*, 159–163.

Seligman, M. E. P., Steen, T. A., Park, N., & Peterson, C. (2005). Positive psychology progress: Empirical validation of interventions. *American Psychologist, 60*, 410–421.

Sheldon, K. M., & Elliot, A. J. (1999). Goal striving, need satisfaction, and longitudinal well-being: The self-concordance model. *Journal of Personality and Social Psychology, 76*, 482–497.

Steger, M. F. (2009). Meaning in life. In S. J. Lopez (Ed.), *Oxford handbook of positive psychology* (2nd Ed.) (pp. 679–687). Oxford, UK: Oxford University Press.

Steger, M. F., & Frazier, P. (2005). Meaning in life: One link in the chain from religiousness to well-being. *Journal of Counseling Psychology, 52*, 574–582.

Steger, M. F., Frazier, P., Oishi, S., & Kaler, M. (2006). The Meaning in Life Questionnaire: Assessing the presence of and search for meaning in life. *Journal of Counseling Psychology, 53*, 80–93.

Tugade, M. M., & Fredrickson, B. L. (2004). Resilient individuals use positive emotions to bounce back from negative emotional experiences. *Journal of Personality and Social Psychology, 86*, 320–333.

van Dierendonck, D., & Mohan, K. (2006). Some thoughts on spirituality and eudaimonic well-being. *Mental Health, Religion & Culture, 9*, 227–238.

Wong, P. T. P., Wong, L. C. J., McDonald, M. J., & Klassen, D. W. (2007). The positive psychology of suffering and tragic optimism. *The positive psychology of meaning and spirituality* (pp. 235–256). Abbottsford, BC, Canada: INPM Press.

Wray, I. (1986). Buddhism and psychotherapy: A Buddhist perspective. In G. Claxton, & G. Claxton (Eds.), *Beyond therapy: The impact of Eastern religions on psychological theory and practice* (pp. 153–172). Dorset, England: Prism Press.

Wrosch, C., Scheier, M. F., Carver, C. S., & Schulz, R. (2003). The importance of goal disengagement in adaptive self-regulation: When giving up is beneficial. *Self and Identity, 2*, 1–20.

Yalom, I. D. (1980). *Existential psychotherapy.* New York: Basic Books.

Zebrack, B., & Cella, D. (2005). Evaluating quality of life in cancer survivors. In J. Lipscomb, C. C. Gotay, & C. Snyder (Eds.), *Outcomes assessment in cancer: Measures, methods, and applications* (pp. 241–263). New York: Cambridge University Press.

Zinnbauer, B. J., & Pargament, K. I. (2005). Religiousness and spirituality. In R. F. Paloutzian & C. L. Park (Eds.), *Handbook of the psychology of religion and spirituality* (pp. 21–42). New York: Guilford.

# 22

# Mindfulness and Positive Psychological Functioning

*Ruth A. Baer and Emily L. B. Lykins*

Mindfulness is typically described as a form of nonjudgmental, nonreactive attention to experiences occurring in the present moment, including cognitions, emotions, and bodily sensations, as well as sights, sounds, smells, and other environmental stimuli (Kabat-Zinn, 2005; Linehan, 1993). The cultivation of mindfulness is a central component of Eastern meditation traditions and lies at the heart of Buddhist teachings about the nature of reality and human experience (Goldstein & Kornfield, 1987; Kabat-Zinn, 2003). In recent decades, instruction in mindfulness has become widely available in Western society through meditation centers offering guided retreats in Buddhist traditions and through mental health and stress-reduction programs that include training in secular adaptations of mindfulness practices. In the Buddhist tradition, the regular practice of mindfulness meditation is believed to facilitate both the relief of suffering and the cultivation of strengths and positive characteristics, including well-being, insight, wisdom, openness, compassion, and equanimity (Goldstein & Kornfield, 1987). The current psychological literature suggests that similar outcomes occur in secular Western settings.

Positive psychology is the study of optimal human functioning (Peterson, 2006). Recognizing that psychological health is more than the absence of disease or disorder (Peterson & Seligman, 2004), positive psychology aims to broaden the scope of psychology from a long-standing emphasis on pathology and distress to the study of how individuals and communities can flourish and thrive (Seligman & Csikszentmihalyi, 2000). One of the central concerns of positive psychology is the understanding and cultivation of human virtues, such as wisdom, courage, humanity (caring for others), justice, temperance (avoidance of excess), and transcendence, as well as their associated strengths of character, including open-mindedness, authenticity, kindness, leadership, self-regulation, and gratitude, among others (Peterson, 2006; Seligman, 2002).

Thus, both mindfulness training and positive psychology are concerned with the development and cultivation of human strengths and adaptive characteristics. However, it appears that they use different methods. Positive psychology emphasizes active behavioral exercises designed to develop strengths and virtues. Specific examples include writing letters of appreciation to cultivate gratitude, doing anonymous favors for loved ones to cultivate kindness, organizing social events to cultivate leadership, and attending lectures on unfamiliar topics to cultivate curiosity, among numerous others (Peterson, 2006). In contrast, although mindfulness exercises can take many forms, perhaps the most common practice is sitting meditation, which involves sitting quietly, often with the eyes closed, and directing attention to present-moment stimuli, such as the sensations and movements of breathing. Participants are encouraged to notice when the mind wanders into daydreams or fantasies and to bring it back nonjudgmentally to the present moment. Bodily sensations, emotions, and urges will inevitably arise, and participants are invited to welcome these with an attitude of openness, acceptance, and willingness; to observe them closely; and to refrain from efforts to evaluate, change, or terminate them. Although participants are strongly encouraged to apply mindfulness skills to their activities of daily life, mindfulness training typically does not explicitly teach specific behavior changes, other than those required to engage in the practices themselves.

The mindfulness-based approach to personal development is relatively unfamiliar in Western culture and often seems paradoxical (Kabat-Zinn, 2005) because of its emphasis on nonjudgmental acceptance rather than active striving for change. However, a growing body of empirical literature suggests that mindfulness-based approaches have substantial beneficial effects in many populations. The central thesis of this chapter, therefore, is that mindfulness cultivates human characteristics that are central to positive psychology, including character strengths and virtues and psychological well-being, but that it does so through acceptance-based rather than change-based methods. Because mindfulness training appears to have a broad range of outcomes, including enhancement of positive characteristics, its potential contribution to optimal human functioning warrants substantially increased attention. In this chapter, we examine the literature supporting this view, discuss the processes or mechanisms through which this may occur, and suggest directions for future research.

## Taking Stock

### Conceptualization of Mindfulness

Mindfulness has been described as a state, as a trait-like quality, and as a set of skills. A two-component model of mindfulness as a state was proposed by Bishop et al. (2004). The first component is the deliberate self-regulation of attention so that it remains focused on present-moment experiences. This allows for greater awareness and recognition of mental events (thoughts, feelings, and sensations) as they occur. The second component is a curious, open, and accepting orientation or stance toward observed experience. For example, if a sad feeling arises, the mindful individual will observe it closely, along with any accompanying sensations or cognitions, and will allow these experiences to come and go without attempting to avoid, suppress, or change them. Thus, a person in a mindful state is aware of and attentive to the ongoing stream of experiences and stimuli that are arising in each moment and is bringing an attitude of acceptance and openness to them, regardless of how pleasant or unpleasant they are. Mindfulness of unpleasant thoughts or emotions is not equivalent to passive resignation or hopelessness. Rather, it is believed to facilitate constructive responses, such as taking action to address a problematic situation (when appropriate) or simply allowing thoughts and feelings to run their natural course while recognizing that such experiences are not inherently harmful.

Mindfulness has also been described as a dispositional or trait-like quality. Published definitions and descriptions have many common elements. Most agree that the general tendency to be mindful includes a consistent pattern of noticing or attending to internal stimuli (cognitions, emotions, sensations, urges), external stimuli (sights, sounds, smells), and ongoing behavior. The tendency to be mindful has been contrasted with the tendency to behave mechanically or mindlessly, with attention focused elsewhere, in a manner often called *automatic pilot* (Segal, Williams, & Teasdale, 2002). Trait-like descriptions of mindfulness also include qualities of attention that are brought to bear on present-moment experiences, including acceptance, openness, nonjudging, and nonreactivity. A growing body of literature suggests that individuals vary in their general tendency to be mindful in daily life, and that this tendency is positively correlated with numerous adaptive characteristics, including psychological well-being, openness to experience, emotional intelligence, and self-compassion, and negatively associated with psychological symptoms and maladaptive cognitive and emotional processes, such as rumination, thought suppression, and experiential avoidance (Baer, Smith, & Allen, 2004;

Baer, Smith, Hopkins, Krietemeyer, & Toney, 2006, Brown, Ryan, & Creswell, 2007).

Methods for teaching mindfulness often describe it as a set of skills that can be learned and practiced. A prominent example comes from dialectical behavior therapy (DBT; Linehan, 1993), a cognitive-behavioral treatment for borderline personality disorder that incorporates training in several mindfulness skills. In the DBT framework, *observing* is defined as noticing or attending to internal and external stimuli as they arise. *Describing* refers to noting or labeling them with words (e.g., "here is sadness" or "self-critical thoughts have arisen"). *Participating* is defined as paying attention to the activities of the present moment, rather than behaving automatically or mindlessly, with attention focused elsewhere. Clients in DBT are encouraged to engage in these skills *nonjudgmentally* (without evaluating present-moment experiences as good or bad), *one-mindfully* (with attention focused on one thing at a time), and *effectively* (using skillful means). The skills-training approach to mindfulness suggests that with practice, individuals can learn to be more observant, accepting, and nonjudgmental of their daily experiences and to participate with awareness in their activities; that is, to adopt a mindful state more frequently and more consistently across situations.

An alternative conceptualization of mindfulness described by Langer (1989, 1997) includes alertness and sensitivity to context and perspective, openness to novelty, and orientation in the present. Although this conception of mindfulness is consistent with Eastern meditative traditions in its emphasis on flexible awareness in the present, there are several important differences. Langer's mindfulness interventions often involve working with information to be learned or manipulated and may include active, goal-oriented tasks, such as solving problems. In contrast, approaches derived from Eastern meditative traditions often are focused on the internal experiences of the participants (e.g., cognitions, emotions, sensations) and emphasize a less goal-directed nonjudgmental observation. Langer (1989) has cautioned against drawing unwarranted parallels between the two forms of mindfulness. For this reason, Langer's conception of mindfulness will not be addressed further in this chapter. Interested readers are referred to Langer (2002), which provides an interesting discussion of her conception of mindfulness and its relationship to positive psychology.

## Beneficial Effects of Mindfulness Training

A large and growing body of literature provides strong evidence for the efficacy of mindfulness-based interventions for a wide variety of psychological disorders, stress-related conditions, and maladaptive behaviors (for reviews, see Baer, 2003; Grossman, Niemann, Schmidt, & Wallach, 2004; Hayes, Luoma, Bond, Masuda, & Lillis, 2006; Lynch, Trost, Salsman, & Linehan, 2007). The most commonly studied interventions include acceptance and commitment therapy (ACT; Hayes, Strosahl, & Wilson, 1999), DBT (Linehan, 1993), mindfulness-based cognitive therapy (MBCT; Segal, Williams, & Teasdale, 2002), and mindfulness-based stress reduction (MBSR; Kabat-Zinn, 1982; 1990). In addition, several studies suggest that the practice of mindfulness leads to measurable improvements in objective tests of attentional processes, including sustained attention and working memory (Chambers, Lo, & Allen, 2008; Valentine and Sweet, 1999), the attentional blink (Slagter et al., 2007), executive attentional control (Jha, Krompinger, & Baime, 2007; Tang et al., 2007), and alerting and orienting (Jha et al., 2007).

## Relationships between Mindfulness and Central Constructs in Positive Psychology

### Well-Being

Several studies of mindfulness and psychological functioning have included measures of well-being. Subjective well-being (SWB) is composed of emotional responses (positive and negative affect), satisfaction with life, and satisfaction with various specific domains such as self, family, work, health, and leisure (Diener, Suh, Lucas, & Smith, 1999). Psychological well-being (PWB) entails perception of engagement with the existential challenges of life and includes components of autonomy, environmental mastery, personal growth, positive relations with others, purpose in life, and self-acceptance (Ryff & Keyes, 1995). Quality of life is a related concept that includes subjective evaluations of multiple life dimensions, such as quality of psychological and physical health, social relationships, and environment (Cella, 1994).

Several studies provide evidence of positive relationships between mindfulness and the various forms of well-being. Self-reported mindfulness has been found to relate positively with SWB and with several of its components, such as general affect, day-to-day affect, and life satisfaction (Brown & Kasser, 2005; Brown and Ryan, 2003). Participation in mindfulness- and acceptance-based interventions has been found to elicit increases in self-reported positive affect and quality of life in a variety of nonclinical, medical, and psychiatric populations (Carlson, Speca, Faris, & Patel, 2007; Kuyken et al., 2008; Shapiro, Astin, Bishop, & Cordova, 2005; Shapiro, Brown, & Biegel, 2007). Other studies have shown that individuals higher in dispositional mindfulness, who practice mindfulness meditation, or who have undergone a mindfulness-based intervention report higher levels of PWB (Baer et al., 2008; Brown & Ryan, 2003; Carmody & Baer, 2008; Lykins & Baer, 2009). It has also been suggested that attention to and engagement with present-moment experiences may promote pleasant states of flow, add clarity and vividness to current experience, and encourage sensory contact with life in ways that may be experienced as enjoyable (Brown & Ryan, 2003; Csikszentmihalyi, 1990).

## Character Strengths and Virtues

In order to promote the scientific study of optimal human functioning, the field of positive psychology has developed a framework for defining, classifying, and measuring the strengths and virtues that exemplify good character (Peterson & Seligman, 2004). Virtues are core characteristics that have been recognized and endorsed by numerous philosophical and religious traditions. The six virtues in this classification system are wisdom, courage, humanity, justice, temperance, and transcendence. Each virtue is defined by three to five character strengths through which the virtue is manifested or achieved. For example, the virtue of wisdom is expressed through creativity, curiosity, love of learning, open-mindedness, and perspective (Peterson & Seligman, 2004), and the virtue of humanity is achieved through kindness, love, and social intelligence. All of the 24 currently recognized character strengths within this classification system meet a set of criteria: They (a) contribute to fulfillment for the self or others, (b) are morally valued independently of tangible outcomes they may produce, (c) do not diminish others and tend to elevate those who witness them, eliciting admiration rather than jealousy, (d) have a clear opposite that is negative, (e) are trait-like (occurring across situations and consistently over time), (f) are not redundant with other strengths, (g) are embodied at

strikingly high levels in some individuals, (h) are shown precociously by some children or youth, (i) are absent in some individuals, and (j) have institutions and societal practices that cultivate and sustain them (Peterson, 2006; Peterson & Seligman, 2004).

Relationships between mindfulness and the strengths and virtues of this classification system have not been investigated in a systematic or comprehensive way. However, intersections between these two bodies of literature can be noted and are summarized in the following paragraphs.

As noted earlier, the virtue of *wisdom* includes five specific strengths: creativity, curiosity, open-mindedness, love of learning, and perspective. Theoretical and empirical work suggests interesting connections between mindfulness and some of these strengths. For example, Bishop et al. (2004) described curiosity about one's own sensations, cognitions, and emotions as a central component of mindfulness. The Toronto Mindfulness Scale (Lau et al., 2006) is a self-report instrument based on this conceptualization of mindfulness and includes two factors: curiosity and decentering. Scores on both factors were shown to increase with participation in MBSR, and both were related to the extent of meditation experience in regular practitioners. Meditation practice has also been shown to relate positively to the *openness to experience* domain of personality (Brown & Ryan, 2003; Lykins & Baer, 2009), which includes intellectual curiosity and receptivity to a wide range of ideas, values, and activities (Costa & McCrae, 1992). Sugiura (2004) reported that a self-reported mindful stance toward thoughts was positively related to the perceived quality of problem solving, suggesting that mindfulness may be important in effective critical thinking. Finally, theoretical work has suggested that mindfulness should promote wisdom, learning, and creativity by allowing individuals to disengage from conditioning (Kristeller, 2003) and by stilling the mind, thus promoting optimal conditions for generative thinking and reflection (Fisher, 2006).

Four specific character strengths exemplify the virtue of *courage:* bravery (valor), persistence (perseverance, industriousness), integrity (authenticity, honesty), and vitality (zest, enthusiasm, vigor, energy). Research has demonstrated several connections between mindfulness and these strengths. Self-reported mindfulness has been found to relate positively with a multicomponent measure of authenticity, with higher scores on both mindfulness and authenticity related to lower levels of verbal defensiveness (Lakey, Kernis, Heppner, & Lance, 2008). Heppner and Kernis (2007) also note that higher levels of self-reported mindfulness are related to higher levels of self-esteem, as well as more stable and less contingent self-esteem, meaning that feelings of self-worth are not highly vulnerable to challenge. Thus, authenticity is promoted by reducing the need for excessive self-protection or self-promotion (Heppner & Kernis, 2007). Further, higher levels of autonomously motivated behavior have been found in individuals higher in trait mindfulness, regardless of their implicitly assessed orientation toward autonomy or heteronomy (Levesque & Brown, 2007), again suggesting that mindfulness is associated with more authentic behavior. These findings are consistent with research on self-determination theory (Deci & Ryan, 2000) which shows that autonomous motivation and a focus on intrinsic goals yields greater psychological health than behavior motivated by perceived external pressures (Deci & Ryan, 2008).

Several studies supporting a link between mindfulness and vitality have also been reported, though the concept is often not framed positively. Improvements in self-reported vitality and vigor have been demonstrated following mindfulness-based interventions in both medical and nonclinical populations (Reibel, Greeson, Brainard, & Rosenzweig, 2001; Tang et al., 2007). Multiple studies have demonstrated that such participation leads to self-reported decreases in fatigue (Carlson & Garland, 2005; Kaplan, Goldenberg, & Galvan, 1993; Surawy, Roberts, & Silver, 2005), which may be inversely related to vitality. The strength of persistence has only rarely been addressed. However, high-level canoeists showed increased repetitions in an inclined rowing exercise following intervention with ACT (which includes mindfulness training), though performance was similarly improved by a hypnotic intervention (Garcia, Villa, Cepeda, Cueto, & Montes, 2004).

The virtue of *humanity* includes three specific character strengths: love (close relationships), kindness (generosity, nurturance, care, compassion), and social intelligence (emotional intelligence, understanding of others and social situations). Relationships between mindfulness and these strengths have been demonstrated. For example, self-reported mindfulness has been shown to be related to emotional intelligence (Baer et al., 2004; Brown & Ryan, 2003). Several studies support a link between mindfulness and kindness

toward the self. In fact, the concept of self-compassion (a caring and non-evaluative self-attitude) includes a mindfulness factor, along with components of self-kindness and common humanity (Neff, 2003). Given their conceptual overlap, it is not surprising that mindfulness-based interventions have been shown to increase self-compassion in various populations (Proulx, 2008; Shapiro et al., 2005; Shapiro et al., 2007). Several authors have theorized that mindfulness promotes attunement, connection with others, closeness in relationships, and interaction styles that support healthy relationship functioning (Kabat-Zinn, 1990; Welwood, 1996), and research supports these assertions. For example, Shapiro, Schwartz, & Bonner (1998) reported increases in empathy in premedical and medical students who completed MBSR. In nondistressed couples, a mindfulness-based relationship enhancement intervention has been shown to lead to increased relationship satisfaction, autonomy, relatedness, closeness, and acceptance of one another (Carson, Carson, Gil, & Baucom, 2004), while higher levels of self-reported dispositional mindfulness have been shown to relate to higher levels of relationship satisfaction, a greater ability to respond to relationship stress effectively, and lower levels of emotional stress, both at baseline and during conflict (Barnes, Brown, Krusemar, Campbell, & Rogge, 2007). As some evidence suggests that physiological arousal during conflict is related to subsequent consideration of dissolution, separation, and divorce (Gottman, 1993), this lower level of arousal associated with mindfulness may be an important predictor of long-term relationship success. Finally, studies of ACT, which includes training in mindfulness skills, have shown reduced stigmatizing attitudes (which are probably negatively associated with empathy and compassion) among mental health professionals and students toward people with substance use (Hayes, Bissett et al., 2004) and other psychological disorders (Masuda et al., 2007).

Three specific character strengths comprise the virtue of *justice*: citizenship (social responsibility, loyalty, teamwork), fairness, and leadership. Very little empirical work on relationships between mindfulness and these characteristics has been conducted. Bond and Bunce (2000) showed that a worksite ACT intervention led to increases in the self-reported tendency to innovate at work. Bond, Hayes, & Barnes (2006) provide a theoretical argument that increasing psychological flexibility through ACT should facilitate adaptive organizational behavior (which presumably includes loyalty and teamwork). Boyatzis & McKee (2005) suggest that mindfulness (along with hope and compassion) can lead to enhanced leadership. However, additional empirical examination of these relationships is needed.

The virtue of *temperance* includes four specific character strengths: forgiveness/mercy, humility/modesty, prudence, and self-regulation/self-control. We found no literature assessing relationships between mindfulness and first three of these strengths. However, the relationship between mindfulness and self-regulation has been addressed extensively, both theoretically and empirically. Self-regulation is guided by goals or standards and includes both conscious and unconscious processes that operate through feedback loops to maintain functional stability and adaptability to change (Carver & Scheier, 1981; Shapiro & Schwartz, 2000). Baumeister (2002) describes self-regulation or self-control as the capacity to alter or override responses that various environmental conditions tend to evoke. Attentional control has long been recognized as critical to the processes that underlie regulation of behavior. Dysregulation can occur when internal signals are ignored, suppressed, or cognitively exaggerated (Shapiro & Schwartz, 2000). The intentional cultivation of mindful attention may promote self-regulation by allowing for increased attentional sensitivity to psychological, somatic, and environmental cues (Kabat-Zinn, 1982; Linehan, 1993). It also may encourage awareness of stimulus-response relationships previously associated with mindless, habitual, or overlearned behavior, functionally creating a gap between stimulus and response that allows the individual to choose behavior congruent with values, goals, or needs (Brown et al.; Leary, Adams, & Tate, 2006). In support of these ideas, Wenk-Sormaz (2005) reported that a mindfulness induction in a laboratory setting promoted less automatized and habitual responding in word production and emotional Stroop tasks. Baumeister, Heatherton, & Tice (1994) describe research showing that the intentional direction of attention can allow individuals to override unwanted responses, thus promoting more effective self-regulation. Other research has shown that self-reported dispositional mindfulness is associated with goal setting and goal clarity (Kee & Wang, 2008). Chatzisarantis & Hagger (2007) reported that mindfulness moderated the relationship between intentions and behavior, such that those higher in mindfulness were more likely to behave consistently with their intentions.

Weiss, Nordlie, & Siegel (2005) found that adults who participated in MBSR as an adjunct to individual psychotherapy showed greater gains on a measure of self-directed goal achievement relative to a control group receiving individual therapy only.

While most of the literature linking mindfulness and self-regulatory abilities focuses on effortful self-control, other work suggests that mindfulness may promote hypo-egoic self-regulation in which deliberate, conscious control over one's behavior is relinquished. Leary et al. (2006) suggest that under some circumstances, deliberate efforts to control one's own behavior can be counterproductive. Such efforts may lead to disruption of complex behaviors that can be skillfully performed automatically. Thus, for example, when engaged in sports or music performance, it may be more adaptive to be absorbed in the game or the music than to be consciously trying to control one's performance. During hypo-egoic self-regulation, self-awareness is lowered because attention is focused externally on the task at hand. When self-focused thoughts occur, they tend to be concrete, present-focused, and specific to the immediate task (e.g., shooting the basketball), rather than abstract or ruminative (e.g., "am I really successful at this?" or "am I making a good impression?"). As a result, behavior is more natural, spontaneous, or automatic. An example of a hypo-egoic state is *flow*, in which ongoing activity requires so much concentration that none is available for self-consciousness or self-relevant thoughts (Csikszentmihalyi, Abuhamdeh, & Nakamura, 2005). Such states may occur naturally. However, from the perspective of self-regulation, the critical issue is whether individuals can enter such states voluntarily. The practice of mindfulness is theorized to cultivate the ability to engage in hypo-egoic self-regulation when it would be adaptive to do so, by focusing attention directly on the task at hand and engaging in highly concrete task-relevant thinking, when thinking is required (Leary et al., 2006).

Five specific character strengths exemplify the virtue of *transcendence*: appreciation of beauty and excellence (awe, wonder, elevation), gratitude, hope (optimism, future-mindedness), humor (playfulness), and spirituality (religiousness, faith, purpose). Unfortunately, little research on the relationships between mindfulness and most of these strengths has been conducted. One study demonstrated that participation in a mindfulness-based relationship enhancement intervention led to higher levels of optimism in individual participants (Carson et al., 2004). Leary et al. (2006) suggest that mindfulness practice may cultivate the ability to enter voluntarily into states of transcendence, in which the individual experiences a sense of oneness or unity with nature, the universe, or God, but no empirical study of this question was found. More extensive work has been done on spirituality. Several studies have demonstrated that participation in mindfulness-based interventions leads to increases in self-reported spirituality (Carmody, Reed, Kristeller, & Merriam, 2008; Carson et al., 2004). While some research has demonstrated that mindfulness relates positively with religious values (Heaven & Ciarrochi, 2007), other work has shown that the variables predicting mindfulness overlap little with those explaining variance in church attendance, with the exception of spiritual mindedness (Brinkerhoff & Jacob, 1999). Other research has demonstrated that engaging in a loving-kindness meditation practice led to increases in mindfulness and purpose in life (Fredrickson, Cohn, Coffey, Pek, & Finkel, 2008).

### Is Mindfulness a Character Strength?

Mindfulness meets most of the criteria summarized earlier for defining a character strength. Relationships between mindfulness and well-being suggest that mindfulness contributes to self-fulfillment. In Buddhist traditions, mindfulness is embedded in a system of moral and ethical conduct, and the practice of mindfulness is described as a way of cultivating compassion for all living beings, suggesting that mindfulness should not diminish others. Mindfulness appears to have a nonfelicitous opposite (mindlessness), which is associated with impulsive, automatic, thoughtless behavior that can be harmful to self and others. As noted earlier, mindfulness is often described as trait-like, in that some individuals are consistently more likely than others to be mindful in general daily life. Although mindfulness is significantly correlated with many character strengths, these correlations are not large enough to suggest that it is redundant with any of them. Individuals who embody extremely high levels of mindfulness (typically Buddhist monks with many years of intensive meditation experience) have been studied in laboratory research (Brefczynski-Lewis, Lutz, Schaefer, Levinson, & Davison, 2007; Lutz, Greischar, Rawlings, Ricard, & Davidson, 2004) and shown to have brain functions that differ substantially

from those of the general population. Prodigies in childhood have not been studied in the psychological literature, and it is unclear whether mindfulness is completely absent in some persons. Kabat-Zinn (2003) describes mindfulness as an inherent human capacity and notes that "we are all mindful, to one degree or another, moment by moment" (pp. 145–146). However, institutions and associated rituals for the cultivation of mindfulness have existed for centuries, in the form of meditation centers run by recognized teachers who offer guidance and instruction in meditation practices described in ancient texts that have been preserved, translated, and discussed by generations of scholars in many cultures.

On the other hand, if mindfulness were defined as a character strength, it would be unclear to which virtue it should be assigned. The small body of literature just reviewed includes empirical evidence and theoretical writings suggesting that mindfulness is related to many of the virtues in this classification system. For this reason, we do not propose that mindfulness should be defined as a character strength or a virtue. Rather, we suggest that mindfulness is an attentional stance, or a way of relating to one's present-moment experiences, that probably cultivates a wide range of strengths and virtues.

### How Does Mindfulness Cultivate Optimal Psychological Functioning?

Each of the mindfulness-based interventions mentioned earlier is based on theoretical foundations that suggest mechanisms or processes through which the practice of mindfulness should lead to improved psychological functioning (see Baer & Huss, 2008, for a brief review). In addition, several theories of self-awareness can be useful in understanding the beneficial effects of mindfulness training (Brown et al., 2007). The concept of decentering, also known as distancing, disidentification, defusion (Hayes et al. 1999), or re-perceiving (Shapiro, Carlson, Astin, & Freedman, 2006), is a common element in many of these theoretical approaches. Decentering has been defined as the ability to observe one's thoughts and feelings with the recognition that they are transitory events that do not necessarily reflect on reality, truth, or self-worth; are not necessarily important; and do not require particular behaviors in response (Fresco et al., 2007). Decentering was recognized as an important concept in the early days of cognitive therapy, where it was discussed primarily in relation to thoughts (Hollon & Beck, 1979). Decentering enables clients in cognitive therapy to recognize their negative thoughts as mental phenomena or ideas to be tested, rather than as aspects of the self or as facts. In mindfulness-based interventions, decentering is broadly defined to include all internal experiences (cognitions, sensations, and emotions), rather than just thoughts. Decentering reduces the behavioral impact of cognitions, emotions, and sensations, because people come to see them as events to be noticed but necessarily believed or acted on. Thus, participants in mindfulness-based therapies become better able to behave in accordance with their most deeply held values and associated goals in life, rather than in the service of controlling or avoiding their thoughts and feelings. In ACT, this combination of mindful acceptance of internal experience with commitment to values-consistent behavior is known as psychological flexibility (see Hayes & Strosahl, 2004, for more detail).

Regularly adopting a decentered stance toward internal experiences appears to have outcomes consistent with research literature on the forms and consequences of self-focused attention. Ingram (1990) defines self-focused attention as awareness of internally generated information, including bodily sensations, cognitions, and emotional states. The tendency to engage in excessive and inflexible self-focused attention is associated with many psychological disorders (Harvey, Watkins, Mansell, & Shafran, 2004) and with general negative affect in clinical and nonclinical populations (Mor & Winquist, 2002). Self-focused attention is closely related to rumination, a type of unproductive, repetitive, and self-focused thinking that occurs in several forms of psychopathology (Nolen-Hoeksema, Wisco, & Lyubomirsky, 2008). However, self-focused attention also has positive correlates, including greater self-knowledge and insight (Nasby, 1989), behavioral self-regulation (Carver & Scheier, 1981), and emotion regulation (Stanton, Danoff-Burg, Cameron, & Ellis, 1994). Several authors have noted that different forms of self-focused attention have distinct functional properties (McFarland & Buehler, 1998; Trapnell & Campbell, 1999). Although ruminative self-focus leads to increased distress and pathology, an observational, open-minded, and exploratory self-focus is associated with adaptive outcomes. Mindfulness training encourages an experiential, nonjudgmental, and nondiscursive awareness of

internal stimuli in which they are simply observed (Teasdale, 1999), and recent experimental research suggests that experiential (mindful) self-focus induced in a laboratory setting has beneficial outcomes relative to analytical, ruminative self-focus (Watkins & Teasdale, 2004). Overall, the literature suggests that individuals higher in dispositional mindfulness, or who cultivate mindfulness through meditation or skills training, may learn to engage in adaptive forms of self-focused attention rather than dysfunctional maladaptive forms such as rumination, and that this tendency may be an important mechanism accounting for the relationship between mindfulness and healthy psychological functioning (Baer, 2009).

This formulation can be integrated with other self-awareness theories to help explain how mindfulness facilitates optimal psychological functioning. For example, self-regulation and self-discrepancy theories (Carver & Scheier, 1998; Higgins, Bond, Klein, & Strauman, 1986) suggest that self-awareness leads to recognition of discrepancies between one's current state and a standard, which in turn leads to behavior to minimize the discrepancies. In contrast, mindful awareness encourages nonjudgmental observation of thoughts, including discrepancy-related thoughts, as they come and go. For example, if the thought, "I should be more successful" arises, the mindful individual will recognize this as a thought, observe it nonjudgmentally, and return attention to the present moment, without becoming absorbed in ruminations about this topic or assuming that the thought represents important truths about the self. The mindful individual may or may not change ongoing behavior, depending on what is most consistent with the strengths and virtues that the individual most highly values. Thus, mindfulness facilitates decentered awareness of discrepancy-based thoughts as well as deliberate actions that may not be consistent with automatic discrepancy-reducing behaviors (Evans, Baer, & Segerstrom, 2009).

## Moving Forward

Although the literature showing relationships between mindfulness and character strengths is intriguing and growing, it has limitations. When mindfulness is related to one of the character strengths, it is not always clear that mindfulness is promoting the character strength. It is possible that the character strength promotes increased mindfulness (Masicampo & Baumeister, 2007), that they facilitate each other over time, or that both are due to a third variable. Therefore, we suggest that relationships between mindfulness and optimal psychological functioning should be more systematically investigated, with the goal of clarifying whether (and under what conditions) mindfulness is a causal agent in the cultivation of strengths, virtues, and well-being. Experimental and longitudinal research, using a wide range of measures in varied populations, will be required. The effects of dispositional mindfulness, the regular practice of mindfulness meditation, participation in mindfulness-based interventions, and laboratory-based mindfulness inductions on behaviors that represent positive psychology constructs should be investigated. The developmental course of mindfulness over the lifespan, as well as the effects of mindfulness training in children and adolescents, should be studied. In addition, if mindfulness is more conclusively shown to cultivate optimal psychological functioning, it will be critical to understand the mechanisms through which this occurs. Mediational and process-oriented studies will be required to clarify whether theoretical formulations described earlier are accurate.

We also suggest that this line of research has great potential for facilitating optimal psychological functioning. If mindfulness training has the broad range of positive outcomes supported by the current literature, then its potential contributions to the central constructs of positive psychology are substantial. For example, the positive psychology literature includes the concept of *signature strengths*. These are character strengths that individuals identify as part of their essential, authentic selves. Peterson & Seligman (2004) note that most adults can readily identify from three to seven of the character strengths as inherent parts of themselves, or "the real me" (p. 18). They also suggest that the exercise of signature strengths is fulfilling, exciting, and invigorating. If this is true, then what stops people from exercising their strengths more consistently and experiencing greater fulfillment? Environmental constraints (such as jobs that do not allow people to draw on their strengths) are an important factor. Children who grow up in disadvantaged environments may have limited opportunities to develop inherent strengths. From the perspective of mindfulness training, however, obstacles to engaging in highly valued behavior often take the form of negative thoughts

and feelings, which are probably inevitable in many situations in which strengths might be expressed. Exercising leadership, for example, might involve publically taking an unpopular stand, which risks criticism, disapproval, and potential embarrassment. Thoughts such as "I'll look like an idiot if I do that" or unwillingness to experience the emotional discomfort associated with disapproval can inhibit the expression of leadership, even in individuals whose relevant skills are otherwise well developed and who harbor a desire to engage in more leadership. The practice of mindfulness encourages decentering from thoughts and feelings, rather than suppression or avoidance, allowing individuals to engage in the behavior they value, even while fully acknowledging any unpleasant thoughts and feelings that may be present. Clinical experience shows that people feel empowered when they realize that it is possible to move forward with highly valued behavior consistent with strengths and virtues, even while feeling sad, anxious, or angry and having discouraging thoughts. We suggest that this understanding is the key to the seemingly paradoxical nature of mindfulness training, in which the cultivation of nonjudgmental acceptance of present-moment experience, rather than trying to change it, leads to beneficial changes in psychological functioning.

Mindfulness is a relatively new topic in psychological research and clinical practice and has garnered so much attention and enthusiasm that it may appear to be a fad. We emphasize that mindfulness is not a panacea. The appropriateness of mindfulness training for some clinical disorders is still a matter of debate (Johanson, 2006; Shapiro & Carlson, 2009), and the importance of a sound theoretical foundation for applying mindfulness training to any specific problem has been clearly articulated (Teasdale, Segal, and Williams, 2003). In a few clinical outcome studies, mindfulness-based treatment has been ineffective for some participants (Teasdale et al., 2000) or less effective than an alternative intervention (Koszycki, Benger, Shlik, & Bradwejn, 2007). However, most of the empirical literature supports the utility of mindfulness training in a striking range of populations. From the perspective of positive psychology, we suggest that, if everyone has signature strengths, and if mindfulness training would enhance the ability to use them, then it is quite possible that mindfulness could be beneficial for most people.

Finally, in addition to biological, experiential, personal, and relational functioning, which have been discussed in the mindfulness literature, the scope of positive psychology includes optimal functioning at the institutional, cultural, and global levels (Sheldon, Fredrickson, Czikszentmihalyi, Rathunde, & Haidt, 1999). Similar statements have been made about mindfulness. Kabat-Zinn (2005) suggests that, "when cultivated and refined, mindfulness can function effectively on every level, from the individual to the corporate, the societal, the political, and the global" (p. 11). The empirical literature on mindfulness does not yet shed much light on societal, political, or global effects of mindfulness training. However, we suggest that the cultivation of optimal human functioning on a broad scale may have far-reaching outcomes, and that mindfulness training could make substantial contributions to this endeavor.

## References

Baer, R. A. (2003). Mindfulness training as a clinical intervention: A conceptual and empirical review. *Clinical Psychology: Science and Practice, 10*, 125–143.

Baer, R. A. (2009). Self-focused attention and mechanisms of change in mindfulness-based treatment. *Cognitive Behaviour Therapy, 38*, 15–20.

Baer, R. A., & Huss, D. B. (2008). Mindfulness- and acceptance-based therapy. In J. L. Lebow (Ed.), *Twenty-first century psychotherapies: Contemporary approaches to theory and practice* (pp. 123–166). Hoboken, NJ: John Wiley & Sons.

Baer, R. A., Smith, G. T., & Allen, K. A. (2004). Assessment of mindfulness by self-report: The Kentucky Inventory of Mindfulness Skills. *Assessment, 11*, 191–206.

Baer, R. A., Smith, G. T., Hopkins, J., Krietemeyer, J., & Toney, L. (2006). Using self-report assessment methods to explore facets of mindfulness. *Assessment, 13*, 27–45.

Barnes, S., Brown, K. W., Krusemark, E., Campbell, W. K., & Rogge, R. D. (2007). The role of mindfulness in romantic relationship satisfaction and responses to relationship stress. *Journal of Marital and Family Therapy, 33*, 482–500.

Baumeister, R. F. (2002). Ego depletion and self-control failure: An energy model of the self's executive function. *Self and Identity, 1*, 129–136.

Baumeister, R. F., Heatherton, T. F., & Tice, D. M. (1994). *Losing control: How and why people fail at self-regulation.* San Diego, CA: Academic Press.

Bishop, S. R., Lau, M., Shapiro, S., Carlson, L., Anderson, N., Carmody, J., et al., (2004). Mindfulness: A proposed operational definition. *Clinical Psychology: Science and Practice, 11*, 230–241.

Bond, F. W., & Bunce, D. (2000). Mediators of change in emotion-focused and problem-focused work-site stress management interventions. *Journal of Occupational Health Psychology, 5*, 156–163.

Bond, F. W., Hayes, S. C., & Barnes, H. D. (2006). Psychological flexibility, ACT, and organizational behavior. *Journal of Organizational Behavior Management, 26*, 25–54.

Boyatzis, R., & McKee, A. (2005). *Resonant leadership: Renewing yourself and connecting with others through mindfulness, hope, and compassion.* Boston, MA: Harvard Business School Publishing.

Brefczynski-Lewis, J. A., Lutz, A., Schaefer, H. S., Levinson, D. B., & Davidson, R. J. (2007). Neural correlates of attentional expertise in long-term meditation practitioners. *Proceedings of the National Academy of Sciences, 104*, 11483–11488.

Brinkerhoff, M. B., & Jacob, J. C. (1999). Mindfulness and quasi-religious meaning systems: An empirical exploration within the context of ecological sustainability and deep ecology. *Journal for the Scientific Study of Religion, 38*, 524–542.

Brown, K. W., & Kasser, T. (2005). Are psychological and ecological well-being compatible? The role of values, mindfulness, and lifestyle. *Social Indicators Research, 74*, 349–368.

Brown, K. W., & Ryan, R. M. (2003). The benefits of being present: Mindfulness and its role in psychological well-being. *Journal of Personality and Social Psychology, 84*, 822–848.

Brown, K. W., Ryan, R. M., & Creswell, J. D. (2007). Mindfulness: Theoretical foundations and evidence for its salutary effects. *Psychological Inquiry, 18*, 211–237.

Carlson, L. E., & Garland, S. N. (2005). Impact of mindfulness-based stress reduction (MBSR) on sleep, mood, stress and fatigue symptoms in cancer outpatients. *International Journal of Behavioral Medicine, 12*, 278–285.

Carlson, L. E., Speca, M., Faris, P., & Patel, K. D. (2007). One year pre-post intervention follow-up of psychological, immune, endocrine and blood pressure outcomes of mindfulness-based stress reduction (MBSR) in breast and prostate cancer outpatients. *Brain, Behavior, and Immunity, 21*, 1038–1049.

Carmody, J., & Baer, R. A. (2008). Relationships between mindfulness practice and levels of mindfulness, medical and psychological symptoms, and well-being in a mindfulness-based stress reduction program. *Journal of Behavioral Medicine, 31,* 23–33.

Carmody, J., Reed, G., Kristeller, J., & Merriam, P. (2008). Mindfulness, spirituality, and health-related symptoms. *Journal of Psychosomatic Research, 64,* 393–403.

Carson, J. W., Carson, K. M., Gil, K. M., & Baucom, D. H. (2004). Mindfulness-based relationship enhancement. *Behavior Therapy, 35,* 471–494.

Carver, C. S., & Scheier, M. F. (1981). *Attention and self-regulation: A control-theory approach to human behavior.* New York: Springer-Verlag.

Carver, C. S., & Scheier, M. F. (1998). *On the self-regulation of behavior.* NY: Cambridge University Press.

Cella, D. F. (1994). Quality of life: Concepts and definition. *Journal of Pain and Symptom Management, 9,* 186–192.

Chambers, R., Lo, B. C. Y., & Allen, N. B. (2008). The impact of intensive mindfulness training on attentional control, cognitive style, and affect. *Cognitive Therapy and Research, 32,* 303–322.

Chatzisarantis, N. L. D., & Hagger, M. S. (2007). Mindfulness and the intention-behavior relationship within the theory of planned behavior. *Personality and Social Psychology Bulletin, 33,* 663–676.

Costa, P. T., & McCrae, R. R. (1992). *NEO PI-R professional manual.* Odessa, FL: PAR.

Csikszentmihalyi, M. (1990). *Flow: The psychology of optimal experience.* NY: Harper Collins.

Csikszentmihalyi, M., Abuhamdeh, S., & Nakamura, J. (2005). Flow. In C. S. Dweck & A. J. Elliot (Eds.), *Handbook of competence and motivation* (pp. 589–608). NY: Guilford.

Deci, E. L., & Ryan, R. M. (2000). The "what" and "why" of goal pursuit: Human needs and the self determination theory of behavior. *Psychology Inquiry, 11,* 227–268.

Deci, E. L., & Ryan, R. M. (2008). Self-determination theory: A macrotheory of human motivation, development, and health. *Canadian Psychology, 49,* 182–185.

Diener, E., Suh, E. M., Lucas, R. E., & Smith, H. L. (1999). Subjective well-being: Three decades of progress. *Psychological Bulletin, 125,* 276–302.

Evans, D. R., Baer, R. A., & Segerstrom, S. C. (2009). The effects of mindfulness and self-consciousness on persistence. *Personality and Individual Differences, 47,* 379–382.

Fisher, R. (2006). Still thinking: The case for meditation with children. *Thinking Skills and Creativity, 1,* 146–151.

Fredrickson, B. L., Cohn, M. Coffey, K., Pek, J., & Finkel, S. (2008). Open hearts build lives: Positive emotions, induced through loving-kindness meditation, build consequential personal resources. *Journal of Personality and Social Psychology, 95,* 1045–1062.

Fresco, D. M., Moore, M. T., van Dulmen, M., Segal, Z. V., Ma, S. H., Teasdale, J. D. et al. (2007). Initial psychometric properties of the Experiences Questionnaire: Validation of a self-report measure of decentering. *Behavior Therapy, 38,* 234–246.

Garcia, R. F., Villa, R. S., Cepeda, N. T., Cueto, E. G., & Montes, J. M. G. (2004). Effect of hypnosis and Acceptance and Commitment Therapy (ACT) on physical performance in canoeists. *International Journal of Clinical and Health Psychology, 4,* 481–493.

Goldstein, J., & Kornfield, J. (1987). *Seeking the heart of wisdom: The path of insight meditation.* Boston: Shambhala.

Gottman, J. M. (1993). A theory of marital dissolution and stability. *Journal of Family Psychology, 7,* 57–75.

Grossman, P., Neimann, L., Schmidt, S., & Walach, H. (2004). Mindfulness-based stress reduction and health benefits: A meta-analysis. *Journal of Psychosomatic Research, 57,* 35–43.

Harvey, A., Watkins, E., Mansell, W., & Shafran, R. (2004). *Cognitive behavioural processes across psychological disorders: A transdiagnostic approach to research and treatment.* Oxford, UK: Oxford University Press.

Hayes, S. C., Bissett, R., Roget, N., Padilla, M., Kohlenberg, B. S., Fisher, G., et al. (2004). The impact of acceptance and commitment training and multicultural training on the stigmatizing attitudes and professional burnout of substance abuse counselors. *Behavior Therapy, 35,* 821–835.

Hayes, S. C., Luoma, J. B., Bond, F. W., Masuda, A., & Lillis, J. (2006). Acceptance and commitment therapy: Model, processes, and outcomes. *Behaviour Research and Therapy, 44,* 1–25.

Hayes, S. C., & Strosahl, K. D. (2004). *A clinical guide to acceptance and commitment therapy.* NY: Springer.

Hayes, S. C., Strosahl, K. D., & Wilson, K. G. (1999). *Acceptance and commitment therapy.* NY: Guilford Press.

Heaven, P. C. L, & Ciarrochi, J. (2007). Personality and religious values among adolescents: A three-wave longitudinal analysis. *British Journal of Psychology, 98,* 681–694.

Heppner, W. L., & Kernis, M. H. (2007). "Quiet ego" functioning: The complementary roles of mindfulness, authenticity, and secure high self-esteem. *Psychological Inquiry, 18,* 248–251.

Higgins, E. T., Bond, R. N., Klein, R., & Strauman, T. (1986). Self-discrepancies and emotional vulnerability: How magnitude, accessibility, and type of discrepancy influence affect. *Journal of Personality and Social Psychology, 51,* 5–15.

Hollon, S. D. & Beck, A. T. (1979). Cognitive therapy of depression. In P. C. Kendall & S. D. Hollon (Eds.), *cognitive-behavioral interventions: Theory, research, and procedures* (pp. 153–203). New York: Academic Press.

Ingram, R. E. (1990). Self-focused attention in clinical disorders: Review and a conceptual model. *Psychological Bulletin, 107,* 156–176.

Jha, A. P., Krompinger, J., & Baime, M. J. (2007). Mindfulness training modifies subsystems of attention. *Cognitive, Affective, and Behavioral Neuroscience, 7,* 109–119.

Johanson, G. (2006). A survey of the use of mindfulness in psychotherapy. *Annals of the American Psychotherapy Association, 9,* 15–24.

Kabat-Zinn, J. (1982). An outpatient program in behavioral medicine for chronic pain patients based on the practice of mindfulness meditation: Theoretical considerations and preliminary results. *General Hospital Psychiatry, 4,* 33–47.

Kabat-Zinn, J. (1990). *Full catastrophe living: Using the wisdom of your mind and body to face stress, pain, and illness.* NY: Delacorte.

Kabat-Zinn, J. (2003). Mindfulness-based interventions in context: Past, present, and future. *Clinical Psychology: Science and Practice, 10,* 144–156.

Kabat-Zinn, J. (2005). *Coming to our senses: Healing ourselves and the world through mindfulness.* NY: Hyperion.

Kaplan, K. H., Goldenberg, D. L, & Galvin, N. M. (1993). The impact of a meditation-based stress reduction program on fibromyalgia. *General Hospital Psychiatry, 15,* 284–289.

Kee, Y. H., & Wang, C. K. (2008). Relationships between mindfulness, flow dispositions and mental skills adoption: A cluster analytic approach. *Psychology of Sport and Exercise, 9,* 393–411.

Koszycki, D., Benger, M., Shlik, J., & Bradwejn, J. (2007). Randomized trial of a meditation-based stress reduction program and cognitive behavior therapy in generalized social anxiety disorder. *Behaviour Research and Therapy, 45,* 2518–2526.

Kristeller, J. L. (2003). Mindfulness, wisdom, and eating: Applying a multi-domain model of meditation effects. *Constructivism in the Humans Sciences, 8,* 107–118.

Kuyken, W., Byford, S., Taylor, R. S., Watkins, E., Holden, E., White, K. et al. (2008). Mindfulness-based cognitive therapy to prevent relapse in recurrent depression. *Journal of Consulting and Clinical Psychology, 76,* 966–978.

Lakey, C. E., Kernis, M. H., Heppner, W. L., & Lance, C. E. (2008). Individual differences in authenticity and mindfulness as predictors of verbal defensiveness. *Journal of Research in Personality, 42,* 230–238.

Langer, E. J. (1989). *Mindfulness.* Reading, MA: Addison Wesley.

Langer, E. J. (1997). *The power of mindful learning.* Reading, MA: Addison Wesley.

Langer, E. J. (2002). Well-being: Mindfulness vs. positive evaluation. In C. Snyder & S. Lopez (Eds.), *Handbook of positive psychology* (pp. 214–230). NY: Oxford University Press.

Lau, M. A., Bishop, S. R., Segal, Z. V., Buis, T., Anderson, N. D., Carlson, L., et al. (2006). The Toronto Mindfulness Scale: Development and validation. *Journal of Clinical Psychology, 62,* 1445–1467.

Leary, M. R., Adams, C. E., Tate, E. B. (2006). Hypo-egoic self-regulation: Exercising self-control by diminishing the influence of the self. *Journal of Personality, 74,* 1803–1831.

Levesque, C., & Brown, K. W. (2007). Mindfulness as a moderator of the effect of implicit motivational self-concept on day-to-day behavioral motivation. *Motivation and Emotion, 31,* 284–299.

Linehan, M. M. (1993). Cognitive-behavioral treatment of borderline personality disorder. New York: Guilford Press.

Lutz, A. Greischar, L. L., Rawlings, N. B., Ricard, M., & Davidson, R. J. (2004). Long-term meditators self-induce high-amplitude gamma synchrony during mental practice. *Proceedings of the National Academy of Sciences, 101,* 16369–16373.

Lykins, E., & Baer, R. (2009). Psychological functioning in a sample of long-term practitioners of mindfulness meditation. *Journal of Cognitive Psychotherapy, 23,* 226–241.

Lynch, T. R., Trost, W. T., Salsman, N., & Linehan, M. M. (2007). Dialectical behavior therapy for borderline personality disorder. *Annual Review of Clinical Psychology, 3,* 181–205.

Masicampo, E. J., & Baumeister, R. F. (2007). Relating mindfulness and self-regulatory processes. *Psychological Inquiry, 18,* 255–258.

Masuda, A., Hayes, S., Fletcher, L., Seignourel, P., Bunting, K., Herbst, S., et al. (2007). Impact of acceptance and commitment therapy versus education on stigma toward people with psychological disorders. *Behaviour Research and Therapy, 45,* 2764–2772.

McFarland, C., & Buehler, R., (1998). The impact of negative affect on autobiographical memory: the role of self-focused attention to moods. *Journal of Personality and Social Psychology,* 75, 1424–1440.

Mor, N. & Winquist, J. (2002). Self-focused attention and negative affect: A meta-analysis. *Psychological Bulletin, 128,* 638–662.

Nasby, W. (1989). Private and public self-consciousness and articulation of the self-schema. *Journal of Personality and Social Psychology, 56,* 117–123.

Neff, K. D. (2003). Self-compassion: An alternative conceptualization of a healthy attitude toward oneself. *Self and Identity, 2,* 85–101.

Nolen-Hoeksema, S., Wisco, & Lyubomirsky, S. (2008). Rethinking rumination. *Perspectives on Psychological Science, 3,* 400–424.

Peterson, C. (2006). *A primer in positive psychology.* NY: Oxford University Press.

Peterson, C., & Seligman, M. E. P. (Eds.) (2004). *Character strengths and virtues: A handbook and classification.* Washington, DC: American Psychological Association.

Proulx, K. (2008). Experience of women with bulimia nervosa in a mindfulness-based eating disorder treatment group. *Eating Disorders: The Journal of Treatment and Prevention, 16,* 52–72.

Reibel, D. K., Greeson, J. M., Brainard, G. C., & Rosenzweig, S. (2001). Mindfulness-based stress reduction and health-related quality of life in a heterogeneous patient population. *General Hospital Psychiatry, 23,* 183–192.

Ryff, C. D., & Keyes, C. L. (1995). The structure of psychological wellbeing revisited. *Journal of Personality and Social Psychology, 69,* 719–727.

Segal, Z. V., Williams, J. M. G., & Teasdale, J. D. (2002). *Mindfulness-based cognitive therapy for depression: A new approach to preventing relapse.* NY: Guilford Press.

Seligman, M. E. P. (2002). *Authentic happiness.* New York: Free Press.

Seligman, M. E. P., & Csikszentmihalyi, M. (2000). Positive psychology: An introduction. *American Psychologist, 55,* 5–14.

Shapiro, S. L., Astin, J. A., Bishop, S. R., & Cordova, M. (2005). Mindfulness-based stress reduction for health care professionals: Results from a randomized trial. *International Journal of Stress Management, 12,* 164–176.

Shapiro, S. L., Brown, K. W., & Biegel, G. M. (2007). Teaching self-care to caregivers: Effects of mindfulness-based stress reduction on the mental health of therapists in training. *Training and Education in Professional Psychology, 1,* 105–115.

Shapiro, S. L., & Carlson, L. E. (2009). *The art and science of mindfulness: Integrating mindfulness into psychology and the helping professions.* Washington, DC: APA.

Shapiro, S. L., Carlson, L. E., Astin, J. A., & Freedman, B. (2006). Mechanisms of mindfulness. *Journal of Clinical Psychology, 62,* 373–386.

Shapiro, S. L., & Schwartz, G. E. (2000). Intentional systemic mindfulness: An integrative model for self-regulation and health. *Advances in Mind-Body Medicine, 16,* 128–134.

Shapiro, S. L., Schwartz, G., & Bonner, G. (1998). Effects of mindfulness-based stress reduction on medical and premedical students. *Journal of Behavioral Medicine, 21,* 581–599.

Sheldon, K., Fredrickson, B., Rathunde, K., Csikszentmihalyi, M., & Haidt, J. (1999). *Positive psychology manifesto.* Presented at the Akumal 1 Conference, Akumal, Mexico.

Slagter, H., Lutz, A., Greishar, L., Francis, A., Nieuwenhuis, S., Davis, J., et al. (2007). Mental training affects distribution of limited brain resources. *PLoS Biology, 5,* e138.

Stanton, A. L., Danoff-Burg, S., Cameron, C. L., & Ellis, A. P. (1994). Coping through emotional approach: Problem of conceptualization and confounding. *Journal of Personality and Social Psychology, 66,* 350–362.

Sugiura, Y. (2004). Detached mindfulness and worry: A meta-cognitive analysis. *Personality and Individual Differences, 37,* 169–179.

Surawy, C., Roberts, J., & Silver, A. (2005). The effects of mindfulness training on mood and measures of fatigue, activity, and quality of life in patients with chronic fatigue syndrome on a hospital waiting list. *Behavioral and Cognitive Psychotherapy, 33,* 103–109.

Tang, Y., Ma, Y., Wang, J., Fan, Y., Feng, S., Lu, Q., et al. (2007). Short-term meditation training improves attention and self-regulation. *PNAS, 104,* 17152–17156.

Teasdale, J. D., (1999). Emotional processing, three modes of mind and the prevention of relapse in depression. *Behavior Research Therapy, 37,* S53–S77.

Teasdale, J. D., Segal, Z. V., & Williams, J. M. G. (2003). Mindfulness training and problem formulation. *Clinical Psychology: Science and Practice, 10,* 157–160.

Teasdale, J. D., Segal, Z. V., Williams, J. M. G., Ridgeway, V., Soulsby, J., & Lau, M. (2000). Prevention of relapse/recurrence in major depression by mindfulness-based cognitive therapy. *Journal of Consulting and Clinical Psychology, 68,* 615–623.

Trapnell, P. D., & Campbell, J. D. (1999). Private self-consciousness and the five-factor model of personality: Distinguishing rumination from reflection. *Journal of Personality and Social Psychology, 76,* 284–304.

Valentine, E. R., & Sweet, P. L. G. (1999). Meditation and attention: A comparison of the effects of concentrative and mindfulness meditation on sustained attention. *Mental Health, Religion, & Culture, 2,* 59–70.

Watkins, E., & Teasdale, J. D. (2004). Adaptive and maladaptive self-focus in depression. *Journal of Affective Disorders, 82,* 1–8.

Weiss, M., Nordlie, J. W., & Siegel, E. P. (2005). Mindfulness-based stress reduction as an adjunct to outpatient psychotherapy. *Psychotherapy and Psychosomatics, 74,* 108–112.

Welwood, J. (1996). Reflection and presence: The dialectic of self-knowledge. *Journal of Transpersonal Psychology, 28,* 107–128.

Wenk-Sormaz, H. (2005). Meditation can reduce habitual responding. *Alternative Therapies in Health and Medicine, 11,* 42–58.

# VIII

## Organizational Perspectives

# 23

# Positive Psychological Capital in the Workplace: Where We Are and Where We Need to Go

*Carolyn M. Youssef and Fred Luthans*

In order to restore more balance to the prevailing negativity, the positive psychology movement has emphasized positive character strengths, emotions, values, virtues, and cognitions at both self and interpersonal levels (e.g., see Lopez & Snyder, 2009; Peterson & Seligman, 2004; Snyder & Lopez, 2002). Although the initial research recognized the benefits of positivity on work performance outcomes, the vast majority of studies were concerned with relationships and health (e.g., see the meta-analysis by Lyubomirsky, King & Diener, 2005). Even though the field of management and organizational behavior over the years has given relatively more attention to the value of a positive perspective and constructs (see Luthans & Avolio, 2009 and Luthans & Youssef, 2009, which trace this history), the advent of positive psychology has also stimulated a refocus and testing of the applicability of new positive constructs in the development and effective management of human resources in today's workplaces.

Luthans (2002a, 2002b) introduced this positive organizational behavior, or simply POB, as "the study and application of positively oriented human resource strengths and psychological capacities that can be measured, developed, and effectively managed for performance improvement in today's workplace" (2002b, p. 59). POB is thus clearly distinguished not only from the positively oriented, faddish self-help literature in the popular business press but also from most of the other traditionally recognized positive constructs and approaches in the academic field of organizational behavior. This differentiation is attained through the definitional inclusion criteria that require a psychological capacity or resource to be theoretically grounded, measurable, state-like, open to development and management, and have performance impact (Luthans, 2002a, 2002b). To date, the psychological resources of efficacy, hope, resilience, and optimism have been identified to best meet these inclusion criteria and, when combined, have been termed psychological capital or simply PsyCap (Luthans, Luthans & Luthans, 2004; Luthans & Youssef, 2004; Luthans, Youssef & Avolio, 2007). This PsyCap is defined as "an individual's positive psychological state of development that is characterized by: (1) having confidence (self-efficacy) to take on and put in the necessary effort to succeed at challenging tasks; (2) making a positive attribution (optimism) about succeeding now and in the future; (3) persevering toward goals and, when necessary, redirecting paths to goals (hope) in order to succeed; and (4) when beset by problems and adversity, sustaining and bouncing back and even beyond (resilience) to attain success" (Luthans, Youssef, Avolio, 2007, p. 3).

The purpose of this chapter is to first assess where we are ("Taking Stock") with the theory, research, and application of positivity in the workplace in general and POB/PsyCap in particular. Special attention is initially given to the traditional role of positivity in organizational research. Next, an overview of a parallel development to POB/PsyCap as covered in this chapter that is called positive organizational scholarship, or simply POS, is given attention. The similarities and differences between POB/PsyCap and POS are discussed. This is followed by a brief critique of the positively oriented self-help fads found in the popular literature. Then an in-depth examination and assessment of where we are on all aspects of positive psychological capital (PsyCap) is made. The balance of the chapter uses this platform of where we are to launch into where PsyCap needs to go, needed future theory building, research, and practice.

## Taking Stock

As indicated, the importance of positivity in general and in the workplace in particular has deep historical roots. For example, the contents of Abraham Maslow's seminal works (e.g., his 1954 classic on Motivation and Personality had a chapter titled "Toward a Positive Psychology") and his final unpublished papers (see Hoffman, 1996) clearly indicate close similarities to the contents of this volume and other recent positive psychology references. From a psychology of health, happiness, and well being, to peak experiences and transcendence, and passing through creativity, gratitude, justice, and even realistic optimism, this historical legacy by no means reflects a "negative" psychology, but indeed attests to the fact that positive psychology is in fact at least decades, if not centuries, old. Similarly, from the recognized very beginning of the field of organizational behavior, the Hawthorne studies revealed that positive group dynamics, supervisory style, worker participation, and increased care and attention (i.e., the "Hawthorne effect") can influence workers' productivity and attitudes. These initiatives at

Hawthorne clearly went beyond simply fixing what was wrong with employees and with the work environment in terms of improving physical working conditions such as light intensity or implementing rest pauses. The same can be said for Douglas McGregor's (1960) pioneering Theory Y, a very positive alternative to the negatively oriented Theory X assumptions and approach to managing human resources.

In other words, it is not that positive psychology or the field of POB discovered the importance of positivity, but rather is simply calling for a refocus on positivity that cannot take place by solely extrapolating what is known based on a deficiency model. Positive and negative constructs are not simply polar opposites, neither in psychology (e.g., optimism vs. pessimism, Chang, D'Zurilla, & Maydeu-Olivares, 1994) nor in organizational behavior (e.g., job satisfaction vs. job dissatisfaction, Herzberg, Mausner, & Snyderman, 1959; organizational citizenship behaviors vs. counterproductive work behaviors, Sackett, Berry, Wiemann, & Laczo, 2006). We refer to this positive refocus as "old wine, old bottles... but perhaps a new restaurant" (Luthans & Avolio, 2009). This metaphor of a "new restaurant" is used to indicate that, although positivity has a long historical legacy in the organization sciences ("old wine, old bottles"), we would argue for a refocus with resulting new theory building, research, and application. This is opposed to the many management fads that tend to be surrounded with unsubstantiated claims of being "new wine," or the common criticism of positivity movements in general as "old wine in new bottles." With this "new restaurant" perspective (i.e., new context, under-recognized positive constructs) serving as a point of departure, we now take stock and assess some of the established as well as the recently emerging positively oriented constructs in the study of organizational behavior and human resource management.

## The Role of Positivity in Traditional Organizational Behavior Research and Practice

Before the emergence of POB, over the years there were many established streams of research based on positive constructs (see Wright & Quick, 2009 for a comprehensive history of positive organizational research). These can be classified into positive traits, states, attitudes, and behaviors. Positive traits used in organizational behavior research included stable characteristics that do not significantly vary over time or across situations such as intelligence or general mental abilities (e.g., Schmidt & Hunter, 2000), positive affectivity (e.g., George, 1991), the Big Five personality traits (Conscientiousness, Agreeableness, Extraversion, Emotional Stability, and Openness to Experience; e.g., Barrick & Mount, 1991), and core self-evaluations (self-esteem, generalized efficacy, locus of control, and emotional stability; e.g., Judge & Bono, 2001). Positive states are highly transient and situational, such as positive moods (e.g., George, 1991) or experiences of flow (Csíkszentmihályi, 2003), which contribute to the better understanding of organizational behavior. Positive work attitudes such as job satisfaction (e.g., see Wright, 2005) and organizational commitment (Allen & Meyer, 1990) incorporate the cognitions, emotions, and evaluations that can drive behavioral intentions and actual behaviors in the workplace. Positive behaviors are actions that are conducive to higher work productivity in general but also include organizational citizenship behaviors that represent those who go above and beyond the call of duty (Organ, 1988), as well as moral behavioral choices based on effective moral evaluations in ethically challenging situations (Jones, 1991). Behavioral management through positive reinforcement has also been established in organizational behavior research (Stajkovic & Luthans, 2003). This sampling is merely indicative of the widespread use of positive constructs in organizational behavior research over the years.

Stimulated by positive psychology and the perceived need to refocus on the positive in organizational studies, as indicated two parallel initiatives emerged—positive organizational scholarship (POS, Cameron, Dutton & Quinn, 2003) and positive organizational behavior (POB, Luthans, 2002a, 2002b). POS is defined as "the study of that which is positive, flourishing, and life-giving in organizations. Positive refers to the elevating processes and outcomes in organizations. Organizational refers to the interpersonal and structural dynamics activated in and through organizations, specifically taking into account the context in which positive phenomena occur. Scholarship refers to the scientific, theoretically derived, and rigorous investigation of that which is positive in organizational settings" (Cameron & Caza, 2004, p. 731). POB was defined in the introductory discussion and, despite the apparent similarities between POS and POB (e.g., positivity, scientific rigor, and organizational context), there are several differences at least in emphasis

if not substance. First, POS primarily emphasizes group and organizational-level variables and processes, while POB tends to focus more on individual-level psychological resources, a perspective that it shares with positive psychology. Again, this distinction on the unit of analysis does not preclude either approach from moving between levels (e.g., see the recent studies by Peterson & Zhang, in press; Walumbwa, Luthans, Avey & Oke, in press, on collective psychological capital and many individual level studies in POS). Second, although POS and POB share several positive constructs, POB emphasizes in its inclusion criteria the measurability and performance impact (broadly defined) of its constituent psychological resources, while POS utilizes a wider variety of organizational phenomena as indicators of positivity and its outcomes, lending itself to a more qualitative or mixed-methods study approach and making it more of an umbrella term for an emerging domain of study and application.

In addition to the expanding positive organizational research in the academic domain, there is accelerating growth in the popular positive self-help literature. Again, positivity is not new here either, with classics such as Norman Vincent Peale's *Power of Positive Thinking* or Dale Carnegie's *How to Win Friends and Influence People*. Representative of the more recent blockbuster, best-selling self-help books are Steven Covey's *Seven Habits of Highly Effective People* and Spencer Johnson's *Who Moved My Cheese?* These positive messages have found their way to practicing managers' minds, hearts, and bookshelves. They present intuitively appealing positive answers and practical guidelines to people-oriented challenges in the workplace. Management consultants have also utilized many of these approaches in employee selection, corporate training, and leadership and organizational development programs. Generally lacking evidence from theory and scientifically based research, these popular approaches too often lack sustainability and arguably take on the properties of a fad or "silver bullet" mentality.

On the other hand, the popular self-help literature does share some common characteristics with the academic literature in positive psychology, POS, POB, and PsyCap. Both tend to emphasize the internalization or mindset of positivity through self-awareness, self-evaluation, and self-development. At least implicitly, both tend to have an underlying cognitive-affective-social model advocating the importance of a holistic approach to understanding human behavior.

Most importantly, both are not only aimed at self-help, but they also share the goals and aspirations of increasing overall well-being and performance.

Despite these commonalities, on balance we would argue that the popular self-help literature suffers from a lack of scientific-based evidence. From reliance on anecdotal evidence, to flawed research design, to use of non-validated measures, to simplistic interpretation of survey data from convenience samples, to non-substantiated generalizations to populations that are significantly different from those studied, many management fads promoted by the popular literature at best lack sustainable impact and at worst have led practicing managers astray. However, a notable exception to this criticism of the practice literature is the Gallup Organization's strengths-based management and employee engagement integrated stream of research, publication, and consulting practice (e.g., Wagner & Harter, 2006). The Gallup research has found its way to the academic positivity literature due to scientific rigor (e.g., see Harter, Schmidt & Hayes, 2002). This literature advocates that stable, hard-wired talents should be emphasized in selection and placement to enhance the fit between employees and their jobs. It promotes key factors such as clear expectations, recognition, social support, participation, learning and growth opportunities, and others. These factors, when practiced within a strengths framework where employees are positioned to work, learn, and grow along their areas of strength, can increase employee engagement, leading to increased productivity and well-being (Harter, Schmidt & Hayes, 2002).

## Positive Organizational Behavior (POB) and Psychological Capital (PsyCap)

Besides recognizing the established and alternative positive approaches in the academic and practitioner literatures, the main intent of this chapter is to take stock of POB and PsyCap. As we indicated, POB focuses on theory-based positive constructs that can be validly measured, that are open to development and management in the workplace, and that have a measurable performance impact (Luthans, 2002a, 2002b). PsyCap combines the four criteria-meeting positive psychological resources of efficacy, hope, optimism, and resilience into a multidimensional core construct supported by theory (Luthans, Youssef & Avolio, 2007) and research (Luthans, Avolio, Avey & Norman, 2007). A 24-item PsyCap questionnaire (PCQ) has also been adapted from

published measures and developed (see Luthans, Youssef & Avolio, 2007, pp. 237–238 for the full PCQ and go to www.mindgarden.com for free permission to use for research purposes) and validated (Luthans, Avolio et al., 2007).

First, the positive constructs selected for inclusion in PsyCap are deeply rooted in several well-established theoretical traditions (Luthans, Youssef & Avolio, 2007). For example, PsyCap efficacy draws from Bandura's (1997) social cognitive theory and refers to "one's conviction (or confidence) about his or her abilities to mobilize the motivation, cognitive resources, and courses of action needed to successfully execute a specific task within a given context" (Stajkovic & Luthans, 1998, p.66). Following Bandura's (1997) emphasis on social cognitive capacities of symbolizing, forethought, observation, self-regulation, and self-reflection, efficacy or confidence can be built in a specific domain through mastery experiences, modelling and vicarious learning, social persuasion, and physiological and psychological arousal. Interestingly, while research supports that personal success, followed by vicarious (and modelling) success of relevant others, is most effective in building self-efficacy, more feel-good approaches that tend to rely on social persuasion (e.g., encouraging managers to support their employees with a "you can do it" attitude and language), physical arousal (e.g., eating right and exercising to increase physical fitness), and psychological arousal (e.g., listening to motivational speakers) are much more popular in practice.

PsyCap hope builds on the foundations of Snyder's (2000) hope theory and is defined as "a positive motivational state that is based on an interactively derived sense of successful (1) agency (goal-directed energy) and (2) pathways (planning to meet goals)" (Snyder, Irving, & Anderson, 1991, p. 287). While the agency component, also referred to as willpower, may have some conceptual and practical similarities to self-efficacy, hope's pathways or "waypower" component, which refers to the ability to generate alternative ways to achieve goals when faced with obstacles, is unique to hope. This goal-oriented and alternative pathways view is also unique to the research-based definitions of hope and stands in clear contrast to the everyday use of the word "hope" to indicate uncertainty (e.g., I hope I can do this) or unsubstantiated positivity (e.g., stay hopeful), which is finding its way to the practicing manager's language as well.

PsyCap optimism primarily draws from the positive psychology movement but is also rooted in established attribution and expectancy work motivation theories. It integrates positive general expectancies about the future (Carver & Scheier, 2002) with a positive explanatory style of past and current situations. Optimists attribute positive situations to internal, permanent, and pervasive causes and negative situations to external, temporary, and situational ones (Seligman, 1998). Optimism certainly shares some characteristics with efficacy and hope, e.g., positivity and psychological ownership or internalization (especially in relation to success). However, optimism is also distinguished by its generality, both in terms of scope, because it includes overarching positive future expectations (as opposed to efficacy being context specific, or hope being directed toward specific goals), and in terms of agency, since it utilizes both internal and external attributions. The external attributions are especially critical in negative situations in order for the individual to maintain positivity in times of failure. It is this latter aspect of externalizing negative events that has caused optimism to be particularly challenging in its applications to the workplace, due to its contradiction with notions of responsibility and accountability. This is why the qualifiers of "realistic" and "flexibility" are associated with PsyCap optimism (Luthans, Youssef et al., 2007).

PsyCap resilience draws from a long tradition in developmental and clinical psychology (Masten, 2001) and is defined as "the capacity to rebound or bounce back from adversity, conflict, failure, or even positive events, progress, and increased responsibility" (Luthans, 2002a, p. 702). Resilience is particularly distinguished from efficacy, hope, and optimism by being primarily reactionary in nature, but several aspects are also shared. For example, perseverance in resiliency is shared with efficacy, the emphasis on adaptive processes is shared with hope, and the balance between internal and external resources is shared with optimism. Although PsyCap resilience has been recognized as important, both in times of adversity and in positive events, the increased frequency and magnitude of economic setbacks suffered by organizations in recent times, and the resulting impact on personal and professional lives, have made resiliency surface as a very critical positive psychological resource.

The convergent and discriminant validity of the four constructs that constitute PsyCap support it as a multidimensional core construct

(see Luthans, Avolio et al., 2007), and by the same token the convergence and divergence between PsyCap and other related positive constructs also support its overall construct validity (see Avey, Luthans & Youssef, 2010, for a comprehensive review and research support for the value-added contribution of PsyCap over other positive constructs). Three critical attributes of PsyCap distinguish it from other positive constructs and approaches. The first is that PsyCap's level of analysis to date has been primarily the individual. Although PsyCap and its related models (e.g., authentic leadership, Avolio & Luthans, 2006) take into consideration organizational factors, such as those studied in POS (Cameron et al., 2003), these macro-level factors are primarily viewed as contextual variables that can facilitate, accelerate, or hinder PsyCap development. Also, recent research has demonstrated that PsyCap may play a mediating role in the supportive organizational climate-employee performance relationship (Luthans, Norman et al., 2008) and between authentic leadership and work groups' performance and citizenship behavior (Walumbwa et al., in press). This latter study also indicated the positive impact that collective PsyCap has on group-level performance.

A second major differentiation is PsyCap's state-like or developmental potential, which places it toward the state end of the much-debated trait-state continuum. On the trait end of the continuum, many of the "pure" traits discussed earlier or emphasized by much of the positive psychology literature may be genetically determined, "hard-wired," or can be developed only through lifelong development or exceptional trigger (or jolting) experiences. On the other hand, PsyCap has been shown to readily lend itself to development and management through relatively short training interventions (Luthans, Avey, Avolio, Norman, & Combs, 2006; Luthans, Avey, Avolio, & Peterson, 2010; Luthans, Avey, & Patera, 2008). On the state end of the continuum, "pure" states (e.g., pleasures, moods or emotions), which continuously fluctuate over time and across situations, can be found. On the other hand, unlike these pure states, PsyCap has some evidence of relative stability (e.g., see Luthans, Avolio et al., 2007). Effective human resources management training needs to have a reasonable time span impact (about six months, according to Wright, 2007) in order to capitalize on PsyCap's development and management, hence the term "state-like." This positioning of PsyCap as "state-like" is also in line with recent findings that, although an individual's positivity may have a nature- and nurture-determined baseline or "set point," and aside from the relatively small portion of positivity that is highly transient and circumstantial (e.g., income or location), there is significant room for managing one's positivity through intentional everyday cognitive, affective, social, and spiritual activities that can alter attention, interpretation, and retention processes (Diener & Biswas-Diener, 2008; Lyubomirsky, 2007).

Third, and perhaps most critical to organizational behavior as an applied field, is PsyCap's performance impact criterion. Positivity in general has been shown to improve performance in most life domains, including work (e.g., see Biswas-Diener & Dean, 2007; Diener & Biswas-Diener, 2008; Lyubomirsky, King, & Diener, 2005 for reviews). Most of the research to date on PsyCap has been devoted to testing the relationship with employees' work-related outcomes. Even after controlling for various individual differences such as demographics, personality traits, core self-evaluations, person-organization fit, and person-job fit, PsyCap has been shown to positively relate to a wide range of desirable outcomes such as in-role performance, job satisfaction, work happiness, organizational commitment, organizational citizenship behaviors, psychological well-being over time, job search behaviors, and negatively to undesirable stress, counterproductive work behaviors, cynicism, absenteeism, and turnover (Avey, Luthans & Jensen, 2009; Avey, Luthans, Smith & Palmer, 2010; Avey, Luthans & Youssef, 2010; Avey, Wernsing & Luthans, 2008; Larson & Luthans, 2006; Luthans, Avey, Clapp-Smith & Li, 2008; Luthans, Avolio et al., 2007; Luthans, Avolio, Walumbwa, & Li, 2005; Luthans, Norman et al., 2008) and at the group level citizenship behaviors and performance (Walumbwa et al., in press) and business unit performance (Peterson & Zhang in press).

Not only has this growing body of research established the relationship between PsyCap and employee performance and desirable attitudes and behaviors, but preliminary utility analysis has also indicated robust (over 200%) return on investment in PsyCap development, or what we refer to as "Return on Development" (ROD; see Luthans, Avey et al., 2006 and Luthans, Youssef & Avolio, 2007, for quantitative utility analysis based on realistic corporate data). Furthermore, the return on PsyCap development is not limited to immediate in-role performance but has also been shown to impact a wide range of work-related outcomes,

with established relationships to various long-term indicators of individual and organizational effectiveness and change (Avey, Wernsing et al., 2008; Avey, Luthans & Youssef, 2010). This broader, more holistic perspective of outcomes conceptualized for PsyCap (Youssef & Luthans, 2009) is in line with the essence of the positive psychology movement's emphasis on the whole person, positive organizational scholarship's emphasis on the contextualization and wider impact of positivity, and the increased emphasis on long-term effectiveness in management practice. For example, we have recently proposed that PsyCap can contribute to organizational virtuousness and can help virtuous business organizations in maintaining their success through crises, as well as during ordinary and even exemplary times (Youssef & Luthans, 2008).

## When PsyCap Is Not the Answer

Positivity in general, and positive organizational research in particular, has not been without its critics (e.g., see Fineman, 2006; George, 2004; Hackman, 2009; Lazarus, 2003). From underlying assumptions of human benevolence, to cross-cultural differences in valuing positivity and what is considered positive, organizational behavior research and practice may find some of the tenets of positivity at least questionable, if not disproved. Indeed, extreme positivity has been shown to have disadvantages (Diener & Biswas-Diener, 2008). Illusions and self-deceit can result from overconfidence, false hope, or unrealistic optimism, leading to wasted resources, faulty strategies, threats to the survival of the organization, and even to the physical or financial safety and well-being of its employees (see Luthans & Avolio, 2009; Luthans, Youssef, & Avolio, 2007, which have a potential "pitfalls" section at the end of each chapter).

On the other hand, the value of a balanced perspective of workplace positivity is clearly evident. Similar to the field of psychology, a deficit approach (e.g., emphasis on employee incompetence, disengagement, stress, and other forms of negative deviance) is far too common but can be argued as justifiable to the problem-oriented decision-making and resource allocation processes in traditional management practice. In other words, it is not that negativity per se is necessarily wrong or hurtful to performance. Instead, it is the emphasis and the ratio of negativity to positivity that needs to be revisited. For example, positive psychologist Barbara Fredrickson's "tipping point" ratio of three positives to one negative for effective performance needs to be recognized in the management field (Fredrickson & Losada, 2005). She uses the analogy of a sailing ship where the mast must be at least three times the length/depth of the keel (i.e., 3 : 1) to perform well. However, without the keel the ship would flounder and fall flat. "Without negativity you become Pollyanna. You lose touch with reality. You're not genuine" (Fredrickson, 2009, p.136).

Positivity alone is certainly not *the* answer and is *not* going to solve all individual, group, or organizational problems. Moreover, PsyCap per se cannot be expected to make employees happier and more productive when developed in isolation of its context. This context incorporates organizational-level variables such as the structure, strategy, and culture; employee-level factors such as personality traits and individual states; social interactions and relationships among managers and employees and their implications on effective leadership and social support; and the organization-employee interface that impacts perceptions of fit, work-life balance, and other critical determinants of personal fulfillment (and effectiveness) at work. Integration with the established organizational behavior literature on various constructs and approaches that may appear at least on the surface to be "negatively oriented" (e.g., unethical behavior, risk aversion, bureaucracy, stress, and negative attitudes) is also indispensable for a better understanding and effective management of positivity in the workplace (Avey et al., 2010; Youssef & Luthans, 2009).

**Moving Forward**

One clear direction for POB and PsyCap in moving ahead on their journey (not destination) is to heed the critics' warnings about becoming exclusive, elitist endeavors. They cannot afford to be just fads and instead must be founded on and/or build upon the decades of existing research. They cannot become elusive exercises in chasing ill-defined emotions with only the feel-good appearance of positivity. Indeed, it is easy for positivity research to fall into these pitfalls, especially given today's post-modern emphasis on hedonism. However, in line with our inquiry (rather than advocacy) position that we have taken with POB (see Luthans & Avolio, 2009), these warnings and criticisms have

promoted further theory building and the development and testing of integrated conceptual frameworks in the POB/PsyCap literature (e.g., see Avey et al., 2010; Youssef & Luthans, 2009).

**Future Directions for PsyCap Research**

Although, as indicated above, a PsyCap measure has been determined and validated, has been clearly demonstrated to be related to important outcomes, and development interventions have been successfully implemented, as with any relatively new domain of study, these research results should be viewed as only the first steps. There remains the need for better understanding of the work-life interface that may hinder or facilitate, accelerate, or otherwise help shape an individual's level of positivity, both in terms of and beyond PsyCap. Individual employees' PsyCap levels are also likely to represent the building blocks of PsyCap in groups, organizations, and communities. In other words, future research needs to explore alternative approaches to measuring and developing PsyCap in various contexts and at multiple levels of analysis.

With respect to measurement, in most academic disciplines researchers tend to build expertise in one or a very few research methods. These methods tend to then become strongly associated with the areas of research interest of those researchers. So far, PsyCap research has been almost exclusively cross-sectional designs and quantitative analysis. However, with positivity being a complex integration of cognitive, affective, and social evaluations, many of which are subjective in nature (e.g., subjective well-being, see Biswas-Diener & Dean, 2007; Diener & Biswas-Diener, 2008; Lyubomirsky, 2007; Wright, 2005, 2007), it becomes critical to account for that complexity through qualitative methods or through methods that integrate both quantitative and qualitative approaches (i.e., mixed methods). While harder to "sell" in management research and practice, where the emphasis is on quantifying return on investment, qualitative methods may facilitate a richer understanding of the antecedents, processes, and consequences of positivity in general and workplace PsyCap in particular. Qualitative, alternative methodologies may help in the further development of more viable theoretical understanding of positivity and workplace PsyCap.

To date, PsyCap development has been empirically demonstrated in short workshop training interventions (Luthans, Avey et al.,2010) and even when delivered online (Luthans, Avey & Patera, 2008). Preliminary experimental research has also demonstrated that such PsyCap training has a casual impact on improving participants' performance (Luthans, Avey et al., 2010). The familiarity of corporate trainers and trainees with this type of "micro-intervention" has facilitated the initial acceptance and testing of developing PsyCap in employees and leaders. On the other hand, the salience of the context within which positivity in general and PsyCap in particular develops over time—including leadership effectiveness, supervisor and coworker support, employee job responsibilities and challenges, and the interface between work and other life domains—seems to indicate much untapped potential that can be realized from a broader range of PsyCap development approaches (see Avolio & Luthans, 2006). For example, given the effectiveness of one-on-one approaches in developing PsyCap's constituent resources (e.g., vicarious learning or modelling in developing self-efficacy), the coaching approach that has been developed and implemented in developing happiness (Biswas-Diener & Dean, 2007) may also lend itself to PsyCap development. Moreover, positivity in general, and PsyCap in particular, should be taken into consideration and fully integrated in various human resource management programs such as job design, compensation, performance appraisal, succession planning, and team building.

In addition to future training and development opportunities, a critical aspect that is yet to be explored in positive organizational behavior research are the possible discontinuities. Although empirical findings to date are consistent in supporting desirable relationships between PsyCap and an increasing number of employee outcomes, various biases (e.g., systematic self-selection into or out of training interventions by participants who are higher or lower on PsyCap) may disguise the realities of those relationships. For example, occasional negative relationships, especially at high levels of PsyCap, may indicate curvilinear relationships in which extreme PsyCap may be "too much of a good thing," a possibility that has been found in the positivity (see Fredrickson, 2009) and in particular the happiness (see Diener & Biswas-Diener, 2008) literature. Moreover, even though some studies may yield no statistically significant findings, especially at restricted ranges of PsyCap, such findings may indicate the existence of thresholds, saturation points, tipping points, trigger events, or other discontinuities that the sampling approach utilized may have missed. These discontinuities are worth studying in and of themselves for a better understanding of the role of positivity in general and the contribution of PsyCap in the workplace in particular.

Levels of analysis need to also be carefully considered, especially since PsyCap is now being studied at the group (e.g., collective PsyCap, Walumbwa et al., in press; Peterson & Zhang, in press) and organizational (e.g., virtuous organizations, Youssef & Luthans, 2008) levels. Although now underway, considerable cross-level collaboration potential is still untapped for researchers in positive psychology, positive organizational behavior, and positive organizational scholarship (e.g., see Wright & Goodstein, 2007). This research should take into account not only the co-presence of various levels of analysis but also the interaction across those levels.

Because of the state-like nature of PsyCap and the need for more evidence of a causal link between PsyCap and outcomes, a call has recently been made for longitudinal PsyCap research (Avey, Luthans, & Mhatre, 2008), and initial longitudinal research has found a relationship between employees' PsyCap and their objective performance at multiple points in time (Peterson, Luthans, Avolio, Walumbwa, & Zhang, 2010). Such longitudinal research can facilitate the better understanding of the various discontinuities outlined earlier, as well as clarifying the trait-state distinction (e.g., the initial longitudinal study found within-person PsyCap variability over time, Peterson et al., 2010). This apparent malleability of PsyCap over time would in turn increase the effectiveness of human resource management initiatives by shedding more light on the most appropriate courses of action, e.g., the recruitment and selection of those with certain stable traits versus development of state-like PsyCap. This research on developable PsyCap could also lead to anticipation and even proactive design of trigger events that can foster and accelerate PsyCap. Over time PsyCap could be integrated within the larger framework of organizational strategy, structure, and culture. As for establishing a causal relationship between PsyCap and outcomes, the longitudinal studies can contribute, but of course true experimental designs are still needed. Like with the group- and organizational-level analyses of PsyCap, although research has started, more PsyCap longitudinal and experimental designed research is needed for the future.

Finally, PsyCap has never been intended to be exclusive to the four psychological resources of efficacy, hope, optimism, and resilience. Other positive psychological capacities have also been investigated for their fit with the inclusion criteria, and some have been shown to be promising for future research (see Chapters 6 and 7 in Luthans, Youssef & Avolio, 2007). It is critical for PsyCap, and the positivity domain in general, especially at their current stages, to maintain openness and inclusiveness in order for these approaches to further develop toward their full potential. In light of the current economic turmoil and seeming ethical meltdown in the business environment, there is an unprecedented need for openness to new ideas and approaches that can enhance corporate effectiveness in general and that can specifically accomplish this goal through increased emphasis on the importance of human resources and their performance, attitudes, and behaviors (e.g., see Cascio & Cappelli, 2009). Expanding PsyCap research to include relevant positive constructs such as creativity, courage, wisdom, flow, spirituality, authenticity, gratitude, forgiveness, and others, as well as the relationships, interactions, and discontinuities within and between these and other constructs, will likely enhance our understanding of positivity in the workplace and help meet the daunting challenges that lie ahead.

## Future Directions for the Application of Positivity and Psycap

Since positivity and PsyCap are relatively new to actual organizational practice, they may be approached by managers and decision makers with caution, faced with doubts, or most commonly just paid lip service to give an impression of openness to new ideas and a caring, humanistic attitude toward the people-side of the organization. Yet, especially in these turbulent times, it seems critical for managers to genuinely recognize the untapped potential of positivity in the workplace and to design ways of integrating positivity into the structures, strategies, and cultures of their organizations by investing in the PsyCap of their people. Recruitment, selection and placement, job design, reward systems, and training and development are all possible vehicles for the promotion of positivity and PsyCap in the workplace. The same is true for organizational-level processes such as organizational development and change, communication systems, and decision-making processes. Failing to recognize

the importance of this "big picture" may result in losing the most positive employees to the competition or to entrepreneurial opportunities, leaving an organization with a rigid status quo and a cynical workforce that is resistant to change. In other words, as a recent study indicated, positive employees may lead to positive organizational change (Avey, Wernsing et al., 2008).

On the other hand, similar to the points raised earlier, it is also important for practicing managers to realize the contextual nature of positivity in actual practice. Some practical examples may help illustrate the opportunities and challenges in applying positivity and PsyCap. For instance, the positive impact of optimism on insurance sales employees has been recognized in the positive psychology literature (Seligman, 1998). On the other hand, consider the negative impact of a highly optimistic explanatory style in jobs that require high levels of financial prudence (e.g., auditors) or physically hazardous jobs where strict adherence to safety regulations is paramount. Only mild levels of optimism are desirable in such jobs, and managers may have to find ways to discourage extreme levels of optimism without appearing to be uncaring or callous.

Similarly, high levels of hope pathways may be conducive to creativity and innovation, especially in research and development. On the other hand, managers may have to put a stop to an endless stream of ideas to avoid false hope, to prevent escalation of commitment, or to reallocate resources toward more effective uses. High levels of confidence in marketing, sales, or customer service employees and the tools and approaches they utilize may also have to be toned down, for example, when managing in cultures that place a higher value on modesty and deference. A highly resilient employee may continue to bounce back and recover from setbacks that should have indicated to that employee that a job or a career change is warranted. In other words, the discontinuities and situational idiosyncrasies of positivity and PsyCap research are also likely to translate into challenges for the realities of organizational practice that managers need to recognize and manage.

There may be situations where employees may even need to learn to express different levels of positivity and PsyCap. For example, funeral home employees may need to learn to display less positivity, without allowing their solemn expressions to take reign over their emotional well-being in other life domains. Nurses and other helping professionals may need to convey optimism when dealing with patients and families, but may need a more pessimistic explanatory style when attempting diagnosis and contemplating alternative treatment procedures. Lawyers may choose different approaches depending on their defense strategies. They may prepare themselves and their clients to appear more confident, hopeful, and resilient, or they may instruct them to express hesitation, sadness, or remorse. The literature on emotional labor is rich with examples where display rules force employees to express unfelt emotions, which can over time lead to estrangement or to "deep acting" where the expressed emotions eventually become internalized (Morris & Feldman, 1996). Parallels can be drawn between such display rules in emotional labor and what can become a stereotype of positivity that can take its toll on employees due to unreasonable expectations of expressing certain levels of positivity and PsyCap that may not match those actually experienced.

## Linking Positivity and PsyCap Research and Practice

One of the most critical challenges facing management practice today is the significant discrepancy between managers' knowledge and expressed beliefs and the behaviors they truly exhibit regarding human resources, or what is now commonly called the "knowing-doing gap" (Pfeffer, 1998; Pfeffer & Sutton, 2000). Unlike in psychology, where the primary emphasis is on humans, today's managers may or may not believe (but they most often say they do) that human resources are vital and provide competitive advantage. Despite what they say, they may still question whether human resources make enough of a significant contribution to organizational effectiveness to justify the costs involved in planning, implementing, or evaluating human-oriented initiatives. Furthermore, even if they do believe in the importance of human resources, what they actually do about those beliefs, and the consistency with which they hold onto and act upon those beliefs, too often turns out to be a different matter. The analogous situation occurs in health care. Medical doctors may know the evidence concerning the significant impact that positivity has on health outcomes (Lyubomirsky et al., 2005) and even length of life (e.g., the famous Nun Study, Danner, Snowden & Friesen, 2001), yet they most often ignore this research in doing check-ups or

diagnoses (e.g., Diener & Biswas-Diener, 2008). Despite the evidence indicating organizations that value their human resources rank higher on a multitude of efficiency and effectiveness criteria (e.g., see Pfeffer, 1998), many practicing managers are tempted to forego human-oriented initiatives and practices. Unfortunately, this is especially true when economic problems such as in recent times drive tighter budgets, or when organizational politics favor more readily quantifiable, financially visible initiatives.

There is a major gap between organizational behavior research and management practice. Frequently, practicing managers invest valuable time and resources implementing initiatives that are not necessarily consistent with established research findings. What many practicing managers perceive to be "best practices" may be unrelated, or unfortunately even contradictory, to solid research evidence. Reasons for this gap may include ignorance, fear, or resistance to change on the practice side, as well as perceptions that academic research may be too theoretical and thus inapplicable to everyday management practice. Limited access or motivation to establish linkages between research and practice may further drive academics to their "ivory tower," or at least exacerbate the perception of such attitudes in the eyes of practicing managers with limited training on the scientific process. This has recently triggered the call for "evidence-based management" (Pfeffer & Sutton, 2006; Rousseau, 2006), where those missing linkages can be created, urging academic researchers to become "scientist-practitioners" and helping practicing managers become "practitioner-scientists."

Positive organizational behavior research and practice represent a case-in-point for the above challenges. Over the years, organizational behavior research supports the importance of positively oriented human characteristics and constructs such as positive personality traits, positive work attitudes such as job satisfaction and organizational commitment, and positive organizational actions such as organizational citizenship behaviors. However, similar to mainstream psychology, management practitioners focus on problem, dysfunctional employees' poor performance and on containing stress, conflict, absenteeism, and turnover. Too often they ignore the "soft" side of management altogether. Moreover, despite the exponential increase in positive organizational research, even positively oriented management practitioners continue to be led by an explosion of popular management literature, which promotes a plethora of intuitively appealing "best practices" with limited if any grounding in scientific research or validated evidence.

## Ways to Close the Knowledge–Practice Gap

Drawing from Pfeffer and Sutton (2006), we propose a three-dimensional action plan to help narrow the existing gap between positivity and PsyCap research and actual practice. First, positive organizational researchers need to work on translating their findings into a language that management practitioners can readily understand and use. This should not be such a daunting endeavor. This is because most academicians have already mastered such language through their daily teaching in the classroom, especially with MBA students, who in most cases are full-time managers and employees, being their primary audience. Unfortunately, there is often a clear dichotomy between teaching and research languages. Such language differences may be contributing to the dilemma that many academic researchers may be providing an inferior product and an outdated knowledge base to students in the classroom in order to keep their attention, appear relevant, and get good evaluations. It should not come as a surprise that many MBA-qualified managers lack knowledge of cutting-edge research. While scientific jargon may be necessary for communication in academic circles, a more amiable language may facilitate the transfer of research knowledge to practicing managers and reduce their "ivory tower" perceptions of academicians. The classroom would seem to be an excellent vehicle for the development of such language and the practice of its communication.

Second, unlike many character strengths in positive psychology, which may have terminal value, human-oriented positive organizational behavior constructs are primarily pursued due to their instrumental value. Although valuable in their own right, especially for socially responsible organizations, unless positively oriented human resource initiatives can show a quantifiable return on investment, limited financial resources are likely to be allocated to other more objectively measurable investments. Management research on quantifying the return on investment in various human resource practices has been open to criticism (Latham & Whyte, 1994). Additional research needs to be conducted on quantifying the return on investment in and development of human resources in general, and

in positively oriented interventions in particular. Furthermore, positive organizational behavior research needs to emphasize the linkages with productivity, retention, stress reduction, and other quantifiable outcomes that would render the findings of such research directly useful for organizational decision making and resource allocation.

Third, it is unfortunate that human resource (HR) professionals often lack the research methods and statistical analysis skills to speak the language, let alone use the methods, of their more financially oriented counterparts. This deficiency leaves HR managers in an inferior position in terms of their power and decision-making scope, the budget allocations they receive, and even their personal compensation. In order for HR managers to be involved in strategic decision making and resource allocation, they need to enhance their methodological and quantitative skills (i.e., they must become practitioner-scientists). Unlike many professions, most management education, training, and development programs, especially those oriented toward human resource professionals, overemphasize the "soft" side of management (e.g., leadership, motivation, communication), at the expense of the "hard," data-driven aspects of decision making (e.g., research methodology, statistical analysis, financial analysis). This may have further contributed to the commonly observed intimidation of human resource professionals with and resistance to quantitative measurement and assessment of human resource initiatives. This reluctance of HR professionals to use quantitative assessment tools may come across to more financially oriented decision makers as aversion to accountability and responsibility, and worse that there is no hard evidence of validity or real value to the organization. Professional human resource management education, training, and certification standards are slowly catching up but need to be more cognizant of the new realities of the demands and challenges found in today's highly competitive environment.

Other venues for bridging the research-practice gap include initiatives that promote academic-practitioner interactions such as practitioner-oriented conferences, non-academic speaking engagements, and consulting opportunities. However, motivating academicians to actively engage in such initiatives would require significant structural and cultural changes by academic institutions to enhance the status of (and rewards from) practice-oriented activities and publications.

In the final analysis, the positive force, now backed by an evidence-based, scientific process, is too important for organizations and management practitioners to ignore or write off as too soft or even "Pollyannaish." Positivity in general and PsyCap in particular is certainly not the answer or "silver bullet" for today's embattled organizations, but it can no longer be ignored if they expect to compete and even survive in the increasingly negative environment.

*References*

Allen, N. J., & Meyer, J. P. (1990). The measurement and antecedents of affective, continuance and normative commitment to the organization. *Journal of Occupational Psychology, 63,* 1–18.

Avey, J. B., Luthans, F., & Jensen, S. M. (2009). Psychological capital: A positive resource for combating employee stress and turnover. *Human Resource Management, 48,* 677–693.

Avey, J., Luthans, F., & Mhatre, K. (2008). A call for longitudinal research in positive organizational behavior. *Journal of Organizational Behavior, 29,* 705–711.

Avey, J. B., Luthans, F., Smith, R., & Palmer, N. (2010). Impact of positive psychological capital on employee well-being over time. *Journal of Occupational Health Psychology, 12,* 17–28.

Avey, J., Luthans, F., & Youssef, C. M. (2010). The additive value of psychological capital: Predicting positive and negative work attitudes and behaviors. *Journal of Management, 36,* 430–452.

Avey, J., Wernsing, T. S., & Luthans, F. (2008). Can positive employees help positive organizational change? *The Journal of Applied Behavioral Science, 44,* 48–70.

Avolio, B. J., & Luthans, F. (2006). *The high impact leader: Moments matter in accelerating authentic leadership development.* New York: McGraw-Hill.

Bandura, A. (1997). *Self-efficacy: The exercise of control.* New York: Freeman.

Barrick, M. R., & Mount, M. K. (1991). The big five personality dimensions and job performance: A meta-analysis. *Personnel Psychology, 44,* 1–26.

Biswas-Diener, R., & Dean, B. (2007). *Positive psychology coaching: Putting the science of happiness to work for your clients.* Hoboken, NJ: Wiley.

Cameron, K. S., & Caza, A. (2004). Contributions to the discipline of positive organizational scholarship. *American Behavioral Scientist, 47,* 731–739.

Cameron, K., Dutton, J., & Quinn, R. (Eds.) (2003). *Positive organizational scholarship.* San Francisco: Berrett-Koehler.

Carver, C., & Scheier, M. (2002). Optimism. In C.R. Snyder & S. Lopez (Eds.), *Handbook of positive psychology* (pp. 231–243). Oxford, UK: Oxford University Press.

Cascio, W. F., & Cappelli, P. (2009). Lessons from the financial services crisis. *HR Magazine, 54(1),* 47–50.

Chang, E., D'Zurilla, T., & Maydeu-Olivares, A. (1994). Assessing the dimensionality of optimism and pessimism using a multimeasure approach. *Cognitive Therapy and Research, 18,* 143–160.

Csikszentmihalyi, Mihaly (2003). *Good business: Flow, leadership and the making of meaning.* New York: Viking.

Danner, D. D., Snowden, D. A., & Friesen, W. (2001). Positive emotions in early life and longevity: Findings from the Nun Study. *Journal of Personality and Social Psychology, 80,* 804–813.

Diener, E. & Biswas-Diener, R. (2008). *Happiness: Unlocking the mysteries of psychological wealth.* Oxford: Blackwell.

Fineman, S. (2006). On being positive: Concerns and counterpoints. *Academy of Management Review, 31,* 270–291.

Fredrickson, B. L. (2009). *Positivity.* New York: Crown.

Fredrickson, B. L., & Losada, M. F. (2005). Positive affect and the complex dynamics of human flourishing. *American Psychologist, 60,* 678–686.

George, J. M. (1991). State or trait: Effects of positive mood on prosocial behaviors at work. *Journal of Applied Psychology, 76,* 299–307.

George, J. M. (2004). Book review of positive organizational scholarship. *Administrative Science Quarterly, 49,* 325–330.

Hackman, J. R. (2009). The perils of positivity. *Journal of Organizational Behavior, 30,* 309-319.

Harter, J., Schmidt, F., & Hayes, T. (2002). Business-unit-level relationship between employee satisfaction, employee engagement, and business outcomes: A meta-analysis. *Journal of Applied Psychology, 87,* 268–279.

Herzberg, F., Mausner, B., & Snyderman, B. B. (1959) *The motivation to work.* New York: Wiley.

Hoffman, E. (Ed.) (1996). *Future visions: The unpublished papers of Abraham Maslow.* Thousand Oaks, CA: Sage.

Jones, T. (1991). Ethical decision-making by individuals in organizations: An issue-contingent model. *Academy of Management Review, 16,* 363–375.

Judge, T. A., & Bono, J. E. (2001). Relationship of core self-evaluations traits—self-esteem, generalized self-efficacy, locus of control, and emotional stability—with job satisfaction and job performance: A meta-analysis. *Journal of Applied Psychology, 86*, 80–92.

Larson, M., & Luthans, F. (2006). Potential added value of psychological capital in predicting work attitudes. *Journal of Leadership & Organizational Studies, 13*, 45–62.

Latham, G. P., & Whyte, G. (1994). The futility of utility analysis. *Personnel Psychology, 47*, 31–46.

Lazarus, R. S. (2003). Does the positive psychology movement have legs? *Psychological Inquiry, 14*, 93–109.

Lopez, S., & Snyder, C. R. (Eds.). (2009). *Handbook of positive psychology*, 2nd ed. Oxford, UK: Oxford University Press.

Luthans, F. (2002a). The need for and meaning of positive organizational behavior. *Journal of Organizational Behavior, 23*, 695–706.

Luthans, F. (2002b). Positive organizational behavior: Developing and managing psychological strengths. *Academy of Management Executive, 16*, 57–72.

Luthans, F., Avey, J.B., Avolio, B.J., Norman, S.M. & Combs, G. M. (2006). Psychological capital development: Toward a micro-intervention. *Journal of Organizational Behavior, 27*, 387–393.

Luthans, F., Avey, J.B., Avolio, B.J., & Peterson, S.J. (2010). The development and resulting performance impact of positive psychological capital. *Human Resource Development Quarterly, 21*, 41–67.

Luthans, F., Avey, J.B., Clapp-Smith, R., & Li, W. (2008). More evidence on the value of Chinese workers' psychological capital: A potentially unlimited competitive resource? *International Journal of Human Resource Management, 19*, 818–827.

Luthans, F., Avey, J.B., & Patera, J.L. (2008). Experimental analysis of a web-based training intervention to develop positive psychological capital. *Academy of Management Learning and Education, 7*, 209–221.

Luthans, F., & Avolio, B. J. (2009). The point of positive organizational behavior. *Journal of Organizational Behavior, 30*, 291–307.

Luthans, F., Avolio, B. J., Avey, J. B., & Norman, S. M. (2007). Psychological capital: Measurement and relationship with performance and satisfaction. *Personnel Psychology, 60*, 541–572.

Luthans, F., Avolio, B., Walumbwa, F., & Li, W. (2005). The psychological capital of Chinese workers: Exploring the relationship with performance. *Management and Organization Review, 1*, 247–269.

Luthans, F., Luthans, K., & Luthans, B. (2004). Positive psychological capital: Going beyond human and social capital. *Business Horizons, 47(1)*, 45–50.

Luthans, F., Norman, S. M., Avolio, B. J., & Avey, J. B. (2008). The mediating role of psychological capital in the supportive organizational climate-employee performance relationship. *Journal of Organizational Behavior, 29*, 219–238.

Luthans, F., & Youssef, C. M. (2004). Human, social and now positive psychological capital management: Investing in people for competitive advantage. *Organizational Dynamics, 33*, 143–160.

Luthans, F., & Youssef, C. M. (2007). Emerging positive organizational behavior. *Journal of Management, 33*, 321–349.

Luthans, F., & Youssef, C. M. (2009). Positive workplaces. In S. Lopez, & C.R. Snyder (Eds.), *Handbook of positive psychology*, 2nd edition. Oxford, UK: Oxford University Press.

Luthans, F., Youssef, C. M., & Avolio, B. J. (2007). *Psychological capital: Developing the human competitive edge.* Oxford, UK: Oxford University Press.

Lyubomirsky, S. (2007). *The how of happiness: A scientific approach to getting the life you want.* New York: Penguin Press.

Lyubomirsky, S., King, L., & Diener, E. (2005). The benefits of frequent positive affect: Does happiness lead to success? *Psychological Bulletin, 131*, 803–855.

Maslow, A. (1954). *Motivation and personality.* New York: Harper.

Masten, A. S. (2001). Ordinary magic: Resilience process in development. *American Psychologist, 56*, 227–239.

McGregor, D. (1960). *The human side of enterprise.* New York: McGraw-Hill.

Morris, J. A., & Feldman, D. C. (1996). The dimensions, antecedents, and consequences of emotional labor. *Academy of Management Review, 21*, 986–1010.

Organ, D. W. (1988). *Organizational citizenship behavior: The good soldier syndrome.* Lexington, MA: Lexington Books.

Peterson, C., & Seligman, M. (2004). *Character strengths and virtues: A handbook and classification.* New York: Oxford University Press.

Peterson, S. J., Luthans, F., Avolio, B. J., Walumbwa, F. O., & Zhang, Z. (2010). The impact of psychological capital on employee performance: A latent growth modeling approach. Under journal review.

Peterson, S. J., & Zhang, Z. (in press). Examining the relationships beteeen top management team psychological characteristics, transformational leadership, and business unit performance. In M.A. Carpenter (Ed.), *Handbook of top management research*. New York: Edward Elgar Publishing.

Pfeffer, J. (1998). *The human equation*. Boston: Harvard Business School Press.

Pfeffer, J., & Sutton, R. I. (2000). *The knowing-doing gap*. Boston: Harvard Business School Press.

Pfeffer, J., & Sutton R. I. (2006). Evidenced-based management. *Harvard Business Review, 84(1)*, 63–74.

Rousseau, D. (2006). Is there such a thing as evidence-based management? *Academy of Management Review, 311*, 256–269.

Sackett, P. R., Berry, C. M., Wiemann, S. A., & Laczo, R. M. (2006). Citizenship and counterproductive behavior: Clarifying relations between the two domains. *Human Performance, 19*, 441–464.

Schmidt, F., & Hunter, J. (2000). Select on intelligence. In E. Locke (Ed.), *The Blackwell handbook of principles of organizational behavior* (pp. 3–14). Oxford, UK: Blackwell.

Seligman, M. E. P. (1998). *Learned optimism*. New York: Pocket Books.

Snyder, C.R. (2000). *Handbook of hope*. San Diego: Academic Press.

Snyder, C. R., Irving, L., & Anderson, J. (1991). Hope and health: Measuring the will and the ways. In C. R. Snyder & D. R. Forsyth (Eds.), *Handbook of social and clinical psychology* (pp. 285–305). Elmsford, NY: Pergamon.

Snyder, C. R., & Lopez, S. (Eds.) (2002). *Handbook of positive psychology*. Oxford, UK: Oxford University Press.

Snyder, C. R., & Lopez, S. (Eds.) (2009). *Handbook of positive psychology*, 2nd ed. Oxford, UK: Oxford University Press.

Stajkovic, A. D., & Luthans, F. (1998). Social cognitive theory and self-efficacy: Going beyond traditional motivational and behavioral approaches. *Organizational Dynamics, 26*, 62–74.

Stajkovic, A., & Luthans F. (2003). Behavioral management and task performance in organizations: Conceptual background, meta-analysis, and test of alternative models. *Personnel Psychology, 56*, 155–194.

Wagner, R., & Harter, J. (2006). *12: The elements of great managing*. New York: Gallup Press.

Walumbwa, F. O., Luthans, F., Avey, J. B., & Oke, A. (in press). Authentically leading groups: The mediating role of collective psychological capital and trust. *Journal of Organizational Behavior*.

Wright, T. A. (2005). The role of "happiness" in organizational research: Past, present and future directions. In P. L. Perrewe & D. C. Ganster (Eds.), *Research in occupational stress and well-being* (vol. 4, pp. 221–264). Amsterdam: JAI Press.

Wright, T. A. (2007). A look at two methodological challenges for scholars interested in positive organizational behavior. In D. Nelson & C. L. Cooper (Eds.), *Positive organizational behavior: Accentuating the positive at work*. Thousand Oaks, CA: Sage.

Wright, T. A., & Goodstein, J. (2007). Character is not "dead" in management research. *Journal of Management, 33*, 928–958.

Wright, T. A., & Quick, J. C. (2009). The emerging positive agenda in organizations. *Journal of Organizational Behavior, 30*, 147–159.

Youssef, C. M., & Luthans, F. (2008). Leveraging psychological capital in virtuous organizations: Why and how. In C. Manz, K. Cameron, K. Manz, & R. Marx (Eds.), *The virtuous organization* (pp. 141–162). Hackensack, NJ: World Scientific Publishers.

Youssef, C. M., & Luthans, F. (2009). An integrated model of psychological capital in the workplace. In A. Linley, S. Harrington, & N. Garcea (Eds.), *Handbook of positive psychology and work* (pp. 277–288). New York: Oxford University Press.

# 24

# Organizational Applications of Positive Psychology: Taking Stock and a Research/ Practice Roadmap for the Future

*P. Alex Linley, Nicky Garcea, Susan Harrington, Emma Trenier, and Gurpal Minhas*

## Organizational Applications of Positive Psychology

As we write this chapter, it is 10 years since the "positive psychology" movement as we know it was founded (Seligman, 1999) and five years since the field of "applied positive psychology" was christened with the publication of *Positive Psychology in Practice* (Linley & Joseph, 2004). Wow—how much has happened in that time! As an eagle-eye overview of developments, consider this: The positive psychology special issue of the *American Psychologist* (Seligman & Csikszentmihalyi, 2000) had nothing to say about organizational applications (with respect, this may not be surprising, since many of the founding figures of positive psychology emanated from the clinical and social psychology disciplines). *Positive Psychology in Practice*, which purported to introduce the field of applied positive psychology, included a mere four chapters on organizational applications—and they were typically speculative or making connections with other bodies of work, rather than empirical reviews of published positive psychology

research in the area. Yet, things had already started to change.

In 2004, *Harvard Business Review* listed positive psychology as one of the 20 breakthrough ideas for organizational management, and within five years, an entire 26-chapter volume has been completed that is focused exclusively on the organizational applications of positive psychology—the *Oxford Handbook of Positive Psychology and Work* (Linley, Harrington, & Garcea, 2010a). Journal special issues have been dedicated to the topic—including the *International Coaching Psychology Review* (Linley & Kauffman, 2007), the *Journal of Positive Psychology* (Fredrickson & Dutton, 2008), and *Organisations and People* (Page & Linley, 2008)—and an increasing number of practitioners are infusing positive psychology into their work with organizations, led by our work at the Centre of Applied Positive Psychology, which we go on to discuss further below.

Outside of the tightly defined positive psychology field, other positive trends were also emerging and shifting the nature of organizational focus. For at least a decade previous to positive psychology, David Cooperrider's work on Appreciative Inquiry was changing the way in which organizational change was viewed (Cooperrider & Srivastva, 1987). The work of the Gallup Organization on strengths-based approaches started a new management paradigm (Buckingham & Clifton, 2001), and a sister discipline to positive psychology, positive organizational scholarship, emerged through leading scholars at the University of Michigan (Cameron, Dutton, & Quinn, 2003). Clearly, positive psychology was one part—but a very significant part—of a wider emerging trend toward accentuating the positive.

As is almost always the case, however, the essence of these ideas was not new—it had been around for some time but had become lost, laying dusty on library shelves until a changing zeitgeist breathed new life into it. As we look back over the history of management and organization, it's not unduly difficult to find great management thinkers who shared the ideas espoused by positive psychologists today.

In *The Effective Executive*, for example, Peter Drucker argued that "to make strength productive is the unique purpose of organization" (Drucker, 1967, p. 60). Aubrey Daniels professed the power of positive reinforcement and what this means for managers in *Bringing Out the Best in People: How to Apply the Astonishing Power of Positive Reinforcement* (Daniels, 1994). And possibly the best known of them all, Douglas McGregor (1960/2006), challenged management orthodoxy by distinguishing between Theory X assumptions about workers (i.e., that they are inherently lazy and will avoid work if they can) and Theory Y assumptions (i.e., that individuals are motivated to do their best and fulfill their potential). The deep implication of McGregor's work was that organizations with Theory X mindsets would treat their employees very differently from those with Theory Y mindsets—and that employees would respond in kind to how they were being treated. Indeed, we can go further and note the work of some of the great early "positive psychologists," such as Abraham Maslow—for example, *Maslow on Management* (originally published as *Eupsychian Management*) has gone on to influence the thinking of managers to this day (Maslow, 1998).

In the current day, leading management thinkers such as Gary Hamel and Dave Ulrich have similarly started to tap the essence of what positive psychology could bring to management and organizations. Hamel (2007) has focused on the role of management innovation, together with how organizations could be very different if they tapped the inherent potential of their people (Hamel, 2009). Ulrich (2008) makes the case as to why HR professionals should be "using their strengths to strengthen others" and subsequently goes on to outline his thoughts on the "abundant organization," which he believes will become the necessary organizational model for the future—drawing heavily from positive psychology (Ulrich, 2010). Whether positive psychology is referenced explicitly, the themes are the same—a finding which speaks to the infusion of a more positive mindset across management thinkers and beyond, further evidence of the changing zeitgeist of which positive psychology is both cause and effect.

## The Plan for this Chapter

In this chapter, we will do three things. First, we will provide a brief overview of what is known about organizational applications of positive psychology—but we will do so through the lens of the practitioner who is actually doing the applying. In this way, we will review what is known about the organizational applications of positive psychology at each stage of the employee life cycle, demonstrating that, in many cases, there is little empirical research directed in these areas, but there is a growing trend toward applied experience and case-study evidence. We note explicitly that we have not cast our net more widely to consider research studies more broadly in these areas—which are not specific to positive psychology—since this is the explicit focus of our chapter and this volume. Notwithstanding this, we acknowledge openly that there is much that could be learned from a broader consideration of these literatures, some of which the interested reader will find in the *Oxford Handbook of Positive Psychology and Work* (Linley, Harrington, & Garcea, 2010a).

Second, we will briefly review and answer critiques that have been made of positive psychology both through the lens of organizational science particularly and also more generally. In doing so, we address the three critiques that positive psychology is inappropriate for organizations that are focused on and driven by profit, rather than any consideration of human concerns; that positive psychology is focused on the positive at the expense and exclusion of the negative; and that positive psychology is focused on strengths at the expense and exclusion of weaknesses. In each of these cases, we demonstrate comprehensively that the critique is either misguided, a misunderstanding, or simply wrong.

Third, we will turn our attention to the presentation of our *Research/Practice Roadmap for the Organizational Applications of Positive Psychology*, presenting therein our view on *how* the future of organizational positive psychology applications should be developed, and *why* we believe that they should be developed in this way. In doing so, we draw from the first author's experience of being a leading positive psychology academic and making the transition into the world of organizational applications and management consulting, thereby giving us license, we believe, to have a solid view about how positive psychology as an applied discipline—especially as applied to organizations—might be developed.

This Roadmap lays out the key challenges that we believe are faced by positive psychology as an applied discipline in organizations, together with how we recommend those challenges can be overcome. Fundamentally, however, our Roadmap is designed to be about our desired future of the organizational applications of positive psychology, including its influence into the practitioner field of occupational (I/O) psychology, where such a positive shift is sorely needed (Anderson, Herriot, & Hodgkinson, 2001; Cascio, 1995; Hill, 2003). We also explore how organizations can be developed to make work more of a place where people love to be and a thing that people love to do. Finally, we examine the imperative for organizations to become more effective agents of social change, in ways that blend profit and market capitalism with positive social impact and sustainability. Let us begin, however, by surveying what is known and where we are now.

## Taking Stock: Positive Psychology Applications across the Employee Life Cycle

The employee life cycle is an organizational concept that is used to describe the major elements of an employee's journey in working with an organization. The employee life cycle could be described in headline form as the cycle of Attract/Select-Retain-Develop-Exit. We use this as our overall sub-structure for the section, but as we go on to demonstrate below, there may be often multiple further sub-elements of the employee life cycle nested under each of these broad domains.

### Attract/Select

The attraction element of the employee life cycle is concerned with why employees would want to work with that organization in the first place. It is fundamentally concerned with employer brand (Barrow & Mosley, 2005), a domain of marketing, and so perhaps it is not so surprising that there is little—if any—empirical positive psychology work in these areas. We turn, however—as we will throughout this chapter—to examples of organizational case studies and evidence from our own practice, as a means to illustrate some of the ways in which positive psychology is being applied in organizations. While the work we describe may not fall under the remit of "empirical research," it still squarely speaks to organizational applications, and we find ourselves typically operating at the intersection of the two.

As such, our consulting experience with the Centre of Applied Positive Psychology provides two examples of how positive psychology is being used in the attraction element of the employee life cycle. In both the insurance company Norwich Union (now Aviva) and Ernst & Young, the professional services firm, the strengths approach has been used as a means to attract and select new employees. Norwich Union has used strengths-based recruitment across its UK businesses, leading to the removal of their pre-existing competency frameworks (Stefanyszyn, 2007).

Ernst & Young has used strengths-based graduate recruitment as a means to differentiate its offering in the highly competitive professional services graduate marketplace (Isherwood, 2008). Further, Ernst & Young has gone on to use a bespoke version of Realise2, CAPP's online strengths assessment and development tool, as a way of positioning itself in the graduate marketplace and to attract candidates for whom the prospect of working for an organization that builds on their strengths appeals—a key aspiration, even requirement, for members of the so-called Generation Y or Generation Me (Twenge, 2007; Twenge & Campbell, 2010).

Both of these are examples of strengths-based recruitment, an application of positive psychology developed and pioneered by the Centre of Applied Positive Psychology. Strengths-based recruitment identifies the strengths that would deliver the key outcomes of a role and then recruits individuals who demonstrate these strengths. The critical distinction here with traditional competency approaches is that strengths are both authentic and energizing (Linley, 2008), and they are mapped more specifically to the role outcomes that an individual needs to deliver rather than to generic competency frameworks that have no predictive validity (Barrett & Depinet, 1991; Shippman et al., 2000). The results are that people are likely to be far more engaged and effective in using their strengths, with attendant business results—Norwich Union has been able to demonstrate that candidates learn the role faster, perform better, and are more highly engaged at work—key organizational outcomes (Stefanyszyn, 2007; Stefanyszyn & Garcea, 2009).

Other recruitment approaches that draw from elements of positive psychology include the role of core self-evaluations in recruitment and the role of person-organization fit on hiring decisions. Garcia, Triana, Peters, and Sanchez (2009) investigated the role of self-enhancement in a job search context and found that it was positively related to preparatory job search and mediated the relationship between core self-evaluations and perceived job alternatives, such that people with higher core self-evaluations presented themselves more effectively and so perceived that they had more job opportunities available to them. Chen, Lee, and Yeh (2008) examined how candidates ingratiated themselves with interviewers, thus increasing the feeling of similarity with the manager and increasing their chances of receiving a job offer.

### Retain

Under the broad heading of *Retain* in the employee life cycle, we consider such topics as employee engagement, employee well-being, diversity, and performance management.

*Engagement* is perhaps one area where there is a more solid body of evidence from a positive psychology perspective. Recent work by Stairs and Galpin (2010) highlights the shift that may be recommended in organizational thinking, which they describe as being from employee engagement to employee happiness. Indeed, the UK department store and Waitrose food hall owner, the John Lewis Partnership, has as one of its founding premises the "happiness of Partners [i.e., employees] as the ultimate purpose [of the business]" (John Lewis Partnership, 2009). More traditionally, the empirical work of the Gallup

Organization has highlighted the significant business benefits that flow from employee engagement, including productivity, quality, reduced sickness absence, and better employee and business performance (Harter, Schmidt, & Keyes, 2003). In our own work looking at the positive psychology-inspired question of "What engages the most highly engaged?" we were able to demonstrate the central role of an individual's own personal responsibility for engagement, the revolutionary finding that highly engaged employees consciously decided whether to give their engagement or not (Galpin, Stairs, & Page, 2008).

It's also worth noting that engagement is a topic that has longevity within organizations, having been steadily on the organizational radar for many years. This is undoubtedly because of a wealth of evidence that engagement drives performance benefits (MacLeod & Clarke, 2009), but, even with the onset of the global economic recession, employee engagement has remained a significant priority. This is likely because of the role of engagement in retaining employees in organizations (Harter & Blacksmith, 2010), which becomes an ever more critical consideration in times of economic downturn, redundancies, and layoffs, where talent retention—holding on to the people that you want to hold on to—is key.

*Employee well-being* is also becoming increasingly studied under the banner of the positive psychology movement. There is a long-lasting recognition that happier workers are more productive workers (Judge, Thoreson, Bono, & Patten, 2001) and that employees with higher levels of positive emotion score more highly across all performance indicators (Marks, 2006), but more recent work demonstrates that employee well-being also impacts on physical health through such media as blood pressure and heart disease—which in turn of course also play through to impact on individual and organizational performance (Wright, 2010). Organizations are also increasingly recognizing the importance of their employees' well-being and commissioning well-being audits to guide their interventions in this area (nef consulting, 2009).

*Diversity* is perhaps often regarded as a compliance issue within organizations, yet positive psychology research and applications are increasingly suggesting how embracing diversity can actually be more of a critical performance driver than it ever was a legislative compliance issue. For example, Hamel (2007) argues that organizations that embrace diversity are also far more innovative, a result driven by the inevitable mixing of different experiences, assumptions, and views that a diverse workforce entails. From the perspective of positive emotions, it has been shown that people experiencing higher levels of positive emotion are less biased and more inclusive (Johnson & Fredrickson, 2005), and more likely to develop deeper and more meaningful relationships with their colleagues (Waugh & Fredrickson, 2006)—findings that have implications for how positive psychology might be used to inform second-generation diversity interventions with organizations.

Similarly, organizations are also recognizing how interventions to build engagement can be equally as effective in diversity, and that engagement and diversity outcomes may indeed be two sides of the same coin. More engaged employees are more likely to demonstrate inclusive behaviors, and in doing so to create an environment where diversity is valued if not positively encouraged. This is critical in ensuring the longevity of diversity, since one of the key factors in determining the retention of minority group staff is the perception of the diversity climate (McCay, Avery, Tonidandel, Morris, Hernandez, & Hebl, 2007), which is in turn positively influenced by higher levels of engagement.

*Performance management* is concerned with how employees are managed on a day-to-day basis and the effect that this has on their performance. Work from the Corporate Leadership Council (2002) surveying 19,187 employees from 34 organizations in 29 countries examined 50 different performance drivers. Notable from their findings was that when a manager focused on the strengths of the employee, performance increased by up to 36.4%. In contrast, when the manager focused on the weaknesses of the employee, performance declined by up to 26.8%.

As an example of positive psychology principles applied to performance management, CAPP worked with Ellie Roberts of Imago Services at Loughborough University to develop a performance management system for the cleaners, cooks, drivers, and administrators employed by Imago Services (Roberts, 2009). Called *"Celebrating You,"* it was built around the strengths that individuals needed to demonstrate to deliver the outcomes for each of these roles, with builds into a strengths hierarchy at each level of the organization, such that employees could see a clear line of sight between their strengths, successful performance in their current role, and what they would need to be able to

deliver in order to progress—all the way up to Director level within the organization, as has happened with employees who joined initially as unqualified cooks and cleaners.

## Develop

*Talent management and development* is arguably at the very core of the "Develop" dimension of the employee life cycle—and yet, it is very difficult to find explicit work on positive psychology applied to talent management and talent development. This may well be because the field of talent management is broadly defined, meaning different things to different people (CIPD, 2006)—or it may be that the work simply has not yet been done. Notwithstanding this, there are, we believe, a multitude of areas in which positive psychology could be applied to issues of talent management and development in organizations—and indeed the latest thinking on talent seems to be including much more that is aligned with a positive psychology perspective (Centre for Tomorrow's Company, 2009).

First, there is the question of "who is talent?" Many talent management approaches define talent exclusively, for example as the "top X%" of people at particular levels of the organization. Yet in doing so, they risk disenfranchising and disengaging the much larger proportion of the population that is not now classified as talent. Second, they run the risk of the archetypal "hero to zero" syndrome, whereby someone is a talented high-flyer this year but doesn't make the cut next time round and so becomes a "nobody."

In contrast to this, building on what we believe a positive psychology understanding of talent would look like, we have developed an approach that we call "total talent management" (Page, 2007). This approach is premised on three assumptions. First, that we work with the total pool of talent available (including everyone in the organization and those who are not yet in the organization but may be attracted to join it), while recognizing that there may be occasions where it is legitimate to focus limited resource on a particular sub-section of the talent population (but even in doing so, the fundamental assumptions about everyone being talent remain the same). Second, that we are focused on harnessing the total talent of each individual, which means realizing all the strengths and qualities that they bring, rather than just those that may be relevant to this specific role at this specific time. Third, that we recognize and act with the assumption that talent management and development should permeate the whole of an organization's people processes, rather than being restricted simply to career and succession planning, as may sometimes be the case.

In this way, we recognize and position total talent management as being a holistic, inclusive, and integrative approach to realizing the total talent of the total population of the organization. Strengths-based approaches will be at the heart of any total talent management approach, but equally the approach is broader than focusing only on an individual's strengths, also encompassing the wider vista of their passions, abilities, experiences, and expertise.

Individual development has also been considered through the lens of positive psychology in relation to what Luthans calls "psychological capital," which is a combination of hope, optimism, efficacy, and resilience. Taken together, these four characteristics can be subsumed as a positive core for individuals, with evidence showing that it is both possible to develop psychological capital (Luthans, Avey, & Patera, 2008) and that such psychological capital development has a potential for financial impact in organizations and a high return on investment (Luthans, Avey, Avolio, Norman, & Combs, 2006; Youssef & Luthans, 2007). In similar veins, hope has been shown to be a predictor of higher job performance (Peterson & Byron, 2008), and optimistic managers were shown to be more likely to have employees who were engaged, optimistic, and high performing (Arakawa & Greenberg, 2007).

*Coaching* is an area that has received extensive attention from positive psychology researchers and practitioners, quite likely because of the numerous links that exist between the two disciplines (Linley & Harrington, 2005; 2006). This attention has included both authored volumes on *Positive Psychology Coaching* (Biswas-Diener & Dean, 2007) and a special issue of the *International Coaching Psychology Review* on coaching psychology and positive psychology (Linley & Kauffman, 2007).

Empirically, Tony Grant's work has lead the field, being focused on how lessons from positive psychology can be evaluated through the context of coaching, and showing that coaching is associated with significant increases in goal striving, well-being, and hope, which were maintained up to 30 weeks post-coaching (Green, Oades, & Grant, 2006), and that working with a professional coach relative to a peer coach led to higher levels of goal commitment, attainment, and environmental mastery (Spence & Grant, 2007).

Further, there has been a marked interest in strengths coaching, with a number of publications describing both the research underpinnings and practice of this approach. For example, Linley and Harrington (2006) drew out the links between strengths coaching and coaching psychology, while Govindji and Linley (2007) showed that strengths use was associated with higher levels of happiness and well-being, even when controlling for self-esteem and self-efficacy. Linley, Woolston, and Biswas-Diener (2009) provided practical case studies and insights into strengths coaching with leaders, and Carter and Page (2009) provided an overview of the field for the Encyclopedia of Positive Psychology.

The outcomes of strengths coaching typically include a greater client understanding and internalization of their strengths; recognizing how strengths can be used to overcome and mitigate weaknesses; greater effectiveness in linking strengths to the delivery of goal outcomes; more effective working with others through harnessing strengths and complementary partnering; and learning how to use the golden mean of strengths use—"the right strength, to the right amount, in the right way, and at the right time" (Linley, 2008, p. 58).

*Leadership development* is similarly an area where positive psychology scholars and others whose work is supportive of the positive psychology approach have been active in their contributions. These include work on transformational leadership (Sivanathan, Arnold, Turner, & Barling, 2004), authentic leadership (Gardner, Avolio, & Walumbwa, 2005), and the key question of whether leaders are born or made—and, if made, through what particular experiences and developments (Avolio, Griffith, Wernsing, & Walumbwa, 2010). More broadly, attention has been paid to the question of strengths development in leaders (Morris & Garrett, 2010; Rath & Conchie, 2009), especially in relation to using strengths appropriately for the situation and context (Kaplan & Kaiser, 2010; Linley et al., 2009).

Across these complementary approaches, the key themes of leadership development from a positive psychology perspective revolve around making the best of what one already has as a leader (i.e., building on one's strengths) rather than trying to become all things to all people; recognizing and harnessing strengths effectively both in oneself and in teams; understanding the emotional climate that they create and their role as "climate engineers"; and delivering both positive and negative feedback authentically and positively, such that it retains the greatest traction and outcomes.

In relation to the identification and development of strengths, CAPP's development of the Realise2 model is salutary (see www.realise2.com). From our experience of working as practitioners in the field, we were (and are) often asked what the first step is in introducing a strengths approach into an organization. For us, the key to this is in seeding the language of strengths (Page & Carter, 2009). To do so, however, we were left frustrated by the absence of a sufficiently developed language of strengths, or the existence of models of strengths that actually captured and included what we considered to be the key determinants of a strength (Linley, 2008).

It was for these reasons that we set about developing Realise2, which assesses the 60 most prevalent attributes according to the three dimensions of energy, performance, and use. Ratings on each of these dimensions are then combined to determine whether an attribute falls into the category of a Realized Strength, an Unrealized Strength, a Learned Behavior, or a Weakness. Depending on the development that is right for the individual in context, he or she may be recommended to one or more of the four areas of the Realise2 4-M Development model: to *marshal* Realized Strengths, to *maximize* Unrealized Strengths, to *moderate* Learned Behaviors, or to *minimize* Weaknesses (see Linley, Willars, & Biswas-Diener, 2010).

*Team development* has been examined from a positive psychology perspective by Richardson and West (2010). They present a positive team "IPO" (Input-Process-Outcome) model, which includes team diversity, attachment, and role clarity as inputs; optimism, potency, and leadership as processes; and performance, engagement, and flourishing as outcomes. Examining team development from a strengths perspective, Miles and Watkins (2007) argued that leadership teams are most effective when they capitalize on the strengths of each of their members in relation to the outcomes that the team needs to deliver. In practice, this is illustrated in work undertaken by CAPP with the leadership team of a major business unit of BAE Systems (Smedley, 2007).

In an empirical study of high-performing teams, Losada and Heaphy (2004) showed that the best-performing teams moved between inquiry, asking questions to understand, and advocacy, putting forward their own point of view—and that as they did so, they demonstrated positive to negative emotion ratios of 6 to 1 or greater. In stark contrast, medium- and low-performing teams tended to get more stuck in advocacy and to have much lower ratios of positive to negative emotion.

## Exit

Broadly speaking, there may be three reasons why employees will ultimately exit from their organization: through redundancy and outplacement, through retirement, or to pursue career opportunities elsewhere. Again, there is little positive psychology research that speaks to these domains of the employee life cycle, although in our consulting work we have developed and delivered organizational restructure and outplacement services using insights from the science of positive psychology. It is from these that we will draw our case examples.

Examining U.S. airline industry reactions to the September 11, 2001, terrorist attacks, Gittell, Cameron, Lim, and Rivas (2006) found that organizations with stronger relational resources were more likely to have better financial resources, and that these two combined served to predict greater organizational resilience—with Southwest Airlines being their case in point because they avoided layoffs in the aftermath of 9/11 and within six months had announced plans to hire another 4,000 employees, mainly from those who had been laid off by other airlines. Similarly, in *Making the Impossible Possible*, Kim Cameron and Marc Lavine (2006) tell the story of how the Rocky Flats nuclear facility was decommissioned and closed down fully 60 years and $30bn dollars ahead of budget—a feat that they attributed to the "abundance mindset" of those responsible for managing the closure.

In our own work, we have used lessons from positive psychology to inform the development and delivery of outplacement services for organizations. These include helping people to manage their emotions during organizational transitions (Mossholder, Settoon, Armenakis, & Harris, 2000), particularly through emotion-focused coping (Stanton, Kirk, Cameron, & Danoff-Burg, 2000) and through using the pathways thinking of hope theory to help them in constructing desired future alternatives (Snyder, 1994), as well as providing strengths-based transition coaching to enable people to build a view of their personal future that is constructed through recognition and development of their strengths (Linley, Biswas-Diener & Trenier, in press). More widely, work is highlighting the importance of allowing employees to move into roles more aligned to their strengths at times of organizational restructure (Corporate Leadership Council, 2009), and positive psychology is being used to inform the evidence base for new approaches to the evaluation of career development programs (Preskill & Donaldson, 2008).

## Answering the Critiques of Positive Psychology in Organizational Contexts

This chapter would not be complete without an examination and answering of the critiques of positive psychology in organizations (e.g. Fineman, 2006; Kaiser, 2009a; Lazarus, 2003; Warren, 2010). There are three broad critiques that have been put forward and that bear mention and correction: first, that positive psychology presumes a view of organizations as places of potential positivity that is no longer tenable in today's economic climate; second, that positive psychology's approach is fundamentally based on separating positive emotions from negative emotions "so that positive feelings and outcomes can be understood in their own right" to the exclusion of the negative (Fineman, 2006, p. 274); and third, that positive psychology approaches are predicated and focused exclusively on "strengths" at the exclusion of "weaknesses." We shall address each critique in turn.

In making the first challenge, Fineman (2006) argues that the reality of current organizational cultures is one of profit and competition as a result of our modern world of capitalism, consumerism, corporate power, and transient jobs, with the result that humanistic values (positivity) are rejected. Hence, he argues that a major challenge for positive psychology in such a climate is deciding *what* constitutes "good" or "right," for *whom*, and *who* should be making such decisions, that is, "whose positiveness is really being served, and to what ends?" (Fineman, 2006, p. 283).

Warren (2010) expands on Fineman's (2006) last point. She argues that there is an imbalance in the benefits realized from applying positive psychology at work and that it is predominantly the organization that benefits from encouraging positivity in employees' increased productivity and performance.

We agree that contemporary organizational climates may have a strong focus on competitive advantage and profit, but we do not accept—fundamentally—that this automatically renders positive psychology impotent or unimportant. In contrast, we would argue that it makes the case for positive psychology even more strongly, because organizations of the future will need to do *ever more* to release and realize the best of what their people have to offer (e.g., Hamel, 2007), and positive psychology, as we have demonstrated above, has a major and increasing role to play in this.

For example, Linley, Harrington, and Garcea (2010b) differentiate between the traditional "problem-solving" approach that organizations have historically adopted, whereby optimal solutions are sought to overcome organizational deficits and problems, and the "abundance approach," which involves organizations identifying and harnessing the highest potential of their people, thereby enabling optimal performance and sustainable impact. Hence, even in the modern economic climate, there is a real opportunity for positive psychology to enable organizations to embrace the positive potential of their employees to meet the present and future challenges more effectively than a negatively focused problem-solving approach.

The second challenge for positive psychology within these critiques is the charge that the fundamental tenets of positive psychology seek to focus on the positive aspects of human behavior and organizational life, explicitly aiming to understand what makes individuals happy and flourishing to the exclusion of the negativity of human experience, such as stress, loss, anger, and anxiety. Lazarus (2003, p. 94) argues that positive and negative emotions are "two sides of the same coin of life"; they are in an ongoing dialectical relationship, mutually informing each other. For example, hope and optimism would not be possible without experiencing disappointment.

This charge belies a naive understanding of positive psychology, since numerous scholars and practitioners have been at great pains to demonstrate that positive psychology is concerned with the positive as well as the negative, rather than at exclusion to it—as evidenced by our opening article for the *Journal of Positive Psychology* (Linley, Joseph, Harrington, & Wood, 2006). For example, in their model of moral courage in organizations, Sekerka and Bagozzi (2007) argue that, by reflecting on the negative emotions of fear, anxiety, and the self-conscious emotions of shame and guilt associated with possible future actions, individuals are able to develop and exercise positive morally courageous behavior at work—the positive comes from an awareness and experience of the negative. This rebuttal is eloquently captured by Roberts (2006, p. 297) in her response to Fineman: "rather than draw the line between what is bad and what is good, the positive lens encourages scholars to explore what may be positive about seemingly neutral or even negative states, and how to transform conditions that are truly negative into those that are positive." Further, this challenge largely ignores the evidence that positivity does benefit organizations, as well as the individuals within those organizations (Linley et al., 2009; Muse, Harris, Giles, & Feild, 2008; Ramlall, 2008; Youssef & Luthans, 2007), and as such has a moral imperative to be given due consideration in organizational research and practice. To separate out the organizational benefits of positive approaches and criticize them on this basis, while ignoring the attendant individual benefits of these positive approaches, is akin to "throwing the baby out with the bathwater."

The third challenge to positive psychology in organizations is similarly premised on the idea that a positive psychology approach is exclusively focused on strengths and has no time for weaknesses (Kaiser, 2009a). This is similar in intent to Lazarus' (2003) charge that positive psychology is focused only on positive emotions, but also needs to address negative emotions. While we dispute that this is actually the case, we agree wholeheartedly with the intent. Specific to strengths approaches, our experience as *practitioners* is that it is never appropriate to focus *only* on strengths, and that appropriate attention to weaknesses is always needed for a holistic and integrative view, as our Realise2 model shows (Linley, Willars, & Biswas-Diener, 2010). This is borne out by evidence showing that optimal strengths use (neither too much nor too little) is most effective for performance, making up to 43% difference in effectiveness (Kaiser, Lindberg, & Craig, 2007).

Overall, then, it seems like the arguments against positive psychology in organizations are typically premised on either misunderstandings or limited understandings of the approaches that positive psychology practitioners may employ. By shifting the focus from problem solving to abundance, organizations have the potential to develop an approach that allows employees to excel at what they do best, to create a sustainable,

positive, and rewarding culture, for both individuals and the organization. This does not translate into an exclusive focus on the positive, but rather provides the potential for an integrative understanding of how we can create organizations as places that may ultimately serve as instruments for the magnification and development of all that is best about the human spirit—a theme to which we turn in our Roadmap, next.

## Moving Forward: A Research/Practice Roadmap for the Organizational Applications of Positive Psychology

In developing this Roadmap, we have reflected on some of the biggest challenges and the biggest questions that we face as practitioner-researchers in the organizational applications of positive psychology. The field is nascent, and so we don't have all the answers, but instead we pose a series of questions that we intend will shape the direction of the field in moving forward, and deliver the benefits of positive psychology applications more widely for everyone working in organizations. In setting our six questions for the *Research/ Practice Roadmap for the Organizational Applications of Positive Psychology*, we start with those that are close to home—the nature of what we do and who does it—before moving on to those questions that actually fire us up much more on a daily basis—the questions of *why* we should be doing this in the first place.

### Inspiring Collaboration and Integration

If we believe (as *we* do) that society is better served by the integration of research and practice in organizational life, and in the collaborations that lead to this integration, then we must begin by paying attention to the types of research that are conducted and the reasons for which they are conducted. Anderson, Herriott, and Hodgkinson (2001) provide a superb 2X2 matrix (the 2X2 matrix would be considered by many to be the doyen of the consulting world) along the dimensions of research quality and research audience for occupational psychology. These two dimensions intersect to define research that is *Puerile* (poor quality and of little interest to any audience), *Populist* (poor quality but appeals to a popular audience), *Pedantic* (high quality but of very limited circulation and interest, only to one's professional peers), and *Pragmatic* (high-quality research that has a broad circulation and relevance to both other researchers and practitioners).

Clearly, one should be desirous of *Pragmatic* research, yet also recognize the multitude of barriers that exist to its inception and delivery. These barriers include the research interests of researchers (who typically write for other researchers, rather than for practitioners); the academic reward systems for those researchers (which typically reward pedantic research at the expense of pragmatic research); the intellectual barrier that is created between researchers and practitioners when researchers write in a scientific language that is opaque to all but their initiated peers (a seeming prerequisite for pedantic research); and massive discrepancies in time horizons between academic institutions (where course accreditations and promotion panels can typically take upward of a year) and commercial organizations (where, in reflection of the exponential pace of change, time horizons are measured in minutes, hours, and days in the short term, months and quarters in the medium term, and years only in the very long term). Clearly, a visitor from another planet may well conclude that research and practice had been explicitly designed *not* to support each other.

Yet, as much of the research and practice reviewed in this chapter attests, positive psychology—and especially positive psychology researcher/practitioners—are doing much to surmount these barriers and to create communities of practice where research is translated into practice and where practical concerns are used to shape research questions of interest. This is what we do every day in blending our research and consulting work at the Centre of Applied Positive Psychology—and this chapter serves as one example of doing so. As such, in taking a positive psychology mindset to the challenge, we ask:

1. *What can we learn from the successful integration of research and practice that can be used to inform and develop further successful integration of research and practice on a much wider scale? Specific research projects that could address this question include: What is the evidence to show that empirically informed organizational interventions deliver better outcomes than experientially informed interventions? Such a question might be approached by having two groups presented with the same issue, and one group designing an empirically informed*

*intervention, while the second group designs an intervention based on their own experience. The effectiveness of the two interventions would then be compared.*

## Creating Communities of Practice

The people who are enabled to serve in this integration of research and practice will come, by definition, from a variety of backgrounds—academia, consulting, private practice, organizations large and small, commercial, and public sector. There are, however, two key constituencies where we might effectively intervene in order to leverage the future of the organizational applications of positive psychology: occupational (I/O) psychology training and business school training.

In our discussions with UK practitioners of occupational (I/O) psychology, there is a real sense that occupational psychology has lost its way and needs to be refreshed in its thinking and approach. Organizational purchasers of traditional occupational psychology services (assessment centers, development retreats, diversity audits) are increasingly taking this work in-house as a means of reducing costs and realizing the benefits of the talent and expertise they already employ. This trend means that traditional occupational psychology practices are having to redefine what they do to position themselves as shapers of the game once again, rather than as chasers of the game. Positive psychology applications in organizations have tremendous potential in this way and provide one of the reasons we see such an explosion of interest across organizational consulting firms in this area.

Similarly, business school graduates are increasingly turning their attention to what they need to know—and hence what should be included in their curricula—that goes beyond the traditional business school content of strategy, marketing, economics, finance, and accounting. Organizational Behavior (OB) is often included, but for many, "OB" stood for a less-than-flattering alternative term. With the science of positive psychology, and an increasing evidence base for the critical role of human engagement and innovation in organizations, OB has the potential to take an increasingly critical differentiating role in management and organizational innovation (see Hamel, 2007). As such, the question we pose for our Roadmap is:

2. *How do we need to shape and design occupational (I/O) psychology and business*

*school training, such that developing practitioners are inspired to infuse the lessons of positive psychology applications in organizations in their work? A specific research project to assess this question would be to compare and contrast the professional effectiveness of I/O psychologists and business school graduates who (a) had had no experience with OB materials and (b) had had significant exposure to OB materials. The outcome variables of interest would be whether the practitioners were differentially effective in their outcomes achieved, and whether this effectiveness varied according to the nature of the outcomes, for example, people outcomes relative to business strategy outcomes, as two comparison points.*

## Making the Business, Research, and Social Case for Positive Psychology Applications in Organizations

Why should organizations give credence to positive psychology applications? Why should practitioners invest their valuable training time in attending to it? Why should consulting teams consider that a knowledge of positive psychology may be a key part of their consulting arsenal? It is imperative that we, as a discipline, are able to answer these questions affirmatively. Otherwise we have no call whatsoever on the time and attention of those we seek to serve in an increasingly information-crowded world.

Positive psychology is about the study of the "positive" but is also fundamentally about changing the nature of the questions that we ask (Linley, Joseph, Harrington, & Wood, 2006). When we ask the right questions, we are far more likely to arrive at the right answers—and yet, so often, we unwittingly ask the wrong questions, shaped and conditioned as we are by the fundamental assumptions, cultural norms, organizational codes, and behavioral experiences that define the lenses through which we see the world. As Robert Sternberg (1999; in Morgeson, Seligman, Sternberg, Taylor, & Manning, 1999) insightfully recognized, knowing which question to ask in the first place is key. We should be absolutely clear on the "so what" of what we discover, and yet too often our experience is that the implications of research are literally "so what?" Life would typically have been no different—and certainly no worse—had we not known the answer to this particular research question.

As such, we must strive to ensure that the questions we ask as researchers and practitioners are worthy of being asked in the first place. Do they not only advance knowledge but do so in a way that will make a fundamental difference, or provide powerful insights, into how we might improve the lot of human beings in the world of work? Our Roadmap question is thus:

3. *What do we need to demonstrate to make the business, research, and social case for positive psychology? Are the questions that we are asking, and the interventions that we are undertaking, really going to help us in making this case? Specific research questions that we are often asked include, "What is the business value of positivity?" or "What is the bottom-line impact of employing strengths-based approaches?" In each case, we should be striving to provide specific evidence that answers these questions. For example, is strengths-based recruitment more effective than traditional competency-based recruitment? Is a positive psychology approach to talent management better at developing people than a traditional deficit-based model? Do outplaced employees fare better when they have experienced strengths-based outplacement relative to traditional CV-building workshops? Ultimately, as this evidence builds and we are able to collate it by literature reviews and meta-analyses, we will be able to answer the questions in the broad terms that they are asked, but in the short term, our focus should be on answering specific research questions about specific outcome needs that will ultimately form the evidence base on which later applications can be built.*

### Redefine the Nature of Work

Work is, for many, still an "industrial age" activity, despite the fact that we have been in the information age for at least a decade. Organizations, and the management of organizations, are very slow to catch up. As Studs Terkel (1972, p. xi) put it:

"… work is, by its very nature, about violence—to the spirit as well as to the body. It is about ulcers as well as accidents, about shouting matches as well as fistfights, about nervous breakdowns as well as kicking the dog around… It is about a search too, for daily meaning as well as daily bread, for recognition as well as cash, for astonishment rather than torpor; in short, for a sort of life rather than a Monday through Friday sort of dying."

Conduct a thesaurus search for the synonyms of work, and this is representative of what you find: *drudge, grind, servitude sweat, toil*. Even worse, its antonyms: *entertainment, fun, pastime* (search conducted at www.thesaurus.com). Is work really so bad? As positive psychologists, we don't think so, but lay definitions and vocabulary seem to suggest that for many people it is. Given this, it seems that one cannot talk about the organizational applications of positive psychology without first recognizing the fundamental that the experience of work for so many people could be so much more—and that, as positive psychologists, we have both a deep responsibility and a major opportunity to take on the mantle of expanding and sharing our knowledge of what makes work fulfilling, and then, most important of all, helping to shape workplaces so that they are conducive to this general experience, for both organizational and individual ends.

In essence, it is our view that positive psychology—and especially positive psychology practitioners working with and within organizations—have before them a remarkable opportunity to help shape work as something that people want to *do*, and to create organizations as communities where people want to *be*. There is already a wealth of knowledge from positive psychology research that speaks to how we can create environments that allow people to give of the best of themselves, and how we can both identify and harness the best of what people have to offer.

We see organizations that inculcate the key principles of positive psychology as being organizations where employees know for themselves what their greatest contribution can be and how they can make it, where they know what their strengths are and how they can use them most effectively, and where they have a clear view on what does and doesn't engage them in their work—and have the opportunity to do something about it. This vision speaks to a different sort of organizing than most of us have experienced, but it is one of which we have (hopefully) all had a sight—if only fleetingly—at some point in time. This vision requires a simplification, rather than a complication, of HR processes and practices, since it speaks to employees being in the driver's seat for their own contributions and

their own careers, rather than being mere passengers across the employee life cycle. This leads us to the fourth question of our Roadmap:

4. *How can we create work as something that people love to do, and organizations as places where people love to be? Specific research projects in this area would be focused on questions of whether organizations that adopt a more positive approach score higher than others on employee engagement and corporate responsibility scores, and whether they ultimately are able to deliver better business performance. Anecdotally, evidence suggests that this is the case, but in the complex world of organizational life, it is increasingly difficult to untangle cause and effect and establish meaningful predictors of outcomes—but we should still be striving to do so!*

### Redefine Our Definition and Assumptions about Organizations

Our views of organizations and how they ought to be "organized" have not really changed since the industrial revolution. Henri Fayol, a management theorist, described some of the essential functions of management in organizations thus in 1917: planning, organizing, commanding, coordinating, and controlling. Approaching a century later, the same list could largely apply. Can we really claim that the world—and the world of *organizations*—has changed so little in this time? We think *not*.

As such, where might we turn to try and understand more modern ideas for the structure of organizations, or indeed the process of organizing? There are two great lessons that are all around us. The first is evolution, and the lesson of how we as human beings have consistently evolved to defend ourselves against threats and to take advantage of opportunities. Organizations need to do the same, developing an organizational change agility that reflects the evolutionary adaptiveness of the humans who make up organizations—but at a much, *much* faster pace.

The second, in our modern age, is the lesson of the Internet. It has become a cliché to say that the Internet has revolutionized our lives and continues to do so. But the principles of the Internet—distributed leadership, greater open-source technologies, networked organizing, parallel processing, almost no hierarchies—have yet to revolutionize how we think about and organize in organizations. But change is coming, and practitioner-researchers in the organizational applications of positive psychology would do well to develop a view on how organizations could learn from the power of harnessing the collective talents that exist around them—the open-source operating system Linux, and the online encyclopedia Wikipedia being but two of the most well-known examples (Tapscott & Williams, 2007).

There is but one organization that has truly adapted the principles of evolution and the distributed efficacy of the Internet into its management structures from the beginning. It is the largest organization in the world. Almost everyone has heard of it, almost all of us will have used it, but few of us would recognize its accolade as World No. 1—in large part because it is, like evolution and the Internet, all around us. The company is VISA, and its history and rise is charted movingly by its Founding CEO, Dee Hock (2005). There is much that we can all learn from this new way of conceptualizing organizations, as our fifth Roadmap question attests:

5. *If we were to design organizations that are fit for the challenges of the 21st century and beyond, how would we do so? How can the organizational applications of positive psychology help realize this field of inquiry? Here specific research projects would be focused on whether positivity allows organizations to be more agile, adaptive, and resilient, all three being qualities that will define the successful organizations of the future. Can researchers conduct studies of organizational agility, adaptiveness, and resilience that can then predict how those organizations will fare over the course of differing social, economic, technological, and demographic challenges? These are the issues faced by organizations in the modern world, and by grasping this need, positive psychology has the opportunity to contribute to their design and practice in the future.*

### Redefine our View of "How Organizations Ought to Be"

Well before the global recession and financial crisis that prompted a questioning of our model of increasingly globalized capitalism, prescient thinkers were raising the question of "how ought organizations to be?"—in fact, none other than the VISA Founding CEO, Dee Hock (2005).

There are many things about our current organizational structures that work at the level of efficiency and profit but that are woefully lacking at the level of human engagement and social contribution. Equally, organizations are the most powerful entities on Earth, and so we rightly should attend to the question of how organizations can be used as a force for positive social change (see also Biswas-Diener, Linley, Govindji & Woolston, this volume). Peter Senge and colleagues (2008) describe this as *The Necessary Revolution*, while Howard Gardner (2007) focuses on *Responsibility at Work* and the nature of *Good Work* (Gardner, Csikszentmihalyi, & Damon, 2001). In a close link to the positive psychology field, David Cooperrider and his colleagues lead the way in adopting a positive approach to answering the question of how organizations can be used to positive social ends, through their work at the Center for Business as an Agent of World Benefit (see http://worldbenefit.case.edu).

Whatever one's view of organizations, it is *our* view that two things are fundamental givens and need to be harnessed to effect the change the world so desperately requires: first, organizations are not the enemy, but rather the single greatest means we have to effect this necessary social, economic, and environmental change; and second, the imperative of that change is becoming ever greater—and as it does, so does the imperative for us to find more satisfying answers to the question of *how organizations ought to be*, in service of creating a world that is environmentally sustainable, economically developing, technologically advanced, and socially inclusive. This leads us to the final—and arguably most important—question for our Roadmap:

6. *How ought organizations to be, if we are to redefine them as agents for positive social change in a way that blends the driving forces of profit and market capitalism with the imperative outcomes of positive social impact and sustainability? On this basis, positive psychology researchers can be looking to provide the evidence that organizations that are agents of positive social change are making a tangible and sustainable difference in their worlds. Here the challenge is a slightly different one, since many know in their hearts that they are, yet they lack the empirical evidence to demonstrate it. Here positive psychology researchers can serve the future of the discipline by bringing the rigor of their*

scientific training and methods to evaluation and outcome studies that are not intervention-based but instead seek to provide the evidence for good works that are already underway. In doing so, positive psychology researchers may be doing one of the greatest services for their field and for humankind, by shining the light of empirical evidence in support of the good works that are happening already but which require scientific support for their defense and continuation.

Overall in this chapter, we have set out to take stock of what is known so far about the organizational applications of positive psychology, but also, perhaps more importantly, to turn our minds, and your thoughts, toward what a future Roadmap for the discipline may be. We have cast our perspectives well beyond the academic library and the consultant's office, ultimately to take on our responsibility as citizens of the world, asking ourselves how the discipline that we love can become even more of a force for good in the world we all share. We hope we have inspired you to join us on this journey.

## References

Anderson, N., Herriot, P., & Hodgkinson, G. P. (2001). The practitioner-researcher divide in industrial, work, and organizational (IWO) psychology: Where are we now, and where do we go from here? *Journal of Occupational and Organizational Psychology, 74*, 391–411.

Arakawa, D., & Greenberg, M. (2007). Optimistic managers and their influence on productivity and employee engagement in a technology organization: Implications for coaching psychologists. *International Coaching Psychology Review, 2* (1), 78–89.

Avolio, B. J., Griffith, J., Wernsing, T. S., & Walumbwa, F. O. (2010). What is authentic leadership development? In P. A. Linley, S. Harrington, & N. Garcea (Eds.), *Oxford handbook of positive psychology and work* (pp. 39–51). New York: Oxford University Press.

Barrett, G. V., & Depinet, R. L. (1991). A reconsideration of testing for competence rather than for intelligence. *American Psychologist, 46*, 1012–1024.

Barrow, S., & Mosley, R. (2005). *The employer brand: bringing the best of brand management to people at work.* Chichester, UK: Wiley.

Biswas-Diener, R., & Dean, B. (2007). *Positive psychology coaching: Putting the science of happiness to work for your clients.* Hoboken, NJ: Wiley.

Buckingham, M., & Clifton, D. O. (2001). *Now, discover your strengths.* New York: Simon & Schuster.

Cameron, K. S., Dutton, J. E., & Quinn, R. E. (Eds.). (2003). *Positive organizational scholarship: Foundations of a new discipline.* San Francisco, CA: Berrett-Koehler.

Cameron, K., & Lavine, M. (2006). *Making the impossible possible: Leading extraordinary performance—the Rocky Flats story.* San Francisco, CA: Berrett-Koehler.

Carter, D., & Page, N. (2009). Strengths coaching. In S. J. Lopez (Ed.), *The encyclopaedia of positive psychology.* Oxford: Blackwell.

Cascio, W. F. (1995). Whither industrial and organizational psychology in a changing world of work? *American Psychologist, 50*, 928–939.

Centre for Tomorrow's Company (2009). *Tomorrow's global talent: How will leading global companies create value through people?* London: Author.

Chen, V. C., Lee, H., & Yeh, Y. Y. (2008). The antecedent and consequence of person-organization fit: Ingratiation, similarity, hiring recommendations, and job offer. *International Journal of Selection and Assessment, 16* (3), 210–219.

CIPD (2006). *Talent management: Understanding the dimensions.* London: Chartered Institute for Personnel and Development.

Cooperrider, D. L., & Srivastva, S. (1987). Appreciative inquiry in organizational life. In R. W. Woodman & W. A. Pasmore (Eds.), *Research in organizational change and development* (vol. 1, pp. 129–169). Greenwich, CT: JAI Press.

Corporate Leadership Council (2002). *Performance management survey.* Washington, DC: Author.

Corporate Leadership Council (2009). *Rebuilding the employment value proposition: Four strategies to improve employee effort and retention.* Washington, DC: Author.

Daniels, A. C. (1994). *Bringing out the best in people: How to apply the astonishing power of positive reinforcement.* New York: McGraw Hill.

Drucker, P. F. (1967). *The effective executive.* London: Heinemann.

Fayol, H. (1917). *Industrial and general administration* (Trans. J. A. Coubrough) [1930]. Geneva: International Management Institute.

Fineman, S. (2006). On being positive: Concerns and counterpoints. *Academy of Management Review, 31* (2), 270–291.

Fredrickson, B. F., & Dutton, J. E. (Eds.). (2008). Positive organizing [special issue]. *Journal of Positive Psychology, 3 (1)*, 1–75.

Galpin, M., Stairs, M., & Page, N. (2008). Whose engagement is it anyway? *Organisations and People, 15 (2)*, 37–43.

Garcia, M. F., Triana, M. C., Peters, A. N., & Sanchez, M. (2009). Self-enhancement in a job search context. *International Journal of Selection and Assessment, 17 (3)*, 290–299.

Gardner, H. (Ed.) (2007). *Responsibility at work: How leading professionals act (or don't act) responsibly*. San Francisco, CA: Jossey Bass.

Gardner, H., Csikszentmihalyi, M., & Damon, W. (2001). *Good work: Where excellence and ethics meet*. New York: Basic Books.

Gardner, W. L., Avolio, B. J., & Walumbwa, F. O. (Eds.). (2005). *Authentic leadership theory and practice: Origins, effects and development*. Greenwich, CT: JAI Press.

Gittell, J. H., Cameron, K., Lim, S., & Rivas, V. (2006). Relationships, layoffs, and organizational resilience: Airline industry responses to September 11. *Journal of Applied Behavioral Science, 42*, 300–329.

Govindji, R., & Linley, P. A. (2007). Strengths use, self-concordance and well-being: Implications for strengths coaching and coaching psychologists. *International Coaching Psychology Review, 2 (2)*, 143–153.

Green, L. S., Oades, L. G., & Grant, A. M. (2006). Cognitive-behavioral, solution-focused life coaching: Enhancing goal striving, well-being and hope. *Journal of Positive Psychology, 1*, 142–149.

Hamel, G. (2007). *The future of management*. Boston, MA: Harvard Business School Press.

Hamel, G. (2009, *February*). Moon shots for management. *Harvard Business Review*, 91–98.

Harter, J. K., & Blacksmith, N. (2010). Employee engagement and the psychology of joining, staying in, and leaving organizations. In P. A. Linley, S. Harrington, & N. Garcea (Eds.), *Oxford handbook of positive psychology and work* (pp. 121–130). New York: Oxford University Press.

Harter, J. K., Schmidt, F. L., & Keyes, C. L. M. (2003). Well-being in the workplace and its relationship to business outcomes: A review of the Gallup studies. In C. L. M. Keyes & J. Haidt (Eds.), *Flourishing: Positive psychology and the life well-lived* (pp. 205–224). Washington, DC: American Psychological Association.

Hill, J. (2003). Bleak future or new dawn? *The Psychologist, 16*, 137–138.

Hock, D. (2005). *One from many: VISA and the rise of chaordic organization*. San Francisco, CA: Berrett-Koehler.

Isherwood, S. (2008). Flaws exposed in talent spotting models. *Financial Times, October*, 13.

John Lewis Partnership (2009). Our employees. Retrieved October 5, 2009, from: http://www.johnlewispartnership.co.uk/Display.aspx?&MasterId=aa8998ed–9ef3–4d14–8264–f62b2a218dc1&NavigationId=632

Johnson, K. J., & Fredrickson, B. L. (2005). "We all look the same to me": Positive emotions eliminate the own-race bias in face recognition. *Psychological Science, 16*, 875–881.

Judge, T. A., Thoresen C. J., Bono, J. E., & Patton, G. K. (2001). The job satisfaction–job performance relationship: A qualitative and quantitative review. *Psychological Bulletin, 127*, 376–407.

Kaplan, R., & Kaiser, R. B. (2010). Toward a positive psychology for leaders. In P. A. Linley, S. Harrington, & N. Garcea (Eds.), *Oxford handbook of positive psychology and work* (pp. 107–117). New York: Oxford University Press.

Kaiser, R. B., Lindberg, J. T., & Craig, S. B. (2007). Assessing the flexibility of managers: A comparison of methods. *International Journal of Selection and Assessment, 16*, 40–55.

Lazarus, R. S. (2003). Does the positive psychology movement have legs? *Psychological Inquiry, 14 (2)*, 93–109.

Linley, A. (2008). *Average to A+: Realising strengths in yourself and others*. Coventry, UK: CAPP Press.

Linley, P. A., Biswas-Diener, R., & Trenier, E. (in press). *Positive psychology and strengths coaching through transition*. In S. Palmer & S. Panchal (Eds.), *Developmental coaching: Life transitions and generational perspectives*. London: Routledge.

Linley, P. A., & Harrington, S. (2005). Positive psychology and coaching psychology: Perspectives on integration. *The Coaching Psychologist, 1 (1)*, 13–14.

Linley, P. A., & Harrington, S. (2006). Strengths coaching: A potential-guided approach to coaching psychology. *International Coaching Psychology Review, 1*, 37–46.

Linley, P. A., Harrington, S. & Garcea, N. (Eds.) (2010a). *Oxford handbook of positive psychology and work*. New York: Oxford University Press.

Linley, P. A., Harrington, S. & Garcea, N. (2010b). Finding the positive in the world of work. In P. A. Linley, S. Harrington, & N. Garcea (Eds.), *Oxford handbook of positive psychology and work* (pp. 3–9). New York: Oxford University Press.

Linley, P. A., & Joseph, S. (Eds.) (2004). *Positive psychology in practice*. Hoboken, NJ: Wiley.

Linley, P. A., & Kauffman, C. (Eds.) (2007). Positive psychology and coaching psychology [special issue]. *International Coaching Psychology Review, 2* (1).

Linley, P. A., Joseph, S., Harrington, S., & Wood, A. M. (2006). Positive psychology: Past, present, and (possible) future. *The Journal of Positive Psychology, 1*, 3–16.

Linley, A., Willars, J., & Biswas-Diener, R. (2010). *The strengths book: Be confident, be successful, and enjoy better relationships by realising the best of you*. Coventry, UK: CAPP Press.

Linley, P. A., Woolston, L., & Biswas-Diener, R. (2009). Strengths coaching with leaders. *International Coaching Psychology Review, 4*, 37–48.

Losada, M., & Heaphy, E. (2004). The role of positivity and connectivity in the performance of business teams: A nonlinear dynamics model. *American Behavioral Scientist, 47*(6), 740–765.

Luthans, F., Avey, J. B., Avolio, B. J., Norman, S. M., & Combs, G. M. (2006). Psychological capital development: Toward a micro-intervention. *Journal of Organizational Behavior, 27*, 387–393.

Luthans, F., Avey, J. B., & Patera, J. L. (2008). Experimental analysis of a web-based training intervention to develop positive psychological capital. *Academy of Management Learning and Education, 7*, 209–221.

MacLeod, D., & Clarke, N. (2009). *Engaging for success: Enhancing performance through employee engagement*. London: Department for Business, Innovation and Skills.

Marks, N. (2006). Happiness is a serious business. In CIPD (Ed.), *Reflections on employee engagement*. London: Chartered Institute for Personnel and Development.

Maslow, A. (1998). *Maslow on management* (revised ed.). Hoboken, NJ: Wiley.

McCay, P. F., Avery, D. R., Tonidandel, S., Morris, M. A., Hernandez, M., & Hebl, M. R. (2007). Racial differences in employee retention. Are diversity climate perceptions the key? *Personnel Psychology, 60*, 35–62.

McGregor, D. (1960/2006). *The human side of enterprise* (annotated edition). New York: McGraw-Hill.

Miles, S. A., & Watkins, M. D. (2007, April). The leadership team: Complementary strengths or conflicting agendas?. *Harvard Business Review*, 90–98.

Morgeson, F., Seligman, M., Sternberg, R., Taylor, S., & Manning, C. (1999). Lessons learned from a

life in psychological science. *American Psychologist, 54*, 106–116.

Morris, D., & Garrett, J. (2010). Strengths: Your leading edge. In P. A. Linley, S. Harrington, & N. J. Garcea (Eds.), *Oxford handbook of positive psychology and Work* (pp. 95–105). New York: Oxford University Press.

Mossholder, K. W., Settoon, R. P., Armenakis, A. A., & Harris, S. G. (2000). Emotion during organizational transformations. *Group and Organization Management, 25, 3*, 220–243.

Muse, L., Harris, S. G., Giles, W. F., & Feild, H. S. (2008). Work-life benefits and positive organizational behavior: Is there a connection? *Journal of Organizational Behavior, 29*, 171–192.

nef consulting (2009). *Well-being@Work*. London: nef consulting.

Page, N. (20 July 07, 10). *Strengths-based approaches to talent management*. Invited presentation to the Corporate Research Forum, London.

Page, N., & Linley, P. A. (Eds.) (2008). Positive psychology at work [special issue]. *Organisations and People, 15* (1).

Peterson, S. J., & Byron, K. (2008). Exploring the role of hope in job performance: Results from four studies. *Journal of Organizational Behavior, 29*, 785–803.

Preskill, H., & Donaldson, S. I. (2008). Improving the evidence base for career development programs: Making use of the evaluation profession and positive psychology movement. *Advances in Developing Human Resources, 10*, 104–121.

Ramlall, S. J. (2008). Enhancing employee performance through positive organizational behavior. *Journal of Applied Social Psychology, 38*, 1580–1600.

Rath, T., & Conchie, B. (2009). *Strengths-based leadership: A landmark study of great leaders, teams, and the reasons why we follow*. New York: Gallup Press.

Richardson, J., & West, M. A. (2010). Dream teams: A positive psychology of team working. In P. A. Linley, S. Harrington, & N. Garcea (Eds.), *Oxford handbook of positive psychology and work* (pp. 235–249). New York: Oxford University Press.

Roberts, E. (2009, April). *Imago Services' strengths-based performance management*. Presentation at the 2nd Applied Positive Psychology Conference, University of Warwick, UK.

Roberts, L. M. (2006). Shifting the lens on organizational life: The added value of positive scholarship. *Academy of Management Review, 31* (2), 292–305.

Sekerka, L. E., & Bagozzi, R. P. (2007). Moral courage in the workplace: Moving to and from the desire and decision to act. *Business Ethics: A European Review, 16* (2), 132–149.

Seligman, M. E. P. (1999). The president's address. *American Psychologist, 54,* 559–562.

Seligman, M. E. P., & Csikszentmihalyi, M. (2000). Positive psychology: An introduction. *American Psychologist, 55,* 5–14.

Senge, P., Smith, B., Kruschwitz, N., Laur, J., & Schley, S. (2008). *The necessary revolution: How individuals and organizations are working together to create a sustainable world.* London: Nicholas Brealey.

Shippmann, J. S., Ash, R. A., Battista, M., Carr, L., Eyde, L. D., Hesketh, B., et al. (2000). The practice of competency modeling. *Personnel Psychology, 53,* 703–740.

Sivanathan, N., Arnold, K. A., Turner, N., & Barling, J. (2004). Leading well: Transformational leadership and well-being. In P. A. Linley & S. Joseph (Eds.), *Positive psychology in practice* (pp. 741–755). Hoboken, NJ: Wiley.

Smedley, T. (2007). The powers that BAE. *People Management, 13* (22), 40–43.

Snyder, C. R. (1994). *The psychology of hope: You can get there from here.* New York: Free Press.

Stefanyszyn, K. (2007, November). Norwich Union changes focus from competencies to strengths. *Strategic HR Review, 7,* 10–11.

Stefanyszyn, K., & Garcea, N. (2009, May). *Strengthening Aviva in the face of adversity.* Presentation at the Association of Business Psychologists Annual Conference, Wyboston, UK.

Spence, G. B., & Grant, A. M. (2007). Professional and peer life coaching and the enhancement of goal striving and well-being: An exploratory study. *Journal of Positive Psychology, 2,* 185–194.

Stairs, M., & Galpin, M. (2010). Positive engagement: From employee engagement to workplace happiness? In P. A. Linley, S. Harrington & N. Garcea (Eds.), *Oxford handbook of positive psychology and work* (pp. 155–172). New York: Oxford University Press.

Stanton, A. L., Kirk, S. B., Cameron, C. L., & Danoff-Burg, S. (2000). Coping through emotional approach: Scale construction and validation. *Journal of Personality and Social Psychology, 66,* 350–362.

Tapscott, D., & Williams, A. D. (2007). *Wikinomics: How mass collaboration changes everything.* London: Atlantic Books.

Terkel, S. (1972/1997). *Working: People talk about what they do all day and how they feel about what they do.* New York: The New Press.

Twenge, J. M. (2007). *Generation me: Why today's young Americans are more confident, assertive, entitled–and more miserable than ever before.* New York: Free Press.

Twenge, J. M., & Campbell, S. M. (2010). Generation me and the changing world of work. In P. A. Linley, S. Harrington & N. Garcea (Eds.), *Oxford handbook of positive psychology and work* (pp. 25–35). New York: Oxford University Press.

Ulrich, D. (2008). Use your strengths to strengthen others. *Workforce Management, 87* (5), 28–29.

Ulrich, D. (2010). The abundant organization [foreword]. In P. A. Linley, S. Harrington & N. Garcea (Eds.), *Oxford handbook of positive psychology and work* (pp. xvii–xxi). New York: Oxford University Press.

Warren, S. (2010). What's wrong with being positive? In P. A. Linley, S. Harrington & N. Garcea (Eds.), *Oxford handbook of positive psychology and work* (pp. 313–322). New York: Oxford University Press.

Waugh, C. E., & Fredrickson, B. L. (2006). Nice to know you: Positive emotions, self-other overlap, and complex understanding in the formation of a new relationship. *Journal of Positive Psychology, 1,* 93–106.

Wright, T. A. (2010). More than meets the eye: The role of employee well-being in organizational research. In P. A. Linley, S. Harrington & N. Garcea (Eds.), *Oxford handbook of positive psychology and work* (pp. 143–154). New York: Oxford University Press.

Youssef, C. M., & Luthans, F. (2007). Positive organizational behavior in the workplace: The impact of hope, optimism, and resilience. *Journal of Management, 33,* 774–800.

# IX

---

## Societal Perspectives

# 25

# Place and Well-Being

*Richard Florida and Peter J. Rentfrow*

Place is a fundamental feature of human existence. Jane Jacobs (1969, 1984) long ago argued that cities are the fundamental building blocks of economic progress. Cities are vital to economic growth, as they vary markedly in natural resources, human capital, and market demands. Politicians and social scientists have long known that systems of power, the rise and fall of nations, and electoral outcomes all hinge on geography. And recent research has found that human civilization and the birth of language itself can be traced to early cities (Powell, Shennan, & Thomas, 2009). Thus, the scientific study of cities has provided terrific insight into the nature of human behavior.

But cities are not just containers comprising crops and fossil fuels, businesses and industries, or voting blocks and town halls. They are places where people live—where people come together, where they fall in love, where they raise their families, where they go to school and work, where they worship, and where they spend their free time. They are locations of human existence, human creativity, and human energy. These are fundamental aspects of human life that contribute to psychological health. And if we are to develop

an understanding of the factors that contribute to the prosperity of cities, we must consider the factors that contribute to the psychological well-being of the people who live in them.

Psychologists and the field of positive psychology in particular have made a huge contribution in shifting attention away from the factors that promote negative affect and psychological distress, toward the things that contribute to our positive affect and psychological well-being. There is now a large and robust literature on well-being; the results of which are clear. We know that well-being is positively associated with marital satisfaction, income, productivity, sociability, creativity, and physical health (Lyubomirsky, King, & Diener, 2005). Although the causal directions of those relationships are not clear, there are good reasons to believe that success in each of those domains contributes to well-being. And given that the places in which people live affect their opportunities for finding a partner, a good job, and rewarding hobbies, it is necessary to consider the impact that place has on psychological well-being.

Curiously, little attention has been given to the geography of well-being and the role of place and community in it. Psychologists and social scientists have by and large overlooked the impact that place can have on a person's happiness and satisfaction with life. More often than not, it seems as though place is merely the backdrop against which all the "real" stuff that causes people happiness or misery occurs; a stage where love is found or lost and where careers begin or end. Rarely has place been considered a source of meaning in its own right. Perhaps social scientists have gravitated away from questions about place and well-being toward other questions because place is not necessarily easy to operationalize or measure systematically. Or perhaps little attention has been paid to it because we take for granted the places in which we live. Whatever the reason is, place remains a great unknown in positive psychology.

In this chapter, we hope to redress the neglect of place by making a case for its importance in positive psychology. The primary question motivating our work is: Does where people live affect their psychological well-being? We believe there is a fair amount of research already available to help us answer that question. And we have some ideas about which aspects of places are most important. But to really develop an understanding of the interplay between place and well-being, more research is desperately needed. In the final section of the chapter, we develop a research agenda for further exploring the relation between place and well-being.

## Taking Stock: What Do We Know about Place and Well-Being?

*National differences in well-being.* Most of the research that has anything to say about place and well-being has focused on national differences (Diener & Diener, 1995; Diener, Diener, & Diener, 1995; Diener & Lucas, 2000; Diener, Oishi, & Lucas, 2003; Inglehart & Klingemann 2000; Lynn & Steel, 2006; Steel & Ones, 2002; Veenhoven, 1993). Results from several international studies converge showing consistent mean differences in well-being across nations. For example, Canada, Denmark, Switzerland, and the U.S. invariably have the highest well-being scores compared to other nations, while many nations in Eastern Europe and Africa score near the bottom (Diener, 2000; Diener et al., 1995; Veenhoven, 1993). What accounts for these national differences?

Several studies have linked national levels of well-being to a range of social indicators. By and large, the results indicate that nations where

people are happy tend to be individualistic and value independence and autonomy (Diener et al., 1995; Hofstede, 2001). Explanations for the links suggest that in individualistic societies people have a wide variety of options for how to live their lives, success is usually attributed to personal ability, and people have more freedom to express themselves than do people in more collectivistic societies. Nations that score high on measures of well-being also score high on indexes of human rights and social equality. In line with explanations for the happiness and individualism link, nations that protect the rights of people of a different gender, race, nationality, religion, or sexual orientation afford a greater proportion of their population the freedom to pursue a life that is satisfying and rewarding. A number of studies have also found a connection between national levels of well-being and income (Diener et al., 1995, 2003; Diener & Suh, 1997; Schyns, 1998). For example, Stevenson and Wolfers (2008) recently showed that happiness and income are closely related—people with high incomes are happier than people with lower incomes, both in absolute and relative terms. However, it should be noted that this link has not been found consistently (see Easterlin, 1995; Veenhoven, 1991). The inconsistency may depend on the nations that are studied, as Diener and colleagues (1995) have found that the relationship between national levels of well-being and income plateau once personal wealth reaches a certain point. The explanation for the happiness and income association is straightforward: for people to be happy, basic needs for food, water, and shelter must be met. Once the basics are taken care of, most everything else is a luxury.

As interest in national differences in well-being has taken off, so too has interest in national differences in personality. Armed with a consensually shared and empirically valid model of personality structure, teams of psychologists have started investigating national differences in the Big Five (Allik & McCrae, 2004; Hofstede & McCrae, 2004; McCrae, 2001; McCrae & Terracciano, 2007; McCrae, Terracciano et al., 2005; Schmitt, Allik, McCrae, & Benet-Martínez, 2007; Steel & Ones, 2002). In an impressive series of studies, McCrae and colleagues have amassed a database of personality scores for more than 70 nations. The results from that work show robust national personality differences and that national levels of personality are associated with rates of cancer, life expectancy, substance abuse, and obesity (McCrae & Terracciano, 2007).

Interest in national personality differences has also helped shed more light on the interplay of place and well-being. For example, Steel and Ones (2002) found that national levels of happiness and satisfaction were negatively related to levels of Neuroticism and positively related to Extraversion and Openness. McCrae et al. (2005) also found relationships between well-being and personality. Their work showed that national levels of well-being were positively related to Extraversion, Openness, and Agreeableness. Curiously, however, no relationship between Neuroticism and well-being was found. Taken together, this research indicates that the psychological dispositions common to a geographic region contribute to levels of well-being.

In summary, there is a considerable amount of evidence that well-being is not uniformly distributed around the globe but is geographically clustered. In nations where people's basic needs are taken care of, where people have the freedom to be themselves, and where differences are tolerated, people are generally happy. So we now have some clues about which aspects of place are related to psychological well-being. But is nationality a sufficient proxy for place? Is it enough for understanding the impact place has on well-being?

The nations in which people live obviously have a profound effect on their lives, but when we think and talk about where we live, it is not our home country that comes to mind, but the cities, towns, and neighborhoods in which we live. Moreover, when people are considering places to live, places to settle down, find a job, and start a family, they tend not to look outside their home country but within it. Thus, if we are going to develop an understanding of the interplay between place and well-being, we really need to look within nations.

*Intra-national differences in well-being.* There are good reasons to expect the interplay of place and well-being to go deeper than the national level. Regions within nations vary on many of the same indicators that are associated with national levels of well-being.

Perhaps the only study that has directly investigated intra-national differences in well-being was conducted by Plaut, Markus, and Lachman (2002). Using a nationally representative sample of U.S. residents, they compared each of the nine U.S. Census divisions on psychological, social, and physical well-being. Their results revealed high levels of well-being in the New England, Great Plain, Southwest, and Mountain regions,

and comparatively lower levels in the Mid-Atlantic, Midwest, and especially Southeastern and South Central regions. The results from this work demonstrate that there are intra-national differences in well-being. But because the regional differences in well-being were not compared to any social indicators or outcome variables, it is hard to know how much importance or meaning to place on those differences.

A recent study of personality differences within the U.S. provides reasons to believe that regional differences in well-being probably vary at the state level and, more importantly, are related to important state-level outcomes. Using a sample of more than three-quarters of a million U.S. residents, Rentfrow, Gosling, and Potter (2008) mapped the distribution of the Big Five personality dimensions and examined their connections with a variety of social indicators. Their results revealed some very clear patterns. For example, Extraversion was highest in the central states and lowest in the Northwest and most of the East Coast states. Agreeableness was higher in the Midwest and Southern states than in the Northeastern states. Conscientiousness was highest in the Southern and Midwest states and lowest in the Northeastern states. The map of Neuroticism revealed a "stress belt" dividing the East and West, with states from Maine to Louisiana being highest, states to the immediate Northwest and Southeast having slightly lower levels, and states in the West having the lowest levels of Neuroticism. And a clear geographic divide emerged for Openness, such that states in the Northeast and West Coast were higher than those in the Midwest and South. But what do these differences mean? How important are they?

It turns out that they are very important. Statewide personality differences were associated with a wide array of social indicators, from crime and social involvement to political ideology and mortality. For instance, Rentfrow and colleagues (2008; Rentfrow, Jost, Gosling, & Potter, 2009) found that regional differences in Extraversion were positively related to social involvement, religiosity, and life expectancy. Statewide differences in Neuroticism were negatively related to social involvement, health-promoting behavior, and longevity. And differences in Openness were positively related to liberal values, tolerating diversity, and creativity, but negatively related to social involvement. It is also worth noting that the geographic distribution of Neuroticism was very similar to the inverse of the well-being pattern reported by Plaut and colleagues (2002). The strong relationships between personality and the social indicators make it reasonable to suppose that statewide differences in well-being might be connected to important outcome variables too. Indeed, given that well-being has been shown to relate to Extraversion and Neuroticism at both individual and aggregate levels of analysis (Diener, 2000; Diener et al., 2003; McCrae et al., 2005; Steel & Ones, 2002), the state-level research suggests that regional differences in well-being may be related to rates of community involvement, spending time with family and friends, healthy behavior, and mortality.

In summary, the research reviewed thus far makes a compelling case that there are national and regional differences in well-being. The so-called "good life" is not available to just anyone, but mainly to those who live in developed countries and in places where people are allowed to be themselves. Moreover, the research indicates that the differences in well-being are associated with cultural and societal processes. In places with strong communities, where people are able to work together and are open and accepting of those from different walks of life, individuals are generally happy and healthy. However, in places that lack such values and ideologies, people are unhappy, tense, and emotionally unstable, and physically unhealthy.

So where people live can have a dramatic effect on their psychological well-being. But all of the research covered thus far has focused on the characteristics common to places where people are happy and satisfied. As we try to develop an understanding of the connections between place and well-being, we also need to focus on the characteristics of individuals. Aside from the basics, what is it that people want from a place? Are there specific characteristics of a place that determine whether people are happy? Are certain aspects of a place more important to some people than other people? What determines whether a person stays someplace or moves away? Understanding what people want and need from where they live and whether where they live satisfies those wants and needs will further inform our knowledge of the connections between place and well-being.

*What do people want from a place?* When people are deciding where to live, what determines where they settle? Is it jobs? What about "quality of place"—outdoor attractions, historic buildings, culture, and nightlife? What about the social climate—the values, political views, and religious beliefs of those who already live there? Tiebout (1956) suggested that when people are choosing a place to live (e.g., a neighborhood), they are evaluating places in terms of how well the places can provide the services they need. Is it a safe area? Are the schools good? How far away is it from the office? People with children naturally pick neighborhoods with good school systems, whereas young, single professionals have different sets of needs and therefore choose different places to settle. But what exactly is it about place that contributes to our happiness?

Using data from a Gallup survey, Florida (2008) examined the characteristics of places that are most important to people, which included proximity to family and friends, career options, and amenities. For some people, the most important aspect of where they lived was its proximity to family and friends. Such people placed considerable importance on tight social relationships and therefore derive a tremendous sense of belonging from where they live. For some, the most important aspect of where they lived depended on career opportunities and, in particular, having a meaningful career. Such people reported deriving higher levels of satisfaction from their work than from their social lives and communities. For others, a great deal of their happiness was derived from the quality of the place itself. Of course, preferences vary, with some people craving outdoor amenities such as trails, mountains, and beaches, and others preferring city amenities such as museums, cultural events, and nightlife.

The results from the Gallup survey also revealed that people who live in different types of places derive happiness from different things. For example, people who lived in suburban areas placed considerable importance on safety, the quality of the school systems, the local economy, and career opportunities. Residents of rural areas reported deriving satisfaction from their relationships with their family and friends, as well as from the clean air and water, and physical and natural beauty of their surroundings. People living in large urban centers reported deriving happiness from their ability to constantly meet new people, as well as the easy access to diverse cultural opportunities like theaters, museums, art galleries, restaurants, and live music venues (Florida, 2008).

That research provides ideas about the key aspects of a place that are important to people and indicates that people who live in different locales derive satisfaction from different things.

There appears to be an interaction between people and the environments in which they live. Not everyone derives happiness from the same place; finding happiness turns on finding a place that fits with a person's wants and needs. Thus, people seem to seek out places that they think will meet their needs.

This idea is consistent with a lot of social scientific research. For instance, there is a considerable amount of evidence from psychological research indicating that people seek out social environments in which their attitudes, beliefs, and personalities are valued by others and can be easily expressed (Buss, 1987; Emmons & Diener, 1986; Ickes, Snyder, & Garcia, 1997; McCrae, 2001; Swann, Rentfrow, & Guinn, 2003). For example, extraverts tend to seek out socially stimulating environments, whereas people high in Neuroticism tend to avoid highly stimulating environments (e.g., Furnham, 1981). Furthermore, when people find social environments where their psychological needs and wants are met, they are more satisfied than are people in environments that do not meet their needs (e.g., Swann, De La Ronde, & Hixon, 1994).

The notion that people seek out environments that will satisfy their needs is consistent with research in demography and economics that is concerned with the factors that influence migration patterns. Traditionally, research on migration has pointed to economic concerns as the primary factor determining whether or not people move. For example, a classic study by Rossi (1955) investigated the factors underlying families' decisions to move and concluded that the most important factors were based on housing and income. Families moved to different areas when their needs for space and amenities could no longer be met, but only to areas they could afford. That research highlighted that the motive to escape from living in a dissatisfactory place is greater than the motive to leave purely for hedonic purposes. In other words, people are more likely to migrate when their current living conditions are deeply unsatisfying than they are to move to a "better" place when their current living conditions are satisfactory.

In addition to satisfying economic needs, researchers have also considered the role that psychological needs play in people's decisions to migrate. A number of researchers have suggested that regional amenities and the extent to which places provide residents with the amenities they want and need are critical in determining people's migration decisions (Clark & Hunter, 1992, 2002;

Glaeser et al. 2001; Florida, 2002; Landale & Guest, 1985; Rosen, 1979; Roback, 1982; Wolpert, 1965). For instance, Roback (1982) argued that the availability of amenities leads to such a sufficient increase in quality of life that people are willing to accept lower salaries, higher taxes, and increased housing expenses.

It turns out that certain amenities are sufficiently important that people claim they would move away from a place if they were absent from a place. Using data from a nationally representative sample of U.S. residents, Florida, Mellander, and Stolarick (2009) found that the strongest determinants of whether people planned to stay where they lived or to move elsewhere was their perception of how aesthetically pleasing and beautiful their city was, whether they felt a sense of community there, the degree of traffic and congestion, the quality of the local schools, and whether there were ample job opportunities in their line of work.

The research on place preferences and migration indicates that there are particular aspects of places that are important to people—so important that they will leave if those aspects are not present. However, that work does not necessarily indicate that the presence or absence of those features has an impact on personal well-being. Below, we draw from theory and research to develop some ideas about how particular features of place might affect well-being.

## Place and Well-Being (or How Place Affects Well-Being)

Florida (2008) suggests that there appear to be four basic qualities that are very important to people's sense of place: basic needs, community, stimulation, and freedom. Basic needs refer to education and learning, crime and safety, shelter, health care, and transportation. Community refers to social support, a sense of social connection, and local government and councils. Stimulation refers to the perceived physical beauty and aesthetics of a place, as well as types and variety of amenities. Freedom refers to the ability for individuals from all walks of life to be themselves, to express themselves however they please and for others in the area to be respectful and tolerant of each person's individuality. In addition to the very basics (food, water, and shelter), we believe each of these place features can have a profound affect on personal well-being.

*Basic needs.* Having basic needs met is critical. In developed countries, places cannot sustain themselves if they do not deliver safe streets, good schools, quality health care, and the like to their residents. Indeed, how can people find happiness if they are preoccupied with their health and safety?

Countless studies have shown strong and stable relationships between psychological well-being and physical health (e.g., Futterman, Kemeny, Shapiro, & Fahey, 1992; Salovey, Rothman, Detweiler, & Steward, 2000; Stone, Cox, Valdimarsdottier, Jandorf, & Neale, 1987). Moreover, certain characteristics of places also have effects on health and well-being. For example, neighborhood characteristics, such as housing quality and proximity to food markets and hospitals, have been shown to influence rates of depression over and above the effects of family income (Cutrona, Wallace, & Wesner, 2006; Evans, Wells, Chan, & Saltzman, 2000). Furthermore, rates of all-cause mortality and psychological stress tend to be higher in densely populated regions than in sparsely populated regions (Fleming, Baum, Davidson, Rectanus, & McArdle, 1987; Levy & Herzog, 1978). Characteristics of places also contribute to the lifestyles of the people who live in them, which, in turn, can contribute to physical health and well-being (Banks, Marmot, Oldfield, & Smith, 2006; Marmot & Wilkinson, 2005).

Living in a place that is safe is also vital for well-being (Black & Krishnakumar, 1998). Families with young children need very safe streets. Urbanites have different coping strategies. Young men worry less about this and are able to tolerate neighborhoods that may be rough around the edges. Some artsy types even say they're inspired by such urbanity. And young women say they often locate in upscale or gay neighborhoods, not just for the architecture or amenities, but because they are safe (Florida, 2002).

Affordable housing is a key part of happiness and well-being. In places where middle-class families can still afford a home, housing is not a big issue. However, affordable housing is a huge dilemma in most major metropolitan areas, like the Bay Area, New York City, Los Angeles, Austin, and Seattle. Those places are becoming unaffordable for middle-class families and even more so for young people starting out in their careers. Add to that the increased amount of traffic. Schrank and Lomax (2004) found that the average urban motorist was stuck in traffic for almost two whole days (46 hours) in 2002. Los Angeles topped the list, with an average annual delay of 93 hours, followed by San Francisco (73 hours) and Washington, DC (67 hours). Although housing may be cheaper and neighborhoods safer in areas bordering large cities, what effect do the long and unpredictable commutes have on personal well-being? Surely the lack of control and unpredictability over the daily commute to work wears some people down.

*Community.* In places where people are connected to one another, they are less isolated and live more fulfilling lives. Jacobs (1961) stressed the importance of city communities as instrumental in helping people meet their needs. People are fulfilled by being able to go out their door and see other people, by interacting on front stoops or porches, by the hustle and bustle of urban life. Indeed, the neighbors and friends that live nearby can provide support and bring satisfaction on a regular basis.

But increasingly, people are feeling less and less connection to the people in their areas. Indeed, a growing number of studies have begun to reveal a decline in the number and quality of social ties people have. For instance, McPherson, Smith-Lovin, and Brashers (2006) found that the percentage of Americans who felt "socially isolated" in their communities (defined by having no one to talk to about personal matters) increased from 25% in 1985 to more than 50% in 2004. The largest change since 1985, however, was the momentous decline in ties among neighbors—the percentage of people who reported being close to someone in their neighborhood dropped from 19% in 1985 to 8% in 2004. Thus, an increasing number of people live alone, lack friends or family nearby, and have no one to talk to about important personal, career, and life matters. This helps explain why so many people want to live in places that make it easy for them to connect with others and form new relationships.

There is also evidence that people are happier in places where the local leadership is positive and forward-looking, and where it acts with ethics and integrity (Florida, 2008). It is not only top-down forms of leadership that matter; bottom-up leadership, which reflects an active and engaged citizenry, is also important. Indeed, communities where people are more engaged and feel that their voices and energy matter see that translate into higher rates of satisfaction and happiness (Putnam, 2007). Volunteerism is most closely linked to people's satisfaction with where they live as well as with overall happiness (Thoits & Hewitt, 2001). In an era when so many people feel alone and isolated, many of us take joy from volunteering for a cause we believe in, helping our community, and connecting with other similarly motivated people.

*Stimulation.* Everyone has a favorite activity for blowing off steam. Some people enjoy time outside, hiking, running, or cycling; others enjoy the company of others, at the local park, watering hole, or community center; and others like cultural events, like museums, food festivals, or music concerts. And when the leisure activities people enjoy are readily available where they live, it can provide satisfaction and fulfillment. Indeed, the extent to which a place provides people with sufficient stimulation is critical for personal well-being because it provides things to do and look forward to. Several studies indicate that proximity to preferred leisure activities is among the most common reasons people give for settling in a particular area, and that people who live in areas where they can easily pursue their hobbies are considerably happier than are people who do not (Barcus, 2004; Frey, Liaw, & Lin, 2000; Rowles & Watkins, 1993).

Places can also be a major source of creative stimulation. For example, Florida (2008) found that the "symbolic amenities"—parks and open space, cultural offerings—afforded by certain places can provide residents with visual and cultural stimulation. This is important because having space and resources to pursue leisure activities can provide fulfillment and satisfaction. Indeed, Csikszentmihalyi (1990) found that engaging in creative activities like writing, playing music, computer programming, mountain climbing, or chess can provide a major source of enjoyment and productivity. Such activities can facilitate "flow," or intense, unfettered focus and concentration. Thus, when the places in which people live have the physical, social, or cultural offerings that fit with their tastes and leisure interests, people should pursue more often the activities they enjoy, and feel a sense of fulfillment and satisfaction as a result.

*Freedom.* It is important that people live in places that allow them to follow their dreams and express their identities. Places need to provide the space necessary for personal discovery and self-actualization. As the research reviewed indicates, a large part of happiness comes from people's ability to pursue their interests and be themselves.

Several studies indicate that in nations where people are free, importance is placed on self-expression, human rights, and discrimination. They also show high levels of well-being, good

health, and equal rights (Inglehart & Oyserman, 2004; Kuppens, Realo, & Diener, 2008). Self-expression, tolerance, and openness are important at local levels too. People place considerable importance on living in a place where individuals are free to be themselves (Florida, 2008).

In places where diversity is tolerated, where people are open and accepting of people from different cultures, more people are free to pursue their own interests. As a result, more people should be able to live fulfilling and satisfying lives. For example, members of certain groups may choose to live in particular places precisely because the residents are believed to be tolerant of their lifestyles.

Happiness and the freedom to self-express go hand in hand. Research by Johnson and Fredrickson (2005) found that happy people are more open-minded and less racially biased than unhappy people. They are also more likely to see the "bigger picture" and are more creative. This is consistent with work by Florida (2002), which indicates that places that are more open and tolerant are also more innovative and creative.

*Summary.* The available research makes it clear that where people live can have a profound effect on their psychological well-being. We propose that one mechanism that contributes to the impact of place on well-being is identity. A considerable amount of empirical research has examined the notion that where people live shapes their self-views and identity (e.g., Cuba & Hummon, 1993; Lewicka, 2005; Proshansky, 1978; Twigger-Ross & Uzzell, 1996). Much of that work indicates that people derive a sense of who they are, a sense of community, and a sense of belonging from where they are from. For example, Cuba & Hummon (1993) found that place identity is based on individuals' connections with people in the community and that particular social amenities facilitate making contact with people in the community. Furthermore, research indicates that when a place is drastically altered, residents may experience grief and a profound sense of loss (Fried, 1963). Thus, the basic needs, community, stimulation, and freedom that places afford must affect how people see themselves, their relation to the world around them, and how they navigate through life.

## Moving Forward: Developing an Agenda for Research on Place and Well-Being

Although very few studies have directly examined connections between place and psychological well-being, the available evidence makes it clear that there is a strong connection between the two. We must now begin to broaden our research foci and start looking more carefully at the specific aspects of places that contribute to well-being. As we see it, there are two areas that need serious consideration. First, we need to develop good social indicators of well-being. Second, we need to develop a better idea of how people perceive and experience places.

The robust national differences in well-being and the obvious importance of psychological health led Diener (2000) to propose the development of a national subjective well-being index. This index would track the population's happiness over time and provide a sort of barometer for assessing the psychological climate of a nation. The index could also inform policy-making decisions and be used as an outcome measure to assess the efficacy of policy reforms. We share Diener's enthusiasm for a national well-being index, but go one step further by proposing that the index should be developed at more local levels. Indeed, state and local governments have more direct and immediate effects on people's lives than do national policies. So tracking the well-being of people at state or metropolitan levels would provide far more sensitive measurements of a place's level of well-being. Additionally, state and local indexes would provide valuable information for comparing the efficacy of policy reforms between regions. Such information would not only inform our understanding of the interplay between place and well-being but could also lead to more effective policies. Thus, our understanding of the links between place and well-being will be informed by developing valid and reliable outcome measures.

With a well-being index that is administered regularly, time-lagged analyses could be performed to evaluate just how influential particular place-factors are to psychological well-being. For example, changes in regional characteristics, such as reductions in crime, revitalized local economies, or the introduction of new amenities, could be compared with local levels of well-being. Such work would not only inform our understanding of the impact certain factors have on well-being but also help us develop more effective local policies. It would also provide insight into the amount of time it takes for changes in the environment to effect individuals' levels of happiness and satisfaction.

The other research direction that deserves serious consideration is people's perceptions and experiences of places. Just as individuals form impressions of other people, so too do they form impressions of places. Some places may be perceived as friendly and relaxing, while others may be perceived as vibrant and upbeat. Talk about a city's energy, its vibe, its hustle-and-bustle, or its ethos is common, but we know very little about how people perceive and experience places, or whether people perceive and experience the same places similarly. From our view, the psychological qualities that a place possesses, what we refer to as energy, are very important to residents' well-being. Future research should explore this idea with the aim of developing a grasp of what underlies people's perceptions of places. How do features of the physical environment, like mountains, vistas, skyscrapers, or open space affect perceptions? What about amenities, like cafes, shops, and parks? Does ethnic diversity shape impressions of places? What about the pace of life, population density, or foot traffic?

Understanding the energy of a place would benefit from investigating connections between perceptions of a place's energy and characteristics common to that place. For instance, people could report the extent to which they perceive certain cities (e.g., New York, San Francisco, Austin, Portland) as vibrant, peaceful, relaxed, or exciting. Those perceptions could be examined in terms of inter-judge agreement in order to gauge the extent to which people perceive those cities as having similar characteristics. And those characteristics could then be related to specific characteristics of the cities, such as population density, ethnic diversity, and amenities, for instance.

Developing a theory of place and well-being should revolve around a theory of human energy—of the inter-subjective (sharing and development) of this human energy. It is this quest for inter-subjective human energy, the energy we feed off from one another—whether in a band, a sports team, an organization, or a community—that inspires people to do more and to be more, which contributes to our sense of well-being. After all, why else would people with the ability to live elsewhere tolerate the hassles, frustrations, and high costs (economic and personal) that come with living in places like New York, Shanghai, or London? From our view, research concerned with the perceived energy of places will greatly inform our understanding of the ways in which place and psychological well-being interact.

*References*

Allik, J., & McCrae, R. R. (2004). Toward a geography of personality traits: Patterns of profiles across 36 cultures. *Journal of Cross-Cultural Psychology, 35*, 13–28.

Banks, J., Marmot, M., Oldfield, Z., & Smith, J. P., (2006). Disease and disadvantage in the United States and in England. *Journal of American Medical Association, 295*, 2037–2045.

Barcus, H. R. (2004). Urban-rural migration in the USA: An analysis of residential satisfaction. *Regional Studies, 38*, 643–657.

Black, M., & Krishnakumar, A. (1998). Children in low-income, urban settings: Interventions to promote mental health and well-being. *American Psychologist, 53*, 635–646.

Buss, D. M. (1987). Selection, evocation, and manipulation. *Journal of Personality and Social Psychology, 53*, 1214–1221.

Clark, D. E., & Hunter, W. J. (1992). The impact of economic opportunity, amenities and fiscal factors on age-specific migration rates. *Journal of Regional Science, 32*, 349–365.

Clark, T. N., Lloyd, R., Wong, K. K., & Jain, P. (2002). Amenities drive urban growth. *Journal of Urban Affairs, 24*, 493–515.

Csikszentmihalyi, M. (1990). *Flow: The psychology of optimal experience.* New York: Harper & Row.

Cuba, L., & Hummon, D. M. (1993). A place to call home: Identification with dwelling, community, and region. *The Sociological Quarterly, 34*, 111–131.

Cutrona, C. E., Wallace, G., & Wesner, K. A. (2006). Neighborhood characteristics and depression: An examination of stress processes. *Current Directions in Psychological Science, 15*, 188–192.

Diener, E. (2000). Subjective well-being: The science of happiness, and a proposal for a national index. *American Psychologist, 55*, 34–43.

Diener, E., & Diener, M. (1995). Cross-cultural correlates of life satisfaction and self-esteem. *Journal of Personality and Social Psychology, 68*, 653–663.

Diener, E., Diener, M., & Diener, C. (1995). Factors predicting the subjective well-being of nations. *Journal of Personality and Social Psychology, 69*, 851–864.

Diener, E., & Lucas, R. (2000). Explaining differences in societal levels of happiness: Relative standards, need fulfillment, culture, and evaluation theory. *Journal of Happiness Studies: An Interdisciplinary Periodical on Subjective Well-Being, 1*, 41–78.

Diener, E., Oishi, S., & Lucas, R. E. (2003). Personality, culture, and subjective well-being: Emotional and cognitive evaluations of life. *Annual Review of Psychology, 54*, 403–425.

Diener, E., & Suh, E. (1997). Measuring quality of life: Economic, social, and subjective indicators. *Social Indicators Research, 40*, 189–216.

Easterlin, R. A. (1995). Will raising the income of all increase the happiness of all? *Journal of Economic Behavior and Organization, 27*, 35–47.

Emmons, R. A., & Diener, E. (1986). Situation selection as a moderator of response consistency and stability. *Journal of Personality and Social Psychology, 51*, 1013–1019.

Evans, G. W., Wells, N. M., Chan, H. Y. E., & Saltzman, H. (2000). Housing quality and mental health. *Journal of Consulting and Clinical Psychology, 68*, 526–530.

Fleming, I., Baum, A., Davidson, L. M., Rectanus, E., & McArdle S. (1987). Chronic stress as a factor in physiologic reactivity to challenge. *Health Psychology, 6*, 221–237.

Florida, R. L. (2002). *The Rise of the creative class: And how it's transforming work, leisure, community, and everyday life.* New York: Basic Books.

Florida, R. (2008). *Who's your city? How the creative economy is making where to live the most important decision of your life.* New York: Basic Books.

Florida, R., Mellander, C., & Stolarick K. (2009). Here to Stay—The Effects of Community Satisfaction on the Decision to Stay. Spatial Economic Analysis (Manuscript under review).

Fried, M. (1963). Grieving for a lost home. In L. Duhl (Ed.), The Urban Condition. New York: Basic Books.

Frey, W. H., Liaw, K. L., & Lin, G. (2000). State magnets for different elderly migrant types in the United States. *International Journal of Population Geography, 6*, 21–44.

Furnham, A. (1981). Personality and activity preferences. *British Journal of Social Psychology, 20*, 57–68.

Futterman, A. D., Kemeny, M. E., Shapiro, D., Polonsky, W., & Fahey, J. L. (1992). Immunological variability associated with experimentally-induced positive and negative affective states. *Psychology and Medicine, 22*, 231–238.

Glaeser, E. L., Kolko, J., & Saiz, A. (2001). Consumer city. *Journal of Economic Geography, 1*, 27–50.

Hofstede, G. (2001). *Culture's consequences: Comparing values, behaviors, institutions, and organizations across nations* (2nd ed.). Thousand Oaks, CA: Sage.

Hofstede, G., & McCrae, R. R. (2004). Personality and culture revisited: Linking traits and dimensions of culture. *Cross-Cultural Research, 38*, 52–88.

Ickes, W., Snyder M., Garcia, S. (1997). Personality influences on the choice of situations. In R. Hogan, J. Johnson, & S. Briggs (Eds.), *Handbook of personality psychology* (pp. 165–195). New York: Academic Press.

Inglehart, R., & Klingemann, H. (2000). Genes, culture, democracy, and happiness. In E. Diener and E. M. Suh (Eds.), *Culture and subjective well-being* (pp. 165–183). Cambridge, MA: The MIT Press.

Inglehart, R., & Oyserman, D. (2004). Individualism, autonomy, and self-expression. In H. Vinken, J. Soeters, & P. Ester (Eds.), *Comparing cultures: Dimensions of culture in a comparative perspective* (pp. 74–96). Leiden, the Netherlands: Brill.

Jacobs, J. (1961). *The death and life of great American cities*. New York: Random House.

Jacobs, J. (1969). *The economy of cities*. New York: Random House.

Jacobs, J. (1984). *Cities and the wealth of nations*. New York: Random House.

Johnson, K. J., & Fredrickson, B. L. (2005). We all look the same to me: Positive emotions eliminate the own-race bias in face recognition. *Psychological Science, 16*, 875–881.

Kuppens, P., Realo, A., & Diener, E. (2008). The role of positive and negative emotions in life satisfaction judgment across nations. *Journal of Personality and Social Psychology, 95*, 66–75.

Landale, N. S., & Guest, A. M. (1985). Constraints, satisfaction, and residential mobility: Speare's model reconsidered. *Demography, 22*, pp 199–222.

Levy L., & Herzog, A. (1978). Effects of crowding on health and social adaptation in the city of Chicago. *Human Ecology, 3*, 327–354.

Lewicka, M. (2005). Ways to make people active: The role of place attachment, cultural capital, and neighborhood ties. *Journal of Environmental Psychology, 25*, 381–395.

Lyubomirsky, S., King, L., & Diener, E. (2005). The benefits of frequent positive affect: Does happiness lead to success? *Psychological Bulletin, 131*, 803–855.

Lynn, M., & Steel, P. (2006). National differences in subjective well-being: The interactive effects of extraversion and neuroticism. *Journal of Happiness Studies, 7*, 155–165.

Marmot, M. G., & Wilkinson, R. G. (Eds.) (2005). *Social Determinants of Health* (2nd ed.). London, England: Oxford University Press.

McPherson, M., Smith-Lovin, L., & Brashears, M. E. (2006). Social isolation in America: Changes in core discussion networks over two decades. *American Sociological Review, 71*, 353–375.

McCrae, R. R. (2001). Trait psychology and culture: Exploring intercultural comparisons. *Journal of Personality, 69*, 819–846.

McCrae, R. R., & Terracciano, A. (2007). *The five-factor model and its correlates in individuals and cultures.* In F. J. R. van de Vijver, D. A. van Hemert, & Y. Poortinga (Eds.), Individuals and cultures in multi-level analysis. Mahwah, NJ: Erlbaum.

McCrae, R. R., Terracciano, A., & 79 Members of the Personality Profiles of Cultures Project. (2005). Personality profiles of cultures: Aggregate personality traits. *Journal of Personality and Social Psychology, 89*, 407–425.

Plaut, V. C., Markus, H. R., & Lachman, M. E. (2002). Place matters: Consensual features and regional variation in American well-being and self. *Journal of Personality and Social Psychology, 83*, 160–184.

Powell, A., Shennan, S., & Thomas, M. G. (2009). Late Pleistocene demography and the appearance of modern human behavior. *Science, 324*, 1298–1301.

Proshansky, H. M. (1978). The city and self-identity. Environment and Behavior, 10, 147–169.

Putnam, R. D. (2007). E Pluribus Unum: Diversity and community in the twenty-first century. *Scandinavian Political Studies, 30*, 137–174.

Rentfrow, P. J., Gosling, S. D., & Potter, J. (2008). A theory of the emergence, persistence, and expression of geographic variation in psychological traits. *Perspectives on Psychological Science, 3*, 339–369.

Rentfrow, P.J., Jost, J.T., Gosling, S.D., & Potter, J. (2009). Statewide differences in personality predict voting patterns in 1996–2004 U.S. Presidential Elections. In J.T. Jost, A.C. Kay, & H. Thorisdottir (Eds.), *Social and psychological bases of ideology and system justification* (pp. 314–347). Oxford, United Kingdom: Oxford University Press.

Roback, J. (1982). Wages, rents, and the quality of life. *The Journal of Political Economy, 90*, 1257–1278.

Rosen, S. (1979). Wage-based indexes of urban quality of life. In P. Mieszkowski & M. Straszheim (Eds.), *Current issues in urban economics.* Baltimore: Johns Hopkins University.

Rossi, P. (1955). *Why families move.* New York: The Free Press.

Rowles, G. D., & Watkins, J. F. (1993). Elderly migration and development in small communities. *Growth and Change, 24*, 509–538.

Salovey, P., Rothman, A. J., Detweiler, J. B., & Steward, W. T. (2000). Emotional states and physical health. *American Psychologist, 55,* 110–121.

Schmitt, D. P., Allik, J. A., McCrae, R. R., & Benet-Martínez, V. (2007). The geographic distribution of Big Five personality traits: Patterns and profiles of human self-description across 56 nations. *Journal of Cross-Cultural Psychology, 38,* 173–212.

Schrank, D., & Lomax, T. (2004). The 2004 urban mobility report. Texas Transportation Institute, The Texas A&M University System. (http://mobility.tamu.edu)

Schyns, P. (1998). Cross-national differences in happiness: Economic and cultural factors explored. *Social Indicators Research, 43,* 3–26.

Steel, P., & Ones, D. S. (2002). Personality and happiness: A national-level analysis. *Journal of Personality and Social Psychology, 83,* 767–781.

Stevenson, B., & Wolfers, J. (2008). Economic growth and subjective well-being: Reassessing the Easterlin Paradox. *Brookings Papers on Economic Activity,* Spring.

Stone, A. A., Cox, D. S., Valdimarsdottir, H., Jandorf, L., & Neale, J. M. (1987). Evidence that secretory IgA antibody is associated with daily mood. *Journal of Personality and Social Psychology, 52,* 988–993.

Swann, W. B., Jr., De La Ronde, C., & Hixon, G. (1994). Authenticity and positivity strivings in marriage and courtship. *Journal of Personality and Social Psychology, 66,* 857–869.

Swann, W. B. Jr., Rentfrow, P. J., & Guinn, J. (2003). Self-verification: The search for coherence. In M. Leary & J. Tangney (Eds.), *Handbook of self and identity* (pp. 367–383). New York, NY: Guilford Press.

Thoits, P. A., & Hewitt, L. N. (2001). Volunteer work and well-being. *Journal of Health and Social Behavior, 42,* 115–131.

Tiebout, C. M. (1956). A pure theory of local expenditures. *The Journal of Political Economy, 64,* 416–424.

Twigger-Ross, C. L., & Uzzell, D. L. (1996). Place and identity processes. *Journal of Environmental Psychology, 16,* 205–220.

Veenhoven, R. (1991). Is happiness relative? *Social Indicators Research, 24,* 1–34.

Veenhoven, R. (1993). *Happiness in nations: Subjective appreciation of life in 56 nations 1946–1992.* Rotterdam, the Netherlands: Risbo.

Wolpert, J. (1965). Behavioral aspects of the decision to migrate. *Papers and Proceedings of the Regional Science Association, 15,* 159–169.

# 26

## Greater Happiness for a Greater Number: Is That Possible? If So, How?

*Ruut Veenhoven*

### Introduction

Positive psychology is the scientific study of optimal human functioning (Sheldon et al. 2000). Happiness is not the same as optimal functioning but is a closely related phenomenon. Happiness is a major manifestation of optimal functioning, since we are hard-wired to feel good when functioning well (e.g. Balcombe 2006). Happiness is also a determinant of optimal functioning, since happiness "broadens" our behavioral repertoire and "builds" resources (Fredrickson 2004). Consequently, happiness is a major topic in positive psychology. Much research in positive psychology aims at understanding why some people are happier than others and tries to find ways for making people happier. As such, the *science* of positive psychology links up with the *ideology* that we should foster human happiness.

The idea of a moral obligation to advance human happiness is a fruit of the European "Enlightenment," an intellectual movement that took position against religious views that had dominated thinking in the Middle Ages. One of the contested views was that happiness can be found only in the afterlife and that earthly life serves as an entrance test to Heaven. Enlightened opinion was rather that happiness is possible on Earth and that we should not renounce it. Another contested view was that the basis of morality is in divine revelation, and in particular in the 10 Commandments. Enlightened thinkers came to see morality more as a matter of human agreement and discussed the intellectual foundations for social contracts. Much of this thought was voiced by Jeremy Bentham (1789) in his famous book *On Morals and Legislation*, in which he argued that the good and bad of actions should be judged by their effects on human happiness. In this view, the best thing to do is what results in the "greatest happiness, for the greatest number." This moral creed is called "the greatest happiness principle."[1]

This secular ideology met much resistance. In the 18the century the opposition came mainly from the churches, which were still quite powerful in those days. In the 19th century there was also opposition from the liberal and socialist emancipation movements that were more interested in freedom and equality than in happiness. In the early 20th century much opposition came from the then-virulent nationalism that laid more emphasis on glory of the nation than on the happiness of its inhabitants. All these ideologies lost power in the late 20th century, and partly for that reason the greatest happiness principle made a comeback. The recent emergence of positive psychology is part of that long-term ideological shift.

The ideological opposition against the greatest happiness principle gave rise to several intellectual arguments, some of which draw on assumptions about reality. One of these arguments is that "great happiness" is hardly possible in the human condition and that "great*er* happiness" is fully out of reach. Another argument holds that attempts to further happiness nevertheless will bring us from the frying pan into the fire because of the various negative side effects of happiness and its pursuit.

In this chapter I will first deal with the question as to *whether* greater happiness is possible, and I will do so by taking stock of the available evidence. Next I will deal with the question of *how* happiness can be furthered, and this requires a look ahead. Before entering these questions I must first explain what I mean by the word "happiness."

## What Happiness?

The word "happiness" has different meanings, also in the realm of positive psychology. In the widest sense, "happiness" is an umbrella term for all that is good. In this meaning it is often used interchangeably with terms like "well-being" or "quality of life." Below I will delineate four qualities of life and show that my concept of happiness fits only one of these.

### Four Qualities of Life

Quality-of-life concepts can be sorted using two distinctions, which together provide a fourfold matrix. That classification is discussed in more detail in Veenhoven (2000a). The first distinction is between chances and outcomes, that is, the difference between opportunities for a good life and the good life itself. A second difference is between outer and inner qualities of life, in other words between "external" and "internal" features. In the first case the quality is in the environment, in the latter it is in the individual. The combination of these two dichotomies yields a fourfold matrix. This classification is presented in Table 26.1.

TABLE 26.1   Four qualities of life

|  | Outer qualities | Inner qualities |
| --- | --- | --- |
| *Life-chances* | Livability of Environment | Life-ability of the person |
| *Life-results* | Utility of life | Satisfaction |

### Livability of the Environment

The left top quadrant denotes the meaning of good living conditions, shortly called "livability." Ecologists see livability in the natural environment and describe it in terms of pollution, global warming, and degradation of nature. City planners see livability in the built environment and associate it with such things as sewer systems, traffic jams, and ghetto formation. In the sociological view, society is central. Livability is associated with the quality of society as a whole and also with the position one has in society.

Livability is not what is called happiness here. It is rather a precondition for happiness, and not all environmental conditions are equally conducive to happiness.

### Life-Ability of the Person

The right top quadrant denotes inner life-chances. That is, how well we are equipped to cope with the problems of life Sen (1992) calls this quality-of-life variant "capability." I prefer the simple term "life-ability," which contrasts elegantly with "livability."

The most common depiction of this quality of life is absence of functional defects. This is "health" in the limited sense, sometimes referred to as "negative health." Next to absence of disease, one can consider excellence of function. This is referred to as "positive health" and associated with energy and resilience. A further step is to evaluate capability in a developmental perspective and to include acquisition of new skills for living. This is commonly denoted by the term "self-actualization." Since abilities do not develop alongside idleness, this quality of life is close to the "activity" in Aristotle's concept of eudaimonia.

Ability to deal with the problems of life will mostly contribute to happiness as defined here, but it is not identical. If one is competent in living, one has a good chance at happiness, but this endowment does not guarantee an enjoyable outcome.

### Utility of Life

The left bottom quadrant represents the notion that a good life must be good for something more than itself. This assumes some higher values. There is no current generic for these external outcomes of life. Gerson (1976: 795) refers to these effects as "transcendental" conceptions of quality of life. Another appellation is "meaning of life," which then denotes "true" significance instead of mere subjective sense of meaning. I prefer the simpler "utility of life," while admitting that this label may also give rise to misunderstanding.

When evaluating the external effects of a life, one can consider several aspects. One aspect is what that life does to the quality of life of other people, such as how well a mother raises her children. Another aspect is contribution to human civilization, such as in inventions or moral behavior. Still another aspect is what a life does to the ecological system. An individual's life can have many environmental effects that may differ on the short term and in the long term, which cannot be meaningfully added.

Leading an objectively useful life may contribute to the subjective appreciation of life, but may also go at the cost of that.

### Core Meaning: Subjective Enjoyment of Life

Finally, the bottom right quadrant represents the inner outcomes of life. That is the quality in the eye of the beholder. As we deal with conscious humans, this quality boils down to subjective enjoyment of life. This is commonly referred to by terms such as "subjective well-being," "life satisfaction," and "happiness" in a limited sense of the word. This is the kind of happiness Jeremy Bentham had in mind, and it is also the kind of happiness addressed here.

### Four Kinds of Satisfaction

Even when we focus on subjective satisfaction with life, there are still different meanings

associated with the word happiness. These meanings can also be charted in a fourfold matrix. In this case, that classification is based on the following dichotomies: life-aspects versus life-as-a-whole, and passing delight versus enduring satisfaction. These distinctions produce the fourfold matrix presented in Table 26.2.

### Pleasure

The top-left quadrant represents passing enjoyments of life-aspects. Examples would be delight in a cup of tea at breakfast, the satisfaction of a chore done, or the enjoyment of a piece of art. I refer to this category as "pleasures." Kahneman (1997) calls it "instant-utilities."

The concept of happiness used here is broader and concerns "overall satisfaction" with life-as-a-whole. Though fleeting enjoyment obviously contributes to a positive appreciation of life, it is not the whole of it.

### Domain Satisfaction

The top right quadrant denotes enduring appreciation of life-aspects, such as marriage satisfaction and job satisfaction. This is currently referred to as domain satisfactions. Though domain satisfactions depend typically on a continuous flow of pleasures, they have some continuity of their own. For instance, one can remain satisfied with one's marriage even if one has not enjoyed the company of the spouse for quite some time.

Domain satisfactions are often denoted with the term happiness: a happy marriage, happy with one's job, etc. Yet I use the term happiness in the broader sense of satisfaction with life-as-a-whole. One would not call a person happy who is satisfied with marriage and job but still dissatisfied on the whole because his health is failing. It is even possible that someone is satisfied with all the domains one can think of but nevertheless feels depressed.

### Peak-Experience

The bottom right quadrant denotes the combination of passing experience and appraisal of life-as-a-whole. That combination occurs typically in peak-experiences, which involve short-lived but quite intense feelings and the perception of wholeness. This is the kind of happiness poets write about.

Again, this is not the kind of happiness aimed at here. A moment of bliss is not enduring

TABLE 26.2   Four kinds of satisfaction

|  | Passing | Enduring |
| --- | --- | --- |
| Part of life | Pleasure | Domain satisfaction |
| Life-as-a-whole | Peak-experience | Life satisfaction (happiness) |

appreciation of life. In fact, such top-experiences even seem detrimental to lasting satisfaction, possibly because of their disorientating effects (Diener et al., 1991).

### Core Meaning: Lasting Satisfaction with One's Life-as-a-Whole

Lastly, the bottom-right quadrant represents the combination of enduring satisfaction with life-as-a-whole. This is what I mean with the word happiness. A synonym is "life satisfaction." This is the meaning at stake in Jeremy Bentham's "greatest happiness principle." When speaking about the "sum" of pleasures and pains, he denoted a balance over time and thus a durable matter.

### Definition of Happiness

In this line I define happiness as *the degree to which an individual judges the overall quality of his/her own life-as-a-whole favourably*. In other words: how much one likes the life one leads. I have elaborated this concept elsewhere (Veenhoven, 1984, ch. 2).

### Different Use of the Word in Positive Psychology

Martin Seligman (2002) uses the word happiness in a broader sense. In his "Authentic Happiness," he distinguishes between: the *engaged life*, the *meaningful life* and the *pleasant life*. His notion of the "engaged life" belongs in the top right quadrant of Table 26.1, and his notion of the "meaningful life" fits the bottom left quadrant. His notion of the "pleasant life" belongs in the bottom right quadrant and fits my concept of happiness.

Another common distinction in positive psychology is between *eudaimonic happiness* and *hedonic happiness* (Ryan & Deci 2001). The notion of "eudaimonic" happiness concerns the use and development of human capabilities and as such in belongs in the top right quadrant of Table 26.1. The notion of "hedonic happiness" belongs in the bottom right quadrant of Table 26.1. As such it fits my concept of happiness. Yet when reduced to mere "pleasure," the notion of "hedonic happiness" belongs in the top left quadrant of Table 26.2 and does not fit my concept of happiness as life satisfaction in the bottom right quadrant of that scheme.

### Taking Stock

Is the pursuit of greater happiness for a greater number illusionary indeed? And are attempts to foster happiness doomed to be counterproductive? By lack of data these questions could not be answered in Bentham's days. Today we can do better. Social scientists have found that happiness can be measured using questions about life satisfaction and have applied such questions in large-scale surveys of the general population. In this section I take stock of the evidence for and against using the research findings gathered in the World Database of Happiness[2] (Veenhoven, 2009).

### Great Happiness Possible?

Several philosophers have claimed that enduring happiness is not possible in the human condition, e.g. Schopenhauer (1851), who maintains that we can at best reduce suffering somewhat. Freud (1948) saw little chance for happiness either, in particular not in modern society that requires inhibition of primitive urges. Likewise, several social scientists believe that happiness depends on comparison and infer on that basis that happiness will oscillate around a neutral level (e.g. Unger 1970, Brickman & Campbell 1971).

### Empirical Indications

Research findings do not support these pessimistic theories. Most people are happy, at least in modern society (Diener & Diener 1996). That appears from their responses to the question: "All things considered, how satisfied are you with your life as a whole nowadays? Please indicate in a number from 0 to 10, where 0 is 'extremely dissatisfied' and 10 'extremely satisfied.'" The responses to this question in the UK are depicted in Figure 26.1. More than 40% of the British rate their life with a number of 7 or higher and less than 20% with a 5 or lower. Studies that use slightly different questions have yielded similar results. The average "school mark" the British give for their life is currently 7,2.

How does British happiness rank in comparison to other nations? Some illustrative findings are presented in Table 26.3. Though the UK is in the middle of this list, it is actually in the top range of the world. As one can see, average happiness varies between 8,4 (Denmark) and 3,3 (Zimbabwe), and with 7,0 the USA ranks high in that five-point interval.

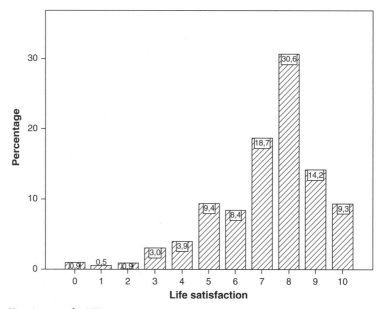

Figure 26.1. *Happiness in the UK.*
ESS Round 3: European Social Survey Round 3 Data (2006). Data file edition 3.2. Norwegian Social Science Data Services, Norway–Data Archive and distributor of ESS data.

Average happiness is much lower in developing nations, and in particular in African "failed states" such as Zimbabwe. As a result the world average is also lower. Though full data are lacking, the current world average is between 5 and 6 on a scale of 0 to 10. This is not great happiness, but the cases of Denmark and Switzerland indicate that great happiness is possible.

### Theoretical Plausibility

In a functional perspective, it is also unlikely that we are doomed to unhappiness. Happiness is part of our monitoring system and typically tells us whether we are doing well or not. As such, we feel happy when our basic needs are being met and unhappy when these are thwarted (Veenhoven 2009b). In this view happiness must be the rule rather than an exception.

### Greater Happiness Possible?

Can we become happier than we are now? Again, several scientists think not. Some psychologists maintain that happiness is largely inborn or at least embedded in stable personality. Hence education for happiness will not make citizens any happier, and neither will social progress. This view is known as the "set-point" theory (e.g., Lykken 1999). Some sociologists draw the same

conclusion because they think that happiness depends on social comparison and that you are not better off than the neighbours if conditions for everybody improve. In that vein, the case of the USA is often mentioned as an example; material wealth would have doubled there since the 1950s while average happiness seems to have remained at the same level (e.g., Easterlin 1995). Yet these scientists are wrong, both empirically and theoretically.

### Empirical Indications

There is a clear relation between average happiness and societal quality. Think of the case of Zimbabwe in Table 26.1, where this country is at the bottom with an average of 3.3. Apparently, people cannot live happy in a failed state, even if their neighbours suffer the same. The correlations in Table 26.4 show that this is no exception, with differences in quality of society explaining about 80% of the variation in average happiness in the present-day world.

Average happiness *has* changed in most nations, and typically for the better (Veenhoven & Hagerty, 2006). Figure 26.2 depicts a gradual rise of happiness in Denmark over the last 30 years and a dramatic fall of average happiness in Russia following the ruble crisis in 1995. Clearly, happiness is not fixed to a set point!

TABLE 26.3 Happiness in nations around 2005:
Average on scale 0–10

| | |
|---|---|
| Denmark | 8.4 |
| Switzerland | 8.1 |
| Mexico | 8.0 |
| Sweden | 7.7 |
| Canada | 7.6 |
| UK | 7.3 |
| Germany | 7.2 |
| USA | 7.0 |
| France | 6.5 |
| China | 6.3 |
| Japan | 6.2 |
| India | 5.9 |
| Russia | 4.4 |
| Iraq | 4.3 |
| Zimbabwe | 3.3 |

Adapted from Veenhoven, R., World Database of Happiness, Happiness in Nations, Rank Report Average Happiness (2009), Erasmus University Rotterdam. Available at: http://worlddatabaseofhappiness.eur.nl/hap_nat/findingreports/RankReport_AverageHappiness.php

Figure 26.2 illustrates also that greater happiness is possible in most nations of the world. Average happiness is currently highest in Denmark, with an average of 8.2. What is possible in Denmark should also be possible in other countries. Don't object that Danish happiness is a matter of genetic endowment or national character, because Figure 26.2 shows that happiness has improved in Denmark since 1973.

Present-day happiness in Denmark may be close to the maximally possible level. If so, there is still a long way to go for most nations of this world, since the world's average is now lower than 6. If we might ever reach the maximum of average happiness, there is still the possibility to extend its duration and create more happy life years for a greater number (Veenhoven, 2005).

So much for average happiness of all citizens in society—how about the chances of an individual getting happier in the given societal conditions? Follow-up research has shown that some people get happier over their lifetime and others less (e.g., Erhardt et al., 2000). Lyubomirsky et al. (2005b) estimate that about 40% of the differences in happiness within modern society is due to intentional activity of individuals, and only some 10% to circumstances beyond their control.

*Theoretical Underpinning*

The erroneous idea that greater happiness is not possible has roots in erroneous theories about the nature of happiness. One of these mistaken theories is that happiness is merely a matter of outlook on life and that this outlook is set in fixed dispositions, which are part of individual personality as well as of national character. Another faulty theory is that happiness results from cognitive comparison, in particular from social comparison. Elsewhere I have shown that these theories are wrong (Veenhoven, 1991, 1995).

My alternative theory of happiness holds that we appraise life on the basis of affective information in the first place. We experience positive as well as negative affects; in appraising how much we like the life we live, we assess to what extent the former outbalance the latter. This theory fits Bentham's concept of happiness as "the sum of pleasures and pains." In my view, positive and negative affects signal the gratification of basic human needs, so in the end happiness is determined by need gratification. I have discussed this theory in more detail elsewhere (Veenhoven, 2009b).

**Greater Happiness Desirable?**

Not everything that is possible is also desirable, so the next question is whether we should try to create greater happiness for a greater number. In Bentham's view this is a moral obligation, but his view is contested, as we have seen.

Some of the objections come from preachers of penitence who like to see us suffer for cleansing our sinful souls. Yet there are also objections from scientists who believe that the pursuit of happiness will bring us from the frying pan into the fire. One of their qualms is that mass happiness will be achieved at the cost of freedom. Another misgiving is that happy people tend to be passive and uncreative. These notions figure in Huxley's (1932) science fiction novel *Brave New World*, in which happiness for everybody is achieved using genetic manipulations and mind control and where the happy citizens are short-sighted consumer slaves.

Yet research on the consequences of happiness shows another picture. It appears that happiness typically fosters activity, creativity, and an open mind. Happy people do better as spouses and parents. They are also better citizens; they typically inform themselves better than unhappy compatriots, and they involve more in social

TABLE 26.4 Societal correlates of happiness

| Condition in nation | Correlation with average happiness | | |
| --- | --- | --- | --- |
| | Zero-order | Wealth Controlled | N |
| Wealth | | | |
| • Purchasing power per head | +.65 | | 88 |
| Freedom | | | |
| • Economic | +.60 | +.26 | 88 |
| • Political | +.48 | +.17 | 90 |
| • Personal* | +.35 | −.13 | 83 |
| Equality | | | |
| • Inequality of incomes | +.05 | +.42 | 82 |
| • Discrimination of women | −.52 | −.25 | 58 |
| Brotherhood | | | |
| • Tolerance | +.52 | +.40 | 76 |
| • Trust in compatriots | +.39 | +.17 | 79 |
| • Social security | +.35 | −.16 | 66 |
| Justice | | | |
| • Rule of law | +.64 | +.20 | 90 |
| • Respect of civil rights | +.47 | +.09 | 90 |
| • Corruption | −.56 | −.03 | 62 |
| Explained variance | 83% | | 60 |

Adapted from Veenhoven, R, World Database of Happiness, data file "States of Nations_2008," Erasmus University Rotterdam. Available at: http://worlddatabaseofhappiness.eur.nl/statnat/statnat_fp.htm

* = not included in regression due to limited number of cases

action while being more moderate in their political views (Lyubomirsky et al., 2005). Happiness also lengthens life considerably, the effect of happiness is comparable to smoking or not (Veenhoven, 2008). A negative effect of happiness is that it may make us less perceptive of risks and/or criticism by others. The evidence is about minor things, and it is not yet established whether happiness makes us also prone to a too-rosy outlook of major things.

These findings on effects of happiness fit well with the theory that feeling good works as a "go-signal"—it tells the organism that the situation is OK and that it can go ahead. Consequently, happy people "broaden" their behavioral scope and "build" more resources (Fredrickson, 2004). So happiness is not only worth pursuing for its own sake, but also for its positive side effects.

## Moving Forward

### How Can Happiness Be Raised?

So, greater happiness for a greater number is possible, how then can that be achieved? I see possibilities at three levels: (1) at the macro-level of society, (2) at the meso-level of organizations, and (3) at the micro-level of individual citizens.

### Macro-Level: Improving the Livability of Society

Happiness depends heavily on the quality of society. As we have seen in scheme 4, there are wide differences in happiness across nations, and these difference are clearly linked to societal qualities, some of which are presented in scheme 5.

#### Wealth

Will further economic growth make us happier? Table 26.4 suggests so, because happiness is strongly correlated with wealth of the nation. Yet material affluence appears to be subject to the law of diminishing returns, and economic growth yields more happiness in poor nations than in rich nations. This is not to say that economic development does not add to happiness at all in rich nations. Happiness is still on the rise in affluent nations, and it is well possible that this rise is linked to economic growth, directly or indirectly. We simply don't know yet.

Still another reason to keep the economy going is that the play may be as important as the prizes. Happiness is found not only in consumption but also in productive activity. Like most animals, we have an innate need to use our potentials. The biological function is to keep us sharp, in the human case in particular to keep the brain in shape. The human species evolved in the conditions of hunter-gatherer existence that involved a lot of challenge. In the conditions of present-day industrial society, we still need some challenge and we find that now mainly in work life. In this perspective, we had better not follow Layard's (2005) advice to discourage economic competition, though there is a point in keeping that competition nice and leaving room for other arenas in society.

#### Equality

The data in Table 26.4 do not suggest that reduction of income differences will add to happiness;

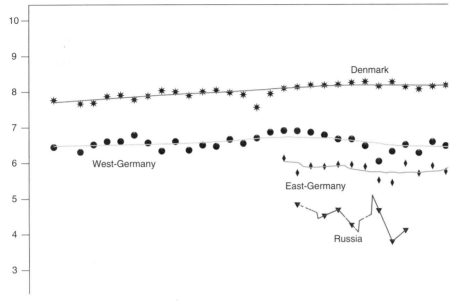

Figure 26.2. *Trend average happiness in three nations.*
Adapted from Veenhoven, R., World Database of Happiness, data file TrendsInNations_2007, Erasmus
University Rotterdam. Available at: http://worlddatabaseofhappiness.eur.nl

the correlation is close to zero, and when wealth of the nation is taken into account we see even a positive effect of inequality. Though income inequality may be unfair, we can apparently live with it (Berg & Veenhoven, 2010). This is not to say that income inequality does not affect happiness at all; it most likely means that the evident negative effects of income inequality are balanced, by not so evident positive effects.[3]

Likewise, the data do not suggest that happiness can be advanced by more welfare state. At first glance there is some correlation between expenditures for social security and happiness in nations, but the statistical relationship disappears when we take into account that big-spending nations tend to be richer. For illustration: happiness is fairly high in Sweden, which is known for its extended welfare state, yet equally high in Iceland, which spends much less on social security (Veenhoven, 2000b; Ouweneel, 2002).

This is not to say that happiness is insensitive to all inequalities, since Table 26.4 also shows a strong negative relationship between average happiness and gender-inequality in nations. This latter kind of inequality links up with differences in freedom across nations.

## Freedom

The case of freedom fits better with intuition, Table 26.4 showing sizable correlations with three kinds of freedom. The effects differ between poor and rich nations: Among poor nations, happiness appears to be most affected by economic freedom. Hence, in these nations, open-market policies will probably add to happiness. Among rich nations, the correlation with political freedom is more pronounced, and this suggests that there is happiness to win by further democratization. Illustrative in this vein is that in Switzerland, average happiness was found to be somewhat higher in the cantons, where the threshold for referenda is lowest (Frey & Stutzer, 2000).

## Institutional Quality

The greatest gains seem to be possible in the realms of justice and good governance. The correlations in Table 26.4 show that people live happier in nations where human rights are respected and where there is rule of law. Reversely, people live less happy in nations where corruption is common, even in cultures where favouritism is morally accepted. Likewise, people live happier in nations where government institutions function properly, irrespective of the colour of the political parties in the saddle. This effect is also independent of culture; rather than a Western ideology, good governance appears to be a universal prerequisite for happiness (Ott, 2009).

## Meso-Level: Improving the Livability of Institutions

Another source of happiness is the institutional settings in which we spend most of our time, such as work and school. Systematic improvements in those realms will probably add to the happiness of a great number of people.

This requires that we know what settings produce the most happiness, e.g., in what kind of schools pupils enjoy their school years most. Curiously, that has hardly been investigated as yet, not even in nursing homes, the prime product of which is happy life years. There is a lot of talk about quality of life in institutions, but hardly any hard research. This is probably because there is little incentive to bother about happiness of pupils and residents.

Governments can create an incentive by instigating research on the happiness output of institutions. Once differences are visible, the market will do its work. For instance, parents will prefer a school where most children are happy over a school where the majority are not, even if the latter school produces higher grades.

There is some research on happiness in work organizations, much of which is summarized by Warr (2007). Still, this strand is small compared to the large literature on job satisfaction and health at work. Another limitation is that most of the research is cross-sectional, and for that reason does not inform us about cause and effect in the relation between happiness and work. What we need is follow-up studies of comparable people in different institutional settings. Research on "positive institutions" is on the agenda of positive psychology, and I hope that we will know more in a couple of years.

## Micro-Level: Helping Individuals to Live Happier

Happiness can be furthered at the individual level in at least three ways: (1) training art-of-living skills, (2) informing people about the probable outcomes of major life choices, and (3) professional guidance in self-development and life choice. Below I will expand on these possibilities, since they are particularly relevant for positive psychology. My aim is to sketch the options, and for that reason I will not review all that is going on in the fields.

### Training Art-of-Living Skills

Many people think that they would be happier if they had more money or a higher position on the social ladder. However, research shows that these things do not matter very much, at least not in affluent and egalitarian societies. Differences in income and social status explain only some 5% of the differences in Table 26.1. Current images about conditions for happiness are misleading.

What then does matter for happiness? About 10% of the differences can be attributed to social relations, in particular to a good marriage. Another 10% is due to good or bad luck, probably more so in countries where life is less predictable. Most of the difference appears to be due to personal characteristics; about 30% can be attributed to variation in life-ability (Heady & Wearing, 1990).

The relative importance of inner strengths should not be surprising if we realize that living conditions are typically very good in modern nations; the better the external conditions, the less they account for differences in happiness. In paradise, all the differences in happiness will be due to inner competence, neurotics quarreling with angels. In Hell, the differences in happiness (if any) will largely be determined by closeness to the fire, because nobody can stand that environment. So the most evident way to advance happiness is to strengthen life-abilities.

Some of these abilities are genetically determined or hardly alterable for other reasons. Still, there are also capabilities that can be improved though therapy and training. Psychotherapy is now well established in modern nations, but still underutilized. There is also an emerging field of training in art-of-living. "Art-of-living" is the knack of leading a satisfying life and, in particular, the ability to develop a rewarding lifestyle (Veenhoven, 2003). This involves various aptitudes, some of which seems to be susceptible to improvement using training techniques. There is a growing literature on that matter. Four of these aptitudes are: (1) the ability to enjoy, (2) the ability to choose, (3) the ability to keep developing, and (4) the ability to see meaning.

## Learning to Enjoy

The ability to take pleasure from life is partly inborn (trait negativity-positivity) but can to some extent be cultivated. Learning to take pleasure from life was part of traditional leisure-class education, which emphasized prestigious pleasures, such as the tasting of exquisite wines and the appreciation of difficult music. Yet it is also possible to develop an enjoyment of the common things in life, such as eating breakfast or watching the sunset. Training in savoring simple pleasures is part of some religious practices.

Hedonic enjoyment is valued in present-day modern society and figures prominently in advertisements. Yet techniques that help us to gain the ability to enjoy are underdeveloped. There are no professional enjoyment trainers, at least no trainers aiming at improving our general level of enjoyment. There is professional guidance for specific types of pleasures, such as how to appreciate fine arts; often the main goal is to sell a particular product.

Still, it would seem possible to develop wider enjoyment training techniques. One way could be to provide training in "attentiveness," possibly using meditation techniques. This approach fits current programs on "mindfulness" (e.g. Jacob & Brinkerhoff, 1999). Another option could be the broadening of one's repertoire of leisure activities, which could link up with expertise in various stimulation programs. A third way could be looking at ways to remove inner barriers to enjoy, which could be linked to clinical treatment of a-hedonie.

## Learning to Choose

Happiness depends also the choices one makes in life and hence on one's ability to choose. The art of choosing involves several skills.

One such skill is getting to know what the options are. This aptitude can be improved by learning, and this is one of the things we do in consumer education. Expertise in this field can be used for training in the charting of wider life options. Another requirement is an ability to estimate how well the various options would fit one's nature. This requires self-knowledge, and that is also something that can be improved, self-insight being a common aim in training and psychotherapy. Once one knows what to choose, there is often a problem of carrying through. This phase requires aptitudes such as persever-

ance, assertiveness, and creativity, all of which can be strengthened and are in fact common objectives in vocational trainings.

The next step in the choice process is assessing the outcomes in term of the above-mentioned distinction, assessing whether "expected utility" fits "experienced utility." This phase calls for openness to one's feelings and a realistic view of one's overall mood pattern. Training in mood monitoring is a common practice in psychotherapy and could possibly be improved using techniques of experience sampling.

## Learning to Grow

Happiness depends largely on the gratification of innate "needs," and an important class of needs is "growth needs" (Maslow, 1970), also referred to as "functioning needs" or "mastery needs." These needs are not restricted to higher mental functions but also concern the use and development of the body and senses. In animals, the gratification of these needs is largely guided by instinct, but in humans it requires conscious action. Cultures typically provide standard action patterns for this purpose, such as providing for vocational career scripts, but people must also make choices of their own, in particular in multiple-choice societies. Failure to involve oneself in challenging activities may lead one into diffuse discontent or even depression; this, for example, happens regularly after retirement from work. Thus another art-of-living is to keep oneself going and developing. This approach fits a strand of research on goal setting and happiness (e.g. Sheldon & Elliot, 1999).

Intervention would also seem possible in this case. Mere information will probably be useful, and one can also think of various ways to get people going. Once again training techniques can build on available experience, in this case experience in various activation programs. There is already an ample supply of "growth trainings" on the peripheries of psychology, but as yet little evidence for the effectiveness of such interventions and certainly no proof of long-term effects on happiness.

## Helping to See Meaning

There are indications that happiness also depends on one seeing meaning in one's life (e.g., King et al., 2006). Though it is not sure that we have an innate need for meaningfulness as such,[4] the idea of it provides at least a sense of coherence.

Seeing meaning in one's life requires that one develops a view of one's life and that one can see worth in it. These mental knacks can also be strengthened, and one can learn to live with the philosophical uncertainties that surround this issue.

There is experience on this matter in existential counselling and in practices such as "life reviewing" (Erlen et al. 2002) and "logo therapy" (Frankl, 1946). As far as I know, the impact of such interventions on happiness has yet to be investigated.

The problem is not so much to develop such training techniques, but to separate the chaff from the corn. That will require independent effect studies, but effect studies are scarce in this field and are typically not carried out independently of the trainers. Reports of this research are highly selective and tell more about short-term success than about long-term significance. As a result, consumers are uncertain about the quality of trainings and for that reason are reluctant to buy such services. In economic terms: the (poor) market supply does not meet the (large) consumer demand. Once training techniques have been proven to be effective, a viable market will develop that will generate income for many psychologists and enhance the happiness of many people.

### Information: Enabling More Informed Choice

Happiness depends to some extent on the choices we make in life, in particular in modern "multiple-choice societies". Life choices are for the most part based on expected happiness; for instance, we typically choose a profession we think we will like. Economists call this "expected utility" or "decision utility" and acknowledge that this may differ from later "experienced utility," because decisions are made mostly on the basis of incomplete information (e.g., Wilson & Gilbert, 2005). An example of mal-informed choice is the decision to accept a higher-paying job that requires more commuting. People typically accept such jobs in the expectation that the extra money will compensate for the travel time, but follow-up research has shown that they are mostly wrong and that happiness went down (Frey & Stutzer, 2004).

Research of this kind can help people to make more informed choices. Though there is no guarantee that things will pan out in the same way for you, it is still useful to know how it has worked out for other people. Such research

is particularly useful if it concerns similar people.

This approach to the furthering of happiness is similar to current evidence-based health education. As in the case of happiness, we are often not sure about the consequences of lifestyle choices on our health. How much drinking is too much? Is eating raw vegetables really good for your health? We cannot answer such questions on the basis of our own experience, and common wisdom is often wrong. Hence, we increasingly look to the results of scientific studies.

As yet, the information basis for such a way of furthering happiness is still small. Although there is a considerable body of research on happiness, this research is typically cross-sectional and does not inform us about cause and effect. What we need is panel data that allow us to follow the effects of life choices over time. Still another problem is that current happiness research deals mainly with things over which we have little control, such as personality and social background. What we need is research on things we can choose, for example, working part-time or full-time or raising a family or not. For this purpose the "Happiness Monitor" project (www.risbo.org/happinessmonitor) follows a large number of people in The Netherlands, using an attractive internet site and yearly calls. Parallel studies in other countries are welcome.

Once such information becomes available, it will quickly be disseminated to the public through the lifestyle press and self-help literature. It can also be included in organized health education, broadened to become education for "living well." The problem is not in the dissemination of knowledge, but in the production of it.

This way of promoting happiness does not involve paternalism; it does not push people into a particular way of life, but it provides them with information for making a well-informed autonomous decision. Paternalism would be involved only if research is manipulated or its results communicated selectively—for instance, if the observed negative effects of parenthood on happiness are disguised.

### Life Coaching

If we feel unhealthy, we go to a medical general practitioner, who makes a diagnosis and either prescribes a treatment or refers us to a medical specialist. If we feel unhappy, there is no such generalist. We have to guess about the possible causes ourselves and on that basis consult a specialist who may be a psychologist, a marriage counsellor, or a lawyer. This is a remarkable market failure, given the large number of people who feel they could be happier. The size of the demand is reflected in the booming sales of self-help books and the willingness to pay for things that promise greater happiness, such as cosmetic surgery and second homes.

Currently, there are quite a few people who present themselves as life coaches or counselors, and many of them are members of organizations affiliated with the positive psychology movement. Yet their clientele is quite small and their impact on average happiness is negligible. Why doesn't the life coach equal the medical general practitioner? In my view, the main reason is in the above-mentioned lack of a knowledge base. Since we do not really know what trainings work for what kind of people, life coaches cannot refer to a specialist and therefore treat clients themselves on the basis of intuition. Likewise, coaches cannot provide evidence-based advice on matters of life choice, since follow-up research on this matter is still in its infancy.

What can life coaches do to foster the development of the required knowledge base? One of the ways is following the effects of their own practices. This would require that a substantial number of life coaches agree to refer all their clients to a long-term follow-up study by a university or an otherwise respected and impartial scientific body. Clients should provide some basic information at intake, among which their current state of happiness and the things for which they seek advice. Next, clients should periodically report their happiness, e.g., every month for a couple of years. This can be done on the Internet, and clients should be sure that their responses are not communicated to the counselor. Counselors in turn should report their diagnosis, treatment, and prognosis, without their clients knowing. The resulting database will allow us to see what interventions work for what kind of people and is likely to stimulate more focused research. Participation in such a study could be one of the requirements for chartering in this profession. The above mentioned "Happiness Monitor" can be used in that context.

## In Short

Professional furthering of the happiness of individuals requires more research, long-term follow-up studies in particular.

## Notes

1. In academic philosophy, this moral principle is known as "utilitarianism."

2. The World Database of Happiness is a collection of research findings on happiness as defined in this chapter.

3. Though inequality in incomes is not related to *average* happiness in nations, it is slightly related to *inequality* of happiness in nations, the standard deviation of happiness tending to be greater in nations where income differences are greatest.

4. The search for meaning seems to be universal, but this does not necessarily mean that this is an innate need. The quest for meaning can also be a consequence of the fact that we can think and therefore cannot avoid wondering what our life is good for. If so, that would explain why we can live without a convincing answer to that question.

## References

Balcombe, J. (2006). *Pleasurable kingdom: Animals and the nature of feeling good.* New York, USA: MacMillan.

Bentham, J. (1789). *Introduction to the principles of morals and legislation* (Original Payne London, 1789 Reprinted by Althone Press, London 1970)

Berg, M., & Veenhoven R. (2010). Income inequality and happiness in nations: When does it hurt? In B. Greve (Ed.), *Social policy and happiness in Europe.* (pp. 174–194) Edgar Elger Cheltenham, UK.

Brickman, P., & Campbell, D. T. (1971). Hedonic relativism and planning the good society. In M. H. Appley (Ed.), *Adaptation level theory* (pp. 287–302). New York, USA: Academic Press.

Diener, E., Pavot, W. & Sandvik, E. (1991) Happiness is the frequency, not intensity of positive versus negative affect. In: Strack, F. et al. (Eds.), *Subjective Wellbeing.* Pergamon, UK.

Diener, E., & Diener, C. (1996). Most people are happy. *Psychological Science, 7,* 181–185.

Easterlin, R. A. (1995). Will raising the incomes of all increase the happiness of all? *Journal of Economic Behavior and Organization, 27,* 35–47.

Ehrhardt, J., Saris, W. & Veenhoven, R. (2000). Stability of life-satisfaction over time: Analysis of change in ranks in a national population, *Journal Of Happiness Studies, 1,* 177–205.

Erlen, J.A., Cook, C., Mellors, M.P. & Sereika, S.M. (2001) The use of life review to enhance the quality of life of people living with AIDS, *Quality of Life Research,* 10, 453–464.

Frankl, V. (1946). *Man's search for meaning,* 2006 English edition, Beacon Press, Boston, USA.

Fredrickson, B. L. (2004). The broaden-and-build theory of positive emotions. *Philosophical Transactions, Biological Sciences, 359*, 1367–1377.

Freud, S. (1948). *Das Unbehagen in der Kultur (Civilization and Its Discontents).* In Gesammelte Werke, Werke aus dem Jahren 1925–1931, S. Fischer Verlag, Germany.

Frey, B., & Stutzer, A. (2000). Happiness prospers in democracy. *Journal of Happiness Studies, 1,* 79–102.

Frey, B., & Stutzer, A. (2004). *Economic consequences of mispredicting utility.* Working Paper, Institute for Empirical Research in Economics, 2004, Zürich, Switzerland.

Gerson, E.M. (1976) On quality of life, *American Sociological Review, 41,* 793–806.

Headey, B., & Wearing, A. (1992). *Understanding happiness: A theory of subjective well-being.* Melbourne Australia: Longman Cheshire.

Huxley, A. (1932). *Brave New World.* London: Shatto & Windus.

Jacob, J. C., & Brinkerhoff, M. B. (1999). Mindfulness and subjective well-being in the sustainability movement: A further discrepancies theory. *Social Indicators Research, 46,* 341–368.

Kahneman, D, Wakker, P.P. & Sarin, R. (1997) Back to Bentham? Explorations of experienced utility, *The Quarterly Journal of Economics, 112,* 375–405.

King, L. A., Hicks, J. A., & Krull, J. L. (2006). Positive affect and the experience of meaning of life. *Journal of Personality and Social Psychology, 90,* 179–196.

Layard, R. (2005). *Happiness: Lessons of a new science.* New York: Penguin.

Lykken, David T. (1999). *Happiness: What studies on twins show us about nature, nurture and the happiness set-point.* New York, USA: Golden Books.

Lyubomirsky, S., King, L. A., & Diener, E. (2005). The benefits of frequent positive affect: Does happiness lead to success? *Psychological Bulletin, 131,* 803–855.

Lyubomirsky, S., Sheldon, K. M., & Schkade, D. (2005b). Pursuing happiness: The architecture of sustainable change. *Review of general psychology, 9,* 111–131.

Maslow, A.H. (1970) *Motivation and personality,* 2e edition, Harper & Row, New York, USA.

Ouweneel, P. (2002). Social security and well-being of the unemployed in 42 nations. *Journal of Happiness Studies, 3,* 167–192.

Ott, J. (2009). Good governance and happiness in nations: Technical quality precedes democracy and quality beats size. *Journal of Happiness Studies, 11,* 353–368.

Ryan, R. M., & Deci, E. L. (2001). On happiness and human potentials. A review of research on hedonic and eudaimonic well-being. *Annual Revue of Psychology, 52,* 141–166.

Schopenhauer, A. (1851). *Parerga und Paralipomena.* Leipzig.

Seligman, M. E. (2002). *Authentic Happiness.* New York, USA: The Free Press.

Sen, A. (1992) Capability and wellbeing. In Sen, A & Nussbaum, M. (Eds.) *The quality of life,* Clarendon Press, Oxford, UK.

Sheldon, K. M., & Elliot, A. J. (1999). Goal striving, need satisfaction, and longitudinal well-being: The self-concordance model. *Journal of Personality and Social Psychology, 76,* 482–497.

Sheldon, K., Frederickson, B., Rathunde, K., Csikszentmihalyi, M., & Haidt, J. (2000). *Positive Psychology Manifesto.* http://www.ppc.sas. upenn.edu/akumalmanifesto.htm

Sheldon, K., & Lyubomirsky, S. (2004). Achieving sustainable new happiness: prospects, practices and prescriptions. In P.A. Linley & S. Joseph (Eds.), *Positive psychology in practice* (pp. 127–145). NJ, USA: Wiley.

Unger, H. F. (1970). The feeling of happiness. *Psychology, 7,* p.27–33.

Veenhoven, R. (1984) *Conditions of Happiness,* Reidel (now Springer), Dordrecht, The Netherlands.

Veenhoven, R. (1991) Is happiness relative? *Social Indicators Research, 24,* 1–34.

Veenhoven, R. (1995) The cross-national pattern of happiness. Test of predictions implied in three theories of happiness, *Social Indicators Research, 34,* 33–68

Veenhoven, R. (2000a) The four qualities of life: Ordering concepts and measures of the good life. *Journal Of Happiness Studies, 1,* 1–39

Veenhoven, R. (2000b). Well-being in the welfare state: Level not higher, distribution not more equitable. *Journal of Comparative Policy Analysis, 2,* 91–125.

Veenhoven, R. (2003). Arts of living. *Journal of Happiness Studies, 4,* 373–384.

Veenhoven, R. (2005). Apparent quality of life: How long and happy people live. *Social Indicators Research, 71,* 61–86.

Veenhoven, R., & Hagerty, M. (2006). Rising happiness in nations 1946–2004. A reply to Easterlin. *Social Indicators Research, 77,* 1–16.

Veenhoven, R. (2008). Healthy happiness: Effects of happiness on physical health and the consequences for preventive health care. *Journal of Happiness Studies, 9,* 449–464.

Veenhoven, R. (2009). *World database of happiness: Continuous register of scientific research on subjective enjoyment of life*. Erasmus Universiteit Rotterdam, The Netherlands. Available at: http://worlddatabaseofhappiness.eur.nl

Veenhoven, R. (2009b). How do we assess how happy we are? In A. Dutt & B. Radcliff (Eds.), *Happiness, economics and politics*. (pp. 45–69), USA: Edward Elger Publishers.

Warr, P. (2007). *Work, happiness and unhappiness*. London: Routledge.

Wilson, T., & Gilbert, D. (2005). Affective forecasting: Knowing what to want. *Current Directions in Psychological Science, 14*, 131–134.

# 27

# Positive Psychology as a Force for Social Change

*Robert Biswas-Diener, P. Alex Linley, Reena Govindji,*
*and Linda Woolston*

## Taking Stock: The Negative Side of Positive Psychology

Positive psychology is the name given to a relatively recent movement within psychology, a trend in which researchers focus on positive topics such as happiness and optimism. In their recent text on the subject, Snyder and Lopez (2007) define positive psychology as "the science and applications related to the study of psychological strengths and positive emotions" (p 22). Although the antecedents of positive psychology can be found in philosophy and the humanistic movement, pioneers of this modern phenomenon claim that it is distinct from past approaches in that rigorous scientific methods are emphasized (Seligman & Csikszentmihalyi, 2000). In its modern guise, positive psychology is a decade old and has evolved from a handful of loosely connected researchers with a professional interest in positive topics to an organized infrastructure including an international professional body, annual conferences around the world, a journal dedicated to this line of study, and graduate-level programs training future generations of positive psychologists (Biswas-Diener &

Dean, 2007; Linley, Joseph, Harrington, & Wood, 2006). These institutions are suggestive of the durability of the movement and offer proof that positive psychology is likely to outlast its charismatic leaders.

Further testament to the power and usefulness of positive psychology comes from the growing body of research, assessment, and intervention produced under this conceptual umbrella. For example, the book *Positive Psychological Assessment* (Lopez & Snyder, 2003) includes dozens of widely used and well-validated surveys for measuring positive constructs. Similarly, a number of positive psychology interventions—principally those intended to increase happiness—have been tested and validated (e.g., Seligman, Steen, Peterson, & Park, 2005; Lyubomirsky, 2008). Most notably, the research on positive topics such as strengths and happiness has grown dramatically in recent years. There is now a *Journal of Happiness Studies, Applied Research in Quality of Life, Journal of Positive Psychology,* and new coaching journals that are, arguably, influenced by positive psychological science. To take a single example—happiness—a recent PsycInfo search revealed that more articles

(1,358) were published with the keyword "happiness" in the last decade than were published in the preceding hundred-year period (1,095 published from 1900–1999). Clearly, there has been an increase in the research attention given to positive topics, which has, presumably, yielded new insights and better theories.

Among the most important and fundamental questions related to this new field is that which asks whether positive psychology is, or should be, prescriptive. Some scholars have argued that positive psychology is, by definition, ideologically based and that the emphasis on concepts such as "the good life" is necessarily reflective of prescriptive values (Woolfolk & Wasserman, 2005). Seligman (2002), recognized as the founder of positive psychology, has argued the opposite, insisting that "science must be descriptive and not prescriptive. It is not the job of Positive Psychology to tell you that you should be optimistic, or spiritual, or kind or good humored; it is rather to describe the consequences of these traits" (p. 129). Here, it is easy to draw corollaries with clinical psychology, itself a prescriptive science. Clinical psychologists are not concerned only with understanding the etiology of depression and other mental disorders but also with designing effective interventions to promote psychological quality of life, broadly speaking. In this respect, positive psychology shares with clinical psychology a primary focus on the welfare of the individual (with apologies to group counselors and couples therapists).

We contend that the heavy emphasis in positive psychology on individual flourishing is the unintended by-product of the overreliance on happiness-related variables as outcome measures. In their "progress report" on positive psychology, for example, Seligman and colleagues (2005) suggest that character strength-related interventions are effective in buffering people against depression and promoting happiness. Similarly, interventions tested by Lyubomirsky (2008), Bryant, and colleagues (2005) and Otake and colleagues (2006) all use happiness as the primary outcome measure. Because happiness is, by definition, a subjectively felt experience, it follows that this science has been able to "prove" its effectiveness most readily at the individual level. A second possibility is that positive psychology is heavily influenced by a personality perspective. Indeed, relatively few published positive psychology articles look at classic situational influences on personal thought or behavior. It could be that an emphasis on situational influences

undermines the explicit positive psychology idea that individuals are not mere "victims of circumstance." Regardless of the origins of an individualistic focus, it is our view that positive psychology has, in general, favored the individual as the basic unit of analysis. Widely used organizational interventions such as Appreciative Inquiry (Cooperrider, Whitney, & Stavros, 2008), by contrast, are conspicuously absent from encyclopedic sources on positive psychology such as the *Handbook of Positive Psychology* (Snyder & Lopez, 2002), just as positive community psychology theories and interventions are frequently overlooked.

Nowhere is this individualistic concern more apparent than in the case of character strengths. The study of strengths has been a major thrust of positive psychology research and forms the basis for many commonly used positive psychology interventions. It is noteworthy that the prevailing conceptual model, the so-called VIA strengths (Peterson & Seligman, 2004), was developed as an intellectual counterpoint to the Diagnostic and Statistical Manual of Mental Disorders (APA, 1994), itself a taxonomy intended for use with individuals. Peterson and Seligman (2004) explicitly submit the cultivation of individual character as the ultimate aim of their work. Strengths are often viewed in terms of stable personality traits (Peterson & Seligman, 2004) or evolutionary adaptations (Linley, 2008), which appear to lend themselves to an individualized appreciation of this construct. In all fairness, however, there is some evidence that major figures in positive psychology are beginning to turn their attention toward group, organization, and society-level intervention. Linley (2008), for example, includes discussion of strengths as integral to marriages and organizations, and Peterson (2006), similarly, has been vocal about creating "strengths-based institutions." In our own work at the Centre for Applied Positive Psychology, we have also been working since 2006 to take positive psychology into practice with both organizations (Linley & Page, 2007), and Jenny Fox Eades has been working since 2004 to take positive psychology into schools (Fox Eades, 2008).

Thus, we find ourselves at a crucial turning point in the evolution of positive psychology. The initial period in which it was necessary for apologists of positive psychology to establish the validity and effectiveness of this new science is past. Now, we are at a point where we can begin expanding our research, assessments, and interventions to reach larger groups. In this regard, positive psychology is a vehicle for positive social change. In this chapter, we will highlight the instances in which positive psychology research and programs have been focused on addressing pressing societal issues. We will also outline the specific mechanisms by which positive psychology can positively influence societies. Finally, we will argue that positive psychology presents a unique opportunity to address social ills with new tools.

## How Positive Psychology Can Be Used as a Tool for Social Change

Since its inception, thought leaders in positive psychology have understood that, in the long term, the discipline must evolve from a basic to an applied science. As our collective insights into happiness, optimism, morality, and other positive topics become more sophisticated and useful, there is a mandate for social responsibility. While scientists do not necessarily feel the onus of that responsibility personally, they are the gatekeepers of knowledge that, arguably, can promote positive psychological change on a widespread basis. Sherman (2007) describes a program of transformative change:

Transformative activists should not only work toward tearing down the old society, but should also work toward building the foundations of a new society. It's not just about closing down toxic landfills, stopping incinerators from moving into the neighborhood, and battling against polluting industries. Instead, it is also a proactive approach of constructing better alternatives—creating a new vision of the community that is both economically strong and environmentally healthy.

To Sherman's comments we would add an emphasis on psychological flourishing. It is in this spirit that positive psychology findings and interventions can contribute to the development of new organizations and institutions to promote higher quality of life. In this section, we will discuss four distinct ways positive psychology may be a force for social change, and supply case illustrations for each.

### Case 1—Beyond Money: Well-Being Indicators and Public Policy

The first case of positive psychology research being used as a force for social change is to be found in the subjective well-being (SWB) research. SWB is the widely accepted scientific

name for happiness, and its research constitutes a major pillar of positive psychology. Although early research on the topic focused largely on demographic factors associated with and explanatory theories of happiness (Diener, 1984), more recent studies have focused on the outcomes or benefits of happiness. Fredrickson (2001), for instance, advanced the "broaden-and-build" theory, which states that positive emotions are associated with the expansion of physical, social, and psychological resources. Evidence for this theory can be found in a wide range of benefits of feeling frequent positive affect, including enhanced creativity, improved social relationships, better health, and better organizational citizenship behaviors (Lyubomirsky, King, & Diener, 2005). In the end, happiness is not something that simply feels good, it *is* good... for individuals, families, and organizations (Diener & Biswas-Diener, 2008). Because happiness is so widely beneficial, some researchers have argued that measures of well-being are necessary to compliment traditional economic indicators of quality of life (e.g., Diener & Seligman, 2004; Michaelson, Abdallah, Steuer, Thompson, & Marks, 2009). In fact, because many measures of well-being are subjective, their use as national indicators may be seen as "part of the democratic process in which citizens and their leaders are given information that can be useful in policy debates" (Diener, 2006, p. 399; Donovan & Halpern, 2001). Thus, positive psychology assessment, itself, can be used as an instrument of social change.

One modern example of this is "State of Global Well-being" a comprehensive poll conducted by the Gallup Organization. The so-called "Gallup World Poll," initiated in 2005 with recurrent sampling cycles, was designed to provide "a broad and deep context within which to study well-being among populations around the world" (Gallup, 2007, p. 9). The poll is noteworthy in that it includes demographically representative samples (N = 1,000 per country approximately) of more than 100 countries. As such, it is able to provide in-depth and reliable information on well-being, law and order, health, and other topics that are important to governors, policy makers, and community developers. Also noteworthy is the poll's clear foundation in positive psychology, as the introduction to the 2007 report suggests:

The science of subjective well-being fills this lacuna by providing a representative measure based on self-reported survey data and, in doing so, it offers a broader alternative to the income/social indicators view of welfare that has been in favor with economists (p. 5).

## Case 2—Environmental Awareness and Change

Another area of potential social impact for positive psychology research is in environmental concerns, especially as they relate to consumption behaviors and psychological health. There is now a body of research literature that suggests that materialism—the active valuing of and desire to acquire material and luxury goods—is toxic to individual well-being (Kasser & Ryan, 1993). Nickerson and colleagues (2003) demonstrated that emphasizing financial success could have deleterious effects on both overall life satisfaction and on relationship satisfaction. Not only is an emphasis on money and material goods associated with psychological costs, there are environmental costs as well. Brown and Kassser (2005) demonstrated that the more materialistic an individual is, on average, the higher his or her ecological footprint. Kasser (2003) concludes that "Earth's health suffers when these [materialistic] values lead individuals to consume at unsustainable and damaging rates" (p. 95).

One example of positive psychology research being used to address environmental concerns such as overconsumption is "The Happy Planet Index (HPI)" published by the New Economics Foundation (Marks, Simms, Thompson, & Abdallah, 2006). Rather than sampling the well-being of nations, as is commonly done in international comparisons of happiness, Marks and colleagues divided national well-being scores (satisfaction and longevity) by scores of environmental consumption, resulting in a ratio that illustrates "the ecological efficiency with which nations deliver happy and long lives to their populations" (p. 9). For instance, the United States—the richest country in the world and one that consistently ranks in the top 20 on measures of happiness (see Biswas-Diener, Vitterso, & Diener, 2010, for further discussion)—has a "poor" HPI rating because of the high levels of consumption and amount of natural resources needed to sustain this level of happiness. The HPI is, arguably, a new and dramatic way to present such information and an effective method of informing the public about the relation between positive psychology topics such as happiness and larger social concerns such as environmental degradation. It is noteworthy that the Happy Planet Index received a large amount of popular media attention, highlighting the usefulness of public education as a positive psychology social change tool.

## Case 3—Strengths-Based Organizations

Just as identifying and using strengths has been found to be effective in promoting individual happiness (Seligman, Steen, Peterson, & Park, 2005), there is increasing awareness that strengths-based interventions may have organizational benefits. Clifton and Harter (2003) apply the concept of strengths to the business environment, arguing that strengths play an important role in employee engagement and superior management practices. The best managers, for example, "were more likely to indicate that they spend time with high producers, match talents to tasks, and emphasize individual strengths versus seniority in making personnel decisions" (p. 116). Linley (2008) takes this idea a step further when he promotes the notion that strengths are not merely an individual, but collective, phenomenon. In his "strengths-based teamworking" approach, Linley argues that allocating tasks, roles, and responsibilities according to strengths is more productive than what can be achieved by an individual.

The "Celebrating Strengths" school-based program by Fox Eades (2008) is an example of how positive psychology can be used to enact social change at the organizational level. Eades uses strengths as a thematic foundation to promote individual and cultural change in schools through fesitvals, discussions, building teacher skills, storytelling, and other techniques. In her "Treasure Chest" approach to strengths-building, for example, Eades suggests that classes keep a photo album or similar record of their collective successes and moments of strengths. Here, the emphasis is shifted from individual achievement to the collective good. The Celebrating Strengths program differs from other strengths intervention programs in that it is explicitly geared toward organizations (schools, in this case) and, therefore, includes attention to transformation at the individual, classroom, and whole school levels.

## Case 4—Initiatives for Addressing Poverty Through Enabling Human Talent and Potential

Perhaps the most pressing of all social problems is poverty. A 2002 United Nations Human

Development Report reveals that about half the people in sub-Saharan Africa and more than a third of the people in Southeast Asia live on less than a dollar a day. Not only is poverty a matter of material deprivation, but studies suggest that there are psychological consequences related to poverty including higher incidence of trauma (Hein & Bukszpan, 1999) and elevated rates of sadness, anger, and worry (Biswas-Diener & Diener, 2006). The recognition that poverty is associated with more than material deprivation is at the heart of a vigorous new dialogue on poverty reduction. Narayan (2002), for example, frames poverty in terms of empowerment. She writes:

> Empowerment refers broadly to the expansion of freedom of choice and action to shape one's life. It implies control over resources and decisions. For poor poeple, that freedom is severely curtailed by their voicelessness and powerlessness... (p. xvii).

Thus, it may be that the true evil of poverty lies not in the health complications associated with poor water or inadequate health care (notwithstanding that these are serious issues) but in the inability of dynamic, intelligent, motivated individuals to reach their own potential. Indeed, Nobel Laureate Amartya Sen (1992) claims that "poverty is better seen in terms of capability failure than in terms of the failure to meet 'basic needs'" (p.109). To the extent that this is true, addressing poverty dovetails nicely with the underlying ideology of positive psychology, which, itself, is primarily concerned with potential.

A number of programs developed to alleviate poverty directly address the issue of personal empowerment. The Nobel Prize-winning Grameen Bank, for example, is a pioneering institution in microfinance programs aimed at providing low-income men and women opportunities for increased participation in their own financial, social, and psychological affairs (Yunus, 2008). Similarly, our own charitable project, The Strengths Project (see www.thestrengthsproject. org), is—perhaps—the world's first explicitly positive psychology charitable project with the goal of addressing problems associated with poverty. Sen (1993) argues that poor people adapt too easily to their low-class status, and that their self-reported life satisfaction is based on unreasonably low standards of comparisons. To intervene in such a way as to improve the quality of their lives, then, it is necessary to create programs that focus on psychological empowerment as well as material needs. The Strengths Project uses a motivational interviewing technique called the Individual Strengths Assessment to promote a sense of worth, efficacy, and community pride among people living in impoverished areas of Kolkata, India. By shifting attention away from daily struggles to an appreciation of personal strengths and social successes, the people associated with The Strengths Project have experienced a positivity they might not have otherwise.

## Moving Forward: A Positive Psychology Mandate for Social Change

In thinking about the potential of positive psychology to usher in social change, it makes sense to ask fundamental questions about our responsibilities—personally and collectively—in using this new science to shape a better society. Whether we are researchers, educators, coaches, consultants, or therapists, if our work is informed by positive psychology, do we bear the burden of enacting social change? Certainly there is no explicit directive for social change activism in our professional codes of ethics or in our job descriptions. But, it is fair to say that such a mandate is embedded in the very ideology of positive psychology itself. Linley (2008) suggests that, for those wishing to make the greatest possible contribution, there are "three pillars" of responsibility: 1) personal responsibility to use and develop our individual strengths, 2) collective responsibility to create conditions that enable the strengths of others, and 3) social responsibility to harness strengths for the benefit of wider society. It is our intent to argue in this paper that, as gatekeepers of positive psychology, we are all called upon to live up to these three responsibilities.

The best route to social change is, however, not a clear path, and the best use of our resources is not always certain. Take the example of environmental degradation: As people involved in a social science, do we have a preemptive responsibility to help other people (as opposed to focusing our energies on addressing environmental problems)? An argument could be made that patterns of development and consumption affect human psychology and, therefore, environmental matters fall directly under the purview of positive psychologists. On the other hand, it could be that the tools of our trade—psychological assessments, counseling interventions, education— are more appropriate to a type of transformative change that is directly linked to organizations and societies; that is, to people. Obviously, there is no single correct answer to this question, and the type and method of social change pursued will largely be a matter of individual preference. That said, we believe positive psychology offers mechanisms by which people can achieve an improved quality of life and therefore ought to be used toward this end. In closing, we outline what we believe to be the goals and tools of social change in a positive psychology context.

## Goals of Social Change

To some degree, the idea of social change underscores all of the work of psychology. We study human thought and behavior because we believe that a better understanding of ourselves will lead to better self-control, relationships, and decisions. We try to intervene in the lives of people who struggle with painful mental illness or to promote health and wellness behaviors because we believe it will feel better and result in outcomes we value. In each case psychology is, itself, about change. But when we talk about social change we mean transforming existing social structures to improve the lives of many. Social change need not be anchored in liberal or conservative ideologies, and we show no favor to either here. Instead, we have identified broad goals of social change that meet two criteria: first, they must be widely appealing to people regardless of politics, ethnicity, nationality, religion, or other personal factors; second, they must be directly tied to the technologies of positive psychology, either in its current form or in some reasonably predictable future form. These goals include:

1. Economic possibility: We have a responsibility to disseminate information about the toxic effects of focusing too heavily on material aspirations (Nickerson et al, 2003) and bringing to light the psychological mechanisms by which people make responsible and irresponsible financial decisions (e.g., Stewart, 2009). By the same token, we have an obligation to educate policy makers on the relation between income and well-being, especially at the national level of analysis (Diener & Biswas-Diener, 2002). This extends to the many benefits of income on happiness (see Hagerty & Veenhoven, 2003).

2. Human potential: Human potential has been of central interest to psychologists since Maslow (1954) introduced his famous "hierarchy of needs." Positive psychology is, itself, about unleashing talent, developing strengths, and increasing the capabilities of all people. The psychological science of human potential is especially germane to social transformation to the extent that it can be applied to members of disenfranchised groups.

3. Community capability: From a community psychology standpoint, those interested in positive psychology are well poised to research and intervene with community health and welfare initiatives. It is possible to extend beyond a traditional focus on social ills such as drug abuse, homelessness, and violence and shift a focus to prevention, volunteerism, and community regeneration programs that are highly inclusive. Narrow and colleagues (1993) note that nearly half the people who seek ambulatory mental health services do not qualify for an official diagnosis. To the extent that positive psychology is about promoting health, even among the healthy there is much that this new science has to offer communities.

## Mechanisms for Social Change

We close with practical suggestions for using positive psychology in the service of social change. First, we believe it is imperative that positive psychological science be widely accessible. Lazarus (2003) suggests that, perhaps, positive psychology is too popular in nature and scientists in this discipline need more time to investigate and define concepts of interest. While his point is well taken, it also seems responsible to make those conclusions about which we are confident available to the public. A cottage industry has sprung up around positive psychology books, coaching seminars, and consultancies. It would be a shame, in our view (and we speak as part of that industry), if the potential benefits of positive psychology were limited to middle- or upper-class individuals or to those living in industrialized nations. We suggest experimenting with methods for giving positive psychology away for free. One excellent example of this is the VIA assessment of strengths, which is available free of charge to anyone who can access the Internet. Similarly, it is possible to establish methods by which relatively affluent people purchasing positive psychological assessments or services help subsidize comparable services for a counterpart in an impoverished area of the world. A portion of the revenue from coaching clients, for instance, might be placed in a kitty that could later be used to fund coaching for community leaders in India, South America, or other areas where these services might not be affordable. Similar programs could be developed in any instance where positive psychology consultation, assessment, or interventions are sold.

Next, we believe that positive psychology can be used effectively as an educational tool that affects social change. Sherman (2007) claims that one of the fundamental tenets of transformative action is "exposing injustice." At the core of this argument is a tacit understanding of the power of knowledge. Proctor (2008) argues that ignorance—such as the instances when businesses mount campaigns to cast doubt on the harmful effects of their products—can lead to social ills. It follows that using positive psychology to educate people about promising routes to happiness, factors that promote resilience, and other positive topics can be helpful in creating a good society. In the so-called "information age" some people have been concerned about a perceived "information gap," in which people without access to Internet resources or mobile technology are at a disadvantage in higher education, industry, and health. In our opinion, we must ensure that positive psychology information is available to all people. As an example of this, one of us (RBD) has sometimes arranged to give lectures in severely impoverished areas in India so that the local population may have the same access to research findings on subjective well-being as their counterparts in countries where popular books on happiness are widely available. Similar dissemination of positive psychology research results is possible with a number of target audiences using a wide variety of media and presentation tools.

Finally, positive psychology has the greatest potential for social change in interventions at the group level. Admittedly, a number of programs aimed at group change such as *Appreciative Inquiry* or *Celebrating Strengths* are already in use and are effective. Despite this fact, counseling and community psychologists have largely been left outside the strategic development of the field of positive psychology (Cowen & Kilmer, 2002, Mollen, Ehtington & Ridley, 2006). As a result, positive psychology is largely influenced by

an individual-intervention mindset. Community-based approaches to social change would not only be a welcome addition to positive psychology but are, arguably, its greatest area of growth.

Ultimately, positive psychology is a science that is concerned with human betterment, community flourishing, and the good life, broadly defined. In the last decade we have been successful in establishing this ideological movement as a viable science with lasting institutions and worthwhile intellectual products. We now find ourselves at the advent of a new phase in the evolution of positive psychology. We are now called to reach our own personal and professional potential by using our knowledge and technologies not just for good, but for the good of many.

*References*

American Psychiatric Association (1994). *Diagnostic and statistical manual of mental disorders* (4th ed.). Washington, DC: APA.

Biswas-Diener, R., & Dean, B. (2007). *Positive psychology coaching: Putting the science of happiness to work for your clients.* Hoboken, NJ: John Wiley & Sons.

Biswas-Diener, R., & Diener, E. (2008). *Happiness: Unlocking the mysteries of psychological wealth.* Malden, MA: Blackwell.

Biswas-Diener, R., & Diener, E. (2006). Subjective well-being of the homeless, and related lessons for happiness. *Social Indicators Research, 76,* 185–205.

Biswas-Diener, R., Vitterso, J., & Diener, E. (2010). The Danish effect: Beginning to explain the high happiness of Denmark. *Social Indicators Research, 97,* 229–246.

Brown, K. W., & Kasser, T. (2005). Are psychological and ecological well-being compatible? The role of values, mindfulness, and lifestyle. *Social Indicators Research, 74,* 349–368.

Bryant, F. B., Smart, C. M., & King, S. P. (2005). Using the past to enhance the present: Boosting happiness through positive reminiscence. *Journal of Happiness Studies, 6,* 227–260.

Clifton, D., & Harter, J. (2003). Investing in strengths. In K. Cameron, J. Dutton, & R. Quinn (Eds.), *Positive organizational scholarship: Foundations of a new discipline.* San Francisco: Barrett-Koehler Publishers.

Cooperrider, D., Whitney, D., & Stavros, J. M. (2008). *Appreciative inquiry handbook: For leaders of change* (2nd ed.). San Francisco: Barrett-Koehler Publishers.

Cowen, E. L., & Kilmer, R. P. (2002). "Positive psychology": Some plusses and some open issues. *Journal of Community Psychology, 30*, 449–460.

Diener, E., & Biswas-Diener, R. (2002). Will money increase subjective well-being? A literature review and guide to needed research. *Social Indicators Research, 57*, 119–169.

Diener, E., & Seligman, M. E. P. (2004). Beyond money: Toward an economy of well-being. *Psychological Science in the Public Interest, 5*, 1–31.

Diener, E. (2006). Guidelines for national indicators of subjective well-being and ill-being. *Journal of Happiness Studies, 7*, 397–404.

Diener, E. (1984). Subjective well-being. *Psychological Bulletin, 95*, 542–575.

Donovan, N., & Halpern, D. (2001). *Life satisfaction: The state of knowledge and implications for government*. London: Downing Street Strategy Unit.

Fox Eades, J. M. (2008). *Celebrating strengths: Building strengths-based schools*. Coventry, England: CAPP Press.

Fredrickson, B. (2001). The role of positive emotions in positive psychology: The broaden-and-build theory of positive emotions. *American Psychologist, 56*, 218–226.

Gallup (2007). *The state of global well-being*. New York: Gallup Press.

Hagerty, M. R., & Veenhoven, R. (2003). Wealth and happiness, revisited—growing national income *does* go with greater happiness. *Social Indicators Research, 64*, 1–27.

Hein, D., & Bukszpan, C. (1999). Interpersonal violence in "normal" low-income groups. *Women & Health, 29*, 1–16.

Kasser, T. (2003). *The high price of materialism*. Cambridge, MA: MIT Press.

Kasser, T., & Ryan, R. M. (1993). A dark side of the American Dream: Correlates of financial success as a central life aspiration. *Journal of Personality & Social Psychology, 65*, 410–422.

Lazarus, R. (2003). The Lazarus manifesto for positive psychology and psychology in general. *Psychological Inquiry, 14*, 173–189.

Linley, A. (2008). *Average to A+: Realising strengths in yourself and others*. Coventry, England: CAPP Press.

Linley, P. A., Joseph, S., Harrington, S., & Wood, A. M. (2006). Positive psychology: Past, present, and (possible) future. *The Journal of Positive Psychology, 1*, 3–16.

Linley, P. A., & Page, N. (2007, October). Positive approaches to human resource management: Outlines of a strengths-based approach. *PersonalFuhrung, 10*, 22–30.

Lopez, S., & Snyder, C. R. (2003). *Positive psychological assessment*. Washington, DC: American Psychological Association.

Lyubomirsky, S. (2008). The how of happiness: A scientific approach to getting the life you want. New York: Penguin.

Lyubomirsky, S., King, L. A., & Diener, E. (2005). The benefits of frequent positive affect. *Psychological Bulletin, 131*, 803–855.

Marks, N., Simms, A. Thompson, S., & Abdallah, S. (2006). *The happy planet index*. London: new economics foundation.

Maslow, A. (1954). Motivation and personality. New York: Harper.

Michaelson, J., Abdallah, S., Steuer, N., Thompson, S., & Marks, N. (2009). *National accounts of well-being: Bringing real wealth onto the balance sheet*. London: new economics foundation.

Mollen, D., Ehtington, L. L., & Ridley, C. R. (2006). Positive psychology: Considerations and implications for counseling psychology. *The Counseling Psychologist, 34*, 304–312.

Narayan, D. (2002). *Empowerment and poverty reduction: A sourcebook*. Washington, DC: World Bank.

Narrow, W. E., Regeir, D. A., Rae, D. S., Manderscheid, R. W., & Locke, B. Z. (1993). Use of services by persons with mental and addictive disorders: Findings from the National Institute of Mental Health Epidemiological Catchment Area program. *Archives of General Psychiatry, 50*, 95–107.

Nickerson, C., Schwarz, N., Diener, E., & Kahneman, D. (2003). Zeroing in on the dark side of the American dream: A closer look at the negative consequences of the goal for financial success. *Psychological Science, 14*, 531–536.

Otake, K., Shimai, S., Tanaka-Matsumi, J., Otsui, K, & Fredrickson, B. L. (2006). Happy people become happier through kindness: A counting kindnesses intervention. *Journal of Happiness Studies, 7*, 361–375.

Peterson, C. (2006). *A primer in positive psychology*. Oxford: Oxford University Press.

Peterson, C., & Seligman, M. E. P. (2004). *Character strengths and virtues: A handbook and classification*. Washington, DC: APA Press and Oxford University Press.

Proctor, R. (2008). Agnotology: A missing piece to describe the cultural production of ignorance (and its study). In R. Proctor & L. Schiebinger (Eds.), *Agnotology: The making and unmaking of ignorance* (pp. 1–36). Stanford, CA: Stanford University Press.

Seligman, M. E. P. (2002). *Authentic happiness: Using the new positive psychology to realize your potential for lasting fulfillment.* New York, NY: Free Press.

Seligman, M. E. P., & Csikszentmihalyi, M. (2000). Positive psychology: An introduction. *American Psychologist, 55,* 5–14.

Seligman, M. E. P., Steen, T., Park, N., & Peterson, C. (2005). Positive psychology progress: Empirical validation of interventions. *American Psychologist, 60,* 410–421.

Sen, A. (1992). *Inequality re-examined.* New York: Russell Sage Foundation.

Sen, A. (1993). Capability, well-being. In M. C. Nussbaum & A. Sen (Eds.), *The quality of life* (pp. 30–53). Oxford: Clarendon Press.

Sherman, S. 2007, October. Positive psychology and social change activism. Paper presented at the Sixth International Positive Psychology Summit, Washington, DC.

Snyder, C. R., & Lopez, S. (2007). *Positive psychology: The scientific and practical explorations of human strengths.* Thousand Oaks, CA: Sage.

Snyder, C. R., & Lopez, S. (2002). *Handbook of positive psychology.* Oxford: Oxford University Press.

Stewart, N. (2009). *The costs of anchoring on credit card minimum payments. Psychological Science,* 20, *39–41.*

Woolfolk, R. L., & Wasserman, R. H. (2005). Count no one happy: A critique of second generation positive psychology. *Journal of Theoretical and Philosophical Psychology, 25,* 81–90.

United Nations (United Nations Human Development Program, 2002). Human development report: Deepening democracy in a fragmented world. New York: United Nations.

Yunus, M. (2008). *Creating a world without poverty: Social business and the future of capitalism.* New York: Public Affairs.

# X

**Summary Perspectives**

# 28

# What's Positive about Positive Psychology? Reducing Value-Bias and Enhancing Integration within the Field

*Kennon M. Sheldon*

In this book we have invited a host of notewor-thy scientists to take stock of the field of positive psychology and to give their suggestions about how the field may move forward. In this chapter I (the lead editor) will take my own shot at these questions. What are the key issues facing posi-tive psychology?

## Taking Stock: Has the Value-Laden Nature of Positive Psychology Detracted from Positive Psychological Science?

In taking stock, I'd like to begin by focusing on an interesting tension within positive psychology: the very fact that it contains the word "positive" in its title. Already this seems a violation of the proper scientific attitude, which says that science must be value-free and unbiased (Kendler, 1999). According to this view, the scientist should be a neutral observer, carefully documenting what exists in reality, not what he or she wishes existed. Indeed, it is difficult and almost ludicrous to imagine a field of "positive physics" or "positive chemistry"—aren't these hard sciences whose purview is objective physical reality, independent

of our subjective feelings about that reality? Shouldn't psychology (including positive psy-chology) also be "hard"?

In this section I hope to unpack and evaluate this aspect of positive psychology—the fact that it seems to presuppose that its subject matter is positive or desirable according to some value system. What is that value system, and is it justifiable? Does it get in positive psychology's way as a science? Can positive psychology even *be* a science, given its potential bias?

### Positive Psychology as a Positive Science

In considering the matter, it becomes apparent that the "positive" in positive psychology can be, and has been, conceptualized and applied in a vari-ety of different ways. One way simply involves doing what we might call "positive science," which can be defined as a mixture of basic and applied research in which the search for basic knowledge is influenced by the desire to improve or optimize human life. Of course, there are many topics that a scientist could choose to study within his or her field; the positive scientist chooses topics that have direct relevance for making things better for people. By this definition, many physicists and chemists could be classified as positive scientists; for example, a molecular biologist who seeks to change the by-products of a certain chemical reaction so that a drug with fewer side effects may be produced, or a nuclear physicist who seeks to understand fusion reactions in order to solve human energy problems. Similarly, a positive psychologist might research how to best communicate with participants during a life-skills intervention, so that participants gain the most from the intervention. Here, the psychologist's search for basic knowledge (concerning fundamental principles of communication and persuasion) takes place within a particular type of applied context (improving a skills intervention). From this perspective, the value judgments or biases implied by positive psychology seem non-problematic, as long as the goal of improving life does not bias or cloud the broader goal of understanding objective reality in order to do that.

## Positive Psychology as an Ideological Stance

However, it seems that positive psychologists are doing more than this. Some of us seem to be thinking that our subject matter itself (people) is generally positive or admirable. This brings us to a second possible understanding of the "positive" within positive psychology: that the scientist's subject matter is inherently good, desirable, or valuable (relative to an opposing perspective, that the subject matter might be inherently bad, undesirable, or not valuable). One example is the book, *Born to Be Good: The Science of a Meaningful Life* (Keltner, 2009). Keltner makes an argument that humans evolved to be more cooperative and interconnected than selfish and destructive, and that these positive characteristics are a prominent part of humanity's adaptive toolkit. Of course, such arguments can be evaluated on their empirical merits, and Keltner does a very reasonable job of defending his optimistic thesis. Still, it is difficult to imagine a chemist or physicist saying that chemical or physical processes are "more good than bad" (except perhaps from the perspective that if they did not occur, life could not exist).

It seems to me that this is where positive psychology is most vulnerable to going wrong, as the belief that humans are more good than bad could be a self-serving illusion or an ideological bias that clouds or completely blocks our view of half of human nature (i.e., the not-so-good part).

Indeed, many "noble human" movements in the past (Rousseau's romantic humanism, 1960s Third Force psychology) seem to have lost favor precisely because their view seemed, at least to some, to be too naïve or Pollyannaish. This does not mean that those making such positive assumptions are *necessarily* wrong; again, it may be possible to make an empirical case that humans are more positive than negative with respect to carefully specified value-categories (i.e., maybe we *do* cooperate more than we compete, smile more than we frown, grow more than we contract). Indeed, it does seem that people are more happy than unhappy (Myers, 2000). But researchers should tread very cautiously in this area!

As a personal example, I work extensively with Deci and Ryan's self-determination theory (Deci & Ryan, 1985; Ryan & Deci, 2008), a very "positive" theory that assumes that an orientation toward growth and integration is the default state of humans. However, I strive to remain critical of the idea that humans are inherently growth-seeking and intrinsically motivated until social forces derail them. There is plenty of evidence that humans are also inherently small-minded, defensive, and susceptible to greed and venality, and this fact needs to be reconciled with the positive view. In fact, an exciting trend within contemporary self-determination theory is to explore the exact mechanisms by which thwarted positive motivations can become twisted into substitute, compensatory, and unhealthy negative motivations (Ryan & Deci, 2008).

## Positive Psychology as an Appreciative View

However, many positive psychologists do not go quite so far as to assume that "humans are basically good." Instead, they are merely trying to take an "appreciative" view of their subject matter (King, 2008). As one considers the data and their implications, one pauses to admire the admirable, praise the praiseworthy, and like the likeable. Also, one is open to the fact that most people function rather well despite their problems, and one is attentive to "what works" more so than "what doesn't work" (Sheldon & King, 2001). There seems to be nothing wrong with such an attitude: of course, many physicists, chemists, and biologists have a fascination for the intricacies of their topic (that's why they went into the field) and experience great enthusiasm regarding their discoveries. Such enthusiasm and appreciation is doubtless a large part of why some academics write books for lay audiences—to communicate the wonders of their field to a broader audience.

I suggest that the latter, "appreciative" attitude is a particularly important one for positive psychologists to cultivate, because it can help to rectify and re-balance what I believe has been a negative bias in the field of psychology. This is manifested both in the predominant topics studied by psychologists prior to the year 2000 (mental illness, pathology, conflict, prejudice, aggression, and the like) and by the previous century's implicit assumption that human functioning is predominantly characterized by problems—errors, biases, self-serving motives, hostile instincts, and the like. One notable contribution of positive psychology in the last 10 years has been to begin to counterbalance these dominant foci and assumptions so that the good side of human nature, and our general success in solving the problems of living, are recognized and understood. Of course, the danger always looms that appreciative positive psychologists will be *too* appreciative, fooled by their wishes and preconceptions into seeing humans as better than they really are, a danger noted and discussed by many of the contributors to this volume. However, the danger seems not as great for this third definition of the positive in positive psychology, as it refers more to an attitude toward the topic rather than to an ideological position formally located within theory.

## Positive Psychology as the Study of Positive Topics

An unfortunate implication of the term "positive psychology" is that it suggests that some areas or eras of psychology may be "negative" psychology. This can lead to an unfortunate dynamic: nobody wants to think they are a negative psychologist, so they must either join the bandwagon ("I too am a positive psychologist!") or deny it ("Positive psychology is wrong and harmful!"). My position is that *all* fields of psychology are positive sciences to the extent that the derived knowledge can be used to solve problems and to improve what is in need of improvement. After all, clinical researchers studying depression and cognitive researchers studying learning errors are not trying to increase depression and error; they hope their knowledge can be used to reduce these problems. Even military psychologists studying brainwashing or prisoner intimidation techniques could be viewed as positive psychologists, if one accepts their claim that this knowledge is

essential for protecting America's security. This is of course a debatable proposition, and here it may simply become a question of values and interpretations. (Which are correct and worthy?) The main point is that we are (nearly) all proceeding in good faith, doing what we think is right.

Obviously, however, the term "positive psychology" is not very useful if it applies to all psychologists. Thus, I believe that the term positive psychology is best reserved specifically for research into the "good" side of human life—topics such as gratitude (rather than jealousy), forgiveness (rather than revenge), happiness (rather than depression), cooperation (rather than disruptive competition), and longevity (rather than premature death). Positive psychology focuses directly on providing the owner's manual for human optimization—helping people to go not from "awful" to "OK" (the focus of prior, "negative" psychology that in a sense focused primarily on negative topics like depression) but rather, from "OK" to "awesome" (Seligman, 2002). And indeed, "positive topics" does seem to be the way the term is primarily used within the field, as can be seen by scanning any issue of *The Journal of Positive Psychology*. For example, the January 2009 issue contains articles on flourishing, achievement, well-being, pleasure, interest, positive emotions, gratitude, meaning in life, open-mindedness, life purpose, elevation, prosocial behavior, empathy, and thriving. Only two "negative" terms appeared in the title of any of the nine articles in this issue: relationship dissolution (how to cope with it through positive writing) and materialism (how to reduce it by increasing gratitude).

In sum, from a definitional standpoint, positive psychology is a positive science that conducts basic research with an eye to improving human life and functioning; its practitioners try to at least take an appreciative view of the positive aspects of human nature, even if they do not go so far as to assume that human nature is "basically good"; they tend to study topics that are framed in positive terms rather than in polar negative terms; and they try to recognize and correct (when necessary) the negative biases regarding human nature that used to permeate the field, even as they try to remain realistic, so as not to fall prey to wishful thinking and overly rosy visions and so as not to ignore important "negative" aspects of human nature that impact upon their topics. However, as suggested by the canvassing of positive psychology titles in the journal issue above, there may not be enough attention to negative characteristics—how they detract from the positive, and how such detraction may be prevented (22% of articles addressed this).

## The Fragmentation of Positive Psychology

Above, I suggested that most positive psychologists are defined by the fact that they study "positive topics," such as happiness, gratitude, forgiveness, savoring, awe, curiosity, flow, and the like. This brings us to another possible critique of the movement, that it is a grab-bag or smorgasbord of topical research, without sufficient integration between even different positive topics, much less between positive and negative topics. Of course, an important aspect of the movement has been that previously ignored phenomena are finally receiving the attention they deserve. But on the other hand, where should it end? One might form a separate line of inquiry regarding nearly any positive term in the dictionary (strength, virtue, inspiration, charity, chastity, hope, faith, etc.), leading to a near-infinite number of segmented research literatures. A common approach is to devise a scale to measure positive characteristic X, show that it is correlated with positive outcomes (such as well-being), and perhaps later in the program, that it moderates the effect of some other variable on positive outcomes. This type of research is important to do in the early phases of a new science, but I suggest that in a more mature science research should focus on integrating across lines of research and eliminating less useful constructs and measures from further consideration. For example, well-being has been correlated with a near-infinite variety of positive characteristics—but which characteristics are the most cardinal or central, accounting for the most variance? We do not yet know.

## Moving Forward: The Need for an Integrative Model of Human Functioning

As illustrated by the above critique of positive psychology's "topic-ism," it seems that the field of positive psychology (and perhaps psychology more generally) is in need of an integrative conceptual and empirical framework in which to a) conceptually unify diverse topics within positive psychology, and b) determine which positive psychology constructs are most essential for

bringing about the various positive outcomes of interest. I will briefly describe the candidate model and approach offered in *Optimal Human Being: An Integrated Multi-level Perspective* (Sheldon, 2004). The model attempts to provide a framework for achieving consilience (Wilson, 1998) between the different levels of science; this must in principle be possible, because they are all operating within a singular, self-consistent reality.

According to this model, reality is a multi-level nested hierarchy of processes occurring at different scales and levels of analysis, each running off at its own level but also reaching up or down at times to influence or be influenced by processes at other levels. Figure 28.1 presents the basic model, which merely formalizes (in my view) what most scientists already implicitly assume.

As can be seen, atomic processes are assumed to form the building blocks for everything else (although future high-energy particle research might extend this even further down). Atomic processes are entrained in higher-order aggregates (molecular compounds), which themselves interact at their own level by their own, partially independent laws. Thus, chemistry "emerges" from physics as a higher level of organization that is constrained by atomic processes but that also functions somewhat independently of atomic processes (thus, ultimately, both the sciences of physics and chemistry are necessary; chemistry is not reducible to physics).

This process of higher-order emergence continues up the chain, such that in the case of living systems, cells emerge as an aggregate of chemical processes that can reach back down to organize those chemical processes, organ tissues emerge as an aggregate of cellular processes that can reach back down to organize cellular processes, nervous tissue emerges as a special type of organ tissue that can reach down to organize organic processes, and so on. All of these processes are happening simultaneously, all up and down the hierarchy of reality. Perhaps-novel features of the model are that it straddles the brain-mind boundary by postulating that cognitive processes are an aggregate of nervous-tissue processes that can reach back down to organize nervous processes, it straddles the objectivity/subjectivity boundary by postulating that personality (and self in particular) is an aggregate of cognitive processes that can reach back down to organize cognitive and neuronal processes, and it straddles the person-social context boundary by postulating that social relations emerge from the

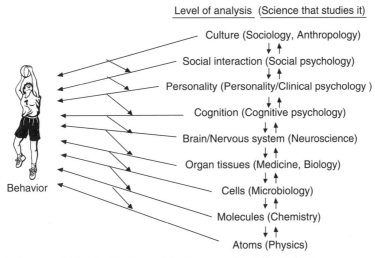

Figure 28.1 An Integrated Model of Reality and the Processes that Affect Behavior.

interactions of particular personalities, the social-relations level containing its own set of laws (i.e., reciprocity norms, turn-taking norms) that in turn can reach back down to affect the personalities embedded within social relations. Finally, the model recognizes that cultural patterns and histories emerge over time from the long-term interactions of personalities existing in close proximity within a bounded geographical region, and further, that cultural patterns can reach down to organize the interactions of those nested within the culture. The hope is that the model contains and acknowledges all of the major categories of influence relevant to understanding human behavior and experience. And indeed, we (the editors) applied this framework as we organized the chapters in this book; a glance at the Table of Contents shows that the chapters herein consider topics ranging from biological to emotions to social-cognitive to personality to relationships to clinical to organizational to societal levels of analysis.

Space does not permit complete explication of the model (see Sheldon, 2004, 2007, 2008), but I will briefly point out several important further features. First, different time-scales operate at each level, such that processes (and changes) occur more slowly at each subsequent level. This provides the primary basis for suggesting that a particular level can be emergent from the level below but also have top-down effects upon that level; namely, the inexorable operation of longer-term processes at a given level can change the operational conditions for the constituent shorter-term processes at the level below, such that two levels might influence each other in a bottom-top-bottom-top sinusoidal-type pattern.

Second, each level is assumed to be irreducible to the level below—each has its own set of laws that must be discovered (thus, molecular biology will never "go away" because it has been reduced to chemistry or physics, and personality psychology will never "go away" because it has been reduced to brain processes). This implies that each level will be important for explaining at least *some* kinds of behavior, phenomena, and outcomes (i.e., the organ-tissue level may take precedence to explain a trip to the refrigerator, whereas the personality level may take precedence to explain a trip to the psychiatrist). This principle of causal plurality is illustrated in Figure 28.1 by the simultaneous arrows leading from every level to "behavior."

Third, many behaviors or outcomes are likely best explained via cross-level interactions, as indicated by the diagonal arrows in Figure 28.1 showing possible moderation of each level's effects by the level above. For example, the personality style of neuroticism may moderate the effects of particular cognitions ("what if something goes wrong?") upon lower-level cortisol (stress) reactions, and the cultural style of collectivism may moderate the effects of particular interaction styles (assertive vs. obeisant) upon the lower-level outcomes of the particular personalities nested within the social interactions.

Fourth, the principle of "scientific reductionism" can be illustrated in the model as the attempt to explain the rules and processes of a particular level of analysis entirely in terms of rules and processes at the level below (i.e., all of chemistry understood as resulting from the properties of atoms alone, or all of personality understood as resulting from the properties of cognitions alone). The principle of "scientific holism" can be illustrated in the model as the attempt to explain the rules and processes of a particular level of analysis entirely in terms of rules and processes at the level above (i.e., cognitive processes as completely determining neural processes, or social role forces as completely determining personality). Both philosophies are likely to bear fruit in most cases, but neither can ever win because both bottom-up and top-down chains of causality flow through the system. It is particularly important to point out that reductionism, although it has paid huge dividends in science, can never win, precisely because of the phenomenon of emergence. Thus, again, neuroscientists will always need personality psychologists to tell them what higher-order processes or aggregates may be lurking in their data, and molecular biologists will always need neuroscientists to tell them what higher-order processes may be conditioning cellular-level processes.

Researchers trying to apply this model to do integrative research would need to be fluent in the concepts and methods of several adjacent levels of analysis, so they are best prepared to conceptualize the full range of processes that may influence the phenomenon of interest; they would also need to be fluent in the possible cross-level interactions that may occur between the levels of analysis close to the phenomenon. Thus, for example, a social dilemma researcher might want to know about the cognitive processes implicated in different ways of calculating expected utilities, the personality processes (values, traits) implicated in biasing or reacting to calculated utilities, the interpersonal processes by which personalities respond to one another when paired within the iterated dilemma, and the cultural-level processes by which different kinds of social interaction patterns are encouraged or discouraged within the person's cultural context. What this implies is a four-level model for data collection: multiple cognitions each nested inside of multiple types of personalities nested inside of multiple types of interaction patterns nested inside of multiple types of cultures. For the study above, one might need an N = 10,000 from 10 different cultural samples, each of which contains 10 different interaction patterns

(whether observed naturally or experimentally assigned), each of which contains 10 personality types or traits, each of which contains 10 different cognitive processes (the latter would be a within-subjects factor). Obviously, such data collections are daunting to even think about, much less actually conduct and analyze. However, I believe that this kind of study may provide the best route to truly comprehensive, integrated knowledge within psychology and across the disciplines related to psychology. Thus, it is worthwhile trying to plot the possible paths to consilience (Wilson, 1998)!

How might such a multi-level model be applied to a positive psychology topic? Sheldon and Tan (2007) provided one example, based on the reasoning of Sheldon (2004), who argued that needs, traits, motivations, and selves constitute four levels of personality *within* the "personality" level of analysis represented in Figure 28.1, and thus that each level of personality needed to be considered simultaneously for a complete understanding of happiness (see McAdams, 1996, and McAdams & Pals, 2006, for similar arguments). Sheldon and Tan considered all of these conceptual levels by measuring the psychological need-satisfaction, personality traits, motivational styles, self-processes, social relations, and subjective well-being (SWB) of 533 participants nested within two different cultures, Singapore and the U.S. They also considered the level of social support experienced by each participant, a social interactions-level construct (notably, there were only two statistical levels in their data, namely, participant nested in culture).

In their data analysis, Sheldon and Tan (2007) took a two-stage approach. First, they tried to identify the most efficacious predictor of SWB *within* each level of the postulated hierarchy. Specifically, they identified two or more candidate predictors of happiness from within each level (i.e., Deci and Ryan's (1985) autonomy, competence, and relatedness needs at the needs level; the Big Five traits at the trait level; goal self-concordance and current goal progress at the motive level; self-esteem and positive possible selves at the self level; perceived social support and autonomy support from important others at the social interactions level) and first compared them as predictors within each level. At each level, a particular construct "won" the initial test and was advanced to the multi-level competition. In the second and final analysis, these winners were entered into the same equation containing every level at once (including cultural membership as a level 2 factor). As a result, high competence need-satisfaction, low neuroticism, high goal progress, high self-esteem, high social support, and membership within the U.S. cultural sample all had independent main effects upon participant well-being, supporting the "irreducibility" postulate discussed above; all levels of information were relevant to understanding this particular phenomenon, namely, SWB. Notably, cultural membership did not moderate the effects of need-satisfaction upon well-being, supporting Deci and Ryan's (2000) claim that the basic psychological needs are universal and should have roughly equivalent effects in any cultural context examined (i.e., there should be no cross-level interactions, illustrated in Figure 28.1, involving psychological needs).

I suggest that this general type of procedure could be used to begin establishing a) which are the most important variables and topics in positive psychology for understanding particular positive outcomes (i.e., is forgiveness, gratitude, or kindness most important for predicting marital longevity?), and b) understanding how these factors' effects may be moderated by type of relationship or cultural context. The main recommendation is to measure as many different (but relevant) constructs simultaneously as possible, both within and between levels, so that the work of paring down to the essentials for each outcome of interest may begin. Obviously, many positive psychology "topics" can be studied both as outcomes (e.g., expressed gratitude results from receiving favors from others; McCullough, 2008) and as predictors in their own right (e.g., expressed gratitude predicts relationship functioning). Thus, researcher's goals will determine which phenomenon is moved to the left side of Figure 28.1 as the outcome of choice, versus which phenomena will be retained on the right side of Figure 28.1, as a possible predictor.

## Positive Psychology Should Focus on "Personality on Up"

Again, positive psychology is the study of positive topics. In terms of Figure 28.1, what levels of analysis should positive psychology address? Might positive psychologists focus on positive biochemical processes, positive cellular functioning, or positive brain function? Or are positive psychology topics best constrained to a higher level or levels? To address this question, I returned to the definition and goals of positive

psychology that were first stated at the Akumal conference in 1999, in the "positive psychology manifesto" (see appendix, this volume). The definition: "Positive Psychology is the scientific study of optimal human functioning. It aims to discover and promote the factors that allow individuals and communities to thrive." Positive psychology's main goal: "to understand optimal functioning at multiple levels, including experiential, personal, relational, institutional, societal, and global." As can be seen, this definition and goal seem to focus "from experience on up." That is, the statement suggests that we should start "above" the body-mind boundary, moving from positive experience on up toward the personal, relational, and cultural. Only from there up do concepts like joy, value, integrity, cooperation, and growth have meaning. Cognition and below all concern the "how" (nuts and bolts) and not the "who" (the person and his/her experiences, relationships, and cultures that we want to optimize).

Of course, one can focus lower, i.e., to find psychotropic drugs that help mood, or to find brain regions that light up when we're happy. Several chapters in this volume do precisely this. Nevertheless, the dependent variable in these cases (i.e., the focal phenomenon at the left of Figure 28.1) is still positive experience on up. Thus, positive psychology is not (directly) about understanding how psychotropic drugs work, or how the brain responds to stimulation, although it may be about how these factors influence positive experience, personality, relationships, or societies.

## Positive Psychology Is Not, in Principle, Overly Individualistic

Notice that the recommendation to focus on "personality on up" enjoins positive psychologists to focus not only on personality but also upon the higher-level contexts in which personality is nested—positive relationships, organizations, and cultures. These are emergent processes that go beyond individual experience. Indeed, there is some work in positive psychology that addresses these higher-order processes (i.e., relationship issues, covered by Gable and Grant in our book; organizational issues, covered by Luthans and Linley in this book; societal issues, covered by Biswas-Diener and Florida in this book), but probably not as much as there needs to be. So, one "moving forward" issue is more research at the higher levels. Of course, this type of research is more difficult and costly to do, and, after all, positive psychologists are psychologists, not sociologists or anthropologists; still, a complete understanding demands such research.

However, this brings us to a frequent criticism of positive psychology that I believe is unfounded: that positive psychology is too individually focused and ignores or de-emphasizes relationships and culture (see Christopher and Hickinbottom, 2008, Richardson and Guignon, 2008, and Becker and Maracek, 2008, all published in a special issue of *Theory & Psychology*; see also Rozin, this volume). Again, in principle, positive psychology is committed to understanding social and cultural diversity, at least because this variation provides grist for the mill of understanding which facets of these levels of analysis are most important for optimal functioning. However, this type of understanding of diversity may not be enough for cultural relativists, many of whom seem to insist that all cultural styles and national systems have equal dignity and are equally worthy of respect. While a respectful attitude should certainly be cultivated when interacting with anyone, it is possible that positive psychology could find that some types of culture, or some types of governmental and societal institutions, are more salubrious than others, just as some management, teaching, or parenting styles might be more salubrious than others. These are empirical questions, questions that can be answered after the researcher specifies the outcome of interest, acknowledges the value system that denotes this outcome as best (Sheldon & Kasser, 2000), and collects the requisite data.

Really, the assumption that seems to be lurking at the heart of the "overly individualistic" critique is this: that the individual and society are necessarily in conflict, and that positive psychology favors the individual in this conflict, when perhaps society ought to be favored. This view sees positive psychology as glorifying the individual and his/her experience at the expense of the relationships and societies in which he/she lives. However, I believe the assumption of inevitable conflict between the pleasure-seeking individual and the responsible restraining society is largely unfounded. For example, in self-determination theory data, autonomy and relatedness need-satisfaction are always very positively correlated, even impossible to disentangle sometimes. And this is what is expected: to feel a healthy sense of self, one must also be engaged in healthy relationships (Ryan & Deci, 2008). What critics

sometimes seem to have in mind is a selfish, self-centered form of individualism, in which individuals are narcissistic and self-gratifying, with no real desire to form meaningful connections with others. I urge that degraded forms of Western individualism (narcissism, consumerism, entitlement, materialism) not be mistaken for, or discourage the pursuit of, the positive potentials of the higher forms of Western individualism (simultaneous connectivity *and* creativity; personal growth *and* personal relationships; individual happiness *and* collective welfare).

## Summary

In this chapter I have considered four possible meanings of the "positive" in positive psychology: that positive psychology involves doing "positive science" (basic and applied research aimed at improving human life), that it involves assuming that human nature is inherently "good" as a theoretical tenet, that it involves merely appreciating formerly unappreciated but admirable aspects of human nature, and that it involves studying the positive rather than the negative extreme of particular topics (i.e., forgiveness, not revenge; elation, not depression). Examples exist of all four definitions, and I cautioned that "assuming that humans are basically good" may at times be problematic for positive psychologists. Next I considered the rampant "topic-ism" in positive psychology and criticized the tendency to invent a new scale to measure every positive term in the dictionary. We need to start paring down and organizing and integrating our constructs, rather than having a continuing proliferation of constructs. To this end, I discussed the multi-level model of human functioning proposed in Sheldon (2004) and suggested that this model provides a framework for achieving such organization and integration. Drawing from this model and also the original "positive psychology manifesto," I recommended that positive psychology should focus on "personality on up"; only there does the term "positive" make sense, because positive has meaning with reference to human experience. In contrast, positive physics, positive chemistry, or positive neuroscience make less sense as fields of study, except insofar as they benefit human experience and life. Finally, I attempted to defend positive psychology against the individualistic bias critique by pointing out that truly positive individuality is also connected individuality, and that only the less admirable forms of Western individualism (materialism, narcissism, egocentrism) work against positive functioning at the relational and cultural levels. These maladaptive forms of individualism are not what positive psychology is trying to enhance.

*References*

Becker, D., & Maracek, J. (2008). Positive psychology: History in the remaking? *Theory & Psychology, 18*, 591–604.

Christopher, J. C., & Hickinbottom, S. (2008). Positive psychology, ethnocentrism, and the disguised ideology of individualism. *Theory & Psychology, 18*, 563–589.

Deci, E. L., & Ryan, R. M. (1985). *Intrinsic motivation and self-determination in human behavior.* New York: Plenum.

Deci, E. L., & Ryan, R. M. (2000). The "what" and "why" of goal pursuits: Human needs and the self-determination of behavior. *Psychological Inquiry, 11*, 227–268.

Kendler, H. (1999). The role of value in the world of psychology. *American Psychologist, 54*, 828–835.

Keltner, D. (2009). Born To Be Good: The science of a meaningful life. New York, NY, USA: W.W. Norton Publishers.

King, L. A. (2008). *The science of psychology: An appreciative view.* Boston: McGraw-Hill.

McAdams, D. P. (1996). Personality, modernity, and the storied self: A contemporary framework for studying persons. *Psychological Inquiry, 7*, 295–321.

McAdams, D. P., & Pals, J. L. (2006). A new Big Five: Fundamental principles for an integrative science of personality. *American Psychologist, 61(3)*, 204–217.

McCullough, M. E. (2008). *Beyond revenge: The evolution of the forgiveness instinct.* San Francisco: Jossey-Bass.

Myers, D. G. (2000). The funds, friends, and faith of happy people. *American Psychologist, 55*, 56–67.

Richardson, F. C., & Guignon, C. B. (2008). Positive psychology and philosophy of social science. *Theory and Psychology, 18*, 605–627.

Ryan, R. M., & Deci, E. L. (2008). Self-determination theory and the role of basic psychological needs in personality and the organization of behavior. In Oliver P. John, Richard W. Robins, & Lawrence A. Pervin (Eds), *Handbook of personality psychology: Theory and research* (3rd ed.) (pp. 654–678). xv, 862 pp. New York, NY: Guilford Press.

Seligman, M. E. P. (2002). *Authentic happiness: Using the new positive psychology to realize your potential for lasting fulfillment.* New York, NY: Free Press.

Sheldon, K. M. (2004). *Optimal human being: An integrated multi-level perspective.* New Jersey: Erlbaum.

Sheldon, K. M. (2008). The interface of motivational science and personology: Self-concordance, quality motivation, multi-level personality integration. In J. Shah and W. Gardner (Eds.), *Handbook of motivational science* (pp. 465–476). New York: Guilford.

Sheldon, K. M. (2007). Considering the optimality of personality: Goals, self-concordance, and multi-level personality integration. In B. Little, K. Salmelo-Aro, J. Nurmi, & S. Phillips (Eds.), *Personal projects pursuit: Goals, action and human flourishing* (pp. 355–374). Mahwah, NJ: Lawrence Erlbaum & Associates.

Sheldon, K. M., & King, L.K. (2001). Why positive psychology is necessary. *American Psychologist, 56*, 216–217.

Sheldon, K. M., Schmuck, P., & Kasser, T. (2000). Is value-free science possible? (commentary). *American Psychologist, 10*, 1152–1153.

Sheldon, K. M., & Tan, H. (2007). The multiple determination of well-being: Independent effects of positive needs, traits, goals, selves, social supports, and cultural contexts. *Journal of Happiness Studies, 8*, 565–592.

Wilson, E. O. (1998). *Consilience: The unity of knowledge.* New York: Alfred A. Knopf.

# 29

# To Celebrate Positive Psychology and Extend Its Horizons

*Gordon Bermant, Charu Talwar, and Paul Rozin*

Most psychologists will agree that the aims of academic psychology are to understand the human mind and behavior and to better the human condition on the basis of improved understanding. But psychologists disagree about the best conceptual or methodological frameworks within which to pursue their aims. Such disagreements are part of the normal development of a discipline. Typically, a successful new movement emphasizes a distinct change from its predecessors while still accepting many of their accomplishments. In other words, movements import most of the baggage of their predecessors. We do not use baggage in a pejorative sense. We intend it to include accumulated knowledge and wisdom as well as errors in approach, content, or framework. Things that are too revolutionary are hard to adopt. Behaviorism was most importantly a change in methodology (objective, observable responses) in comparison to its predecessors, and cognitive science adopted much of the methodological sophistication of behaviorism as it turned the focus from behavior to mind.

Positive psychology appropriately accepts much of the baggage of its predecessors, including the

fundamental aims of understanding and practical improvement; it also emphasizes respect for methodological rigor. On the other hand, positive psychology represents a reaction to the prevailing worldview of clinical psychology. It widens the focus of its enterprise in order to understand and improve the quality of life of all individuals, not only the small proportion who are seriously compromised.

Positive psychology begins with the premise that psychology has focused too narrowly on the "medical model" of dysfunctional, abnormal behavior, and has thereby drained resources from efforts to understand how individuals in the general population can lead more effective, satisfying lives (Seligman and Csikszentmihalyi, 2000; Seligman, 2002). In addition to its critical stance, positive psychology has opened up new areas for study, such as positive emotions, and introduced promising interventions.

It is our view, however, that one of the less promising pieces of baggage that positive psychology has brought on board is the focus of research on Americans as proxies for all the world's citizens. Here we believe that positive psychology might wish to incorporate the innovations of another new branch of psychology, cultural psychology (Fiske, Kitayama, Markus & Nisbett, 1999; Kitayama & Cohen, 2007). If it can nurture a discipline with a more inclusive worldview, positive psychology will enhance its constructive incorporation of the methods and psychological principles that it has inherited without diluting the impact of its unique contributions.

We urge a broadening of positive psychology to include respectful, serious study of the norms of wholesome living in cultures quite different from America's current culture. Inevitably, this leads us to considerations of religion and spirituality, topics that much of positive psychology has eschewed in favor of a traditionally scientific, secular worldview. In other cultures, however, the distinctions among religion, philosophy, and psychology are not maintained as strictly as they are in the European-American context. In our view, exporting American norms and concepts of well-being to other parts of the world should be undertaken, if at all, only after indigenous norms and concepts of well-being have been thoroughly comprehended and demonstrated to be wanting in their own context. Though we believe such a demonstration is highly unlikely, we accept the possibility of the relevant questions being asked in sound empirical fashion. We might discover, after all, that the wiser course is to import rather than export psychological goods. Or at least we may advocate for "psychological free trade" in which the barriers to culturally diverse forms of wholesome living are eliminated.

Perhaps it is instructive to notice that, just as the seriously mentally ill occupy about six percent of the American population (Kessler et al., 2005), Americans occupy less than five percent of the world's population (U.S. Census Bureau, 2010). Perhaps the premise of positive psychology should therefore be extended. Just as psychology has unwisely focused too closely on the 6% who are seriously mentally ill in America, it has also unwisely focused on the less than 5% of the world who happen to live in the USA.

The main message of this paper is that positive psychology should not emulate most of the rest of psychology in its emphasis on Americans, let alone American undergraduates, but should focus on human nature and its growth potential around the world. Of course, a few in positive psychology have already explored outside of the Euro-American world. We are indebted to the insights of Ed Diener, and his collaborators, who have attended to the measurement of subjective well-being across cultures and explored different contributions to the quality of life represented in diverse cultural values (e.g., Diener & Suh, 2000; Suh & Oishi, 2002).

We have also been very fortunate to have Peterson & Seligman's excellent compendium to work with (Peterson & Seligman, 2004). The authors and their collaborators scoured the world's wisdom literature and psychological information to develop their "aspirational classification" of six virtues with 24 character strengths nested under them. Their work is a reference that will serve the field well for decades. The compendium includes several valuable descriptions of Asian moral and religious thought (see especially pp. 40–46). Inevitably, however, the weight and thrust of the work is decidedly western; it could hardly be otherwise, given its dedication to relying on empirical data whenever possible. Also, by explicitly targeting universally acknowledged virtues and character strengths, it has understandably not included some that may be limited to the South and East Asian contexts.

In what follows we make three basic points. First, we present three interrelated goals for wholesome living, based largely on South and East Asian religions and cultures, which stand in some contrast to general normative directions of positive psychology as we understand them. Second, from these same religions and cultures, we will discuss a path (process) for continued personal growth throughout the lifespan. Continued improvement of the mature adult mind is a more important theme in Asian than in Western views of optimal living. Finally, we will discuss the core idea within positive psychology of building on signature strengths, raising some questions about this pillar of the field, again from Asian perspectives.

## Three Additional and Potentially Central Virtues or Strengths

Three virtues or strengths that derive from Asian sources are selflessness, reduced or eliminated concern for personal benefit of action, and nonattachment to entities or outcomes (for a general orientation to the relevant Asian philosophy, see Kupperman, 1999). We believe that these terms label psychological realities that have real effects in the lives of people who live by them or aspire to them as opposed to those who do not. They are specified most clearly in Asian wisdom/religious doctrines and practices, but resonances of the ideas are also present in Western teachings.

Although these virtues/strengths are embedded in religious teaching and practice, they find secular expression in the cultures where they are valued. As mentioned earlier, in India especially, the separation of religious, philosophical, and psychological vocabularies is not nearly as rigid as it is in the U.S. and elsewhere in the West. (For convenience going forward, when we speak of "Asian" religions, we are referring to Hinduism and Buddhism. We occasionally contrast these with the Abrahamic tradition comprising Judaism, Christianity, and Islam).

## Selflessness

Apprehending the correct relationship between the perceived self and the world in actuality is at the core of Asian wisdom doctrine and practice. Famously, Hindu and Buddhist teachings diverge over the metaphysics of the self. It may be, however, irrespective of that doctrinal divide, that there are beneficial psychological consequences associated with the traditional practices developed to reveal the metaphysical truth to the practitioner. For the Hindu, glimpsing the truth relating *atman* and *brahman* may have consequences for daily life much like those awaiting the Buddhist practitioner who apprehends the dissolution of self into aggregates that are decidedly impermanent. The "small self" that is apprehended as one with the universal self is embraced in the world, as is the "small self" that is apprehended as disaggregated into components.

The mental practice leading to this sort of awareness is not available to many—few Asians or Westerners leave their homes for the ashram or monastery. In the West, meditation retreats and similar spiritual luxuries may offer emotional consequences and cognitive insights with wholesome consequences, and numerous clinicians have begun to bring meditation into their therapeutic milieux (e.g., Hayes, Follette & Linehan, 2004). Our emphasis here is somewhat different. In Buddhist traditions, wisdom and compassion are pre-eminent among attainments or realizations of practice, and apprehension of selflessness opens the mind to them as two sides of a single coin. Positive psychology has listed gratitude, humility, and kindness (including compassion) as character strengths arising respectively under the virtues of transcendence, temperance, and humanity. Wisdom is joined to knowledge as a virtue comprising five different character strengths (Peterson & Seligman, 2004). Without at all disputing the historical and analytic accuracy of the

virtue-character strength classification, we wonder whether it creates a guide to wholesome living as simple as a calm focus on the self as composed of aggregates or part of a larger entity. This sense of selflessness is certainly more than just kindness or altruism. It is widening one's focus of consciousness leading to heightened concern for others and their well-being, and a sense of being an integral part of a larger entity—or at least not one among many mutually impenetrable monads. These ideas about selflessness are related to, but not the same as, the prominent idea in cultural psychology of the independent Euro-American self and the interdependent East Asian self (Markus & Kitayama, 1991).

## Subordinating Personal Benefit

A second, related principle is subordination or abandonment of concern for the personal benefits of one's actions. The emphasis is on doing things because they are right, because they are one's sacred and socially appropriate duties, and because they lead to improvement of the relevant society. *Incidentally*, such behavior will also increase the moral worth of the doer (Menon, 2009). The point is to be engaged in the present and animated by improvement of the moral worth of the self and the welfare of the community, to not but be particularly concerned with the personal consequences of one's actions.

Action without concern or desire for benefit, *nishkama karma* in Sanskrit and Hindi, is a core goal of Hindu teaching with a doctrinal foundation in the *Bhagavad-Gita* (Rama, 1985). It is one component of a cluster of wholesome characteristics that together constitute *karma yoga*. This teaching has penetrated deeply into modern Indian life and, indeed, into Indian organizational psychology.

The use of *karma yoga* in current Indian organizational psychology is seen in the work of Venkat Krishnan and colleagues, who call *karma yoga* "the core of the Indian philosophy of work" (Madhu & Krishnan, 2005). This group's work is interesting for several reasons. Some of their language demonstrates the blending of religious, philosophical, and psychological domains that is non-existent in the West. Thus, Madhu & Krishnan (2005) rely on the *Bhagavad-Gita* and Tilak's (1915/2000) interpretation of it to define *karma yoga* as "a technique for intelligently performing actions." They continue that this definition "means the same thing" as "a technique for performing actions in a manner that the soul is not bound by the effects of the action." Mulla & Krishnan (2006) state further that *karma yoga* describes three essential characteristics: "performing action without attachment, doing one's duty, and being neutral to opposites." Being neutral to opposites, a phrase that arises in scripture, we interpret as meaning emotional equipoise across situations. The authors developed a survey for Indian executives that measured self-reported absence of desire for reward and sense of duty but not emotional equipoise. Perhaps the most interesting of their findings was the prevalence among Indian executives of a commitment to hard work accompanied by a relative lack of concern for personal achievement. The notion that one would work hard but be relatively unconcerned about the personal benefits thereof is not one found in American business circles or in American life more generally. Moreover, the issue of "personal benefits" is complex. For example, it is not obvious to us that it is entirely wholesome if the sense of duty is narrowly defined by employees as what is good for the company. Be that as it may, Mulla & Krishnan (2006) observe that the normative separation between hard work and concern for reward led earlier Western observers of Indian workplaces to dismiss the Indians as incapable of operating in a modern business environment. The current rise of Indian commercial successes puts the lie to that misconception even without bringing the characteristics of *karma yoga* into the discussion. Here seems to be a particularly rich area for organizational and positive psychologists to do good work in a nuanced, culturally aware fashion.

## Non-attachment

The English term non-attachment is both accurate and deceptively complicated as a pointer to a psychological reality that is revered in Asian religious traditions. It covers territory that in the original languages is covered by numerous terms that are connected but not identical in their referents. It is related *to nishkama karma* (see above) but not identical to it. While *nishkama karma* addresses the correct relationship between action and reward, non-attachment (e.g., *anasakti* in Sanskrit) carries a sense of letting events go past without negative reactions. The Vedanta tradition speaks of being in the world but not being of it. Traditional Buddhist teaching calls for the practitioner to break the wheel of causality between craving and grasping, and thus to

"let go" of attachment (for a trustworthy introduction to traditional Buddhism, see Rahula, 1959). Craving may be an indelible part of our biological heritage, but grasping/attaching can be controlled. Metaphors of entanglement, as webs of messy attachments, are used to describe the normal human condition of *samsara*. Dispassion or non-attachment is not to be confused with disengagement or apathy. There is no nihilism hiding in the shadows of non-attachment. Calm, focused action is the norm. To the extent that the non-attached actor and her act merge (the dancer becomes the dance), the connection to the idea of flow (Csíkszentmihályi, 1990) is obvious and appropriate.

To conclude this section, we repeat that there are lofty virtues/strengths in the Asian wisdom literature and practice that emphasize decentering of the self, relinquishing concern with personal benefit arising from effort, and acceptance of life without wasteful emotional response. These goals originated among individuals living lives of great renunciation. The practitioner's intent is to achieve liberation from endless cycles of birth and death. Given the seriousness of the stakes, the methods of achieving the goal could be very demanding; more than a single lifetime might be required to arrive at the appropriate states of mind (or no-mind). It is only recently in the history of these religions, for example the last 800 years in the case of Buddhism in Japan, that laypeople had more than supporting roles in the practices that had become normative among monks and nuns. The translation into English of important texts and practice manuals has a very short history, notwithstanding the apparent flood of popular literature now available. It would not be wise to jump quickly to the conclusion that the "wisdom of the East" should trump the values of the Western religious and Enlightenment traditions. But it is also unwise to ignore the depths of these great traditions in searching for the virtues, character strengths, and approaches to the sacred that they provide. Positive psychology should embrace this search and play a leading role in it.

## Adult Development Toward an Ideal Synthesis

In Western traditions, adulthood and maturity are conceived principally as the consequence of prior growth in understanding, resources, and wisdom. This process is seen as substantially complete in early adulthood. By contrast, in the

Hindu tradition especially, there are prescribed "paths" along which the mature man is encouraged to move away from material success and achievement toward renunciation and spiritual attainment. Something related to this type of development in adulthood appears in the view of mature adult development espoused by Erik Erikson (1950) in his eight stages of development. However, the idea of major transformations of the mature adult holds a special prominence in the cultures and religions of East and South Asia. In the Hindu and Buddhist traditions, the cultivation of wisdom, compassion, and equanimity remains an aspiration throughout life.

One feature of the adult path promoted in East and South Asian traditions has to do with emotion. Recent work by Tsai (2007) on ideal affect illustrates the importance of a path of emotional development. Tsai's findings suggest that American and East Asian cultures differ in their valuation of high-arousal positive affective states and low-arousal positive affective states. This would mean that while presence of positive emotions like excitement, thrill, and enthusiasm may give a sense of well-being to individuals of a particular culture in other cultures, the absence of these emotions and the presence of calmness, serenity, and equanimity will be experienced as well-being. In an ancient Indian taxonomy of emotions, the Natyasastra, peace is listed as one of nine basic emotions (Bharata, 1956; Hejmadi, Davidson & Rozin, 2000). Ideals of stimulation and excitement contrast with ideals of peace, contentment, and humility, all of which induce gratitude. In this respect, the popular Positive and Negative Affect Scale (PANAS) may be limited as a fundamental measure in psychology. As Suh, Diener, Oishi, and Triandis (1998) have noted, adjustment to norms may be relatively more important than positive emotions in determining well-being in East Asians. One of the authors of this paper experienced a similar difficulty in her work (Talwar, 2010) when she administered the PANAS to a sample of yogic practitioners in India. Although these practitioners appeared well adjusted and wholesome, their subjective well-being scores were not very high. This calls for designing better outcome measures that acknowledge calmness, peacefulness, and equanimity as indices of subjective well-being. Talwar has collected data in India suggesting that adherence to some of the principles of wholesomeness discussed above, as measured by an instrument developed by Bhushan and Jha (2005), predicts subjective well-being as measured by standard positive psychology measures (Diener, Emmons, Larsen & Griffins, 1985).

Perhaps in the West and Western psychology, development is treated as essentially terminating at about the point where the American focus of research is: the undergraduate years. Freudian and other views envision a level adult pathway from the college years onward in managing basic biological urges and meshing successfully with real-world and cultural demands. In the Hindu tradition in particular, the path from middle age into old age should be a major spiritual quest, in which material concerns are left behind in favor of a steadfast effort to connect the individual self/soul with the world in its entirety. Practical difficulties prevent many Hindu men from fulfilling this ideal, but the ideal remains as an aspiration and inducement to live one's earlier life stages so as to be able to realize the aspiration at the appropriate time. This is certainly a prosocial cultural tradition.

There is no doubt that the metaphor of path is central to religious teaching, both Asian and Western. Indeed, the path metaphor can become a problem in its own right. Some modern Buddhist commentators have begun to spell out the meaning and the problems associated with the metaphor (e.g., Batchelor, 2004; Corless, 1997; Magid, 2008; Trungpa, 1987). As metaphor and lived reality, the spiritual developmental path deserves serious respect and consideration by the positive psychology community. In some significant ways, the positive psychology movement, with its research and interventions, has begun to address the idea of development in mature adults, a "path" to a more open mind, a mind more appreciative of the blessings it has had the fortune to encounter.

## Is It a Good Idea to Build on Signature Strengths?

The excellent taxonomy of human virtues assembled in positive psychology (Peterson & Seligman, 2004) is the basis for the idea of determining how an individual measures up on these virtues (the VIA scale). This scale and procedure are important contributions to self-knowledge. What a person is advised to do as a result of his or her profile of virtues and strengths is debatable on cultural grounds.

Thus, a core idea in the practice of positive psychology is to use the VIA to identify one's "signature strengths" and to organize one's life around building on these strengths. As Seligman (2002) says, "When you read about these strengths, you will also find some that are deeply characteristic of you, whereas others are not. I call the former your *signature strengths,* and one of my purposes is to distinguish these from strengths that are less a part of you. I do not believe that you should devote overly much effort to correcting your weaknesses. Rather, I believe that the highest success in living and the deepest emotional satisfaction comes from building and using your signature strengths" (p. 13). And further, "… I believe in building the good life around polishing and developing your strengths, and then using them to buffer against your weaknesses and the trials that weakness brings" (p. 160).

We consider this to be a *reasonable* life plan, particularly in a Western context, but we are much less certain that it is an *optimal* life plan, even in a Western context.

Seligman (2002) and others in positive psychology appropriately distinguish between talents, on the one hand, and virtues with associated character strengths, on the other hand. Among the virtues, furthermore, some, like the wisdom cluster, have at most a weak moral component, whereas others, like the humanity and love cluster, occupy a central moral position. We need to be careful to distinguish positive personal characteristics with moral content from those without moral content.

We can quickly introduce our concern about the advice to build on one's strengths by observing that it opposes the aphorism that a chain is only as strong as its weakest link. What wisdom, if any, lies in that aphorism? We address this question below. Further, just as the aphorism may apply in some life domains and not others, so the norm of accentuating one's signature strengths at the expense of ameliorating one's weaknesses may also have limited application.

## Ability: The Superstar Ideal

Let us begin with the talent or ability domain, because of the ubiquity of what we will call the superstar ideal. In much of the world influenced by Western mass media and the values they project, income and fame are understood to derive from being exceptionally good at something.

Moreover, income and fame are taken to equal success. Michael Jordan is rich and famous because he was a phenomenal basketball player; Meryl Streep is a phenomenal actress. Michael and Meryl may or may not be skilled at caring for children, creating a PowerPoint presentation, or fixing a leaky faucet, but it doesn't matter. The rewards and esteem they receive don't depend on their being capable "all-round." There is no Oscar category or Hall of Fame niche for the jack-of-all-trades who is master of none. It is even rare for an individual to achieve "world-class" status in two professions or other areas of accomplishment. Michael Jordan's failure at baseball is illustrative.

Individuals who build on a single talent strength have become culture heroes by making sacrifices to elevate their performances to remarkable heights. They typically have built on an initial endowment that is beyond ordinary. The income that results from their great strength allows them to manage the rest of their lives to compensate for shortcomings. They can hire people with other strengths as needed. In the domain of ability, what you are best at is what matters most, especially in the West.

That we honor our superstars comes as no news. The question is whether the model that applies to superstars should be the cultural norm. To put the point briefly, it seems to us that we are already at risk of overemphasizing the development of single skills—at the expense of balance. We cannot expand on the point here, but we note that the critique we propose is aligned with concerns that we are becoming, or have become, a "winner-take-all" society (Frank & Cook, 1996).

Does an emphasis on equanimity and balance lead to more wholesome outcomes? Psychologists have discussed the distinction between harmony and agency for at least two decades (Markus & Kitayama, 1991; Triandis, 1995). There is more recent evidence that in comparison to Euro-Americans, East Asians are more inclined to emphasize self-improvement in abilities or talent arenas where they see themselves as unaccomplished (Heine et al., 2001; Oishi & Diener, 2002). When given the option of continuing a task or switching to another, the likelihood that East Asians will continue with the original task is inversely related to how well they have done on this task. Of course, being versatile was really important in our evolutionary history, and cultures have generally evolved to support more specialization. Cultural institutions have moved in this direction; witness for example the decline of repertory theaters and the scarcity of doctors practicing general medicine.

We acknowledge that our caveat about building on one's strong abilities may represent a nostalgic nod to human history. It seems that increasing population density favors increased personal specialization. In urban environments, which comprise increasing proportions of the world's population, the advantages of specialization may well trump the advantages of versatility. Individuals may need to forgo repairing weak links in their chains of coordinate abilities.

But as we move from talents to virtues, and especially those virtues that fall within the moral domain ("character"), a good case can be made that the chain *is only* as strong as its weakest link. This may be in part because the virtues that make up character are more dependent on one another than the other virtues, or talents. In the ability domain, the focus is on successes, on peak performance. We are not interested in the average 100-meter time of the world champion, but rather his or her world-record performance. We are not interested in the average quality of Mozart's 41 symphonies, but in the great late ones. But as it normally plays out, in the domain of morality and judgments of character, moral failings play a potent role. This is a prime domain of negativity dominance (Rozin & Royzman, 2001). One marital infidelity, one incident of cheating, one crime of any sort can spoil our assessment of the character of an otherwise virtuous person. This is, at least in part, because immoral actions are thought to be relatively rare, and also because one takes them to be diagnostic of a strong tendency to commit other moral errors. Most legal systems are disinclined to discount offenses if the offender also has a record of morally admirable acts.

A few psychologists, in the context of trait inferences, have noted that outstanding performances are more informative or diagnostic in the domain of capacities, whereas failures are more informative in the domain of morality (Reeder, 1993; Skowronski, 2002). Thus, in terms of signature strengths, a person who is "strong" on the virtue of honesty but failing in kindness might be considered to be less worthy than someone with a modest level of both virtues. This, of course, is an empirical question, and one that will no doubt vary by culture. Balance at the expense of focal excellence in abilities may be unwise, but balance in character may be critically important.

Traditional Buddhism is unambiguous in emphasizing the importance of balance in the virtues. For example, the Theravada Abhidhamma warns that emphasizing some faculties at the expense of keeping balance among them is negative and potentially dangerous. This is true even though each of the faculties is a positive trait. The eight faculties in this classification are faith, energy, mindfulness, concentration, wisdom, mind, joy, and vitality. An authoritative commentator on the ancient text says, "if a single faculty is developed exclusively while the others… are neglected or deliberately suppressed, that faculty may come to exercise unbridled control over the entire personality…. As in the macrocosm of human society so in the microcosm of the human mind, those in charge are often tempted to abuse their power… the final result is bad: balance is disturbed and an obstacle sets in to continuous and harmonious development" (Nyanaponika, 1965, p. 63). The critical issue is whether balance, in some or all domains of life, should be considered a major virtue at a level equivalent, for example, to courage or temperance. It is not clear to us that the canonical list of virtues within positive psychology gives unambiguous guidance about the importance of seeking balance in one's moral characteristics. For example, courage might promote building on strength, while temperance (with component strengths of self-control, prudence/discretion/caution and humility/modesty) pushes toward balance.

## Conclusion

We celebrate the reorientation that positive psychology has produced in psychology and applaud many of the specific advances made by this new movement. Furthermore, we note that many of the interventions developed by positive psychologists are oriented to adult development and increasing the meaningfulness of life in the journey from early adulthood to full maturity. We urge positive psychologists to pay more attention to the non-Euro-American world. This larger world comprises the great majority of humanity and offers different perspectives on the good life and how to live it.

*Acknowledgment*   We are grateful to D. C. Rao for his guidance on matters of Hindu doctrine.

*References*

Batchelor, S. (2004). *Living with the devil*. New York: Riverhead.

Bharata (1956). *Natyasastra by Bharatamuni* (M. R. Kavi, Ed.; rev. ed.). Baroda, India: Gaekwad Oriental Series.

Bhushan, L. I., & Jha, M. K. (2005). Developing test of Asakti and Anasakti. *Indian Journal of Psychometrics and Education, 36*, 3–9.

Corless, R. (1997). The pathless path for North America. *The Pure Land, new series*, No. 13–14, 6–18.

Csikszentmihalyi, M. (1990). *Flow: The psychology of optimal experience*. New York: Harper and Row.

Diener, E., Emmons, R. A., Larsen, R.J., & Griffins (1985). The satisfaction with life scale. *Journal of Personality Assessment, 49*, 71–75.

Diener, E., & Suh, E. M. (Eds). (2000). *Culture and subjective well-being*. Cambridge, MA: MIT Press.

Erikson, E. (1950). *Childhood and society*. New York: Norton.

Fiske, A. P., Kitayama, S., Markus, H., & Nisbett, R. E. (1999). The cultural matrix of social psychology. In D. Gilbert, S. Fiske, & G. Lindzey (Eds.), *Handbook of social psychology* (4th ed.). New York: McGraw-Hill.

Frank, R. H., & Cook, P. J. (1996). *The winner-take-all society*. New York: Penguin Books.

Hayes, S. C., Follette, V. M., & Linehan, M. M. (2004). *Mindfulness and acceptance*. New York: Guilford.

Heine, S. J., Kitayama, S., Lehman, D. R., Takata, T., Ide, E., Leung, C., & Matsumoto, H. (2001). Divergent consequences of success and failure in Japan and North America: An investigation of self-improving motivations and malleable selves. *Journal of Personality and Social Psychology, 81*, 599–615.

Hejmadi, A., Davidson, R., & Rozin, P. (2000). Exploring Hindu Indian emotion expressions: Evidence for accurate recognition by Americans and Indians. *Psychological Science, 11*, 183–187.

Kessler, R. C., Chiu W. T., Demler, O., & Walters, E. E. (2005). Prevalence, severity, and comorbidity of twelve-month DSM-IV disorders in the National Comorbidity Survey Replication (NCS-R). *Archives of General Psychiatry, 62*, 617–627.

Kitayama, S., & Cohen, D. (Eds.). *Handbook of cultural psychology*. New York: Guilford.

Kupperman, J. J. (1999). *Learning from Asian philosophy*. New York: Oxford University Press.

Madhu, B., & Krishnan, V. R. (2005). Impact of transformational leadership and karma-yoga on organizational citizenship behavior. *Prestige Journal of Management and Research, 9*, 1–20.

Magid, B. (2008). *Ending the pursuit of happiness*. Boston: Wisdom.

Markus, H., & Kitayama, S. (1991). Culture and the self: Implications for cognition, emotion, and motivation. *Psychological Review, 98*, 224–253.

Menon, U. (2009). Dharma and re-envisioning the Hindu moral code. In G. Misra (Ed.), *Psychology and Psychoanalysis*. New Delhi, India: Delhi University (in press).

Mulla, Z. R., & Krishnan, V. R. (2006). Karma yoga: A conceptualization and validation of the Indian philosophy of work. *Journal of Indian Psychology, 24*, 26–43.

Nyanaponika, V. T. (1965). *Abhidhamma studies: Buddhist explorations of consciousness and time*. Boston: Wisdom Publications.

Oishi, S., & Diener, E. (2002). Culture and well-being: The cycle of action, evaluation, and decision. *Personality and Social Psychology Bulletin, 29*, 939–949.

Peterson, C., & Seligman, M. E. P. (2004). *Character strengths and virtues*. A handbook and classification. Oxford, UK: Oxford University Press.

Rahula, W. (1959). *What the Buddha taught*. New York: Grove.

Rama, S. (1985). *The perennial psychology of the Bhagavad-Gita*. Honesdale, PA: Himlayan Institute Press.

Reeder, G. D. (1993). Trait-behavior relations and dispositional inference. *Personality & Social Psychology Bulletin, 19*, 586–593.

Rozin, P., & Royzman, E. (2001). Negativity bias, negativity dominance, and contagion. *Personality and Social Psychology Review, 5*, 296–320.

Seligman, M. E. P. (2002). *Authentic happiness*. New York: Basic Books.

Seligman, M. E. P., & Csikszentmihalyi, M. (2000). Positive psychology: An introduction. *American Psychologist, 55*, 5–14.

Skowronski, J. J. (2002). Honesty and intelligence judgments of individuals and groups: The effects of entity-related behavior diagnosticity and implicit theories. *Social Cognition, 20*, 136–169.

Suh, E., Diener, E., Oishi, S., & Triandis, H. C. (1998). The shifting basis of life satisfaction judgments across cultures: Emotions versus norms. *Journal of Personality and Social Psychology, 74*, 482–493.

Suh, E., & Oishi, S. (2002). Subjective well-being across cultures. In W. J. Lonner, D. L. Dinnel, S. A. Hayes, & D. N. Sattler (Eds.), *Online Readings in Psychology and Culture* (Unit 7, Chapter 1), (http://www.wwu.edu/~culture), Center for

Cross-Cultural Research, Western Washington University, Bellingham, Washington USA.

Talwar, C. & Banth, C. (2010). Anasakti, the Indian ideal, and its relationship with well-being and orientations to happiness *Journal of Religion & Health*, in press.

Tilak, B. G. (2000). *Srimad Bhagavadgita-Rahasya* (S. lukhantar, Trans.). Poona: Kesari Press. (Originally published 1915)

Triandis, H. C. (1995). *Individualism and collectivism.* Boulder, CO: Westview Press.

Trungpa, C. (1987). *Cutting through spiritual materialism.* Boston & London: Shambala.

Tsai, J. L. (2007). Ideal affect: Cultural causes and behavioral consequences. *Perspectives on Psychological Science, 2*, 242–259.

U.S. Census Bureau (2010). U.S. & World Population Clock.    www.census.gov/main/www/popclock. html - (Accessed January 8, 2010)

# 30

# Are We There Yet? What Happened on the Way to the Demise of Positive Psychology

*Laura A. King*

"My hope is that positive psychology is a
movement that will eventually disappear
because it becomes part of the very fabric of
psychology ... it will fade precisely because it
has been so successful" (Diener, 2003, p. 120).
"...fading need not be taken as a sign of failure.
If positive psychology is a meaningful step
toward a more integrated field of psychology,
one can imagine a time when it will have
served its purpose ..." (King, 2003, p. 131).
"Although the current spate of interest in
positive psychology may fade ... we see the
more important possibility being that
researchers will routinely investigate their world
from a positive along with a negative frame of
reference" (Rand & Snyder, 2003, p. 149).
"... the contribution of positive psychology has
been ... to make the self-conscious argument
that the good life deserves its own field of
inquiry within psychology at least until the day
when all psychology embraces the study of
what is good with the study of what is bad"
(Peterson & Park, 2003, p. 144).

A decade ago in the pages of *American
Psychologist*, Martin Seligman and Mihaly

Csikszentmihalyi (2000), two brilliant scientists
and prominent scholars, announced the arrival of
a new movement in the science of psychology.
Positive psychology was to meant "to catalyze a
change in the focus of psychology from preoccupation only with repairing the worst things in
life to also building positive qualities" (Seligman
& Csikszentmihalyi, 2000, p. 5). The breathtak-
ingly rapid spread of positive psychology surprised even its founders (Csikszentmihalyi,
2003). In a very short time, conferences and
research networks were formed. Scholarly prizes
were announced. Books gave way to handbooks,
and courses and textbooks to full-fledged training
programs, and applied professionals (life coaches
and consultants). Articles and special issues, in
turn, gave way to the *Journal of Positive Psychology*, founded in 2006 by Robert Emmons. In
short order, in many ways, the positive psychology movement gave way to positive psychology,
the scholarly field.

Perhaps a strong indicator of the perceived
power of this movement was that an early critique of positive psychology was produced by no
less a scholar than Richard Lazarus. Among other
things, Lazarus (2003a, b) decried the movement's

bestowal of equal status to positive and negative affective states, the prematurity of its prominence in psychology, and what he perceived to be its shaky empirical foundation. Interestingly, as illustrated in the opening quotes of this chapter, in replies to Lazarus' critique, a few positive psychologists (myself included) asserted that his concern was not entirely justified, in part because the movement would likely go away once its mission was fulfilled. In this chapter, I will review some of the things that happened on the way to this imagined eventual demise of the positive psychology movement. I focus first on what might well be the best predictor of the field of positive psychology's future: its recent past. I address the somewhat surprising relevance of positive psychology in a context that differs greatly from the one that existed at its inception. Second, I examine what happened to happiness and consider the future of happiness and unhappiness in positive psychology. Third, I review the ways that positive psychology has recreated the history of business-as-usual (Rand & Peterson, 2003; Seligman & Pawelski, 2003) psychology, and engage in a bit of wishful thinking in this regard. To conclude, I offer some closing thoughts on the future of the field of positive psychology and its research agenda.

## The Proven Durability of Positive Psychology

It is perhaps no accident that the positive psychology movement first gained a foothold at the turn of a new century, in a particular historical moment: during (what turned out to be the close of) a period of relative peace and economic flourishing. Drawing bold comparisons to Athens circa 5 BCE and Victorian England, Seligman and Csikszentmihalyi (2000) suggested that the U.S. was at a moment of historic opportunity. They described the nation as "wealthy, at peace, and stable" (p. 13), suggesting that "the time is finally right" for a sea change in the values of psychological science. For researchers dedicated to topics such as well-being, optimism, hope, gratitude, and forgiveness (or individuals with healthy 401(k)s), these were heady days indeed.

In some ways positive psychology is like a child born into a family of enormous wealth in the months before the Great Depression. Just as quickly as positive psychology took off, the rest of those rosy times began a precipitous decline. The intervening years have seen the terrorist attacks of September, 11, 2001, the long and

profoundly costly wars in Iraq and Afghanistan, the horror of human suffering in numerous natural disasters, the emergence of any number of saber-rattling dictators with looming nuclear weapon technology, news stories of torture, corruption, greed, and incompetence, and, most recently, nearly unprecedented worldwide economic collapse. In such a context, it is difficult to imagine that anyone, even one as bold as Martin Seligman, would suggest that psychology ought to focus more on the bright side of life. Nevertheless, and importantly, positive psychology has flourished in these difficult times.

This durability is due, in no small part, to the creativity and dedication of scholars in positive psychology whose research has demonstrated the value of human strengths and positive capacities in good times and bad. As an example, after the terrorist attacks of 9/11, Fredrickson, Tugade, Waugh, and Larkin, (2003) demonstrated that positive emotional experiences played a key role in the coping of resilient individuals. Likewise, Peterson and Seligman (2003) reported on changes in character strengths in individuals completing surveys before and after the attacks. Indeed, the vast majority of progress in positive psychology has occurred not in the warm glow of the U.S. in 1999 or 2000, but in the rather more negative context since.

In 2000, because things were generally going so well, it seemed acceptable to talk about the needs of psychologically healthy people and the ways that psychological science might enrich their already pretty good lives. Ironically, for all of Lazarus' concern about overstepping, Seligman and Csikszentmihalyi (2000) may have *underestimated* the enormous relevance of human strengths and positive capacities during the most trying of times. A decade later, one can hardly imagine that there was a time when the value placed on strengths such as hope, optimism, integrity, fairness, and hard work was ever higher. During these myriad crises, when the question of how we could possibly go on has loomed large, positive psychologists have offered empirical answers.

Surely another reason for the durability of positive psychology over the last decade has been the fact that many of the research programs that were included under the umbrella of the movement were ongoing for many years prior to the movement itself being given a name (e.g, Rand & Snyder, 2003). Just as these topics intrigued psychologists (and humanity) long before positive psychology existed, they will likely continue to do so in the future, within positive psychology and otherwise. The true value of human strengths is demonstrated in their relevance to times of enormous struggle and difficulty.

It seems hardly controversial to predict that in the future positive psychologists will continue to explore the functions of human strengths and resources in a variety of positive and negative events and contexts. Among the various psychological resources embraced by positive psychology, one of these, happiness, has (arguably) received the most ambivalent treatment. Indeed, the place of positive feelings in positive psychology represents a crucial issue for the future of the movement and the field.

## What Happened to Happiness?

Despite its widespread and enduring popular appeal, happiness has long been a sore spot for positive psychology. A key talking point in the early days of the movement was that positive psychology is not and would not devolve into "happiology" (e.g., Seligman, 2002). Yet, perhaps smelling blood in the water on this particular point, Lazarus (2003a) claimed that, indeed, the positive psychology movement was little more than Hoagy Carmichael and Norman Vincent Peale *redux*: The power of positive thinking on empirical steroids.

The response of positive psychologists to this particular line of attack was and has been surprisingly conciliatory—implicitly and explicitly agreeing with the central contention that if positive psychology were centrally the science of happiness, this would, indeed, constitute a fatal flaw. For example, some scholars argued that happiness (or positive emotion) is but a very small part of the agenda of positive psychology (e.g., Rand & Snyder, 2003). Others have argued against the value of happiness per se, declaring war on the apparently shallow lives of cheerful people everywhere (Seligman, 2002). Somehow a movement meant to highlight the good things in life developed a severe case of cherophobia— turning away from the central human motivation for pleasure. Oddly enough, in ways big and small, to use the popular phrase, positive psychology threw happiness "under the bus." Over the last few years in the pursuit of not being happiologists, positive psychologists have adopted different names for happiness including thriving, flourishing, zest—essentially anything but happiness.

In their efforts to avoid the dreaded label of happiology, some positive psychologists sought refuge in something *better* than happiness and found their answer in a division that had been brewing in the field of well-being for some years. In the years prior to the founding of positive psychology, scholars in the area of well-being had bifurcated the topic into two different approaches and constructs: hedonic well-being (positive affect, negative affect, and life satisfaction; Kahneman, Diener, Schwarz, 1999) and eudaimonic well-being (everything else, but especially the actualization of potential and the experience of meaning and purpose in life; Ryan & Deci, 2001; Seligman, 2002). Borrowing Aristotle's (350 BCE/1998 CE) term for the happiness that comes from a life of virtue (and to the dismay of some objectivist philosophers, Woolfolk & Wasserman, 2005), many psychologists embraced the notion that the outcome of interest for positive psychologists and others ought not to be simply happiness but a particular kind of happiness, that which emerges as a by-product of good acts, or the fulfillment of organismic needs (Ryan & Deci, 2001). Hedonic well-being has been portrayed as relatively shallow, fleeting, and subjective. Eudaimonic well-being, in contrast, represents something deeper, less morally ambiguous, and, perhaps, more objective (Seligman, 2002).

My colleagues and I (Biswas-Diener, Kashdan, & King, 2009; Kashdan, Biswas-Diener, & King, 2008; King, 2008) have proposed that this war on plain old happiness (ironically from within positive psychology itself) is misguided. Here, I briefly summarize a few of the problems with the rapid emergence of the construct of eudaimonic well-being (as a happiness that is qualitatively distinct from hedonic well-being). First, eudaimonic well-being lacks a specific and widely accepted definition. Second, hedonic and eudaimonic well-being overlap considerably, conceptually but especially empirically. Most importantly, to date, there is no evidence for a *qualitative* difference between the happiness that emerges from so-called eudaimonic activities and the happiness that emerges otherwise. Rather, these activities differ *quantitatively* in terms of their implications for the person's subjective happiness. Essentially, people are happier when engaged in activities that have been labeled eudaimonic (see King, 2008 for a review). What stronger argument could there be for the central role of happiness in human strengths than evidence that this variable (plain old happiness) tracks the engagement of our better natures (King, 2008)? Certainly, naïve scientists recognize the central relevance of happiness to the good life (King & Napa, 1998). Indeed, even a life of difficult and taxing work is perceived as more desirable if the worker nevertheless enjoys him- or herself (Scollon & King, 2004). Further, no evidence has emerged supporting the dangers of hedonic well-being or even a hedonistic approach to happiness (e.g., Peterson, Park, & Seligman, 2005).

At least two aspects of this debate are worth noting in terms of their relevance for the future of positive psychology. First, importantly, much of this debate has occurred within the pages of the *Journal of Positive Psychology*, surely bearing witness to the openness of the movement for divergent views, an enormously healthy sign. Second, in some ways, the rejection of happiness in favor of eudaimonia speaks to a tension in positive psychology between the ordinary and extraordinary, a theme that I will return to at the close of this chapter. To foreshadow, in my view, positive psychology, the field, will be most successful (most enduring and most relevant) if, even as it focuses in some ways on human greatness or the "Good Life," it remains ever-tethered to everyday human existence, and the many good lives that are being lived around us every day.

Certainly a large body of research continues to attest to the salubrious effects of good old happiness. Positive affective states precede many adaptive behaviors and have been shown to predict success (Lyubomirsky, King, & Diener, 2005). Positive affective experiences have been strongly linked to more highfalutin concepts. Enjoyment is a central feature of intrinsic motivation and flow (Csikszentmihalyi, 1990). The strong relationship between positive affect and altruism is all but inescapable (Batson & Powell, 2003). Research has shown that inducing positive mood can increase the sense that life is meaningful (Hicks & King, 2008; King, Hicks, Krull, & Del Gaiso, 2006). A happy day is more often than not a meaningful day (King et al., 2006).

Further, the experience of positive emotions appears to be the glue that connects the strength of resilience to other positive outcomes (Fredrickson, Tugade, Waugh, & Larkin, 2003). Resilient people thrive not in spite of their pleasant feelings but because of them. Significantly, resilient individuals centrally differ from their less resilient counterparts not so much in the level of negative affect they experience, but in their abilities to capitalize on pleasurable experiences when they occur, even in the midst of difficulty. Increasingly, garden-variety positive emotions have been shown to play a crucial role in resilience and well-being (Cohn, Fredrickson, Brown, Mikels, & Conway, 2009; Fredrickson, Cohn, Coffey, Pek, & Finkel, 2008).

At this point, one might well wonder what would be so awful about being happiologists? Rather than shirk the label, positive psychology would likely achieve major and wide impact by unabashedly pursuing the much-maligned research agenda of happiology. If recent political rhetoric has provided any lesson for the larger world, it is that just because an idea can be readily caricatured does not mean it is wrong.

The place of life coaches in positive psychology presents an interesting case in terms of the overarching ambivalence of positive psychology toward happiness. It makes sense that individuals interested in applying positive psychology to helping people improve their lives would seek out evidence-based foundations for practice in the basic findings of positive scholarship. Yet, one wonders if a coach would have much success building a client base with promises devoid of happiness. Perhaps coaches everywhere can take heart that even if the goal is *eudaimonia*, they can assure their clients that they can look forward to feeling happy, in any case.

## The Place of Unhappiness in the Future of Positive Psychology

Clearly, I strongly advocate more research on happiness and positive emotional states as a central focus of positive psychology, in part because I believe that such research brings us closer to the good life as it is lived in the real world. However, beyond happiness, I would suggest that positive psychology ought to study outcomes other than happiness, but in particular ways. Just as positive psychology has courageously confronted the tendency to pathologize everyday human behavior, I would like to see a research agenda built around a positive psychology of unhappiness, de-pathologizing garden-variety negative emotional states. Where is the positive psychology righteous anger? Or legitimate worry? Or the healthy disappointment and sadness that emerge from the valiant, if fruitless, pursuit of important goals? Exploring the role of regret, for example, in healthy maturity and development, or the place of suffering in good lives, are compelling goals for budding positive psychologists.

In addition, it would be vital to understand those moments when human beings do the right thing when it involves the sacrifice of happiness. It is no small irony that the construct of eudaimonic well-being is often legitimized and validated because it relates to hedonic well-being. Far more interesting would be investigations of activities that are virtuous, principled, and difficult that might relate to important outcomes that have nothing to do with happiness or that are, in fact, negatively related to happiness. Where do legitimate losses fit into the positive psychology of topics such as disability, trauma, or illness? Research on resilience illuminates the ways that very good lives are constructed in adversity. What are the hedonic costs of a good life lived by an individual who sacrifices unselfishly for the greater good?

Since its inception, positive psychology has shared with business-as-usual psychology an appropriately strong emphasis on solid empirical research. The positive psychology movement has provided resources, outlets, and forums for scholars interested in topics that might not garner much interest in business-as-usual psychology, not because of lack of rigor but because of the very topics of interest. In some ways, however, positive psychology can be seen to have constructed a parallel psychology, one that shares some of the regrettable (and one hopes not inevitable) features of business-as-usual psychology.

## Business-as-Usual (Positive) Psychology

In their introduction to positive psychology, Seligman and Csikszentmihalyi (2000) traced the emergence of psychology as primarily occupied with psychological disorder. They noted that with the founding of the National Institute of Mental Health, psychologists recognized that their work could be funded if it addressed psychological disorders. Seligman and Csikszentmihalyi (2000) powerfully asserted that psychologists "came to see themselves as part of a mere subfield of the health professions, and psychology became victimology" (p. 6). One consequence of this value shift was the proliferation of practitioners over academic scientists in the American Psychological Association. While the APA certainly remains primarily an organization for practitioners over scientists, positive psychology has adopted its own practitioner guild, life coaches (Seligman, 2007). While business-as-usual psychology has

clinical practitioners, business-as-usual positive psychology has coaches and consultants.

A second, more troubling consequence of the founding of NIMH was the subjugation of broad scholarly interests to the policies and values of federal funding agencies. Certainly this latter issue is, if anything, even more pressing today than it was in 2000, with the well-known changes in funding priorities at NIMH toward severe psychological disorders. As a scholar whose federal funding was attacked on the floor of the U.S. House of Representatives, I speak from experience when I say that this situation is of more than passing concern. How has positive psychology lifted this difficult yoke? By creating another one that surely fits better but is a yoke nevertheless. For, while business-as-usual psychology has federal agencies, business-as-usual positive psychology has benefactors (e.g., the Mayerson and Templeton Foundations).

Although these organizations may have research agendas that are more amenable to positive psychology, they nevertheless do have agendas. Without question, such foundations have every right to support research that serves their missions. Perhaps it was and will be ever thus: the curious scientist straining to fit the square peg of science into the round hole of the interests of whoever is holding the purse strings. And perhaps, from the long view, having funding for research on the breadth of human experience is best regardless of its sources.

It may be too much to ask that positive psychology manage to find its way into the auspices of federal funding because, over time, it will have proven its usefulness in terms of prevention and its wider relevance to human lives. Of course, all of psychology (and the behavioral sciences more generally) would benefit if the value of our basic research were understood and appreciated. Until such time, cultivating such benefactor relationships will likely continue to be a central goal of positive psychology. However, one hopes that individuals are ever mindful of the nature of such relationships, the overarching importance of scientific rigor, and the danger of ideology, a threat recognized, rather ominously, by one of the founders of the positive psychology movement:

"... unfortunately, there is a real danger that positive psychology will become to some extent an ideological movement. Although those of us involved from the beginning are resisting this outcome as much as we can, to a large extent the future is out of our hands" Csikszentmihalyi (2003, p. 114).

The specter of ideology does loom when researchers are funded by organizations with wider agendas that are not in keeping with strong science. To my mind, the hectoring of happiology is much less threatening to the legitimacy of positive psychology than the knowledge that even very fine research is conducted under the auspices of benefactors who support and promote pseudoscience such as intelligent design or religious tenets cloaked as empirical truths.

## Some Concluding Thoughts

In closing, I would like to address a theme I noted earlier, the tension between the extraordinary and the ordinary in positive psychology. When positive psychology first began, there was, in my view, a focus on the far right-hand side of the bell curve of positive traits—an emphasis on the extraordinary and exceptional, the brightest, the most gifted, the genius, not just good lives, but the "Best Lives." To some extent, for Seligman and Csikszentmihalyi (2000), psychology was missing an approach to the reality of human greatness. This may well have been the case and might still be the case today. However, I would suggest that the true future of positive psychology ought to be staked not just on the Greats, but on the near-greats, the also-rans, and even the dreaded underdogs that Seligman and Csikszentmihalyi (2000) worried would preoccupy psychology into the next 50 years.

In our preface to the 2001 special section of the *American Psychologist* devoted to positive psychology, Ken Sheldon and I offered a somewhat humble definition of the movement/field as ". . . nothing more than the psychology of ordinary human strengths and virtues" (p. 216). That definition reflects the kind of positive psychology I would hope to see in the future—research that illuminates the mundane greatness of human behaviors in everyday life, the kinds of good lives that are constructed by our own mothers, fathers, friends, the people whose lives we encounter and take part in every day. If there was a key flaw in business-as-usual psychology, it is that, in its focus on psychopathology, it convinced everyday human beings that it was not centrally about them, that it had nothing to offer people who were keeping their heads above water and their noses clean. Understanding the

extremes of positive human functioning is important, but it likewise misses the many people who provide the big hump in the middle of the frequency distribution and risks the same irrelevance to their lives.

What sort of research agenda am I advocating? Among other things, it is one that incorporates daily life measured in rigorous ways (e.g., Steger, Kashdan, & Oishi, 2008). It allows for the small-time heroes of everyday life to share their wisdom and insights (e.g., King & Hicks, 2007). It incorporates the most sophisticated theories and methods in examining self-regulation, goal pursuit (Fischbach, Friedman, & Kruglanski, 2003), and creativity (Friedman & Forster, 2001). And it serves the potentially small-stakes longings of everyday people to experience fulfillment and a sustainable sense of well-being (Sin & Lyubomirsky, 2009; Sheldon & Lyubomirsky, 2007). This positive psychology maintains a sense of humility and wonder about the everyday folk who provide our data, confident in the knowledge that just as we have something to offer them, they, still, have much more to offer us.

For my part, I would hope that positive psychology stays relevant to everyday human experience, in theory, methods, and applications. Positive psychology would do well to emerge as the scientific study of the ordinary and the simple that are, simultaneously, the graceful, the beautiful, and the wondrous that we see in everyday human life. I offer the following words of wisdom from William James as inspiration for scholars in positive psychology:

"All Goods are disguised by the vulgarity of their concomitants, in this work-a-day world; but woe to him who can only recognize them when he thinks them in their pure and abstract form!" (James, 1890, p. 125)

Future positive psychologists should take James' declaration as a credo. The very best of positive psychology will find those goods, disguised though they may be in their vulgar trappings in everyday life. Woe to positive psychology, indeed, if it cannot recognize and enthusiastically uncover them. By applying rigorous empirical methods to the goods of this work-a-day world, we bring them into sharp relief, providing a richer and more accurate portrait of human lives and behavior. Herein lies a historic opportunity to demonstrate how science can not only reduce but also elevate human experience.

At the beginnings of positive psychology, there was a sense that someday psychology itself would be so transformed by the movement that the movement itself would cease to exist. So, are we there yet? Not quite. In some ways those prognosticators quoted at the beginning of this chapter were correct in that positive psychology, *the movement*, has perhaps begun to fade. To the extent that *the field* of positive psychology promotes rigorous research and good practice, it has outlived the movement and shows every sign of maintaining a healthy relevance to human life. The positive psychology movement is dead! Long live the field of positive psychology! I wish it a long, virtuous, and (especially) *happy* life.

*References*

Aristotle (350 BCE/1998 CE). *Nicomachean Ethics*. J.L. Ackrill, J.O. Urmson, and D. Ross Trans. New York: Oxford University Press.

Batson, C. D., & Powell, A. A. (2003). Altruism and prosocial behavior. In T. Millon & M. J. Lerner (Eds.), *Handbook of psychology, Volume 5: Personality and social psychology* (pp. 463–484). Hoboken, NJ: Wiley.

Biswas-Diener, R., Kashdan, T., & King, L. A. (2009). Two traditions of happiness research, not two distinct types of happiness. *Journal of Positive Psychology, 4*, 208–211.

Diener, E. (2003). What is positive about positive psychology? The curmudgeon and Pollyanna. *Psychological Inquiry, 14*, 115–120.

Csikszentmihalyi, M. (1990). *Flow*. New York, NY: Harper & Row.

Csikszentmihalyi, C. (2003). Legs or wings? A reply to R.S. Lazarus. *Psychological Inquiry, 14*, 113–115.

Cohn, M. A., Fredrickson, B. L., Brown, S.L., Mikels, J. A., & Conway, A.M. (2009). Happiness unpacked: Positive emotions increase life satisfaction by building resilience. *Emotion, 9*, 361–368.

Fishbach, A., Friedman, R.S., & Kruglanski, A.W. (2003). Leading us not into temptation: Momentary allurements elicit overriding goal activation. *Journal of Personality and Social Psychology, 84*, 296–309.

Fredrickson, B. L., Cohn, M. A., Coffey, K. A., Pek, J., & Finkel, S. M. (2008). Open hearts build lives: Positive emotions, induced through loving-kindness meditation, build consequential personal resources. *Journal of Personality and Social Psychology, 95*, 1045–1062.

Fredrickson, B. L., Tugade, M. M., Waugh, C. E., & Larkin, G. R. (2003). What good are positive emotions in crisis? A prospective study of resilience and emotions following the terrorist attacks on the United States on September 11th, 2001. *Journal of Personality and Social Psychology, 84*, 365–376.

Friedman, R. S., & Forster, J. (2001). The effects of approach and avoidance motor actions on the elements of creative insight. *Journal of Personality and Social Psychology, 79*, 477–492.

Hicks, J. A., & King, L. A. (2008). Mood and religion as information about meaning in life. *Journal of Research in Personality, 42*, 43–57.

James, W. (1890). *Principles of psychology, Volume I*. New York: Henry Holt and Company.

Kahneman, D., Diener, E., & Schwarz, N. (1999). *Well-being: The foundations of hedonic psychology*. New York: Russell-Sage.

Kashdan, T. B., Biswas-Diener, R., & King, L. A. (2008). Reconsidering happiness: The costs of distinguishing between hedonics and eudaimonia. *Journal of Positive Psychology, 8*, 219–233.

King, L. A. (2008). Interventions for enhancing SWB: The pursuit of happiness. In R. J. Larsen and M. Eid (Eds.), *The science of subjective well-being* (pp. 431–448). New York: Guilford.

King, L. A. (2003). Some truth behind the trombones? *Psychological Inquiry, 14*, 128–131.

King, L. A., & Hicks, J. A. (2007). Whatever happened to "what might have been"? Regret, happiness, and maturity. *American Psychologist, 62*, 625–636.

King, L. A., Hicks, J. A., Krull, J., & Del Gaiso, A. (2006). Positive affect and the experience of meaning in life. *Journal of Personality and Social Psychology, 90*, 179–196.

King, L. A., & Napa, C. (1998). What makes a life good? *Journal of Personality and Social Psychology, 75*, 156–165.

Lazarus, R. S. (2003a). Does the positive psychology movement have legs? *Psychological Inquiry, 14*, 93–109.

Lazarus, R. S. (2003b). The Lazarus manifesto for positive psychology and psychology in general. *Psychological Inquiry, 14*, 173–189.

Lyubomirsky, S., King, L. A., & Diener, E. (2005). The benefits of frequent positive affect: Does happiness lead to success? *Psychological Bulletin, 131*, 803–855.

Peterson, C., & Park, N. (2003). Positive psychology as the evenhanded positive psychologist views it. *Psychological Inquiry, 14*, 143–146.

Peterson, C., Park, N., & Seligman, M. E. P. (2005). Orientations toward happiness and life satisfaction: The full life and the empty life. *Journal of Happiness Studies, 6*, 25–41.

Peterson, C., & Seligman, M. E. P. (2003). Character strengths before and after September 11. *Psychological Science, 14*, 381–384.

Rand, K. L., & Snyder, C. R. (2003). A reply to Dr. Lazarus, The Evocator Emeritus. *Psychological Inquiry, 14*, 148–153.

Ryan, R. M., & Deci, E. L. (2001). On happiness and human potentials: A review of research on hedonic and eudaimonic well-being. In S. Fiske (Eds.), *Annual Review of Psychology* (vol. 52; pp. 141–166). Palo Alto, CA: Annual Reviews, Inc.

Scollon, C. N., & King, L. A. (2004). Is the good life the easy life? *Social Indicators Research, 68*, 127–162.

Seligman, M. E. P. (2007). Coaching and positive psychology. *Australian Psychologist, 42*, 266–267.

Seligman, M. E. P. (2002). *Authentic happiness.* New York: Free Press.

Seligman, M. E. P., & Csikszentmihalyi, C. (2000). Positive psychology: An introduction. *American Psychologist, 55*, 5–14.

Seligman, M. E. P., & Pawelski, J. O. (2003). Positive psychology FAQs. *Psychological Inquiry, 14*, 110–172.

Sheldon, K., & King, L. A. (2001). Why positive psychology is necessary (foreword to the special section). *American Psychologist, 56*, 216–217.

Sheldon, K. M., & Lyubomirsky, S. (2007). Is it possible to become happier? (And if so, how?). *Social and Personality Psychology Compass, 1*, 129–145.

Sin, N. L., & Lyubomirsky, S. (2009). Enhancing well-being and alleviating depressive symptoms with positive psychology interventions: A practice-friendly meta-analysis. *Journal of Clinical Psychology, 65*, 467–487.

Steger, M. F., Kashdan, T. B., & Oishi, S. (2008). Being good by doing good: Daily eudaimonic activity and well-being. *Journal of Research in Personality, 42*, 22–42.

Woolfolk, R. L., & Wasserman, R. H. (2005). Count no one happy: Eudaimonia and positive psychology. *Journal of Theoretical and Philosophical Psychology, 25*, 81–90.

# 31

# Positive Psychology in Historical and Philosophical Perspective: Predicting Its Future from the Past

*Dean Keith Simonton*

In this evaluative essay, I am going to examine positive psychology from a combined historical and philosophical perspective. Perhaps it might be better said that I will examine the movement from the standpoint of the philosophy of history—the scholarly discipline that examines the source of change in the course of human events. Scholars in this discipline endeavor to tease out the "laws" or "lessons" of history, that is, the abstract principles or regularities that govern the phenomenon. However, my specific approach to discerning such generalizations is decidedly neither historical nor philosophical. Instead, the analyses on which I rely are quantitative rather than qualitative. In fact, almost all of the research reviewed in this chapter will be historiometric, a method that applies measurement and statistical methods to historical and biographical data (Simonton, 1990). Some of these historiometric studies have been applied to the history of science, others to the history of philosophy, and still others to the history of psychology. Taken together they provide a unique perspective on the established past and projected future of positive psychology as a scientific enterprise.

To be specific, below I will discuss (a) the long-term impact of intellectual extremism, (b) the Hegelian dialectic underlying the history of ideas, and (c) the Comtian hierarchy of the sciences. In each case I will review the empirical findings and then discuss how those findings might be applied to positive psychology.

## The Long-Term Impact of Intellectual Extremism

One fact cannot be denied: Philosophers, scientists, and other thinkers vary tremendously in how much impact they exert on the history of ideas. Indeed, some exerted so much influence that they have become well-known eponyms. Thus in the history of Western thought we can speak of ideas that are Socratic, Platonic, Aristotelian, Epicurean, Augustinian, Thomist, Baconian, Cartesian, Lockean, Kantian, Comtist, Marxist, Freudian, Hullian, Piagetian, Skinnerian, and so on. But what are the origins of these phenomenal differences? Why are Aristotle, Descartes, and Kant so much better known than Xenocrates, Henri du Roy, and G. Cocceji?

## Empirical Findings

The issue just raised has been addressed in two separate historiometric investigations. Although these studies examined two rather divergent kinds of intellectual contributions, both studies identified a common predictor of long-term impact.

*Study 1: 2,012 philosophers from Western civilization* (Simonton, 1976). The first investigation began with a very large sample of thinkers from the Western intellectual tradition (from Sorokin, 1937–1941). The sample extended back to the ancient Greeks and extended to the early 20th century—essentially from Thales to Bertrand Russell and virtually everybody between. All 2,012 philosophers were then scored on a highly reliable indicator of long-term influence (see also Murray, 2003; Simonton, 1991). In addition, a team of professional philosophers had already assessed these individuals on the positions they advocated on seven major issues: (a) source of knowledge (empiricism, rationalism, mysticism, skepticism, criticism, or fideism), (b) nature of reality (materialism or idealism), (c) the reality of change (eternalism or temporalism), (d) the status of abstract ideas (nominalism, realism, or conceptualism), (e) the relation between the individual and society (singularism or universalism), (f) the status of freedom (determinism versus indeterminism), and (g) the basis of ethical life (happiness, principles, or love). These assessments were then used to define several potential predictors of a thinker's long-term impact, such as the breadth, consistency, and extremism of the belief system; the fit between the thinker's positions and the prevailing philosophical zeitgeist; and the degree of ideological diversity evinced by the thinker's contemporaries. Furthermore, several contextual factors were created, such as political fragmentation, political instability, and role-model availability (taken from Simonton, 1975).

Although a multiple-regression analysis yielded lots of significant results, I would like to concentrate on just one: intellectual extremism. Those thinkers who had the greatest impact on the history of ideas were those who became known for extreme positions (Simonton, 1976). By "extreme" I mean that they advocated views located at the tails of the distribution. Such ideas are both rare and far above or below the average. For example, rather than argue for a dualistic view that reality consists of both mind and matter, the thinker might defend an extreme monistic idealism (e.g, George Berkeley) or an equally extreme mechanistic materialism (e.g., Thomas Hobbes). Thinkers who attempt to put forward more middle-of-the-road, even conciliatory viewpoints will tend to pay the penalty of greater obscurity. Moderation means mediocrity—at least in terms of long-term impact.

*Study 2: 54 eminent psychologists* (Simonton, 2000). One might be inclined to dismiss the foregoing finding as irrelevant to the matter at hand. After all, this chapter is devoted to the discussion of positive psychology, not positive philosophy (albeit I'll discuss the latter soon). Even so, a second historiometric study conducted almost a quarter century later suggests that high-impact psychologists operate according to the same fundamental principle (Simonton, 2000). The investigation began with a sample of 54 eminent psychologists born between 1801 (Gustav Fechner) and 1919 (William Estes). The sample included representatives of every major subdiscipline (physiological, comparative, cognitive, personality, developmental, educational, social, clinical, etc.) and major school (Structuralism, Functionalism, Behaviorism, Gestalt, Psychoanalytic, Humanistic, etc.).

On the basis of 232 expert evaluations, each of these 54 had been previously assessed on six theoretical and methodological orientations (Coan, 1968, 1979). These dimensions may be described as follows: (a) objectivistic versus subjectivistic (emphasis on observable behavior versus emphasis on subjective experience; e.g., Watson, Pavlov, Skinner, and Hull versus Jung, Brentano, Adler, Piaget, Fechner, and Janet); (b) elementaristic versus holistic (emphasis on molecular or atomistic analysis versus emphasis on molar analysis; e.g., Spence, Titchener, Estes, Hull, Wundt, Pavlov, and Skinner versus Goldstein, Koffka, G. Allport, Lewin, and Rogers); (c) impersonal versus personal (emphasis on the nomothetic, deterministic, abstract, and tightly controlled versus emphasis on the idiographic, emotional, and the unconscious; e.g., Hull, Skinner, Titchener, and G. E. Müller versus Rorschach, Adler, Jung, Janet, G. Allport, and Charcot); (d) quantitative versus qualitative (emphasis on mathematics, statistics, and precision versus emphasis on qualitative attributes and processes; e.g., Estes, Thurstone, Spearman, Binet, and Ebbinghaus versus Freud, Charcot, Wertheimer, Sullivan, and Köhler); (e) static versus dynamic (emphasis on the normative and stable versus emphasis on motivation, emotion, and the self; e.g., Wundt, Mach, Fechner,

Spearman, and Külpe versus McDougall, Mowrer, Freud, and James); and (f) exogenist versus endogenist (emphasis on environmental determinants and social influences versus emphasis on biological determinants and heredity; e.g., Skinner, Angell, Hull, Rogers, and Watson versus Galton, Freud, Hall, McDougall, and Cannon).

Factor analysis revealed that these six orientations can be consolidated into a single dimension that contains a natural-science orientation at one end and a human-science orientation at the other end (Coan, 1979; Simonton, 2000). That is, the factor pits objectivistic, elementaristic, quantitative, exogenist, impersonal, and static psychologists against their subjectivistic, holistic, qualitative, personal, endogenist, and dynamic colleagues.

The big question was then: How does placement along this inclusive factor correspond with a psychologist's long-term impact? The answer clearly required some measure of influence on the field of psychology. This assessment was obtained by means of the number of citations that the 54 had received in the psychological literature in the 1970s and 1980s (Simonton, 2000). Although all of these psychologists are certainly famous, some clearly have more impact than others. At one extreme, Freud averaged 1,271 per year over the period of assessment, whereas at the other extreme Külpe (who?) averaged only 16. Does the natural- versus human-science dimension help explain this differential? If so, which pole is favored?

The answer is pretty amazing: Although there is a tendency for human-science-oriented psychologists to receive more citations than natural-science-oriented psychologists, in fact the relation is best described by a U-shaped curve! Psychologists with the highest impact are those who take an extreme stance on this dimension. Their theories and methods tend to be either extremely objectivistic, elementaristic, quantitative, exogenist, impersonal, and static or extremely subjectivistic, holistic, qualitative, personal, endogenist, and dynamic. As an example, consider the nature-nurture issue, which is a special case of the endogenist-exogenist contrast; psychologists are most likely to exert long-term impact if they argue for either nature or nurture rather than some complex combination of both. Think of Francis Galton versus John B. Watson. Can you conceive a psychologist of equal stature who argued for an integrated nature-nurture perspective?

## Application: The Long-Term Influence of Positive Psychologists?

Two separate historiometric inquiries have shown that the advocacy of extreme positions tends to enhance a thinker's long-term influence. How does this apply to positive psychology? I believe that one can reasonably argue that positive psychologists, from the very outset of the movement, have taken an extremist stance. In essence, proponents have put together a research program that encompasses everything good about *Homo sapiens* while excluding everything bad— or even just plain ordinary—about our species. This distinctive characteristic can be directly inferred from various handbooks and special journal issues (see, e.g., Baumeister & Simonton, 2005; Seligman & Csikszentmihalyi, 2000; Keyes & Haidt, 2002; Seligman & Peterson, 2004; Snyder & Lopez, 2002). More specifically, the standard topics include happiness, all the virtues and upbeat personality traits, and even special abilities like leadership, creativity, giftedness, and genius, all the while excluding psychopathology, stress and hassles, aggression and violence, hatred, prejudice and discrimination, and even such neutral psychological phenomena as attention, memory, and language.

What renders this positive-only emphasis most problematic is the often implicit assumption that these good things all go together. It's as if researchers are endeavoring to discover the recipe for the all-around human greatness. Yet for good or ill, human nature is far more complex and finely nuanced than that. For instance, Bacon (2005) has proposed that positive psychology actually consists of two contrasting cultures, one stressing "balance strengths," such as wisdom, and the other emphasizing "focus strengths," such as creativity. These two strengths may not necessarily co-occur, and even may be antithetical (cf. Simonton, 2008a). Nowhere is this antithesis more apparent than in the creative genius (Simonton, 2008b). Although we cannot exactly say that genius is always associated with madness, that statement contains more truth than to say that genius-level creativity is associated with higher mental health and subjective well-being. The higher the degree of creativity a person displays, the greater is the likelihood that he or she will display symptoms that are more characteristic of psychopathology (Simonton, 2009a, 2009b). That empirical fact cannot be ignored by any comprehensive human psychology.

Positive psychologists may not necessarily agree with the foregoing analysis. Yet if that analysis is correct, then positive psychology's long-term impact will be reinforced rather than undermined. Exclusive focus on the good is itself good.

## The Hegelian Dialectic Underlying the History of Ideas

Now let us turn to an entirely different historical and philosophical question. It is evident that the history of ideas is a narrative of change. Modern thinkers do not advocate the same positions as those advocated by thinkers in the Middle Ages, just as the latter proposed ideas that departed significantly from the philosophies of Classical Greece. Hegel (1832/1952) suggested that such changes can be explicated in terms of a dialectic process. The process begins with a specific thesis. This thesis would then provoke the emergence of the antithesis, an intellectual reaction to the thesis. The juxtaposition of thesis and antithesis would then stimulate the appearance of a synthesis that integrates the two contrary positions. Yet the Hegelian process does not end there. The synthesis then becomes a new thesis, and the history of ideas continues to manifest change as a consequence (albeit Hegel himself saw this process terminating in his own set of beliefs). This Hegelian dialectic has some interesting implications for understanding positive psychology. But before I discuss those implications, let me first examine the available evidence on behalf of this historical mechanism.

### Empirical Findings

The same data on more than two thousand philosophers discussed earlier can be analyzed differently (Simonton, 1978). Rather than scrutinize individual differences in eminence, we can assign the thinkers to 20-year generational periods so as to discern the ups and downs in various philosophical beliefs. This tabulation has already been carried out by Sorokin (1937–1941; who also weighted the counts according to the differential eminence of each thinker). The resulting generational time series can then by subjected to analytical methods that determine how the prevailing beliefs in one generation influence the dominant beliefs in the next (Simonton, 1984). A historiometric investigation applying these methods obtained some suggestive results, namely,

that such cross-generational influences actually operate for a large number of philosophical beliefs (Simonton, 1978).

To offer but one example, suppose that one generation features a large number of philosophers who argue for skepticism, the epistemological position that says that truth cannot be known. Then the next generation tends to display a marked increase in the number of thinkers who espouse fideism, the position that says that knowledge can be based on faith alone, thus bypassing the need for empirical or rational support. Here skepticism can be considered the thesis and fideism the antithesis. Admittedly, because this investigation was not specifically designed to identify occurrences of a Hegelian dialectic, it did not look for a synthesis of these two rival epistemologies. On that possibility I can only cite evidence that great philosophers may be those who synthesize contrary intellectual positions (Simonton, 1976). For instance, Kant integrated Locke's empiricism, Hume's skepticism, and the idealistic rationalism of Kant's continental predecessors. Kantian philosophy was a synthesis.

In any event, it remains true that the philosophical views of one generation can stimulate philosophical reactions in the next. Hence, the above results can be taken as tentative support for the hypothesized Hegelian process.

### Application: From Positive Psychology to Synthesized Psychology?

It is easy to offer concrete illustrations of this historical mechanism. Thus, Plato's otherworldly rationalism was followed by the more this-worldly empiricism of Aristotle, his one-time pupil. The history of psychology is also replete with instances. The introspectionist school of psychology represented by Wilhelm Wundt and Edward Titchener provoked an antithesis known as behaviorism, initially led by James B. Watson. The cognitive revolution that occurred some decades later might even be considered a synthesis, combining the interest in mind with more objective research methods. Another example is the emergence of humanistic psychology, which was a reaction not only to behaviorism but to psychoanalytic theory besides. Behaviorism and psychoanalysis shared a lack of interest in personal freedom, values, and consciousness.

So what about positive psychology? One response is that the very existence of a "positive" psychology implies a "negative" psychology. Presumably, the discipline had placed so much emphasis on the bad that it had become necessary to counter one extremist position with another. By adding human strengths to human failings, psychology would acquire a more balanced view of human nature. If negative psychology is the thesis, and positive psychology the antithesis, then what will be the synthesis? Will it be a neutral psychology that combines and integrates both positive and negative features of human nature?

Yet there's another way to examine this question. Rather than view positive psychology as an antithesis, we might see it as a special kind synthesis: the integration of the concerns of humanistic psychology with the methods of mainstream experimental and correlational psychology. Although the humanistic psychologists tended to emphasize human virtues and strengths, their research was most prone to be qualitative and even holistic—more akin to the human sciences than to the natural sciences. In contrast, positive psychologists have investigated many of the same topics using psychometric, experimental, and survey methodologies. Nevertheless, we still must anticipate some eventual integration with the subject matter of "neutral" and "negative" psychologies. Otherwise positive psychology may become increasingly marginalized within the field, much as happened to humanistic psychology.

## The Comtian Hierarchy of the Sciences

In an earlier remark I mentioned the existence of a positive philosophy. It would make life easier if positive philosophy is to philosophy what positive psychology is to psychology. Unfortunately, the adjective "positive" is used in two different senses. In the philosophical case, positive is the adjective form of positivism. The latter term has a broad- and narrow-sense meaning. Broadly speaking, positivism is the doctrine that sensory data must be the only admissible source for human knowledge. Narrowly speaking, positivism is the philosophical system advanced by the French philosopher Auguste Comte (Martineau, 1853/1893).

Comte's system included a philosophy of history. In that philosophy, history consisted of three stages: the theological (gods and spirits), the metaphysical (abstract rational principles), and the positive (i.e., modern empirical science). More interestingly, in the positive stage the sciences were said to emerge according to a defined hierarchy: astronomy, physics, chemistry, biology, and sociology. To a psychologist, the absence of psychology is conspicuous. Worse still, Comte's specification also was based on analytical rather than empirical considerations (see also Bliss, 1935; Gnoli, 2008). Accordingly, I now wish to report an empirical (positive) inquiry into the placement of psychology within a hierarchy of the sciences (Simonton, 2004).

### Empirical Findings

Cole (1983) was the first researcher to investigate the empirical support for a hierarchy but failed to introduce the appropriate statistical analyses. As a consequence, he incorrectly concluded that there was no evidence for a hierarchical arrangement (Simonton, 2002). Later I conducted a more elaborate analysis that incorporated a large supply of criteria that should distinguish a discipline's place in the hierarchy (Simonton, 2004). These criteria included both positive and negative indicators. The former consisted of citation concentration, citation immediacy, early impact rate, knowledge obsolescence rate, anticipation frequency, peer evaluation consensus, graph prominence, and rated disciplinary hardness, whereas the latter consisted of peer consultation rate, theories-to-laws ratio in textbooks, age at receipt of the Nobel prize, and lecture disfluency in introductory courses (for variable definitions and data sources, see Simonton, 2004). Making suitable provision for missing values, the factor and correlational analyses established a clear-cut hierarchy for the following five sciences: physics, chemistry, biology, psychology, and sociology. Significantly, the two physical sciences are clustered closer together than they are to biology, and biology is closer to psychology than it is to chemistry, but the gap between psychology and sociology is larger than that between any other pair of disciplines.

Later it was shown that a discipline's placement on this hierarchy was correlated with the dispositional traits and developmental experiences of the scientists who practice within that discipline (Simonton, 2009a, 2009b). In other words, the dimension has a psychological basis. For the most part, physical scientists differ psychologically from biologists in the same way that biological scientists differ from psychologists and the latter differ from sociologists. Indeed, there is strong evidence that this hierarchical arrangement can be extended into the humanities and even the arts. Creators at the top of the hierarchy are more likely to be emotionally stable, conventional, and objective; they create products that are more formal, logical, and constrained by a well-defined disciplinary consensus, or paradigm. Creators at the bottom of the hierarchy are more likely to be emotionally unstable, unconventional, and subjective; they create products that are more intuitive, expressive, emotional, and individualistic. Respective developmental experiences reinforce these contrasts. For example, those at the top more likely come from highly conventional, stable homes and demonstrate exceptional academic attainments, whereas those at the bottom more likely come from unconventional, unstable homes and exhibit lesser scholastic success.

What is equally fascinating is that these differences also operate within a given scientific discipline (Simonton, 2009a, 2009b). Each science consists of subdisciplines that may lie higher or lower along the underlying dimension relative to the science as a whole. Within the behavioral sciences, for instance, scientists closer to the natural-science end tend to be realistic, objective, orderly, stable, conventional, conforming, interpersonally dependent, passive, and reactive, whereas those closer to the human-science end tend to be more cognitively complex, imaginative, creative, changing, nonconforming, participative, active, purposive, autonomous, and individualistic (Johnson, Germer, Efran, & Overton, 1988; Suedfeld, 1985). This intradisciplinary contrast within psychology closely matches the inter-disciplinary contrast between the physical sciences and psychology (Chambers, 1964; Roe, 1953). In fact, some subdisciplines of psychology may be more proximate to the physical sciences than to mainstream psychology. This is probably the case for Skinnerian behaviorism (Cole, 1983).

In sum, the hierarchical model handles not just the obvious differences between separate disciplines ranging from the sciences to the arts but also the more subtle contrasts within specific disciplines (Simonton, 2009a, 2009b).

## Application: Positive Psychology's Status as a Scientific Discipline?

In light of the preceding findings, one must inquire where positive psychology fits on the dimension underlying the hierarchical organization of the sciences. The most obvious interpretation is that the movement represents a shift toward the human-science side of psychology.

As such, positive psychology represents a subdiscipline that lies lower in the hierarchy. That is, in comparison to mainstream psychology, the practitioners of positive psychology have moved away from the natural sciences and toward the social sciences and humanities. Because positive psychology incorporates scientific research methods, this shift is certainly not as great as witnessed in the earlier humanistic psychology movement.

To some positive psychologists, the foregoing conclusion may seem like a negative appraisal. I seem to be saying that the movement is less scientific than "negative" or "neutral" psychology. But that judgment is not necessarily negative. To see why, consider the following three points:

First, although the hierarchical model orders disciplines according to rigor, objectivity, and consensus, it also *inversely* ranks disciplines according to other values. Most notably, the disciplines lower in the hierarchy tend to display more creative freedom (Simonton, 2009b). Artists exhibit more creativity than scientists, and social scientists exhibit more than natural scientists. So in this sense positive psychologists should be displaying more creativity than their psychological colleagues farther up in the hierarchy. So long as a practitioner does not suffer from excessive "physics envy," this asset may offset any deficits regarding the criteria underlying the hierarchical arrangement.

Second, it may be useful to cast this assessment in terms of Kuhn's (1970) distinction between the practitioners of normal science, who follow the received disciplinary paradigm, and the revolutionary scientists who challenge that paradigm. If positive psychology can then be viewed as a revolutionary movement rebelling against a negative psychology paradigm, then it would be expected that positive psychologists would move down the hierarchy (Simonton, 2009b). Scientific revolutionaries must be more creative than practitioners of normal science, and thus will have more affinities with creators in disciplines closer to the humanities and arts. For example, scientific revolutionaries are more disposed toward psychopathology than are scientists who conform to the given paradigm (Ko & Kim, 2008).

Third, and last, it must be emphasized that there are good reasons why disciplines array themselves along the hierarchy the way they do. Most strikingly, disciplines lower down the hierarchy must grapple with phenomena that are far more complex and subtle than typically holds for disciplines higher in the hierarchy. This increased complexity and subtlety pose more challenges, reducing the latitude for logical rigor, objectivity, and disciplinary consensus. The only way a psychologist can be as rigorous and objective as a biologist is to introduce some variety of reductionism, such as a focus on the biological bases of behavior (e.g., behavior genetics, cognitive neuroscience, evolutionary psychology). Psychologists who want to study human strengths and virtues do not have this option. These phenomena are inherently more complex and subtle.

## Conclusion: The Future of Positive Psychology

In this chapter I have examined positive psychology from three historical-philosophical perspectives. I began with the research on the long-term impact of a thinker's ideas. Citing historiometric inquiries on both philosophers and psychologists, I showed that high-impact thinkers are more prone to advocate extremist positions. From there I discussed whether positive psychology can be considered to have taken an extremist stance. The next perspective originated in Hegel's philosophy of history. In particular, I discussed a generational time-series analysis that scrutinized how the philosophical commitments of one generation can affect those of the succeeding generation. These tentative findings led to a discussion of whether positive psychology represents an antithesis or a synthesis. The third perspective grew out of Comte's hierarchy of the sciences. After reviewing the evidence for this hierarchy, and indicating how the hierarchy can account for within-discipline contrasts as well as encompass the humanities and the arts, I then addressed the question of where positive psychology is placed in the disciplinary configuration. Although I concluded that positive psychology is positioned lower in the hierarchy than is mainstream psychology, I also presented three reasons why this should not be considered a bad outcome.

So where does all this leave positive psychology? It's difficult to say. A lot depends on exactly how the movement is positioned in the history of psychology. Can it really be considered an extremist position? Should it be viewed as an antithesis or synthesis? Does it count as a scientific revolution? If so, will it motivate a new and more integrative paradigm for psychological inquiry? Perhaps these questions can only be granted secure answers in retrospect, after we learn how the story comes out. Even so, I believe one prediction is secure: Positive psychology is here to stay. It may have a short past, but it will most likely have a long future.

*References*

Bacon, S. F. (2005). Positive psychology's two cultures. *Review of General Psychology, 9,* 181–192.

Baumeister, R. F., & Simonton, D. K. (2005). Positive psychology [Special Issue]. *Review of General Psychology, 9,* 99–102.

Bliss, H. E. (1935). The system of the sciences and the organization of knowledge. *Philosophy of Science, 2,* 86–103.

Chambers, J. A. (1964). Relating personality and biographical factors to scientific creativity. *Psychological Monographs: General and Applied, 78* (7, Whole No. 584, 1–20).

Coan, R. W. (1968). Dimensions of psychological theory. *American Psychologist, 23,* 715–722.

Coan, R. W. (1979). *Psychologists: Personal and theoretical pathways.* New York: Irvington Publishers.

Cole, S. (1983). The hierarchy of the sciences? *American Journal of Sociology, 89,* 111-139.

Gnoli, C. (2008). Categories and facets in integrative levels. *Axiomathes, 18,* 177–192.

Hegel, G. W. F. (1952). *The philosophy of history* (C. F. Atkinson, Trans.). New York: Dover. (Original work published 1832)

Johnson, J. A., Germer, C. K., Efran, J. S., & Overton, W. F. (1988). Personality as the basis for theoretical predilections. *Journal of Personality and Social Psychology, 55,* 824–835.

Keyes, C. L. M., & Haidt, J. (Eds.). (2002). *Flourishing: Positive psychology and the life well-lived.* Washington, DC: American Psychological Association.

Ko, Y., & Kim, J. (2008). Scientific geniuses' psychopathology as a moderator in the relation between creative contribution types and eminence. *Creativity Research Journal, 20,* 251–261.

Kuhn, T. S. (1970). *The structure of scientific revolutions* (2nd ed.). Chicago: University of Chicago Press.

Martineau, H. (1893). *The positive philosophy of August Comte* (3rd ed., vol. 1). London: Kegan Paul, Trench, Trubner. (Original work published 1853)

Murray, C. (2003). Human accomplishment: The pursuit of excellence in the arts and sciences, 800 B.C. to 1950. New York: HarperCollins.

Roe, A. (1953). A psychological study of eminent psychologists and anthropologists, and a comparison with biological and physical scientists. *Psychological Monographs, 67* (2, Whole No. 352, 1–54).

Seligman, M. E. P., & Csikszentmihalyi, M. (Eds.). (2000). Happiness, excellence, and optimal human functioning [Special issue]. *American Psychologist, 55* (1).

Seligman, M. E. P., & Peterson, C. (Eds.). (2004). *Character strengths, virtues: A handbook and classification.* Washington, DC: American Psychological Association; New York: Oxford University Press.

Simonton, D. K. (1975). Sociocultural context of individual creativity: A transhistorical time–series analysis. *Journal of Personality and Social Psychology, 32,* 1119–1133.

Simonton, D. K. (1976). Philosophical eminence, beliefs, and zeitgeist: An individual–generational analysis. *Journal of Personality and Social Psychology, 34,* 630–640.

Simonton, D. K. (1978). Intergenerational stimulation, reaction, and polarization: A causal analysis of intellectual history. *Social Behavior and Personality, 6,* 247–251.

Simonton, D. K. (1984). Generational time–series analysis: A paradigm for studying sociocultural influences. In K. Gergen & M. Gergen (Eds.), *Historical social psychology* (pp. 141–155). Hillsdale, NJ: Lawrence Erlbaum.

Simonton, D. K. (1990). Psychology, science, and history: An introduction to historiometry. New Haven, CT: Yale University Press.

Simonton, D. K. (1991). Latent–variable models of posthumous reputation: A quest for Galton's G. *Journal of Personality and Social Psychology, 60,* 607–619.

Simonton, D. K. (2000). Methodological and theoretical orientation and the long–term disciplinary impact of 54 eminent psychologists. *Review of General Psychology, 4,* 1–13.

Simonton, D. K. (2002). Great psychologists and their times: Scientific insights into psychology's history. Washington, DC: APA Books.

Simonton, D. K. (2004). Psychology's status as a scientific discipline: Its empirical placement within an implicit hierarchy of the sciences. *Review of General Psychology, 8,* 59–67.

Simonton, D. K. (2008a). Creative wisdom: Similarities, contrasts, integration, and application. In A. Craft, H. Gardner, & G. Claxton (Eds.), *Creativity, wisdom, and trusteeship: Exploring the role of education* (pp. 68–76). Thousand Oaks, CA: Corwin Press.

Simonton, D. K. (2008b). Genius and creativity. In O. P. John, R. W. Robins, & L. A. Pervin (Eds.), *Handbook of personality: Theory and research* (3rd ed., pp. 679–698). New York: Guilford Press.

Simonton, D. K. (2009a). Varieties of perspectives on creativity. *Perspectives on Psychological Science, 4,* 466–467.

Simonton, D. K. (2009b). Varieties of (scientific) creativity: A hierarchical model of disposition, development, and achievement. *Perspectives on Psychological Science, 4,* 441–452.

Snyder, C. R., & Lopez, S. J. (Eds.). (2002). *The handbook of positive psychology.* New York: Oxford University Press.

Sorokin, P. A. (1937–1941). *Social and cultural dynamics* (vols. 1–4). New York: American Book.

Suedfeld, P. (1985). APA presidential addresses: The relation of integrative complexity to historical, professional, and personal factors. *Journal of Personality and Social Psychology, 47,* 848–852.

# Appendix

## Akumal Manifesto

Authors: Ken Sheldon, Barbara Fredrickson, Kevin Rathunde, Mike Csikszentmihalyi, and Jon Haidt. This manifesto was originally created during the Akumal 1 meeting in January 1999. See http://www.ppc.sas.upenn.edu/akumalmanifesto.htm for more information.

### 1. Definition

Positive Psychology is the scientific study of optimal human functioning. It aims to discover and promote the factors that allow individuals and communities to thrive. The positive psychology movement represents a new commitment on the part of research psychologists to focus attention upon the sources of psychological health, thereby going beyond prior emphases upon disease and disorder.

### 2. Goals

To meet these objectives, we must consider optimal functioning at multiple levels, including biological, experiential, personal, relational, institutional, cultural, and global. It is necessary to study a) the dynamic relations between processes at these levels, b) the human capacity to create order and meaning in response to inevitable adversity, and c) the means by which "the good life," in its many manifestations, may emerge from these processes.

### 3. Applications

Potential applications of positive psychology include:

Improving child education by making greater use of intrinsic motivation, positive affect, and creativity within schools
Improving psychotherapy by developing approaches that emphasize hope, meaning, and self-healing
Improving family life by better understanding the dynamics of love, generativity, and commitment

455

Improving work satisfaction across the lifespan by helping people to find authentic involvement, experience states of flow, and make genuine contributions in their work

Improving organizations and societies by discovering conditions that enhance trust, communication, and altruism between persons

Improving the moral character of society by better understanding and promoting the spiritual impulse within humans.

## 4. Implementation of Goals

In order to create the optimal conditions for the flourishing of positive psychology, we propose the following: 1) The circle of researchers who call themselves positive psychologists should be broadened, funded, nurtured in their career development, and kept in close contact. 2) We must produce useful and inspiring products, such as articles, books, and effective interventions. Specific strategies for bringing about these ends include:

a)  The formation of "Positive Science" research networks. Each network would include members from several social sciences. Below are three emerging network foci:
    • Positive subjective states. What characterizes and promotes optimal experiencing?
    • The good life/good person. What characterizes and promotes admirable persons and lives?
    • The good society (including groups such as families, corporations, and communities). What characterizes and promotes fully functioning groups?

It is recommended that networks have a chairperson, but no permanent members. Potentially interested scientists will be invited to participate in specific activities. Networks will select concrete tasks to work on, such as designing interventions to foster moral development in late childhood.

b)  Fostering contact among positive scientists:
    • Holding at least one large meeting per year in a positive location conducive to the development of new insights and collaborations

    • Maintaining a current positive psych listserv: positive-psychology@lists.apa.org
    • Supporting special topical meetings (in addition to those of the networks described above). It may be useful to schedule more than one subgroup meeting in the same time and place to facilitate cross-fertilization.

c)  Facilitation of funding for positive psychology researchers. Senior members of the Akumal group are taking the lead in identifying and contacting interested foundations. As one example, the Templeton Foundation has created a yearly prize for the most innovative research done in positive psychology by young scientists.

d)  Finding high-profile outlets for promoting positive approaches. Current and upcoming publications include:
    • A special issue of the *American Psychologist*, which appeared in January 2000, in which senior researchers explore the applicability of positive perspectives within their work (edited by Seligman & Csikszentmihalyi)
    • A special section of the *American Psychologist* on positive psychology, to appear in March 2001, in which researchers describe their emerging research findings that are relevant to positive psychology (edited by Sheldon & King)
    • A forthcoming book series on subtopics within positive psychology (edited by Aspinwall & Staudinger)
    • A forthcoming *Handbook of Positive Psychology* (edited by Snyder & Lopez)

e)  Fostering the careers of positive psychologists: As practitioners of positive psychology rise in prominence, so does the field. Positive psychologists should:
    • Be willing to host graduate students from other universities in post-docs or short-term visits
    • Invite positive psychologists to present colloquia at their universities

f)  Spreading positive psychological principles and perspectives to the broader public. For example, positive psychology might be incorporated into high school psychology curricula or within public health initiatives.

# Index

Note: Page numbers followed by " *f* ", " *t* " and " *n* " denote figures, tables, and notes respectively.

ability, 435–36
abundance mindset, 371
academic psychology, aims of, 430
acceptance, mindfulness and, 152
acceptance-based approaches, goal of, 11
accommodation, 268, 330
accreditation, 295–96
acculturation, 198
achievement, 423
acoustic startle reflex, 31
action-oriented responses, 162
active-constructive reactions, 268–69
active-destructive reactions, 268–70
active management, 33
Actor-Partner Interdependence Model (APIM), 285
adaptive responses, mindfulness and, 152–55
ADHD. *See* attention deficit hyperactivity disorder
Adult Self-Transcendence Inventory (ASTI), 142
adversarial growth, 331
affect. *See also* negative affect; positive affect
    ideal, 434
    personal projects and, 237
    raw, 70, 78n2
affect-as-information hypothesis, 106–7
affective dimensions, 237
affective experiences, 66–67, 249
    neurobiological nature of, 75
affective feelings, 51, 65–66
Affective Neuroscience Personality Scales, 65
affective thermostat model, 125
affordances, 237–39
agenda
    of positive psychology, 160–61
    science v., 161
agreeableness, 14, 210, 230, 387
Akumal I, 5–6
Akumal II, 5
Allport, Gordon, 208
    on personality traits, 209–10
altruism, 140–41, 432, 442

American Constitution, 4
American Psychological Association, 3, 5, 443
anabolic hormones, 42
anger, 54, 60–61
    confrontation and, 93–94
    magnitude ratings of, 125
animal/culture interface, conscious thought at, 181–85
antiphonal laughter, 120
anxiety, 10, 61–62
    mood disorders and, 164
    self-focus and, 163
    self-induced, 139
APIM. *See* Actor-Partner Interdependence Model
appreciation of beauty, 214*t*
appreciative inquiry, 366
approach motivation, 162, 167
Aron, Arthur, 104, 272
Aronson, Elliot, 104
arousal, 122, 274, 434
    tonic, 45*f*
ARP. *See* Association for Research in Personality
art-of-living skills, 404
assimilation, 18, 330
Association for Research in Personality (ARP), 242n1
ASTI. *See* Adult Self-Transcendence Inventory
atomic processes, 424
attentional control, blood glucose and, 29
attention deficit hyperactivity disorder (ADHD), 65
    frontal lobe executive functions and, 77
attitude assessment, 287
authenticity, 335, 339
automatic-controlled processing distinction, 167
automatic pilot, 336
autonomic nervous system, 27
avoidance motivation, 162

balance, 326, 435–36
    focus v., 449
    of mind, 156
basic orientations, 231–37

basic tendencies, 197, 198f
Baumeister, Roy, 17, 320–21
behavior(s), 12–14. *See also* organizational behavior
    adaptive, 148
    automatic initiation of, 177
    conscious thought and, 180–81
    initiation of, 178
    marital, 281
    modification of, 177
    moral, 253
    problematic, 268
    processes affecting, 425f
    simulation and, 182
    unconscious mind and, 177
behavioral affirmation, 271
behavioral measures, need for, 288
behavioral neuroscience, 54
behaviorism, 3, 104
benefit(s)
    of gratitude, 253
    of happiness, 401–2
    of positive psychological processes, 47
    of self-awareness, 135–36
    of socialization, 65
    of task-focus, 166
benefit-finding, 331
benevolence, 251
Bentham, Jeremy, 51, 396
between-person approaches, 13
Big Five Inventory, 201, 208–11, 214t, 241
    as orthogonal, 218
    well-being and, 230
biological adaptation, to repeated stress, 42
biological perspectives, integrating, 16–18
biological processes, positive psychological states and,
        43–44
blood glucose tolerance, 26. *See also* glucose
body-mind boundary, 427
Borderline Personality Disorder, 31, 196
Bowlby, John, 75–76
bracket creep, 10
brain
    as demanding organ, 34
    epigenetic construction of, 73–75
    frontal lobe executive functions of, 77
    MFB, 58
    play and, 73–75
    primary process emotions and, 54
    stimulation of, 72
BrainMind, 51, 54. *See also* MindBrain
    emotional-affective, 55
    evolutionary controls in, 68–72
BrainMindBody functions, 51
bravery, 214t
broaden-and-build theory, 116, 124–25, 140, 303, 412
Buddhism, 436
Buddhist psychology, 328–29
buffering model, 267
bulimic symptoms, self-verification and, 319–20
burdensomeness, perceived, 318–19

capitalization, 267
    as both interpersonal/intrapersonal, 268
    perceived responsiveness to self and, 270–71
    PRCA and, 268–69
    relationships and, 282
    research on, 271

care/maternal nurturance system, 63
catabolic hormones, 42
causal structure, 15
CFA. *See* confirmatory factor analysis
chance, impact of, 242
chaotic systems, 126
characteristic adaptations, 198f, 199–200
    trait influence on, 197–98
character strengths, 215–16, 223, 343
    interrelatedness of, 217–18
    mindfulness as, 341
    personality traits v., 207–8
    VIA classification of, 211–12
    virtues and, 338–41
cheerfulness, 10, 195
    optimal level of, 105
chemical stimulation of brain (CSB), 72
child development
    optimal, 59
    primary-process emotions and, 75–76
circumplex model, 125
citizenship, 214t
clinical psychology, 7, 411, 425f
    positive psychology v., 430
coaching, 370, 406–7
    academic status of, 296
    between-subjects studies of, 298t–299t
    credentialing, 295–96
    depression and, 301
    developmental, 305
    emergence of, 293–94
    organizational change and, 303–4
    outcome studies of, 297
    problems/possibilities of, 305–6
    professional status of, 295–96
    randomized controlled studies of, 297, 298t–299t,
        300
    research on, 296–305
    ROI of, 301–2
    systems change and, 304–5
    therapy v., 301
    use of, 293, 302–5
coaching psychology, 293, 302
coarse feeling states, 68
cognitive deconstruction, 136. *See also* hypo-egoic
        states
cognitive/emotional relations, 150–52
cognitive functions, regulation of, 29–30
cognitive psychology, 7, 425f
cognitive sophistication, epigenetic neocortical sources
        of, 67–68
cognitive therapies, variants of, 11
collaboration, 373–74
communities of practice, creation of, 374–75
community, 207, 390, 415
compassion, 10, 140–41, 432
compassionate goals, 140–41
Comtian hierarchy of sciences, 451–53
conceptual perspectives, 52–54
Conditioned Place Aversion (CPA), 72
Conditioned Place Preference (CPP), 72
confirmatory factor analysis (CFA), 211–12
conflict management, accumulated positive deposits
        and, 283–85
confrontation, anger and, 93–94
conscientiousness, 14, 198, 210, 230
    life satisfaction and, 199

conscious awareness, 176
conscious mind, 178–81
consciousness, 185
    levels/types of, 176
conscious processing, 137
conscious thought
    at animal/culture interface, 181–85
    behavior and, 180–81
    complex social life and, 179
    contribution of, 175–76
    function of, 176, 178
    interpersonal aspects of, 184–85
    intrapersonal aspects of, 182–84
    reason and, 180
    social/cultural information and, 179
    as uniquely human, 175, 178
conscious will, 178
contentment, in relationships, 275
content validity, 219
context
    boundary, 424
    culture as, 109–10
    emotions and, 93–94, 119
    importance of, 13
    well-being and, 97
cooperation, 423
coping. See also emotion-focused coping; problem-
        focused coping
    meaning making and, 326
    positive experiences and, 440
    research, 200–201
core affects, 78n2
core project sustainability, 243n13
core SELF, 56–57
correlational studies, 201
Corticotrophin Releasing Factor (CRF), 61
cortisol
    emotions and, 31
    executive cognitive functions and, 29
    measurement/meaning of, 27
    release of, 41
    response monitors for, 42
courage, 214t, 335, 338–39
CPA. See Conditioned Place Aversion
CPP. See Conditioned Place Preference
creativity, 214t, 452
creatureliness, 16
credibility, loss of, 7
CRF. See Corticotrophin Releasing Factor
cross-method replication, 201
CSB. See chemical stimulation of brain
Csikszentmihalyi, Mihaly, on optimal states, 162
cultural change, perception of, 4
cultural information, conscious thought and, 179
cultural norms, 425
    conforming to, 92–93
    emotion and, 118–19
Cultural Orientation Inventory, 241
cultural therapy, 193, 202n1
cultural values, role of, 122
culture
    as context, 109–10
    emotions and, 94–95, 118–19, 122
    interpersonal aspects of, 184–85
    intrapersonal aspects of, 182–84
culture/animal interface, conscious thought at, 181–85
culture wars, 68–69

curiosity, 14, 214t
current concerns, 233
current major depressive disorder, 31
cytokine production, stimulation of, 43

dACC. See dorsal anterior cingulate
        cortex
daily relationship deposits, 281–82, 289
    positive, accumulated, 283–85
DBT. See dialectical behavior therapy
decentering, 341–42
deficit-orientation, 4
dehydroepiandrosterone (DHEA), 42
deindividuation, 141
delayed gratification paradigm, 104
depression, 31, 163, 315–16
    coaching and, 301
    gratitude and, 257
descriptive psychology, 196–97
detection-and-response system, 121
developmental coaching, 305
developmental psychology, 7
DHEA. See dehydroepiandrosterone
diabetes
    insulin-dependent, 30
    non-insulin-dependent, 29
dialectical behavior therapy (DBT), 337
direction of inquiry, 314
dispositional gratitude, 249–50, 255
dispositional mindfulness, 150
dispositions, positive, 230
diversity, 368, 428
dlPFC. See dorsolateral prefrontal cortex
dogma, 4
domain(s), 6
    life, 275
    psychology as, 7
    satisfaction, 398
domestic violence, forgiveness and, 283
dopamine availability, as task-focus, 166
dorsal anterior cingulate cortex (dACC), 154
dorsolateral prefrontal cortex (dlPFC), 168
    lesions to, 165–66
    task-focus as, 165–66
drug addictions, operation of, 59
dual-aspect monism ontology, 72
dual-process theories, 137
dyadic interventions, 256
dyadic relationships, 285
dynamic modeling
    of emotions, 125–26
    nonlinear, 126
dynamic understanding, 325, 327, 329–30
dysfunction, medical model of, 430

efficacious interventions, 9
efficacy, 235–36, 359
    introspective, 183
ego depletion, 26
egoic state, characterization of, 136
ego identity, 149
ego identity contextualization, experiential processing
        and, 149–50
ego-involvement, hypo-egoic states and, 138
ego threats, adaptive responses to, 152–55
electrical stimulation of brain (ESB), 72
embarrassment, function of, 121–22

EMCC. *See* European Mentoring and Coaching Council
Emmons, Robert, 101–2
emotion(s), 51, 96, 117. *See also* negative emotions; positive emotions; *specific emotions*
  coarse, 102
  context and, 93–94, 119
  cortisol and, 31
  culture and, 94–95, 118–19, 122
  dynamic modeling of, 125–26
  families, 119–20
  functional theories of, 121–22
  glucose and, 30–31
  as hedonic states, 91
  HRV and, 31
  interpersonal, 94–95
  primary-process, 52–54, 67, 75–76
  read-out theories of, 66–67
  self-conscious, 119
  social-functional model of, 272
  sub-neocortical foundations of, 65–66
  subtle, 102
  toxic, 250–51
  unpleasant, 97
  utility of, 91
  within groups, 121–22
  within relationships, 120–21
emotional affects, 51, 56–57, 79n4
  core, 72
emotional distress, self-relevant thoughts, 139
emotional experiences, 162–63
emotional networks, sub-neocortical, 71
emotional primes, 57–65
emotional reactivity, 123–24
emotional stability, 210
emotion-focused coping, 43, 162, 167
emotion regulation, 30–32, 96–97, 125
  effective, 151–52
  instrumental approach to, 92–95
  mindfulness and, 151
  outcomes of, 150–51
  short-term hedonic approach limitations to, 90–91
  short-term hedonic approach to, 89–90
empathy, 72–73, 77
empiricism, 450
employee, life cycle of
  attract/select, 367–68
  develop, 369–71
  exit, 371–72
  retain, 368–69
employee well-being, 368
empowerment, 414
endocrine activity, positive psychological states and, 44
endocrine markers, 42
energy metaphor, 28–29
enhanced allostasis model, 41, 44–46, 45f
enjoyment, 398, 442
  dimensions of, 240
  learning, 405
environmental awareness, change and, 413
environmental livability, 397
environmental mastery, 202
environment-gene interactions, 75, 123–24
envy, 250
equality, 402–3, 402t, 407n3
Eriksson, Erik, 434

ESB. *See* electrical stimulation of brain
*eudaimonia* (happiness/flourishing in life), 110
eudaimonic happiness, 399
eudaimonic states, 44, 91
eudaimonic well-being, 229
European Mentoring and Coaching Council (EMCC), 295
evaluative threat
  on self-regulation, 35
  on stress, 35
evolved functions, 67
executive cognitive functions, 77
  cortisol and, 29
  HRV and, 29–30
existential psychology, 328
experiential processing, contextualization of ego identity and, 149–50
exposure process, 267
expressions, 117. *See also* emotion(s)
expressive writing, 108
external influences, 198f, 200
external validity, 219–20
extraversion, 199, 202, 210, 223, 387
  change in, 198
  stable, 230–31
extreme monistic idealism, 448
extrinsic motivation, 167

fairness, 214t
fear, 54
  as positive, 315
  unconditioned, 55
fear/anxiety system, 61–62
feeling(s). *See also* emotion(s)
  affective, 51, 65–66
  coarse, 68
  control of, 10
feelings-in-action, 71
FFT. *See* Five-Factor Theory
fight or flight response, 27, 54
find, remind, and bind, 273
Five-Factor Theory (FFT), 197, 198f
5-HTT. *See* serotonin transporter genes
Five Remembrances of Buddha, 328–29, 329t
flourishing, 423
  unified concept of, 229
flow, 6
  levels of, 162
forgiveness, 6, 214t, 423
  domestic violence and, 283
  gratitude and, 257
  relationships and, 283
fortuity, 242
Four Existential Givens, 329t
Fourth European Conference on Positive Psychology, 8
Fredrickson, Barbara, 6, 356–57
freedom, 391, 402t, 403
free will, 183
friendship, 120
  compassionate goals in, 140–41

GAS. *See* goal attainment scaling
gene-environment interactions, 75, 123–24
generalizability, 218–19
gestalt therapy, 18
GH. *See* growth hormone

gift-giving, function of, 122
glucoregulatory processes, 30, 33
glucose
  attentional control and, 29
  emotions and, 30–31
  self-regulation and, 26, 28–29, 33
glucose transporters (GLUT), 28
GLUT. *See* glucose transporters
goal attainment scaling (GAS), 301
goals, 331
  absence of, 257
  compassionate, 140–41
  gratitude and, 254
  personal, 92, 97
  pursuit of, 177
  self-ascribed, 272
  short-term v. long-term, 93
  for social change, 415
  stress and, 149
golden mean, 10
the good, complexity/contestability of, 229–30
GQ. *See* Gratitude Questionnaire
GRAT. *See* Gratitude Resentment and
    Appreciation Test
gratitude, 8, 102, 121, 214*t*, 256, 335, 423, 432
  benefits of, 253
  depression and, 257
  dispositional, 249–50, 255
  forgiveness and, 257
  goals and, 254
  health and, 254
  hypotheses 1-10 of, 254
  materialistic strivings and, 251
  memory and, 252
  moral behavior and, 253
  relational function of, 273
  relationships and, 272–73, 282–83
  self-esteem and, 251–52
  social benefits of, 253
  social function of, 122
  spirituality and, 253–54
  stress and, 250
  value of, 248
  well-being and, 249, 258
gratitude interventions, 254
  comparison groups for, 255
  dose-effect relationship of, 256
  enhancing retention in self-guided programs for,
    257
  gender and, 256–58
  trait moderators for, 255
Gratitude Questionnaire (GQ), 249
Gratitude Resentment and Appreciation Test
  (GRAT), 249
group-based egocentrism, 143
growth
  learning, 405
  positive emotions and, 117
  post-traumatic, 331
growth hormone (GH), 42
growth hormone axis, 42
guilt, function of, 107

habituation, rapid, 45*f*
Haidt, Jonathan, 6, 102
Hamel, Gary, 366
HAP. *See* high arousal positive

happiness, 10, 53, 109–10, 116, 397, 410–11, 423,
    441–43. *See also* hedonic happiness
  benefits of, 401–2
  as conscious, 185
  eudaimonic v. hedonic, 399
  fundamentals of, 199
  increasing, 400–407
  levels of, 105
  mindfulness v., 11
  as monitoring system, 400
  by nation, 401*t*
  national levels of, 387
  optimal human functioning v., 396
  of pursuit, 239–40
  pursuit of, 11, 149
  societal correlates of, 402*t*
  sustainable, 243n13
  theories of, 4, 401
  well-being and, 220–22
happiness obsession, 10–12
Happy Planet Index (HPI), 413
Hawthorne effect, 352
health, general, 216*t*, 221
  gratitude and, 254
  relationships and, 265
  well-being and, 265, 274
health outcomes, positive psychological
    states and, 44
heart, as demanding organ, 34
heart rate variability (HRV), 27
  emotions and, 31
  executive cognitive functions and, 29–30
  insecurity and, 32
  in relationships, 32–33
  repetitive thought and, 30
  self-regulation and, 33
hedonic approach, short-term, 89
  limitations of, 90–91
  predictions of, 95
hedonic experiences, subjective, 90
hedonic happiness, 399, 441–42
hedonic states, 44
  emotions as, 91
hedonic tone, hypoglycemia and, 30
hedonic view, of optimal human functioning, 89–90
hedonism, 251
hedonistic well-being, 229
Hegelian dialectic, 450–51
hemispheric asymmetry, 17
heuristic principles, 320–21
hierarchical model, 451–52
high arousal positive (HAP), 122, 434
higher-order emergence, 424
hindrance, 236
history of ideas, 447–49
  Hegelian dialectic and, 450–51
HIV/AIDS, positive psychological states and, 43–44
Hock, Dee, 377
homeostatic affects, 51, 55–57
homeostatic systems, cumulative toll on, 44
hope, 8, 214*t*, 359
hope theory, 354
hormones, anabolic/catabolic/growth, 42
HPA. *See* hypothalamic-pituitary-adrenal
HPI. *See* Happy Planet Index
HR. *See* human resources
HRV. *See* heart rate variability

human beings, 4
  conscious thought and, 175, 178
  evolution of, 422
  nature of, 451
  optimal, 9
  potential of, 415
  as social creatures, 120
  as unit of analysis, 16
human choice, 3
human functioning. *See* optimal human functioning
human infrastructure, creation of, 6
humanistic psychology, 5
humanity, 214*t*, 335, 338–39, 432
human psyche, dark v. light sides of, 147–56
human resources (HR), 361
human-science orientation, 449
Hume's skepticism, 450
humility, 432
  hypo-egoic states and, 138–39
humor, 6, 214*t*
hunger, homeostatic affect of, 55
hypnosis, 317
hypo-egoic states
  ego-involvement and, 138
  humility and, 138–39
  as integrative heuristic, 144
  open-mindedness and, 142
  perspective and, 142
  positive emotions and, 139
  positive psychology and, 136–38
  spirituality and, 142–43
  transcendence and, 142–43
  wisdom and, 142
hypoglycemia, hedonic tone and, 30
hypothalamic-pituitary-adrenal (HPA) axis, 27
  dysregulation of, 41
  positive psychological states and, 42
hypothalamic-pituitary-adrenal (HPA)
    processes, 41

ICF. *See* International Coach Federation
ideal affect, 434
idealistic rationalism, 450
identity, 137. *See also* ego identity
  challenges to, 152–55
  individuated, 141
  traits and, 195
IGF. *See* insulin-like growth factor
immediate pleasure, 93
immune system, 34
  positive psychological states and, 43–44
implementation intention, 181
implicit measures, of positive relationships, 287–88
impulsive responding, 169
individualism, 428–29
inflammatory processes, 41
influences
  external, 198*f*, 200
  macro-level, 239
  social/physical, 238
information
  sharing of, 179, 184–85
  simulated, 182
  types of, 184
in-group, 154
initiation, 236
  appraisal dimension of, 235

Input-Process-Outcome (IPO), 371
insecurity, HRV and, 32
Institute for Personality and Social Research (IPSR),
    209
Institute of Personality Assessment and Research
    (IPAR), 209
institutional quality, 403–4
insulin-dependent diabetes, 30
insulin-like growth factor (IGF), 42
  play and, 74
insulin resistance, 29
integration, 373–74
integrity, 214*t*
intellectual extremism, 447–50, 453
intentional activities, 199
inter-individual comparison, 12
International Coach Federation (ICF), 295
interoceptive monitoring, 51
Interpersonal Theory of Suicide, 318–19
intimacy, 274
  daily relationship deposits and, 282
intimacy projects, 239
intra-individual comparison, 12
intrinsic motivation, 162, 167
*Introduction to Social Psychology* (McDougall), 70
introspection, 182–83
introspective efficacy, 183
IPAR. *See* Institute of Personality Assessment and
    Research
IPO. *See* Input-Process-Outcome
IPSR. *See* Institute for Personality and Social
    Research

James, William, 102, 314, 444
Johnson, Spencer, 353
joy, 54
  effects of, 103
judgment, 214*t*
  situation-based, 12
justice, 214*t*, 335, 338, 339–40, 402*t*

Kantian philosophy, 450
karma yoga, 432–33
kidneys, as demanding organs, 34
kindness, 214*t*, 335, 432
kindness intervention, 110
King, Laura, 115
knowledge, 214*t*
knowledge-practice gap, 361
Kuhn, Thomas, 5, 452

language, 179
LAP. *See* low arousal positive
Lazarus, Richard, 439–40
leadership, 184, 214*t*, 335
  development, 370–71
  local, 390–91
learned optimism, 3
Leary, M.R., 17, 320–21
left prefrontal cortex, hypoactivation of, 163
leukocyte telomere length, positive
    emotions and, 124
life-ability, 397
life coaching. *See* coaching
life experiences, positive v. negative, 281
life narratives, 15, 179
life plan, reasonable v. optimal, 435

life satisfaction, 216*t*
  conscientiousness and, 199
life tasks, 233–34
life utility, 398
livability, 404
  of environment, 397
liver, as demanding organ, 34
Locke's empiricism, 450
longevity, 423
  good living and, 35
long-term goals, short-term goals v., 93
Lopez, Shane, 6, 18
love, 140–41, 214*t*, 221
  biological underpinnings of, 274
  companionate, 273–74
  passionate, 273–74
  relationships and, 273–74
love of learning, 214*t*
loving-kindness meditation, 116, 199
low arousal positive (LAP), 122, 434
lust/sexual system, 62–63
lymphocyte proliferation, 48
Lyubomirsky, Sonja, 6, 115

MAAS. *See* Mindful Attention Awareness Scale
macro-level influences, 239
main effects model, 267
manageability, 235–36
management
  active, 33
  conflict, 283–85
  organizational, 365
  performance, 369
  practice, 360
  talent, 369, 435–36
  of terror, 16, 154
marital behavior, 281
Marital Convention Scale, 287
*markarion* (fortune), 110
Maslow, Abraham, 208, 352, 366, 415
materialism, 423
materialistic strivings, gratitude and, 251
MBSR. *See* mindfulness-based stress reduction
McDougall, William, 70, 102–3
meaning, 329
  approaches to, 326–27
  coping and, 326
  global, 330*f*
  learning to see, 405–6
  making, 326, 330*f*, 331
  in positive psychology, 325–26
  search for, 407n4
  spirituality and, 328
  subjective sense of, 331
  systems of, 330–31
mean response tendencies, 13
mechanistic materialism, 448
Medial Forebrain Bundle (MFB), 58
medial prefrontal cortex (mPFC), 150, 154
meditation
  loving-kindness, 116, 199
  practice, 338
memory
  abnormal v. normal, 317–18
  gratitude and, 252
  retrieval, 317
  short-term v. long-term, 318

mental content
  mindful contextualization of, 155
  well-being and, 149
mental illness, 431
MFB. *See* Medial Forebrain Bundle
Michelangelo phenomenon, 271
mind. *See* BrainMind; conscious mind; MindBrain;
    unconscious mind
MindBrain, 78n1. *See also* BrainMind
  evolution of, 71
  functions of, 52
  organization of, 75
  secondary/tertiary processes of, 56
Mindful Attention Awareness Scale (MAAS), 151,
    153–54
mindfulness, 6, 216*t*
  acceptance and, 152
  adaptive responses and, 152–55
  balance of mind and, 156
  as character strength, 341
  cultivation of, 335–36, 344
  dispositional, 150
  emotion regulation and, 151
  happiness v., 11
  induction exercises for, 151
  mental content and, 155
  optimal psychological functioning and, 341–42
  positive cognitive/emotional relations and, 150–52
  as processing mode, 150
  self-focus v., 168
  self-regulation and, 340
  self-report measures of, 151
  social exclusion and, 153–54
  training, 337
  well-being and, 152
  worldview defense and, 154–55
mindfulness-based approaches, goal of, 11
mindfulness-based stress reduction (MBSR), 337–38
minding, 274–75
Mini-Mental State Examination, 29
Minnesota Multiphasic Personality Inventory, 196
mirror neurons, 72–73, 119
moderation, 10
modesty, 214*t*
moods, 51
mood disorders, anxiety and, 164
moral behavior, gratitude and, 253
morale, 200
moral emotions, 119
  positive, 102
moral obligation, 396
mortality risk, social isolation and, 265
motherese, 68
mPFC. *See* medial prefrontal cortex
multi-level model, 424–28
multiple-choice societies, 406

NA. *See* negative affect
narrative, 15, 179
National Institute of Mental Health
    (NIMH), 443
natural-science orientation, 449
need(s)
  basic, 389–90
  to belong, 17
  to contribute, 318–19
  economic, 389

satisfaction of, 389
negative affect (NA), 125
 in project pursuit, 236–37
negative emotions
 disputing/challenging, 10
 function of, 107
 positive role of, 106–7
 potency of, 118
 relevance of, 117–18
 self-focus and, 163
 self-induced, 139–40
 themes regarding, 120
negative life events, function of, 107
negative psychological processes, independence from,
 46
negativity biases, 148
neocortex, expansion of, 71
neocortical awareness functions, 66–67
neural matrix, extended, 56
neuroendocrine function, positive psychological states,
 41–43
neuropeptide Y (NPY), 42
neuropsychic entities, 208
neuroscience, 425*f*
neuroticism, 14, 198, 230, 387
Neurovisceral Integration Model, 28
NIMH. *See* National Institute of Mental Health
*nishkama karma* (action without concern for benefit),
 432–33
noble human movements, 422
non-attachment, 433
nonconscious processing, 137
nonindividualted phenomenal self, 137–38
non-insulin-dependent diabetes, 29
nonlinear dynamic models, 126
northern tilt, 228, 231, 234, 242
 as natural inclination, 230
 as personal action, 233
NPY. *See* neuropeptide Y

OB. *See* organizational behavior
objective biography, 198, 198*f*
observational data, need for, 288–89
occupational (I/O) psychology, 374–75
Olds, Jim, 58–59
open-mindedness, 335
 hypo-egoic states and, 142
openness, 14, 387
 change in, 198
 to experience, 210, 230, 338
 to fantasy, 196
opioids
 endogenous, 63
 release through touch of, 64
optimal human being, 9. *See also*
 human beings
optimal human functioning, 166, 335
 happiness v., 396
 hedonic view of, 89–90
 integrative model of, 424–27
 motivated view of, 92, 97
 views of, 95
optimal life plan, 435
optimal states, 162
optimism, 8, 359
 initial positive effects of, 229
optimistic disposition, 3

organizational applications
 of positive psychology, 365, 372–73
 research/practice roadmap for, 373–78
organizational behavior (OB), 374–75. *See also*
 positive organizational behavior
 research, 352–54, 360
 traditional, 352–54
organizational change, coaching as
 means to, 303–4
organizational management, 365
organizational psychology, 7
organizations, redefining, 376–78
orientations, traits and, 240–41
other-condemning, 119
other-praising, 119
out-group, 154
oxytocin, 42, 62
oxytocinergic tone, 73

PA. *See* positive affect
PAC. *See* personal action constructs
PAG. *See* Periaqueductal gray
PANAS. *See* Positive and Negative Affect Scale
panic disorder, 321
panic/grief/separation distress system, 63–64
 social bonds and, 76–77
paradigm shift, adoption of, 5
parasympathetic nervous system, 27
partner affirmation, 271–72
passive-constructive reactions, 268–70
passive-destructive reactions, 268–70
past-negative, 216*t*
past-positive, 216*t*
peak-experience, 398–99
Peale, Norman Vincent, 353, 441
perceived burdensomeness, 318–19
Perceived Responses to Capitalization Attempts
 (PRCA), 268–69
perceived responsiveness
 capitalization and, 270–71
 in relationships, 271
 support and, 266–67
perceptual affirmation, 271
perfectionism, 105–6
performance management, 369
Periaqueductal gray (PAG), 60
persistence, 214*t*
personal action constructs (PAC) units, 233–34,
 243n11
personal coaching. *See* coaching
personal construct theory, 231
personal goals
 investment in, 97
 pursuit of, 92
personality, 425*f*
 changes in, 196
 conceptions of, 15
 consistency of, 217
 disorder, 31, 196
 as field, 209
 national differences in, 387
 nature/assessment of, 12–14
 personality within, 426
 positive psychology and, 207–8
 signature pattern of, 13
 situation and, 13
 social indicators and, 388

stability of, 195–96
variation in, 14
personality psychology, 207
personality science, 228
  advancing, 239–42
  positive psychology and, 231
  summary of, 231
  themes in, 229–30
personality system, 198*f*
personality traits. *See also* trait(s)
  Allport on, 209–10
  character strengths v., 207–8
  as inherited, 193–94
  stability of, 193, 195
  VIA-IS and, 212–15
  well-being and, 193, 215
personal projects, 233, 241
  affect and, 237
  PA/NA in, 236–37
  predictive paradox of, 234–35
  social ecology of, 237–39
  well-being and, 234
person-centered approach, 15–16
person-situation debate, 229
person-social context boundary, 424
person specialists, 232, 243n8
perspective(s), 214*t*
  biological, 16–18
  conceptual, 52–54
  historical, 447
  hypo-egoic states and, 142
  negative/positive, 5
  social ecological, 236–39, 241–42
  on time, 216*t*
  on traits, 197–200
Peterson, Chris, 6, 8, 101
  VIA-IS creation by, 12
phenomenal self, 137
philosophers, impact of, 447–48
philosophy of history, 451, 453
phobia, 181
phronesis, 56, 58, 61, 67, 78
physical influences, 238
physiological psychology, 54
place, 385
  desires and, 388
  energy of, 392
  key aspects of, 388–89
  perception of, 392
  research on, 391–92
  role of, 385–86
  safety and, 390
  well-being and, 386–92
plasticity, 231
play, 77–78
  brain and, 73–75
  IGF-1 and, 74
  social system of, 64–65
play/joyful rough-and-tumble physical social-engagement system, 64–65
pleasure, 59, 76, 398
  immediate, 93
POB. *See* positive organizational behavior
Polyvagal Theory, 28
POS. *See* Positive Organizational Scholarship
positive affect (PA), 125, 442
  prediction of, 255

in project pursuit, 236–37
research on, 68–72
Positive and Negative Affect Scale (PANAS), 434
positive character traits, 207. *See also* personality traits; trait(s)
positive cognitive/emotional relations, mindfulness and, 150–52
positive constructs, theory-based, 354
positive dispositions, 230
positive emotions, 8
  as buffer, 125
  build effect of, 126
  cultivation of, 123
  decline in, 196
  enhancing, 25
  as foundation of society, 102–3
  growth and, 117
  hypo-egoic states and, 139
  increasing, 10
  leukocyte telomere length and, 124
  moral, 102
  progesterone and, 124
  as worthy intervention target, 115
positive illusion, 106
positive institutions/communities, 207
positive interventions, 7, 116
  long-term effects of, 107–9
positive memories, accessibility to, 252
positive moral emotions, 102. *See also* moral emotions
positive organizational behavior (POB), 351, 353
  future of, 357
  human-oriented, 361
  PsyCap and, 354–56
  research, 360–61
Positive Organizational Scholarship (POS), 304, 353
positive psychological processes
  benefits of, 47
  differing pathways for, 47
  enhancement interventions for, 47–48
  on physiology, 46–47
  positive physiological functioning markers and, 46
positive psychological states, 41
  biological processes and, 43–44
  as cortisol response moderators, 42
  endocrine activity and, 44
  health outcomes and, 44
  HIV/AIDS and, 43, 44
  HPA axis activity and, 42
  immune function and, 43
  neuroendocrine function and, 41–43
positive psychology, 5–7, 9, 15, 96–97, 116, 324–25, 410–12, 427
  agenda of, 160–61
  as appreciative view, 422–23
  breadth/depth of focus of, 325–29
  clinical psychology v., 430
  critique of, 284–85
  durability of, 440–41
  dynamic understanding in, 325, 327, 329–30
  extraordinary v. ordinary in, 444–45
  fragmentation of, 424
  hedonic approach to, 90–92
  historical perspective of, 447
  hypo-egoic states and, 136–38
  as ideological stance, 422
  long-term influence of, 449–50
  on the market, 18–19

on meaning, 325–26
mission of, 314–16
organizational applications of, 365, 372–78
personality science and, 231
of positive emotion, 110*t*
as positive science, 421–22
potential applications of, 8
rapid assimilation of, 18
relationships in, 428
social change and, 412–14
status of, 452–53
as study of positive topics, 423–24
subjects of, 160
traits and, 194–97
unhappiness in, 442–43
universality of, 109–10
value-laden nature of, 421
Positive Relationship Science (PRS), 284
positive subjective experience, 207
positivity
internalization of, 353–54
PsyCap and, 359–61
in workplace, 351–52, 356–57
positivity offset, 118
positivity ratios, 118, 281
post-traumatic growth, 331
poverty initiatives, 413–14
power, 251
PPA, 235–36
practice
communities, 374–75
knowledge and, 361
management, 360
meditation, 338
organizational application roadmap for, 373–78
task performance and, 165
PRCA. *See* Perceived Responses to Capitalization Attempts
present-fatalistic, 216*t*
present-hedonistic, 216*t*
pride, 109
in social conditions, 120
primary control strategies, 162, 167
primary orientations, 231–37, 240–41
primary particulars, 232
primary-process affects
nature of, 72
role of, 73
primary-process emotions, 52–53, 67
child development and, 75–76
in mammalian brains, 54
primary-process issues, 52
*The Principles of Psychology* (James), 102
problem-focused coping, 162, 167
problem-oriented decision making, 356
processing. *See also* self-focused processing; task-focused processing
accuracy of, 169
conscious, 137
correlates/consequences of, 162–64, 163*f*
experiential, 149–50
integrative potential of, 161–62
nonconscious, 137
speed of, 165, 169
progesterone, positive emotions and, 124
prosocial orientations, 140–41
PRS. *See* Positive Relationship Science

prudence, 214*t*
PsyCap. *See* psychological capital
psychic energy, 59
psychological capital (PsyCap), 351–52, 370
application of, 359–60
future of, 357–60
limitations of, 356–57
optimism of, 355
performance impact criterion of, 356
POB and, 354–56
positivity and, 359–61
research, 357–59
resilience of, 355
psychological stress, acute, 43
psychological variables, importance of, 15
psychological well-being (PWB), 337. *See also* well-being
psychology. *See also* specific subdisciplines
as domain, 7
negative/positive perspectives in, 5
virtues/strengths/values in, 6
psychology of emotions, 7
psychology of personality, 7
psychoneuroimmunology, 43
psychopathology, 163–64
as exaggeration, 321
mission of, 314–16
universality and, 320–21
psychophysiological theories, of self-regulation, 28–29
psychophysiology, study of, 33
PWB. *See* psychological well-being

quality of life, 337, 397, 397*t*
improvement in, 3
self-focus and, 136

rage/anger system, 60–61
random access memory, 67–68, 71
rational emotive behavioral therapy, 18
raw affect, 70, 78n2
raw emotional feelings, sub-neocortical foundations of, 65–66
reactivity process, 267
reality, integrated model of, 425*f*
reason, conscious thought and, 180
reasonable life plan, 435
recovery, rapid, 45*f*
recruitment approaches, 367–68
regret, 216*t*, 251
relationship(s)
as bank accounts, 281–85, 289
capitalization and, 282
close, 265, 280
conflict in, 152–53
contentment in, 275
dyadic, 285
emotions within, 120–21
forgiveness and, 283
gratitude and, 272–73, 282–83
health and, 265
HRV and, 32–33
implicit measures of, 287–88
initiation, 273
interdependent, 271
love and, 273–74
marital behavior and, 281

negative biases in, 148
other life domains and, 275
perceived responsiveness in, 271
positive, 287–88
positive/negative interactions in, 35
in positive psychology, 428
regulation of, 32–33
satisfaction, 105–6, 287
well-being and, 265
religiosity, 15–16
remitted major depressive disorder, 31
repetitive thought. See also thoughts
HRV and, 30
research, 9–10
on capitalization, 271
on coaching, 296–305
on coping, 200–201
designs, 285–86
longitudinal, 285–86, 300
organizational application roadmap for, 373–78
on organizational behavior, 352–54, 360
on PA, 68–72
on place, 391–92
on POB, 360–61
on positive affect, 68–72
on PsyCap, 357–59
specialization theory and, 232
on stress, 200–201
research questions, 12
resilience, 355, 359, 440
self-regulation and, 25
respiratory sinus arrhythmia (RSA), 27
restorative processes, 25–26
return on development (ROD), 356
return on investment (ROI), 301–2
reward motivation, 274
reward/pleasure/reinforcement system, 59
seeking/desire system v., 76
ROD. See return on development
ROI. See return on investment
romantic relationship conflict, 152–53
RSA. See respiratory sinus arrhythmia
rules, systems of, 179–80, 183
Ryff's Psychological Well-Being scales, 196–97

sadness, function of, 106
safety, place and, 390
satisfaction, 400f
domain, 398
kinds/levels of, 105, 398–99, 398t
lasting, 399
life, 199, 216t
of needs, 389
in relationships, 105–6, 287
schizophrenia, 163
science, agenda v., 161
scientific holism, 426
secondary behavioral processes, 52
secondary control strategies, 162, 167
secondary emotional processes, 53
secondary-process emotions, 75
seeking/desire system, 58–60
reward/pleasure/reinforcement system v., 76
selective attunement, 231
self
expansion of, 272
ideal, 271–72

self-as-knower, 150
self-awareness. See also hypo-egoic states
benefits of, 135–36
capacity for, 136, 148–49
emergence of, 135
functional aspects of, 149
high v. low, 136
low, 136–37, 141, 144
self-compassion, 10, 141
self-concept, 197, 198f
self-concern, disengagement from, 155
self-confirmation motive, 319–20
self-conscious emotions, 119
self-consciousness distinction, public v.
private, 167
self-conscious states, 107
self-critical motivation, 105
self-deceit, 356
self-determination theory, 235, 303, 422
self-esteem, 43
gratitude and, 251–52
volunteering and, 184
self-expansion, 272
self-focus, 139
anxiety and, 163
mindfulness v., 168
negative emotional experiences and, 163
quality of life and, 136
self-focused processing, 161, 163f
as adaptive, 167–68
as aversive, 163
task-focused processing v., 162
self-fulfillment, 97
self-image, compassionate goals and, 141
self-improvement, 105–6
selflessness, 431–32
self-monitoring, of thoughts, 11
self-regulation, 14, 16, 96, 214t, 335
autonomic nervous system and, 27
the body and, 25–35
capacity for, 33
cortisol and, 27
demands of, 34
evaluative threat on, 35
failure of, 25
glucose and, 26, 28–29, 33
HRV and, 33
limitations in, 26
mindfulness and, 340
physiological parameters of, 26–27
psychophysiological correlates of, 33
psychophysiological theories of, 28–29
resilience and, 25
summary of, 33
self-regulatory fatigue, 26, 29, 32
self-relevant thoughts, emotional distress
and, 139
self-report data, limitations of, 286–87
self-verification, bulimic symptoms
and, 319–20
Seligman, Marty, 3–6, 101, 242n1, 411
VIA-IS creation by, 12
sensitive dependence on initial conditions, 126
sensory affects, 51, 55–56
serotonin transporter genes (5-HTT), 75, 123
shared laughter, 120
short-term goals, long-term goals v., 93

short-term hedonic approach, 89
  limitations of, 90–91
  predictions of, 95
signature strengths, 108, 343, 434–35
simulation, 183
  behavior change and, 182
situation, personality and, 13
situational themes, 217
situation-based judgments, 12
skepticism, 450
social acceptance, 124
social behaviors, automatic
    initiation of, 177
social bonds, deficient, 76–77
social brain, play and, 73–75
social change
  goals for, 415
  mandate for, 414–15
  mechanisms for, 415–16
  positive psychology and, 412–14
social cognitive theory, 354
social conditions, 14
  pride in, 120
social cues, 177
Social Darwinism, 103
social ecological perspective, 236
  of personal project pursuit, 237–39
  well-being and, 241–42
social exclusion, mindfulness and, 153–54
social indicators
  personality and, 388
  of well-being, 392
social influences, 238
social information, conscious thought and, 179
social intelligence, 214*t*
social interactions, antagonistic, 32
social isolation, all-cause mortality risk and, 265
socialization, benefits of, 65
social life, conscious thought and, 179
social norms, conforming to, 92–93
social play system, 64–65
social psychology, 7, 161, 425*f*
social resources, building of, 252–53
social support, 16, 266. *See also* support
social vitality, 223
societal change, 4
societal conditions, 8
societal progress, assessment of, 9
socioemotional selectivity, 123
specialists, 232, 243n8
specialization, 435–36
specialization theory, 231, 233, 243n7
  research agenda of, 232
spirituality, 214*t*
  gratitude and, 253–54
  hypo-egoic states and, 142–43
  meaning and, 328
spirituality scale, 65
spontaneous self-concept, 137
stability, 231
  emotional, 210
  of personality, 195–96
  of traits, 193, 195
state cheerfulness, 10
state-oriented responses, 162
states. *See also specific states*
  assessment of, 13

positive, 353
pure, 355–56
temporary, 14
stimulation, 72, 391
  of cytokine production, 43
strength-orientation, 4
strengths, 411. *See also* character strengths;
    signature strengths
  balance v. focus, 449
  functions of, 441
  at global level, 12
  nature/assessment of, 12–14
  personal, 14
  possessing v. using, 13
  value of, 440
  well-being and, 12
strengths-based approaches, 370, 411
strengths-based organizations, 413
strengths-based recruitment, 367–68
strengths coaching, 370
stress, 42–44
  evaluative threat on, 35
  goals and, 149
  gratitude and, 250
  physiological responses to, 45*f*
  research, 200–201
stressfulness, dimensions of, 34
structural validity, 219
structured narrative, 15, 179
subjective enjoyment of life, 398
subjective experience, positive, 207
subjective well-being (SWB), 90, 221, 337–38, 412–13.
    *See also* well-being
  predictors of, 426–27
sub-neocortical affective mind, 74
subordinating personal benefit, 431–33
substantive validity, 220–22
suffering, vulnerability to, 148–49
suffocation alarm system, 321
suicide, theory of, 318–19
support, 236, 238
  cost of, 266
  perceived responsiveness and, 266–67
  social, 16, 266
SWB. *See* subjective well-being
symbolic representation, 135
sympathetic nervous system, activation of, 34
systems change, coaching as means to, 304–5

tabula rasa, 71, 74
tailoring interventions, 201–2
talent management/development, 369, 435–36
task-focus
  benefits of, 166
  as dopamine availability, 166
  as dorsolateral prefrontal cortex
      activation, 165–66
  as response speed, 165
task-focused processing, 161, 163*f*, 169
  self-focused processing v., 162
  task performance and, 164–65
task-involvement, increased, 166
task performance, 164
  practice and, 165
team development, 371
temperance, 214*t*, 335, 338, 340, 432
Terkel, Studs, 375–76

terror management theory (TMT), 16, 154
tertiary-process affects, 52, 75
tertiary processes, 53, 56
theory-based positive constructs, 354
Theory Y assumptions, 366
therapy, coaching v., 301
Thing-Person orientation scale
    (T-P scale), 232
thing specialists, 232
thoughts. *See also* conscious thought;
    repetitive thought
  control of, 10
  self-monitoring of, 11
time perspective, 216*t*
tipping point ratio, 357
Titchener, Edward, 450
TMT. *See* terror management theory
tonic arousal, lower, 45*f*
tool-based discipline, prevention of, 14
Toronto Mindfulness Scale, 338
total talent management, 369
touch, opioid release through, 64
T-P scale. *See* Thing-Person orientation scale
Trail Making Test, 29
trait(s). *See also* personality traits
  as biologically based, 197
  centrality of, 201
  change in, 198–99
  in FFT, 197
  as fixed, 194
  identity and, 195
  interventions and, 199–200
  orientations and, 240–41
  positive, 196, 208–10
  positive psychology and, 194–97
  role of, 195
  self-reports of, 201
  stability of, 193, 195
  in theoretical perspective, 197–200
  as universal, 197
  value of, 195
  well-being and, 230–31
trait approach, 12–13
trait gratitude, 255–56, 258
trait psychology, 194
  limitations imposed by, 200
  offerings of, 201
transcendence, 214*t*, 251, 335, 338, 340–41, 432
  hypo-egoic states and, 142–43
transformative activists, 412
trust, 184
twilight state, 66

UCRs. *See* unconditioned responses
UCSs. *See* unconditioned stimuli
ultrasonic vocalizations (USVs), 61
unconditioned responses (UCRs), 53, 69–70,
    73, 78n3
unconditioned stimuli (UCSs), 52, 69–70, 73
unconscious mind
  as behavioral guide, 177
  capabilities of, 176, 178
universalism, 251
universality
  of positive psychology, 109–10
  psychopathology and, 320–21
USVs. *See* ultrasonic vocalizations

utilitarianism, 51, 407n1
utility of life, 398

vagal inhibition, 30
validity
  content, 219
  external, 219–20
  structural, 219
  substantive, 220–22
value congruency, 240
Values in Action Inventory of Strengths (VIA-IS), 8,
    12, 415–16, 435
  critical evaluation of, 211–15
  development of, 209
  evaluation of, 218
  personality traits and, 212–15
  prediction of, 214*t*
  studies of, 218
  translation of, 218–19
  well-being and, 215, 216*t*
variable-centric universe, 14–16
Ventral Tegmental Area (VTA), 58
ventral vagus complex, 28
ventromedial portion of prefrontal cortex
    (vmPFC), 165
veridical unconditional signaling, 69
VIA-IS. *See* Values in Action Inventory
    of Strengths
virtues, cultivation of, 335, 338–41, 434–35
visceral organs, demands of, 34
visualization, of best possible self, 108
vmPFC. *See* ventromedial portion of
    prefrontal cortex
volition, 183
volunteering, 390–91
  self-esteem and, 184
VTA. *See* Ventral Tegmental Area
vulnerability, 284
  to suffering, 148–49

Watson, James B., 450
wealth, 402, 402*t*
well-being, 11, 242n2, 412–13. *See also* subjective
    well-being
  Big Five Inventory and, 230
  complexity/contestability of, 229–30
  context and, 97
  of employee, 368
  gratitude and, 249, 258
  happiness and, 220–22
  health and, 265, 274
  hedonistic v. eudaimonic, 229
  hypotheses 1-10 of, 250–54
  intra-national differences in, 387–89
  mental content and, 149
  mindfulness and, 152
  national differences in, 386–89
  national indicators of, 7
  personality traits and, 193, 215
  personal projects and, 234
  place and, 386–92
  psychological contributions to, 15
  relationships and, 265
  social ecology and, 241–42
  social indicators of, 392
  strengths and, 12
  temperamental explanation of, 199

traits and, 230–31
variables involved in, 91–92
varieties of, 239–40
VIA-IS and, 215, 216*t*
well-being dimensions, matrix of, 10–12
willpower, role of, 104
wisdom, 107, 214*t*, 335, 338, 432
  hypo-egoic states and, 142

within-person approaches, 13–14
work, 222
  nature of, 375–76
working self-concept, 137
worldview defense, mindfulness and, 154–55
Wundt, Wilhelm, 450

zest, 214*t*